Web Database Applications
with PHP and MySQL

Web Database Applications
with PHP and MySQL

Hugh E. Williams and David Lane

O'REILLY®

Beijing · Cambridge · Farnham · Köln · Paris · Sebastopol · Taipei · Tokyo

Web Database Applications with PHP and MySQL
by Hugh E. Williams and David Lane

Published by O'Reilly & Associates, Inc., 1005 Gravenstein Highway North,
Sebastopol, CA 95472.

O'Reilly & Associates books may be purchased for educational, business, or sales promotional
use. Online editions are also available for most titles (*safari.oreilly.com*). For more information,
contact our corporate/institutional sales department: (800) 998-9938 or *corporate@oreilly.com*.

Editor:	Lorrie LeJeune
Production Editor:	Mary Anne Weeks Mayo
Cover Designer:	Ellie Volckhausen
Interior Designer:	Melanie Wang

Printing History:

March 2002:	First Edition.

ISBN: 0-596-00041-3
[M]

Table of Contents

Preface

Web database applications integrate databases and the Web. Well-known web destinations such as online auction sites, retail stores, news sites, discussion forums, and personalized home pages are all examples of web database applications. The popularity of these applications stems from their accessibility and usability: thousands of users can access the same data at the same time without the need to install additional software on their machines.

What This Book Is About

This book is for developers who want to build database applications that are integrated with the Web. It presents the principles and techniques of developing small- to medium-scale web database applications that store, manage, and retrieve data, as well as the basic techniques for securing an application. The architecture we describe is a successful framework for applications that can run on modest hardware and process more than a million hits per day from users.

An important feature of this book is our ongoing case study, *Hugh and Dave's Online Wines*. It's a complete but fictional online retail store that allows users to browse and search a database of wines, add items to a shopping cart, manage their membership, and purchase wines. Searching, browsing, storing user data, validating user input, managing user transactions, and security are each the subject of a chapter, and each topic is illustrated with examples from the case study. The completed winestore scripts are presented and briefly discussed at the end of the book.

We use open source software. Our database management system (DBMS) is MySQL, a system known for its suitability to applications that require speed but low resource overheads. Our scripting language is PHP, which is best known for its function libraries that interact with more than 15 relational database systems, the web environment, and many other services. We use PHP to develop the application logic that brings together the Web and the relational database management system (RDBMS). Apache is our web server of choice.

What You Need to Know

This book is about understanding and developing application logic that brings databases and the Web together. We introduce database systems over the course of the book, but our discussions don't replace a book or class dedicated to relational database theory, or a book about a specific relational database system such as MySQL. Likewise, we assume you are already familiar with the Web. We introduce but don't delve deeply into the three key web protocols, HTML, HTTP, and TCP/IP.

We also assume you can program in a third-generation programming language such as C, C++, Java, Perl, FORTRAN, or Visual Basic. Our introduction to the PHP web scripting language doesn't assume you are familiar with web scripting or are an expert programmer, but we do assume you understand the basic HTML constructs and are familiar with the popular web browsers. If you can author an HTML document with a text editor that contains a `<form>` and a `<table>` element, you have sufficient HTML skills to use this book. It is the principles of structure in the markup process that are important, not the attractiveness or usability of the presentation in the web browser. We introduce advanced HTML concepts as required, but an HTML guide such as O'Reilly's *HTML and XHTML: The Definitive Guide*, by Chuck Musciano and William Kennedy, is a useful resource for understanding and building web database applications. You may also find O'Reilly's *Programming PHP*, by Rasmus Lerdorf and Kevin Tatroe useful as well.

You don't need a detailed understanding of relational databases to use this book, but a working knowledge is helpful. We present the relational database theory needed for developing simple applications, and we cover many other basic concepts, including how to tell when a database is the method of choice to store data, the architecture of a DBMS, the database query language SQL, and a case study that models system requirements and converts the model to a database design. This book isn't a substitute for the many good resources on database theory, however, it's enough to begin developing the underlying databases for many web database applications.

We briefly introduce web servers and networking in Chapter 1 and provide additional material in Appendix B. Both web servers and networking are important to a web database application but aren't the focus of this book. We present enough information to set up a web server and to understand how it fits in the architecture of a web database application. For many applications, this is sufficient. Likewise, we present sufficient detail so that you will understand what networking and network protocol issues impact web database application design.

How This Book Is Organized

There are 13 chapters and 5 appendixes in this book. Chapters 1 to 3 introduce web database applications, PHP, MySQL, and SQL:

Chapter 1, *Database Applications and the Web*

Discusses the three-tier architecture commonly used in web database applications and in those that we discuss in this book. We introduce each of the three tiers and the features of each, and we introduce the software tools that we use. We also briefly introduce web protocols. The chapter concludes with an introduction to our case study example, Hugh and Dave's Online Wines. We discuss the components of the winestore, the system requirements, and where in the book the techniques to develop each component are covered.

Chapter 2, *PHP*

Introduces the PHP scripting language. It covers programming in PHP and discusses the basic programming constructs, variables, types, functions, techniques, and common sources of bugs. We include many short code examples to illustrate how to program with PHP.

Chapter 3, *MySQL and SQL*

Introduces the MySQL DBMS and how to interact with it using the database query language SQL. Using examples from the online winestore, we introduce the SQL commands for creating, deleting, and updating data and databases. We also present a longer, example-driven section on querying the online winestore. The chapter concludes with discussion of advanced topics, including MySQL database tuning and configuration.

Chapters 4 to 9 cover the principles and practice of developing web database application logic.

Chapter 4, *Querying Web Databases*

Introduces the basics of connecting to the MySQL DBMS with PHP. We explain the querying process used in most interactions with the DBMS and present examples that use most of the PHP MySQL library functions. We also show how results from database queries can be formatted as HTML for delivery in a web browser. The chapter is supported by the online winestore case study example, which shows how to build a moderately complex querying module.

Chapter 5, *User-Driven Querying*

Continues the principles and practice of querying web databases. Here we focus on user-driven querying, in which the user provides parameters to the querying process. We show how data is encoded, sent in requests from a web browser to a web server, and decoded for processing in PHP. We discuss the security implications in processing user data and show steps to secure interactive querying systems. Our discussion is supported by a user-driven querying example with results that can be browsed page by page.

Chapter 6, *Writing to Web Databases*

Covers writing data to web databases. There are several reasons why writing data is different from reading it. For example, reloading or printing a page from a web browser can cause data to be written to a database more than once.

Multiple users accessing the same database introduces other problems, such as data unexpectedly being changed by one user while it's being read by another. We discuss how to solve problems related to the nature of the Web and multiple users. We illustrate the principles with an example that adds and edits customer details in the online winestore.

Chapter 7, *Validation on the Server and Client*
This chapter is related to Chapter 6 and presents the principles and techniques for user-input validation. We introduce validation models and reporting methods that work in web database applications and show how these are implemented using PHP and supported by client-side, browser-based JavaScript.

Chapter 8, *Sessions*
Covers the principles of adding session management to web database applications. Session management allows the interactions between a user and the application to be related so that, for example, a user can log in and log out of an application and be guided through a series of steps in a process. We show how PHP manages sessions and illustrate the techniques with a case study of managing error feedback to users who are joining as customers of the winestore.

Chapter 9, *Authentication and Security*
Presents topics in web security. We show how PHP can be used for basic authentication, how databases can manage many users, and how communications can be secured with the network-level secure sockets layer. Our case study is the login and logout process for the online winestore. This extends our discussion of session management in Chapter 8.

Chapter 10 to 13 present and outline the completed winestore case study. The outlines aren't comprehensive: we assume you have completed Chapters 4 to 9 and understand the principles of developing web database applications. We recommend that you view, edit, and use the winestore PHP scripts while reading Chapters 10 through 13.

Chapter 10, *Winestore Customer Management*
Presents the code for customer management in the winestore, as well as the general-purpose functions that are used throughout the application. The code presented is based on the examples developed throughout Chapters 4 to 8. We present the scripts for collecting, validating, and modifying customer details. We also include the code for the user login and logout processes based on the material presented in Chapter 9.

Chapter 11, *The Winestore Shopping Cart*
Presents the code for the shopping cart at the winestore. The shopping cart is stored in a database, and each user's cart is tracked using the session techniques from Chapter 8. The cart module allows a user to view her cart, add items to the cart, update item quantities, delete items, and empty the cart.

Chapter 12, *Ordering and Shipping at the Winestore*

Presents the code for the ordering and shipping modules of the winestore. The ordering process shows how the complex database-processing techniques discussed in Chapters 3 and 6 are used to convert a shopping cart into a customer order. We also show how email confirmations of the order are sent to the user, and an order confirmation is presented as an HTML page.

Chapter 13, *Related Topics*

Concludes the case study examples and presents related web database topics. We present the complete searching and browsing winestore module based on the techniques discussed in Chapter 5. We also discuss automating queries and using templates to separate script code from HTML markup.

There are five appendixes in this book:

Appendix A, *Installation Guide*

A concise guide to installing the Apache web server, PHP, and MySQL under the Linux operating system; includes resource pointers to more detailed installation guides for Linux and other operating systems.

Appendix B, *Internet and Web Protocols*

Builds on Chapter 1 and describes the workings of the Web in greater detail.

Appendix C, *Modeling and Designing Relational Databases*

Contains a case study that models the system requirements for the winestore using entity-relationship database modeling. It shows how this model can be converted to a design. It also details the SQL commands used to create the winestore database.

Appendix D, *Managing Sessions in the Database Tier*

An extension of Chapter 8, this appendix shows how the default PHP method for session handling can be moved to the more scalable underlying database tier.

Appendix E, *Resources*

Lists useful resources, including web sites and books containing more information on the topics presented throughout this book.

How to Use This Book

This book is designed as a tutorial-style introduction to web database applications.

If you haven't installed the Apache web server, the PHP scripting engine, or the MySQL database management system, begin with Appendix A. Appendix A lists possible methods for obtaining the software and includes instructions for those who wish to install from source code. Appendix A also shows how the examples used in this book can be downloaded and installed locally. We recommend obtaining the code and databases used in this book, as they will help you understand the concepts as they are presented. The database configuration steps are included at the beginning of Chapter 3.

Each chapter covers a different topic. Chapters through 3 can be read independently. Chapter 1 introduces web database applications and the case study application. We recommend reading Chapter 1 first. Chapters 2 and 3 are designed as introductions to PHP and SQL, respectively; both can be used as references when reading the later chapters.

Chapter 4 through 9 are a major section with a tutorial style that follows through the principles and practice of web database applications. Chapters 4, 5, and 6 begin with basic principles and components. Chapter 7, 8, and 9 contain more sophisticated examples that rely on concepts from the earlier chapters. These chapters are designed to be read sequentially. By the conclusion of Chapter 9, you should have mastered the principles of developing web database applications.

Chapter 10 to 13 present and briefly discuss the completed scripts developed for the online winestore case study. The scripts show how the techniques from Chapter 4 to 9 are applied in practice and, as such, are most useful after mastering the content of the earlier chapters. The material in these later chapters is also particularly useful when the example application has been downloaded and installed on a local server, allowing the scripts to be modified and tested as the chapters are read.

Appendixes B and C are also in a tutorial style. We recommend Appendix B if you are interested in or are unfamiliar with the web environment and its underlying protocols. Appendix C is a brief introduction to entity-relationship modeling for databases and shows the steps we took in designing the winestore database. We recommend reading Appendix C after completing Chapter 3, and only if a detailed understanding of the winestore database is desired.

Conventions Used in This Book

The following conventions are used in this book:

Italic
> Used for program names, URLs, and database entities, and for new terms when they are defined

`Constant width`
> Used for code examples, functions, statements, and attributes, and to show the output of commands

`Constant width italic`
> Used to indicate variables within commands and functions

This icon designates a note, which is an important aside to the nearby text.

This icon designates a warning relating to the nearby text.

How to Contact Us

Please address comments and questions concerning this book to the publisher:

O'Reilly & Associates, Inc.
1005 Gravenstein Highway North
Sebastopol, CA 95472
(800) 998-9938 (in the United States or Canada)
(707) 829-0515 (international or local)
(707) 829-0104 (fax)

There is a web page for this book, which lists errata, examples, or any additional information. You can access this page at:

http://www.oreilly.com/catalog/webdbapps/

To comment or ask technical questions about this book, send email to:

bookquestions@oreilly.com

For more information about books, conferences, Resource Centers, and the O'Reilly Network, see the O'Reilly web site at:

http://www.oreilly.com

The authors can be reached at:

hugh@computer.org
dave@simdb.com

Web Site and Code Examples

Code examples from this book, data used to create the online winestore database, and the completed winestore application can be found at this book's web site, *http://www.oreilly.com/catalog/webdbapps/* or at the authors' web site, *http://www.webdatabasebook.com.*

Acknowledgments

We thank our technical reviewers, Justin Zobel, Harry Williams, S.M.M. (Saied) Tahaghoghi, and Rasmus Lerdorf, for their expertise and diligence in helping to improve this book. We also thank our editor, Lorrie LeJeune, and her editorial assistant, Sarmonica Jones. We acknowledge the support of our employer, RMIT University; Hugh thanks the School of Computer Science and Information Technology, and David thanks the Multimedia Database Systems group. We also thank our colleagues, who throughout this project have provided ideas, suggestions, and help. In particular, we thank Abhijit Chattaraj for his help with the MySQL implementation of session support, and Derryn Grabowski and Jakub Korab for their help with an initial prototype of the winestore application.

Last, but most importantly, we thank our wives, Selina Williams and Louise Excell. Very little of this book would exist without Selina's support of Hugh's hectic schedule; he's now looking forward to supporting her through the birth of their first child. Louise has been especially patient with David throughout this project, and looks forward to his support in bringing up their second child, William. David also thanks his daughter Beth; the wisdom of her advice in dealing with a troublesome PC was far beyond her three years: "now, just press one key at a time."

Database Applications and the Web

With the growth of the Web over the past decade, there has been a similar growth in services that are accessible over the Web. Many new services are web sites that are driven from data stored in databases. Examples of web database applications include news services that provide access to large data repositories, e-commerce applications such as online stores, and business-to-business (B2B) support products.

Database applications have been around for over 30 years, and many have been deployed using network technology long before the Web existed. The point-of-service systems used by bank tellers are obvious examples of early networked database applications. Terminals are installed in bank branches, and access to the bank's central database application is provided through a wide area network. These early applications were limited to organizations that could afford the specialized terminal equipment and, in some cases, to build and own the network infrastructure.

The Web provides cheap, ubiquitous networking. It has an existing user base with standardized web browser software that runs on a variety of ordinary computers. For developers, web server software is freely available that can respond to requests for both documents and programs. Several scripting languages have been adapted or designed to develop programs to use with web servers and web protocols.

This book is about bringing together the Web and databases. Most web database applications do this through three layers of application logic. At the base is a database management system (DBMS) and a database. At the top is the client web browser used as an interface to the application. Between the two lies most of the application logic, usually developed with a web server-side scripting language that can interact with the DBMS, and can decode and produce HTML used for presentation in the client web browser.

We begin by discussing the three-tier architecture model used in many web database applications. We then introduce the nature of the Web and its underlying protocols and then discuss each of the three tiers and their components in detail. Hugh and Dave's Online Wines, our case study application, is introduced at the end of this chapter. We refer to it frequently throughout the course of the book and use it as a model to illustrate the construction of a web database application.

Three-Tier Architectures

This book describes web database applications built around a *three-tier architecture* model, shown in Figure 1-1. At the base of an application is the *database tier,* consisting of the *database management system* that manages the database containing the data users create, delete, modify, and query. Built on top of the database tier is the complex *middle tier*, which contains most of the application logic and communicates data between the other tiers. On top is the *client tier*, usually web browser software that interacts with the application.

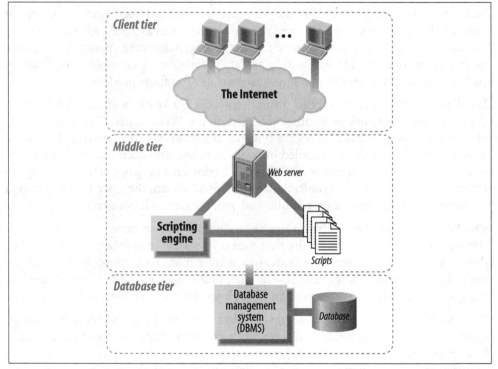

Figure 1-1. The three-tier architecture model of a web database application

The formality of describing most web database applications as three-tier architectures hides the reality that the applications must bring together different protocols and software. The majority of the material in this book discusses the middle tier and the application logic that brings together the fundamentally different client and database tiers.

When we use the term "the Web," we mean three major, distinct standards and the tools based on these standards: the Hypertext Markup Language (HTML), the Hypertext Transfer Protocol (HTTP), and the TCP/IP networking protocol suite. HTML works well for structuring and presenting information using a web browser application. TCP/IP is an effective networking protocol that transfers data between applications over the Internet and has little impact on web database application developers. The problem in building web database applications is interfacing traditional database applications to the Web using HTTP. This is where the complex application logic is needed.

Hypertext Transfer Protocol

The three-tier architecture provides a conceptual framework for web database applications. The Web itself provides the protocols and network that connect the client and middle tiers of the application; that is, it provides the connection between the web browser and the web server. HTTP is one component that binds together the three-tier architecture. A detailed knowledge of HTTP isn't necessary to understand the material in this book, but it's important to understand the problems HTTP presents for web database applications. The HTTP protocol is used by web browsers to request resources from web servers, and for web servers to return responses. (A longer introduction to the underlying web protocols—including more examples of HTTP requests and responses—can be found in Appendix B.)

HTTP allows resources to be communicated and shared over the Web. From a network perspective, HTTP is an *applications-layer protocol* that is built on top of the TCP/IP networking protocol suite. Most web servers and web browsers communicate using the current version, HTTP/1.1. Some browsers and servers use the previous version, HTTP/1.0, but most HTTP/1.1 software is backward-compatible with HTTP/1.0.

HTTP communications dominate Internet network traffic. In 1997, HTTP accounted for about 75% of all traffic.[*] We speculate that this percentage is now even higher due to the growth in the number and popularity of HTTP-based applications such as free email services.

HTTP example

HTTP is conceptually simple: a client web browser sends a *request* for a resource to a web server, and the web server sends back a *response*. The HTTP response carries the resource—the HTML document, image, or output of a program—back to the web browser as its payload. This simple request-response model is shown in Figure 1-2.

---

[*] From K. Thompson, G. J. Miller, and R. Wilder. "Wide-area internet traffic patterns and characteristics," *IEEE Network*, 11(6):10-23, November/December 1997.

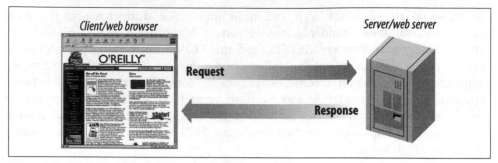

Figure 1-2. A web browser makes a request and the web server responds with the resource

An HTTP request is a textual description of a resource and additional header information. Consider the following example request:

```
GET /index.html HTTP/1.0
From: hugh@computer.org (Hugh Williams)
User-agent: Hugh-fake-browser/version-1.0
Accept: text/plain, text/html
```

This example uses a GET method to request an HTML page index.html with HTTP/1.0. In this example, three additional header lines identify the user and the web browser and define what data types can be accepted by the browser. A request is normally made by a web browser and may include other headers; the previous example was created manually by typing the request into Telnet software.

An HTTP response has a response code and message, additional headers, and usually the resource that has been requested. An example response to the request for index.html is as follows:

```
HTTP/1.0 200 OK
Date: Sat, 21 Jul 2002 03:44:25 GMT
Server: Apache/1.3.20
Content-type: text/html
Content-length: 88
Last-modified: Fri, 1 Feb 2002 03:40:03 GMT

<html><head>
<title>Test Page</title></head>
<body>
<h1>It Worked!</h1>
</body></html>
```

The first line of the response agrees to use HTTP/1.0 and confirms that the request succeeded by reporting the response code 200 and the message OK; another common response is 404 Not Found. In this example, five lines of additional headers identify the current date and time, the web server software, the data type, the length of the response, and when the resource was last modified. After a blank line, the resource itself follows. In this example the resource is the requested HTML document, index.html.

State

Traditional database applications are *stateful*. In traditional database applications, users log in, run related transactions, and then log out when they are finished. For example, in a bank application, a bank teller might log in, use the application through a series of menus as he serves customer requests, and log out when he's finished for the day. The bank application has state: once the teller is logged in, he can interact with the application in a structured way using menus. When the teller has logged out, he can no longer use the application.

HTTP is *stateless*. Statelessness means that any interaction between a web browser and a web server is independent of any other interaction. Each HTTP request from a web browser includes the same header information, such as the security credentials of the user, the types of pages the browser can accept, and instructions on how to format the response. Statelessness has benefits: the most significant are the resource savings from not having to maintain information at the web server to track a user, and the flexibility to allow users to move between unrelated pages or resources.

Because HTTP is stateless, it is difficult to develop stateful web database applications. What is needed is a method to maintain state in HTTP so that information flows and structure can be imposed. A common solution is to exchange a token between a web browser and a web server that uniquely identifies the user and her *session*. Each time a browser requests a resource, it presents the token, and each time the web server responds, it returns the token to the web browser. The token is used by the middle-tier software to restore information about a user from her previous request, such as which menu in the application she last accessed. Exchanging tokens allows stateful structure such as menus, steps, and workflow processes to be added to the application.

Thin Clients

Given that a web database application built with a three-tier architecture doesn't fit naturally with HTTP, why use that model at all? The answer mostly lies in the benefits of the *thin client*. Web browsers are very thin clients: little application logic is included in the client tier. The browser simply sends HTTP requests for resources and then displays the responses, which contain mostly HTML documents.

A three-tier model means you don't have to build, install, or configure the client tier. Any user who has a web browser can use the web database application, usually without needing to install additional software, be using a specific operating system, or own a particular hardware platform. This means an application can be delivered to any number of diverse, geographically dispersed users. The advantage is so significant that our focus in this book is entirely on three-tier solutions with this thin-client web browser architecture.

But what are the alternatives to a thin client? A custom-built Java applet is an example of a thicker client that can still fit the three-tier model: the user downloads an applet and runs more of the overall application logic on her platform. The applet still interacts with a middle tier that, in turn, provides an interface to the database tier. The advantage is customization: rather than using the generic browser solution, a custom solution can eliminate many problems inherent in the statelessness, security, and inflexibility of the Web. The applet might not even use HTTP to communicate with the middle-tier application logic.

A thick client is also part of a traditional two-tier solution, also known as a *client/server architecture*. Most traditional database applications—such as those in the bank—have only two tiers. The client tier has most of the overall application logic, and the server tier is the DBMS itself. The advantage is that a customized solution can be designed to meet the exact application requirements without any compromises. Disadvantages are the lack of hardware and operating system flexibility and the requirement to provide software to each user.

The Client Tier

The client tier in the three-tier architecture model is usually a web browser. Web browser software processes and displays HTML resources, issues HTTP requests for resources, and processes HTTP responses. As discussed earlier, there are significant advantages to using a web browser as the thin-client layer, including easy deployment and support on a wide range of platforms.

There are many browser products available, and each browser product has different features. The two most popular windowing-based browsers are Netscape and Internet Explorer. While we won't describe all the features of web browsers, they have a common basic set:

- All web browsers are HTTP clients that send requests and display responses from web servers (usually in a graphical environment).
- All browsers interpret pages marked up with HTML when rendering a page; that is, they present the headings, images, hypertext links, and so on to the user.
- Some browsers display images, play movies and sounds, and render other types of objects.
- Many browsers can run JavaScript that is embedded in HTML pages. JavaScript is used, for example, to validate a <form> or change how a page is presented based on user actions.
- Selected web browsers can run components developed in the Java or ActiveX programming languages. These components often provide additional animation, tools that can't be implemented in HTML, or other, more complex features.

- Several browsers can apply Cascading Style Sheets (CSS) to HTML pages to control the presentation of HTML elements.

There are subtle—and sometimes not so subtle—differences between the capabilities different browsers have in rendering an HTML page. Lynx, for example, is a text-only browser and doesn't display images or run JavaScript. MultiWeb is a browser that renders the text on a page as sound—the spoken word—providing web access for the vision-impaired. Many subtle but annoying differences are in the support for CSS and the features of the latest HTML standard, HTML 4.

Web browsers are the most obvious example of a *user agent*, a software client that requests resources from a web server. Other user agents include *web spiders*—automated software that crawls the Web and retrieves web pages—and *proxy caches*, software systems that retrieve and locally store web pages on behalf of many other user agents.

While this book isn't a guide to writing HTML, we discuss HTML features as they are used throughout the book. Pointers to resources that describe HTML, how to author web pages, and the direction of web page standards are included in Appendix E. We introduce JavaScript client-side scripting for validation of data entry and manipulating the web browser in Chapter 7.

The Middle Tier

In most three-tier web database systems, the majority of the application logic is in the middle tier. The client tier presents data to and collects data from the user; the database tier stores and retrieves the data. The middle tier serves most of the remaining roles that bring together the other tiers: it drives the structure and content of the data displayed to the user, and it processes input from the user as it is formed into queries on the database to read or write data. It also adds state management to the HTTP protocol. The middle-tier application logic integrates the Web with the database management system.

In the application framework used in this book, the components of the middle tier are a web server, a web scripting language, and the scripting language engine. A web server processes HTTP requests and formulates responses. In the case of web database applications, these requests are often for programs that interact with an underlying database management system. The web server we use throughout this book is the Apache Software Foundation's Apache HTTP server, the open source web server used by more than 60% of Internet connected computers.*

We use the PHP scripting language as our middle-tier scripting language. PHP is an open source project of the Apache Software Foundation and, not surprisingly, it is

---

* From *The Netcraft Web Server Survey*, *http://www.netcraft.com/survey/* (April 2001).

the most popular Apache HTTP server add-on module, with around 40% of the Apache HTTP servers having PHP capabilities.* PHP is particularly suited to web database applications because of its integration tools for the Web and database environments. In particular, the flexibility of embedding scripts in HTML pages permits easy integration with the client tier. The database-tier integration support is also excellent, with more than 15 libraries available to interact with almost all popular database management systems.

Web Servers

Web servers are often referred to as *HTTP servers*. The term "HTTP server" is a good summary of their function: their basic task is to listen for HTTP requests on a network, receive HTTP requests made by user agents (usually web browsers), serve the requests, and return HTTP responses that contain the requested resources.

There are essentially two types of request made to a web server: the first asks for a file—often a static HTML web page or an image—to be returned, and the second asks for a program to be run and its output to be returned to the user agent. Simple requests for files are further discussed in Appendix B.

Requests for web scripts that access a database are examples of HTTP requests that require a server to run a program. With the software used in this book, the HTTP requests are for PHP script resources, which require that the PHP Zend engine be run, a script retrieved and processed, and the script output captured.

The Apache HTTP server, Version 1.3

Like most users of the Apache HTTP server, we call it *Apache*. Apache is an open-source web server. The current release at the time of writing is 1.3.20.

The installation and configuration of Apache for most web database applications is straightforward. A concise installation guide for the Linux operating system is presented in Appendix A. Apache can be downloaded from *http://www.apache.org*; other Apache resources are listed in Appendix E.

Apache is fast and scalable. It can handle simultaneous requests from user agents and is designed to run under multitasking operating systems, such as Linux and 32-bit variants of Microsoft Windows. It's also lightweight, has low per-process requirements, can effectively handle changes in request loads, and can run fast on even modest hardware.

Apache—at least conceptually—isn't complicated. The web server is actually several processes, where one process coordinates the others. The coordinating process

---

* From the Security Space web server survey, Apache module report, *http://www.securityspace.com/s_survey/data/index.html* (April 2001).

usually runs with the permissions of the *superuser* or root user on a Unix machine and doesn't serve requests itself. The other processes, which usually run as more secure, permissionless users, notify their availability to handle requests to the coordinating server. If too few servers are available to handle incoming requests, the coordinating server may start new servers; if too many are free, it may kill spare servers to save resources.

How Apache listens on the network and serves requests is controlled by its configuration file. The server administrator controls the behavior of Apache through more than 150 directives that affect resource requirements, response time, flexibility in dealing with request load variability, security, how HTTP requests are handled and logged, and most other aspects of its operation. Careful adjustment of these parameters is important for performance, and more details of Apache configuration can be found in the resources listed in Appendix E.

The Apache HTTP server, Version 2.0

Version 1.3 of Apache has some limitations that will be addressed in Version 2.0. Version 2.0 is available for download, but at the time of writing remains in the beta-testing phase. Only around 20 sites are known to be using the beta version.

The significant enhancements in Apache 2.0 are:

- Use of lighter-weight processes or *threads* in conjunction with the process model on the older versions. This will most likely offer significant performance improvement in starting new servers and reduce the overall memory requirements of running servers.
- Better support, performance, and stability on non-Unix machines.
- Addition of filtering modules so that data can be modified as it is processed by the web server.
- Support for IPv6, the new version of the IP protocol in the TCP/IP networking suite.

Web Scripting with PHP

PHP has emerged as a component of many medium- and large-scale web database applications. This isn't to say that other scripting languages don't have excellent features. However, there are many reasons that make PHP a good choice, including:

- PHP is open source, meaning it is entirely free. As such, community efforts to maintain and improve it are unconstrained by commercial imperatives.
- One or more PHP scripts can be embedded into static HTML files and this makes client-tier integration easy. On the down side, this can blend the scripts with the presentation; however the template techniques described in Chapter 13 can solve most of these problems.

- There are over 15 libraries for native, fast access to the database tier.

- Fast execution of scripts. With the new innovations in the Zend engine for script processing, execution is fast, and all components run within the main memory space of PHP (in contrast to other scripting frameworks, in which components are in distinct modules). Empirical evidence suggests that for tasks of at least moderate complexity, PHP is faster than other popular scripting tools.

- Platform and operating-system flexibility. Apache runs on many different platforms and under selected operating systems; PHP runs on all these and more when integrated with other web servers.

- PHP is suited to complex systems development. It is a fully featured programming language, with more than 50 function libraries.

The current version of PHP is Version 4—we call this PHP throughout most of this book—and the current release at the time of writing is PHP 4.0.6.

PHP4 represents a complete rewrite of the underlying scripting engine used in PHP3. The significant difference is a change in the model used to run scripts with the scripting engine. The PHP3 scripting engine was an *interpreter*. Each line of code in a script was read, parsed, and executed. If a statement in the body of a loop is executed 100 times, the line of code is reinterpreted 100 times using PHP3. This model is slow for complex scripts, but fast for short scripts.

The PHP4 script-processing model is different and designed for larger applications. A script is read, parsed, and compiled into an intermediate format, and then the intermediate code is executed by the PHP4 Zend engine script *executor*. This means that each line in the script is interpreted from its raw form only once, even if it is executed hundreds of times. Moreover, compilation allows optimization of code segments. The result is a performance improvement in PHP4 for all but very simple scripts.

The architecture of the PHP4 scripting environment is shown in Figure 1-3 (image from Zend Technologies Inc.). As shown, PHP4 is a module of the web server software. The PHP software itself is divided into two components: the function libraries or modules, and the Zend engine.

When a user agent makes a request to the web server for a PHP script, six steps occur:

1. The web server passes the request to the Zend engine's web server interface.

2. The web server interface calls the Zend engine and passes parameters to the engine.

3. The PHP script is retrieved from disk by the engine.

4. The script is compiled by the runtime compiler.

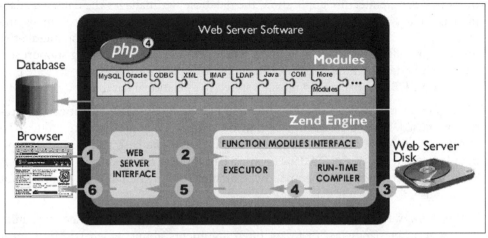

Figure 1-3. The architecture of the PHP4 scripting environment

5. The compiled code is run by the engine's executor and may include calls to function modules. The output of the executor is returned to the web server interface.

6. The web server interface returns output to the web server (which, in turn, returns the output as an HTTP response to the user agent).

How the PHP scripting engine is managed and run depends on how the PHP module is included in the Apache web server installation process. In the instructions provided in Appendix A, the PHP module library is *statically* linked with the Apache httpd binary executable. This means that the PHP scripting engine is loaded into main memory when Apache runs, making the PHP engine run faster. The drawbacks are that Apache with a static PHP library consumes more memory than if the module is loaded *dynamically*, and that the module upgrade process is less flexible.

Pointers to web resources, books, and commercial products for PHP development are listed in Appendix E.

The Database Tier

The database tier is the base of a web database application. Understanding system requirements, choosing database-tier software, designing databases, and building the tier are the first steps in successful web database application development. We discuss techniques for modeling system requirements, converting a model into a database, and the principles of database technology in Appendix C. In this section, we focus on the components of the database tier and introduce database software by contrasting it with other techniques for storing data. Chapter 3 covers the standards and software we use in more detail.

In a three-tier architecture application, the database tier manages the data. The data management typically includes storage and retrieval of data, as well as managing updates, allowing simultaneous, or *concurrent,* access by more than one middle-tier process, providing security, ensuring the integrity of data, and providing support services such as data backup. In many web database applications, these services are provided by a RDBMS system, and the data stored in a relational database.

Managing relational data in the third tier requires complex RDBMS software. Fortunately, most DBMSs are designed so that the software complexities are hidden. To effectively use a DBMS, skills are required to design a database and formulate commands and queries to the DBMS. For most DBMSs, the query language of choice is SQL. An understanding of the underlying architecture of the DBMS is unimportant to most users.

In this book, we use the MySQL RDBMS to manage data. Much like choosing a middle-tier scripting language, there are often arguments about which DBMS is most suited to an application. MySQL has a well-deserved reputation for speed, and it is particularly well designed for applications where retrieval of data is more common than updates and where small, simple updates are the general class of modifications. These are characteristics typical of most web database applications. Also, like PHP and Apache, MySQL is open source software. However, there are down sides to MySQL we'll discuss later in this section.

There are other, nonrelational DBMS software choices for storing data in the database tier. These include search engines, document management systems, and simple gateway services such as email software. Our discussions in this book focus on relational database technology in the database tier.

Database Management Systems

A database management system stores, searches, and manages data.

A *database* is a collection of related data. The data stored can be a few entries, or *rows,* that make up a simple address book of names, addresses, and phone numbers. In contrast, the database can also contain millions of records that describe the catalog, purchases, orders, and payroll of a large company. The database behind our case study, Hugh and Dave's Online Wines, is an example of a medium-sized database that falls between these two extremes.

A DBMS is a set of components for defining, constructing, and manipulating a database. When we refer to a database management system, we generally mean a relational DBMS or RDBMS. Relational databases store and manage relationships between data—for example, customers placing orders, customer orders containing line items, or wineries being part of a wine-growing region.

Figure 1-4 shows the simplified architecture of a typical DBMS.

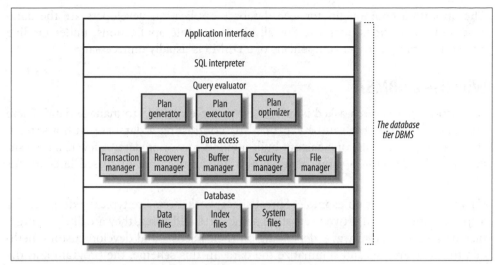

Figure 1-4. The architecture of a typical DBMS

A DBMS consists of several components:

Applications interface
   Libraries for communicating with the DBMS. Most DBMSs have a simple command-line interpreter that often uses these libraries to relay requests typed from the keyboard to the DBMS and to display responses. In a web database application, the command-line interpreter is usually replaced by a function library that is part of the middle-tier scripting language.

SQL interpreter
   A parser that checks the syntax of incoming query statements and translates these into an internal representation.

Query evaluator
   Generates different plans for evaluating a query by considering database statistics and properties, selects one of these plans, and translates the plan into low-level actions that are executed.

Data access
   The modules that manage access to the data stored on disk, including a transaction manager, a recovery manager, the main-memory buffer manager, data security manager, and the file and access method manager.

Database
   The physical data itself stored in data files. The data also contains *index* files for fast access to data, and database and system summary statistics primarily used for query plan generation and optimization.

The important components for web database application developers are the database and applications interface. For all but large-scale applications, understanding and configuring the other components of a DBMS is usually unnecessary.

Why Use a DBMS?

A question that is often asked is: why use a complex DBMS to manage data? There are several reasons that can be explained by contrasting a database with a spreadsheet, a simple text file, or a custom-built method of storing data. A few example situations where a DBMS should and should not be used are discussed later in this section.

Take spreadsheets as an example. Spreadsheet worksheets are typically designed for a specific application. If two users store names and addresses, they are likely to organize data in a different way—depending on their needs—and develop custom methods to move around and summarize the data. In this scheme, the program and the data aren't independent: moving a column might mean rewriting a macro or formula, while exchanging data between the two users' applications might be complex. In contrast, a DBMS and a database provide data-program independence, where the method for storing the data, the order of the stored information, and how the data is managed on disk are independent of the software that accesses it.

Managing complex relationships is difficult in a spreadsheet or text file. For example, consider our online winestore: if we want to store information about customers, we might allocate a few spreadsheet columns to store each customer's residential address. If we were to add business addresses and postal addresses, we'd need more columns and complex processing to, for example, process a mail-out to customers. If we want to store information about the purchases by our customers, the spreadsheet becomes wider still, and problems start to emerge. For example, it is difficult to determine the maximum number of columns needed to store orders and to design a method to process these for reporting.

Spreadsheets or text files don't work well when there are associations or relationships between stored data items. In contrast, DBMSs are designed to manage complex *relational* data. DBMSs are also a complete solution: if you use a DBMS, you don't need to design a custom spreadsheet or file solution. The methods that access the data—most often the query language SQL—are independent of how the data is physically stored and actually processed.

A DBMS usually permits multiuser transactions. Medium- and large-scale DBMSs include features that control the writing of data by multiple users in a methodical way. In contrast, a spreadsheet should be opened and written only by one user; if another user opens the spreadsheet, she won't see any updates being made at the same time by the first user. At best, a shared spreadsheet or text file permits very limited concurrent access.

An additional benefit of a DBMS is its speed. It isn't totally true to say that a database provides faster searching of data than a spreadsheet or a custom filesystem. In many cases, searching a spreadsheet or a special-purpose file might be perfectly acceptable, or even faster if it is designed carefully and the volume of data is small. However, for managing large amounts of related information, the underlying search structures in a DBMS can permit fast searching, and if information needs are complex, a DBMS should optimize the method of retrieving the data.

There are also other advantages of DBMSs, including data-oriented and user-oriented security, administration software, and data recovery support. A practical benefit is reduced application development time: the system is already built, it needs only data and queries to access the data.

Examples of when to use a DBMS

In any of these situations, a DBMS should probably be used to manage data:

- There is more than one user who needs to access the data at the same time.
- There is at least a moderate amount of data. For example, we may need to maintain information about a few hundred customers.
- There are relationships between the stored data items. For example, customers may have any number of related purchase orders.
- There is more than one kind of data record. For example, there might be information about customers, orders, inventory, and other data in an online store.
- There are constraints that must be rigidly enforced on the data, such as field lengths, field types, uniqueness of customer numbers, and so on.
- New or consolidated information must be produced from basic, related information; that is, the data must be queried to produce reports or results.
- There is a large amount of data that must be searched quickly.
- Security is important. There is a need to enforce rules as to who can access the data.
- Adding, deleting, or modifying data is a complex process.

Examples of when not to use a DBMS

There are some situations where a relational DBMS is probably unnecessary or unsuitable. Here are some examples:

- There is one type of data item, and the data isn't searched. For example, if a log entry is written when a user logs in and logs out, appending the entry to the end of a simple text file may be sufficient.
- The data-management task is trivial. In this case, the data might be coded into a web script in the middle tier, rather than adding the overhead of a database access each time the data is needed.

- The data requires complex analysis. For analysis, a spreadsheet package or statistical software may be more appropriate.

The MySQL DBMS

MySQL is a medium-scale DBMS, with most of the features of a large-scale system and the ability to manage very large quantities of data. Its design is ideally suited to managing the databases that are typical of many web database applications.

The difference between MySQL and some other systems is that MySQL is missing some querying support and has limited concurrency-handling abilities. In terms of concurrency, tens of middle-tier processes can access a database at the same time but not hundreds. Two querying techniques—specifically *nested querying* and *views*—aren't supported, but support is planned for the near future in MySQL Version 4. There are other, more minor limitations that don't typically affect web development.

The limitations of MySQL usually have a very minor impact on web database application development. However, for high-throughput systems, large numbers of concurrent users, or applications that modify the database frequently, other DBMSs may be considered. Our second choice would be PostgreSQL, which is known to be slower but supports more concurrent users. More information on PostgreSQL can be found at *http://www.postgresql.org*.

At the time of writing, the current version of MySQL is 3.23, and the current release is 3.23.38. MySQL resources are listed in Appendix E.

SQL

SQL is the standard relational database interaction language. Almost all relational database systems, including MySQL, support SQL as the tool to create, manage, secure, and query databases. Indeed, this is an important point about SQL: it is much more than just a query language; it is a fully fledged tool for all aspects of database management.

History

SQL has had a complicated life. It began at the IBM San Jose Research Laboratory in the early 1970s, where it was known as *Sequel*; some users still call it Sequel, though it's more correctly referred to by the three-letter acronym, SQL. After almost 16 years of development and differing implementations, the standards organizations ANSI and ISO published an SQL standard in 1986. IBM published a different standard one year later!

Since the mid-1980s, three subsequent standards have been published by ANSI and ISO. The first, SQL-89, is the most widely, completely implemented SQL in popular database systems. Many systems implement only some features of the next release,

SQL-2 or SQL-92, and almost no systems have implemented the features of the most recently approved standard, SQL-99 or SQL-3.

We focus on features found in the MySQL DBMS. MySQL supports the entry-level SQL-92 standard.

SQL components

SQL has four major parts, and we discuss two of them—the Data Definition Language (DDL) and the Data Manipulation Language (DML)—in detail in Chapter 3. The four major components of SQL are:

Data Definition Language
> DDL is the set of SQL commands that create and delete a database, add and remove tables, create indexes, and modify each of these. DDL commands are generally used only during the construction of the database. Indexes are structures for fast access and updates of data.

Data Manipulation Language
> DML is the set of commands that work with a DBMS and a database. DML commands include those to search, insert, and delete data. These commands are the tools that interact with a database during its normal use.

Transaction management
> SQL includes commands for treating a set of commands as a unit, or *transaction*. Using these tools, transactions can be undone, or *rolled back*.

Advanced features
> DML and DDL include advanced features for embedding SQL into general-purpose programming languages (in much the same way you can see SQL commands embedded in PHP in Chapter 4) and defining special-purpose views of the underlying data, and granting and removing access rights to the DBMS and databases. They also include commands for ensuring the integrity of the system; that is, ensuring the data is correct and that relational constraints are maintained correctly.

Transaction management and advanced features of SQL are discussed briefly in Chapters 3 and 6, and in Appendix C. Pointers to references on SQL can be found in Appendix E.

Our Case Study

The principles of web database applications are illustrated in practice throughout this book with the running example of Hugh and Dave's Online Wines. We refer to it as the *winestore* throughout the book.

The winestore application has many components of a typical web database application, including:

- Web pages populated with data from a database
- User-driven querying and browsing, in which the user provides the parameters that limit the searching or browsing of the database
- Data entry and validation. HTML <form> widgets collect data, and JavaScript client-side scripts and PHP server-side scripts perform validation.
- User tracking; that is, session management techniques that add state to HTTP
- User authentication and management
- Reporting

Let's take a look at the scope of the winestore and the system functional requirements. (The process of modeling these requirements with relational database entity-relationship (ER) modeling and converting this model to SQL statements is the subject of Appendix C. The completed winestore ER model and the SQL statements to create the database can be found in Chapter 3. We use the winestore components as examples beginning in Chapter 4. Completed components of the winestore application are discussed in Chapters 10 to 13.)

What Is Hugh and Dave's Online Wines?

Hugh and Dave's Online Wines is a fictional online wine retailer. In this section, we briefly detail the aims and scope of the winestore and then discuss the system requirements derived from these. We also introduce the technical components of the winestore and point to the chapters in the book where these components are discussed in detail. We conclude with a discussion of the shortcomings of the winestore and what isn't covered in this book. The completed winestore described in this section can be accessed via this book's web site.

The winestore is open to the public: anonymous users have limited access to the system, and users can make purchases if they become members. The site aims to be attractive, simple, and usable; however, since it was designed by two computer scientists, we failed to make it attractive! It succeeds better in its technical aims: the winestore manages over 1,000 wines, stock information, and a database of around 1,000 customers and their orders.

Any user with a web browser can access the site, browse or search for wines that are in stock, and view the details. The details of wines include the name, year of release, wine type, grape varieties, and, in some cases, an expert review of the wine. Anonymous users can add selected wines to a shopping cart. Users can also be members, and the membership application process collects details about the customer in the same way as at most online sites.

To purchase wines, users must log in using their membership details. If a user has just joined as a member, he is logged in automatically. After selecting wines for purchase, the user can place an order. An order is shipped immediately and a confirmation sent by email.

Behind the scenes, the system also allows the stock managers of the winestore to add new shipments of wines to the database. The web site manager can also add new wines, wineries, winery regions, and other information to the winestore. Limited reporting features are available.

System requirements

The following requirements can typically be gathered from a scope document, customer interviews, and so on. But, of course, this book isn't about software engineering processes, and we present here the general requirements that form a basis for the examples in this book. Some aspects of our requirements are simplified, some aspects of a commercial store are omitted, and some details are real-world and comprehensive.

The requirements listed here are an overview; a real-world commercial application would present these facts in detailed functional and system requirements. A production application would also have an accompanying design document discussing the database design, screen layouts, and information flows.

Here's a summary of the functional and systems requirements:

- The online winestore is primarily aimed as an e-commerce site to sell wine.
- The system doesn't manage accounting, stock control, payroll, ordering, and other tasks.
- Users may select wines and add them to a shopping basket. Users may purchase the items in their shopping baskets for up to one day after the first item is added to the basket. Users have only one shopping basket each and may empty their basket at any time.
- Users of the site may be anonymous and can remain anonymous until they agree to purchase the items in the shopping basket.
- To purchase items in a shopping basket, the user must log in to the system. To log in, a user must have an account. To get an account, a user must provide at least his surname, first name, one address line, a city, a zip code, a country, his birth date, an email address, and a password. The email address is used as the user's login name. The user may also optionally provide a middle initial, a title, two additional address lines, a state, a telephone number, and a fax number.
- When a user purchases wines, his order is archived.

- A user may receive a percentage discount on the price of an order. A discount can be levied on a particular day, a minimum threshold quantity, or given to a regular customer.

- An order may have a delivery charge that is levied according to the user's location and the delivery mode. Delivery modes include sea mail, regular mail, and express mail. An order may also have a note that is directed to the delivery company; for example, a note might indicate to "leave the wines at the back door of the house."

- Wines are classified into broad types of red, white, sparkling, sweet, and fortified. Wines also have a name, a vintage, and a description; descriptions are optional free-form text that are typically a review of the wine similar to that found on the label.

- Wines are made with different grape varieties, including Chardonnay, Semillon, Merlot, and so on. A wine can be made of any number of grape varieties, and the order of these grape varieties is important. For example, for a wine made of two varieties, Cabernet and Merlot, a Cabernet Merlot is different from a Merlot Cabernet.

- Users may browse wines at the winestore by type or wine region.

- Wines are produced by one winery.

- Wineries have a description—which is typically a review—as well as a phone and fax number.

- Wineries are in one region. A region is an area—for example, the Barossa Valley in South Australia—and each region has a description and, possibly, an image or map of the area.

- A shopping basket is an incomplete order that contains items. It can be converted to a completed order after the user logs in. Each item in an order is for a particular wine, a quantity of that wine to be purchased, and a price per bottle. The price of the wine is always the price of the first bottle of wine added to the shopping cart, which in turn is always the cheapest available inventory price.

- The quantities of wines in the shopping basket can be updated by the user, and items can be removed from the shopping basket.

- The wines available for sale are stored in an inventory. Each inventory record has a date added and is for a particular wine. The inventory contains a stock quantity available at a particular per-bottle and per-case price. There can be several inventory records for a wine, representing different shipments that arrived at the winestore on different dates or that have a different price.

- The user will always be advertised prices from the cheapest inventory for each wine. When a user adds a wine to her shopping basket, she is guaranteed this price.

- A user can purchase only wines that are in stock.

- When a user converts his shopping basket to an order, the availability of sufficient inventory to complete the order is checked. If insufficient wine is available, the user is alerted, and the quantities in the shopping basket are updated; this situation can occur if a user adds more wine to his basket than is available.

- When sufficient inventory is available to complete an order, the quantity of wine in the inventory is reduced as the order is finalized. The inventory reduced is always the oldest inventory of that wine.

Components of the Winestore

This section outlines where the principles and practical techniques to develop each component of the winestore are covered throughout this book. The completed winestore application is the subject of Chapters 10 through 13.

Database-driven querying

In Chapter 4, we introduce the techniques to connect to a DBMS, run a moderately complex SQL query, retrieve results, and process these results. To illustrate these techniques, we implement the Hot New Wines panel on the front page of the winestore. The completed panel is shown in Figure 1-5. The panel shows the newest three wines added to the database that have been reviewed by a wine expert. The completed shopping cart component is described in Chapter 11 and includes the panel code developed in Chapter 4.

User-driven querying and browsing

Users can display selected wines stocked at the winestore by entering simple search criteria.

The result of clicking Search after selecting wines of type "Red" in the "Margaret River" region is shown in Figure 1-6. The results screen shows the first 12 of 38 wines that match the criteria and has links at the base of the screen to allow users to move through the results.

The techniques for collecting user input with HTML <form> widgets, query formulation with user input, and results browsing are presented in Chapter 5. There we also introduce the basics of securing a web database application by preprocessing user input. The completed code for this module is in Chapter 13.

Data entry and saving records to a database

Chapter 6 introduces techniques to write data to a database. We illustrate the principles of writing data by developing a simple customer membership <form> in Chapters 6, 7, and 8. The complete implementation of the customer membership process is discussed in Chapter 10, and the completed <form> is shown in Figure 1-7.

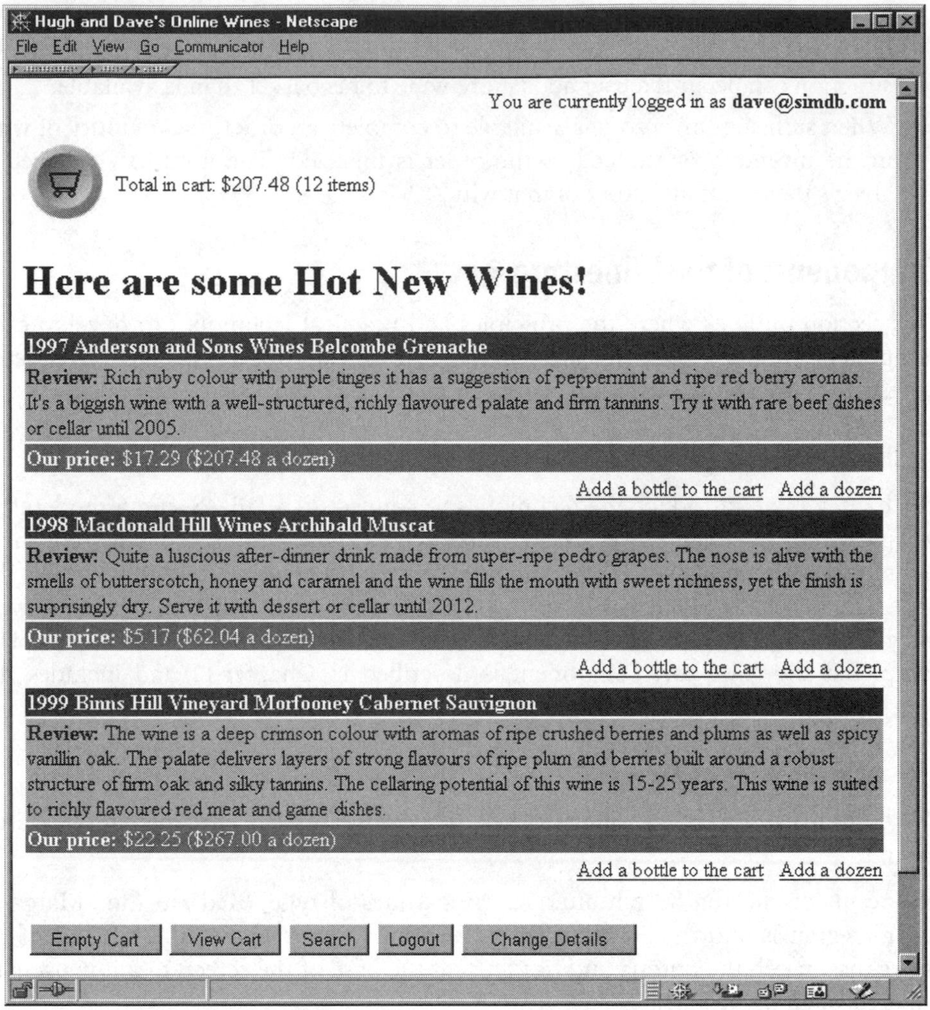

Figure 1-5. The completed front page panel with the Hot New Wines panel

Writing data requires careful consideration of how other users are interacting with the database at the same time. We introduce the theory and practice of writing to databases in Chapter 6, as well as the PHP functions to manage and report on the writing process.

Validation in the client and middle tiers

We continue our development of the simplified customer <form> in Chapter 7, where we introduce validation in the client and middle tiers. Validation in both tiers is important. Client-side validation with JavaScript lightens the web-server load in the middle tier, is fast for the user, and has no network overhead. Server-side validation

```
┌──────────────────────────────────────────────────────────────────────────┐
│ ☼ Hugh and Dave's Online Wines - Netscape                        _ □ ☒    │
│ File  Edit  View  Go  Communicator  Help                                   │
│ ▶···········/ ▶······/ ▶······/                                            │
├──────────────────────────────────────────────────────────────────────────┤
```

🛒 Total in cart: $207.48 (12 items)

Red wines of the Margaret River region.

1984 Anderson Daze Vineyard Titshall Shiraz Cabernet
Our price: $14.51 ($174.12 a dozen)   Add a bottle to the cart Add a dozen

1998 Anderson Daze Vineyard Tonkin Shiraz Cabernet Merlot
Our price: $22.32 ($267.84 a dozen)   Add a bottle to the cart Add a dozen

1982 Beard Daze Winery Ruscina Shiraz
Our price: $12.09 ($145.08 a dozen)   Add a bottle to the cart Add a dozen

1977 Beard Daze Winery Sears Cabernet Merlot
Our price: $27.94 ($335.28 a dozen)   Add a bottle to the cart Add a dozen

1975 Bell Daze Wines Nancarral Cabernet Sauvignon
Our price: $7.95 ($95.40 a dozen)   Add a bottle to the cart Add a dozen

1975 Bell Daze Wines Oaton Cabernet Merlot
Our price: $12.74 ($152.88 a dozen)   Add a bottle to the cart Add a dozen

1988 Bell Daze Wines Taggendharf Pinot Noir
Our price: $16.21 ($194.52 a dozen)   Add a bottle to the cart Add a dozen

1990 Borg Hill Premium Wines Leramonth Cabernet Merlot
Our price: $19.36 ($232.32 a dozen)   Add a bottle to the cart Add a dozen

1997 Borg Hill Premium Wines Lombardi Shiraz
Our price: $8.58 ($102.96 a dozen)   Add a bottle to the cart Add a dozen

1999 Buettner Station Vineyard Mellili Shiraz Cabernet
Our price: $17.52 ($210.24 a dozen)   Add a bottle to the cart Add a dozen

1991 Buettner Station Vineyard Sorrenti Shiraz
Our price: $24.39 ($292.68 a dozen)   Add a bottle to the cart Add a dozen

1978 Buettner Station Vineyard Woodburne Cabernet Sauvignon Add a bottle to the cart Add a dozen
Our price: $8.43 ($101.16 a dozen)

1-12 of 38 wines found matching your criteria
Previous 1 2 3 4 Next

Choose a wine region: | Margaret River ▾ |

Choose a wine type: | Red ▾ |

[Search] [Home] [Empty Cart] [View Cart] [Logout] [Change Details]

W3C HTML 4.01 ✓

```
├──────────────────────────────────────────────────────────────────────────┤
│ ⊡ ⊐⊨         Document: Done                    ▤ ☼ ▚ ⊟ ⊟ ✎            │
└──────────────────────────────────────────────────────────────────────────┘
```

Figure 1-6. Links at the bottom of the browse page allow users to move through the results set

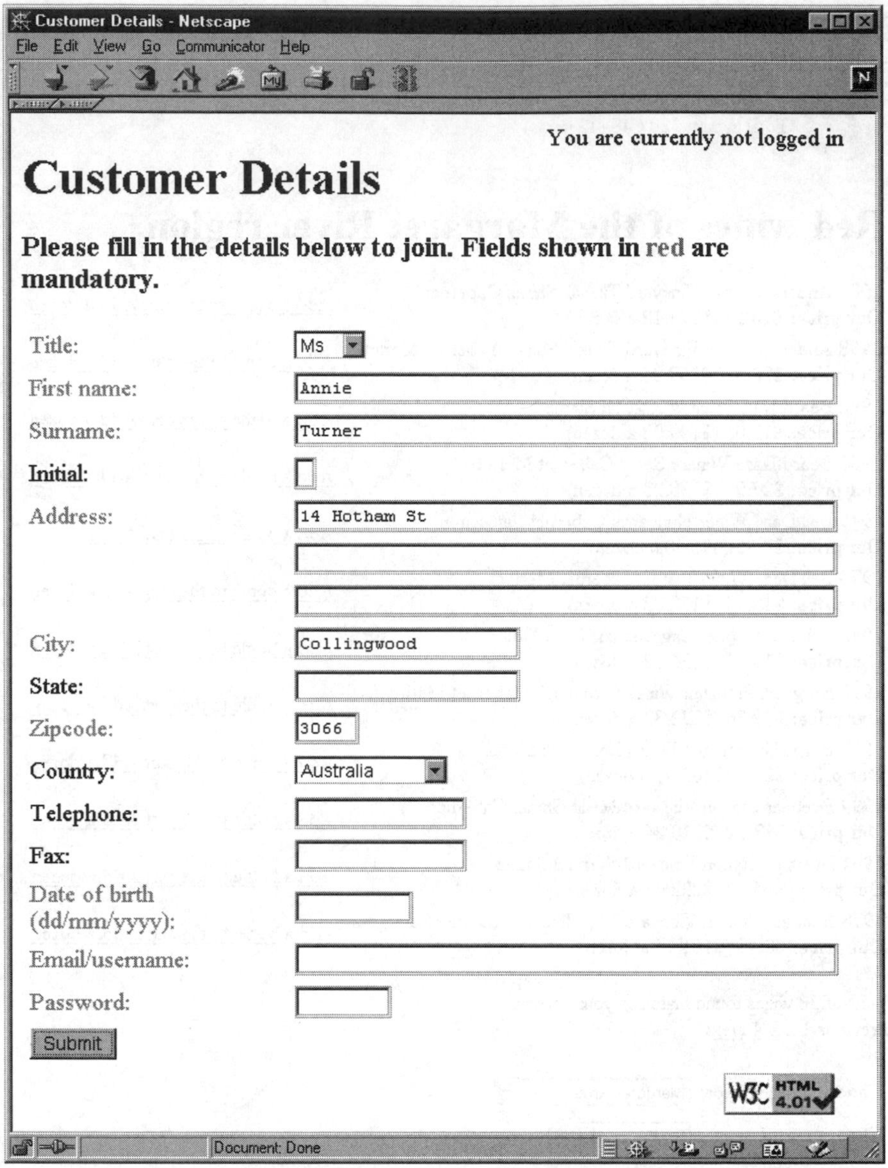

Figure 1-7. The customer <form> collects and updates member information

is also important: users can bypass client-tier validation or may not have it configured correctly, it may not be supported by the browser, and complete and complex validation might be possible only in the middle tier.

Figure 1-8 shows a customer <form> validation error message produced using the client-side JavaScript techniques discussed in Chapter 7.

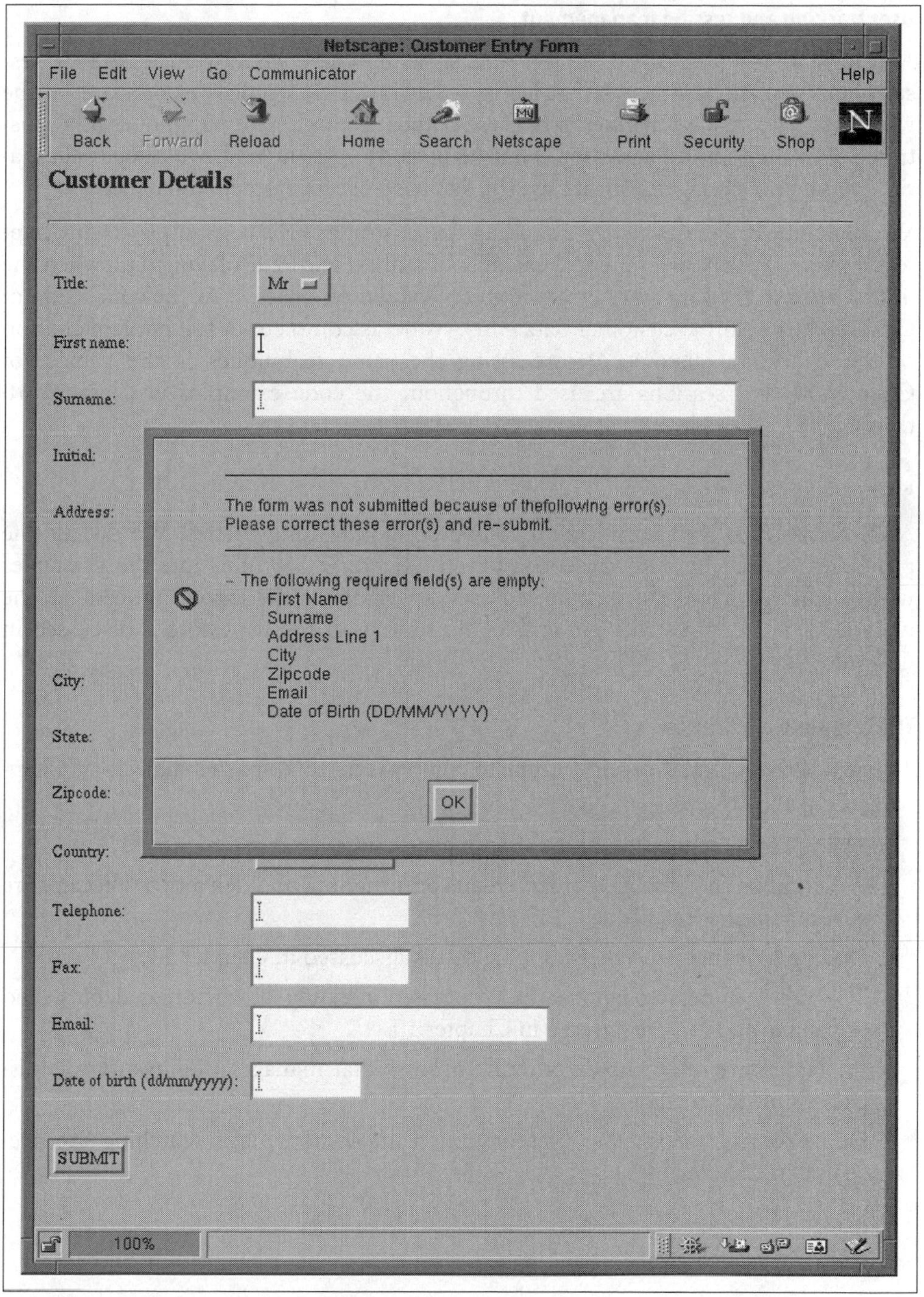

Figure 1-8. A JavaScript validation error for the winestore customer <form>

User tracking and session management

Adding state to HTTP is the subject of Chapter 8, where we introduce the PHP session-management techniques that manage the transaction processes of a user at the winestore. We discuss the merits of these session management techniques and illustrate when they should and should not be used. In Appendix D, we discuss alternatives to session management that use the database tier for state maintenance.

We illustrate PHP sessions by extending the customer <form> example from Chapters 6 and 7. We show a practical example of storing and redisplaying data when the user returns to fix data entry errors from the validation process. At the conclusion of Chapter 8, the simple customer data entry <form> is complete. A full implementation of the winestore customer <form> using the same techniques is the subject of Chapter 10, and sessions are used throughout the code examples in Chapters 10 through 13.

Authentication

Authentication is the identification of two communicating parties. We discuss the principles of security and authentication in Chapter 9. We illustrate the principles with examples from the customized customer login and logout process at the winestore. The completed login and logout process at the winestore is discussed in Chapter 10.

The complete application

The winestore includes several complete components that are the subjects of Chapters 10 through 13:

- The full implementation of the shopping cart is covered in Chapter 11.
- Presentation of a finalized order, email confirmation, and delivery of a receipt are covered in Chapter 12.
- Updating quantities in the shopping cart is discussed in Chapter 11.
- The full membership application process, amending of customer details, and logging in and out are covered in Chapter 10.
- Implementing the complex ordering process that manages the inventory is discussed in Chapter 12.
- Housekeeping, separating presentation from content, and searching are presented in Chapter 13.

PHP

In this chapter, we introduce the PHP scripting language. PHP is similar to high-level languages such as C, Perl, Pascal, FORTRAN, and Java, and programmers who have experience with any of these languages should have little trouble learning PHP. This chapter serves as an introduction to PHP; it's not a programming guide. We assume you are already familiar with programming in a high-level language.

The topics covered in this chapter include:

- PHP basics, including script structure, variables, supported types, constants, expressions, and type conversions
- Condition and branch statements supported by PHP, including if, if...else, and the switch statements
- Looping statements
- Arrays and array library functions
- Strings and string library functions
- Regular expressions
- Date and time functions
- Integer and float functions
- How to write functions, reuse components, and determine the scope and type of variables
- An introduction to PHP object-oriented programming support
- Common mistakes made by programmers new to PHP, and how to solve them

Programmers new to PHP should read the section "Introducing PHP," which describes the basic structure of a PHP script and its relationship to HTML, and includes discussion of how PHP handles variables and types. The two sections that follow, "Conditions and Branches" and "Loops," deal with conditional statements and looping structures and should be familiar material. We then present a short example that puts many of the basic PHP concepts together.

The remainder of the chapter expands on the more advanced features of PHP, presents a reference to selected library functions, and discusses some of the common mistakes that programmers make when learning PHP. This material can be examined briefly, and used later as a reference while reading Chapter 4 to 13 and while programming in PHP. However, programmers new to PHP should consider reading the beginning of the "Arrays" and "Strings" sections to understand the way PHP supports these concepts, as there are important differences from other languages.

We don't attempt to cover every function and every library that are supported by PHP. However, we provide brief descriptions of the supported libraries in Appendix E. In later chapters, we discuss more specialized library functions that support the topics and techniques presented here.

Introducing PHP

The current version of PHP is PHP4, which we call PHP throughout this book. The current release at the time of writing is 4.0.6.

PHP is a recursive acronym that stands for *PHP: Hypertext Preprocessor*; this is in the naming style of *GNU*, which stands for *GNU's Not Unix* and which began this odd trend. The name isn't a particularly good description of what PHP is and what it's commonly used for. PHP is a scripting language that's usually embedded or combined with HTML and has many excellent libraries that provide fast, customized access to DBMSs. It's an ideal tool for developing application logic in the middle tier of a three-tier application.

PHP Basics

Example 2-1 shows the first PHP script in this book, the ubiquitous "Hello, world." When requested by a web browser, the script is run on the web server and the resulting HTML document sent back to the browser and rendered as shown in Figure 2-1.

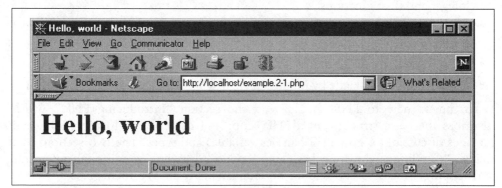

Figure 2-1. The rendered output of Example 2-1 shown in the Netscape browser

Example 2-1. The ubiquitous Hello, world in PHP

```
<!DOCTYPE HTML PUBLIC
    "-//W3C//DTD HTML 4.0 Transitional//EN"
    "http://www.w3.org/TR/html4/loose.dtd" >
<html>
<head>
  <title>Hello, world</title>
</head>
<body bgcolor="#ffffff">
  <h1>
  <?php
    echo "Hello, world";
  ?>
  </h1>
</body>
</html>
```

Example 2-1 illustrates the basic features of a PHP script. It's a mixture of HTML—in this case it's mostly HTML—and a PHP script. The script in this example:

```
<?php
  echo "Hello, world";
?>
```

simply prints the greeting, "Hello, world."

The PHP script shown in Example 2-1 is rather pointless: we could simply have authored the HTML to include the greeting directly. Because PHP integrates so well with HTML, using PHP to produce static strings is far less complicated and less interesting than using other high-level languages. However, the example does illustrate several features of PHP:

- The begin and end script tags are `<?php` and `?>` or, more simply, just `<?` and `?>`. The longer begin tag style `<?php` avoids conflicts with other processing instructions that can be used in HTML. We use both styles in this book.

  Other begin and end tag styles can also be configured, such as the HTML style that is used with JavaScript or other embedded scripts: `<script language="PHP">` and `</script>`.

- Whitespace has no effect, except to aid readability for the developer. For example, the script could have been written succinctly as `<?php echo "Hello, world";?>` with the same effect. Any mix of spaces, tabs, carriage returns, and so on in separating statements is allowed.

- A PHP script is a series of statements, each terminated with a semicolon. Our simple example has only one statement: `echo "Hello, world";`.

- A PHP script can be anywhere in a file and interleaved with any HTML fragment. While Example 2-1 contains only one script, there can be any number of PHP scripts in a file.

- When a PHP script is run, the entire script including the start and end script tags <?php and ?> is replaced with the output of the script.

 When we present a few lines of code that are sections of larger scripts, we usually omit the start and end tags.

The freedom to interleave any number of scripts with HTML is one of the most powerful features of PHP. A short example is shown in Example 2-2; a variable, $outputString="Hello, world", is initialized before the start of the HTML document, and later this string variable is output twice, as part of the <title> and <body> elements. We discuss more about variables and how to use them later in this chapter.

Example 2-2. Embedding three scripts in a single document

```
<?php $outputString = "Hello, world"; ?>
<!DOCTYPE HTML PUBLIC
    "-//W3C//DTD HTML 4.0 Transitional//EN"
    "http://www.w3.org/TR/html4/loose.dtd" >
<html>
<head>
  <title><?php echo $outputString; ?></title>
</head>
<body bgcolor="#ffffff">
  <h1><?php echo $outputString; ?></h1>
</body>
</html>
```

The flexibility to add multiple scripts to HTML can also lead to unwieldy, hard-to-maintain code. Care should be taken in modularizing code and HTML; we discuss how to separate code and HTML using templates in Chapter 13.

Creating PHP scripts

A PHP script can be written using plain text* and can be created with any text editor, such as *joe*, *vi*, *nedit*, *emacs*, or *pico*. If you save a PHP script in a file with a *.php* extension under the directory configured as Apache's document root, Apache executes the script when a request is made for the resource. Following the installation instructions given in Appendix A, the document root is:

```
/usr/local/apache/htdocs/
```

---

* While printable characters with the most significant bit are allowed, PHP scripts are usually written using characters from the 7-bit ASCII character set.

Consider what happens when the script shown in Example 2-1 is saved in the file:

```
/usr/local/apache/htdocs/example.2-1.php
```

Apache—when configured with the PHP module—executes the script when requests to the URL *http://localhost/example.2-1.php* are made, assuming the web browser is running on the same machine as the web server.

If directory permissions don't permit creation of files in the document root, it's also possible to work in the user home directories. If the installation instructions in Appendix A have been followed, a directory can be created by a user beneath her home directory and the permissions set so that the directory is readable by the web server:

```
mkdir ~/public_html
chmod a+rx ~/public_html
```

The example file can then be created with the filename:

```
~/public_html/example.2-1.php
```

The file can then be retrieved with the URL *http://localhost/~user/example.2-1.php*, where *user* is the user login name.

Comments

Comments can be included in code using familiar styles from other high-level programming languages. This includes the following styles:

```
// This is a one-line comment

#  This is another one-line comment style

/* This is how you
   can create a multi-line
   comment */
```

Outputting data with echo and print

The echo statement used in Examples 2-1 and 2-2 is frequently used and designed to output any type of data. The print statement can be used for the same purpose. Consider some examples:

```
echo "Hello, world";

// print works just the same
print "Hello, world";

// numbers can be printed too
echo 123;

// So can the contents of variables
echo $outputString;
```

The difference between `print` and `echo` is that `echo` can output more than one argument:

```
echo "Hello, ", "world";
```

There is also a shortcut that can output data. The following very short script outputs the value of the variable $temp:

```
<?=$temp; ?>
```

The `print` and `echo` statements are also often seen with parentheses:

```
echo "hello";

// is the same as
echo ("hello");
```

Parentheses make no difference to the behavior of `print`. However, when they are used with `echo`, only one output parameter can be provided.

The `echo` and `print` statements can be used for most tasks and can output any combination of static strings, numbers, arrays, and other variable types discussed later in this chapter. We discuss more complex output with `printf` in the "Strings" section later in this section.

String literals

PHP can create double- and single-quoted string literals. If double quotation marks are needed as part of a string, the easiest approach is to switch to the single-quotation style:

```
echo 'This works';
echo "just like this.";

// And here are some strings that contain quotes
echo "This string has a ': a single quote!";
echo 'This string has a ": a double quote!';
```

Quotation marks can be escaped like this:

```
echo "This string has a \": a double quote!";
echo 'This string has a \': a single quote!';
```

One of the convenient features of PHP is the ability to include the value of a variable in a string literal. PHP parses double-quoted strings and replaces variable names with the variable's value. The following example shows how:

```
$number = 45;
$vehicle = "bus";
$message = "This $vehicle holds $number people";

// prints "This bus holds 45 people"
echo $message;
```

To include backslashes and dollar signs in a double-quoted string, the escaped sequences \\ and \$ can be used. The single-quoted string isn't parsed in the same way as a double-quoted string and can print strings such as:

```
'a string with a \ and a $'
```

We discuss parsing of string literals in more detail in the "Strings" section.

Variables

Variables in PHP are identified by a dollar sign followed by the variable name. Variables don't need to be declared, and they have no type until they are assigned a value. The following code fragment shows a variable $var assigned the value of an expression, the integer 15. Therefore, $var is defined as being of type integer.

```
$var = 15;
```

Because the variable in this example is used by assigning a value to it, it's implicitly declared. Variables in PHP are simple: when they are used, the type is implicitly defined—or redefined—and the variable implicitly declared.

The variable type can change over the lifetime of the variable. Consider an example:

```
$var = 15;
$var = "Sarah the Cat";
```

This fragment is acceptable in PHP. The type of $var changes from integer to string as the variable is reassigned. Letting PHP change the type of a variable as the context changes is very flexible and a little dangerous.

Variable names are case-sensitive in PHP, so $Variable, $variable, $VAriable, and $VARIABLE are all different variables.

One of the most common sources of bugs in PHP is failing to detect that more than one variable has accidentally been created. The flexibility of PHP is a great feature but is also dangerous. We discuss later how to set the error reporting of PHP so that it creates warning messages sensitive to unassigned variables being used.

Types

PHP has four scalar types—boolean, float, integer, and string—and two compound types, array and object.

In this book, and particularly in this chapter, we present function prototypes that specify the types of arguments and return values. There are many functions that allow arguments or return values to be of different types, which we describe as *mixed*.

Variables of a scalar type can contain a single value at any given time. Variables of a compound type—array or object—are made up of multiple scalar values or other compound values. Arrays and objects have their own sections later in this chapter. Other aspects of variables—including global variables and scope—are discussed later, with user-defined functions.

Boolean variables are as simple as they get: they can be assigned either true or false. Here are two example assignments of a Boolean variable:

```
$variable = false;
$test = true;
```

An *integer* is a whole number, while a *float* is a number that has an exponent and a fractional part. The number 123.01 is a float, and so is 123.0. The number 123 is an integer. Consider the following two examples:

```
// This is an integer
$var1 = 6;

// This is a float
$var2 = 6.0;
```

A float can also be represented using an exponential notation:

```
// This is a float that equals 1120
$var3 = 1.12e3;

// This is also a float that equals 0.02
$var4 = 2e-2
```

You've already seen examples of strings earlier, when echo( ) and print( ) were introduced, and string literals are covered further in the "Strings" section. Consider two example string variables:

```
$variable = "This is a string";
$test = 'This is also a string';
```

Constants

Constants associate a name with a simple, scalar value. For example, the Boolean values true and false are constants associated with the values 1 and 0, respectively. It's also common to declare constants in a script. Consider this example constant declaration:

```
define("pi", 3.14159);

// This outputs 3.14159
echo pi;
```

Constants aren't preceded by a $ character; they can't be changed once they have been defined; they can be accessed anywhere in a script, regardless of where they are declared; and they can only be simple, scalar values.

Constants are useful because they allow parameters internal to the script to be grouped. When one parameter changes—for example, if you define a new maximum number of lines per web page—you can alter this constant parameter in only one place and not throughout the code.

Expressions, Operators, and Variable Assignment

We've already described simple examples of assignment, in which a variable is assigned the value of an *expression* using an equals sign. Most numeric assignments and expressions that work in other high-level languages also work in PHP. Here are some examples:

```
// Assign a value to a variable
$var = 1;

// Sum integers to produce an integer
$var = 4 + 7;

// Subtraction, multiplication, and division
// that might have a result that is a float or
// an integer, depending on the initial value of $var
$var = (($var - 5) * 2) / 3;

// These all add 1 to $var
$var = $var + 1;
$var += 1;
$var++;

// And these all subtract 1 from $var
$var = $var - 1;
$var -= 1;
$var--;

// Double a value
$var = $var * 2;
$var *= 2;

// Halve a value
$var = $var / 2;
$var /= 2;

// These work with float types too
$var = 123.45 * 28.2;
```

There are many mathematical functions available in the math library of PHP for more complex tasks. We introduce some of these in the "Integer and Float Functions" section.

String assignments and expressions are similar:

```
// Assign a string value to a variable
$var = "test string";
```

```
// Concatenate two strings together
// to produce "test string"
$var = "test" . " string";

// Add a string to the end of another
// to produce "test string"
$var = "test";
$var = $var . " string";

// Here is a shortcut to add a string to
// the end of another
$var .= " test";
```

Expressions

Expressions in PHP are formulated in much the same way as other languages. An expression is formed from literal values (integers, strings, floats, Booleans, arrays, and objects), operators, and function calls that return values. An expression has a value and a type; for example, the expression 4 + 7 has the value *11* and the type *integer,* and the expression "Kelpie" has the value *Kelpie* and the type *string*. PHP automatically converts types when combining values in an expression. For example, the expression 4 + 7.0 contains an integer and a float; in this case, PHP considers the integer as a floating-point number, and the result is a float. The type conversions are largely straightforward; however, there are some traps, which are discussed later in this section.

Operator precedence

The precedence of operators in an expression is similar to the precedence defined in any other language. Multiplication and division occur before subtraction and addition, and so on. However, reliance on evaluation order leads to unreadable, confusing code. Rather than memorize the rules, we recommend you construct unambiguous expressions with parentheses, because parentheses have the highest precedence in evaluation.

For example, in the following fragment $variable is assigned a value of 32 because of the precedence of multiplication over addition:

```
$variable = 2 + 5 * 6;
```

The result is much clearer if parentheses are used:

```
$variable = 2 + (5 * 6);
```

Type Conversion

PHP provides several mechanisms to allow variables of one type to be considered as another type. Variables can be explicitly converted to another type with the following functions:

```
string strval(mixed variable)
integer intval(mixed variable)
float floatval(mixed variable)
```

The function settype(mixed variable, string type) can explicitly set the type of *variable* to *type*, where *type* is again one of *array, boolean, float, integer, object*, or *string*.

PHP supports *type-casting* in much the same way as C, to allow the type of an expression to be changed. By placing the type name in parentheses in front of a variable, PHP converts the value to the desired type:

(int) $var or (integer) $var	Cast to integer
(bool) $var or (boolean) $var	Cast to Boolean
(float) $var, (double) $var or (real) $var	Cast to float
(string) $var	Cast to string
(array) $var	Cast to array
(object) $var	Cast to object

The rules for converting types are mostly common sense, but some conversions may not appear so straightforward. Table 2-1 shows how various values of $var are converted using the (int), (bool), (string), and (float) casting operators.

Table 2-1. Examples of type conversion in PHP using casting operators

Value of $var	(int) $var	(bool) $var	(string) $var	(float) $var
null	0	false	""	0
true	1	true	"1"	1
false	0	false	""	0
0	0	false	"0"	0
3.8	3	true	"3.8"	3.8
"0"	0	false	"0"	0
"10"	10	true	"10"	10
"6 feet"	6	true	"6 feet"	6
"foo"	0	true	"foo"	0

Automatic type conversion

Automatic type conversion occurs when two differently typed variables are combined in an expression or when a variable is passed as an argument to a library function that expects a different type. When a variable of one type is used as if it were another type, PHP automatically converts the variable to a value of the required type.

The same rules are used for automatic type conversion as are demonstrated in Table 2-1.

Some simple examples show what happens when strings are added to integers and floats and when strings and integers are concatenated:

```
// $var is set as an integer = 115
$var = "100" + 15;

// $var is set as a float = 115.0
$var = "100" + 15.0;

// $var is set as a string = "39 Steps"
$var = 39 . " Steps";
```

Not all type conversions are so obvious and can be the cause of hard-to-find bugs:

```
// $var is set as an integer = 39
$var = 39 + " Steps";

// $var is an integer = 42
$var = 40 + "2 blind mice";

// $var is a float, but what does it mean
$var = "test" * 4 + 3.14159;
```

Automatic type conversion can change the type of a variable. Consider the following example:

```
$var = "1"; // $var is a string == "1"
$var += 2;  // $var is now an integer == 3
$var /= 2;  // $var is now a float == 1.5
$var *= 2;  // $var is still a float == 3
```

Care must be taken when interpreting non-Boolean values as Boolean. Many library functions in PHP return values of different types: false if a valid result could not be determined, or a valid result. A valid return value of 0, 0.0, "0", an empty string, null, or an empty array is interpreted false when used as a Boolean value.

The solution is to test the type of the variable using the functions described in the next section.

Examining Variable Type and Content

Because PHP is flexible with types, it provides the following functions that can check a variable's type:

```
boolean is_int(mixed variable)
boolean is_float(mixed variable)
boolean is_bool(mixed variable)
boolean is_string(mixed variable)
boolean is_array(mixed variable)
boolean is_object(mixed variable)
```

All the functions return a Boolean value of true or false for the variable *variable,* depending on whether it matches the variable type that forms the name of the function. For example, the following prints 1, that is, true:

```
$test = 13.0;
echo is_float($test); // prints 1 for true
```

Debugging with print_r( ) and var_dump( )

PHP provides the print_r( ) and var_dump( ) functions, which print the type and value of an *expression* in a human-readable form:

```
print_r(mixed expression)
var_dump(mixed expression [, mixed expression ...])
```

These functions are useful for debugging a script, especially when dealing with arrays or objects. To test the value and type of $variable at some point in the script, the following code can be used:

```
$variable = 15;
var_dump($variable);
```

This prints:

```
int(15)
```

While the var_dump( ) function allows multiple variables to be tested in one call, and provides information about the size of the variable contents, print_r( ) provides a more concise representation of arrays and objects. These functions can be used on variables of any type, and we use them throughout this chapter to help illustrate the results of our examples.

Testing, setting, and unsetting variables

During the running of a PHP script, a variable may be in an unset state or may not yet be defined. PHP provides the isset( ) function and the empty( ) language construct to test the state of variables:

```
boolean isset(mixed var)
boolean empty(mixed var)
```

isset( ) tests if a variable has been set with a non-null value, while empty( ) tests if a variable has a value. The two are different, as shown by the following code:

```
$var = "test";

// prints: "Variable is Set"
if (isset($var)) echo "Variable is Set";

// does not print
if (empty($var)) echo "Variable is Empty";
```

A variable can be explicitly destroyed using unset( ):

```
unset(mixed var [, mixed var [, ...]])
```

After the call to unset in the following example, $var is no longer defined:

```
$var = "foo";

// Later in the script
unset($var);

// Does not print
if (isset($var)) echo "Variable is Set";
```

Another way to test that a variable is empty is to force it to the Boolean type using the (bool) cast operator discussed earlier. The example interprets the $var variable as type Boolean, which is equivalent to testing for !empty($var):

```
$var = "foo";

// Both lines are printed
if ((bool)$var)   echo "Variable is not Empty";
if (!empty($var)) echo "Variable is not Empty";
```

Table 2-2 show the return values for isset($var), empty($var), and (bool)$var when the variable $var is tested. Some of the results may be unexpected: when $var is set to "0", empty( ) returns true.

Table 2-2. Expression values

State of the variable $var	isset($var)	empty($var)	(bool)$var
$var = null;	false	true	false
$var = 0;	true	true	false
$var = true	true	false	true
$var = false	true	true	false
$var = "0";	true	true	false
$var = "";	true	true	false
$var = "foo";	true	false	true
$var = array( );	true	true	false
unset $var;	false	true	false

Conditions and Branches

The control structures in PHP are similar in syntax to those in other high-level programming languages.

Conditionals add control to scripts and permit branching so that different statements are executed depending on whether expressions are true or false. There are two branching statements in PHP: if, with the optional else clause, and switch, usually with two or more case clauses.

if...else Statement

The `if` statement conditionally controls execution and its use in PHP is as in any other language. The basic format of an `if` statement is to test whether a condition is true and, if so, to execute one or more statements.

The following `if` statement executes the echo statement and outputs the string when the conditional expression, $var is greater than 5, is true:

```
if ($var > 5)
    echo "The variable is greater than 5";
```

The `if` statement executes only the one, immediately following statement.

Multiple statements can be executed as a block by encapsulating the statements within braces. If the expression evaluates as `true`, the statements within braces are executed. If the expression isn't true, none of the statements are executed. Consider an example in which three statements are executed if the condition is true:

```
if ($var > 5)
{
    echo "The variable is greater than 5.";
    // So, now let's set it to 5
    $var = 5;
    echo "In fact, now it is equal to 5.";
}
```

The `if` statement can have an optional `else` clause to execute a statement or block of statements if the expression evaluates as `false`. Consider an example:

```
if ($var > 5)
    echo "Variable greater than 5";
else
    echo "Variable less than or equal to 5";
```

It's also common for the `else` clause to execute a block of statements in braces, as in this example:

```
if ($var > 5)
{
    echo "Variable is less than 5";
    echo "-----------------------";
}
else
{
    echo "Variable is equal to or larger than 5";
    echo "------------------------------------";
}
```

Consecutive conditional tests can lead to examples such as:

```
if ($var < 5)
    echo "Value is very small";
else
    if ($var < 10)
```

```
      echo "Value is small";
    else
      if ($var < 20)
        echo "Value is big";
      else
        if ($var < 30)
          echo "Value is very big";
```

If consecutive, cascading tests are needed, the elseif statement can be used. The choice of which method to use is a matter of personal preference. This example has the same functionality as the previous example:

```
if ($var < 5)
  echo "Variable is very small";
elseif ($var < 10)
  echo "Variable is small";
elseif ($var < 20)
  echo "Variable is big";
elseif ($var < 30)
  echo "Variable is very big";
```

switch Statement

The switch statement can be used as an alternative to if to select an option from a list of choices:

```
switch ($menu)
{
  case 1:
    echo "You picked one";
    break;
  case 2:
    echo "You picked two";
    break;
  case 3:
    echo "You picked three";
    break;
  case 4:
    echo "You picked four";
    break;
  default:
    echo "You picked another option";
}
```

This example can be implemented with if and elseif, but the switch method is usually more compact, readable, and efficient to type. The use of break statements is important: they prevent execution of statements that follow in the switch statement and continue execution with the statement that follows the closing brace.

If break statements are omitted from a switch statement, you get a bug. If the user chooses option 3, the script outputs not just:

```
"You picked three"
```

but also:

```
"You picked three. You picked four. You picked another option"
```

The fact that break statements are needed is sometimes considered to be a feature but is more often a source of difficult-to-detect bugs.

Conditional Expressions

The most common conditional comparison is to test the equality of two expressions with the Boolean result of true or false. Equality is tested with the double-equal operator, ==. Consider an example:

```
$var = 1;

if ($var == 1)
    echo "Equals one!";
```

If $var is equal to 1, the example evaluates as true and prints the message. If the example evaluates as false, nothing is printed.

Inequality can be tested with the != inequality operator:

```
$var = 0;

if ($var != 1)
    echo "Does not equal one!";
```

This evaluates as true and prints the message if $var isn't equal to 1. The operator != is usually referred to as the *not equals operator*, because the exclamation mark character negates an equality expression.

If the equality operator == and the assignment operator = are unfamiliar beware: they are easy to inadvertently interchange. This is a very common bug and hard to detect.

The incorrectly formed conditional expression ($var = 1) always evaluates as true, because the assignment that actually occurs always succeeds and, therefore, is always true.

The error of incorrectly replacing an assignment with == is a far less common mistake. However, it's also difficult to detect because an incorrectly written assignment of $var == 1; is quietly evaluated as true or false with no effect on $var.

Expressions can be combined with parentheses and with the Boolean operators && (and) and || (or). For example, the following expression returns true and prints the message if $var is equal to either 3 or 7:

```
if ($var == 3) || ($var == 7)
    echo "Equals 3 or 7";
```

The following expression returns true and prints the message if $var equals 2 and $var2 equals 6:

```
if ($var == 2) && ($var2 == 6)
    echo "The variables are equal to 2 and 6";
```

Interestingly, if the first part of the expression ($var == 2) evaluates as false, PHP doesn't evaluate the second part of the expression ($var2 == 6), because the overall expression can never be true; both conditions must be true for an && (and) operation to be true. This *short-circuit* evaluation property has implications for design; to speed code, write the expression most likely to evaluate as false as the left-most expression, and ensure that computationally expensive operations are as right-most as possible.

Never assume that expressions combined with the Boolean operators && and || are evaluated. PHP uses short-circuit evaluation when determining the result of a Boolean expression.

More complex expressions can be formed through combinations of the Boolean operators and the liberal use of parentheses. For example, the following expression evaluates as true and prints the message if one of the following is true: $var equals 6 and $var2 equals 7, or $var equals 4 and $var2 equals 1.

```
if ((($var == 6) && ($var2 == 7)) ||
    (($var == 4) && ($var2 == 1)))
    echo "Expression is true";
```

As in assignment expressions, parentheses ensure that evaluation occurs in the required order.

Equality and inequality are the two basic comparisons, but numbers are also compared to determine which is greater or lesser. Consider the following examples:

```
// Returns true if $var is less than 5
if ($var < 5)
    echo "Less than 5";

// Returns true if $var is less than or equal to 5
if ($var <= 5)
    echo "Less than or equal to 5";

// Returns true if $var is greater than 5
if ($var > 5)
    echo "Larger than 5";

// Returns true if $var is greater than or equal to 5
if ($var >= 5)
    echo "Equal to or larger than 5";
```

There is a new operator in PHP4, the is-identical operator ===. This isn't found in other languages and returns true only if the expression evaluates as equal and the arguments are of the same type. Consider an example:

```
// Returns true, since both are integers and equal
if (5 === 5)
  echo "Same types and value";

// Returns false, since there are mixed types
// (5.0 is a float, and 5 is an integer)
if (5.0 === 5)
  echo "This never prints!";

// The normal equality check would return true
if (5.0 == 5)
  echo "This always prints";
```

 The conditional expressions described here can compare strings but usually not with the expected results. If strings need to be compared— a common requirement—use the PHP string library function strcmp( ).

The strcmp( ) function is a string function used in this book and is discussed in more detail later in the "Strings" section.

Any of the Boolean expressions we have discussed can be negated with an exclamation mark !, the *unary not operator*. The following two expressions are equivalent:

```
if (!($var != 1))
  echo "variable is one";

if ($var == 1)
  echo "variable is one";
```

So are the following:

```
if ($var < 10)
  echo "less than 10";

if (!($var >= 10))
  echo "less than 10";
```

Probably the most common use of the unary not operator is to check if a function call fails, and we often use this with the database functions in later chapters.

Loops

Loops in PHP have the same syntax as other high-level programming languages.

Loops add control to scripts so that statements can be repeatedly executed as long as a conditional expression remains true. There are four loop statements in PHP: while, do...while, for, and foreach. The first three are general-purpose loop constructs, and foreach is used exclusively with arrays.

while

The while loop is the simplest looping structure but sometimes the least compact to use. The while loop repeats one or more statements—the loop body—as long as a condition remains true. The condition is checked first, then the loop body is executed. So, the loop never executes if the condition isn't initially true. Just as in the if statement, more than one statement can be placed in braces to form the loop body.

The following fragment illustrates the while statement by printing out the integers from 1 to 10 separated by a space character:

```
$counter = 1;
while ($counter < 11)
{
  echo $counter;
  echo " ";
  // Add one to $counter
  $counter++;
}
```

do...while

The difference between while and do...while is the point at which the condition is checked. In do...while, the condition is checked after the loop body is executed. As long as the condition remains true, the loop body is repeated.

You can emulate the functionality of the while example as follows:

```
$counter = 1;
do
{
  echo $counter;
  echo " ";
  $counter++;
} while ($counter < 11);
```

The contrast between while and do...while can be seen in the following example:

```
$counter = 100;
do
{
  echo $counter;
  echo " ";
  $counter++;
} while ($counter < 11);
```

This example outputs 100, because the body of the loop is executed once before the condition is evaluated as false.

The do...while loop is the least-frequently used loop construct, probably because executing a loop body once when a condition is false is an unusual requirement.

for

The for loop is the most complicated of the loop constructs, but it also leads to the most compact code.

Consider this fragment that implements the example used to illustrate while and do...while:

```
for($counter=1; $counter<11; $counter++)
{
  echo $counter;
  echo " ";
}
```

The for loop statement has three parts separated by semicolons, and all parts are optional:

Initial statements
Statements that are executed once, before the loop body is executed.

Loop conditions
The conditional expression that is evaluated before each execution of the loop body. If the conditional expression evaluates as false, the loop body is not executed.

End-loop statements
Statements that are executed each time after the loop body is executed.

The previous code fragment has the same output as our while and do...while loop count-to-10 examples. $counter=1 is an initial statement that is executed only once, before the loop body is executed. The loop condition is $counter<11, and this is checked each time before the loop body is executed; when the condition is no longer true—i.e., when $counter reaches 11—the loop is terminated. The end-loop statement $counter++ is executed each time after the loop body statements.

Our example is a typical for loop. The initial statements sets up a counter, the loop condition checks the counter, and the end-loop statement increments the counter. Most for loops used in PHP scripts have this format.

Conditions can be as complex as required, as in an if statement. Moreover, several initial and end-loop statements can be separated by commas. This allows for complexity:

```
for($x=0,$y=0; $x<10&&$y<$z; $x++,$y+=2)
```

However, complex for loops can lead to confusing code.

foreach

The foreach statement was introduced in PHP4 and provides a convenient way to iterate through the values of an array. Like a for loop, the foreach statement executes the loop body once for each value in an array. The following code fragment converts an array of centimeter values to inches for each value in the array:

```
// Construct an array of integers
$lengths = array(0, 107, 202, 400, 475);

// Convert an array of centimeter lengths to inches
foreach($lengths as $cm)
{
  $inch = (100 * $cm) / 2.45;
  echo "$cm centimeters = $inch inches\n";
}
```

The foreach loop is an extremely useful and convenient method of processing arrays and is discussed in detail in the "Using foreach Loops with Arrays" section.

Changing Loop Behavior

To break out of a loop early—before the loop condition becomes false—the break statement is useful. This example illustrates the idea:

```
for($x=0; $x<100; $x++)
{
  if ($x > $y)
    break;
  echo $x;
}
```

If $x reaches 100, the loop terminates normally. However, if $x is (or becomes) greater than $y, the loop is terminated early, and program execution continues after the loop body. The break statement can be used with all loop types.

To start again from the top of the loop without completing all the statements in the loop body, use the continue statement. Consider this example:

```
$x = 1;

while($x<100)
{
  echo $x;
  $x++;
  if ($x > $y)
    continue;
  echo $y;
}
```

The example prints and increments $x each time the loop body is executed. If $x is greater than $y, the loop is begun again from the top; otherwise, $y is printed, and the loop begins again normally. Like the break statement, continue can be used with any loop type.

A Working Example

In this section, we use the techniques described so far to develop a simple, complete PHP script. The script doesn't process input from the user, so we leave some of the best features of PHP as a web scripting language for discussion in later chapters.

Our example is a script that produces a web page containing the times tables. Our aim is to output the 1–12 times tables. The first table is shown in Figure 2-2 as rendered by a Netscape browser.

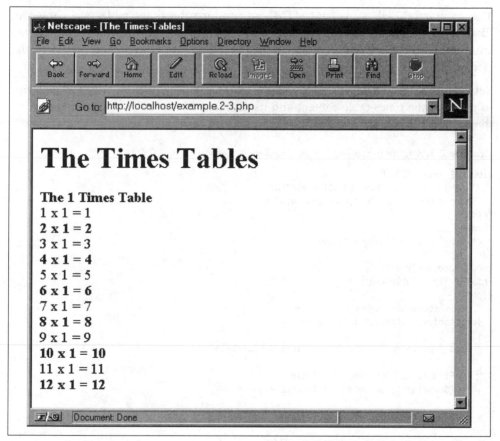

Figure 2-2. The output of the times-tables script shown rendered in a Netscape browser

To begin the development, we need to design how the output should appear and, therefore, what HTML needs to be produced. If we use simple HTML markup, the first 12 lines of the HTML produces Example 2-3 as follows:

```
<html>
<head>
  <title>The Times-Tables</title>
</head>
```

```
<body bgcolor="#ffffff">
<h1>The Times Tables</h1>
<p><b>The 1 Times Table</b>
<br>1 x 1 = 1
<br><b>2 x 1 = 2</b>
<br>3 x 1 = 3
<br><b>4 x 1 = 4</b>
<br>5 x 1 = 5
```

The script produces this output using a mixture of HTML and an embedded PHP script.

The completed PHP script and HTML to produce the times tables are shown in Example 2-3. The first nine lines are HTML that produces the <head> components and the <h1>The Times Tables</h1> heading at the top of the web page. Similarly, the last two lines are HTML that finishes the document: </body> and </html>.

Between the two HTML fragments that start and end the document is a PHP script to produce the times-table content and its associated HTML. The script begins with the PHP open tag <?php and finishes with the close tag ?>.

Example 2-3. A script to produce the times tables

```
<!DOCTYPE HTML PUBLIC
    "-//W3C//DTD HTML 4.0 Transitional//EN"
    "http://www.w3.org/TR/html4/loose.dtd" >
<html>
<head>
  <title>The Times-Tables</title>
</head>
<body bgcolor="#ffffff">
<h1>The Times Tables</h1>
<?php
  // Go through each table
  for($table=1; $table<13; $table++)
  {
    echo "<p><b>The " . $table . " Times Table</b>\n";

    // Produce 12 lines for each table
    for($counter=1; $counter<13; $counter++)
    {
      $answer = $table * $counter;

      // Is this an even-number counter?
      if ($counter % 2 == 0)
        // Yes, so print this line in bold
        echo "<br><b>$counter x $table = " .
             "$answer</b>";

      else
        // No, so print this in normal face
        echo "<br>$counter x $table = $answer";
```

Example 2-3. A script to produce the times tables (continued)

```
    }
  }
?>
</body>
</html>
```

The script is designed to process each times table and, for each table, to produce a heading and 12 lines. To do this, the script consists of two nested loops: an outer and inner for loop.

The outer for loop uses the integer variable $table, which is incremented by 1 each time the loop body is executed until $table is greater than 12. The body of the outer loop prints the heading and executes the inner loop that actually produces the body of each times table.

The inner loop uses the integer variable $counter to generate the lines of the times tables. Inside the loop body, the $answer to the current line is calculated by multiplying the current value of $table by the current value of $counter.

Every second line of the tables and the times-table headings are encapsulated in the bold tag `<b>` and bold end tag `</b>`, which produces alternating bold lines in the resulting HTML output. After calculating the $answer, an if statement follows that decides whether the line should be output in bold tags. The expression the if statement tests uses the modulo operator % to test if $counter is an odd or even number.

The modulo operation divides the variable $counter by 2 and returns the remainder. So, for example, if $counter is 6, the returned value is 0, because 6 divided by 2 is exactly 3 with no remainder. If $counter is 11, the returned value is 1, because 11 divided by 2 is 5 with a remainder of 1. If $counter is even, the conditional expression:

```
    ($counter % 2 == 0)
```

is true, and bold tags are printed.

Comments on Example 2.3

Example 2-3 is complete but isn't especially interesting. Regardless of how many times the script is executed, the result is the same web page. In practice, you might consider running the script once, capturing the output, and saving it to a static HTML file. If you save the output as HTML, the user can retrieve the same page, with less web-server load and a faster response time.

In Chapter 4, we introduce more PHP scripts that don't support input from the user. However, the difference is that the scripts interact with the MySQL DBMS and run SQL queries. The result is that the pages can change if the underlying data in the database is updated. Therefore, unlike our simple example here, the scripts in Chapter 4 may not be readily replaced with static HTML pages.

Arrays

Arrays in PHP are sophisticated and more flexible than in many other high-level languages. An *array* is an ordered set of variables, in which each variable is called an *element*. Technically, arrays can be either *numbered* or *associative*, which means that the elements of an array can be accessed by a numeric index or by a textual string, respectively.

In PHP, an array can hold scalar values—integers, Booleans, strings, or floats—or compound values—objects and even other arrays, and can hold values of different types. In this section, we show how arrays are constructed and introduce several useful array functions from the PHP library.

Creating Arrays

PHP provides the array( ) language construct that creates arrays. The following examples show how arrays of integers and strings can be constructed and assigned to variables for later use:

```
$numbers = array(5, 4, 3, 2, 1);
$words = array("Web", "Database", "Applications");

// Print the third element from the array
// of integers: 3
echo $numbers[2];

// Print the first element from the array
// of strings: "Web"
echo $words[0];
```

By default, the index for the first element in an array is 0. The values contained in an array can be retrieved and modified using the bracket [] syntax. The following code fragment illustrates the bracket syntax with an array of strings:

```
$newArray[0] = "Potatoes";
$newArray[1] = "Carrots";
$newArray[2] = "Spinach";

// Oops, replace the third element
$newArray[2] = "Tomatoes";
```

Numerically indexed arrays can be created to start at any index value. Often it's convenient to start an array at index 1, as shown in the following example:

```
$numbers = array(1=>"one", "two", "three", "four");
```

Arrays can also be sparsely populated, such as:

```
$oddNumbers = array(1=>"one", 3=>"three", 5=>"five");
```

An empty array can be created by assigning a variable with no parameters with array( ). Values can then be added using the bracket syntax. PHP automatically assigns the next numeric index—the largest current index plus one—when an index isn't supplied. Consider the following example, which creates an empty array $errors and tests whether that array is empty at the end of the script. The first error added with $errors[] is element 0, the second is element 1, and so on:

```
$errors = array();

// later in the code ..
$errors[] = "Found an error";

// ... and later still
$errors[] = "Something went horribly wrong";

// Now test for errors
if (empty($errors))
  // Phew. We can continue
  echo "Phew. We can continue";
else
  echo "There were errors";
```

Associative arrays

An associative array uses string indexes—or *keys*—to access values stored in the array. An associative array can be constructed using array(), as shown in the following example, which constructs an array of integers:

```
$array = array("first"=>1, "second"=>2, "third"=>3);

// Echo out the second element: prints "2"
echo $array["second"];
```

The same array of integers can also be created with the bracket syntax:

```
$array["first"] = 1;
$array["second"] = 2;
$array["third"] = 3;
```

There is little difference between using numerical or string indexes to access values. Both can reference elements of an associative array, but this is confusing and should be avoided in practice.

Associatively indexed arrays are particularly useful for interacting with the database tier. Arrays are used extensively in Chapters 4, 5, and 6, and more examples and array-specific functions are presented there.

Heterogeneous arrays

The values that can be stored in a single PHP array don't have to be of the same type; PHP arrays can contain *heterogeneous* values. The following example shows the heterogeneous array $mixedBag:

```
$mixedBag = array("cat", 42, 8.5, false);

var_dump($mixedBag);
```

The function var_dump( ) displays the contents (with a little whitespace added for clarity):

```
array(4) { [0]=> string(3) "cat"
           [1]=> int(42)
           [2]=> float(8.5)
           [3]=> bool(false) }
```

Multidimensional arrays

PHP arrays can also hold other arrays creating multidimensional arrays. Example 2-4 shows how multidimensional arrays can be constructed.

Example 2-4. Examples of multidimensional arrays in PHP

```
<!DOCTYPE HTML PUBLIC
    "-//W3C//DTD HTML 4.0 Transitional//EN"
    "http://www.w3.org/TR/html4/loose.dtd" >
<html>
<head>
  <title>Multi-dimensional arrays</title>
</head>
<body bgcolor="#ffffff">
<h2>A two dimensional array</h2>
<?php

  // A two dimensional array using integer indexes
  $planets = array(array("Mercury", 0.39, 0.38),
                   array("Venus", 0.72, 0.95),
                   array("Earth", 1.0, 1.0),
                   array("Mars", 1.52, 0.53) );

  // prints "Earth"
  print $planets[2][0]
?>

<h2>More sophisticated multi-dimensional array</h2>
<?php

  // More sophisticated multi-dimensional array
  $planets2 = array(
    "Mercury"=> array("dist"=>0.39, "dia"=>0.38),
    "Venus"  => array("dist"=>0.39, "dia"=>0.95),
    "Earth"  => array("dist"=>1.0,  "dia"=>1.0,
                "moons"=>array("Moon")),
    "Mars"   => array("dist"=>0.39, "dia"=>0.53,
                "moons"=>array("Phobos", "Deimos")),
  );
```

Example 2-4. Examples of multidimensional arrays in PHP (continued)

```
  // prints "Moon"
  print $planets2["Earth"]["moons"][0];
?>
</body>
</html>
```

The first array constructed in Example 2-4 is two-dimensional and is accessed using integer indexes. The array `$planets` contains four elements, each of which is an array that contains three values: the planet name, the distance from the Sun, and the planet diameter relative to the Earth.

The second array in Example 2-4 is a little more sophisticated: the array `$planets2` uses associative keys to identify an array that holds information about a planet. Each planet has an array of values that are associatively indexed by the name of the property that is stored; the array is effectively acting like a property list. For those planets that have moons, an extra property is added that holds an array of the moon names.

As stated in the introduction to this section, PHP arrays are very flexible. Many data structures—such as property lists, stacks, queues, and trees—can be created using arrays. We limit our usage of arrays to simple structures; the examination of more complex data structures is outside the scope of this book.

Using foreach Loops with Arrays

As we discussed earlier, the easiest way to iterate through—or traverse—an array is using the foreach statement. The foreach statement was specifically introduced in PHP4 to make working with arrays easier.

The foreach statement has two forms:

```
foreach(array_expression as $value) statement
foreach(array_expression as $key => $value) statement
```

Both iterate through an *array expression*, executing the body of the loop for each element in the array. The first form assigns the value from the element to a variable identified with the as keyword; the second form assigns both the key and the value to a pair of variables.

The following example shows the first form in which the array expression is the variable $lengths, and each value is assigned to the variable $cm:

```
  // Construct an array of integers
  $lengths = array(0, 107, 202, 400, 475);

  // Convert an array of centimeter lengths to inches
  foreach($lengths as $cm)
  {
    $inch = $cm / 2.54;
    echo "$cm centimeters = $inch inches\n";
  }
```

The example iterates through the array in the same order it was created:

```
0 centimeters = 0 inches
107 centimeters = 42.125984251969 inches
202 centimeters = 79.527559055118 inches
400 centimeters = 157.48031496063 inches
475 centimeters = 193.87755102041 inches
```

The first form of the foreach statement can also iterate through the values of an associative array, however the second form assigns both the key and the value to variables identified as $key => $value. The next example shows how the key is assigned to $animal, and the value is assigned to $sound to generate verses of "Old Mac-Donald":

```
// Old MacDonald
$sounds = array("cow"=>"moo", "dog"=>"woof",
                "pig"=>"oink", "duck"=>"quack");

foreach ($sounds as $animal => $sound)
{
    echo "<p>Old MacDonald had a farm EIEIO";
    echo "<br>And on that farm he had a $animal EIEIO";
    echo "<br>With a $sound-$sound here";
    echo "<br>And a $sound-$sound there";
    echo "<br>Here a $sound, there a $sound";
    echo "<br>Everywhere a $sound-$sound";
}
```

This prints a verse for each $animal/$sound pair in the $sounds array:

```
Old MacDonald had a farm EIEIO
And on that farm he had a cow EIEIO
With a moo-moo here
And a moo-moo there
Here a moo, there a moo
Everywhere a moo-moo

Old MacDonald had a farm EIEIO
And on that farm he had a dog EIEIO
With a woof-woof here
And a woof-woof there
Here a woof, there a woof
Everywhere a woof-woof
```

When the second form of the foreach statement is used with a nonassociative array, the index is assigned to the key variable and the value to the value variable. The following example uses the index to number each line of output:

```
// Construct an array of integers
$lengths = array(0, 107, 202, 400, 475);

// Convert an array of centimeter lengths to inches
foreach($lengths as $index => $cm)
{
    $inch = $cm / 2.54;
```

```
    $item = $index + 1;
    echo $index + 1 . ". $cm centimeters = $inch inches\n";
}
```

The foreach statement is used throughout Chapters 4 to 13.

Using Array Pointers

Along with the keys and the associated values stored in an array, PHP maintains an internal index that points to the current element in the array. Several functions use and update this array index to provide access to elements in the array. To illustrate how this internal index can be used, consider the following example:

```
$a = array("a", "b", "c", "d", "e", "f");
echo current($a);      // prints "a"

// Array ( [1]=> a [value]=> a [0]=> 0 [key]=> 0 )
print_r each($a);

// Array ( [1]=> b [value]=> b [0]=> 1 [key]=> 1 )
print_r each($a);

// Array ( [1]=> c [value]=> c [0]=> 2 [key]=> 2 )
print_r each($a);

echo current($a);      // prints "d"
```

The internal index is set to point at the first element when a new array is created, and the function current( ) returns the value pointed to by the array's internal index. The function each( ) returns an array that holds the index key and the value of the current element, and then increments the internal index of the array to point at the next element. The array each( ) returns has four elements: two that hold the key, accessed by the numeric index 0 and the associative key key; and two that hold the value, accessed by the numeric index 1 and the associative key value.

Other functions that use the array's internal pointer are end( ), next( ), prev( ), reset( ), and key( ).

Before the foreach statement was introduced to the PHP language, a common way to iterate through an associative array was to use a while loop with the each( ) function to get the key/value pairs for each element and the list( ) function to assign these values to variables. The following example shows how such an iteration is performed through the $sounds array to generate verses of "Old MacDonald":

```
$sounds = array ("pig"=>"oink", "cow"=>"moo",
                 "duck"=>"quack", "dog"=>"woof");

while (list($animal, $sound) = each($sounds))
{
   echo "<p>Old MacDonald had a farm EIEIO";
   echo "<br>And on that farm he had a $animal EIEIO";
```

```
    echo "<br>With a $sound-$sound here";
    echo "<br>And a $sound-$sound there";
    echo "<br>Here a $sound, there a $sound";
    echo "<br>Everywhere a $sound-$sound";
  }
```

The foreach statement is clearer and should be used in most cases. However we include the while loop example here because many existing scripts use this structure to iterate through an associative array.

The list() function isn't really a function, but a language construct that assigns multiple variables from an array expression:

```
list($var1, $var2, ...) = array_expression
```

list() appears on the left side of an assignment and an array expression appears on the right. The arguments to list() must be variables. The first variable is assigned the value of the first element in the array, the second variable the value from the second element, and so on. We avoid using the list() construct, because its use leads to assumptions about the number of elements in an array. The need to use list() to access the key/value pairs returned from each() is avoided with the foreach statement.

Basic Array Functions

In this section, we introduce selected basic PHP array library functions.

Counting elements in arrays

The count() function returns the number of elements in the array *var*:

```
integer count(mixed var)
```

The following example prints 7 as expected:

```
$days = array("Mon", "Tue", "Wed", "Thu",
              "Fri", "Sat", "Sun");

echo count($days);  // 7
```

The count() function works on any variable type and returns 0 when either an empty array or a variable that isn't set is examined. If there is any doubt, isset() and is_ array() should be used to check the variable being considered.

Finding the maximum and minimum values in an array

The maximum and minimum values can be found from an array *numbers* with max() and min(), respectively:

```
number max(array numbers)
number min(array numbers)
```

If an array of integers is examined, the returned result is an integer, if an array of floats is examined, min( ) and max( ) return a float:

```
$var = array(10, 5, 37, 42, 1, -56);
echo max($var);   // prints 42
echo min($var);   // prints -56
```

Both min( ) and max( ) can also be called with a list of integer or float arguments:

```
number max(number arg1, number arg2, number arg3, ...)
number min(number arg1, number arg2, number arg3, ...)
```

Both max( ) and min( ) work with strings or arrays of strings, but the results may not always be as expected.

Finding values in arrays with in_array( ) and array_search( )

The in_array( ) function returns true if an array *haystack* contains a specific value *needle*:

```
boolean in_array(mixed needle, array haystack [, boolean strict])
```

The following example searches the array of integers $smallPrimes for the integer 19:

```
$smallPrimes = array(3, 5, 7, 11, 13, 17, 19, 23, 29);

if (in_array(19, $smallPrimes))
   echo "19 is a small prime number"; // Always printed
```

A third, optional argument can be passed that enforces a strict type check when comparing each element with the *needle*. In the following example in_array( ) by default returns true; however, with strict type checking, the string "19" doesn't match the integer 19 held in the array and returns false:

```
$smallPrimes = array(3, 5, 7, 11, 13, 17, 19, 23, 29);

if (in_array("19", $smallPrimes, true))
   echo "19 is a small prime number"; // NOT printed
```

The array_search( ) function—introduced with PHP 4.0.5—works the same way as the in_array( ) function, except the key of the matching value *needle* is returned rather than the Boolean value true:

```
mixed array_search(mixed needle, array haystack [, boolean strict])
```

However, if the value isn't found, array_search( ) returns false. The following fragment shows how array_search( ) works with both associative and indexed arrays:

```
$measure = array("inch"=>1, "foot"=>12, "yard"=>36);

// prints "foot"
echo array_search(12, $measure);

$units = array("inch", "centimeter", "chain", "furlong");
```

```
// prints 2
echo array_search("chain", $units);
```

Because array_search( ) returns a mixed result—the Boolean value false if the value isn't found or the key of the matching element—a problem is encountered when the first element is found. PHP's automatic type conversion treats the value 0—the index of the first element—as false in a Boolean expression.

 Care must be taken with functions, such as array_search( ), that return a result or the Boolean value false to indicate when a result can't be determined. If the return value is used as a Boolean—in an expression or as a Boolean parameter to a function—a valid result may be automatically converted to false. If such a function returns 0, 0.0, "c", an empty string, or an empty array, PHP's automatic type conversion converts the result to false when a Boolean value is required.

The correct way to test the result is to use the is-identical operator ===, as shown in the following example:

```
$index = array_search("inch", $units);

if ($index === false)
  echo "Unknown unit: inch";
else
  // OK to use $index
  echo "Index = $index";
```

Reordering elements in arrays with array_reverse( )

Often it's useful to consider an array in reverse order. The array_reverse( ) function creates a new array by reversing the elements from a *source* array:

```
array array_reverse(array source [, bool preserve_keys])
```

The following example shows how to reverse an indexed array of strings:

```
$count = array("zero", "one", "two", "three");

$countdown = array_reverse($count);
```

Setting the optional *preserve_keys* argument to true reverses the order but preserves the association between the index and the elements. For a numerically indexed array, this means that the order of the elements is reversed, but the indexes that access the elements don't change. This might seem a bit weird, but the following example shows what is happening:

```
$count = array("zero", "one", "two", "three");
$countdown = array_reverse($count, true);
print_r($countdown);
```

This prints:

```
Array ([3] => three [2] => two [1] => one [0] => zero)
```

Sorting Arrays

In the previous section we showed how to reverse the elements of an array. In this section we show how to sort arrays. Unlike the array_reverse( ) function that returns a copy of the source array in the new order, the sorting functions rearrange the elements in the source array itself. Because of this behavior, the sort functions must be passed a variable, not an expression.

Sorting with sort( ) and rsort( )

The simplest array-sorting functions are sort( ) and rsort( ), which rearrange the elements of the *subject* array in ascending and descending order, respectively:

```
sort(array subject [, integer sort_flag])
rsort(array subject [, integer sort_flag])
```

Both functions sort the *subject* array based on the values of each element. The following example shows the sort( ) function on an array of integers:

```
$numbers = array(24, 19, 3, 16, 56, 8, 171);
sort($numbers);

foreach($numbers as $n)
  echo $n . " ";
```

The output of the example prints the elements sorted by value:

```
3 8 16 19 24 56 171
```

Another way to examine the contents of the sorted array is to use the print_r( ) function described in the "Examining Variable Type and Content" section. The output of the statement print_r($numbers) shows the sorted values with the associated index:

```
Array ( [0] => 3
        [1] => 8
        [2] => 16
        [3] => 19
        [4] => 24
        [5] => 56
        [6] => 171 )
```

The following example shows the rsort( ) function on the same array:

```
$numbers = array(24, 19, 3, 16, 56, 8, 171);
rsort($numbers);
print_r($numbers);
```

The output of the example shows the elements sorted in reverse order by value:

```
Array ( [0] => 171
        [1] => 56
        [2] => 24
        [3] => 19
```

```
[4] => 16
[5] => 8
[6] => 3 )
```

By default, PHP sorts strings in alphabetical order and numeric values in numeric order. An optional parameter, sort_flag, can be passed to force the string or numeric sorting behavior. In the following example, the PHP constant SORT_STRING sorts the numbers as if they were strings:

```
$numbers = array(24, 19, 3, 16, 56, 8, 171);
sort($numbers, SORT_STRING);
print_r($numbers);
```

The output of the example shows the result:

```
Array ( [0] => 16
        [1] => 171
        [2] => 19
        [3] => 24
        [4] => 3
        [5] => 56
        [6] => 8 )
```

Many of the array sorting functions accept a sort_flag parameter. Other sort flags are SORT_REGULAR to compare items in the array normally and SORT_NUMERIC that forces items to be compared numerically.

sort( ) and rsort( ) can be used on associative arrays, but the keys are lost. The resulting array contains only the values in the sorted order. Consider the following example:

```
$map =
    array("o"=>"kk", "e"=>"zz", "z"=>"hh", "a"=>"rr");

sort($map);
print_r($map);
```

The print_r( ) output shows the modified array without the key values:

```
Array ( [0] => hh [1] => kk [2] => rr [3] => zz )
```

Sorting associative arrays

It's often desirable to keep the key/value associations when sorting associative arrays. To maintain the key/value association the asort( ) and arsort( ) functions are used:

```
asort(array subject [, integer sort_flag])
arsort(array subject [, integer sort_flag])
```

Like sort( ) and rsort( ), these functions rearrange the elements in the *subject* array from lowest to highest and highest to lowest, respectively. The following example shows a simple array sorted by asort( ):

```
$map =
    array("o"=>"kk", "e"=>"zz", "z"=>"hh", "a"=>"rr");

asort($map);
print_r($map);
```

The print_r( ) function outputs the structure of the sorted array:

```
Array ( [z] => hh
        [o] => kk
        [a] => rr
        [e] => zz )
```

When assort( ) and arsort( ) are used on nonassociative arrays, the order of the elements is arranged in sorted order, but the indexes that access the elements don't change. This might seem a bit weird; effectively the indexes are treated as association keys in the resulting array. The following example shows what is happening:

```
$numbers = array(24, 19, 3, 16, 56, 8, 171);
asort($numbers);
print_r($numbers);
```

This outputs:

```
Array ( [2] -> 3
        [5] => 8
        [3] => 16
        [1] => 19
        [0] => 24
        [4] => 56
        [6] => 171 )
```

Sorting on keys

Rather than sort on element values, the ksort( ) and krsort( ) functions rearrange elements in an array by sorting on the keys or the indexes:

```
integer ksort(array subject [, integer sort_flag])
integer krsort(array subject [, integer sort_flag])
```

ksort( ) sorts the elements in the *subject* array from lowest key to highest key, and krsort( ) sorts in the reverse order. The following example demonstrates the ksort( ) function:

```
$map =
    array("o"=>"kk", "e"=>"zz", "z"=>"hh", "a"=>"rr");

ksort($map);
print_r($map);
```

The sorted array $map is now:

```
Array ( [a] => rr
        [e] => zz
        [o] => kk
        [z] => hh )
```

There is little point in using ksort( ) on an integer-indexed array because the keys are already in order. When krsort( ) is used on an indexed array, it reverses the order of the elements.

Sorting with user-defined element comparison

The sorting functions described so far in this section sort elements in alphabetic, numeric, or alphanumeric order. To sort elements based on user-defined criteria, PHP provides three functions:

```
usort(array subject, string compare_function)
uasort(array subject, string compare_function)
uksort(array subject, string compare_function)
```

usort( ) sorts the *subject* array based on the value of each element, uasort( ) pre-serves the key/value associations as described earlier for the asort( ) function, and uksort( ) rearranges the elements based on the key of each element. When these functions sort the *subject* array, the user-defined compare function is called to deter-mine if one element is greater than, lesser than, or equal to another. The compare function can be written to implement any sort order, but the function must conform to the prototype:

```
integer my_compare_function(mixed a, mixed b)
```

We discuss how to write functions in more detail in the "User-Defined Functions" section. The compare function takes two arguments, *a* and *b*, and returns −1 if *a* is less than *b*, 1 if *a* is greater than *b*, and 0 if *a* and *b* are equal. How the function deter-mines that one value is less than, greater than, or equal to another depends on the requirements of sorting. The following example shows how usort( ) sorts an array of strings based on the length of each string:

```
// Compare two string values based on the length
function cmp_length($a, $b)
{
  if (strlen($a) < strlen($b)) return -1;
  if (strlen($a) > strlen($b)) return 1;

  // String lengths must be equal
  return 0;
}

$animals =
  array("cow", "ox", " hippopotamus", "platypus");

usort($animals, "cmp_length");

print_r($animals);
```

The array $animals is printed:

```
Array ([0]=>ox [1]=>cow [2]=>platypus [3]=>hippopotamus)
```

In this example, cmp_length( ) is defined as the compare function, but it isn't called directly by the script. The name of the function, "cmp_length", is passed as an argument to usort( ), and usort( ) uses cmp_length( ) as part of the sorting algorithm. User-defined functions used in this way are often referred to as *callback functions.*

PHP has several library functions that allow user-defined behavior through user-defined callback functions. The array_map( ) and array_walk( ) functions allow user-defined functions to be applied to the elements of an array. We provide another example in Appendix D where we implement user-defined session management.

Strings

A string of characters—a string—is probably the most commonly used data type when developing scripts, and PHP provides a large library of string functions to help transform, manipulate, and otherwise manage strings. We introduced PHP strings earlier, in the "PHP Basics" section. Here, we examine string literals in more detail and describe some of the useful string functions PHP provides.

String Literals

As already shown in previous examples, enclosing characters in single quotes or double quotes can create a string literal. Single-quoted strings are the simplest form of string literal; double-quoted strings are parsed to substitute variable names with the variable values and allow characters to be encoded using escape sequences. Single-quoted strings don't support all the escape sequences, only \' to include a single quote and \\ to include a backslash.

Tab, newline, and carriage-return characters can be included in a double-quoted string using the escape sequences \t, \n, and \r, respectively. To include a backslash, a dollar sign, or a double quote in a double-quoted string, use the escape sequences \\, \$, or \".

Other control characters and characters with the most significant bit set can be included using escaped octal or hexadecimal sequences. For example, to include the umlauted character ö, the octal sequence \366 or the hexadecimal sequence \xf6 are used:

```
//Print a string that includes a lowercase
//o with the umlaut mark
echo "See you at the G\xf6teborg Film Festival";
```

PHP uses eight-bit characters in string values, so the range of characters that can be represented is \000 to \377 in octal notation or \x00 to \xff in hexadecimal notation.

Unlike many other languages, PHP allows newline characters to be included directly in a string literal. The following example show the variable $var assigned with a string that contains a newline character:

```
// This is Ok. $var contains a newline character
$var = 'The quick brown fox
        jumps over the lazy dog';
```

This feature is used in later chapters to construct SQL statements that are readable in the source code, for example:

```
$query = "SELECT max(order_id)
          FROM orders
          WHERE cust_id = $custID";
```

Other control characters, such as tabs and carriage returns, and characters with the most significant bit set—those in the range \x80 to \xff—can also be directly entered into a string literal. We recommend that escape sequences be used in practice to aid readability and portability of source files.

Variable substitution

Variable substitution provides a convenient way to output variables embedded in string literals. When PHP parses double-quoted strings, variable names are identified when a $ character is found and the value of the variable is substituted. We have already used examples earlier in this chapter such as:

```
$cm = 127;
$inch = $cm / 2.54;

// prints "127 centimeters = 50 inches"
echo "$cm centimeters = $inch inches";
```

When the name of the variable is ambiguous, braces {} can delimit the name as shown in the following example:

```
$memory = 256;

// Fails: no variable called $memoryMbytes
$message = "My computer has $memoryMbytes of RAM";

// Works: Curly braces are used delimit variable name
$message = "My computer has {$memory}Mbytes of RAM";

// This also works
$message = "My computer has ${memory}Mbytes of RAM";
```

Braces are also used for more complex variables, such as multidimensional arrays and objects:

```
echo "Mars is {$planets['Mars']['dia']} times the diameter of the Earth";

echo "There are {$order->count} green bottles ...";
```

Example 2-4 shows how the multidimensional array $planets is assigned, and objects and the member access operator -> are discussed in the "Objects" section.

Length of a string

The length property of a string is determined with the strlen() function, which returns the number of eight-bit characters in the *subject* string:

```
integer strlen(string subject)
```

Consider an example that prints 16:

```
print strlen("This is a String");  // prints 16
```

Printing and Formatting Strings

Earlier we presented the basic method for outputting text—with echo and print—and the functions print_r() and var_dump(), which can determine the contents of variables during debugging.

PHP provides several other functions that allow more complex and controlled formatting of strings.

Creating formatted output with sprintf( ) and printf( )

Sometimes more complex output is required than can be produced with echo or print. For example, a floating-point value such as 3.14159 might need to be truncated to 3.14 as it is output. For complex formatting, the sprintf() or printf() functions are useful:

```
string sprintf (string format [, mixed args...])
integer printf (string format [, mixed args...])
```

The operation of these functions is modeled on the identical C programming language functions, and both expect a string with optional conversion specifications, followed by variables or values as arguments to match any formatting conversions. The difference between sprintf() and printf() is that the output of printf() goes directly to the output buffer PHP uses to build a HTTP response, whereas the output of sprintf() is returned as a string.

Consider an example printf statement:

```
printf("Result: %.2f\n", $variable);
```

The format string Result: %.2f\nis the first parameter to the printf statement. Strings like Result: are output the same as with echo or print. The %.2f component is a conversion specification:

- All conversion specifications begin with a % character.
- The f indicates how the type of value should be interpreted. The f means the value should be interpreted as a floating-point number, for example, 3.14159 or

128.23765. Other possibilities include b, c, d, and s, where b means binary, c means a single character, d means integer, and s means string.

- The .2 is an optional width specifier. In this example, .2 means two decimal places, so the overall result of %.2f is that a floating-point number with two decimal places is output. A specifier %5.3f means that the minimum width of the number before the decimal point should be five (by default, the output is padded on the left with space characters and right-aligned), and three digits should occur after the decimal point (by default, the output on the right of the decimal point is padded on the right with zeros).

In the example, the value that is actually output using the formatting string %.2f is the value of the second parameter to the printf function—the variable $variable.

To illustrate other uses of printf, consider the examples in Example 2-5.

Example 2-5. Using printf to output formatted data

```
<!DOCTYPE HTML PUBLIC
    "-//W3C//DTD HTML 4.0 Transitional//EN"
    "http://www.w3.org/TR/html4/loose.dtd" >
<html>
<head>
  <title>Examples of using printf( )</title>
</head>
<body bgcolor="#ffffff">
<h1>Examples of using printf( )</h1>
<pre>
<?php
  // Outputs "3.14"
  printf("%.2f\n", 3.14159);

  // Outputs "      3.14"
  printf("%10.2f\n", 3.14159);

  // Outputs "3.1415900000"
  printf("%.10f\n", 3.14159);

  // Outputs "halfofthe"
  printf("%.9s\n", "halfofthestring");

  // Outputs "    3.14 3.141590       3.142"
  printf("%5.2f %f %7.3f\n", 3.14159, 3.14159, 3.14159);

  // Outputs "1111011 123 123.000000 test"
  printf("%b %d %f %s\n", 123, 123, 123, "test");
?>
</pre>
</body>
</html>
```

Padding strings

A simple method to space strings is to use the str_pad( ) function:

```
string str_pad(string input, int length [, string padding [, int pad_type]])
```

Characters are added to the input *string* so that the resulting string is characters in *length*. The following example shows the simplest form of str_pad( ) that adds spaces to the end of the input string:

```
// prints "PHP" followed by three spaces
echo str_pad("PHP", 6);
```

An optional string argument *padding* can be supplied that is used instead of the space character. By default, *padding* is added to the end of the string. By setting the optional argument pad_type to STR_PAD_LEFT or to STR_PAD_BOTH, the padding is added to the beginning of the string or to both ends. The following example shows how str_pad( ) can create a justified index:

```
$players =
    array("DUNCAN, king of Scotland"=>"Larry",
          "MALCOLM, son of the king"=>"Curly",
          "MACBETH"=>"Moe",
          "MACDUFF"=>"Rafael");

echo "<pre>";

// Print a heading
echo str_pad("Dramatis Personae", 50, " ", STR_PAD_BOTH) . "\n";

// Print an index line for each entry
foreach($players as $role=>$actor)
  echo str_pad($role, 30, ".")
      . str_pad($actor, 20, ".", STR_PAD_LEFT) . "\n";

echo "</pre>";
```

The example prints:

```
                Dramatis Personae
DUNCAN, king of Scotland....................Larry
MALCOLM, son of the king....................Curly
MACBETH.......................................Moe
MACDUFF....................................Rafael
```

Changing case

The following PHP functions return a copy of the *subject* string with changes in the case of the characters:

```
string strtolower(string subject)
string strtoupper(string subject)
string ucfirst(string subject)
string ucwords(string subject)
```

The following fragment shows how each operates:

```
print strtolower("PHP and MySQL"); // php and mysql
print strtoupper("PHP and MySQL"); // PHP AND MYSQL
print ucfirst("now is the time");  // Now is the time
print ucwords("now is the time");  // Now Is The Time
```

Trimming whitespace

PHP provides three functions that trim leading or trailing whitespace characters—null, tab, vertical-tab, newline, carriage-return, and space characters—from strings:

```
string ltrim(string subject)
string rtrim(string subject)
string trim(string subject)
```

The three functions return a copy of the *subject* string: trim( ) removes both leading and trailing whitespace characters, ltrim( ) removes leading whitespace characters, and rtrim( ) removes trailing whitespace characters. The following example shows the effect of each:

```
$var = trim(" Tiger Land\n");  // "Tiger Land"
$var = ltrim(" Tiger Land\n"); // "Tiger Land\n"
$var = rtrim(" Tiger Land\n"); // " Tiger Land"
```

Rendering newline characters with

Whitespace characters generally don't have any significance in HTML, but it's often useful to preserve newlines when a page is rendered. The nl2br( ) function generates a string by inserting the HTML break element
* before all occurrences of the newline character in the *source* argument:

```
string nl2br(string source)
```

The following example shows how nl2br( ) works:

```
// A short poem
$verse = "Isn't it funny\n";
$verse .= "That a bear likes honey.\n";
$verse .= "I wonder why he does?\n";
$verse .= "Buzz, buzz, buzz.\n";

// The four lines are rendered as one
echo $verse;

// Renders the poem on four lines in HTML as intended
echo nl2br($verse);
```

---

* From PHP Version 4.0.5 onwards, nl2br( ) inserts the XHTML-compliant <br /> markup that includes the shorthand way of closing an empty element. Earlier versions inserted <br>, which isn't valid XML.

Comparing Strings

PHP provides the string comparison functions strcmp( ) and strncmp( ) that safely compare two strings, *str1* and *str2*:

```
integer strcmp(string str1, string str2)
integer strncmp(string str1, string str2, integer length)
```

While the equality operator == can compare two strings, the result isn't always as expected when the strings contain characters with the most significant bit set. Both strcmp( ) and strncmp( ) take two strings as arguments, *str1* and *str2*, and return 0 if the strings are identical, 1 if *str1* is less than *str2*, and −1 if *str1* is greater that *str2*. The function strncmp( ) takes a third argument *length* that restricts the comparison to *length* characters. These examples show the results of various comparisons:

```
print strcmp("aardvark", "zebra");       // -1
print strcmp("zebra", "aardvark");       // 1
print strcmp("mouse", "mouse");          // 0
print strncmp("aardvark", "aardwolf", 4); // 0
print strncmp("aardvark", "aardwolf", 5); // -1
```

The functions strcasecmp( ) and strncasecmp( ) are case-insensitive versions of strcmp( ) and strncmp( ).

The functions strncmp( ), strcasecmp( ), or strncasecmp( ) can be used as the callback function when sorting arrays with usort( ).

Finding and Extracting Substrings

PHP provides several simple and efficient functions that can identify and extract specific substrings of a string.

Extracting a substring from a string

The substr( ) function returns a substring from a *source* string:

```
string substr(string source, integer start [, integer length])
```

When called with two arguments, substr( ) returns the characters from the *source* string starting from position *start*—counting from zero—to the end of the string. With the optional *length* argument, a maximum of *length* characters are returned. The following examples show how substr( ) works:

```
$var = "abcdefgh";

print substr($var, 2);      // "cdefgh"
print substr($var, 2, 3);   // "cde"
print substr($var, 4, 10);  // "efgh"
```

If a negative *start* position is passed, the starting point of the returned string is counted from the end of the *source* string. If the *length* is negative, it's treated as the index, and the returned string ends *length* characters from the end of the *source* string. The following examples show how negative indexes can be used:

```
$var = "abcdefgh";

print substr($var, -1);      // "h"
print substr($var, -3);      // "fgh"
print substr($var, -5, 2);   // "de"
print substr($var, -5, -2);  // "def"
```

Finding the position of a substring

The strpos( ) function returns the index of the first occurring substring *needle* in the string *haystack*:

```
integer strpos(string haystack, string needle [, integer offset])
```

When called with two arguments, the search for the substring *needle* is from the start of the string *haystack* at position zero. When called with three arguments, the search occurs from the index *offset* into the *haystack*. The following examples show how strpos( ) works:

```
$var = "To be or not to be";

print strpos($var, "T");    // 0
print strpos($var, "be");   // 3

// Start searching from the 5th character in $var
print strpos($var, "be", 4); // 16
```

The strrpos( ) function returns the index of the last occurrence of the single character *needle* in the string *haystack*:

```
integer strrpos(string haystack, string needle)
```

Unlike strpos( ), strrpos( ) searches for only a single character, and only the first character of the *needle* string is used. The following examples show how strrpos( ) works:

```
$var = "To be or not to be";

// Prints 13: the last occurrence of "t"
print strrpos($var, "t");

// Prints 0: Only searches for "T" which
// is found at position zero
print strrpos($var, "Tap");

// False: "Z" does not occur in the subject
onlyprint strrpos($var, "Zoo");
```

If the substring *needle* isn't found by strpos( ) or strrpos( ), both functions return false. The is-identical operator === should be used when testing the returned value from these functions against false. If the substring *needle* is found at the start of the string *haystack*, the index returned is zero and is interpreted as false if used as a Boolean value.

Extracting a found portion of a string

The strstr( ) and stristr( ) functions search for the substring *needle* in the string *haystack* and return the portion of *haystack* from the first occurrence of *needle* to the end of *haystack*:

```
string strstr(string haystack, string needle)
string stristr(string haystack, string needle)
```

The strstr( ) search is case-sensitive; the stristr( ) search isn't. If the *needle* isn't found in the *haystack* string, both strstr( ) and stristr( ) return false. The following examples show how the functions work:

```
$var = "To be or not to be";

print strstr($var, "to");    // "to be"
print stristr($var, "to");   // "To be or not to be"
print stristr($var, "oz");   // false
```

The strrchr( ) function returns the portion of *haystack* by searching for the single character *needle*; however, strrchr( ) returns the portion from the last occurrence of *needle*:

```
string strrchr(string haystack, string needle)
```

Unlike strstr( ) and stristr( ), strrchr( ) searches for only a single character, and only the first character of the *needle* string is used. The following examples show how strrchr( ) works:

```
$var = "To be or not to be";

// Prints: "not to be"
print strrchr($var, "n");

// Prints "o be": Only searches for "o" which
// is found at position 14
print strrchr($var, "oz");
```

Extracting multiple values from a string

PHP provides the explode( ) and implode( ) functions, which convert strings to arrays and back to strings:

```
array explode(string separator, string subject [, integer limit])
string implode(string glue, array pieces)
```

The explode( ) function returns an array of strings created by breaking the *subject* string at each occurrence of the *separator* string. The optional integer *limit* determines the maximum number of elements in the resulting array; when the *limit* is met, the last element in the array is the remaining unbroken *subject* string. The implode( )

function returns a string created by joining each element in the array *pieces*, inserting the string *glue* between each piece. The following example shows both the implode( ) and explode( ) functions:

```
$guestList = "Sam Meg Sarah Ben Jess May Adam";
$name = "Fred";

// Check if $name is in the $guestList
if (strpos($guestList, $name) === false)
{
  $guestArray = explode(" ", $guestList);
  sort($guestArray);
  echo "Sorry '$name' is not on the guest list.\n";
  echo "Guest list: " . implode(", ", $guestArray)
}
```

When the string $name isn't found in the string $guestList using strpos( ), the fragment of code prints a message to indicate that $name isn't contained in the list. The message includes a sorted list of comma-separated names: explode( ) creates an array of guest names that is sorted and then, using implode( ), is converted back into a string with each name separated by a comma and a space. The example prints:

```
Sorry 'Fred' is not on the guest list.
Guest list: Adam, Ben, Jess, May, Meg, Sam, Sarah
```

Replacing Characters and Substrings

PHP provides several simple functions that can replace specific substrings or characters in a string with other strings or characters. In the next section we discuss powerful tools for finding and replacing complex patterns of characters. The functions described in this section, however, are more efficient than regular expressions and are often the better choice when searching and replacing strings.

Replacing substrings

The substr_replace( ) function replaces a substring identified by an index with a replacement string:

```
string substr_replace(string source, string replace, int start [, int length])
```

Returns a copy of the *source* string with the characters from the position *start* to the end of the string replaced with the *replace* string. If the optional *length* is supplied, only *length* characters are replaced. The following examples show how substr_replace( ) works:

```
$var = "abcdefghij";

// prints "abcDEF";
echo substr_replace($var, "DEF", 3);

// prints "abcDEFghij";
```

```
echo substr_replace($var, "DEF", 3, 3);

// prints "abcDEFdefghij";
echo substr_replace($var, "DEF", 3, 0);
```

The str_replace( ) function returns a string created by replacing occurrences of the string *search* in *subject* with the string *replace*:

```
mixed str_replace(mixed search, mixed replace, mixed subject)
```

In the following example, the *subject* string, "old-age for the old", is printed with both occurrences of old replaced with new:

```
$var = "old-age for the old.";

echo str_replace("old", "new", $var);
```

The result is:

```
new-age for the new.
```

Since PHP Version 4.0.5, str_replace( ) allows an array of search strings and a corresponding array of replacement strings to be passed as parameters. The following example shows how the fields in a very short form letter can be populated:

```
// A short form-letter for an overdue account
$letter = "Dear #title #name, You owe us $#amount.";

// Set-up an array of three search strings that
// will be replaced in the form-letter
$fields = array("#title", "#name", "#amount");

// An array of debtors. Each element is an array that
// holds the replacement values for the form-letter
$debtors = array(
    array("Mr", "Cartwright", "146.00"),
    array("Ms", "Yates", "1,662.00"),
    array("Dr", "Smith", "84.75"));

foreach($debtors as $debtor)
  echo "<p>" . str_replace($fields, $debtor, $letter);
```

The output of this script is as follows:

```
Dear Mr Cartwright, You owe us $146.00.
Dear Ms Yates, You owe us $1,662.00.
Dear Dr Smith, You owe us $84.75.
```

If the array of replacement strings is shorter than the array of search strings, the unmatched search strings are replaced with empty strings.

Translating characters and substrings

The strtr( ) function translates characters or substrings in a *subject* string:

```
string strtr(string subject, string from, string to)
string strtr(string subject, array map)
```

When called with three arguments, strtr( ) translates the characters in the *subject* string that match those in the *from* string with the corresponding characters in the *to* string. When called with two arguments, a *subject* string and an array *map*, occurrences of the *map* keys in *subject* are replaced with the corresponding *map* values.

The following example uses strtr( ) to replace all lowercase vowels with the corresponding umlauted character:

```
$mischief = strtr("command.com", "aeiou", "äëïöü");
print $mischief;  // prints cömmänd.cöm
```

When an associative array is passed as a translation map, strtr( ) replaces substrings rather than characters. The following example shows how strtr( ) can expand acronyms:

```
// Short list of acronyms used in e-mail
$glossary = array("BTW"=>"by the way",
                  "IMHO"=>"in my humble opinion",
                  "IOW"=>"in other words",
                  "OTOH"=>"on the other hand");

// Maybe now I can understand
print strtr($geekMail, $glossary);
```

Regular Expressions

In this section we show how *regular expressions* can achieve more sophisticated pattern matching to find, extract, and even replace complex substrings within a string.

While regular expressions provide capabilities beyond those described in the last section, complex pattern matching isn't as efficient as simple string comparisons. The functions described in the last section are more efficient than those that use regular expressions and should be used if complex pattern searches aren't required.

This section starts with a brief description of the POSIX regular expression syntax. This isn't a complete description of all the capabilities, but we do provide enough details to create quite powerful regular expressions. The second half of the section describes the functions that use POSIX regular expressions. Examples of regular expressions can be found in this section and in Chapter 7.

Regular Expression Syntax

A regular expression follows a strict syntax to describe patterns of characters. PHP has two sets of functions that use regular expressions: one set supports the Perl Compatible Regular Expression (PCRE) syntax, while the other supports the POSIX extended regular expression syntax. In this book we use the POSIX functions.

To demonstrate the syntax of regular expressions, we introduce the function ereg():

```
boolean ereg(string pattern, string subject [, array var])
```

ereg( ) returns true if the regular expression *pattern* is found in the *subject* string. We discuss how the ereg( ) function can extract values into the optional array variable *var* later in this section.

The following trivial example shows how ereg() is called to find the literal pattern "cat" in the subject string "raining cats and dogs":

```
// prints "Found a cat"
if (ereg("cat", "raining cats and dogs"))
  echo "Found 'cat'";
```

The regular expression "cat" matches the *subject* string, and the fragment prints "Found 'cat'".

Characters and wildcards

To represent any character in a pattern, a period is used as a wildcard. The pattern "c.." matches any three-letter string that begins with a lowercase "c"; for example, "cat", "cow", "cop", etc. To express a pattern that actually matches a period, use the backslash character \—for example, "\.com" matches ".com" but not "xcom".

The use of the backslash in a regular expression can cause confusion. To include a backslash in a double-quoted string, you need to escape the meaning of the backslash with a backslash. The following example shows how the regular expression pattern "\.com" is represented:

```
// Sets $found to true
$found = ereg("\\.com", "www.ora.com");
```

It's better to avoid the confusion and use single quotes when passing a string as a regular expression:

```
$found = ereg('\.com', "www.ora.com");
```

Character lists

Rather than using a wildcard that matches any character, a list of characters enclosed in brackets can be specified within a pattern. For example, to match a three-character string that starts with a "p", ends with a "p", and contains a vowel as the middle letter, the expression:

```
ereg("p[aeiou]p", $var)
```

can be used. This returns true for any string that contains "pap", "pep", "pip", "pop", or "pup". A range of characters can also be specified; for example, "[0-9]" specifies the numbers 0 through 9:

```
// Matches "A1", "A2", "A3", "B1", ...
$found = ereg("[ABC][123]", "A1 Quality");  // true

// Matches "00" to "39"
$found = ereg("[0-3][0-9]", "27");  //true
```

A list can specify characters that aren't matches using the not operator ^ as the first character in the brackets. The pattern "[^123]" matches any character other than 1, 2, or 3. The following examples show more regular expressions that make use of the not operator in lists:

```
// true for "pap", "pbp", "pcp", etc. but not "php"
$found = ereg("p[^h]p", $val);

// true if $var does not contain
// alphanumeric characters
$found = ereg("[^0-9a-zA-Z]", $val);
```

The ^ character can be treated as normal by placing it in a position other than the start of the characters enclosed in the brackets. For example, "[0-9^]" matches the characters 0 to 9 and the ^ character. The - character can be matched by placing it at the start or the end of the list; for example, "[-123]" matches characters -, 1, 2, or 3.

Anchors

A regular expression can specify that a pattern occur at the start or end of a subject string using *anchors*. The ^ anchors a pattern to the start, and the $ character anchors a pattern to the end of a string. For example, the expression:

```
ereg("^php", $var)
```

matches strings that start with "php" but not others. The following code shows the operation of both:

```
$var = "to be or not to be";

$match = ereg("^to", $var); // true
$match = ereg('be$', $var); // true
$match = ereg("^or", $var); // false
```

Both anchors can be used in one regular expression to match a whole string. The following example illustrates this:

```
// Must match "Yes" exactly
$match = ereg('^Yes$', "Yes");      // true
$match = ereg('^Yes$', "Yes sir"); // false
```

Optional and repeating characters

By following a character in a regular expression with a ?, *, or + operator, the pattern matches zero or one, zero to many, or one to many occurrences of the character, respectively.

The ? operator allows zero or one occurrence of a character, so the expression:

```
ereg("pe?p", $var)
```

matches either "pep" or "pp", but not the string "peep". The * operator allows zero or many occurrences of the "o" in the expression:

```
ereg("po*p", $var)
```

and matches "pp", "pop", "poop", "pooop", and so on. Finally, the + operator allows one to many occurrences of "b" in the expression:

```
ereg("ab+a", $var)
```

so while strings such as "aba", "abba", and "abbba" match, "aa" doesn't.

The operators ?, *, and + can also be used with a wildcard or a list of characters. The following examples show how:

```
$var = "www.rmit.edu.au";

// True for strings that start with "www"
// and end with "au"
$matches = ereg('^www.*au$', $var); // true


$hexString = "x01ff";

// True for strings that start with 'x'
// followed by at least one hexadecimal digit
$matches = ereg('x[0-9a-fA-F]+$', $hexString); // true
```

The first example matches any string that starts with "www" and ends with "au"; the pattern ".*" matches a sequence of any characters, including a blank string. The second example matches any sequence that starts with the character "x" followed by one or more characters from the list [0-9a-fA-F].

A fixed number of occurrences can be specified in braces. for example, the pattern "[0-7]{3}" matches three-character numbers that contain the digits 0 through 7:

```
$valid = ereg("[0-7]{3}", "075"); // true
$valid = ereg("[0-7]{3}", "75");  // false
```

The braces syntax also allows the minimum and maximum occurrences of a pattern to be specified as demonstrated in the following examples:

```
$val = "58273";

// true if $val contains numerals from start to end
// and is between 4 and 6 characters in length
$valid = ereg('^[0-9]{4,6}$', $val); // true

$val = "5827003";
$valid = ereg('^[0-9]{4,6}$', $val); // false

// Without the anchors at the start and end, the
// matching pattern "582768" is found
```

```
$val = "582768986456245003";

$valid = ereg("[0-9]{4,6}", $val);    // true
```

Groups

Subpatterns in a regular expression can be grouped by placing parentheses around them. This allows the optional and repeating operators to be applied to groups rather than just a single character. For example, the expression:

```
ereg("(123)+", $var)
```

matches "123", "123123", "123123123", etc. Grouping characters allows complex patterns to be expressed, as in the following example that matches a URL:

```
// A simple, incomplete, HTTP URL regular expression that doesn't allow numbers
$pattern = '^(http://)?[a-zA-Z]+(\.[a-zA-z]+)+$';

$found = ereg($pattern, "www.ora.com"); // true
```

The regular expression assigned to $pattern includes both the start and end anchors, ^ and $, so the whole *subject* string, "www.ora.com" must match the pattern. The start of the pattern is the optional group of characters "http://", as specified by "(http://)?". This doesn't match any of the subject string in the example but doesn't rule out a match, because the "http://" pattern is optional. Next the "[a-zA-Z]+" pattern specifies one or more alpha characters, and this matches "www" from the *subject* string. The next pattern is the group "(\.[a-zA-z]+)". This pattern must start with a period—the wildcard meaning of . is escaped with the backslash—followed by one or more alphabetic characters. The pattern in this group is followed by the + operator, so the pattern must occur at least once in the subject and can repeat many times. In the example, the first occurrence is ".ora" and the second occurrence is ".com".

Groups can also define subpatterns when ereg( ) extracts values into an array. We discuss the use of ereg( ) to extract values later in this section.

Alternative patterns

Alternatives in a pattern are specified with the | operator; for example, the pattern "cat|bat|rat" matches "cat", "bat", or "rat". The | operator has the lowest precedence of the regular expression operators, treating the largest surrounding expressions as alternative patterns. To match "cat", "bat", or "rat" another way, the following expression can be used:

```
$var = "bat";
$found = ereg("(c|b|r)at", $var);   // true
```

Another example shows alternative beginnings to a pattern:

```
// match some URLs
$pattern = '(^ftp|^http|^gopher)://';

$found = ereg($pattern, "http://www.ora.com"); // true
```

Escaping special characters

We've already discussed the need to escape the special meaning of characters used as operators in a regular expression. However, when to escape the meaning depends on how the character is used. Escaping the special meaning of a character is done with the backslash character as with the expression "2\+3, which matches the string "2+3". If the + isn't escaped, the pattern matches one or many occurrences of the character 2 followed by the character 3. Another way to write this expression is to express the + in the list of characters as "2[+]3". Because + doesn't have the same meaning in a list, it doesn't need to be escaped in that context. Using character lists in this way can improve readability. The following examples show how escaping is used and avoided:

```
// need to escape ( and )
$phone = "(03) 9429 5555";
$found = ereg("^\([0-9]{2,3}\)", $phone); // true

// No need to escape (*.+?)| within parentheses
$special = "Special Characters are (, ), *, +, ?, |";
$found = ereg("[(*.+?)|]", $special); // true

// The back-slash always needs to be quoted to match
$backSlash = 'The backslash \ character';
$found = ereg('^[a-zA-Z \\]*$', $backSlash); //true

// Don't need to escape the dot within parentheses
$domain = "www.ora.com";
$found = ereg("[.]com", $domain); //true
```

Another complication arises due to the fact that a regular expression is passed as a string to the regular expression functions. Strings in PHP can also use the backslash character to escape quotes and to encode tabs, newlines, etc. Consider the following example, which matches a backslash character:

```
// single-quoted string containing a backslash
$backSlash = '\ backslash';

// Evaluates to true
$found = ereg("^\\\\ backslash\$", $backSlash);
```

The regular expression looks quite odd: to match a backslash, the regular expression function needs to escape the meaning of backslash, but because we are using a double-quoted string, each of the two backslashes needs to be escaped. The last complication is that PHP interprets the $ character as the beginning of a variable name, so we need to escape that. Using a single-quoted string can help make regular expressions easier to read and write.

Metacharacters

Metacharacters can also be used in regular expressions. For example, the tab character is represented as \t and the carriage-return character as \n. There are also shortcuts: \d means any digit, and \s means any whitespace. The following example returns true as the tab character, \t, is contained in the $source string:

```
$source = "fast\tfood";

$result = ereg('\s', $source); // true
```

Regular Expression Functions

PHP has several functions that use POSIX regular expressions to find and extract substrings, replace substrings, and split a string into an array. The functions to perform these tasks come in pairs: a case-sensitive version and a case-insensitive version. While case-sensitive regular expressions can be written, the case-insensitive versions of these functions allow shorter regular expressions.

Finding and extracting values

The ereg( ) function, and the case-insensitive version eregi( ), are defined as:

```
boolean ereg(string pattern, string subject [, array var])
boolean eregi(string pattern, string subject [, array var])
```

Both functions return true if the regular expression *pattern* is found in the *subject* string. An optional array variable *var* can be passed as the third argument; it is populated with the portions of *subject* that are matched by up to nine grouped subexpressions in *pattern*. Both functions return false if the *pattern* isn't found in the *subject*.

To extract values from a string into an array, patterns can be arranged in groups contained by parentheses in the regular expression. The following example shows how the year, month, and day components of a date can be extracted into an array:

```
$parts = array( );
$value = "2001-09-07";
$pattern = '^([0-9]{4})-([0-9]{2})-([0-9]{2})$';

ereg($pattern, $value, $parts);

// Array ([0]=> 2001-09-07 [1]=>2001 [2]=>09 [3]=>07
print_r($parts);
```

The expression:

```
'^([0-9]{4})-([0-9]{2})-([0-9]{2})$'
```

matches dates in the format YYYY-MM-DD. After calling ereg( ), $parts[0] is assigned the portion of the string that matches the whole regular expression—in this case, the whole string 2001-09-07. The portion of the date that matches each group in the expression is assigned to the following array elements: $parts[1] contains the year

matched by ([0-9]{4}), $parts[2] contains the month matched by ([0-9]{2}), and
$parts[3] contains the day matched by "([0-9]{2})".

Replacing substrings

The following functions create new strings by replacing substrings:

```
string ereg_replace(string pattern, string replacement, string source)
string eregi_replace(string pattern, string replacement, string source)
```

They create a new string by replacing substrings of the *source* string that match the
regular expression *pattern* with a *replacement* string. These functions are similar to
the str_replace( ) function described earlier in the "Strings" section, except that the
replaced substrings are identified using a regular expression. Consider the examples:

```
$source = "The  quick\tbrown\n\tfox jumps";

// prints "The quick brown fox"
echo ereg_replace("[ \t\n]+", " ", $source);

$source = "\xf6 The  quick\tbrown\n\tfox jumps\x88";

// replace all non-printable characters with a space
echo ereg_replace("[^ -~]+", " ", $source);
```

The second example uses the regular expression "[^ -~]+" to match all characters
except those that fall between the space character and the tilde character in the
ASCII table. This represents almost all the printable 7-bit characters.

Splitting a string into an array

The following two functions split strings:

```
array split(string pattern, string source [, integer limit])
array spliti(string pattern, string source [, integer limit])
```

They split the *source* string into an array, breaking the string where the matching *pattern* is found. These functions perform a similar task to the explode( ) function
described earlier and as with explode( ), a *limit* can be specified to determine the
maximum number of elements in the array.

The following simple example shows how split( ) can break a sentence into an array
of "words" by recognizing any sequence of nonalphabetic characters as separators:

```
$sentence = "I wonder why he does\nBuzz, buzz, buzz!";
$words = split("[^a-zA-Z]+", $sentence);
```

When complex patterns aren't needed to break a string into an array, the explode( )
function makes a better choice.

Date and Time Functions

There are several PHP library functions that work with dates and times. Most either generate a Unix timestamp or format a Unix timestamp in a human-readable form.

Generating a Timestamp

Date and time is generally represented as a Unix timestamp: the number of seconds since 1 January 1970 00:00:00 Greenwich Mean Time. Most systems represent a timestamp using a signed 32-bit integer, allowing a range of dates from December 13, 1901 through January 19, 2038. While timestamps are convenient to work with in scripts, care must be taken when manipulating timestamps to avoid integer overflow errors. A common source of errors is to compare two timestamps in which the date range is greater than the largest positive integer—a range just over 68 years for a signed 32-bit integer.

 PHP gives unexpected results when comparing two integers that differ by an amount greater than the largest positive integer, typically $2^{31}-1$. A safer way to compare large integers is to cast them to floating-point numbers. The following example illustrates this point:

```
$var1 = -2106036000;  // 16/08/1902
$var2 = 502808400;    // 24/08/1984

// $result is assigned false
$result = $var1 < $var2;

// $result is assigned true as expected
$result = (float) $var1 < (float) $var2;
```

Even floating-point numbers can overflow. To manipulate numbers of arbitrary precision, the BCMath library should be considered.

Current time

PHP provides several functions that generate a Unix timestamp. The simplest:

```
integer time( )
```

returns the timestamp for the current date and time, as shown in this fragment:

```
// prints the current timestamp: e.g., 1008553254
echo time( );
```

Creating timestamps with mktime( ) and gmmktime( )

To create a timestamp for a past or future date in the range December 13, 1901 through January 19, 2038, the mktime( ) and gmmktime( ) functions are defined:

```
int mktime(int hour, int minute, int second, int month, int day, int year
    [, int is_dst])
```

```
int gmmktime(int hour, int minute, int second, int month, int day, int year
    [, int is_dst])
```

Both create a timestamp from the supplied components; the parameters supplied to gmmktime( ) represent a GMT date and time, while the parameters supplied to mktime( ) represent the local time. This example creates a timestamp for 9:30 A.M. on June 18, 1998:

```
$aDate = mktime(9, 30, 0, 6, 18, 1998);
```

Both functions are reasonably tolerant of zero values, and both correctly handle values out-of-range, allowing scripts to add a quantum of time without range checking. If the components of a date are outside the range of dates the function is defined for, −1 is returned. The following example shows how 30 days can be added to a date and time:

```
$paymentPeriod = 30;  // Days

// generates a timestamp for 26 June 2002 by
// adding 30 days to 27 May 2002
$paymentDue =
    mktime(0, 0, 0, 5, 27 + $paymentPeriod, 2002);

// A different approach adds the appropriate number
// of seconds to the timestamp for 27 May 2002
$paymentDue = mktime(0, 0, 0, 5, 27, 2002)
    + ($paymentPeriod * 24 * 3600);
```

Both functions allow the supplied date to be interpreted as daylight savings time by setting the flag is_dst to 1.

The order of the arguments to these functions is unusual and easily confused. While the mktime( ) and gmmktime( ) functions are similar to the Unix mktime( ) function, the arguments aren't in the same order.

String to timestamp

This function generates a timestamp by parsing the human-readable date and time— between December 13, 1901 and January 19, 2038—from the string *time*:

```
integer strtotime(string time)
```

The function interprets several standard representations of a date, as shown here:

```
// Absolute dates and times
$var = strtotime("25 December 2002");
$var = strtotime("14/5/1955");
$var = strtotime("Fr1, 7 Sep 2001 10:28:07 -1000");

// The current time: equivalent to time( )
$var = strtotime("now");

// Relative times
echo strtotime("+1 day");
```

```
echo strtotime("-2 weeks");
echo strtotime("+2 hours 2 seconds");
```

Care should be taken when using `strtotime()` with user-supplied dates. It's better to limit the use of `strtotime()` to cases when the string to be parsed is under the control of the script, for example, checking a minimum age using a relative date:

```
// date of birth: timestamp for 16 August, 1983
$dob = mktime(0, 0, 0, 16, 8, 1982);

// Now check that the individual is over 18
if ((float)$dob < (float)strtotime("-18 years"))
    echo "Legal to drive in the state of Victoria";
```

Note that both timestamps are cast to floating-point numbers before comparing them to avoid the integer overflow problem highlighted earlier. A different solution to this problem is presented in Chapter 7.

Subsecond times

While a Unix timestamp represents a date and time accurate to the second, many applications require times to be represented to the subsecond. PHP provides the function:

```
string microtime()
```

This returns a string that contains both a Unix timestamp in seconds and a microsecond component. The returned string begins with the microsecond component, followed by the integer timestamp:

```
// prints the time now in the format "usec sec"
// e.g., 0.34783800 1008553410
echo microtime();
```

One common use of the function `microtime()` is to generate the seed for a random-number generator:

```
// Generate a seed.
$seed = (float)microtime() * 100000000;

srand($seed);
```

Because the microsecond component appears at the start of the string returned from `microtime()`, the returned value can be converted to a float with the `(float)` cast operator. Multiplying the float result by 100,000,000 ensures that you pass a suitably varying integer to the seeding function `srand()`. Random-number generation is covered in more detail in the "Integer and Float Functions" section.

Formatting a Date

While the Unix timestamp is programmatically useful, it isn't a convenient display format. The date( ) and gmdate( ) functions return a human-readable formatted date and time:

```
string date(string format [, integer timestamp])
string gmdate(string format [, integer timestamp])
```

The format of the returned string is determined by the *format* argument. A predetermined date can be formatted by passing in the optional *timestamp* argument. Otherwise, both functions format the current time. The format string uses the formatting characters listed in Table 2-3 to display various components or characteristics of the timestamp. To include the characters from the table, the backslash character is used. The following examples show various combinations:

```
// Set up a timestamp for 08:15am 24 Aug 1964
$var = mktime(8, 15, 25, 8, 24, 1964);

// "24/08/1964"
echo date('d/m/Y', $var);

// "08/24/64"
echo date('m/d/y', $var);

// "Born on Thursday 24th of August"
echo date('\B\o\r\n \o\n l jS \of F", $var);
```

Table 2-3. Formatting characters that represent various date and time components

Formatting character	Meaning
a, A	"am" or "pm"; "AM" or "PM"
S	Two-character English ordinal suffix: "st", "nd", "rd", "th"
d, j	Day of the month: with leading zeros: "01"; without: "1"
D, l	Day of the week: as three letters: "Mon"; spelled out: "Monday"
M, F	Month: as three letters: "Jan"; spelled out: "January"
m, n	Month: with leading zeros: "01"–"12"; without: "1"–"12"
h, g	Hour, 12-hour format: with leading zeros: "09"; without: "9"
H, G	Hour, 24-hour format: with leading zeros: "01"; without: "1"
i	Minutes: "00" to "59"
s	Seconds: "00" to "59"
Y, y	Year: four digits "2002"; two digits "02"
r	RFC-2822 formatted date: e.g., "Tue, 29 Jan 2002 09:15:33 +1000" (added in PHP 4.0.4)
w	Day of the week as number: "0" (Sunday) to "6" (Saturday)
t	Days in the month: "28" to "31"
z	Days in the year: "0" to "365"

Table 2-3. Formatting characters that represent various date and time components (continued)

Formatting character	Meaning
B	Swatch Internet time
L	Leap year: "0" for normal year; "1" for leap-year
I	Daylight savings time: "0" for standard time; "1" for daylight savings
O	Difference to Greenwich Mean Time in hours: "+0200"
T	Time zone setting of this machine
Z	Time zone offset in seconds: "-43200" to "43200"
U	Seconds since the epoch: 00:00:00 1/1/1970

PHP also provides the equivalent functions:

```
string strftime(string format [, integer timestamp])
string gmstrftime(string format [, integer timestamp])
```

The *format* string uses the same formatting character sequences as the C library function `strftime( )`.

Validating a Date

The function `checkdate( )` returns true if a given *month, day,* and *year* form a valid Gregorian date:

```
boolean checkdate(integer month, integer day, integer year)
```

This function isn't based on a timestamp and so can accept a larger range of dates: basically any dates in the years 1 to 32767. It automatically accounts for leap years.

```
// Works for a wide range of dates
$valid = checkdate(1, 1, 1066); // true
$valid = checkdate(1, 1, 2929); // true

// Correctly identify bad dates
$valid = checkdate(13, 1, 1996); // false
$valid = checkdate(4, 31, 2001); // false

// Correctly handles leap years
$valid = checkdate(2, 29, 1996); // true
$valid = checkdate(2, 29, 2001); // false
```

Integer and Float Functions

Apart from the basic operators +, -, /, *, and %, PHP provides the usual array of mathematical library functions. In this section, we present some of the library functions that are used with integer and float numbers.

Absolute Value

The absolute value of an integer or a float can be found with the abs( ) function:

```
integer abs(integer number)
float abs(float number)
```

The following examples show the result of abs( ) on floats and integers:

```
echo abs(-1);        // prints 1
echo abs(1);         // prints 1
echo abs(-145.89);   // prints 145.89
echo abs(145.89);    // prints 145.89
```

Ceiling and Floor

The ceil( ) and floor( ) functions can return the integer value above and below a fractional *value*, respectively:

```
float ceil(float value)
float floor(float value)
```

The return type is a float because an integer may not be able to represent the result when a large value is passed as an argument. Consider the following examples:

```
echo ceil(27.3);   // prints 28
echo floor(27.3);  // prints 27
```

Rounding

The round( ) function uses 4/5 rounding rules to round up or down a *value* to a given *precision*:

```
float round(float value [, integer precision])
```

Rounding by default is to zero decimal places, but the precision can be specified with the optional *precision* argument. The 4/5 rounding rules determine if a number is rounded up or down based on the digits that are lost due to the rounding *precision*. For example, 10.4 rounds down to 10, and 10.5 rounds up to 11. The following examples show rounding at various precisions:

```
echo round(10.4);          // prints 10
echo round(10.5);          // prints 11
echo round(2.40964, 3);    // prints 2.410
echo round(567234.56, -3); // prints 567000
echo round(567234.56, -4); // prints 570000
```

Number Systems

PHP provides the following functions that convert numbers between integer decimal and the commonly used number systems, binary, octal, and hexadecimal:

```
string decbin(integer number)
integer bindec (string binarystring)
string dechex(integer number)
integer hexdec(string hexstring)
string decoct(integer number)
integer octdec(string octalstring)
```

The decimal numbers are always treated as integers, and the numbers in the other systems are treated as strings. When converting to decimal, care must be taken that the source number isn't greater than the maximum value an integer can hold. Here are some examples:

```
echo decbin(45);         // prints "101101"
echo bindec("1001011");  // prints 75
echo dechex(45);         // prints "2D"
echo hexdec("5a7b");     // prints 23163
echo decoct(45);         // prints "55"
echo octdec("777");      // prints 511
```

Basic Trigonometry Functions

PHP supports the basic set of trigonometry functions and are listed in Table 2-4.

Table 2-4. Trigonometry functions supported by PHP

Function	Description
float sin(float arg)	Sine of arg in radians
float cos(float arg)	Cosine of arg in radians
float tan(float arg)	Tangent of arg in radians
float asin(float arg)	Arc sine of arg in radians
float acos(float arg)	Arc cosine of arg in radians
float atan(float arg)	Arc tangent of arg in radians
float atan2(float y, float x)	Arc tangent of x/y where the sign of both arguments determines the quadrant of the result
float pi( )	Returns the value 3.1415926535898
float deg2rad(float arg)	Converts arg degrees to radians
float rad2deg(float arg)	Converts arg radians to degrees

Powers and Logs

The PHP mathematical library includes the exponential and logarithmic functions listed in Table 2-5.

Table 2-5. Exponential and logarithmic functions

Function	Description
float exp(float arg)	e to the power of arg
float pow(float base, number exp)	Exponential expression base to the power of exp
float sqrt(float arg)	Square root of arg
float log(float arg)	Natural logarithm of arg
float log10(float arg)	Base-10 logarithm of arg

Random Number Generation

PHP provides the function rand( ), which returns values from a generated sequence of *pseudo-random* numbers. Well-known algorithms generate sequences that appear to have random behavior but aren't truly random. The srand( ) function seeds the algorithm and needs to be called before the first use of the rand( ) function in a script. Otherwise, the function returns the same numbers each time a script is called. The prototypes of the functions are:

```
void srand(integer seed)
integer rand( )
integer rand(integer min, integer max)
```

The srand( ) function is called by passing an integer seed that is usually generated from the current time. When called with no arguments, rand( ) returns a random number between 0 and the value returned by getrandmax( ). When rand( ) is called with two arguments—the *min* and *max* values—the returned number is a random number between *min* and *max*. Consider this example:

```
// Generate a seed.
$seed = (float) microtime( ) * 100000000;

// Seed the pseudo-random number generator
srand($seed);

// Generate some random numbers
print rand();       // between 0 and getmaxrand( )
print rand(1, 6);   // between 1 and 6 (inclusive)
```

User-Defined Functions

Functions provide a way to group together related statements into a cohesive block. For reusable code, a function saves duplicating statements and makes maintenance of the code easier.

We've already presented many examples of function calls in this chapter. Once written, a user-defined function is called in exactly the same way. Consider an example of a simple user-developed function as shown in Example 2-6.

Example 2-6. A user-defined function to output bold text

```
<!DOCTYPE HTML PUBLIC
  "-//W3C//DTD HTML 4.0 Transitional//EN"
  "http://www.w3.org/TR/html4/loose.dtd">
<html>
<head>
  <title>Simple Function Call</title>
</head>
<body bgcolor="#ffffff">
<?php

function bold($string)
{
  echo "<b>" . $string . "</b>\n";
}

// First example function call (with a static string)
echo "this is not bold\n";
bold("this is bold");
echo "this is again not bold\n";

// Second example function call (with a variable)
$myString = "this is bold";
bold($myString);
?>
</body></html>
```

The script defines the function bold( ), which takes one parameter, $string, and prints that string prefixed by a bold <b> tag and suffixed with a </b> tag. The bold( ) function, defined here, can be used with a string literal expression or a variable, as shown.

Functions can also return values. For example, consider the following code fragment that declares and uses a function heading( ), which returns a string using the return statement:

```
function heading($text, $headingLevel)
{
  switch ($headingLevel)
  case 1:
    $result = "<h1>" . ucwords($text) . "</h1>";
    break;

  case 2:
    $result = "<h2>" . ucwords($text) . "</h2>";
    break;

  case 3:
    $result = "<h3>" . ucfirst($text) . "</h3>";
    break;
```

```
      default:
        $result = "<p><b>" . ucfirst($text) . "</b>";

    return($result);
  }

  $test = "user defined functions";
  echo heading($test, 2);
```

The function takes two parameters: the text of a heading and a heading level. Based on the value of $headingLevel, the function builds the HTML suitable to display the heading—changing the case of the $text appropriately. The previous fragment generates the string:

```
  <h2>User Defined Functions</h2>
```

The variable that is returned by a return statement can optionally be placed in parentheses: the statements return($result) and return $result are identical.

Argument Types and Return Types

The argument and return types of a function aren't declared when the function is defined. PHP allows arguments of any type to be passed to the function, and as with variables, the return type is determined when a result is actually returned. Consider a simple function that divides two numbers:

```
  function divide($a, $b)
  {
      return ($a/$b);
  }

  $c = divide(4, 2);    // assigns an integer value = 2
  $c = divide(3, 2);    // assigns a float value = 1.5
  $c = divide(4.0, 2.0); // assigns a float value = 2.0
```

If the types of arguments passed to the function are critical, they should be tested as shown earlier in the "Types" section.

Variable Scope

Variables used inside a function are different from those used outside a function. The variables used inside the function are limited to the *scope* of the function (there are exceptions to this rule, which are discussed later in this section). Consider an example that illustrates variable scope:

```
  function doublevalue($var)
  {
    $temp = $var * 2;
  }
```

```
$variable = 5;
doublevalue($variable);
echo "\$temp is: $temp";
```

This example outputs the string:

```
$temp is:
```

and no value for $temp. The scope of the variable $temp is local to the function doublevalue( ) and is discarded when the function returns.

The PHP script engine doesn't complain about undeclared variable being used. It just assumes the variable is empty. However, this use of an undefined variable can be detected using the error-reporting settings discussed later, in the "Common Mistakes" section.

If you want to use a value that is local to a function elsewhere in a script, the easiest way to do so is to return the value of the variable. This example achieves this:

```
function doublevalue($var)
{
  $returnVar = $var * 2;
  return($returnVar);
}

$variable = 5;
$temp = doublevalue($variable);
echo "\$temp is: $temp";
```

The example prints:

```
$temp is: 10
```

You could have still used the variable name $temp inside the function doublevalue( ). However, the $temp inside the function is a different variable from the $temp outside the function. The general rule is that variables used exclusively within functions are local to the function, regardless of whether an identically named variable is used elsewhere. There are two exceptions to this general rule: variables passed by reference and those declared global in the function aren't local to the function.

Global variables

If you want to use the same variable everywhere in your code, including within functions, you can do so with the global statement. The global statement declares a variable within a function as being the same as the variable that is used outside of the function. Consider this example:

```
function doublevalue( )
{
  global $temp;
  $temp = $temp * 2;
}
```

```
$temp = 5;
doublevalue( );
echo "\$temp is: $temp";
```

Because $temp is declared inside the function as global, the variable $temp used in doublevalue( ) is a global variable that can be accessed outside the function. Because the variable $temp can be seen outside the function, the script prints:

```
$temp is: 10
```

A word of caution: avoid overuse of global as it makes for confusing code.

The global variable declaration can be a trap.

In some other languages, global variables are usually declared global outside the functions and then used in the functions.

In PHP, it's the opposite: to use a global variable inside a function, declare the variable as global inside the function.

An alternative to using global is to return more than one variable from a function by creating and returning an array of values. A better approach is to pass parameters by reference instead of by value. We discuss the latter approach in the next section.

How Variables Are Passed to Functions

By default, variables are passed to functions by value, not by reference. The following example:

```
function doublevalue($var)
{
    $var = $var * 2;
}

$variable = 5;
doublevalue($variable);
echo "\$variable is: $variable";
```

has the output:

```
$variable is: 5
```

The parameter $variable that is passed to the function doublevalue( ) isn't changed by the function. What actually happens is that the value 5 is passed to the function, doubled to be 10, and the result lost forever! The value is passed to the function, not the variable itself.

Passing arguments by reference

An alternative to returning a result or using a global variable is to pass a *reference* to a variable as an argument to the function. This means that any changes to the variable within the function affect the original variable. Consider this example:

```
function doublevalue(&$var)
{
  $var = $var * 2;
}

  $variable - 5;
  doublevalue($variable);
  echo "\$variable is: $variable";
?>
```

This prints:

```
$variable is: 10
```

The only difference between this example and the last one is that the parameter $var to the function doublevalue( ) is prefixed with an ampersand character: &$var. The ampersand means that a reference to the original variable is passed as the parameter, not just the value of the variable. The result is that changes to $var in the function affect the original variable $variable outside the function.

Functions that are defined with arguments that are references to variables can't be called with literal expressions, because the function expects a variable to modify. PHP reports an error when such a call is made.

Assigning by reference

Referencing with the ampersand can also be used when assigning variables, which allows the memory holding a value to be accessed from more than one variable. This example illustrates the idea:

```
$x = 10;
$y = &$x;
$y++;
echo $x;
echo $y;
```

Here's how it prints:

```
11
11
```

Because $y is a reference to $x, any change to $y affects $x. In effect, they are the same variable. So, by adding 1 to $y, you also add 1 to $x, and both are equal to 11.

The reference $y can be removed with:

```
unset($y);
```

This has no effect on $x or its value.

Default argument values

PHP allows functions to be defined with default values for arguments. A default value is simply supplied in the argument list using the = sign. Consider the modified heading( ) function described earlier:

```
function heading($text, $headingLevel = 2)
{
  switch ($level)
  case 1:
    $result = "<h1>" . ucwords($text) . "</h1>";
    break;

  case 2:
    $result = "<h2>" . ucwords($text) . "</h2>";
    break;

  case 3:
    $result = "<h3>" . ucfirst($text) . "</h3>";
    break;

  default:
    $result = "<p><b>" . ucfirst($text) . "</b>";

  return($result);
}

$test = "user defined functions";
echo heading($test);
```

When calls are made to the heading( ) function, the second argument can be omitted, and the default value 2 is assigned to the $headingLevel variable.

Reusing Functions with Include and Require Files

To use functions across many PHP scripts, PHP supports the include statement and the require directive.

If you decide you wish to reuse the bold( ) function from Example 2-6 in more than one script, you can store it in an include file. For example, you can create a file called *functions.inc* and put the bold( ) function in the file:

```
<?php
function bold($string)
{
  echo "<b>" . $string . "</b>\n";
}
?>
```

Any PHP code in an include file must be surrounded by the PHP start and end script tags. The PHP script engine treats the contents of include files as HTML unless script tags are used.

In a script, you can then use the `include` statement to provide access to the function `bold( )`:

```
<html>
<head>
  <title>Simple Function Call</title>
</head>
<body bgcolor="#ffffff">
<?
include "functions.inc";

// First example function call (with a static string)
echo "this is not bold\n";
bold("this is bold");
echo "this is again not bold\n";

// Second example function call (with a variable)
$myString = "this is bold";
bold($myString);
?>
</body></html>
```

The script works as before, but the function `bold( )` can now be reused across several scripts by including *functions.inc*. We use include files throughout Chapters 4 through 13.

 Be careful when using the `include` statement. Including the same file twice or declaring a function in the script that is already in an include file causes PHP to complain about the function being redefined.

The `include` statement is treated in the same way as other statements. For example, you can conditionally include different files using the following code fragment:

```
if ($netscape == true)
{
  include "netscape.inc";
}
else
{
  include "other.inc";
}
```

The file is included only if the `include` statement is executed in the script. The braces used in this example are necessary: if they are omitted, the example doesn't behave as expected.

If a file must always be included, the `require` directive should be used instead of `include`. The require directive is processed before the script is executed, and the contents of the required file are always inserted in the script. This is useful for creating reusable HTML. For example, if you want to add the same header or footer to every page on a site—regardless of errors or other problems—require makes this easy and simple to maintain.

Consider the following HTML fragment:

```
<hr><br>(c) 2001 Hugh E. Williams and David Lane
```

If you want this fragment at the base of every page, the fragment can be stored in a file *footer.inc* and the directive added to the bottom of every script you develop:

```
require "footer.inc";
```

The benefit is that if you want to update the HTML footer, you need to do so in only one file.

Objects

PHP has limited support for object-oriented programming and allows programmers to define their own classes and create object instances of those classes. We make little use of objects in this book, and this section serves as an introduction to PHP's support of object-oriented features. The subject of object-oriented programming is extensive, and we don't provide a complete explanation of the subject here.

Classes and Objects

A class defines a compound data structure made up of member variables and a set of functions—known as methods or member functions—that operate with the specific structure. Example 2-7 shows how a class *Counter* is defined in PHP. The class *Counter* contains two member variables—the integers $count and $startPoint—and four functions that use these member variables. Collectively, the variables and the functions are members of the class *Counter*.

Example 2-7. A simple class definition of the user-defined class Counter

```php
<?php
  // A class that defines a counter.
  class Counter
  {
    // Member Variables
    var $count = 0;
    var $startPoint = 0;

    // Methods
    function startCountAt($i)
    {
```

```
      $this->count = $i;
      $this->startPoint = $i;
    }

    function increment()
    {
      $this->count++;
    }

    function reset()
    {
      $this->count = $this->startPoint;
    }

    function showvalue()
    {
      print $this->count;
    }
  }
?>
```

To use the data structures and functions defined in a class, an *instance* of the class—an object—needs to be created. Like other data types—integers, strings, arrays, and so on—objects are held by variables. However, unlike other types, objects are created using the new operator. An object of class *Counter* can be created and assigned to a variable as follows:

```
$aCounter = new Counter;
```

Once the variable $aCounter is created, the member variables and functions of the new object can be used. Members of the object, both variables and functions, are accessed using the -> operator. Consider the following example:

```
echo $aCounter->count;  // prints 0
$aCounter->increment();
echo $aCounter->count;  // prints 1

// Bypass the function that updates count
$aCounter->count = 101;
```

In the class definition, the code that defines member functions can access the member variables with the variable $this as can be seen in the *Counter* function implementations in Example 2-7. The variable $this has special meaning and acts as a placeholder until a real object is created. For example, when the function $aCounter->increment() is called, the variable $this acts as $aCounter.

By placing the code shown in Example 2-7 in the file *counter.inc*, the class *Counter* can be used by other scripts to create new objects, as shown in Example 2-8.

Example 2-8. Creating and using objects of class Counter

```
<!DOCTYPE HTML PUBLIC
    "-//W3C//DTD HTML 4.0 Transitional//EN"
    "http://www.w3.org/TR/html4/loose.dtd">
<html>
<head><title>Counter</title></head>
<body>
<?php
  include "counter.inc";

  // Create a new object of type "counter"
  $temp = new Counter;

  // Set the counter to 10
  $temp->startCountAt(10);

  // Increment the counter
  $temp->increment();
  $temp->increment();
$temp->increment();

  // Print out the value of the counter
  echo "<p>Counter is now: ";
  $temp->showvalue();

  // Reset the counter
  $temp->reset();

  // Print out the value of the counter
  echo "<p>Counter is now: ";
  $temp->showvalue();
?>
</body></html>
```

Many objects of the same class can be created. For example, you can use the following fragment to create three objects and assign them to three variables:

```
$a = new Counter;
$b = new Counter;
$c = new Counter;
```

The variables $a->count, $b->count, and $c->count are different. Each variable is of type object and references an object of the class *Counter*, but the objects themselves are independent.

Inheritance

One of the powerful concepts in object-oriented programming is inheritance. *Inheritance* allows a new class to be defined by extending the capabilities of an existing base *class*. PHP allows a new class to be created by extending an existing class with the extends keyword. Example 2-9 shows how the class *Counter* is extended to create the new class *BottleCounter* that can determine the number of cases of wine to be shipped.

Example 2-9. A new class BottleCounter is defined by extending the base class Counter

```
<!DOCTYPE HTML PUBLIC
    "-//W3C//DTD HTML 4.0 Transitional//EN"
    "http://www.w3.org/TR/html4/loose.dtd">
<html>
<head><title>Bottle Counter</title></head>
<body>
<?php
 include "counter.inc";

 class BottleCounter extends Counter
 {
  // Add 12 bottles to the counter
  function addCase()
  {
   $this->count += 12;
  }

  // Return the number of cases to be shipped
  function caseCount()
  {
   return ceil($this->count / 12);
  }

  // A Constructor that sets the initial count
  function BottleCounter($startCount)
  {
   $this->count = $startCount;
  }
 }

 // Create a new object of type "BottleCounter"
 // and pass the initial count of 12
 $temp = new BottleCounter(12);

 // Increment the counter
 $temp->increment();

 // Add another Case
 $temp->addCase();

 // Print out the value of the counter: 24
 echo "<p>Counter is now: ";
```

Example 2-9. A new class BottleCounter is defined by extending the base class Counter (continued)

```
$temp->showvalue( );

// Print the number of cases
$cases = $temp->caseCount( );
echo "<p>The number of cases to ship: $cases";
?>
</body></html>
```

The new class *BottleCounter* doesn't add any new member variables but does add three new member functions. The functions of the class *BottleCounter* use the member variables of the base class *Counter* in ways appropriate to *BottleCounter*. The function addCase( ) increments the $count variable by 12, and the function caseCount( ) returns the total number of cases that need to be shipped, including any partially filled cases.

The final function, BottleCounter( ), is the *constructor* of the class *BottleCounter*. Member functions with the same name as the class are treated differently. PHP uses these functions as constructors, and they are called when new objects of that class type are created. A constructor function can include arguments that can be used to initialize member variables when a new object is created. Example 2-9 showed how a new *BottleCounter* object is created:

```
// Create a new object of type "BottleCounter"
// and pass the initial count of 12
$temp = new BottleCounter(12);
```

The power of inheritance doesn't come from simply reusing code. Objects created from the extended class can be used as if they were created from the existing base class. This ability to use an object as if it were an instance of the base class is known as *polymorphism*. You can use the class *Counter* as a base for other new classes, such as a *CanCounter* class in which a case is 24 cans, not 12 bottles. Code that uses an object of class *Counter* can then be used with objects of type *BottleCounter* or *CanCounter*. Consider this example, which defines the function volumeDiscount( ), designed to return a discount factor based on a *Counter* object:

```
// Return a discount factor based on
// the value of the Counter $var
function volumeDiscount($var)
{
  // use $var as a Counter
  if ($var->count > 24)
    return 0.95;
  else
    return 1.0;
}

$bottles = new BottleCounter(10);
$cans = new CanCounter(24);
```

```
$bottleDiscountFactor = volumeDiscount($bottles);
$canDiscountFactor = volumeDiscount($cans);
```

If both the *BottleCounter* and *CanCounter* classes are defined as extensions of
Counter, the function `volumeDiscount( )` can be called on objects of those classes.

Common Mistakes

When switching to PHP, there are several common mistakes even experienced programmers make. In this short section, we highlight some of these mistakes and the
basics of how to rectify them.

A Page That Produces Partial or No Output

One of the most common problems in debugging PHP scripts is seeing:

- No page rendered by the web browser when much more is expected
- A pop-up dialog box stating that the "Document Contains No Data"
- A partial page when more is expected

Most of these problems are caused not by a bug in script-programming logic, but by
a bug in the HTML produced by the script. For example, if the `</table>`, `</form>`, or
`</frame>` closing tags are omitted, the page may not be rendered.

The HTML problem can usually be identified by viewing the HTML page source
using the web browser. With Netscape, the complete output of the erroneous example is shown in the page-source view, and the HTML problem can hopefully be easily identified.

For compound or hard-to-identify HTML bugs, the W3C validator at *http://
validator.w3.org* retrieves a page, analyzes the correctness of the HTML, and issues a
report. It's an excellent assistant for debugging and last-minute compliance checks
before delivery of an application.

If the problem still proves hard to find, consider adding calls to the `flush( )` function
after `echo`, `print`, or `printf` statements. `flush( )` empties the output buffer maintained by the PHP engine, sending all currently buffered output to the web server.
The function has no effect on buffering at the web server or the web browser, but it
ensures that all data output by the script is available to the web server to be transmitted and rendered by a browser. Remember to remove the `flush( )` function calls after
debugging, because unnecessary flushing may prevent efficient buffering of output
by the PHP scripting engine.

A common problem that shouldn't be confused with those described here is not
receiving a response from the web server and getting a "no response" error message.
This problem is a symptom of the bugs described in the next section, and can be distinguished from the problems described here by observing the web browser. Most of

the popular graphical browsers show they are waiting for a response by animating the logo in the top-right corner. For the HTML problems described here, the page loading process will be complete, the logo animation will have stopped, and the HTML page source can be viewed through the web browser menus.

Variable Problems

In this section, we discuss problems that cause a page never to arrive at the web browser, or complete pages to appear with missing output from variables.

Variable naming

Making a mistake with a variable name sometimes inadvertently creates never-ending loops. The result of a never-ending loop is that the web browser eventually times out and alerts the user that the web server isn't responding to an HTTP request.

The following loop never ends, and no output is produced:

```
for($counter=0; $counter<10; $Counter++)
  myFunction();
```

The variable $counter is never incremented. Instead, another variable, $Counter, is, so $counter is always less than 10. Common bugs result from subtle changes in variable names through changing case, omitting or including underscores, or simple typographic errors.

Never-ending loops can also produce unexpected output. The following loop can render thousands of greetings in a web browser in a very short time:

```
for($counter=0; $Counter<10; $counter++)
  echo "<br>hello";
```

These errors can sometimes be detected by setting the PHP error-reporting level to a higher sensitivity. Adding the following code fragment to the top of each PHP script or to a file included with the require directive reports undefined variable errors:

```
error_reporting(E_ALL);
```

This forces variables to be declared by assigning a value before they can be used. Consider the following example:

```
error_reporting(E_ALL);
for($counter=0; $Counter<10; $counter++)
  echo "<br>hello";
```

This produces an unending number of warning messages stating:

```
Warning: Undefined variable: Counter in /var/lib/apache/htdocs/winestore/a.php on
line 2
```

The script keeps on running, because it's only a warning. A custom error handler can be incorporated that stops the script when an error or warning is encountered by using the set_error_handler( ) function. We discuss error handlers in Chapter 10.

Missing output

An uninitialized variable produces no output. This seems obvious, but it can be hard to identify if the problem is a subtle typographic error. Consider this example of a change in case:

```
$testvariable = "hello";
echo "The value of test is $testVariable";
```

This produces the string:

```
The value of test is
```

The problem can be much harder to identify by visual inspection if the variable is part of a complex operation, such as being used as an array element index, part of `<table>` output, or as a parameter to a database query.

If output appears but isn't as expected, an uninitialized variable is a possibility. The simplest approach to detecting the error is then to check for a bug by setting `error_reporting(E_ALL)` at the top of the script as discussed in the last section.

The function `isset()` can also control execution and debug code, because it returns `true` if the variable exists (even if it's set to `NULL` or an empty string) and `false` if it has never been used.

Another related problem involves variable names appearing where values should. This is usually the simple problem of an omitted dollar sign and is easy to fix. For example:

```
echo "the value of test is test";
```

This should have been:

```
echo "the value of test is $test";
```

If a dollar sign is omitted in a statement such as an assignment or conditional, the PHP interpreter reports a specific parse error with its default error-reporting level.

A similar problem can also occur when single quotes are used instead of double quotes, because single-quoted strings are always output directly, and the string isn't interpreted like a double-quoted string is. For example:

```
echo 'the value of test is $test';
```

This produces:

```
the value of test is $test
```

It doesn't output the value of the variable $test.

Complaints About Headers

We have not introduced the functions `header()` and `setcookie()` in this chapter. Both functions can output HTTP headers that are sent by the web server back to the web browser, and they are used frequently in web database applications. The functions are introduced and discussed in Chapters 5, 6, 8, and 9.

A common problem seen in producing HTTP headers with PHP is the error message beginning:

```
Warning: Cannot add header information - headers already sent...
```

Headers can be sent only before any HTML is output, and this includes any whitespace at the top of the file. So, for example, if there is a blank line or single space character before the script open tag `<?php`, HTML has been output—albeit not very interesting HTML—and the call to `header( )` or `setcookie( )` reports this error.

It's possible to avoid header problems by altering how PHP buffers data using the output control library functions. These functions are outside the scope of this book.

Other Common Problems

The three problem categories we have outlined so far are the most infuriating and common mistakes programmers make in PHP. We outline a few less common and less PHP-specific problems here.

Omitting a semicolon at the end of a statement is usually easy to detect. The PHP interpreter continues to parse the script and, when it reaches a threshold of confusion or exceeds the maximum statement length, it reports an error one or more lines later that indicates a semicolon has been missed. In most cases, this is easy to fix, and the line missing the semicolon is identified in the error message.

In some cases, a missing semicolon can be as hard to identify as a missing closing brace or a missing quotation mark. The following erroneous code is missing a closing brace:

```
<?
for($x=0; $x<100 ;$x++)
{
  for($y=0; $y<100; $y++) {
    echo "test1";
    for($z=0; $z<100; $z++)
      echo "test2";
}
?>
```

The error reported is:

```
Parse error: parse error in bug.php on line 9
```

Line 9 is the last line of the script, so the nature and cause of the problem aren't immediately clear. However, parse errors that aren't immediately obvious on the reported line in the error message are usually on the line above, or there may be a missing brace or quotation mark.

It takes only a minute or so to identify the missing brace in this example, but more complex functions can take much longer to fix. This highlights the importance of indentation in code and also of avoiding the practice of placing opening braces at the ends of lines. Braces should always be placed on lines of their own.

Missing open and close script tags can cause similar problems, but these are much easier to identify. If an open script tag is missing, it's obvious because some portion of the code—if not all—is displayed in the browser. A missing close tag usually causes a parse error, because the PHP script engine is confused when it tries to parse HTML and interpret it as PHP.

If script source is always displayed and never run, it's likely that Apache is misconfigured. Specifically, it's likely that the AddType directive for processing PHP scripts was not uncommented in the Apache installation process; this seems to be the default in recent RedHat Linux distributions.

Another possible cause of scripts being displayed and not run is that the PHP scripts aren't saved in files ending with the *.php* suffix. This problem often occurs with legacy PHP3 code, because PHP3 scripts usually use the *.php3* suffix. The problem can be corrected by renaming the script files so they end in the *.php* suffix or by adding an additional AddType directive to the Apache *httpd.conf* file:

```
AddType application/x-httpd-php .php3
```

In some rare cases, a PHP3 script might require minor modifications to run under PHP4.

MySQL and SQL

In this chapter, we introduce the MySQL database management system (DBMS) and the SQL database query language for defining and manipulating databases. Using our case study, Hugh and Dave's Online Wines, as a guide, we illustrate examples of how to use SQL. The techniques that we discuss are used to interact with a DBMS after a database has been designed. An introduction to relational modeling and design can be found in Appendix C, and a more comprehensive introduction to MySQL and SQL can be found in many of the resources that are listed in Appendix E.

In this chapter, we cover the following topics:

- A short introduction to relational databases and relational modeling
- A quick start guide to the *winestore* database and its full entity-relationship model
- The MySQL command interpreter and the basic features of MySQL
- Using SQL to create and modify databases, tables, and indexes
- Using SQL to insert, delete, and update data
- The SQL SELECT statement for querying, with examples of simple and advanced queries
- Functions and operators in SQL and MySQL
- Advanced features, including managing indexes and keys, tuning the MySQL DBMS, security, and the limitations of MySQL

We assume that you have already installed MySQL. If not, the guide in Appendix A will help you. Chapter 6 covers other selected advanced database topics that arise when writing to databases, such as supporting multiple users, transactions, and locking in MySQL. Complete examples of SQL queries and MySQL in use in a web database application can be found in Chapters 10 to 13.

Database Basics

The field of databases has its own terminology. Terms such as database, table, attribute, row, primary key, and relational model have specific meanings and are used throughout this chapter. In this section, we present an example of a simple database to introduce the basic components of relational databases, and we list and define selected terms used in the chapter. More detail can be found in Appendix C.

Introducing Relational Databases

An example relational database is shown in Figure 3-1. This database stores data about wineries and the wine regions they are located in. A relational database manages data in tables, and there are two tables in this example: a *winery* table that manages wineries, and a *region* table that manages information about wine regions.

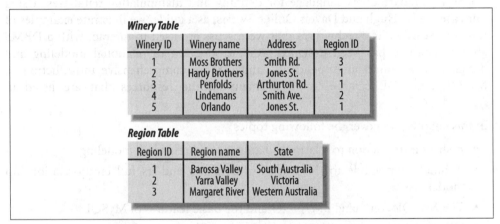

Winery Table

Winery ID	Winery name	Address	Region ID
1	Moss Brothers	Smith Rd.	3
2	Hardy Brothers	Jones St.	1
3	Penfolds	Arthurton Rd.	1
4	Lindemans	Smith Ave.	2
5	Orlando	Jones St.	1

Region Table

Region ID	Region name	State
1	Barossa Valley	South Australia
2	Yarra Valley	Victoria
3	Margaret River	Western Australia

Figure 3-1. An example relational database containing two related tables

Databases are managed by a relational database management system (RDBMS). An RDBMS supports a database language to create and delete databases and to manage and search data. The database language used in almost all DBMSs is SQL, a set of statements that define and manipulate data. After creating a database, the most common SQL statements used are INSERT, UPDATE, DELETE, and SELECT, which add, change, remove, and search data in a database, respectively.

A database table may have multiple columns, or *attributes*, each of which has a name. For example, the *winery* table in Figure 3-1 has four attributes, winery ID, winery name, address, and region ID. A table contains the data as rows or records, and a row contains attribute values. The *winery* table has five rows, one for each winery managed by the database, and each row has a set of values. For example, the first winery has a winery ID value of 1, the winery name value Moss Brothers, and an address of Smith Rd., and is situated in the region ID numbered 3. Region 3 is a row in the *region* table and is Margaret River in Western Australia.

The relationship between wineries and regions is maintained by assigning a region ID to each winery row. Managing relationships in this way is fundamental to relational database technology, and different types of relationship can be maintained. In this example, more than one winery can be situated in a region—three wineries in the example are situated in the Barossa Valley—but a winery can be situated in only one region.

Attributes have data types. For example, in the *winery* table, the winery ID is an integer, the winery name and address are strings, and the region ID is an integer. Data types are assigned when a database is designed.

Tables usually have a *primary key*, which is one or more values that uniquely identify each row in a table. The primary key of the *winery* table is winery ID, and the primary key of the *region* table is region ID. Primary keys are usually indexed to provide fast access to rows when they are searched by the primary key value. For example, an index is used to find the details of the region row that matches a given region ID in a *winery* table row.

Figure 3-2 shows the example database modeled using *entity-relationship (ER) modeling*. The *winery* and *region* tables or entities are shown as rectangles. Each entity has attributes, and the primary key is shown underlined. The relationship between the tables is shown as a diamond that connects the two tables, and in this example the relationship is annotated with an M at the *winery*-end of the relationship. The M indicates that there are potentially many winery rows associated with each region. Because the relationship isn't annotated at the other end, this means that there is only one region associated with each winery. ER modeling is discussed in more detail in Appendix C.

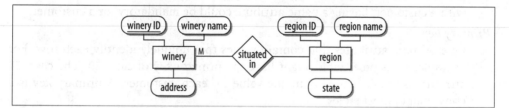

Figure 3-2. An example relational model of the winery database

Terminology

Database

A repository to store data.

Table

The part of a database that stores the data. A table has columns or attributes, and the data stored in rows.

Attributes

The columns in a table. All rows in table entities have the same attributes. For example, a customer table might have the attributes name, address, and city. Each attribute has a data type such as string, integer, or date.

Rows

The data entries in a table. Rows contain values for each attribute. For example, a row in a customer table might contain the values "Matthew Richardson," "Punt Road," and "Richmond." Rows are also known as records.

Relational model

A model that uses tables to store data and manage the relationship between tables.

Relational database management system

A software system that manages data in a database and is based on the relational model. DBMSs have several components described in detail in Chapter 1.

SQL

A query language that interacts with a DBMS. SQL is a set of statements to manage databases, tables, and data.

Constraints

Restrictions or limitations on tables and attributes. For example, a wine can be produced only by one winery, an order for wine can't exist if it isn't associated with a customer, having a name attribute could be mandatory for a customer.

Primary key

One or more attributes that contain values that uniquely identify each row. For example, a customer table might have the primary key of cust ID. The cust ID attribute is then assigned a unique value for each customer. A primary key is a constraint of most tables.

Index

A data structure used for fast access to rows in a table. An index is usually built for the primary key of each table and can then be used to quickly find a particular row. Indexes are also defined and built for other attributes when those attributes are frequently used in queries.

Entity-relationship modeling

A technique used to describe the real-world data in terms of entities, attributes, and relationships. This is discussed in Appendix C.

Normalized database

A correctly designed database that is created from an ER model. There are different types or levels of normalization, and a third-normal form database is generally regarded as being an acceptably designed relational database. We discuss normalization in Appendix C.

Quick Start Guide

This section is a quick start guide to loading the sample *winestore* database and understanding the design of the *winestore* database that is used in examples throughout this book.

Loading the Winestore Database

A local copy of the *winestore* database is required to test the examples in this and later chapters. MySQL must be installed and configured before the *winestore* database can be loaded. MySQL installation instructions can be found in Appendix A.

The steps to load the *winestore* database are as follows:

1. Download a copy of the *winestore* database from this book's web site; look for *winestore.database.tar.gz.*

2. Uncompress the winestore database package in any directory by running:

   ```
   gzip -d winestore.database.tar.gz
   ```

3. Untar the tape archive file by running:

   ```
   tar xvf winestore.database.tar
   ```

   A list of files extracted is output.

4. Check that MySQL is running using:

   ```
   /usr/local/bin/mysqladmin -uroot -ppassword version
   ```

   where *password* is the root user password. If MySQL isn't running, log in as the Linux root user, and start the MySQL server using:

   ```
   /usr/local/bin/safe_mysqld --user=mysql &
   ```

5. Run the MySQL command-line interpreter using the username and password created when MySQL was installed, and load the *winestore* data. The login name is *username,* and the password is *password:*

   ```
   /usr/local/bin/mysql -uusername -ppassword < winestore.database
   ```

6. After the loading is complete—it may take a few seconds—the database can be tested by running a query. Type the following command on one line:

   ```
   /usr/local/bin/mysql -uusername -ppassword -e 'USE winestore; SELECT * FROM
   region;'
   ```

This should produce the list of wine regions as output:

```
+-----------+--------------------+-------------+------+
| region_id | region_name        | description | map  |
+-----------+--------------------+-------------+------+
|         1 | Goulburn Valley    | NULL        | NULL |
|         2 | Rutherglen         | NULL        | NULL |
|         3 | Coonawarra         | NULL        | NULL |
|         4 | Upper Hunter Valley | NULL       | NULL |
|         5 | Lower Hunter Valley | NULL       | NULL |
|         6 | Barossa Valley     | NULL        | NULL |
|         7 | Riverland          | NULL        | NULL |
|         8 | Margaret River     | NULL        | NULL |
|         9 | Swan Valley        | NULL        | NULL |
+-----------+--------------------+-------------+------+
```

The *winestore* database has now been loaded and tested.

The Winestore Database

To complete the introduction to the *winestore* database, we include in this section a summary of the entity-relationship model of the winestore and the SQL statements that create the winestore using the MySQL DBMS. This section is included for easy reference.

The winestore entity-relationship model

Figure 3-3 shows the completed entity-relationship model for the online winestore derived from the system requirements listed in Chapter 1. Appendix C includes a description of the meaning of each shape and line type used in the figure.

The *winestore* model can be summarized as follows:

- A *customer* at the online winestore purchases wines by placing one or more *orders*.
- Each *customer* has exactly one set of *user* details.
- Each *order* contains one or more *items*.
- Each *item* is for a specific quantity of *wine* at a specific price.
- A *wine* is of a type such as "Red," "White," or "Sparkling."
- A *wine* has a vintage year; if the same wine has two or more vintages from different years, these are treated as two or more separate, distinct wines.
- Each *wine* is made by one *winery*.
- Each *winery* is located in one *region*.
- Each *wine* has one or more *grape_variety* entries. For example, a wine of wine_name "Archibald" might be made of the *grape_variety* entries "Sauvignon" and "Cabernet." The order of the entries is important. For example, a "Cabernet Sauvignon" is different from a "Sauvignon Cabernet."

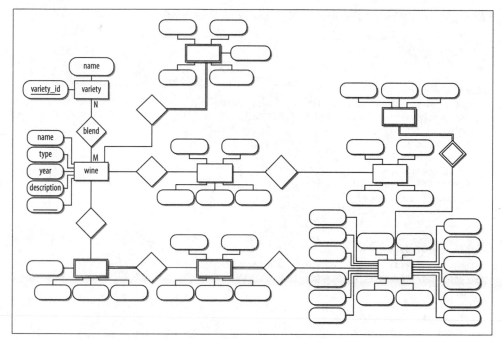

Figure 3-3. The winestore ER model

- Each *wine* may have one or more *inventories*.
- Each *inventory* for a *wine* represents the on-hand stock of a wine that is available at a particular cost or case_cost (a case is 12 bottles of wine). If a wine is available at two prices, there are two inventories.

Creating the winestore with SQL

The CREATE TABLE SQL statements that build the *winestore* database are shown for reference in Example 3-1.

The statements in Example 3-1 are derived from the entity-relationship model in Figure 3-1, and the process of converting this model to CREATE TABLE statements is described in Appendix C. An electronic copy of the statements can be found in the *winestore.database* file used to create the *winestore* database earlier in this section.

Example 3-1. The complete winestore DDL statements

```
CREATE TABLE wine (
  wine_id int(5) DEFAULT '0' NOT NULL auto_increment,
  wine_name varchar(50) DEFAULT '' NOT NULL,
  winery_id int(4),
  type varchar(10) DEFAULT '' NOT NULL,
  year int(4) DEFAULT '0' NOT NULL,
  description blob,
  PRIMARY KEY (wine_id),
```

Example 3-1. The complete winestore DDL statements (continued)

```
  KEY name (wine_name)
  KEY winery (winery_id)
);

CREATE TABLE winery (
  winery_id int(4) DEFAULT '0' NOT NULL auto_increment,
  winery_name varchar(100) DEFAULT '' NOT NULL,
  region_id int(4),
  description blob,
  phone varchar(15),
  fax varchar(15),
  PRIMARY KEY (winery_id),
  KEY name (winery_name)
  KEY region (region_id)
);

CREATE TABLE region (
  region_id int(4) DEFAULT '0' NOT NULL auto_increment,
  region_name varchar(100) DEFAULT '' NOT NULL,
  description blob,
  map mediumblob,
  PRIMARY KEY (region_id),
  KEY region (region_name)
);

CREATE TABLE customer (
  cust_id int(5) NOT NULL auto_increment,
  surname varchar(50) NOT NULL,
  firstname varchar(50) NOT NULL,
  initial char(1),
  title varchar(10),
  addressline1 varchar(50) NOT NULL,
  addressline2 varchar(50),
  addressline3 varchar(50),
  city varchar(20) NOT NULL,
  state varchar(20),
  zipcode varchar(5),
  country varchar(20),
  phone varchar(15),
  fax varchar(15),
  email varchar(30) NOT NULL,
  birth_date date( ),
  salary int(7),
  PRIMARY KEY (cust_id),
  KEY names (surname,firstname)
);

CREATE TABLE users (
  cust_id int(4) DEFAULT '0' NOT NULL,
  user_name varchar(50) DEFAULT '' NOT NULL,
  password varchar(15) DEFAULT '' NOT NULL,
  PRIMARY KEY (user_name),
```

Example 3-1. The complete winestore DDL statements (continued)

```
  KEY password (password)
);

CREATE TABLE grape_variety (
  variety_id int(3),
  variety_name varchar(20),
  PRIMARY KEY (variety_id),
  KEY var (variety)
);

CREATE TABLE inventory (
  wine_id int(5) DEFAULT '0' NOT NULL,
  inventory_id int(3) NOT NULL,
  on_hand int(5) NOT NULL,
  cost float(5,2) NOT NULL,
  case_cost float(5,2) NOT NULL,
  dateadded timestamp(12) DEFAULT NULL,
  PRIMARY KEY (wine_id,inventory_id)
);

CREATE TABLE orders (
  cust_id int(5) DEFAULT '0' NOT NULL,
  order_id int(5) DEFAULT '0' NOT NULL,
  date timestamp(12),
  discount float(3,1) DEFAULT '0.0',
  delivery float(4,2) DEFAULT '0.00',
  note varchar(120),
  PRIMARY KEY (cust_id,order_no)
);

CREATE TABLE items (
  cust_id int(5) DEFAULT '0' NOT NULL,
  order_id int(5) DEFAULT '0' NOT NULL,
  item_id int(3) DEFAULT '1' NOT NULL,
  wine_id int(4) DEFAULT '0' NOT NULL
  qty int(3),
  price float(5,2),
  date timestamp(12),
  PRIMARY KEY (cust_id,order_no,item_id)
);

CREATE TABLE wine_variety (
  wine_id int(5) DEFAULT '0' NOT NULL,
  variety_id int(3) DEFAULT '0' NOT NULL,
  id int(1) DEFAULT '0' NOT NULL,
  PRIMARY KEY (wine_id, variety_id)
);
```

MySQL Command Interpreter

The MySQL command interpreter is commonly used to create databases and tables in web database applications and to test queries. Throughout the remainder of this chapter we discuss the SQL statements for managing a database. All these statements can be directly entered into the command interpreter and executed. The statements can also be included in server-side PHP scripts, as discussed in later chapters.

Once the MySQL DBMS server is running, the command interpreter can be used. The command interpreter can be run using the following command from the shell, assuming you've created a user *hugh* with a password *shhh*:

```
% /usr/local/bin/mysql -uhugh -pshhh
```

The shell prompt is represented here as a percentage character, %.

Running the command interpreter displays the output:

```
Welcome to the MySQL monitor.  Commands end with ; or \g.
Your MySQL connection id is 36 to server version: 3.22.38

Type 'help' for help.

mysql>
```

The command interpreter displays a mysql> prompt and, after executing any command or statement, it redisplays the prompt. For example, you might issue the statement:

```
mysql> SELECT NOW( );
```

This statement reports the time and date by producing the following output:

```
+---------------------+
| NOW( )              |
+---------------------+
| 2002-01-01 13:48:07 |
+---------------------+
1 row in set (0.00 sec)

mysql>
```

After running a statement, the interpreter redisplays the mysql> prompt. We discuss the SELECT statement later in this chapter.

As with all other SQL statements, the SELECT statement ends in a semicolon. Almost all SQL command interpreters permit any amount of whitespace—spaces, tabs, or carriage returns—in SQL statements, and they check syntax and execute statements only after encountering a semicolon that is followed by a press of the Enter key. We have used uppercase for the SQL statements throughout this book. However, any mix of upper- and lowercase is equivalent.

On startup, the command interpreter encourages the use of the help command. Typing help produces a list of commands that are native to the MySQL interpreter and that aren't part of SQL. All non-SQL commands can be entered without the terminating semicolon, but the semicolon can be included without causing an error.

The MySQL command interpreter allows flexible entry of commands and SQL statements:

- The up and down arrow keys allow previously entered commands and statements to be browsed and used.

- The interpreter has command completion. If you type the first few characters of a string that has previously been entered and press the Tab key, the interpreter automatically completes the command. For example, if wines is typed and the Tab key pressed, the command interpreter outputs winestore, assuming the word winestore has been previously used.

  If there's more than one option that begins with the characters entered, or you wish the strings that match the characters to be displayed, press the Tab key twice to show all matches. You can then enter additional characters to remove any ambiguity and press the Tab key again for command completion.

  Several common statements and commands are pre-stored, including most of the SQL keywords discussed in this chapter.

- To use the default text editor to create SQL statements, enter the command edit in the interpreter. This invokes the editor defined by the EDITOR shell environment variable. When the editor is exited, the MySQL command interpreter reads, parses, and runs the file created in the editor.

- When the interpreter is quit and run again later, the history of commands and statements is kept. It is still possible to scroll up using the up arrow and to execute commands and statements that were entered earlier.

- You can run commands and SQL statements without actually launching the MySQL command interpreter. For example, to run SELECT now() from the Linux shell, enter the following command:

  ```
  mysql -ppassword -e "SELECT now();"
  ```

  This is particularly useful for adding SQL commands to shell or other scripts.

Managing Databases, Tables, and Indexes

The *Data Definition Language* (DDL) is the set of SQL statements used to manage a database. In this section, we use the MySQL command interpreter to create databases and tables using the online winestore as a case study. We also discuss the statements that delete, alter, and drop databases and tables, as well as statements for managing indexes.

Creating Databases

The `CREATE DATABASE` statement can create a new, empty database without any tables or data. The following statement creates a database called *winestore*:

```
mysql> CREATE DATABASE winestore;
```

To work with a database, the command interpreter requires the user to be using a database before SQL statements can be issued. Different command interpreters have different methods for using a database and these aren't part of the SQL standard. In the MySQL interpreter, you can issue the command:

```
mysql> use winestore
```

For the rest of this chapter, we omit the `mysql>` prompt from the command examples.

Creating Tables

After issuing the `use winestore` command, you then usually issue commands to create the tables in the database, as shown in Example 3-1. (You already created the tables in the *winestore* database in the "Quick Start Guide" section of this chapter). Let's look at one of these tables, the *customer* table. The statement that created this table is shown in Example 3-2.

Example 3-2. Creating the customer table with SQL

```
CREATE TABLE customer (
  cust_id int(5) DEFAULT '0' NOT NULL auto_increment,
  surname varchar(50) NOT NULL,
  firstname varchar(50) NOT NULL,
  initial char(1),
  title varchar(10),
  addressline1 varchar(50) NOT NULL,
  addressline2 varchar(50),
  addressline3 varchar(50),
  city varchar(20) NOT NULL,
  state varchar(20),
  zipcode varchar(5),
  country varchar(20) DEFAULT 'Australia',
  phone varchar(15),
  fax varchar(15),
  email varchar(30) NOT NULL,
  salary int(7),
  birth_date date(),
  PRIMARY KEY (cust_id),
  KEY names (surname,firstname)
);
```

The `CREATE TABLE` statement has three parts:

- Following the `CREATE TABLE` statement is a free-form table name—in this case customer.

- Following an opening bracket is a list of attribute names, types, and modifiers.
- After the attribute list is a list of keys; that is, information defining what attributes satisfy the uniqueness constraints of a primary key and what attributes are to be indexed for fast access.

A table name may contain any character except a forward slash / or a period, and the name is usually the name of an entity created in the ER model. Attribute names may contain any character, and there are many possible data types for attributes. Details of selected commonly used types are shown in Table 3-1.

Table 3-1. Common SQL data types for attributes

Data type	Comments
int(*length*)	Integer; used for IDs, age, counters, etc.
float(*length*,*decimals*)	Floating-point number; used for currency, measurements, etc.
timestamp(*length*)	Updates each time the row is modified or can be manually set. A length of 14 (the default) displays an attribute containing date and time in the format YYYYMMDDHHMMSS. Length 12 displays YYMMDDHHMMSS, 8 displays YYYYMMDD, and 6 displays YYMMDD.
char(*length*)	A space-padded, fixed-length text string.
varchar(*length*)	An unpadded, variable-length text string with a specified maximum *length*.
blob	An attribute that stores up to 64 KB of data.

For situations where the data stored is always much smaller or larger than the maximum possible value, many attribute types have variants of tiny, small, medium, and big. For example, int has variants smallint, mediumint, and bigint.

Modifiers may be applied to attributes. Two common modifiers are NOT NULL—data can't be added without this attribute having a value—and DEFAULT, which sets the data to the value that follows when no data is supplied.

Identifier attributes—an example in the *customer* table is the cust_id attribute—often have the modifier auto_increment. The auto_increment modifier automatically writes a unique number into an attribute when no value is supplied. For example, if you insert 10 customer rows into the *customer* table, you can automatically generate a cust_id of 11 by inserting NULL (or zero) as the value for cust_id. Only one attribute in each table can have the auto_increment modifier.

All numeric attributes have optional zerofill and unsigned modifiers. The former left-pads a value with zeros up to the size of the attribute type. The latter allows only positive values to be stored and roughly doubles the maximum positive value that can be stored.

Inserting NULL into a TIMESTAMP (or another date or time type) attribute stores the current date and time. What is stored in the attribute depends on its length. For example, if the attribute has the type TIMESTAMP(12), both the time and date are stored in the format YYMMDDHHMMSS. If today is January 3, 2002 and time is 10:43:23, the value stored is 020103104323.

More details on attribute types and modifiers can be found in Section 7.7 of the *manual.html* file distributed with MySQL.

The final component of the CREATE TABLE statement is a specification of key constraints and indexes that are required. In Example 3-2, we specify that the unique identifier is the cust_id attribute by adding the statement PRIMARY KEY (cust_id). The PRIMARY KEY constraint has two restrictions: the attribute must be defined as NOT NULL, and any value inserted must be unique. It is good practice to explicitly state a PRIMARY KEY for all tables; determining primary keys from an ER model is discussed in Appendix C.

We also show in our example another KEY definition; KEY is a synonym for INDEX. In this case, we have defined a KEY names (surname, firstname) to permit fast access to data stored in the *customer* table by a combination of surname and firstname values. In many cases—without yet knowing what kinds of queries will be made on the database—it is difficult to determine what indexes should be specified. MySQL permits up to 16 indexes to be created on any table, but unnecessary indexes should be avoided. Each index takes additional space, and it must be updated as the data stored in the table is inserted, deleted, and modified. We discuss index tuning in the "More on SQL and MySQL" section.

Altering Tables and Indexes

Indexes can be added or removed from a table after creation. For example, to add an index to the *customer* table, you can issue the following statement:

```
ALTER TABLE customer ADD INDEX cities (city);
```

To remove an index from the *customer* table, use the following statement:

```
ALTER TABLE customer DROP INDEX names;
```

The ALTER TABLE statement can also be used to add, remove, and alter all other aspects of the table, such as attributes and the primary index. We don't discuss statements for altering the database in this book; many examples can be found in Section 7.8 of the *manual.html* file that is distributed with MySQL.

Displaying Database Structure with SHOW

Details of databases, tables, and indexes can be displayed with the SHOW command. The SHOW command isn't part of the SQL standard and is MySQL-specific. It can be used in several ways:

SHOW DATABASES
Lists the databases that are accessible by the MySQL DBMS.

SHOW TABLES
> Shows the tables in the database once a database has been selected with the use command.

SHOW COLUMNS FROM tablename
> Shows the attributes, types of attributes, key information, whether NULL is permitted, defaults, and other information for a table. For example:
>
>   SHOW COLUMNS FROM customer
>
> shows the attribute information for the *customer* table. DESCRIBE table produces the same output.

SHOW INDEX FROM tablename
> Presents the details of all indexes on the table, including the PRIMARY KEY. For example:
>
>   SHOW INDEX FROM customer
>
> shows that there are two indexes, the primary index and the names index.

SHOW STATUS
> Reports details of the MySQL DBMS performance and statistics.

Inserting, Updating, and Deleting Data

The *Data Manipulation Language* (DML) encompasses all SQL statements used for manipulating data. There are four statements that form the DML statement set: SELECT, INSERT, DELETE, and UPDATE. We describe the last three statements in this section. While SELECT is also part of DML, we cover it in its own section, "Querying with SQL SELECT." Longer worked examples using all the statements can be found in the section "Modifying the Database."

Inserting Data

Having created a database and the accompanying tables and indexes, the next step is to insert data. Inserting a row of data into a table can follow two different approaches. We illustrate both approaches by inserting the same data for a new customer, Dimitria Marzalla.

Consider an example of the first approach using the *customer* table:

```
INSERT INTO customer
  VALUES (NULL,'Marzalla','Dimitria', 'F','Mrs',
          '171 Titshall Cl','','','St Albans','WA',
          '7608','Australia','(618)63576028','',
          'dimitria@lucaston.com','1969-11-08',35000);
```

In this approach a new row is created in the *customer* table, then the first value listed—in this case, a NULL—is inserted into the first attribute of *customer*. The first attribute of customer is cust_id and—because cust_id has the auto_increment modifier and this is the first row—a 1 is inserted as the cust_id. The value "Marzalla" is then inserted into the second attribute surname, "Dimitria" into firstname, and so on. The number of values inserted must be the same as the number of attributes in the table. To create an INSERT statement in this format, you need to understand the ordering of attributes in the table.

The number inserted by an auto_increment modifier can be checked with the MySQL-specific function last_insert_id(). In this example, you can check which cust_id was created with the statement:

```
SELECT last_insert_id( );
```

This statement reports:

```
+-------------------+
| last_insert_id( ) |
+-------------------+
|                 1 |
+-------------------+
1 row in set (0.00 sec)
```

You can see that the new row has cust_id=1. To check a value, the function should be called immediately after inserting a new row.

When inserting data, nonnumeric attributes must be enclosed in either single or double quotes. If a string contains single quotation marks, the string is enclosed in double quotation marks. For example, consider the string "Steve O'Dwyer". Likewise, strings containing double quotation marks can be enclosed in single quotation marks. An alternative approach is to escape the quotation character by using a backslash character; for example, consider the string 'Steve O\'Dwyer'. Numeric attributes aren't enclosed in quotes.

The same insertion can also be performed using a second approach. Consider this example:

```
INSERT INTO customer
    SET surname = 'Marzalla',
        firstname = 'Dimitria',
        initial='F',
        title='Mrs',
        addressline1='171 Titshall Cl',
        city='St Albans',
        state='WA',
        zipcode='7608',
        country='Australia',
        phone='(618)63576028',
        email='dimitria@lucaston.com',
        birthdate='1969-11-08',
        salary=35000;
```

In this approach, the attribute name is listed, followed by an assignment operator, "=", and then the value to be assigned. This approach doesn't require the same number of values as attributes, and it also allows arbitrary ordering of the attributes. cust_id isn't inserted, and it defaults to the next available cust_id value because of the combination of the auto_increment and DEFAULT modifiers.

The first approach can actually be varied to function in a similar way to the second by including parenthesized attribute names before the VALUES keyword. For example, you can create an incomplete *customer* row with:

```
INSERT INTO customer (surname,city) VALUES ('Smith','Sale');
```

Other approaches to loading data using a similar syntax are also possible. A popular variation is to insert data into a table from another table using a query, and it's discussed briefly in the section "INSERTing with a SELECT Statement."

Bulk loading into a database

Another data insertion method is to bulk-load data from a formatted ASCII text file. A formatted text file is usually a comma-delimited (also known as a comma-separated) or tab-delimited file, where the values to be inserted are separated by comma or tab characters, respectively.

The statement LOAD DATA INFILE can bulk-load data from a file. This is nonstandard SQL. For example, consider the following customer information that has been exported from a legacy spreadsheet program:

```
0,"Marzalla","Dimitria","F","Mrs","171 Titshall Cl","","","St
Albans","WA","7608","Australia", "(618)63576028","","dimitria@lucaston.com",
"1969-08-11","35000"
```

The data might be saved in the file *customer.cdf*. Note that the attribute values are in the same order as the attributes in the *winestore customer* table; most export wizards in spreadsheet software allow data to be reorganized as it is exported. Also, note that the first value is 0 and, because this value will be inserted into the cust_id attribute, the auto_increment feature assigns the next available cust_id value; inserting 0 has the same effect as inserting NULL.

The file can be inserted into the *customer* table using the statement:

```
LOAD DATA INFILE 'customer.cdf' INTO TABLE customer
        FIELDS TERMINATED BY ',' ENCLOSED BY '"'
        LINES TERMINATED BY '\n';
```

If quotation marks form part of an attribute, they must be escaped using backslashes:

```
"RMB 123, \"The Lofty Heights\""
```

Spreadsheet software often automatically escapes quotation marks in strings when data is exported.

Transferring data between databases and DBMSs

For many databases—particularly those in which legacy data is being redeployed into a DBMS—most of the data insertion occurs as the database is created. A common approach is to create a script that contains SQL statements that can be repeatedly replayed; it's the approach we used to create the *winestore* database. This has the advantage that the script can be run on many different DBMSs, and it makes migration easier than with the LOAD DATA INFILE approach.

To remove and partially rebuild the *winestore* database, we might author a script containing the statements shown in Example 3-3.

Example 3-3. Script for creating and inserting winestore data

```
DROP DATABASE winestore;
CREATE DATABASE winestore;
use winestore

CREATE TABLE customer (
    cust_id int(5) NOT NULL auto_increment,
    surname varchar(50) NOT NULL,
    firstname varchar(50) NOT NULL,
    initial char(1),
    title varchar(10),
    addressline1 varchar(50) NOT NULL,
    addressline2 varchar(50),
    addressline3 varchar(50),
    city varchar(20) NOT NULL,
    state varchar(20),
    zipcode varchar(5),
    country varchar(20),
    phone varchar(15),
    fax varchar(15),
    email varchar(30) NOT NULL,
    birthdate date( ),
    salary int(7),
    PRIMARY KEY (cust_id),
    KEY names (surname,firstname)
);

INSERT INTO customer VALUES (NULL,'Marzalla','Dimitria', 'F','Mrs','171 Titshall
Ccl','','','St Albans','WA', '7608','Australia','(618)63576028','', 'Dimitria@Lucaston.
com','1969-08-11',35000);

INSERT INTO customer VALUES (NULL,'LaTrobe','Anthony', 'Y','Mr','125 Barneshaw
St','','','Westleigh','WA','865
5','Australia','(618)73788578','(618)73786674', 'Anthony@Karumba.com','1952-03-10',54000);
```

Example 3-3. Script for creating and inserting winestore data (continued)

```
INSERT INTO customer VALUES (NULL,'Fong','Nicholas','K','Mr','99 Kinsala Pl',
'','','Stormlea','NSW','6400','Australia',
'(612)85534220','(612)85535180','Nicholas@Torquay.com',
'1942-06-29',170000);

INSERT INTO customer VALUES (NULL,'Stribling','James','','Mr','6 Woodburne Pl','','',
'Legana','QLD','6377','Australia','(617)66603522', '','James@Murrabit.com', '1943-11-
22',25000);
```

The script in Example 3-3, which has been saved to a file *winestore.database,* can be replayed using the MySQL command and a shell redirection:

```
% mysql -ppassword < winestore.database
```

This script runs the command interpreter with the statements and commands listed in the file *winestore.database.*

Data that is already managed in a MySQL database can be extracted using the utility *mysqldump*:

```
% mysqldump -ppassword winestore > winestore.database
```

The statements to DROP, CREATE, and use the database can be manually added with an editor to permit replaying of the script. We manually added the first three lines of Example 3-3 after using mysqldump to create the script.

To use the script to create a duplicate database, winestore2, for testing, you can change the first three lines of Example 3-3 to:

```
DROP DATABASE winestore2;
CREATE DATABASE winestore2;
use winestore2
```

Deleting Data

There is an important distinction between dropping and deleting in SQL. DROP is used to remove tables or databases; DELETE is used to remove data.

The statement:

```
DELETE FROM customer;
```

deletes all data in the *customer* table but doesn't remove the table. In contrast, dropping the table removes the data and the table.

A DELETE statement with a WHERE clause can remove specific rows; WHERE clauses are frequently used in querying, and they are explained later in the section "INSERTing with a SELECT Statement." Consider a simple example:

```
DELETE FROM customer WHERE cust_id = 1;
```

This deletes the customer with cust_id=1. Consider another example:

```
DELETE FROM customer WHERE surname = 'Smith';
```

This removes all rows for customers with the surname Smith.

Updating Data

Data can be updated using a similar syntax to that of the INSERT statement. Consider an example:

```
UPDATE customer SET email = lower(email);
```

This replaces the string values of all email attributes with the same string in lower-case. The function lower( ) is one of many functions discussed later in the section "Functions."

The UPDATE statement is also often used with the WHERE clause. For example:

```
UPDATE customer SET title = 'Dr' WHERE cust_id = 7;
```

This updates the title attribute of customer #7. Consider a second example:

```
UPDATE customer SET zipcode = '3001' WHERE city = 'Melbourne';
```

This updates the zipcode of all rows with a city value Melbourne.

Querying with SQL SELECT

We begin this section by covering the basics of using the SELECT statement. We then introduce the WHERE clause for selecting data that matches a condition. The section concludes with an introduction to the more advanced features of SELECT statements.

Basic Querying

The SELECT statement is used to query a database and for all output operations in SQL. Consider an example query:

```
SELECT surname, firstname FROM customer;
```

This outputs the values of the attributes surname and firstname from all rows, or records, in the *customer* table. Assuming we previously inserted four rows when we created the *winestore* database, the output from the MySQL command interpreter is:

```
+-----------+-----------+
| surname   | firstname |
+-----------+-----------+
| Marzalla  | Dimitria  |
| LaTrobe   | Anthony   |
| Fong      | Nicholas  |
| Stribling | James     |
+-----------+-----------+
4 rows in set (0.04 sec)
```

Any attributes of a table may be listed in a SELECT statement by separating each with a comma. If all attributes are required, the shortcut of an asterisk character (*) can be used. Consider the statement:

```
SELECT * FROM region;
```

This outputs all the data from the table *region*:

```
+-----------+--------------------+-------------+------+
| region_id | region_name        | description | map  |
+-----------+--------------------+-------------+------+
|         1 | Goulburn Valley    | NULL        | NULL |
|         2 | Rutherglen         | NULL        | NULL |
|         3 | Coonawarra         | NULL        | NULL |
|         4 | Upper Hunter Valley | NULL       | NULL |
+-----------+--------------------+-------------+------+
4 rows in set (0.07 sec)
```

SELECT statements can also output data that isn't from a database. Consider the following example:

```
SELECT curtime();
```

This example runs a function that displays the current time:

```
+-----------+
| curtime() |
+-----------+
| 08:41:50  |
+-----------+
1 row in set (0.02 sec)
```

The SELECT statement can even be used as a simple calculator, using the mathematical functions described in the later section "Functions":

```
SELECT log(100)*4*pi();
```

This outputs:

```
+-----------------+
| log(100)*4*pi() |
+-----------------+
|       57.870275 |
+-----------------+
1 row in set (0.19 sec)
```

WHERE Clauses

A WHERE clause is used as part of most SELECT queries; it limits retrieval to those rows that match a condition.

Consider this grape-growing *region* table containing the details of nine regions:

```
SELECT * from region;
+-----------+---------------------+-------------+------+
| region_id | region_name         | description | map  |
+-----------+---------------------+-------------+------+
|         1 | Goulburn Valley     | NULL        | NULL |
|         2 | Rutherglen          | NULL        | NULL |
|         3 | Coonawarra          | NULL        | NULL |
|         4 | Upper Hunter Valley | NULL        | NULL |
|         5 | Lower Hunter Valley | NULL        | NULL |
|         6 | Barossa Valley      | NULL        | NULL |
|         7 | Riverland           | NULL        | NULL |
|         8 | Margaret River      | NULL        | NULL |
|         9 | Swan Valley         | NULL        | NULL |
+-----------+---------------------+-------------+------+
9 rows in set (0.00 sec)
```

It is possible to select only a few rows with a SELECT statement by adding a WHERE clause. For example, to show only the first three regions, you can issue the following statement:

```
SELECT * FROM region
  WHERE region_id<=3;
```

This outputs all attributes for only the first three region rows:

```
+-----------+-----------------+-------------+------+
| region_id | region_name     | description | map  |
+-----------+-----------------+-------------+------+
|         1 | Goulburn Valley | NULL        | NULL |
|         2 | Rutherglen      | NULL        | NULL |
|         3 | Coonawarra      | NULL        | NULL |
+-----------+-----------------+-------------+------+
3 rows in set (0.00 sec)
```

You can combine the attribute and row restrictions and select only the region_name and region_id attributes for the first three regions:

```
SELECT region_id, region_name FROM region
  WHERE region_id <= 3;
+-----------+-----------------+
| region_id | region_name     |
+-----------+-----------------+
|         1 | Goulburn Valley |
|         2 | Rutherglen      |
|         3 | Coonawarra      |
+-----------+-----------------+
3 rows in set (0.00 sec)
```

More complex WHERE clauses use the Boolean operators AND and OR, as well as the functions described later in the section "Functions." The Boolean operators AND and OR have the same function as the PHP && and || operators introduced in Chapter 2.

Consider an example query that uses the Boolean operators:

```
SELECT * FROM customer
  WHERE surname='Marzalla' AND
        firstname='Dimitria';
```

This retrieves rows that match both criteria, that is, those customers with a surname Marzalla and a firstname Dimitria.

Consider a more complex example:

```
SELECT cust_id FROM customer
  WHERE (surname='Marzalla' AND firstname LIKE 'M%')
        OR email='john@lucaston.com';
```

This finds rows with either the surname Marzalla and a firstname beginning with M, or customers with the email address *john@lucaston.com*. The OR operator isn't exclusive, so an answer can have an email of *john@lucaston.com*, a surname of Marzalla, and a firstname beginning with M. This query, when run on the *winestore* database, returns:

```
+---------+
| cust_id |
+---------+
|     440 |
|     493 |
+---------+
2 rows in set (0.01 sec)
```

SELECT queries are often sophisticated and a long WHERE clause may include many AND and OR operators. More complex examples of queries are shown in the later section "Join Queries."

The WHERE clause is also a common component of UPDATE and DELETE statements, and we have shown simple examples of using WHERE with these earlier in this chapter. Consider another example of an UPDATE with a WHERE clause:

```
UPDATE wine SET winery_id = 298 WHERE winery_id = 299;
```

In this case, for wines that are made by the winery with winery_id=299, the winery_id is changed to winery_id=298.

The WHERE clause can be used similarly in a DELETE. Consider an example:

```
DELETE FROM wine WHERE winery_id = 299;
```

This removes only selected rows based on a condition; here the wines made by the winery with winery_id=299 are deleted.

Sorting and Grouping Output

We will now discuss techniques to manage the order and grouping of the output.

ORDER BY

The ORDER BY clause sorts the data after the query has been evaluated. Consider an example:

```
SELECT surname, firstname FROM customer
  WHERE title='Mr'
  AND city = 'Portsea'
  ORDER by surname;
```

This query finds all customers who have a title Mr and live in Portsea. It then presents the results sorted alphabetically by ascending surname:

```
+-----------+-----------+
| surname   | firstname |
+-----------+-----------+
| Dalion    | Anthony   |
| Galti     | Jim       |
| Keisling  | Mark      |
| Leramonth | James     |
| Mellili   | Derryn    |
| Mockridge | James     |
| Nancarral | Joshua    |
| Ritterman | James     |
+-----------+-----------+
8 rows in set (0.01 sec)
```

Sorting can be on multiple attributes. For example:

```
SELECT surname, firstname, initial FROM customer
  WHERE zipcode='3001' OR
        zipcode='3000'
  ORDER BY surname, firstname, initial;
```

This presents a list of customers in areas with zipcode='3000' or zipcode='3001', sorted first by ascending surname, then (for those customers with the same surname) by firstname, and (for those customers with the same surname and first name), by initial. So, for example, the output may be:

```
+-----------+-----------+---------+
| surname   | firstname | initial |
+-----------+-----------+---------+
| Keisling  | Belinda   | C       |
| Leramonth | Hugh      | D       |
| Leramonth | Joshua    | H       |
| Leramonth | Joshua    | R       |
| Young     | Bob       | A       |
+-----------+-----------+---------+
5 rows in set (0.11 sec)
```

By default, the ORDER BY clause sorts in ascending order, or ASC. To sort in reverse or descending order, DESC can be used. Consider an example:

```
SELECT * FROM customer
  WHERE city='Melbourne'
  ORDER BY surname DESC;
```

GROUP BY

The GROUP BY clause is different from ORDER BY because it doesn't sort the data for output. Instead, it sorts the data early in the query process, for the purpose of grouping or *aggregation*. An example shows the difference:

```
SELECT city, COUNT(*) FROM customer
    GROUP BY city;
```

This query outputs a sorted list of cities and, for each city, the COUNT of the number of customers who live in that city. The effect of COUNT(*) is to count the number of rows per group. In this example, it doesn't matter what is counted; COUNT(surname) has exactly the same result.

Here are the first few lines output by the query:

```
+--------------+----------+
| city         | COUNT(*) |
+--------------+----------+
| Alexandra    |       14 |
| Armidale     |        7 |
| Athlone      |        9 |
| Bauple       |        6 |
| Belmont      |       11 |
| Bentley      |       10 |
| Berala       |        9 |
| Broadmeadows |       11 |
```

The query aggregates or groups all the rows for each city into sets, and the COUNT(*) operation counts the number in each set. So, for example, there are 14 customers who live in Alexandra.

The GROUP BY clause can find different properties of the aggregated rows. Here's an example:

```
SELECT city, MAX(salary) FROM customer
    GROUP BY city;
```

This query first groups the rows by city and then shows the maximum salary in each city. The first few rows of the output are as follows:

```
+-----------+-------------+
| city      | MAX(salary) |
+-----------+-------------+
| Alexandra |      109000 |
| Armidale  |       75000 |
| Athlone   |       84000 |
| Bauple    |       33000 |
```

 The GROUP BY clause should be used only when the query is designed to find a characteristic of a group of rows, not the details of individual rows.

There are several functions that can be used in aggregation with the GROUP BY clause. Five particularly useful functions are:

AVG( )
> Finds the average value of a numeric attribute in a set

MIN( )
> Finds a minimum value of a string or numeric attribute in a set

MAX( )
> Finds a maximum value of a string or numeric attribute in a set

SUM( )
> Finds the sum total of a numeric attribute

COUNT( )
> Counts the number of rows in a set

The SQL standard places a constraint on the GROUP BY clause that MySQL doesn't enforce. In the standard, all attributes that are selected (i.e., appear after the SELECT statement) must appear in the GROUP BY clause. Most examples in this chapter don't meet this unnecessary constraint of the SQL standard.

HAVING

The HAVING clause permits conditional aggregation of data into groups. For example, consider the following query:

```
SELECT city, count(*), max(salary)
  FROM customer
  GROUP BY city
  HAVING count(*) > 10;
```

The query groups rows by city, but only for cities that have more than 10 resident customers. For those groups, the city, count( ) of customers, and maximum salary of a customer in that city is output. Cities with less than 10 customers are omitted from the result set. The first few rows of the output are as follows:

```
+--------------+----------+-------------+
| city         | count(*) | max(salary) |
+--------------+----------+-------------+
| Alexandra    |       14 |      109000 |
| Belmont      |       11 |       71000 |
| Broadmeadows |       11 |       51000 |
| Doveton      |       13 |       77000 |
| Eleker       |       11 |       97000 |
| Gray         |       12 |       77000 |
+--------------+----------+-------------+
```

The HAVING clause must contain an attribute or expression from the SELECT clause.

The HAVING clause is used exclusively with the GROUP BY clause. It is slow and should never be used instead of a WHERE clause.

DISTINCT

The DISTINCT operator presents only one example of each row from a query. Consider an example:

```
SELECT DISTINCT surname FROM customer;
```

This shows one example of each different customer surname in the *customer* table. This example has exactly the same effect as:

```
SELECT surname FROM customer GROUP BY surname;
```

The DISTINCT clause is usually slow to run, much like the GROUP BY clause. We discuss how indexes and query optimization can speed queries later in this chapter.

Limiting Result Sets in MySQL

An additional operator is available in MySQL that limits the size of the result sets. For example, the following query returns only the first five rows from the *wine* table:

```
SELECT * FROM wine LIMIT 5;
```

This saves query evaluation time and reduces the size of the result set that must be buffered by the DBMS. The LIMIT operator is MySQL-specific.

Join Queries

A *join query* is a querying technique that matches rows from two or more tables based on a join condition in a WHERE clause and outputs only those rows that meet the condition. As part of the process of converting the winestore entity-relationship model to SQL statements, we have included the attributes required in any practical join condition.

To understand which tables can be joined in the *winestore* database, and how the joins are processed, it is helpful to have a copy of the ER model at hand.

Beware of the Cartesian Product

Oddly, the easiest way to introduce join queries is to discuss what not to do. Consider this query, which we might intuitively, but wrongly, use to find all the wineries in a region:

```
SELECT winery_name,region_name FROM winery, region;
```

This query produces—in part—the following results:

```
+------------------------------+-------------+
| winery_name                  | region_name |
+------------------------------+-------------+
| Ryan Ridge Winery            | Victoria    |
| Macdonald Creek Premium Wines | Victoria    |
| Davie's                      | Victoria    |
| Porkenberger Brook Vineyard  | Victoria    |
| Rowley Hill Vineyard         | Victoria    |
```

The impression here is that, for example, Ryan Ridge Winery is located in the Victoria region. This might not be the case. Why? First, you can use the techniques covered so far in this chapter to check which region Ryan Ridge Winery is located in:

```
SELECT region_id FROM winery
  WHERE winery_name='Ryan Ridge Winery';
```

The result is `region_id=2`.

Now query the *region* table to find the name of `region_id=2` using:

```
SELECT region_name FROM region
  WHERE region_id=2;
```

The `region_name` is South Australia. So, Ryan Ridge Winery isn't in Victoria at all!

What happened in the first attempt at a join query? The technical answer is that you just evaluated a *cartesian product*; that is, you produced as output all the possible combinations of wineries and regions. These odd results can be seen if you add an `ORDER BY` clause to the original query:

```
SELECT winery_name, region_name FROM winery, region
  ORDER BY winery_name, region_name;
```

Recall that the `ORDER BY` clause sorts the results after the query has been evaluated; it has no effect on which rows are returned from the query. Here is the first part of the result of the query with the `ORDER BY` clause:

```
+----------------------+-------------------+
| winery_name          | region_name       |
+----------------------+-------------------+
| Anderson Creek Wines | New South Wales   |
| Anderson Creek Wines | South Australia   |
| Anderson Creek Wines | Victoria          |
| Anderson Creek Wines | Western Australia |
| Anderson Group       | New South Wales   |
| Anderson Group       | South Australia   |
| Anderson Group       | Victoria          |
| Anderson Group       | Western Australia |
```

The query produces all possible combinations of the four region names and 300 wineries in the sample database! In fact, the size of the output can be accurately calculated as the total number of rows in the first table multiplied by the total rows in the second table. In this case, the output is 4 × 300 = 1,200 rows.

Elementary Natural Joins

A cartesian product isn't the join we want. Instead, we want to limit the results to only the sensible rows, where the winery is actually located in the region. From a database perspective, we want only rows in which the region_id in the *winery* table matches the corresponding region_id in the *region* table. This is a *natural join.*[*]

Consider a revised example using a natural join:

```
SELECT winery_name, region_name
  FROM winery, region
  WHERE winery.region_id = region.region_id
  ORDER BY winery_name;
```

An ORDER BY clause has been added to sort the results by winery_name but this doesn't affect the join. This query produces—in part—the following sensible results:

```
+----------------------+--------------------+
| winery_name          | region_name        |
+----------------------+--------------------+
| Anderson Creek Wines | Western Australia  |
| Anderson Group       | New South Wales    |
| Beard                | South Australia    |
| Beard and Sons       | Western Australia  |
| Beard Brook          | New South Wales    |
```

Several features are shown in this first successful natural join:

- The FROM clause contains more than one table name. In this example, SELECT retrieves rows from the tables *winery* and *region*.

- Attributes in the WHERE clause are specified using both the table name and attribute name, separated by a period. This usually disambiguates uses of the same attribute name in different tables.

  So, for example, region_id in the *region* table and region_id in the *winery* table are disambiguated as region.region_id and winery.region_id. This procedure can also be used for clarity in queries, even if it isn't required. It can be used in all parts of the query, not just the WHERE clause.

- The WHERE clause includes a join clause that matches rows between the multiple tables. In this example, the output is reduced to those rows where wineries and regions have matching region_id attributes, resulting in a list of all wineries and which region they are located in. This is the key to joining two or more tables to produce sensible results.

---

[*] It isn't quite true to say that the joins described here are natural joins. A true natural join doesn't require you to specify the join condition, because "natural" implies that the system figures this out itself. So, a real natural join doesn't need the WHERE clause; one is automatically included "behind the scenes." The joins described throughout this chapter are actually called *inner joins*, but the results are identical to a those of a natural join.

Examples

The natural join can be used in many other examples in the winestore. Consider another example that finds all the wines made by all the wineries:

```
SELECT winery_name, wine_name, type
   FROM winery, wine WHERE
      wine.winery_id = winery.winery_id;
```

This query finds all wines made by wineries through a natural join of the *winery* and *wine* tables using the `winery_id` attribute. The result is a large table of the 1,028 wines stocked at the winestore, their types, and the relevant wineries.

You can extend this query to produce a list of wines made by a specific winery or group of wineries. To find all wines made by wineries with a name beginning with Borg, use:

```
SELECT winery_name, wine_name, type
   FROM winery, wine WHERE
      wine.winery_id = winery.winery_id AND
      winery.winery_name LIKE 'Borg%';
```

This example extends the previous example by producing not all natural join pairs of wines and wineries, but only those for the winery or wineries beginning with Borg. The `LIKE` clause is covered later, in the "Functions" section.

Here are two more example join queries:

- To find the name of the region Ryan Ridge Winery is situated in:

```
SELECT region.region_name FROM region,winery
   WHERE winery.region_id=region.region_id AND
      winery.winery_name='Ryan Ridge Winery';
```

- To find which winery makes Curry Hill Red:

```
SELECT winery.winery_name FROM winery, wine
   WHERE wine.winery_id=winery.winery_id AND
      wine.wine_name='Curry Hill Red';
```

Table aliases in SQL queries

To save typing and add additional functionality, table aliases are sometimes used in queries. Consider an example that finds all inventory details of wine #183:

```
SELECT * FROM inventory i, wine w
WHERE i.wine_id = 183 AND
      i.wine_id = w.wine_id;
```

In this query, the `FROM` clause specifies aliases for the table names. The alias `inventory i` means than the *inventory* table can be referred to as `i` elsewhere in the query. For example, `i.wine_id` is the same as `inventory.wine_id`. This saves typing in this query.

Aliases are powerful for complex queries that need to use the same table twice but in different ways. For example, to find any two customers with the same `surname`, you can write the query:

```
SELECT c1.cust_id, c2.cust_id FROM
    customer c1, customer c2 WHERE
    c1.surname = c2.surname AND
    c1.cust_id != c2.cust_id;
```

The final clause, c1.cust_id!=c2.cust_id, is essential; without it, all customers are reported as answers. This occurs because all customers are rows in tables c1 and c2 and, for example, a customer with cust_id=1 in table c1 has—of course—the same surname as the customer with cust_id=1 in table c2.

Using DISTINCT in joins

The next join example uses the DISTINCT operator to find red wines that cost less than $10. Wines can have more than one inventory row, and the inventory rows for the same wine can have the same per-bottle cost. The DISTINCT operator shows each wine_name and cost pair once by removing any duplicates. To find which red wines cost less than $10, use:

```
SELECT DISTINCT wine_name, cost
  FROM wine,inventory WHERE
    wine.wine_id=inventory.wine_id AND
    inventory.cost<10 AND
    UPPER(wine.type)='RED';
```

Here are two examples that use DISTINCT to show only one matching answer:

- To find which cities customers live in:

  ```
  SELECT DISTINCT city FROM customer;
  ```

- To find which customers have ordered wines:

  ```
  SELECT DISTINCT surname,firstname FROM customer,orders
    WHERE customer.cust_id = orders.cust_id
    ORDER BY surname,firstname;
  ```

Joins with More than Two Tables

Queries can join more than two tables. In the next example, the query finds all details of each item from each order by a particular customer, customer #2. The example also illustrates how frequently the Boolean operators AND and OR are used:

```
SELECT * FROM customer, orders, items WHERE
  customer.cust_id = orders.cust_id AND
  orders.order_id = items.order_id AND
  orders.cust_id = items.cust_id AND
  customer.cust_id = 2;
```

In this query, the natural join is between three tables, *customer*, *orders*, and *items*, and the rows selected are those in which the cust_id is the same for all three tables, the cust_id is 2, and the order_id is the same in the *orders* and *items* tables.

If you remove the `cust_id=2` clause, the query outputs all items in all orders by all customers. This is a large result set, but still a sensible one that is much smaller than the cartesian product!

Here are two more examples that join three tables:

- To find which wines are made in the Margaret River region:

```
SELECT wine_name FROM wine,winery,region
  WHERE wine.winery_id=winery.winery_id AND
  winery.region_id=region.region_id AND
  region.region_name='Margaret River';
```

- To find which region contains the winery that makes the Red River Red wine:

```
SELECT region_name FROM wine,winery,region
  WHERE wine.winery_id=winery.winery_id AND
  winery.region_id=region.region_id AND
  wine.wine_name='Red River Red';
```

Extending to four or more tables generalizes the approach further. To find the details of customers who have purchased wines from Buonopane Wines, use:

```
SELECT DISTINCT customer.cust_id, customer.surname, customer.firstname
  FROM customer, winery, wine, items
  WHERE customer.cust_id=items.cust_id AND
    items.wine_id=wine.wine_id AND
    wine.winery_id=winery.winery_id AND
    winery.winery_name='Buonopane Wines'
  ORDER BY customer.surname, customer.firstname;
```

This last query is the most complex so far and contains a four-step process. The easiest way to understand a query is usually to start with the WHERE clause and work toward the SELECT clause:

1. The WHERE clause restricts the *winery* rows to those that bear the name Buonopane Wines.

2. The resultant *winery* rows—there is probably only one winery called Buonopane Wines—are joined with *wine* to find all wines made by Buonopane Wines.

3. The wines made by Buonopane Wines are joined with the *items* that have been purchased.

4. The purchases of Buonopane Wines are joined with the *customer* rows of the customers who have purchased the wine. You can leave out the *orders* table, because the *items* table contains a cust_id for the join; if you need the order number, the discount applied, or another *orders* attribute, the *orders* table needs to be included in the query.

5. The result is the details of customers who have purchased Buonopane Wines. DISTINCT is used to show each customer only once. ORDER BY sorts the customer rows into telephone directory order.

Designing a query like this is a step-by-step process. We began by testing a query to find the `winery_id` of wineries with the name Buonopane Wines. Then, after testing the query and checking the result, we progressively added additional tables to the FROM clause and join conditions. Finally, we added the ORDER BY clause.

The next example uses three tables but queries the complex many-to-many relationship in the winestore that exists between the *wines* and *grape_variety* tables via the *wine_variety* table. As outlined in the system requirements in Chapter 1, a wine can have one or more grape varieties and these are listed in a specific order (e.g., Cabernet, then Sauvignon). From the other perspective, a grape variety such as Cabernet can be in hundreds of different wines. The relationship is managed by creating an intermediate table between *grape_variety* and *wine* called *wine_variety*.

Here is the example query that joins all three tables. To find what grape varieties are in wine #1004, use:

```
SELECT variety FROM grape_variety, wine_variety, wine
  WHERE wine.wine_id=wine_variety.wine_id AND
  wine_variety.variety_id=grape_variety.variety_id AND
  wine.wine_id=1004
  ORDER BY wine_variety.id;
```

The result of the query is:

```
+-----------+
| variety   |
+-----------+
| Cabernet  |
| Sauvignon |
+-----------+
2 rows in set (0.00 sec)
```

The join condition is the same as any three-table query. The only significant difference is the ORDER BY clause that presents the results in the same order they were added to the *wine_variety* table (assuming the first variety gets ID=1, the second ID=2, and so on).

We've now covered as much complex querying in SQL as we need to in this chapter. If you'd like to learn more, see the pointers to resources included in Appendix E. SQL examples in web database applications can be found throughout Chapters 4 to 13.

Modifying the Database

In this section, we consider simple examples of writing data to databases. Multiple users writing data, how to manage locking of databases, and more complex transactions with the MySQL DBMS are discussed in Chapter 6.

Adding a New Wine to the Winestore

To illustrate a write transaction with the *winestore* database, consider an example of inserting a new wine. This process can be performed with the MySQL command-line interpreter. Only one user is interacting with the DBMS in this example.

Let's suppose that 24 bottles of a new wine, a Curry Hill Cabernet Merlot 1996 made by De Morton Hill wineries, have arrived, and you wish to add a row to the database for the new wine.

The addition has several steps, the first of which is an `INSERT INTO` statement to create the basic row for the wine in the *wine* table:

```
INSERT INTO wine
  SET wine_name='Curry Hill',
  type='Red',
  year=1996,
  description='A beautiful mature wine. Smooth to taste
               Ideal with red meat.';
```

This creates a new row and sets the basic attributes. The `wine_id` is set to the next available value because of the `auto_increment` and `DEFAULT` modifiers. The remaining attributes to insert require further querying and then subsequent updates.

The second step is to set the `winery_id` for the new wine. We need to search for the De Morton Hill winery to identify the `winery_id`:

```
SELECT winery_id FROM winery
  WHERE winery_name='De Morton Hill';
```

The result returned is:

```
+-----------+
| winery_id |
+-----------+
|       221 |
+-----------+
1 row in set (0.00 sec)
```

We can now update the new wine row to set the `winery_id=221`. However, which row to update? An easy way to find the `wine_id` of the new *wine* row is to use the built-in function `last_insert_id( )`. As discussed in the earlier section "Inserting, Updating, and Deleting Data," this function returns the number created by the most recent `auto_increment` modifier:

```
SELECT last_insert_id( );
```

This returns the `wine_id` of the inserted row:

```
+------------------+
| last_insert_id( ) |
+------------------+
|             1029 |
+------------------+
1 row in set (0.00 sec)
```

You can now issue the UPDATE statement:

```
UPDATE wine SET winery_id = 221
   WHERE wine_id = 1029;
```

The third step is to set the variety information for the new wine. We need the variety_id values for Cabernet and Merlot. These can be found with a simple query:

```
SELECT * FROM grape_variety;
```

In part, the following results are produced:

```
+------------+------------+
| variety_id | variety    |
+------------+------------+
|          1 | Riesling   |
|          2 | Chardonnay |
|          3 | Sauvignon  |
|          4 | Blanc      |
|          5 | Semillon   |
|          6 | Pinot      |
|          7 | Gris       |
|          8 | Verdelho   |
|          9 | Grenache   |
|         10 | Noir       |
|         11 | Cabernet   |
|         12 | Shiraz     |
|         13 | Merlot     |
```

Cabernet has a variety_id=11 and Merlot a variety_id=13. We can now insert two rows into the *wine_variety* table. Because Cabernet is the first variety, set its ID=1, and ID=2 for Merlot:

```
INSERT INTO wine_variety
   SET wine_id=1029, variety_id=11, id=1;
INSERT INTO wine_variety
   SET wine_id=1029, variety_id=13, id=2;
```

The final step is to insert the first *inventory* row into the *inventory* table for this wine. There are 24 bottles, with a per-bottle price of $14.95 and per-case price of $171.99:

```
INSERT INTO inventory VALUES (1029, 1, 24, 14.95, 171.99);
```

We've now completed the process of inserting rows into other tables in the winestore is similar. Adding data to the *winery*, *region*, *inventory*, and *orders* tables follows the same approach. Insertion of rows into the *customer* and *grape_variety* tables is simpler because there are no attributes that require lookups in other tables.

Buying a Bottle of Wine from the Winestore

In this example, we consider the steps required to buy a bottle of wine. Again, assume that there is only one user reading or writing data with the DBMS. The complete process—implemented as part of the winestore web database application—is described in Chapter 12.

To motivate this example, consider a customer, Dimitria Marzalla, who has added two bottles of the new De Morton Wines Curry Hill Cabernet Merlot 1996 to her shopping cart and now wishes to purchase the wines.

Before showing you how the purchase is finalized, let's examine the information recorded in the user shopping cart and what we know about the user.

First, we know that `cust_id=1` is the ID for this customer and that the wine being purchased has `wine_id=1029`. This associated information has been previously determined in the process of collecting data for the purchase in the online winestore.

Second, we need to consider how the shopping cart is managed in the winestore. We use the *orders* and *items* tables to manage the shopping cart for each user. When a user adds the first item to her shopping cart, a new row is created in the *orders* table with a dummy `cust_id=-1` and the next available `order_id` for this dummy customer. We use a dummy customer number because customers don't need to log in to add wine to their shopping carts, and because finalized orders are distinguished by having the `cust_id` of a customer who is a member.

For this example, assume that the shopping cart has `order_id=354`, and the dummy customer is `cust_id=-1`. Also assume that the row in the *items* table that represents the wine in the shopping cart has a `cust_id=-1`, an `order_id=354`, an `item_id=1`, a `wine_id=1029`, a quantity `qty=2`, and the price information for the wine. The price is $14.95 per bottle.

Before finalizing an order, we need to determine if there are two bottles of the wine available. A wine can be added to the shopping cart if there is any stock available, but this doesn't necessarily mean that there is more than one bottle left or that another user has not purchased the wine in the meantime. If there is sufficient wine available to finalize an order, we reduce the on-hand stock by two bottles. Checking if there are two bottles available can be done with the following query:

```
SELECT SUM(on_hand)
  FROM inventory
  WHERE wine_id=1029;
```

A GROUP BY `wine_id` is unnecessary in this case because only one wine is selected.

Assuming there are more than two bottles available, we need to reduce the on-hand stock, beginning with the oldest inventory; this was one of the system requirements defined in Chapter 1. There are several ways to find the oldest inventory and the wine per-bottle price. A simple technique is to inspect the inventories:

```
SELECT inventory_id,cost,on_hand
  FROM inventory
  WHERE wine_id=1029
  ORDER BY date_added;
```

The oldest (and only) `inventory_id=1`, and there is an on-hand stock of 24 bottles. We then reduce the on-hand stock by two:

```
UPDATE inventory
  SET on_hand = on_hand - 2
  WHERE wine_id=1029 AND inventory_id=1;
```

If the on-hand stock in an *inventory* row is reduced to zero—which isn't so in this case—we then remove that row:

```
DELETE FROM inventory
  WHERE wine_id = 1029 AND inventory_id=1;
```

Other possibilities may also occur, such as having to manipulate two inventories because the oldest inventory has only one bottle left. These possibilities are discussed in further detail in Chapter 12.

Having reserved two bottles of the wine for shipping, we can finalize the order for the customer. To do so, we need to store the details of the shopping cart entries in the *orders* and *items* tables. As discussed previously, by tracking the shopping cart of this user we know it has the order_id=354 for the dummy cust_id=-1. We also need to know how many previous orders this customer has made:

```
SELECT max(order_id) FROM orders WHERE customer_id=1;
```

If you find the customer previously made two orders, you update the shopping cart *order* row so that it is now the third order for this customer. Use this statement:

```
UPDATE orders SET cust_id = 1,
                  order_id = 3,
                  date = NULL,
                  delivery = 7.95,
                  discount = 0
    WHERE cust_id = -1 AND order_id = 354;
```

The shopping cart entry is now a customer order. date=NULL sets the date attribute to be the current system time and date. The delivery cost is $7.95, and there is no discount on the order.

To complete the order, we also update the related *items* row in the shopping cart, which contains the two bottles of wine. Use the following UPDATE statement:

```
UPDATE items SET cust_id = 1,
                 order_id = 3,
                 date = NULL
    WHERE cust_id = -1 AND
          order_id = 354 AND
          item_id = 1;
```

There is no need to update the wine_id, price, or qty (quantity).

We can now confirm to the customer the purchase of two bottles of Curry Hill and ship the order.

This isn't quite the whole picture of purchasing wines or updating the database. In Chapter 6, we return to similar examples and discuss the implications and problems of many users interacting with the database at the same time.

INSERTing with a SELECT Statement

We'll now show how insertion and querying can be closely tied together with an INSERT INTO ... SELECT statement. This is useful for copying data and, if needed, modifying the data as it is copied.

Consider an example to create a permanent record of the total sales to each customer up to this month, let's say it's April. First, create a simple table to store the customer and sales details:

```
CREATE TABLE salesuntilapril
(
cust_id int(5) NOT NULL,
surname varchar(50),
firstname varchar(50),
totalsales float(5,2),
PRIMARY KEY (cust_id)
);
```

Now issue a combined INSERT INTO ... SELECT statement to populate the new table with the customer details and the total sales:

```
INSERT INTO salesuntilapril
   (cust_id, surname, firstname, totalsales)
    SELECT customer.cust_id, surname, firstname, SUM(price)
      FROM customer, items
      WHERE customer.cust_id = items.cust_id
      GROUP BY items.cust_id;
```

The four attributes listed in the SELECT statement are mapped to the four attributes listed in the INSERT INTO statement. For example, the customer.cust_id in the SELECT line is mapped into cust_id in the *salesuntilapril* table.

A query on the new table shows part of the results:

```
SELECT * from salesuntilapril;
+---------+-------------+-----------+------------+
| cust_id | surname     | firstname | totalsales |
+---------+-------------+-----------+------------+
|       2 | LaTrobe     | Anthony   |     566.42 |
|       3 | Fong        | Nicholas  |     821.78 |
|       4 | Stribling   | James     |     181.69 |
|       5 | Choo        | Richard   |     534.99 |
|       6 | Eggelston   | Perry     |     657.37 |
|       7 | Mellaseca   | Kym       |    1216.88 |
```

There are two sensible limitations of the INSERT INTO ... SELECT statement: first, the query can't contain an ORDER BY, and second, the FROM clause can't contain the target table of the INSERT INTO.

Functions

Functions and operators can be used in SQL statements. This section lists these functions and operators and provides examples. A full list of functions with examples is available in Section 7.4 of the *manual.html* file distributed with MySQL.

Arithmetic and comparison operators

Table 3-2 shows examples of the basic arithmetic and comparison operators in SELECT statements. The basic arithmetic operators are *, +, /, and -, as well as the parentheses ( ) to control the order of evaluation of an expression.

Table 3-2. Using the arithmetic and comparison operators

Statement	Output
SELECT 8+3*2;	14
SELECT (8+3)*2;	22
SELECT 2=2;	1
SELECT 1!=2;	1
SELECT 2<=2;	1
SELECT 3<=2;	0

The comparison operators include =, !=, <, >, <=, and >=. Four examples are shown in Table 3-2. If an expression evaluates as true, the output is 1; if an expression evaluates as false, the output is 0. To test for equality, a single equals sign is used; this contrasts with PHP, where the double equals (==) is used for equality tests, and a single equals sign is used for assignment.

To test whether two items are equal, the != operator is provided. Less-than-or-equal-to is represented by <=, and greater-than-or-equal-to is represented by >=. Parentheses can explicitly express the evaluation order.

String-comparison operators and functions

Table 3-3 shows examples of the MySQL string-comparison operators and functions. Many of the MySQL string functions shown here are similar to PHP functions, which were introduced in Chapter 2.

Table 3-3. Using string comparison functions and operators

Statement	Output
SELECT 'Apple' LIKE 'A%';	1
SELECT 'Apple' LIKE 'App%';	1
SELECT 'Apple' LIKE 'A%l%';	1
SELECT concat('con','cat');	'concat'
SELECT length('Apple');	5

Table 3-3. Using string comparison functions and operators (continued)

Statement	Output
SELECT locate('pp','Apple');	2
SELECT substring('Apple',2,3);	'ppl'
SELECT ltrim(' Apple');	'Apple'
SELECT rtrim('Apple ');	'Apple'
SELECT trim(' Apple ');	'Apple'
SELECT space(3);	' '
SELECT strcmp('a','a');	0
SELECT strcmp('a','b');	-1
SELECT strcmp('b','a');	1
SELECT lower('Apple');	'apple'
SELECT upper('Apple');	'APPLE'

The string functions work as follows:

- The string-comparison function LIKE is useful. The % character represents any number of unspecified characters, are generally known as wildcards. So, for example, the comparison of the string 'Apple' LIKE 'A%' is 1 (true), as is the comparison of 'Apple' LIKE 'App%'. The underscore character can be used to match a single unspecified, wildcard character; for example, 'Apple' LIKE 'Appl_' is true, while 'Appl' LIKE 'Appl_' is false.

- concat( ) joins or concatenates two strings together, so the result of calling concat( ) with two string parameters is a single string consisting of the parameters.

- length( ) returns the length of the string in characters.

- locate( ) returns the location of the first string parameter in the second string parameter. If the string doesn't occur, the result is 0.

- substring( ) returns part of the string passed as the first parameter. The string that is returned begins at the offset supplied as the second parameter and is of the length supplied as the third parameter.

- ltrim( ) removes any left-padding space characters from the string parameter and returns the left-trimmed string.

- rtrim( ) removes any right-padding space characters from the string parameter and returns the right-trimmed string.

- trim( ) performs the function of both ltrim( ) and rtrim( ); that is, any leading or trailing spaces are removed, and the trimmed string is returned.

- space( ) returns a string consisting of spaces of the length of the integer parameter.

- strcmp( ) compares two string parameters. If they are identical, it returns 0. If the first string is alphabetically less than the second, it returns a negative number. If the first string is alphabetically greater than the second, it returns a positive number. Uppercase characters are less than lowercase characters.

- lower( ) converts the string parameter to lowercase and returns the lowercase string.

- upper( ) converts the string parameter to uppercase and returns the uppercase string.

While not detailed in Table 3-3, regular expressions can be used through the function regexp( ). For more on regular expressions in PHP, see Chapter 2.

Mathematical functions

We make little use of the mathematical functions provided by MySQL in this book. However, Table 3-4 shows selected MySQL mathematical functions and their output.

Table 3-4. Using the MySQL mathematical functions

Statement	Output
SELECT abs(-33);	33
SELECT abs(33);	33
SELECT mod(10,3);	1
SELECT 10 % 3;	1
SELECT floor(3.14159);	3
SELECT ceiling(3.14159);	4
SELECT round(3.14159);	3
SELECT log(100);	4.605170
SELECT log10(100);	2
SELECT pow(2,3);	8
SELECT sqrt(36);	6
SELECT sin(pi( ));	0.000000
SELECT cos(pi( ));	-1.000000
SELECT tan(pi( ));	-0.000000
SELECT rand( );	0.8536
SELECT truncate(3.14159,3);	3.141
SELECT format(12345.23,0);	12,345
SELECT format(12345.23, 1);	12,345.2

Several of the functions in Table 3-4 require some explanation:

- The abs( ) operator returns the absolute value of a number; that is, it removes the negative sign from negative numbers.

- The modulo operator—which has two identical variants, % and mod( )—divides the first number by the second number and outputs the remainder.

- The `floor()` and `ceiling()` functions are complementary: `floor()` returns the largest integer not greater than the parameter; `ceiling()` returns the smallest integer not less than the parameter.

- The `round()` function rounds to the nearest integer.

- Both the natural logarithm, `log()`, and base-10 logarithm, `log10()`, are available.

- The `pow()` function raises the first number to the power of the second.

- `sqrt()` takes the square root of the parameter.

- The trigonometry functions `sin()`, `cos()`, and `tan()` take values expressed in radians as parameters. The complementary arc sin, arc cos, and arc tan are available as `asin()`, `acos()`, and `atan()`.

- The `rand()` function returns a pseudorandom number in the range 0 to 1.

- The `truncate()` function removes decimal places without rounding.

- The `format()` function isn't really a mathematical function but is instead used for returning numbers in a predefined format. The first parameter is the number, and the second parameter is the number of decimal places to return. The first parameter is rounded so that, for example, 123.56 formatted to one decimal place is 123.6. This function is seldom used in web database applications, because formatting is usually performed in PHP scripts.

Date and time functions

Table 3-5 shows sample uses of selected time and date functions available in MySQL. The `date_add()` function can be used to add and subtract times and dates; more details can be found in Section 7.4.11 of the *manual.html* file distributed with MySQL.

Table 3-5. Using the date and time functions

Statement	Output
`SELECT dayofweek('2000-05-03');`	3
`SELECT dayname('2000-05-03');`	Wednesday
`SELECT monthname('2000-05-03');`	May
`SELECT week('2000-05-03');`	18
`SELECT date_add("2000-05-03", INTERVAL 1 DAY);`	2000-05-04
`SELECT curdate();`	2002-01-01
`SELECT curtime();`	11:27:20
`SELECT now();`	2002-01-01 11:27:20

Miscellaneous operators and functions

Miscellaneous operators and functions are shown in Table 3-6.

Table 3-6. Miscellaneous operators and functions

Statement	Output
Control flow functions	
SELECT if(1<0,"yes","no")	no
Encryption functions	
SELECT password('secret')	428567f408994404
SELECT encode('secret','shhh')	"|ï ¨˜
SELECT decode('"|ï ¨˜','shhh')	secret
Other functions	
SELECT database( )	winestore
SELECT user( )	*dimitria@localhost*

The conditional function `if` outputs the first string if the expression is true and the second if it is false. This can be used in complex ways. For example, it could be used in an UPDATE statement for intelligent changes to an attribute:

```
UPDATE customer SET country =
    if(trim(country)='','Australia',country);
```

In this case, the SQL statement replaces blank country attributes with Australia and leaves already filled country attributes unaltered.

Authentication and securing data using `password( )`, `encode( )`, and `decode( )` are discussed in Chapter 9. The functions `database( )` and `user( )` provide the names of the current database and user.

More on SQL and MySQL

In this section we discuss miscellaneous tools and techniques for using SQL and MySQL. We introduce:

- Choosing keys and indexes for fast searching
- Elementary database-tuning techniques
- Adding and deleting users of a DBMS, and changing user permissions
- Limitations of MySQL

Keys, Primary Keys, and Indexes

As discussed earlier in our introduction to SQL, each table should have a PRIMARY KEY definition as part of the CREATE TABLE statement. A primary key is an attribute—or set of attributes—that uniquely identifies a row in a table. Storing two rows with the same primary key isn't permitted and, indeed, an attempt to INSERT duplicate primary keys produces an error.

In MySQL, the attribute values of the primary key are stored in an *index* to allow fast access to a row. The default MySQL index type is fast for queries that find a specific row, a range of rows, for joins between tables, grouping data, ordering data, and finding minimum and maximum values. Indexes don't provide any speed improvement for retrieving all the rows in a table or for other query types.

Indexes are also useful for fast access to rows by values other than those that are associated with attributes in the primary key. For example, in the *customer* table, you might define an index by adding the clause:

```
KEY namecity (surname,firstname,city)
```

to the CREATE TABLE statement. After you define this index, some queries that select a particular customer through a WHERE clause can use it. Consider an example:

```
SELECT * FROM customer
    WHERE surname = 'Marzalla' AND
    firstname = 'Dimitria' AND
    city = 'St Albans';
```

This query can use the new index to locate—in at most a few disk accesses—the row that matches the search criteria. Without the index, the DBMS must scan all the rows in the *customer* table and compare each row to the WHERE clause. This might be quite slow and certainly requires significantly more disk accesses than the index-based approach (assuming the table has more than a few rows).

A particular feature of DBMSs is that they develop a query evaluation strategy and optimize it without any interaction from the user or programmer. If an index is available, and it makes sense to use it in the context of a query, the DBMS does this automatically. All you need to do is identify which queries are common, and make an index available for those common queries by adding the KEY clause to the CREATE TABLE statement or using ALTER TABLE on an existing table.

Careful index design is important. The namecity index we have defined can also speed queries other than those that supply a complete surname, firstname, and city. For example, consider a query:

```
SELECT * FROM customer
    WHERE surname = 'LaTrobe' AND
    firstname = 'Anthony';
```

This query can also use the index namecity, because the index permits access to rows in sorted order first by surname, then firstname, and then city. With this sorting, all "LaTrobe, Anthony" index entries are clustered together in the index. Indeed, the index can also be used for the query:

```
SELECT * FROM customer
    WHERE surname LIKE 'Mar%';
```

Again, all surnames beginning with "Mar" are clustered together in the index. However, the index can't be used for a query such as:

```
SELECT * FROM customer
  WHERE firstname = 'Dimitria' AND
  city = 'St Albans';
```

The index can't be used because the leftmost attribute named in the index, surname, isn't part of the WHERE clause. In this case, all rows in the *customer* table must be scanned and the query is much slower (again assuming there are more than a few rows in the customer table, and assuming there is no other index).

 Careful choice of the order of attributes in a KEY clause is important. For an index to be usable in a query, the leftmost attribute must appear in a WHERE clause.

There are other cases in which an index can't be used, such as when a query contains an OR that isn't on an indexed attribute:

```
SELECT * FROM customer
  WHERE surname = 'Marzalla' OR
  email = 'dimitria@lucaston.com';
```

Again, the *customer* table must be completely scanned, because the second condition, email='dimitria@lucaston.com', requires all rows to be retrieved as there is no index available on the attribute email. Also, the case where the ORed attribute isn't the leftmost attribute in an index requires a complete scan of the *customer* table. The following example requires a complete scan:

```
SELECT * FROM customer
  WHERE firstname = 'Dimitria' OR
  surname = 'Marzalla';
```

If all the attributes in the index are used in all the queries, to optimize index size, the leftmost attribute in the KEY clause should be the attribute with the highest number of duplicate entries.

Because indexes speed up queries, why not create indexes on all the attributes you can possibly search on? The answer is that while indexes are fast for searching, they consume space and require updates each time rows are added or deleted, or key attributes are changed. So, if a database is largely static, additional indexes have low overheads, but if a database changes frequently, each additional index slows the update process significantly. In either case, indexes consume additional space, and unnecessary indexes should be avoided.

One way to reduce the size of an index and speed updates is to create an index on a prefix of an attribute. Our namecity index uses considerable space: for each row in the *customer* table, an index entry is up to 120 characters in length because it is created from the combined values of the surname, firstname, and city attributes.* To reduce space, you can define the index as:

```
KEY namecity (surname(10),firstname(3),city(2));
```

This uses only the first 10 characters of surname, 3 of firstname, and the first 2 characters of city to distinguish index entries. This is quite reasonable, because 10 characters from a surname distinguishes between most surnames, and the addition of a few characters from a first name and the prefix of their city should be sufficient to uniquely identify almost all customers. Having a smaller index with less information can also mean that queries are actually faster, because more index information can be retrieved from disk per second, and disk retrieval speed is almost always the bottleneck in query performance.

The space saving is significant with a reduced index. A new index entry requires only 15 characters, a saving of up to 105 characters, so index insertions, deletions, and modifications are now likely to be much faster. Note that for TEXT and BLOB attribute types, a prefix must be taken when indexing, because indexing the entire attribute is impractical and isn't permitted by the MySQL DBMS.

Tuning the Database System

Careful index design is one technique that improves the speed of a DBMS and can reduce the resource requirements of a database. However, comprehensive database tuning is a complex topic that fills many books. We include in this section only a few additional practical ideas to begin to improve the performance of a database system.

As discussed previously, accessing a hard disk is slow and is usually the bottleneck in DBMS performance. More specifically, disk seeking—moving the disk head to get information from another location of the disk—is the slowest component of disk access. Therefore, most techniques described in this section are also techniques that improve performance by minimizing disk space requirements.†

Here are some ways to improve DBMS performance:

- Carefully choose attribute types and lengths. Where possible, use small variants such as SMALLINT or MEDIUMINT rather than the regular choice INT. When using fixed-length attributes, such as CHAR, specify a length that is as short as practical.

---

* This isn't the space actually required by an index entry, because the data is compressed for storage. However, even with compression, the fewer characters indexed, the more compact the representation, the more space saved, and—depending on the usability of the index—the faster searching and updates are.

† Reducing disk space requirements improves both disk seek and read performance. Disk read performance is improved because less data is required to be transferred, while seek performance is improved because the disk head has to move less on average when randomly accessing a smaller file than when accessing a larger file.

- Use fixed-length attributes; that is, try to avoid types such as VARCHAR or BLOB. While fixed-length text attributes may waste space, scanning fixed-length rows in a query is much faster than scanning variable-length rows.

- Design indexes with care. As discussed in the last section, keep the primary key index as small as possible, create only indexes that are needed, and use prefixes of attributes where possible. Ensure that the leftmost attribute in the index is the most frequently used in queries and, if all attributes are used, make sure the leftmost attribute is the one with the highest number of duplicate entries.

- Create a statistics table if aggregate functions such as COUNT( ) or SUM( ) are frequently used in queries on large tables. A statistics table stores only one row that is manually updated with the aggregate values of another table. For example, if the statistics table maintains the count of rows in a large *customer* table, each time a row is inserted or deleted in the *customer* table, the count is updated in the statistics table. For large tables, this is often faster than calculating aggregate functions with the slow built-in functions that require complete processing of all rows.

- If large numbers of rows are deleted from a table, or a table containing variable-length attributes is frequently modified, disk space may be wasted. MySQL doesn't usually remove deleted or modified data; it only marks the location as being no longer in use. Wasted space can affect access speed.

  To reorganize a table—by copying data to a temporary location and back again—MySQL provides the OPTIMIZE TABLE command, which should be used periodically. For example:

  ```
  OPTIMIZE TABLE customer;
  ```

  The OPTIMIZE command should be run when the DBMS is offline for scheduled maintenance. The command is nonstandard SQL.

- It is possible to create different table types for specific tasks. The default in MySQL is the MyISAM type, and all the tables described so far are this table type. For small, temporary, frequently used lookup tables, a different type, the heap table type, can be used. There are other types, and we briefly discuss alternatives in Chapter 6. More details are provided in Section 9.4 of the MySQL user manual.

- Section 10.7 of the MySQL manual includes other excellent ideas for simple performance improvement.

Another aspect of database tuning is optimizing the performance of the DBMS itself. Included with the MySQL installation is the *mysqladmin* tool for database administration. Details of the system setup can be found by running the following command from a Linux shell:

```
% mysqladmin -ppassword variables
```

This shows, in part, the following selected system parameters:

```
join_buffer        current value: 131072
key_buffer         current value: 8388600
net_buffer_length  current value: 16384
record_buffer      current value: 131072
sort_buffer        current value: 2097144
table_cache        current value: 64
```

The important parameters are those that impact disk use. MySQL has several main-memory buffer parameters that control how much data is kept in memory for processing. These include:

- The record_buffer for scanning all rows in a table
- The sort_buffer for ORDER BY and GROUP BY operations
- The key_buffer for storing indexes in main memory
- The join_buffer for joins that don't use indexes

In general, the larger these buffers, the more data from disk is *cached* or stored in memory and the fewer disk accesses are required. However, if the sum of these parameters is near to exceeding the size of the memory installed in the server, the underlying operating system will start to swap data between disk and memory, and the DBMS will be slow. In any case, careful experimentation based on the application is likely to improve DBMS performance.

Section 10.2.3 of the MySQL manual suggests parameter settings when starting the MySQL server. First, for machines with at least 64 MB of memory, large tables in the DBMS, and a moderate number of users, use:

```
safe_mysqld -O key_buffer=16M -O table_cache=128 \
            -O sort_buffer=4M -O record_buffer=1M &
```

Second, if there is less than 64 MB of memory available, and there are many users, try the following:

```
safe_mysqld -O key_buffer=512k -O sort_buffer=100k \
            -O record_buffer=100k &
```

The following setting might be appropriate for the winestore, because many users are expected, the queries are largely index-based, and the database is small:

```
safe_mysqld -O key_buffer=512k -O sort_buffer=16k \
            -O table_cache=32 -O record_buffer=8k \
            -O net_buffer=1K &
```

Even more conservative settings might also be acceptable.

There are two other parameters we have not discussed. The table_cache parameter manages the maximum number of open tables per user connection, while the net_buffer parameter sets the minimum size of the network query buffer in which incoming queries are kept before they are executed.

The *mysqladmin* utility can report the status of the DBMS:

```
% mysqladmin -ppassword status
```

The output has the following format:

```
Uptime: 5721024  Threads: 14  Questions: 7874982
Slow queries: 6  Opens: 115136  Flush tables: 1
Open tables: 62
```

This gives a brief point-in-time summary of the DBMS status and can help find more about the number of user connections, queries, and table use. Similar output can be generated by running the commands SHOW STATUS and SHOW VARIABLES through the MySQL command interpreter.

Information about query performance can be gained with the benchmark( ) function, which can be used iteratively for tuning when altering table design or DBMS system parameters. The following statement illustrates benchmarking:

```
SELECT benchmark(10000, COUNT(*))
    FROM items;
```

This statement reports the time taken to evaluate 10,000 calls to COUNT( ) on the *items* table.

Adding and Deleting Users

We have not yet discussed adding and deleting users from the MySQL DBMS. Our rationale in leaving this topic until this final section is that DBMS users aren't as important in a web database application as in other applications. Because access to the database and DBMS is generally controlled in the application logic of the middle tier, usually only one or two DBMS users are needed.

A user, *hugh,* who has full control over all aspects of the DBMS and can access the DBMS from the machine that hosts the DBMS, can be created with the statement:

```
GRANT ALL PRIVILEGES ON *.* TO hugh@localhost
    IDENTIFIED BY 'password' WITH GRANT OPTION;
```

Allowing access over a network can be added with:

```
GRANT ALL PRIVILEGES ON *.* TO hugh@"%"
    IDENTIFIED BY 'password' WITH GRANT OPTION;
```

There is no need to allow network access for a web database application if the middle-tier components—the web server and scripting engine—are installed on the same machine as the DBMS.

This user can then connect to the database from the shell with the command:

```
% mysql -ppassword -uhugh
```

The user information is stored in the *mysql* database in the *user* table, which can be explored with:

```
USE mysql;
SELECT * FROM user;
```

The *mysql* database and the *user* table can be managed in the same way as any other database. For example, you can update the password of the new user with the UPDATE statement:

```
UPDATE user
    SET password=password('newpwd')
    WHERE user='hugh';
```

Note the use of the password( ) function we described earlier to encrypt the password for storage in the *user* table.

Permissions

Users can be added to the system with an INSERT INTO the *user* table in the *mysql* database or, as previously illustrated, you can use the GRANT statement. Moreover, privileges can be adjusted with an UPDATE, added with GRANT, or removed with REVOKE.

Consider the following example:

```
GRANT SELECT,INSERT,UPDATE,DELETE,CREATE,DROP
    ON winestore.*
    TO dave@localhost
    IDENTIFIED BY 'password';
```

This adds a new user *dave* and allows him to use only the SQL statements listed in the *winestore* database. The parameter winestore.* means all tables within the *winestore* database.

Privileges can be removed with the REVOKE statement. For example:

```
REVOKE DROP,CREATE ON winestore.* FROM dave@localhost;
```

If the privilege or privileges are to be revoked for all databases in the DBMS, not just a single database, winestore.* can be replaced with *.*.

The following privileges can be used in GRANT and REVOKE statements:

```
ALL PRIVILEGES, FILE, RELOAD, ALTER, INDEX, SELECT,
CREATE, INSERT, SHUTDOWN, DELETE, PROCESS, UPDATE,
DROP, REFERENCES, USAGE
```

Limitations of MySQL

The most significant limitation of MySQL is that it doesn't support nested queries. However, support is planned in MySQL Version 4. *Nested queries* are those that contain another query. Consider an example nested query to find the wines that have inventory stock:

```
SELECT DISTINCT wine_id FROM wine
WHERE wine_id IN
  (SELECT wine_id from inventory);
```

The query returns the wine_id values from the *wine* table that are found in the *inventory* table. Nested queries use the IN, NOT IN, EXISTS, and NOT EXISTS operators.

In many cases, a nested query can be rewritten as a join query. For example, to find the wines that are in stock, you can use the following join query:

```
SELECT DISTINCT wine.wine_id FROM wine, inventory
WHERE wine.wine_id = inventory.wine_id;
```

However, some nested queries can't be rewritten as join queries; for difficult queries, temporary tables are often a useful workaround.

A limitation of DELETE and UPDATE is that only one table can be specified in the FROM clause. This problem is particular to MySQL and related to the lack of support for nested queries. This limitation can make modifications of data difficult. For example, it prevents data being deleted or updated using the properties of another table. A solution involves data being copied to a temporary table using a combined INSERT and SELECT statement that joins together data from more than one table. Then, the data can be deleted or updated in the temporary table and then transferred back to the original table. Another approach, using the concat( ) string function, is discussed in Section 1.4.4.1 in the MySQL manual.

To avoid UPDATE and DELETE problems, consider adding additional attributes to tables at design time. For example, in the winestore we added a DATE attribute to the *items* table so that shopping-cart items can be removed easily if they aren't purchased within one day. Removing rows from the *items* table based on the DATE in the *orders* table is difficult without support for nested queries.

MySQL doesn't support stored procedures or triggers. *Stored procedures* are queries that are compiled and stored in the DBMS. They are then invoked by the middle-tier application logic, with the benefit that the query is parsed only once and there is less communication overhead between the middle and database tiers. *Triggers* are similar to stored procedures but are invoked by the DBMS when a condition is met. Stored-procedure support is planned for MySQL, but trigger support isn't.

Views aren't supported in MySQL. *Views* consolidate read-only access to several tables based on a join condition. For example, a view might allow a user to browse the sales made up to April without the need to create a temporary table, as we did in the example in the section "Modifying the Database." View support is planned for the future.

Limitations that we don't discuss here include the lack of support for foreign keys and cursors. More detail on the limitations of MySQL can be found in Section 1.4 of the manual distributed with MySQL.

CHAPTER 4

Querying Web Databases

This chapter is the first of six that introduce practical web database application development. In Chapter 1, we introduced our case-study application, Hugh and Dave's Online Wines. We use the winestore here to illustrate the basic principles and practice of building commonly used web database components.

In this chapter, we introduce the basics of connecting to the MySQL DBMS with PHP. We detail the key MySQL functions used to connect, query databases, and retrieve result sets, and we present the five-step process for dynamically serving data from a database. Queries that are driven by user input into an HTML <form> or through clicking on hypertext links are the subject of Chapter 5.

We introduce the following techniques in this chapter:

- Using the five-step web database querying approach to develop database-driven queries
- Coding a simple solution to produce HTML <pre> preformatted text
- Using the MySQL library functions for querying databases
- Handling MySQL DBMS errors
- Producing formatted output with the HTML <table> environment
- Using include files to modularize database code
- Adding multiple queries to a script and consolidating the results into one HTML presentation environment
- Performing simple calculations on database data
- Developing basic database-driven scripts incrementally and producing modular code encapsulated in functions

Our case study in this chapter is the front-page panel from the winestore that shows customers the Hot New Wines available at the winestore. The front page of the winestore is shown in Figure 4-1, and the panel is the section of the page that contains the list of the three newest wines that have been added to the database and reviewed by a wine expert.

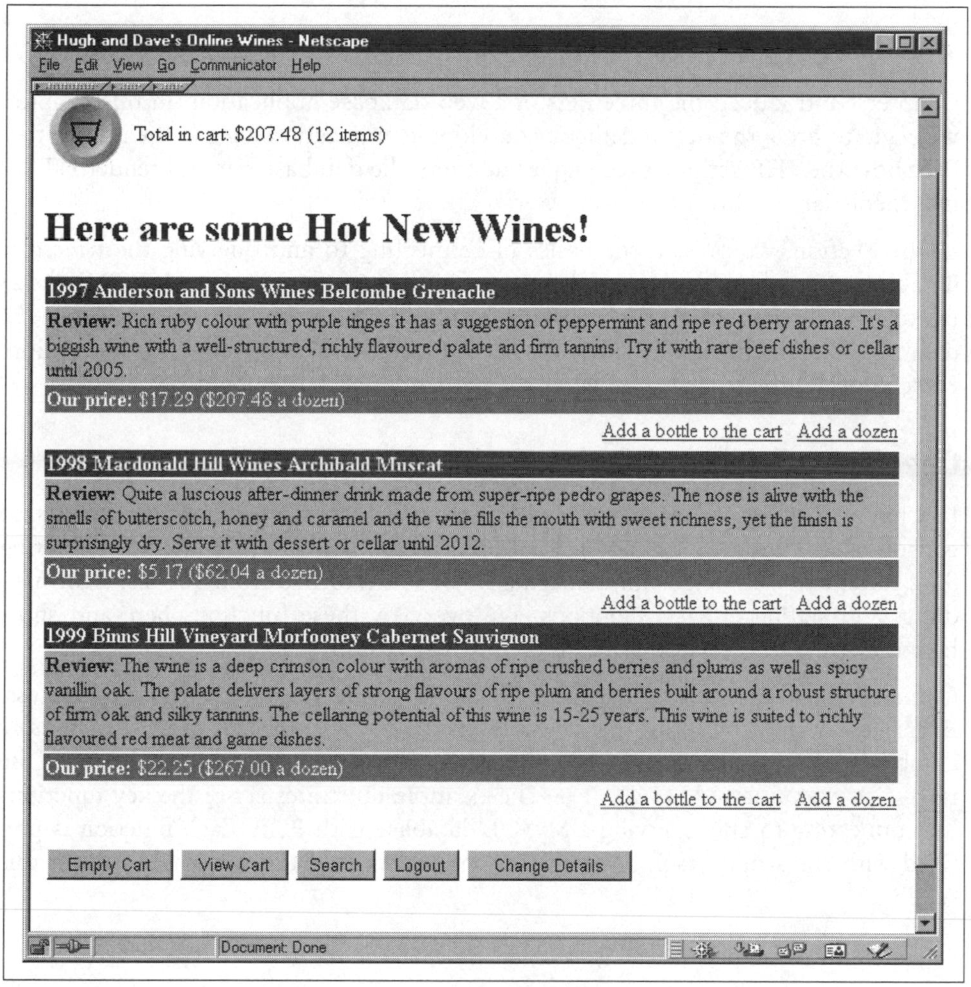

Figure 4-1. The front page of the winestore, showing the front page panel

We begin by introducing the basic principles of web database querying. Our first examples use a simple approach to presenting result sets using the HTML <pre> pre-formatted text tag. We then build on this approach and introduce result presentation with the <table> environment. The panel itself is a complex case study, and we follow its development as natural join queries are introduced, conditional presentation of results included, and the HTML <table> environment used for more attractive presentation. We focus on iterative development, starting simply and progressively adding new functionality. The complete code for the front page of the winestore application is presented in Chapter 11.

For completeness, we conclude this chapter with a brief overview of how other DBMSs can be accessed and manipulated with PHP.

Connecting to a MySQL Database

Chapter 1 introduced the three tiers of a web database application. In this chapter, we begin to bring the tiers together by developing application logic in the middle tier. We show the PHP scripting techniques to query the database tier and render HTML in a client-tier web browser.

In this section, we present the basics of connecting to and querying the *winestore* database using a simple query. The output is also simple: we use the HTML <pre> tag to reproduce the results in the same format in which they are returned from the database. The focus of this section is the DBMS interaction, not the presentation. Presentation is the subject of much of the remainder of this chapter.

Opening and Using a Database Connection

In Chapter 3, we introduced the MySQL command interpreter. In PHP, there is no consolidated interface. Instead, a set of library functions are provided for executing SQL statements, as well as for managing result sets returned from queries, error handling, and setting efficiency options. We overview these functions here and show how they can be combined to access the MySQL DBMS.

Connecting to and querying a MySQL DBMS with PHP is a five-step process. Example 4-1 shows a script that connects to the MySQL DBMS, uses the *winestore* database, issues a query to select all the records from the *wine* table, and reports the results as preformatted HTML text. The example illustrates six of the key functions for connecting to and querying a MySQL database with PHP. Each function is prefixed with the string mysql_. We explain the function of this script in detail in this section.

Example 4-1. Connecting to a MySQL database with PHP

```
<!DOCTYPE HTML PUBLIC
                "-//W3C//DTD HTML 4.0 Transitional//EN"
                "http://www.w3.org/TR/html4/loose.dtd">
<html>
<head>
  <title>Wines</title>
</head>
<body><pre>
<?php
    // (1) Open the database connection and use the winestore
    // database
    $connection = mysql_connect("localhost","fred","shhh");
```

Example 4-1. Connecting to a MySQL database with PHP (continued)

```
      mysql_select_db("winestore", $connection);

      // (2) Run the query on the winestore through the
      // connection
      $result = mysql_query ("SELECT * FROM
                            wine", $connection);

      // (3) While there are still rows in the result set,
      // fetch the current row into the array $row
      while ($row = mysql_fetch_row($result))
      {
        // (4) Print out each element in $row, that is,
        // print the values of the attributes
          for ($i=0; $i<mysql_num_fields($result); $i++)
            echo $row[$i] . " ";

          // Print a carriage return to neaten the output
          echo "\n";
      }
      // (5) Close the database connection
      mysql_close($connection);
?>
</pre>
</body>
</html>
```

The five steps of querying a database are numbered in the comments in Example 4-1, and they are as follows:

1. Connect to the DBMS and use a database. Open a connection to the MySQL DBMS using `mysql_connect( )`. There are three parameters: the hostname of the DBMS server to use, a username, and a password. Once you connect, you can select a database to use through the connection with the `mysql_select_db( )` function. In this example, we select the *winestore* database.

   Let's assume here that MySQL is installed on the same server as the scripting engine and therefore, we can use `localhost` as the hostname.

   The function `mysql_connect( )` returns a connection handle. A *handle* is a value that can be used to access the information associated with the connection. As discussed in Step 2, running a query also returns a handle that can access results.

   To test this example—and all other examples in this book that connect to the MySQL DBMS—replace the username *fred* and the password *shhh* with those you selected when MySQL was installed following the instructions in Appendix A. This should be the same username and password used throughout Chapter 3.

2. Run the query. Let's run the query on the *winestore* database using `mysql_query( )`. The function takes two parameters: the SQL query itself and the DBMS connection to use. The connection parameter is the value returned from

the connection in the first step. The function `mysql_query( )` returns a result set handle resource; that is, a value that can retrieve the output—the result set—of the query in Step 3.

3. Retrieve a row of results. The function `mysql_fetch_row( )` retrieves one row of the result set, taking only the result set handle from the second step as the parameter. Each row is stored in an array `$row`, and the attribute values in the array are extracted in Step 4. A while loop is used to retrieve rows until there are no more rows to fetch. The function `mysql_fetch_row( )` returns `false` when no more data is available.

4. Process the attribute values. For each retrieved row, a `for` loop is used to print with an echo statement each of the attributes in the current row. Use `mysql_num_fields( )` is used to return the number of attributes in the row; that is, the number of elements in the array. For the *wine* table, there are six attributes in each row: `wine_id`, `wine_name`, `type`, `year`, `winery_id`, and `description`.

   The function `mysql_num_fields( )` takes as a parameter the result handle from Step 2 and, in this example, returns 6 each time it is called. The data itself is stored as elements of the array `$row` returned in Step 3. The element `$row[0]` is the value of the first attribute (the `wine_id`), `$row[1]` is the value of the second attribute (the `wine_name`), and so on.

   The script prints each row on a line, separating each attribute with a single space character. Each line is terminated with a carriage return using echo `"\n"` and Steps 3 and 4 are repeated.

5. Close the DBMS connection using `mysql_close( )`, with the connection to be closed as the parameter.

The first 10 wine rows produced by the script in Example 4-1 are shown in Example 4-2. The results are shown marked up as HTML.

Example 4-2. Marked-up HTML output from the code shown in Example 4-1

```
<!DOCTYPE HTML PUBLIC
           "-//W3C//DTD HTML 4.0 Transitional//EN"
           "http://www.w3.org/TR/html4/loose.dtd">
<html>
<head>
  <title>Wines</title>
</head>
<body><pre>
1 Archibald Sparkling 1997 1
2 Pattendon Fortified 1975 1
3 Lombardi Sweet 1985 2
4 Tonkin Sparkling 1984 2
5 Titshall White 1986 2
6 Serrong Red 1995 2
7 Mettaxus White 1996 2
8 Titshall Sweet 1987 3
```

```
9 Serrong Fortified 1981 3
10 Chester White 1999 3
...
</pre>
</body>
</html>
```

Other functions can be used to manipulate the database—in particular, to process result sets differently—and we discuss these later in this chapter. However, the basic principles and practice are shown in the six functions we have used. These key functions are described in more detail in the next section.

Essential Functions for Accessing MySQL with PHP

resource mysql_connect([string *host*], [string *username*], [string *password*])

Establishes a connection to the MySQL DBMS. The function returns a connection resource handle on success that can be used to access databases through subsequent commands. Returns false on failure (error handling is discussed later in this section).

The command has three optional parameters, all of which—*host*, *username*, and *password*—are used in practice. The first permits not only the *hostname*, but also an optional port number; the default port for MySQL is 3306 (ports are discussed in more detail in Appendix B). However, when the DBMS runs on the same machine as the PHP scripting engine and the web server—and you have set up a database user that can access the DBMS from the local machine—the first parameter need only be localhost.

In Example 4-1, the function call:

```
mysql_connect("localhost", "fred", "shhh")
```

connects to the MySQL DBMS on the local machine with the username *fred* and a password of *shhh*. As discussed in the last section, you should replace these with the username and password values you chose in Appendix A and used in Chapter 3. If the connection is successful, the returned result is a connection resource handle that should be stored in a variable for use as a parameter to other MySQL functions.

This function needs to be called only once in a script, assuming you don't close the connection (see mysql_close( ), later in this section). Indeed, subsequent calls to the function in the same script with the same parameters—the same host, username, and password triple—don't return a new connection. They return the same connection handle returned from the first successful call to the function.

int mysql_select_db (string *database,* [resource *connection*])

Uses the specified *database* on a *connection.* In Example 4-1, the database *winestore* is used on the connection returned from mysql_connect( ). If the second parameter is omitted, the last connection opened is assumed, or an attempt is made to open a connection with mysql_connect( ) and no parameters. We caution against omitting the *connection* parameter.

resource mysql_query(string *SQL_command,* [resource *connection*])

Runs the SQL statement *SQL_command.* In practice, the second argument isn't optional and should be a connection handle returned from a call to mysql_connect( ). The function mysql_query( ) returns a resource—a result handle that can fetch the result set—on success, and false on failure.

In Example 4-1, the function call:

```
$result=mysql_query("SELECT * FROM wine", $connection)
```

runs the SQL query SELECT * FROM wine through the previously established DBMS connection resource $connection. The return value is assigned to $result, a result resource handle that is used as a parameter to mysql_fetch_row( ) to retrieve the data.

> The query string passed to mysql_query( ) or mysql_unbuffered_ query( ) doesn't need to be terminated with a semicolon; the latter function is discussed later in this section.

If the second parameter to mysql_query( ) is omitted, PHP tries to use any open connection to the MySQL DBMS. If no connections are open, a call to mysql_ connect( ) with no parameters is issued. In practice, the second parameter should be supplied.

array mysql_fetch_row(resource *result_set*)

Fetches the result set data one row at a time by using as a parameter the result handle *result_set* that was returned from an earlier mysql_query( ) function call. The results are returned as an array, and the elements of the array can then be processed with a loop statement. The function returns false when no more rows are available.

In Example 4-1, a while loop repeatedly calls the function and fetches rows into the array variable $row until there are no more rows available.

int mysql_num_fields(resource *result_set*)

Returns the number of attributes associated with a result set handle *result_set.* The result set handle is returned from a prior call to mysql_query( ).

This function is used in Example 4-1 to determine how many elements to process with the for loop that prints the value of each attribute. In practice, the function might be called only once per query and the returned result assigned to a variable that can be used in the for loop. This is possible since all rows in a result set have the same number of attributes. Avoiding repeated calls to DBMS functions where possible is likely to improve performance.

The array function count( ) can also be used to count the number of elements in an array.

int mysql_close([resource *connection*])

Closes a MySQL connection that was opened with mysql_connect( ). The *connection* parameter is optional. If it is omitted, the most recently opened connection is closed.

As we discuss later, this function doesn't really need to be called to close a connection opened with mysql_connect( ), because all connections are closed when a script terminates. Also, this function has no effect on *persistent* connections opened with mysql_pconnect( ); these connections stay open until they are unused for a specified period. We discuss persistent connections in the next section.

The functions we have described are a contrasting approach for DBMS access to the consolidated interface of the MySQL command line interpreter. mysql_connect( ) and mysql_close( ) perform equivalent functions to running and quitting the interpreter. The mysql_select_db( ) function provides the use database command, and mysql_query( ) permits an SQL statement to be executed. The mysql_fetch_row( ) and mysql_num_fields( ) functions manually retrieve a result set that's automatically output by the interpreter.

More MySQL Functions in PHP

Web database applications can be developed that use only the six functions we have described. However, in many cases, additional functionality is required. For example, database tables sometimes need to be created, information about database table structure needs to be used in reporting or querying, and it is desirable to retrieve specific rows in a result set without processing the complete dataset.

Additional functions for interacting with a MySQL DBMS using PHP are the subject of this section. We have omitted functions that are used to report on insertions, deletions, and updates. These are discussed in Chapter 6.

Frequently used functions

int mysql_data_seek(resource *result_set*, int *row*)

This function retrieves only some results from a query. It allows retrieval from a result set to begin at a row other than the first row. For example, executing the function for a *result_set* with a *row* parameter of 10, and then issuing a mysql_fetch_row( ), mysql_fetch_array( ), or mysql_fetch_object( ), retrieves the tenth row of the result set.

This function can reduce communications between the database and middle tiers in an application.

The parameter *result_set* is the result resource handle returned from `mysql_query()`. The function returns `true` on success and `false` on failure.

`array mysql_fetch_array(resource result_set, [int result_type])`

This function is an extended version of `mysql_fetch_row()` that returns results into an associative array, permitting access to values in the array by their table attribute names.

Consider an example query on the *wine* table using the `mysql_query()` function:

```
$result=mysql_query("SELECT * FROM wine", $connection)
```

A row can then be retrieved into the array `$row` using:

```
$row=mysql_fetch_array($result)
```

After retrieving the row, elements of the array `$row` can be accessed by their attribute names in the *wine* table. For example, `echo $row["wine_name"]` prints the value of the `wine_name` attribute from the retrieved row. Attributes can also be accessed by their element numbers. For example, `echo $row[1]` also works.

There are three tricks to using `mysql_fetch_array()`:

- Even though an attribute might be referenced as `customer.name` in the SELECT statement, it must be referenced as `$row["name"]` in the associative array; this is a good reason to design databases so that attribute names are unique across tables. If attribute names are not unique, aliases can be used in the SELECT statement; we discuss this later in this chapter.

- Aggregates fetched with `mysql_fetch_array()`—for example, SUM(cost)—are associatively referenced as `$row["SUM(cost)"]`.

- NULL values are ignored when creating the returned array. This has no effect on associative access to the array but can change the numbering of the array elements for numeric access.

The second parameter to `mysql_fetch_array()`, *result_type,* controls whether associative access, numeric access, or both are possible on the returned array. Because the default is `MYSQL_BOTH`, there is no reason to supply or change the parameter.

`object mysql_fetch_object(resource result_set, [int result_type])`

This function is another alternative for returning results from a query. It returns an object that contains one row of results associated with the *result_set* handle, permitting access to values in an object by their table attribute names.

For example, after a query to `SELECT * from wine`, a row can be retrieved into the object `$object` using:

```
$object =mysql_fetch_object($result)
```

The attributes can then be accessed in $object by their attribute names. For example:

```
echo $object->wine_name
```

prints the value of the wine_name attribute from the retrieved row. Attributes can also be accessed by their element numbers. For example, echo $object->1 also works.

The second parameter to mysql_fetch_object() controls whether associative access, numeric access, or both are possible on the returned array. The default is MYSQL_BOTH, but MYSQL_ASSOC and MYSQL_NUM can also be specified.

int mysql_free_result(resource *result_set*)

This function frees the resources associated with a *result_set* handle. This process happens when a script terminates, so the function need be called only if repeated querying is performed in one script and MySQL memory use is a concern.

int mysql_num_rows(resource *result_set*)

This function returns the number of rows associated with the *result_set* query result resource handle. This function works only for SELECT queries; queries that modify a database should use mysql_affected_rows(), which is discussed in Chapter 6.

If the number of rows in a table is required but not the data itself, it is more efficient to run an SQL query of the form SELECT count(*) FROM table and retrieve the result, rather than running SELECT * FROM table and then using mysql_num_rows() to determine the number of rows in the table.

resource mysql_pconnect([string *host:port*], [string *user*], [string *password*])

This function is a performance-oriented alternative to mysql_connect() that reuses open connections to the MySQL DBMS. The p in mysql_pconnect() stands for *persistent*, meaning that a connection to the DBMS stays open after a script terminates. Open connections are maintained as a pool that is available to PHP. When a call to mysql_pconnect() is made, a pooled connection is used in preference to creating a new connection. Using pooled connections saves the costs of opening and closing connections.

> Whether persistency is faster in practice depends on the server configuration and the application. However, in general, for web database applications with many users running on a server with plenty of main memory, persistency is likely to improve performance.

This function need be called only once in a script. Subsequent calls to mysql_pconnect() in any script—with the same parameters—check the connection pool for an available connection. If no connections are available, a new connection is opened.

The function takes the same parameters and returns the same results as its non-persistent sibling mysql_connect( ). It returns a connection resource handle on success that can access databases through subsequent commands; it returns false on failure. The command has the same three optional parameters as mysql_connect( ).

 A connection opened with mysql_pconnect( ) can't be closed with mysql_close( ). It stays open until unused for a period of time. The timeout is a MySQL DBMS parameter—not a PHP parameter—and is set by default to five seconds; it can be adjusted with a command-line option to the MySQL DBMS script safe_mysqld. For example, to set the timeout to 10 seconds:

```
safe_mysqld --set-variable connect_timeout=10
```

resource mysql_unbuffered_query(string *query*, [resource *connection*])

This function is available only in PHP 4.0.6 or later. The function executes a query without retrieving and buffering the result set. This is useful for queries that return large result sets or that are slow to execute. The advantage is that no resources are required to store a large result set, and the function returns before the SQL query is complete. In contrast, the function mysql_query( ) doesn't return until the query is complete and the results have been buffered for subsequent retrieval.

The disadvantage of mysql_unbuffered_query( ) is that mysql_num_rows( ) can't be called for the result resource handle, because the number of rows returned from the query isn't known.

The function is otherwise identical to mysql_query( ).

Other functions

int mysql_change_user(string *user*, string *password*, [string *database*, [resource *connection*]])

Changes the logged-in MySQL user to another *user*, using that user's *password* for an optionally specified *database* and *connection*. If omitted, the current database and most recently opened connection are assumed. Returns false on failure and, if it does fail, the previous, successful connection stays current.

int mysql_create_db(string *db*, [resource *connection*])

Creates a database named *db* using the *connection* resource returned from a mysql_connect( ) function call or the last-opened connection if the parameter is omitted.

int mysql_drop_db(string *db*, [resource *connection*])

Drops a database named *db* using the *connection* resource returned from a mysql_connect( ) function call or the last-opened connection if the parameter is omitted.

```
object mysql_fetch_field(resource result_set, [int attribute_number])
```
Returns as an object the metadata for each attribute associated with a *result_set* resource returned from a query function call. An optional *attribute_number* can be specified to retrieve the metadata associated with a specific attribute. However, repeated calls process the attributes one by one.

The properties of the object returned by the function are:

name
> The attribute name

table
> The name of the table that the attribute belongs to

max_length
> The maximum length of the attribute

not_null
> Set to 1 if the attribute can't be NULL

primary_key
> Set to 1 if the attribute forms part of a primary key

unique_key
> Set to 1 if the attribute is a unique key

multiple_key
> Set to 1 if the attribute is a nonunique key

numeric
> Set to 1 if the attribute is a numeric type

blob
> Set to 1 if the attribute is a BLOB type

type
> The type of the attribute

unsigned
> Set to 1 if the attribute is an unsigned numeric type

zerofill
> Set to 1 if the numeric column is zero-filled

Example 4-3 is a script that uses the mysql_fetch_field() function to emulate most of the behavior of the SHOW COLUMNS or DESCRIBE commands discussed in Chapter 3. The code uses the same five-step query process discussed earlier, with the exception that mysql_fetch_field() is used in place of mysql_fetch_row(). Sample output for the table *wine* is shown in Example 4-4. The same result could have been achieved by executing DESCRIBE WINE on the *winestore* database using mysql_query() and retrieving the results with mysql_fetch_object().

This function also has other uses. For example, it can be used in validation—the subject of Chapter 7—to check whether the data entered by a user is longer than the maximum length of the database attribute. Indeed, a script can be developed that automatically performs basic validation based on the table structure.

Example 4-3. Using mysql_fetch_field() to describe the structure of a table

```
<!DOCTYPE HTML PUBLIC
            "-//W3C//DTD HTML 4.0 Transitional//EN"
            "http://www.w3.org/TR/html4/loose.dtd">
<html>
<head>
  <title>Wine Table Structure</title>
</head>
<body><pre>
<?php
    // Open a connection to the DBMS
    $connection = mysql_connect("localhost","fred","shhh");

    mysql_select_db("winestore", $connection);

    // Run a query on the wine table in the
    // winestore database to retrieve one row
    $result = mysql_query ("SELECT * FROM wine LIMIT 1",
                            $connection);

    // Output a header, with headers spaced by padding
    print str_pad("Field", 20) .
          str_pad("Type", 14) .
          str_pad("Null", 6) .
          str_pad("Key", 5) .
          str_pad("Extra", 12) . "\n";

    // for each of the attributes in the result set
    for($i=0;$i<mysql_num_fields($result);$i++)
    {
        // Get the meta-data for the attribute
        $info = mysql_fetch_field ($result);

        // Print the attribute name
        print str_pad($info->name, 20);

        // Print the data type
        print str_pad($info->type, 6);

        // Print a "(", the field length, and a ")" e.g.(2)
        print str_pad("(" . $info->max_length . ")", 8);

        // Print out YES if attribute can be NULL
        if ($info->not_null != 1)
            print " YES ";
        else
            print "      ";
```

Example 4-3. Using mysql_fetch_field() to describe the structure of a table (continued)

```
        // Print out selected index information
        if ($info->primary_key == 1)
            print " PRI ";
        elseif ($info->multiple_key == 1)
            print " MUL ";
        elseif ($info->unique_key == 1)
            print " UNI ";

        // If zero-filled, print this
        if ($info->zerofill)
            print " Zero filled";

        // Start a new line
        print "\n";
    }

    // Close the database connection
    mysql_close($connection);
?>
</pre>
</body>
</html>
```

Example 4-4. HTML output of the DESCRIBE WINE emulation script in Example 4-3

```
<!DOCTYPE HTML PUBLIC
                "-//W3C//DTD HTML 4.0 Transitional//EN"
                "http://www.w3.org/TR/html4/loose.dtd">
<html>
<head>
  <title>Wine Table Structure</title>
</head>
<body><pre>
Field               Type        Null  Key  Extra
wine_id             int    (1)        PRI
wine_name           string(9)         MUL
type                string(9)
year                int    (4)
winery_id           int    (1)        MUL
description         blob   (0)   YES
</pre>
</body>
</html>
```

resource mysql_list_tables(string *database*, [resource *connection*])

Returns a result set resource handle that can be used as input to mysql_tablename( ) to list the names of tables in a *database* accessed through a *connection*. If the *connection* is omitted, the last-opened connection is assumed.

```
string mysql_tablename(resource result, int table_number)
```
Used in combination with `mysql_list_tables()` to produce a list of tables in a database. Returns the name of the table indexed by the numeric value *table_number* using a *result* resource returned from the `mysql_list_tables()` function.

The number of tables in a database can be determined by calling `mysql_num_rows()` with the *result* resource handle returned from `mysql_list_tables()` as a parameter.

Functions to avoid

Several MySQL functions shouldn't be used in practice:

- The functions of `mysql_fetch_field()` are also available in the non-object-based alternatives `mysql_fetch_length()`, `mysql_field_flags()`, `mysql_field_name()`, `mysql_field_len()`, `mysql_field_table()`, and `mysql_field_type()`; as these functions are almost a complete subset of `mysql_fetch_field()`, we don't describe them here.

- The function `mysql_result()` is a slower alternative to fetching and processing a row with `mysql_fetch_row()` or `mysql_fetch_array()` and shouldn't be used in practice.

- `mysql_fetch_assoc()` fetches a row of results as an associative array only, providing half the functionality of `mysql_fetch_array()`. The other half—fetching into an array accessed by numeric index—is provided by `mysql_fetch_row()`. Since `mysql_fetch_array()` provides both sets of functionality—or can provide the same functionality by passing through MYSQL_ASSOC as the second parameter—it should be used instead.

- `mysql_field_seek()` can seek to a specific field for a subsequent call to `mysql_fetch_field()`, but this is redundant because the field number can be supplied directly to `mysql_fetch_field()` as the optional second parameter.

- `mysql_db_query()` combines the functionality of `mysql_select_db()` and `mysql_query()`. This function has been deprecated in recent releases of PHP.

Error Handling of MySQL Database Functions

Database functions can fail. There are several possible classes of failure, ranging from critical—the DBMS is inaccessible or a fixed parameter is incorrect to recoverable, such as a password being entered incorrectly by the user.

The PHP interface functions to MySQL support two error-handling functions for detecting and reporting errors:

```
int mysql_errno(resource connection)
```
Returns the error number of the last error on the *connection* resource

```
string mysql_error(resource connection)
```
Returns a descriptive string of the last error on the *connection* resource

Example 4-5 shows the script illustrated earlier in Example 4-1 with additional error handling. We have deliberately included an error where the name of the database *winestore* is misspelled as "winestor". The error handler is a function, showerror( ), that—with the database name error—prints a phrase in the format:

```
Error 1049 : Unknown database 'winestor'
```

The error message shows both the numeric output of mysql_errorno( ) and the string output of mysql_error( ). The die( ) function outputs the message and then gracefully ends the script.

The functions mysql_query( ) and mysql_unbuffered_query( ) return false only on failure; that is, when a query is incorrectly formed and can't be executed.

A query that executes but returns no results still returns a result resource handle. However, a subsequent call to mysql_num_rows( ) reports no rows in the result set.

The mysql_connect( ) and mysql_pconnect( ) functions don't set either the error number or error string on failure and so must be handled manually. This custom handling can be implemented with a die( ) function call and an appropriate text message, as in Example 4-5.

Example 4-5. Querying a database with error handling

```
<!DOCTYPE HTML PUBLIC
            "-//W3C//DTD HTML 4.0 Transitional//EN"
            "http://www.w3.org/TR/html4/loose.dtd">
<html>
<head>
  <title>Wines</title>
</head>
<body><pre>
<?php

    function showerror()
    {
       die("Error " . mysql_errno() . " : " . mysql_error());
    }

    // (1) Open the database connection
    if (!($connection = @ mysql_connect("localhost",
                                        "fred","shhh")))
       die("Could not connect");

    // NOTE : 'winestore' is deliberately misspelt to
    // cause an error
    if (!(mysql_select_db("winestor", $connection)))
       showerror();
```

Example 4-5. Querying a database with error handling (continued)

```
    // (2) Run the query on the winestore through the
    //  connection
    if (!($result = @ mysql_query ("SELECT * FROM wine",
                                    $connection)))
        showerror();

    // (3) While there are still rows in the result set,
    // fetch the current row into the array $row
    while ($row = mysql_fetch_row($result))
    {
        // (4) Print out each element in $row, that is,
      // print the values of the attributes
        for ($i=0; $i<mysql_num_fields($result); $i++)
            echo $row[$i] . " ";

        // Print a carriage return to neaten the output
        echo "\n";
    }
    // (5) Close the database connection
    if (!mysql_close($connection))
        showerror();
?>
</pre>
</body>
</html>
```

The MySQL error-handling functions should be used with the @ operator that suppresses default output of error messages by the PHP script engine. Omitting the @ operator produces messages that contain both the custom error message and the default error message produced by PHP. Consider an example where the string localhost is misspelled, and the @ operator is omitted:

```
    if (!($connection = mysql_connect("localhos",
                                        "fred",:"shhh") ))
        die("Could not connect");
```

This fragment outputs the following error message that includes both the PHP error and the custom error message:

```
Warning:  MySQL Connection Failed: Unknown MySQL Server
Host 'localhos' (0) in Example 4-5.php on line 42

Could not connect
```

> Don't forget to add an @ operator as the prefix to any function call that is handled manually with a custom error handler. The @ operator prevents PHP from issuing its own internal error message.

Formatting Results

So far in this chapter we have shown the basic techniques for connecting to and querying a MySQL DBMS using PHP. In this section, we extend this to produce results with embedded HTML that have both better structure and presentation.

Let's consider an example that presents results in an HTML <table> environment. Example 4-6 shows a script to query the *winestore* database and present the details of wines. Previously, in Example 4-5, the details of wines were displayed by wrapping the output in HTML <pre> tags. The script in Example 4-6 uses the function displayWines( ) to present the results as an HTML <table>. The main body of the script has a similar structure to previous examples, with the exceptions that the query is stored in a variable, and the username, password, and the showerror( ) function are stored in separate files and included in the script with the include directive. We introduced the include directive in Chapter 2 and discuss it in more detail later in this section.

The displayWines( ) function first outputs a <table> tag, followed by a table row <tr> tag with six <th> header tags and descriptions matching the six attributes of the *wine* table. We could have output these using mysql_fetch_field( ) to return the attribute names rather than hardcoding the heading names. However, in most cases, the headers are hardcoded because attribute names are less meaningful to users than manually constructed textual descriptions.

Example 4-6. Producing simple <table> output with MySQL

```
<!DOCTYPE HTML PUBLIC
            "-//W3C//DTD HTML 4.0 Transitional//EN"
            "http://www.w3.org/TR/html4/loose.dtd">
<html>
<head>
  <title>Wines</title>
</head>
<body>
<?php
  include 'error.inc';
  include 'db.inc';

  // Show the wines in an HTML <table>
  function displayWines($result)
  {

    echo "<h1>Our Wines</h1>\n";

    // Start a table, with column headers
    echo "\n<table>\n<tr>\n" .
        "\n\t<th>Wine ID</th>" .
        "\n\t<th>Wine Name</th>" .
        "\n\t<th>Type</th>" .
        "\n\t<th>Year</th>" .
```

Example 4-6. Producing simple <table> output with MySQL (continued)

```
                "\n\t<th>Winery ID</th>" .
                "\n\t<th>Description</th>" .
                "\n</tr>";

        // Until there are no rows in the result set,
        // fetch a row into the $row array and ...
        while ($row = @ mysql_fetch_row($result))
        {
            // ... start a TABLE row ...
            echo "\n<tr>";

            // ... and print out each of the attributes
            // in that row as a separate TD (Table Data).
            foreach($row as $data)
                echo "\n\t<td> $data </td>";

            // Finish the row
            echo "\n</tr>";
        }

        // Then, finish the table
        echo "\n</table>\n";
    }

    $query = "SELECT * FROM wine";

    // Connect to the MySQL server
    if (!($connection = @ mysql_connect($hostname,
                                        $username,
                                        $password)))
        die("Cannot connect");

    if (!(mysql_select_db("winestore", $connection)))
        showerror( );

    // Run the query on the connection
    if (!($result = @ mysql_query ($query, $connection)))
        showerror( );

    // Display the results
    displayWines($result);

    // Close the connection
    if (!(mysql_close($connection)))
        showerror( );
?>
</body>
</html>
```

After producing the HTML <table> open tag, the displayWines( ) function retrieves the rows in the result set, showing each row as a separate <table> row using the <tr> tag. Each attribute value for each wine—where the attributes match the headings—is displayed within the row as <table> data using the <td> tag. Carriage returns and tab characters are used to lay out the HTML for readability; this has no effect on the presentation of the rendering of the document by a web browser, but it makes the HTML much more readable if the user views the HTML source.

The results of using a <table> environment instead of <pre> tags are more structured and more visually pleasing. The output in a Netscape browser is shown in Figure 4-2, along with a window showing part of the HTML source generated by the script.

Figure 4-2. Presenting wines from the winestore in an HTML <table> environment

Using Include Files in Practice

Examples 4-7 and 4-8 show the two files included with the include directive in Example 4-6. As discussed in Chapter 2, the include directive allows common functions in other files to be accessible from within the body of a script without directly adding the functions to the code.

Example 4-7. The db.inc include file

```
<?
    $hostName = "localhost";
    $databaseName = "winestore";
    $username = "fred";
    $password = "shhh";
?>
```

Example 4-8. The error.inc include file

```
<?
    function showerror()
    {
        die("Error " . mysql_errno() . " : " . mysql_error());
    }
?>
```

Both include files are added to all code developed for the winestore and allow easy adjustment of the database server name, database name, and DBMS username and password. The flexibility to adjust these parameters in a central location allows testing of the system on a backup or remote copy of the data, by changing the database name or hostname in one file. This approach also allows the use of different username and password combinations with different privileges, for testing purposes.

We have chosen to name our include files with the *.inc* extension. This presents a minor security problem. If the user requests the include file, the source of the include file is shown in the browser. This may expose the username and password for the DBMS, the source code, the database structure, and other details that should be secure.

There are three ways to address this problem. First, you can store the include files outside the document tree of the Apache web server installation. For example, store the include files in the directory */usr/local/include/php* and use the complete path in the include directive. Second, you can use the extension *.php* instead of *.inc*. In this case, the include file is processed by the PHP script engine and produces no output because it contains no main body. Third, you can configure Apache so that files with the extension *.inc* are forbidden to be retrieved.

All three approaches to securing include files work effectively in practice. Using the extension *.php* for include files is the simplest solution but has the disadvantage that includes files can't be easily distinguished from other files. In the online winestore, we have configured Apache to disallow retrieval of files with the extension *.inc*.

Case Study: The Front-Page Panel

In this section, we show how to engineer a front-page panel—we call this the *panel*. The completed panel was shown in Figure 4-1. We use the techniques discussed so far in this chapter to present more attractive HTML <table> formatted results, to process multiple query results, and to customize the output based on the data retrieved. No significant new concepts are introduced in the case study.

The panel case study is a progressive development of a script to display the details of new wines. We show the following details in the panel:

- Information about the three wines most recently added to the database, including the vintage year, the winery, the wine name, and the varieties
- The review written by a wine writer
- How much a bottle costs, how much a case of a dozen bottles costs, and any per-bottle discount users receive if they purchase a case

To achieve the outcome of a functional and attractive panel, you need to query the *wine, winery, inventory, grape_variety*, and *wine_variety* tables. You also need to use the structure of the HTML <table> environment to achieve distinct presentation of the three components—the details, the review, and the price—of each newly added wine. Last, you need some mathematics to calculate any savings for buying a case and present these savings to the user.

The panel component developed in this chapter is the basis of the front page of our online winestore. However, shopping cart features that are not discussed in detail here have been added to the production version shown in Figure 4-1. The finalized code that includes the shopping-cart functionality is discussed further in Chapter 5, and the completed code is presented in Chapter 11.

In engineering the panel, we use the following techniques:

- Querying with the MySQL proprietary LIMIT modifier
- Using SQL table aliases in querying
- Using the HTML <table> environment as a presentation tool
- Producing consolidated HTML output from multiple SQL queries
- Presenting data based on calculations
- Using MySQL functions—especially mysql_fetch_array( )—in practice

Script development is an iterative process of adding features. It is almost always easier to start with the skeleton of a component and progressively add functionality to achieve the final goal. The Web is particularly good for this: a click on the Refresh or Reload buttons in a web browser tests a script, without the need for compilation or processing of other components of the system. Moreover, PHP is good at reporting errors to the browser, and the HTML output can easily be viewed. In most browsers, right-clicking on the HTML document in the web browser window offers the option to view the HTML source.

Step 1: Producing Visually Appealing Tables

Example 4-9 shows a script that is the first step in producing the panel. Not surprisingly, the script combines the same querying process described earlier with an HTML <table> environment to wrap the output. The output is more attractive than in previous examples and the output in a Netscape browser is shown in Figure 4-3.

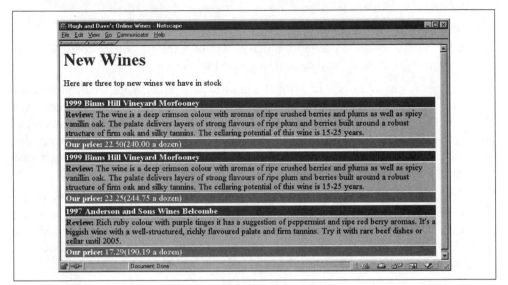

Figure 4-3. The first step in producing a front-page panel that shows more attractive presentation

The basis of the script is a moderately complex SQL query that uses table aliases and the LIMIT operator:

```
SELECT wi.winery_name,
       i.cost,
       i.case_cost,
       w.year,
       w.wine_name,
       w.description
       FROM wine w, winery wi, inventory i
       WHERE w.description != ""
       AND w.winery_id = wi.winery_id
       AND w.wine_id = i.wine_id
       ORDER BY i.date_added DESC LIMIT 3;
```

The table aliases allow the query to be written concisely. For example, the *inventory* table can be referenced throughout the query by the single character *i*.

The query returns one row for each inventory of a wine. If a wine has multiple inventories, the wine appears multiple times. The query also outputs the wine's winery_name, the vintage attribute year, the wine_name, and a descriptive review, description. The WHERE clause ensures that only reviewed wines—those with a description that isn't empty—are returned. The `WHERE` clause also implements a natural join with the *wine* table using the primary keys of the *winery* and *inventory* tables.

The `ORDER BY` clause in the SQL query uses the `DESC` modifier. The date_added isn't an attribute of the *wine*, it is a value from the latest-added *inventory*, and the `LIMIT 3` ensures only the three latest-added inventories are retrieved.

The include files *error.inc* and *db.inc* are included in the script, as discussed in the last section.

Example 4-9. A script to display the three newest wines added to the winestore

```
<!DOCTYPE HTML PUBLIC
            "-//W3C//DTD HTML 4.0 Transitional//EN"
            "http://www.w3.org/TR/html4/loose.dtd">
<html>
<head>
  <title>Hugh and Dave's Online Wines</title>
</head>
<body bgcolor="white">

<h1>New Wines</h1>
Here are three top new wines we have in stock
<br><br>
<?php
    include 'db.inc';
    include 'error.inc';

    $query = "SELECT wi.winery_name,
                     i.cost,
                     i.case_cost,
                     w.year,
                     w.wine_name,
                     w.description
              FROM wine w, winery wi, inventory i
              WHERE w.description != \"\"
              AND w.winery_id = wi.winery_id
              AND w.wine_id = i.wine_id
              ORDER BY i.date_added DESC LIMIT 3";

    // Open a connection to the DBMS
    if (!($connection = @ mysql_connect($hostName,
                                        $username,
                                        $password)))
        die("Could not connect to database");

    if (!mysql_select_db($databaseName, $connection))
        showerror();

    // Run the query created above on the database through
    // the connection
    if (!($result = @ mysql_query ($query, $connection)))
        showerror();
```

```
echo "\n<table border=\"0\">";

// Process the three new wines
while ($row = @ mysql_fetch_array($result))
{
    // Print a heading for the wine
    echo "\n<tr>\n\t<td bgcolor=\"maroon\">" .
        "<b><font color=\"white\">" .
        $row["year"] . " " .
        $row["winery_name"] . " " .
        $row["wine_name"] . " " .
        "</font></b></td>\n</tr>";

    // Print the wine review
    echo "\n<tr>\n\t<td bgcolor=\"silver\">" .
        "<b>Review: </b>" .
        $row["description"] .
        "</td>\n</tr>";

    // Print the pricing information
    echo "\n<tr>\n\t<td bgcolor=\"gray\">" .
        "<b>Our price: </b>" .
        $row["cost"] .
        "(" . $row["case_cost"] . " a dozen)" .
        "</td>\n</tr>";

    // Blank row for presentation
    echo "\n<tr>\n\t<td></td>\n</tr>";
}

echo "\n</table>\n";

if (!mysql_close($connection))
    showerror();
?>
</body>
</html>
```

Besides the moderately complex SQL query, Example 4-9 is only slightly more sophisticated than the examples in previous sections. The code to produce the <table> isn't complex but is a little less readable because:

- The information for each wine is represented over three table rows using three <tr> tags.
- Different background colors for the single <td> element are set in each table row <tr>; the colors are maroon, silver, and gray.
- The color attribute of the <font> tag is set to white for the heading of each wine.
- The bold tag <b> is used for pricing information.
- A blank row between wines is used for spacing in the presentation.

- `mysql_fetch_array()` is used to retrieve rows. This has the advantage that the elements of the `$row` array can be referenced by attribute name. The resultant code is more readable and more query-independent than if `mysql_fetch_row()` is used.

Manipulating presentation by using structure is, unfortunately, part of working with HTML.

Limitations of Step 1

This code is an incomplete solution to the aims we described in the introduction to the case study. Three particular limitations are:

- The varieties of the wines are not shown. For example, you can't tell that the first-listed Binns Hill Vineyard Morfooney is a Cabernet Sauvignon variety.

- The user expects that the dozen price represents a per-bottle saving over purchasing bottles in smaller quantities. However, the front panel doesn't show the saving, and the user needs a calculator to decide whether a dozen bottles is worth the discount.

- The first-listed wine appears twice. There are two *inventory* entries for the same *wine*, and the query has returned two rows for that same *wine*, with the only difference being the prices.

  Another explanation for a double appearance could be that there are two *wines* with the same review and year, but with different *grape_varieties*. This is very unlikely and isn't the case here.

We improve the panel progressively in the next section to address these limitations, while also adding new features.

Step 2: Adding Varieties to the Panel

To add varieties to the panel, you need two SQL queries in a single script. This next step adds an additional query to find the varieties of a wine, and the consolidated varieties are presented together with the vintage, winery, and wine name.

The second addition to the panel in this step is the calculation and conditional display of results. We introduce a new feature to the panel that calculates the savings in buying a dozen bottles and shows the user the per-bottle saving of buying a case of wine, but only when there is such a saving. We don't deal with the situation where a case costs more than 12 single purchases.

The script showing these two new concepts is in Example 4-10. The script improves on Example 4-9 by removing the first two limitations identified in the last section. The output of Example 4-10 is shown in Figure 4-4.

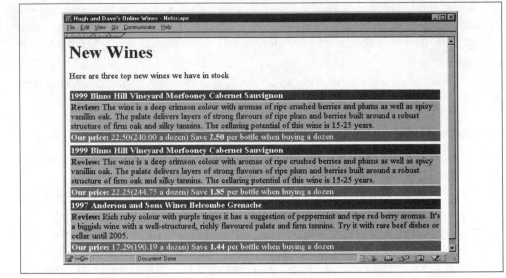

Figure 4-4. Adding wine varieties and discounts to the panel

Example 4-10. An improved display with varieties and the dozen-bottle discount

```
<!DOCTYPE HTML PUBLIC
              "-//W3C//DTD HTML 4.0 Transitional//EN"
              "http://www.w3.org/TR/html4/loose.dtd">
<html>
<head>
  <title>Hugh and Dave's Online Wines</title>
</head>
<body bgcolor="white">

<h1>New Wines</h1>
Here are three top new wines we have in stock
<br><br>
<?php
   include 'db.inc';
   include 'error.inc';

   // Print out the varieties for a wineID
   function showVarieties($connection, $wineID)
   {
     // Find the varieties of the current wine,
     // and order them by id
     $query = "SELECT gv.variety
              FROM grape_variety gv,
                  wine_variety wv, wine w
              WHERE w.wine_id = wv.wine_id
              AND wv.variety_id = gv.variety_id
              AND w.wine_id = $wineID
              ORDER BY wv.id";
```

Example 4-10. An improved display with varieties and the dozen-bottle discount (continued)

```
    // Run the query
    if (!($result = @ mysql_query($query, $connection)))
        showerror( );

    // Retrieve the varieties ...
    while ($row = @ mysql_fetch_array($result))
        // ... and print each one
        echo " " . $row["variety"];
}

// ---------

$query = "SELECT wi.winery_name,
                 i.cost,
                 i.case_cost,
                 w.year,
                 w.wine_name,
                 w.description,
                 w.wine_id
          FROM wine w, winery wi, inventory i
          WHERE w.description != \"\"
          AND w.winery_id = wi.winery_id
          AND w.wine_id = i.wine_id
          ORDER BY i.date_added DESC LIMIT 3";

// Open a connection to the DBMS
if (!($connection = @ mysql_connect($hostName,
                                    $username,
                                    $password)))
    die("Could not connect to database");

if (!mysql_select_db($databaseName, $connection))
    showerror( );

// Run the query created above on the database through
// the connection
if (!($result = @ mysql_query ($query, $connection)))
    showerror( );

echo "\n<table border=\"0\">";
// Process the three new wines
while ($row = @ mysql_fetch_array($result))
{
    // Print a heading for the wine
    echo "\n<tr>\n\t<td bgcolor=\"maroon\">" .
        "<b><font color=\"white\">" .
        $row["year"] . " " .
        $row["winery_name"] . " " .
        $row["wine_name"] . " ";

    // Print the varieties for this wine
    showVarieties($connection, $row["wine_id"]);
```

```
        echo "</font></b></td>\n</tr>";

        // Print the wine review
        echo "\n<tr>\n\t<td bgcolor=\"silver\">" .
            "<b>Review: </b>" .
            $row["description"] .
            "</td>\n</tr>";

        // Print the pricing information
        echo "\n<tr>\n\t<td bgcolor=\"gray\">" .
            "<b>Our price: </b>" .
            $row["cost"] .
            "(" . $row["case_cost"] . " a dozen)";

        // Calculate the saving for 12 or more bottle
        $dozen_saving = $row["cost"] - ($row["case_cost"]/12);

        // If there's a saving, show what it is
        if ($dozen_saving > 0)
            printf(" Save <b>%.2f</b> per bottle when
                    buying a dozen\n", $dozen_saving);

        echo "</td>\n</tr>";

        // Blank row for presentation
        echo "\n<tr>\n\t<td></td>\n</tr>";
    }

    echo "\n</table>\n";

    if (!mysql_close($connection))
        showerror( );
?>
</body>
</html>
```

Adding a second or subsequent query

Often one query isn't enough to gather all the information required for a report or component in a web database application. The panel is a good example: it is difficult to formulate a single query that can retrieve the *wine* details (wine_name, year, and description), the winery_name, the *inventory* data (cost and case_cost), and the varieties (from the *wine_variety* and *grape_variety* tables).

It is possible to write a single query, but the query needs post-processing to remove duplicate information before presentation. A natural join of *wine*, *winery*, *inventory*, *wine_variety*, and *grape_variety* produces one row per variety of each wine. So, for example, a Cabernet Merlot variety wine is two rows in the output, one row for Cabernet and one row for Merlot. The post-processing involves consolidating the two rows into one HTML `<table>` row for presentation by using an `if` statement to check that all other values are identical.

In many cases, more than one query is issued to produce a consolidated result. In the case of the panel, the existing query is used to get most of the information (all the data from *wine*, *winery*, and *inventory*). The second query is nested inside the first; that is, for each row retrieved from the result set of the first query, you run the new query to get the varieties. The result is that the script runs four queries: one to retrieve the three wines, and three queries to get their varieties.

Let's return to Example 4-10. The first query has not changed and still returns one row per inventory of each of the most recently added wines that has a written review. For each wine, the script produces a heading showing the year, `winery_name`, and `wine_name`.

It is after this query is run and the year, `winery_name`, and `wine_name` output that the new functionality of an additional query begins. In this example, a function, `showVarieties()`, is called. This function runs a query to find the varieties of a particular wine with a `wine_id` value that matches the parameter $wineID:

```
$query = "SELECT gv.variety
        FROM grape_variety gv,
            wine_variety wv, wine w
        WHERE w.wine_id = wv.wine_id
        AND wv.variety_id = gv.variety_id
        AND w.wine_id = $wineID
        ORDER BY wv.id";
```

For example, the query identifies that the first-listed 1999 Binns Hill Vineyard Morfooney with `wine_id=191` is a Cabernet Sauvignon. The results are ordered by `wine_variety.id` so that, as in previous examples, a Cabernet Merlot can be distinguished from a Merlot Cabernet.

The subsequent processing of the second query follows a similar pattern to the first. A `mysql_query()` retrieves all result rows with `mysql_fetch_array()` and prints out the only attribute retrieved, `$row["variety"]`, the grape variety of the wine. The connection isn't closed because it's needed, later to find the next wine's varieties.

This multiple-query approach is common and is used throughout the winestore; the approach is used in the panel to produce order receipts for presentation and email confirmation, and in many of the stock and customer reports.

Adding calculations to the result presentation

Often data that is displayed to the user isn't stored directly in the database. For example, the total of an order placed by the user isn't stored. Instead, the following pieces of information are stored: the quantity of each item ordered, the item's price, the delivery cost, and any discount applied. From these, calculating and displaying the total requires some mathematics.

Why isn't such data stored? The answer is usually that it is redundant: storing it adds no more information to the database. The down side is that you need calculations to recreate output when it is needed. In this section, this is illustrated with a simple example that shows the per-bottle saving when a user purchases more than a dozen bottles.

Returning to the script in Example 4-10, having produced a complete heading that now includes the wine variety, we produce the wine review in the script as before. However, rather than finishing with a simple bottle cost and case_cost, we do some calculations that show users any savings through buying a case:

```
$dozen_saving = $row["cost"] - ($row["case_cost"]/12);
if ($dozen_saving > 0)
            printf("Save <b>%-.2f</b> per bottle
            when buying a dozen\n", $dozen_saving);
```

The element $row["cost"] is the cost of a single bottle, and $row["case_cost"] is the cost of a case. Since a case contains 12 bottles, it follows that the cost of 1 bottle in the case is $row["case_cost"]/12. The difference between the price of a single bottle and the price of bottle that comes in a case is then:

```
$row["cost"]-($row["case_cost"]/12)
```

The result is stored in $dozen_saving.

A saving is printed out only if there is one; that is, when $dozen_saving is greater than zero. In the case where buying a dozen bottles at once costs the same as 12 separate purchases (or maybe more!), nothing is shown. printf is used in preference to echo, so that you can include the formatting string %-.2f to show exactly two decimal places (that is, the cents of the $dozen_saving).

There are many examples of calculations that are performed on the raw data from the database to present information to the user in our winestore. These include calculating order totals, discounts, receipt information, delivery charges, and so on. Elementary mathematics is a common component of most web database applications; it's used throughout later examples.

Step 3: Finishing the Panel

We have built a satisfactory component. However, one problem identified earlier still remains. The first-listed wine appears twice. In this case it is because there are two inventory entries for the same wine, with the only difference being the prices. Of course, our user will pick the cheapest.

Fixing the queries

To address the inventory problem—where a wine appears multiple times in the front panel if there are multiple inventories of that wine—you need to modify the initial query.

Only one row should be produced per wine, not one per inventory. To do this, remove the *inventory* table attributes from the SELECT statement and add a DISTINCT to remove the duplicates. However, you can't remove the *inventory* table fully from the query, because you still need to ORDER BY date_added to display the newest wines added to our winestore cellar. The query is now as follows:

```
$query = "SELECT wi.winery_name,
                 w.year,
                 w.wine_name,
                 w.description,
                 w.wine_id
          FROM wine w, winery wi, inventory i
          WHERE w.description != \"\"
          AND w.winery_id = wi.winery_id
          AND w.wine_id = i.wine_id
          GROUP BY winde-id
          ORDER BY i.date_added DESC LIMIT 3";
```

With this modified query, one entry is produced per wine. However, having removed the *inventory* attributes, you no longer have the pricing information.

You need another query and some script reorganization. Example 4-11 shows a substantially rewritten script that adds a second new function, showPricing( ), that has the correct inventory handling. The function showPricing( ) has a similar structure to showVarieties( ).

showPricing( ) adds the cheapest *inventory* price to the panel for each wine and uses a new query. The query is:

```
$query =  SELECT min (cost), min (case_cost)
          FROM inventory
          WHERE wine_id = $wineID;
```

Example 4-11. Script with correct inventory handling for the latest wine display

```
<!DOCTYPE HTML PUBLIC
          "-//W3C//DTD HTML 4.0 Transitional//EN"
          "http://www.w3.org/TR/html4/loose.dtd">
<html>
<head>
  <title>Hugh and Dave's Online Wines</title>
</head>
<body bgcolor="white">

<h1>New Wines</h1>
Here are three top new wines we have in stock
<br><br>
<?php
    include 'db.inc';
    include 'error.inc';
```

```php
// Print out the varieties for a wineID
function showVarieties($connection, $wineID)
{
   // Find the varieties of the current wine,
   // and order them by id                    .
   $query = "SELECT gv.variety
             FROM grape_variety gv,
                  wine_variety wv, wine w
             WHERE w.wine_id = wv.wine_id
             AND wv.variety_id = gv.variety_id
             AND w.wine_id = $wineID
             ORDER BY wv.id";

   // Run the query
   if (!($result = @ mysql_query($query, $connection)))
      showerror();

   // Retrieve the varieties ...
   while ($row = @ mysql_fetch_array($result))
      // ... and print each one
      echo " " . $row["variety"];
}

// Print out the pricing information
function showPricing($connection, $wineID)
{
   // Find the cheapest prices for the wine,
   $query =  SELECT min (cost), min (case_cost)
             FROM inventory
             WHERE wine_id = $wineID

   // Run the query
   if (!($result = @ mysql_query($query, $connection)))
      showerror();

   // Retrieve the cheapest price
   $row = @ mysql_fetch_array($result);

   // Print the pricing information
   echo "\n<tr>\n\t<td bgcolor=\"gray\">" .
        "<b>Our price: </b>" .
        $row["min(case_cost)"] .
        "(" . $row["min(cost)"] . " a dozen)";

   // Calculate the saving for 12 or more bottle
   $dozen_saving = $row["min(cost)"] - ($row["min(case_cost)"]/12);

   // If there's a saving, show what it is
   if ($dozen_saving > 0)
      printf(" Save <b>%.2f</b> per bottle when
               buying a dozen\n", $dozen_saving);
```

```
        echo "</td>\n</tr>";
}

// ---------

$query = "SELECT wi.winery_name,
                 w.year,
                 w.wine_name,
                 w.description,
                 w.wine_id
          FROM wine w, winery wi, inventory i
          WHERE w.description != \"\"
          AND w.winery_id = wi.winery_id
          AND w.wine_id = i.wine_id
          GROUP BY w.wine_id
          ORDER BY i.date_added DESC LIMIT 3";

// Open a connection to the DBMS
if (!($connection = @ mysql_connect($hostName,
                                    $username,
                                    $password)))
   die("Could not connect to database");

if (!mysql_select_db("winestore", $connection))
   showerror( );


// Run the query created above on the database through
// the connection
if (!($result = @ mysql_query ($query, $connection)))
   showerror( );


echo "\n<table border=\"0\">";

// Process the three new wines
while ($row = @ mysql_fetch_array($result))
{
   // Print a heading for the wine
   echo "\n<tr>\n\t<td bgcolor=\"maroon\">" .
        "<b><font color=\"white\">" .
        $row["year"] . " " .
        $row["winery_name"] . " " .
        $row["wine_name"] . " ";

   // Print the varieties for this wine
   showVarieties($connection, $row["wine_id"]);

   echo "</font></b></td>\n</tr>";

   // Print the wine review
   echo "\n<tr>\n\t<td bgcolor=\"silver\">" .
```

```
                    "<b>Review: </b>" .
                    $row["description"] .
                    "</td>\n</tr>";

        // Show the pricing information
        showPricing($connection, $row["wine_id"]);

        // Blank row for presentation
        echo "\n<tr>\n\t<td></td>\n</tr>";
    }

    echo "\n</table>\n";

    if (!mysql_close($connection))
        showerror();
?>
</body>
</html>
```

The difference in producing price information is that the code doesn't retrieve all rows in the result set with a loop. Rather, it retrieves only one row—the row representing the cheapest inventory. It then outputs the min(cost) and min(case_cost) as previously, with the same dozen_saving calculation.

The final panel, with correct inventory handling, calculations, and varieties, is shown in Figure 4-5.

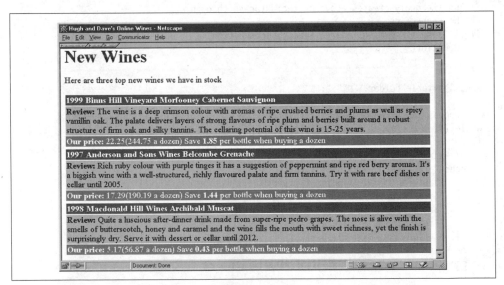

Figure 4-5. Panel with correct inventory handling, calculations, and varieties

Interacting with Other DBMSs Using PHP

Interacting with other relational DBMSs is similar to using MySQL. In this section, we outline the key functions to access Microsoft SQL Server, ODBC-compliant, Oracle, and PostgreSQL DBMSs. We illustrate how to interact with different DBMSs by presenting four rewritten versions of Example 4-1 that include different DBMS functionality.

Functions for accessing other databases, including Informix and Sybase, can be found in the PHP manual. For DBMSs that are not supported natively by PHP, ODBC can usually be used; we discuss ODBC later in this section.

Microsoft SQL Server

Similarly to the MySQL function library, there are many functions for connecting to, querying, and extracting results from Microsoft SQL Server DBMSs.

SQL Server can be used under the Microsoft Windows operating system by making minor changes to THE configuration of PHP in the *php.ini* file; these changes are discussed in the online PHP manual. SQL Server can also be accessed from a Linux platform by installing the FreeTDS package available from *http://www.freetds.org* and recompiling PHP with the *–with-sybase* option; this enables both Sybase and SQL Server support. SQL Server databases can also be accessed using the ODBC library discussed in the next section.

Six functions are listed here, and Example 4-12 shows these implemented in a modified version of Example 4-1.

resource mssql_connect(string *host*, string *username*, string *password*)
> Establishes a connection to a SQL Server DBMS. On success, the function returns a connection resource handle that can access databases through subsequent commands. Returns false on failure.
>
> The parameters (all of which are optional) and their use are identical to those of the mysql_connect( ) function.

int mssql_select_db(string *database*, resource *connection*)
> Uses the *database* on the *connection*, where the *connection* is a resource returned from mssql_connect( ).

resource mssql_query(string *SQL_command*, resource *connection*)
> Runs an SQL command through the *connection* created with mssql_connect( ) on the database selected with mssql_select_db( ). Returns a resource—a result handle used to fetch the result set—on success and false on failure.

array mssql_fetch_row(resource *result_set*)
> Fetches the result set data, row-by-row, following an mssql_query( ) command using the *result_set* resource returned by the query. The results are returned as

an array, and use is again identical to mysql_fetch_row( ). false is returned when no more rows are available.

int mssql_num_fields(resource *result_set*)

Returns the number of attributes in a *result_set* resource handle, where the *result_set* handle is returned from mssql_query( ).

int mssql_close(resource *connection*)

Closes a SQL Server connection opened with mssql_connect( ).

Example 4-12. Connecting to a Microsoft SQL Server database with PHP

```
<!DOCTYPE HTML PUBLIC
             "-//W3C//DTD HTML 4.0 Transitional//EN"
             "http://www.w3.org/TR/html4/loose.dtd">
<html>
<head>
  <title>Wines</title>
</head>
<body><pre>
<?php
<?
   // (1) Open the database connection and select the
   // winestore
   $connection = mssql_connect("localhost","fred","shhh");
   mssql_select_db("winestore", $connection);

   // (2) Run the query on the winestore through the
   // connection
   $result = mssql_query("SELECT * FROM wine",
                         $connection);

   // (3) While there are still rows in the result set
   while ($row = mssql_fetch_row($result))
   {
      // (4) Print out each attribute in the row
      for ($i=0; $i<mssql_num_fields($result); $i++)
        echo $row[$i] . " ";

      // Print a carriage return to neaten the output
      echo "\n";
   }

   // (5) Close the database connection
   mssql_close($connection);
?>
</pre>
</body>
</html>
```

Open DataBase Connectivity (ODBC)

For DBMSs that are not supported natively by PHP—such as Microsoft Access—Open DataBase Connectivity (ODBC) functions are available to connect to, query, and retrieve results. ODBC also offers database-tier flexibility where, for example, a low-end DBMS such as Access can be replaced with a high-end DBMS such as Oracle without modifying the middle-tier PHP scripts. In addition, selected DBMSs—including IBM DB2, Adabas D, and Sybase SQL Anywhere—use ODBC functions for direct access; that is, they don't have their own function libraries but use ODBC natively as a function library.

An ODBC client is required for the DBMS if ODBC is to be used. For example, MySQL can be used with ODBC by installing the MyODBC client described in Section 12 of the MySQL manual; the MyODBC client is available from *http://www.mysql.com*.

Five key ODBC functions are listed here, and Example 4-13 shows these implemented in a modified version of Example 4-1.

resource odbc_connect(string *datasource*, string *username*, string *password*, [int *cursor_type*])

> Establishes a connection to an ODBC data source. On success, the function returns a connection resource handle that can access databases through subsequent commands. The first parameter is a DSN to indicate the data source to connect to. The DSN parameter can require some experimentation; it depends on the DBMS being accessed. The DSN can sometimes be prefixed with DSN= and sometimes this can be omitted. The second and third parameters, as well as the return value (a connection resource), are the same as for mysql_connect( ). The fourth parameter is often unnecessary; however, if problems are encountered using ODBC, try passing through a fourth parameter of SQL_CUR_USE_ODBC.

resource odbc_exec(resource *connection*, string *query*)

> Runs an SQL *query* on the *connection* returned from odbc_connect( ). Returns a result resource handle on success and false on failure.

int odbc_fetch_row(resource *result_set*)

> Fetches the result-set data, row-by-row, following an odbc_exec( ) command using the *result_set* identifier returned by the query. The results are returned as an array, and the use is identical to mysql_fetch_row( ). false is returned when no more rows are available.

int odbc_num_fields(resource *result_set*)

> Returns the number of attributes associated with a *result_set* handle, where the *result_set* handle is returned from odbc_exec( ).

int odbc_close(resource *connection*)

> Closes an ODBC data source opened with odbc_connect( ).

Example 4-13. Connecting to an ODBC data source with PHP

```
<!DOCTYPE HTML PUBLIC
                "-//W3C//DTD HTML 4.0 Transitional//EN"
                "http://www.w3.org/TR/html4/loose.dtd">
<html>
<head>
  <title>Wines</title>
</head>
<body><pre>
<?php
    // (1) Open the database connection
    $connection =
        odbc_connect("DSN=winestore","fred","shhh");

    // (2) Run the query on the winestore through the
    // connection
    $query = odbc_exec($connection, "SELECT * FROM
                            wine");

    // (3) While there are still rows in the result set
    while ($row = odbc_fetch_row($result))
    {

        // (4) Print out each attribute in the row
        for ($i=0; $i<odbc_num_fields($result); $i++)
            echo $row[$i] . " ";

        // Print a carriage return to neaten the output
        echo "\n";
    }

    // (5) Close the connection
    odbc_close($connection);
?>
</pre>
</body>
</html>
```

Oracle 7 and 8 Through the OCI8 Interface

Oracle is well-supported with PHP functions, and seven key functions are listed here. Example 4-14 shows these functions implemented in a modified version of Example 4-1. The functions require that Oracle 8 client libraries be installed and the functions use the Oracle 8 Call Interface (OCI8). Support for previous versions of Oracle is available through a separate function library we don't discuss here.

Oracle access is a six-step process. A connection is opened, and then a query is first prepared with OCIParse( ) and executed with OCIExecute( ). Then, each row is retrieved with OCIFetch( ) and individual attributes are retrieved from the row with OCIResult( ). Last, the connection is closed. Our treatment of Oracle functions is brief, and more detail can be found in the PHP manual.

The key functions are:

resource OCILogon(string *username*, string *password*, string *database*)
> Establishes a connection to an Oracle DBMS. On success, the function returns a connection handle that can access databases through subsequent commands. Parameters are the same as those for mysql_connect( ).

resource OCIParse(resource *connection*, string *SQL_command*)
> Returns a query resource handle that can subsequently be executed, or returns false on error. The *connection* resource created with OCILogon( ) is passed as a parameter, along with an *SQL_command*. The function doesn't execute the query— OCIExecute( ) does that—but this function is required to set up the query for execution.

int OCIExecute(resource *query_handle*)
> Runs the query set up with OCIParse( ), taking the return value of OCIParse( ) as the only parameter. Results are subsequently fetched with OCIFetch( ). Returns true on success and false on failure.

int OCIFetch(resource *query_handle*)
> Buffers a row from the last OCIExecute( ) call specified with the *query_handle* returned from OCIParse( ). Returns true if a row is retrieved and false when no more rows are available. Attributes are fetched from this buffer with OCIResult( ).

int OCINumCols(resource *query_handle*)
> Returns the number of attributes associated with the query specified in OCIParse( ).

mixed OCIResult(resource *query_handle*, int *attribute_number*)
> Fetches the value of *attribute_number* from the current row retrieved with OCIFetch( ). Takes the return result of OCIParse( ) as the first parameter.

int OCILogoff(resource *connection*)
> Closes an Oracle connection opened with OCILogon( ).

Example 4-14. Connecting to an Oracle data source with PHP

```
<!DOCTYPE HTML PUBLIC
            "-//W3C//DTD HTML 4.0 Transitional//EN"
            "http://www.w3.org/TR/html4/loose.dtd">
<html>
<head>
  <title>Wines</title>
</head>
<body><pre>
<?php
    // (1) Open the database connections
    $connection = OCILogon("fred","shhh", "winestore");

    // (2) Setup the query on the winestore through the
    // connection
```

Example 4-14. Connecting to an Oracle data source with PHP (continued)

```
$query = OCIParse($connection, "SELECT * FROM
                                wine");

// (3) Run the query
OCIExecute($query);

// (4) Output the results
while (OCIFetch($query))
{
  // (5) Print out the attributes in this row
  for($x=1;$x<=OCINumCols($query);$x++)
    echo OCIResult($query,$x);

  echo "\n";
}

// (6) Close the database connection
OCILogoff($connection);
?>
</pre>
</body>
</html>
```

PostgreSQL

PostgreSQL DBMSs are accessed in much the same way as MySQL and Microsoft SQL Server DBMSs. Again, there are many—often functionally overlapping—functions for connecting to, querying, and extracting results from a PostgreSQL DBMS.

The five key functions are listed here, and Example 4-15 shows these implemented in a modified version of Example 4-1.

resource pg_connect(string *connection_details*)
> Establishes a connection to a PostgreSQL DBMS. On success, the function returns a connection resource handle that can access databases through subsequent commands. It returns false on failure.

> The parameters are similar to those of the mysql_connect( ) function, but the parameters are concatenated into a single string that usually includes the keywords host, dbname, user, and password. For example, to connect to *localhost*, use the *winestore* database, and log in as *fred* with password *shhh*, the format is:

```
$connection = pg_connect("host=localhost dbname=winestore
            user=fred password=shhh");
```

resource pg_exec(resource *connection*, string *SQL_command*)
> Runs an SQL command through the connection created with pg_connect( ) (the database is selected with pg_connect( )). Returns a resource—a result handle used to fetch the result set—on success, and false on failure.

array pg_fetch_row(resource *result_set*)

Fetches the result-set data, row by row, following a pg_exec( ) command using the *result_set* resource returned by the query. The results are returned as an array, and the use is identical to mysql_fetch_row( ). false is returned when no more rows are available.

int pg_num_fields(resource *result_set*)

Returns the number of attributes in a *result_set* resource handle, where the *result_set* handle is returned from pg_exec( ).

int pg_close(resource *connection*)

Closes a PostgreSQL connection opened with pg_connect( ).

Example 4-15. Connecting to a PostgreSQL server database with PHP

```
<!DOCTYPE HTML PUBLIC
                "-//W3C//DTD HTML 4.0 Transitional//EN"
                "http://www.w3.org/TR/html4/loose.dtd">
<html>
<head>
  <title>Wines</title>
</head>
<body><pre>
<?php
   // (1) Open the database connections
   $connection = pg_connect("host=localhost
            user=fred password=shhh dbname=winestore");

   // (2) Run the query on the winestore through the
   // connection
   $result = pg_exec($connection,"SELECT * FROM wine");

   // (3) While there are still rows in the result set
   while ($row = pg_fetch_row($result))
   {
      // (4) Print out each attribute in the row
      for ($i=0; $i<pg_num_fields($result); $i++)
        echo $row[$i] . " ";

      // Print a carriage return to neaten the output
      echo "\n";
   }

   // (5) Close the database connection
   pg_close($connection);
?>
</pre>
</body>
</html>
```

CHAPTER 5
User-Driven Querying

In this chapter, we build on the querying techniques discussed in Chapter 4 and complete our coverage of techniques that read data from web databases. We focus here on user-driven querying, in which the user provides data that controls the query process. To input parameters into the querying process, the user usually selects or types data into an HTML <form> environment, or clicks on links that request scripts.

We explain user-driven querying by introducing how to:

- Pass data from a web browser to a web server.
- Access user data in scripts.
- Secure interactive query systems.
- Query databases with user data.
- Produce one script that contains an HTML <form> and the code that outputs the query results. We call this a *combined script*.
- Develop results pages with previous page and next page links.
- Use five-step querying to produce components for user input.

Our case-study example in this chapter is the *wine browsing* component of the winestore. Similar to most user-driven modules, the wine browsing component has two subcomponents: first, the *search bar* allows the user to enter a type of wine as a criteria for a database query; and, second, the *results pages* show the user the wines that match the criteria entered in the search bar. The search bar is shown in Figure 5-1 at the base of the winestore search page, and the results of running the query are presented above it in a results page. The results pages allow the user to view the wines in pages of 12 wines each, move between results pages, and add wines to his shopping cart.

The querying just described is a *two-component* user-driven querying process. A less common type of user-driven querying describes a query that doesn't produce output, but instead returns the user directly to the query input component. This

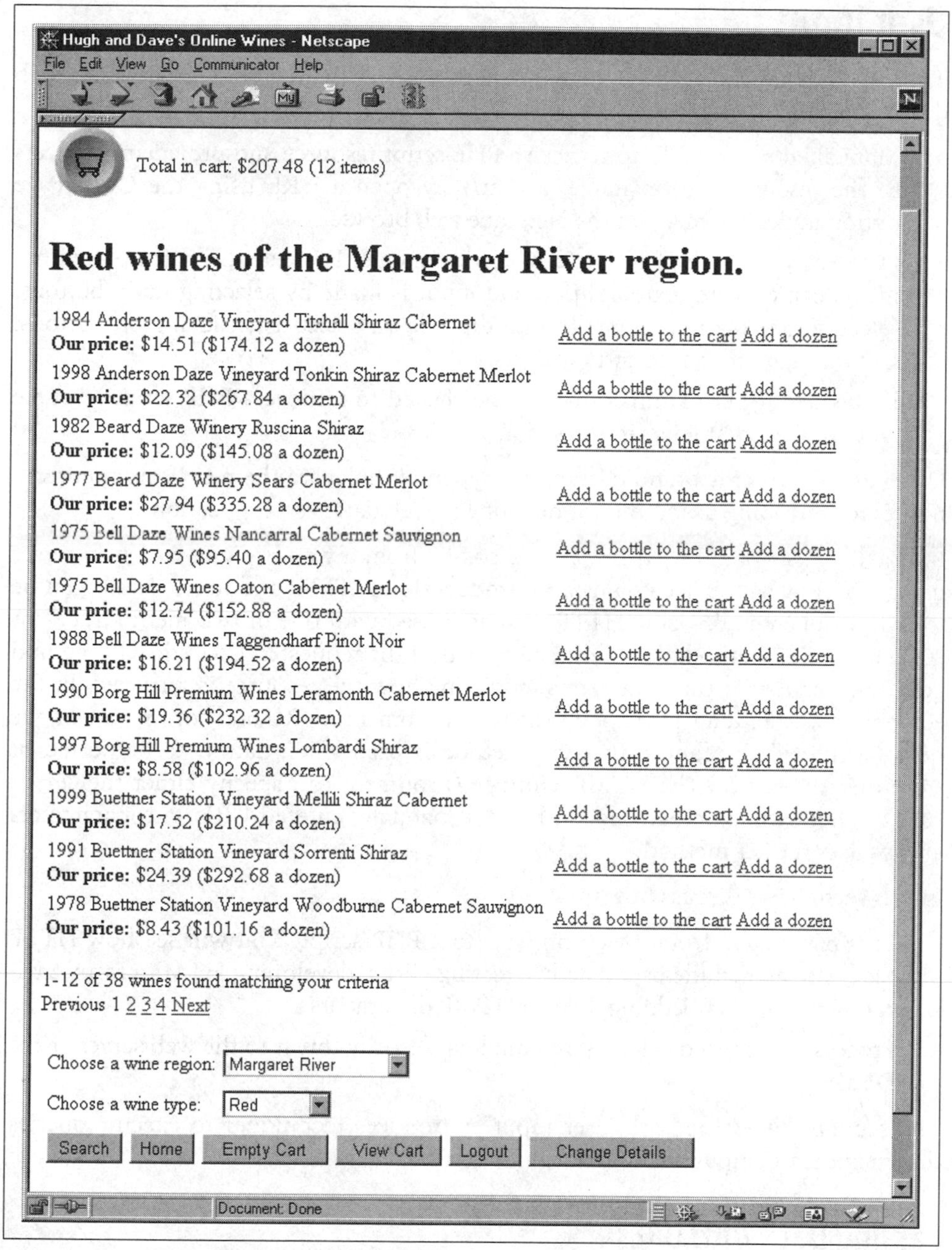

Figure 5-1. The winestore search bar and results page

one-component querying process is often used to add items to a shopping cart. We also explain one-component querying in this chapter.

Extended examples of user-driven querying can be found in Chapters 10 to 13.

User Input

Three techniques can be used to pass data that drives the querying process in a web database application:

- Manual entry of a URL to retrieve a PHP script resource and provide parameters to the resource. For example, a user may open a URL using the Open Page option in the File menu of the Netscape web browser.

- Data entry through HTML <form> environments. For example, <form> environments can capture textual input, and input is made by selecting radio buttons, selecting one or more items from a drop-down select list, clicking on buttons, and through other data entry widgets.

- Embedded hypertext links that can be clicked to retrieve a PHP script resource and provide parameters to the script.

Using an HTML <form> and clicking on hypertext links are the most common techniques for providing user input for querying in web database applications.

In practice, user data or *parameters* are passed from a web browser to a web server using HTTP; Chapter 1 contains an introduction to HTTP and more details can be found in Appendix B. Using HTTP, data is passed with one of two methods, GET or POST. In the GET method, data is passed as part of the requested URL; the GET method gets a resource with the parameters modifying how the resource is retrieved. In the POST method, the data is encoded separately from the URL and forms part of the body of the HTTP request; the POST method is used when data is to be posted or stored on the server. The HTML <form> environment can specify either the GET or POST method, while an embedded link or a manually entered URL with parameters always uses the GET method.

In this section, we discuss how to:

- Pass parameters from a web browser to a PHP script. You will see how HTTP requests can include user data by creating URLs, developing HTML <form> environments, and embedding links in HTML documents.

- Process user data to ensure it is a minimal security threat to the web server or the DBMS.

The section "Querying with User Input" introduces techniques to execute queries that include user input and to present the results.

Passing Data with URLs

The first technique that passes data from a web browser to a web server is manual entry of a URL in a web browser.

Consider an example user request with a parameter. In this example, the user types the following URL directly into the Location box in the Location toolbar of a Netscape browser:

```
http://localhost/example.5-1.php?regionName=Riverland
```

The URL specifies that the resource to be retrieved is example.5-1.php with a query string parameter of regionName=Riverland appended to the resource name. The user then presses the Enter key to issue an HTTP request for the resource and to use the GET method that passes the parameter to the resource. The query string parameter consists of two parts: a parameter name regionName and a value for that parameter of Riverland.

The script resource *example.5-1.php* is shown in Example 5-1. Before the script is processed by the PHP scripting engine, variables associated with any parameters to the resource are initialized and assigned values. In this example, a variable $regionName, which has the same name as the URL parameter name, is automatically initialized by the PHP engine and assigned the value Riverland that was passed in the URL. This variable and its value are then accessible from within the script, making the data passed by the user available in the middle tier.

Example 5-1. Printing the value of a parameter passed to the script with an HTTP request

```
<!DOCTYPE HTML PUBLIC
            "-//W3C//DTD HTML 4.0 Transitional//EN"
            "http://www.w3.org/TR/html4/loose.dtd">
<html>
<head>
  <title>Parameter</title>
</head>
<body>
<?php
  include 'db.inc';

  echo "RegionName is " . $regionName . "\n";
?>
</body>
</html>
```

As a result of running the script, the following HTML document is created with the value of the query string parameter printed as part of the output:

```
<!DOCTYPE HTML PUBLIC
            "-//W3C//DTD HTML 4.0 Transitional//EN"
            "http://www.w3.org/TR/html4/loose.dtd">
<html>
<head>
  <title>Parameter</title>
</head>
<body>
```

```
RegionName is Riverland
</body>
</html>
```

In practice, as discussed later in the section "Querying with User Input," this data might be used as part of a clause in an SQL query.

Automatic variable initialization from parameters is one of the best features of PHP. PHP automatically initializes each variable that has the same name as a parameter in an HTTP request, and the parameter values are automatically assigned to the variables. No additional programming is required to access query string parameters.

More than one parameter can be passed with an HTTP GET request by separating each parameter with an ampersand character. For example, to pass two parameters regionName and Type with the values Yarra and Red, respectively, the following URL can be created:

```
http://localhost/test.php?regionName=Yarra&Type=Red
```

The values of these parameters can then be printed in the script *test.php* using the fragment:

```
echo $regionName;
echo $Type;
```

Passing Data with the HTML <form> Environment

The second technique that captures data passed from a browser to a server is the HTML <form> environment.

Manually entering data as part of a URL is unusual. Instead, users typically enter data into an HTML <form> that is then encoded by the browser as part of an HTTP request. Example 5-2 is an HTML document that contains a <form> in which to enter the name of a wine region. The page, rendered with a Netscape browser, is shown in Figure 5-2.

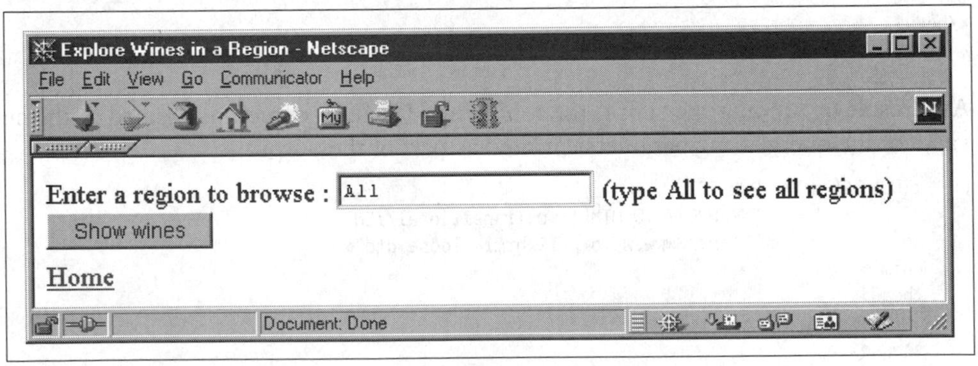

Figure 5-2. A simple page to capture user input

Example 5-2. An HTML <form> for entry of a regionName

```
<!DOCTYPE HTML PUBLIC
              "-//W3C//DTD HTML 4.0 Transitional//EN"
              "http://www.w3.org/TR/html4/loose.dtd">
<html>
<head>
  <title>Explore Wines in a Region</title>
</head>
<body bgcolor="white">
  <form action="example.5-1.php" method="GET">
    <br>Enter a region to browse :
    <input type="text" name="regionName" value="All">
    (type All to see all regions)
    <br>
    <input type="submit" value="Show wines">
  </form>
  <br><a href="index.html">Home</a>
</body>
</html>
```

When the user presses the button labeled Show Wines, the data entered in the
<form> is encoded in an HTTP request for the resource *example.5-1.php*. The
resource to be requested is specified in the action attribute of the <form> tag, as is the
method used for the HTTP request:

```
<form action="example.5-1.php" method="GET">
```

In this <form>, there is only one <input> widget with the attribute type="text" and
name="regionName". When the GET method is used, the name of this attribute and its
value result are appended to the URL as query string parameters. If the user types
Yarra Valley into the text widget and then clicks on Show Wines, the following URL
is requested:

```
http://localhost/example.5-1.php?regionName=Yarra+Valley
```

Submitting the <form> has the same result as manually typing in the URL but the user
need not understand URLs and HTTP requests when using <form>.

After submitting the <form>, the script in Example 5-1 outputs as a response an
HTML document containing the phrase "regionName is Yarra Valley". Note that the
space character entered by the user in the <form> is automatically encoded in the
URL as a plus character by the web browser, then decoded back to a space character
by the PHP scripting engine.

The HTTP POST method can be used in a <form> instead of the GET method by changing the method="GET" attribute of the <form> tag to method="POST"; the merits of POST
versus GET are discussed in more detail in Appendix B. This change of method has no
effect on automatic variable initialization in PHP scripts, and the PHP script engine
initializes variables from the parameters passed in the POST request in the same way it
does for GET requests. The script in Example 5-1 can be used without modification to
process a regionName attribute that is passed with a POST request.

All `<form>` fields—whether passed using the GET or POST methods—are automatically translated into PHP variables for direct use in scripts.

This is one of the best features of PHP, making it far simpler to write web-enabled scripts in PHP than in other languages. However, it introduces a minor security risk discussed later.

Passing Data with Embedded Links

The third technique that passes data from a web browser to a web server is embedding links in an HTML document. This technique runs queries in most web database applications and is conceptually similar to manually entering a URL. We show how to create embedded links using the results of database queries in the section "Querying with User Input."

Embedded links in an HTML document can be authored in the same way a manually created URL is typed into a web browser. Consider the script shown in Example 5-3 that is rendered in a Netscape browser in Figure 5-3.

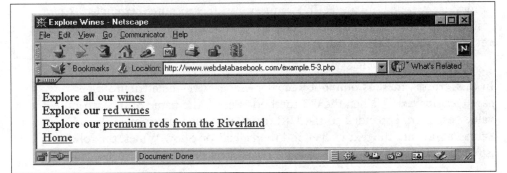

Figure 5-3. The HTML document shown in Example 5-3 rendered in a Netscape browser

Example 5-3. HTML document containing three links that pass two different parameters

```
<!DOCTYPE HTML PUBLIC
          "-//W3C//DTD HTML 4.0 Transitional//EN"
          "http://www.w3.org/TR/html401/loose.dtd">
<html>
<head>
  <title>Explore Wines</title>
</head>

<body bgcolor="#ffffff">

Explore all our
<a href="example.5-4.php?regionName=All&amp;wineType=All">
wines</a>
```

```
<br>Explore our
<a href="example.5-4.php?regionName=All&amp;wineType=Red">
red wines</a>

<br>Explore our
<a href="example.5-4.php?regionName=Riverland&amp;wineType=Red">
premium reds from the Riverland</a>

<br><a href="index.html">Home</a></body>
</html>
```

The script contains three links that can request the resource *example.5-4.php* and pass different parameters to the resource. For example, the first link in the HTML document is:

```
Explore all our <a href-"example.5-4.php? regionName=All&amp;wineType=All">
wines</a>
```

Clicking on this link creates an HTTP request for the URL:

```
http://localhost/example.5-4.php?
regionName=All&wineType=All
```

The result of the request is that the script in Example 5-4 is run, and the following HTML document is created:

```
<!DOCTYPE HTML PUBLIC
            "-//W3C//DTD HTML 4.0 Transitional//EN"
            "http://www.w3.org/TR/html4/loose.dtd">
<html>
<head>
   <title>Parameters</title>
</head>
<body>
regionName is All
<br>wineType is All
</body>
</html>
```

Example 5-4. A simple script to print out HTTP attributes and values

```
<!DOCTYPE HTML PUBLIC
            "-//W3C//DTD HTML 4.0 Transitional//EN"
            "http://www.w3.org/TR/html4/loose.dtd">
<html>
<head>
  <title>Parameters</title>
</head>
<body>
<?php
  include 'db.inc';

  $regionName  = clean($regionName, 30);
  $wineType    = clean($wineType, 10);
```

```
    echo "regionName is "    . $regionName  . "\n";
    echo "<br>wineType is "   . $wineType    . "\n";
?>
</body>
</html>
```

Note that the ampersand characters in the URLs in the HTML document are replaced with &, because the ampersand character has a special meaning in HTML and should not be included directly in a document. When the link is clicked, the encoded & is translated by the browser to & in forming the HTTP request.

Security and User Data

This section introduces simple techniques that preprocess user data to solve many common security holes in web database applications.

> Using the techniques described here doesn't completely secure a system. Remember that securing a web database application is important, and that the advice offered here isn't a complete solution. A discussion of other security issues is presented in Chapter 9.

Data that is passed from a web browser to a web server should be secured using the steps described here. For this purpose, we have authored the clean( ) function to ensure that the data passed to a script is of the correct length and that special characters aren't misused to attack the system. To understand why the clean( ) function is needed, we describe an example attack later in this section. The function is part the include file *db.inc* that is used in all scripts in the online winestore.

Consider the following script. It uses the PHP exec( ) library function to run a program on the web server. The exec( ) function takes two parameters, the program to run and an array populated with any output of the program. In this example, the script uses exec( ) to run the Unix *cal* program and to pass the user-entered parameter $userString to the program. The information in the parameter userString can be provided by using an HTML <form> with a text input widget, by manually creating a URL, or by embedding a link in an HTML document.

```
    <?php
        // DO NOT INSTALL THIS SCRIPT ON A WEB SERVER

        // Run "cal" with the parameter $userString
        // Store the results in the array $result
        exec("/usr/bin/cal $userString", $result);
    ?>
```

```
<!DOCTYPE HTML PUBLIC
                "-//W3C//DTD HTML 4.0 Transitional//EN"
                "http://www.w3.org/TR/html4/loose.dtd">
<html>
  <head>
    <title>Calendar</title>
  </head>
<body>
<pre>
<?php
    // Print out each line of the calendar
    foreach($result as $element)
        echo  "$element\n";
?>
</pre>
</body>
</html>
```

 Never use exec( ) or other commands to run programs from a web
script or to query a database without securing the user data. Do not
install the calendar example on a web server.

The Unix *cal* program is a useful utility that produces monthly or yearly calendars
for any date. For example, to produce a calendar for the whole of 2003, a user could
request the URL:

http://localhost/cal.php?userString=2003

This runs the command /usr/bin/cal 2003 and outputs the complete 2003 calendar,
as shown in Figure 5-4.

To produce a calendar for February 2003, the user requests:

http://localhost/cal.php?userString=2+2003

Requesting the URL without any parameters produces the calendar for the current
month:

http://localhost/cal.php

While this script might seem useful and innocuous, this script is a major security
hole and should never be installed on a web server.

To illustrate why the script should never be installed, consider how it can be misused. If a user wants to enter two or more commands on a single line in a Unix shell,
he can do so by separating the commands with a semicolon character. For example,
to see who is logged in and then to list the files in the current directory, a user can
type the following commands at the shell:

% who ; ls

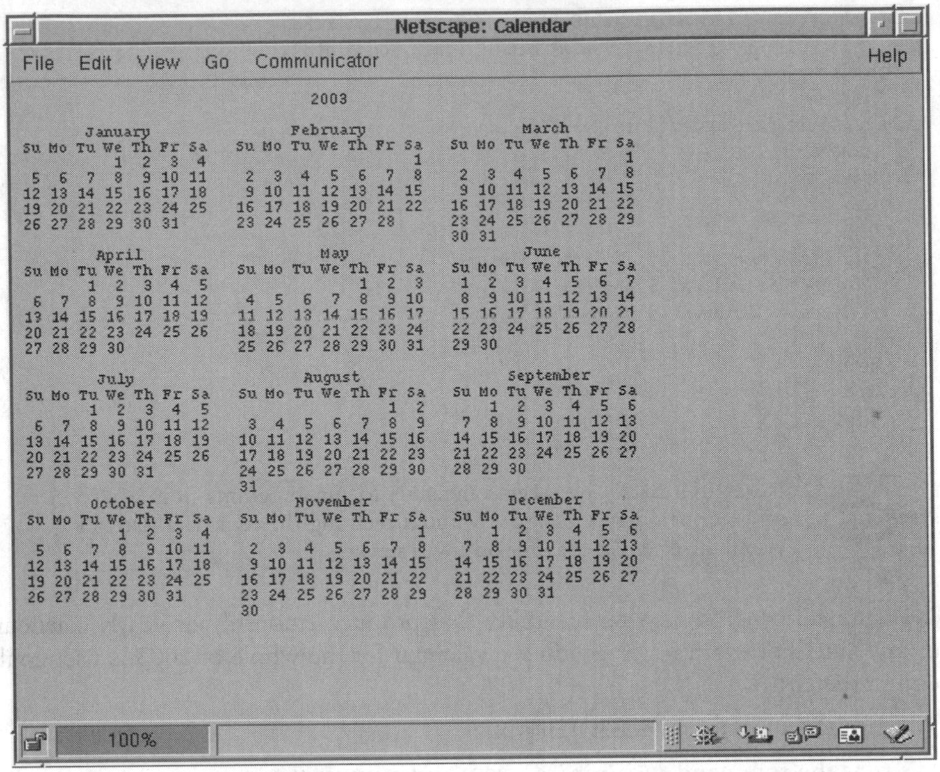

Figure 5-4. Output of the dangerous calendar example when the user requests a 2003 calendar

Now, consider what happens if he exploits this feature by requesting the following URL:

```
http://localhost/cal.php?userString=2001;cat+/etc/passwd
```

The script produces a 2001 calendar, followed by the system password file, as shown in Figure 5-5! The script allows a creative user to do things the web server process can do. The identity of the owner of the web server process affects the severity of the actions that can be performed, but this is at best a major security hole.

Semicolons, colons, greater-than and less-than signs, and other special characters can cause a script or a query to provide undesirable functions, especially if the script executes the library functions system( ) or exec( ) to run server commands. Even if a <form> makes it difficult for a user to enter undesirable data, he can manually create his own request by entering a URL and authoring a query string.

> Never trust anything you don't have control of, that is, anything not in middle or database tiers.

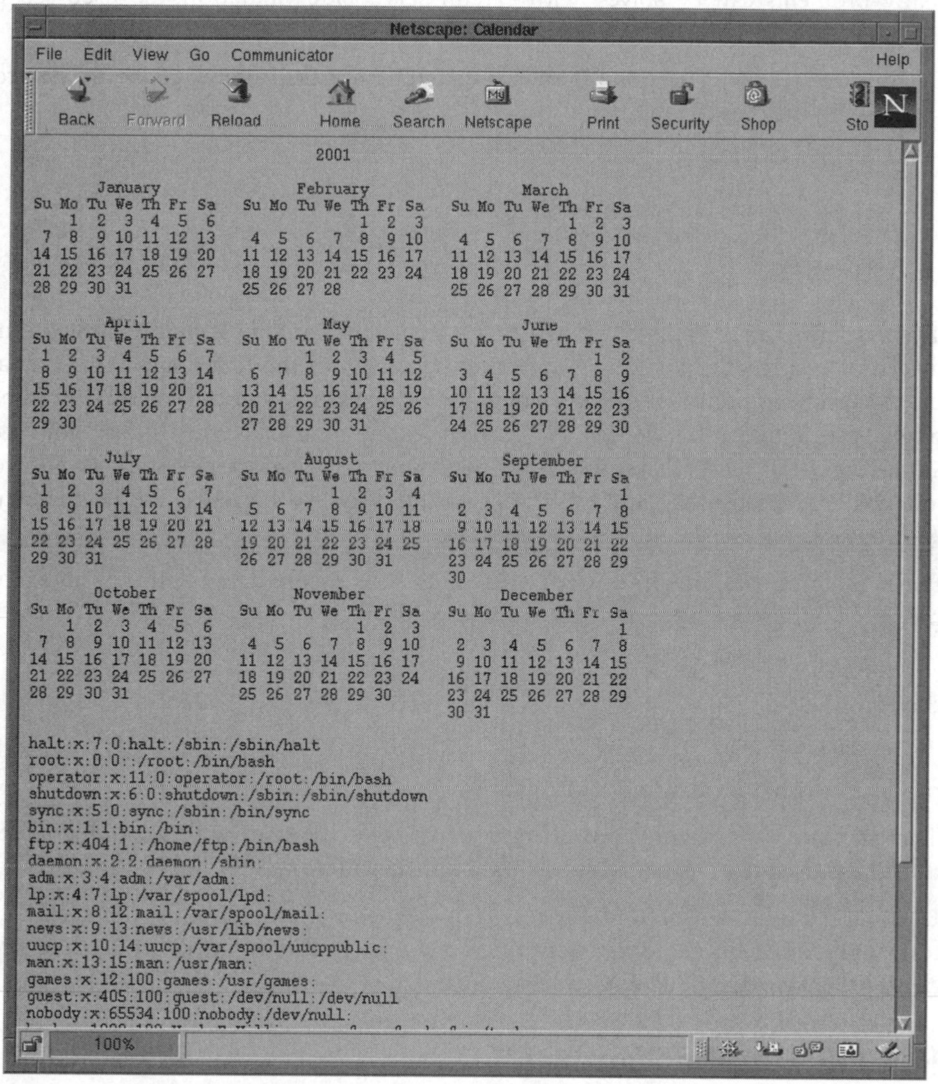

Figure 5-5. Output when the user requests a 2001 calendar and the system password file

SQL querying also has problems. For example, a user can guess the structure of database tables and how a query is formed from user input. A user might guess that a query uses an AND clause and that a particular <form> text widget provides one of the values to the query. The user might then add additional AND and OR clauses to the query by entering a partial SQL query in the text widget. While such tricks may expose data that should remain hidden from the user, problems compound if the user inserts or deletes data with the techniques discussed in Chapter 6. However, many problems can be solved with careful server-side validation, as discussed in Chapter 7 and the approach described next.

To improve security and prevent special-character attacks, user data should be processed with the clean( ) function:

```
function clean($input, $maxlength)
{
  $input = substr($input, 0, $maxlength);
  $input = EscapeShellCmd($input);
  return ($input);
}
```

The first line uses the substr( ) function to reduce the variable $input to a maximum length of $maxlength by taking a substring beginning at the first character. You can use 30 as a maximum $regionName length for Example 5-1, and the calendar example might use a maximum length of 7. The second line calls the library function EscapeShellCmd( ), which escapes any special-purpose characters—such as semicolons, colons, greater-than and less-than signs, and so on—by replacing the character with a single backslash and then the character.

For many purposes, the clean steps are sufficient to ensure data is safe. As an example, if the parameter userString has a value of:

```
2001;cat /etc/passwd
```

then a call of:

```
clean($userString, 7)
```

produces the harmless string 2001\;ca.

This string has no detrimental effect and provides the user with no hidden data. clean( ) is used to preprocess all user data for the winestore.

User data that has not been preprocessed or cleaned is often known as *tainted* data, a term originating from the Perl scripting language. Rectifying this through the processing we have described *untaints* user data.

How PHP Initializes Variables

As we have discussed throughout this section, variables are automatically initialized by PHP from the parameters passed in an HTTP request.

Automatic initialization of variables is an excellent feature for simple scripts, but it has security and processing implications. If required, the automatic initialization can be turned off by setting register_globals=false in the *php.ini* configuration file, usually found in the directory */usr/local/lib/*. The *php.ini* file was copied to this location as part of the PHP installation instructions in Appendix A.

When the PHP script engine is invoked, the engine declares and initializes variables in a predefined order. The automatic initialization feature works in this order:

1. By default, environment variables are initialized first.

2. Variables are initialized from query string parameters passed with the GET method.

3. POST method parameters are initialized.

4. Variables from cookies are initialized.

5. The Apache server internal variables are initialized.

The initialization order can be changed from the default by adjusting the variables_order setting in *php.ini*. The security problem occurs when a user knowingly or inadvertently overrides a previously initialized variable. For example, the PATH environment variable is one of the first initialized when the script engine is invoked. If a GET request contains an attribute named PATH, this overrides the environment variable of the same name, because GET variables are initialized after environment variables. By understanding the initialization process, the user can override previously set variables by passing through parameters. This can change script behavior and possibly lead to a security problem.

If the register_globals feature is turned off, a PHP script must use a different method to access user data. This method is more secure and requires that arrays be accessed to retrieve specific user parameters. For example, the GET variables are stored in an associative array, $HTTP_GET_VARS.

Consider the following URL that is requested by a user:

```
http://localhost/test.php?varname=value
```

The variable $varname can be printed in a PHP script by accessing the associative array $HTTP_GET_VARS using:

```
echo $HTTP_GET_VARS["varname"];
```

The only disadvantage of this approach is that the script is tailored for the GET method. Changing the <form> submission method from GET to POST requires modifying the script. All references to $HTTP_GET_VARS must be replaced with references to $HTTP_POST_VARS, because the array $HTTP_POST_VARS stores all variables passed using the POST method. However, the use of associative arrays is more secure because the script doesn't function if the user maliciously changes the <form> submission method in an attempt to compromise the system.

We often initialize local variables at the beginning of a script from the contents of the $HTTP_GET_VARS or $HTTP_POST_VARS arrays. This emulates the register_globals feature of PHP but without the security issues. Local variables make the code more attractive and readable. For example, the following code fragment initializes three variables from the contents of the $HTTP_GET_VARS array:

```
$surname = $HTTP_GET_VARS["surname"];
$firstname = $HTTP_GET_VARS["firstname"];
$title = $HTTP_GET_VARS["title"];
```

The result is that the script behaves the same as if `register_globals` is on. This also has the advantage that if the `<form>` submission method is changed from `GET` to `POST`, the code need be modified only in one place.

Other external variables can be accessed similarly:

- `POST` variables can found in the array `$HTTP_POST_VARS`.
- Cookie variables can be found in the array `$HTTP_COOKIE_VARS`.
- Environment variables can be found in the array `$HTTP_ENV_VARS`.
- Session variables can be found in the array `$HTTP_SESSION_VARS`.
- Server variables can be found in the array `$HTTP_SERVER_VARS`.

Cookies and sessions are discussed in Chapter 8.

We have set `register_globals=true` in the online winestore application. However, the security implications of automatic initialization should be considered when designing any application.

Querying with User Input

To introduce querying with user input, we begin by explaining a script that retrieves the wines made in a wine region that is specified by a user. This script, shown in Example 5-5, is a companion to the HTML `<form>` in Example 5-2.

Example 5-5. A script to display all wineries in a region

```
<!DOCTYPE HTML PUBLIC
            "-//W3C//DTD HTML 4.0 Transitional//EN"
            "http://www.w3.org/TR/html4/loose.dtd">
<html>
<head>
  <title>Exploring Wines in a Region</title>
</head>

<body bgcolor="white">
<?php

  include 'db.inc';

  // Show all wines in a region in a <table>
  function displayWinesList($connection,
                    $query,
                    $regionName)
  {
    // Run the query on the DBMS
    if (!($result = @ mysql_query ($query, $connection)))
      showerror();

    // Find out how many rows are available
    $rowsFound = @ mysql_num_rows($result);
```

Example 5-5. A script to display all wineries in a region (continued)

```
    // If the query has results ...
    if ($rowsFound > 0)
    {
        // ... print out a header
        echo "Wines of $regionName<br>";

        // and start a <table>.
        echo "\n<table>\n<tr>" .
            "\n\t<th>Wine ID</th>" .
            "\n\t<th>Wine Name</th>" .
            "\n\t<th>Type</th>" .
            "\n\t<th>Year</th>" .
            "\n\t<th>Winery</th>" .
            "\n\t<th>Description</th>\n</tr>";

        // Fetch each of the query rows
        while ($row = @ mysql_fetch_array($result))
        {
            // Print one row of results
            echo "\n<tr>" .
                "\n\t<td>" . $row["wine_id"] . "</td>" .
                "\n\t<td>" . $row["wine_name"] . "</td>" .
                "\n\t<td>" . $row["type"] . "</td>" .
                "\n\t<td>" . $row["year"] . "</td>" .
                "\n\t<td>" . $row["winery_name"] . "</td>" .
                "\n\t<td>" . $row["description"] . "</td>" .
                    "\n</tr>";
        } // end while loop body

        // Finish the <table>
        echo "\n</table>";
    } // end if $rowsFound body

    // Report how many rows were found
    echo "$rowsFound records found matching your
            criteria<br>";
} // end of function


// Secure the user parameter $regionName
$regionName = clean($regionName, 30);

// Connect to the MySQL DBMS
if (!($connection = @ mysql_connect($hostName,
                                    $username,
                                    $password)))
    die("Could not connect");

if (!mysql_select_db($databaseName, $connection))
    showerror();
```

Example 5-5. A script to display all wineries in a region (continued)

```
    // Start a query ...
    $query = "SELECT    w.wine_id,
                        w.wine_name,
                        w.description,
                        w.type,
                        w.year,
                        wry.winery_name
            FROM        winery wry, region r, wine w
            WHERE       wry.region_id = r.region_id
            AND         w.winery_id = wry.winery_id";

    // ... then, if the user has specified a region,
    // add the regionName as an AND clause ...
    if ($regionName != "All")
        $query .= " AND r.region_name = \"$regionName\"";

    // ... and then complete the query.
    $query .= " ORDER BY w.wine_name";

    // run the query and show the results
    displayWinesList($connection, $query, $regionName);

    // Close the DBMS connection
    mysql_close($connection);
?>
</body>
</html>
```

The script in Example 5-5 uses the querying techniques discussed in Chapter 4. This example differs from the others in several ways:

- It expects input of a wine region to be provided through the HTTP attribute regionName.

- The automatically initialized variable $regionName is untainted with the clean( ) function we discussed in the last section.

- The value of the variable $regionName is used in querying.

The script uses the five-step process described in Chapter 4 to provide the following functionality:

1. Connect to the MySQL DBMS. The variable $hostName is set in *db.inc* along with the username $username and password $password. The code then selects the database name set in *db.inc*.

2. Build an SQL query, $query, to find wine and winery information for the region entered by the user through the <form> in Example 5-1.

   The variable $regionName is used to construct a query on the *winestore* database, making the query dependent on the user input and, therefore, a user-driven query. This works as follows: if the user enters a regionName into the <form>, an additional AND clause is added to the query that restricts the `r.region_name` to be equal to the user-supplied region name. For example, if the user enters Margaret River, the clause:

```
AND r.region_name = "Margaret River"
```

is added to the query.

If the `$regionName` is `All`, no restriction on region is made, and the query retrieves wines for all regions.

3. The function `displayWinesList()` is then called to run the query.

4. `displayWinesList()` produces a `<table>` with headings, processes the result set and produces `<table>` rows, and finishes the `</table>` with a message indicating how many records are present in the table. This is similar functionality to the scripts discussed in Chapter 4.

Other than the processing of the user parameter and the handling of the `All` regions option, no significant new functionality is introduced in allowing the user to drive the query process in this example. We improve the processing and develop more modular code in the next section.

Combined Scripts

The approach described in the last section separates the HTML `<form>` and the PHP processing script into two files. It is more common to implement both in the same script where the code can produce a `<form>` or run a query, depending if user parameters are supplied. If the script is called with no parameters, the script produces a `<form>` for user input and, if it is called with input from the `<form>`, it runs the query. This is called a *combined script*.

For wine searching, a combined script is implemented by replacing the main section of Example 5-5 with the code fragment shown in Example 5-6. The difference between the two scripts is that Example 5-6 has the structure:

```
// Has the user provided the parameter?
if (empty($regionName))
{
 // Yes, produce the HTML <form> to collect a regionName
} else
{
 // No, run the query for wines in the region $regionName
}
```

With this structure, when the variable `$regionName` is empty—that is, the user has not yet entered anything—the user `<form>` is produced. When a value has been entered, the query is run and the results are output. Example 5-6 shows you how to replace the main section of the code from Example 5-5 with the `<form>` from

Example 5-2. With this modification, only one file is required to produce the user form and then process the query output.

Example 5-6. A combined <form> and processing script to display wineries in a region

```
<!DOCTYPE HTML PUBLIC
            "-//W3C//DTD HTML 4.0 Transitional//EN"
            "http://www.w3.org/TR/html4/loose.dtd">
<html>
<head>
  <title>Exploring Wines in a Region</title>
</head>

<body bgcolor="white">
<?php

  include 'db.inc';

  // Show all wines in a region in a <table>
  function displayWinesList($connection,
                            $query,
                            $regionName)
  {
      // Run the query on the DBMS
      if (!($result = @ mysql_query ($query, $connection)))
          showerror();

      // Find out how many rows are available
      $rowsFound = @ mysql_num_rows($result);

      // If the query has results ...
      if ($rowsFound > 0)
      {
          // ... print out a header
          echo "Wines of $regionName<br>";

          // and start a <table>.
          echo "\n<table>\n<tr>" .
              "\n\t<th>Wine ID</th>" .
              "\n\t<th>Wine Name</th>" .
              "\n\t<th>Type</th>" .
              "\n\t<th>Year</th>" .
              "\n\t<th>Winery</th>" .
              "\n\t<th>Description</th>\n</tr>";

          // Fetch each of the query rows
          while ($row = @ mysql_fetch_array($result))
          {
              // Print one row of results
              echo "\n<tr>" .
                  "\n\t<td>" . $row["wine_id"] . "</td>" .
                  "\n\t<td>" . $row["wine_name"] . "</td>" .
                  "\n\t<td>" . $row["type"] . "</td>" .
```

```
                    "\n\t<td>" . $row["year"] . "</td>" .
                    "\n\t<td>" . $row["winery_name"] . "</td>" .
                    "\n\t<td>" . $row["description"] . "</td>" .
                    "\n</tr>";
        } // end while loop body

        // Finish the <table>
        echo "\n</table>";
    } // end if $rowsFound body

    // Report how many rows were found
    echo "$rowsFound records found matching your
            criteria<br>";
} // end of function

$scriptName = "example.5-6.php";

// Has the user provided the parameter?
if (empty($regionName))
{
    // No, the user hasn't provided a parameter
?>
    <form action="<?=$scriptName;?>" method="GET">
      <br>Enter a region to browse :
      <input type="text" name="regionName" value="All">
      (type All to see all regions)
      <br>
      <input type="submit" value="Show wines">
    </form><br>
    <a href="index.html">Home</a>
<?php
  } // end of if empty($regionName) body
  else
  {
    // Secure the user parameter $regionName
    $regionName = clean($regionName, 30);

    // Connect to the MySQL DBMS
    if (!($connection = @ mysql_connect($hostName,
                                        $username,
                                        $password)))
        die("Could not connect");

    if (!mysql_select_db($databaseName, $connection))
        showerror();

    // Start a query ...
    $query = "SELECT   w.wine_id,
                       w.wine name,
                       w.description,
                       w.type,
```

Example 5-6. A combined <form> and processing script to display wineries in a region (continued)

```
                  w.year,
                  wry.winery_name
          FROM    winery wry, region r, wine w
          WHERE   wry.region_id = r.region_id
          AND     w.winery_id = wry.winery_id";

      // ... then, if the user has specified a region,
      // add the regionName as an AND clause ...
      if ($regionName != "All")
        $query .= " AND r.region_name = \"$regionName\"";

      // ... and then complete the query.
      $query .= " ORDER BY w.wine_name";

      // run the query and show the results
      displayWinesList($connection, $query, $regionName);

      // Close the DBMS connection
      mysql_close($connection);
  } // end of else if empty($regionName) body
?>
</body>
</html>
```

We use this combined script structure throughout the rest of this book. Output of Example 5-6 with the `Margaret River` parameter is shown in Figure 5-6.

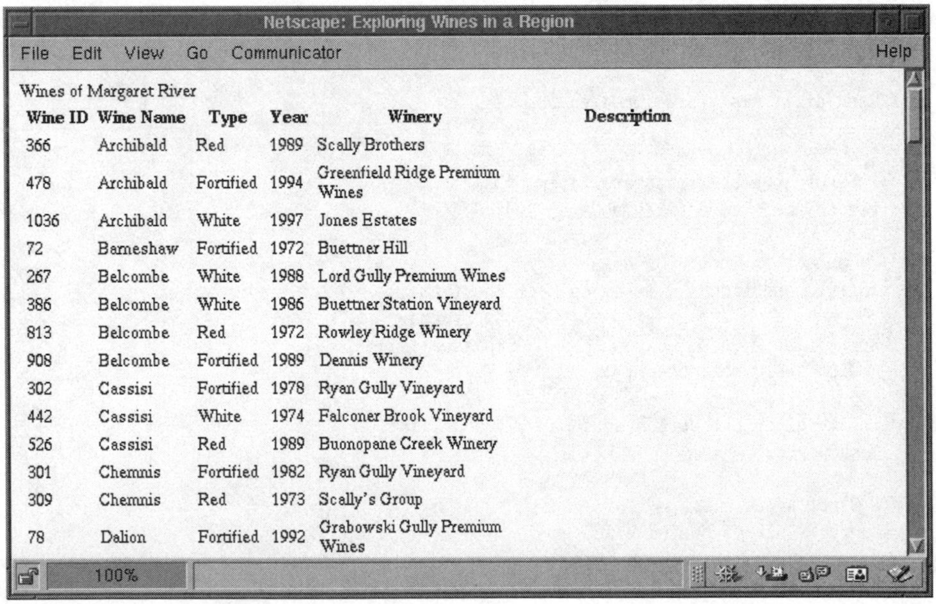

Figure 5-6. Output of the combined script from Example 5-6

Adding Links to Results

As discussed in the earlier section "Passing Data with Embedded Links," scripts can also include embedded URLs with parameters that can run queries. This is a powerful tool, and one that is used in most web database applications. In this section, we show the power of this technique with an example from the winestore. In the next section, we show how embedded URLs can be used in a longer case study.

In Chapter 4, we authored the panel to display the latest wines that have been added to the winestore. We noted that the panel used in the winestore has Add to Cart functionality, in which a user can click on a link, and a bottle or case of wine is added to her shopping cart. This functionality is implemented using an embedded URL that is dynamically created from data in the database. Example 5-7 displays the code used to add the "Add to Cart" link that's embedded in the panel. The code creates a URL with parameters that specify the quantity and the product to add to the shopping cart.

Example 5-7. The code used to add the "Add to Cart" link

```
echo "<tr align=\"right\"><td>" .
    "<a href=\"example.5-8.php?qty=1&amp;wineId=" .
    $row["wine_id"] .
    "\">Add a bottle to the shopping cart</a>" .
    "</td></tr>";
```

The code fragment in Example 5-7 creates a link such as:

```
http://localhost/example.5-8.php?qty=1&wineId=801
```

The URL parameter wineId is formed with the database wine_id attribute value that is associated with the current wine being displayed in the panel. When the user clicks the link, *example.5-8.php* is requested and the parameters are supplied to the script. The user can type the URL directly her their web browser with the same effect, or you can author a <form> for the same purpose. We discuss the script *example.5-8.php* in the next section.

> Be careful what information is embedded in links. For example, never embed the price of an item you later rely on to create an invoice for the user. Remember that the user can manually enter URLs in their browser and can modify any of the parameters. If a price is embedded, a user can create the URL manually and change the price of the item!

One-Component Querying

In many web database applications, functionality is included that allows the user to click on a link that performs an action but allows the user to remain on the same page. This is *one-component* querying, in which the query input component is displayed, but there is no corresponding page that shows output of the query. In this section, we discuss how one-component querying is used and the principles of adding one-component queries to an application.

Figure 5-7 illustrates the principle of one-component querying. When the user selects a link on a page—let's assume this page is named *browse.php* and we refer to this as the *calling* page—an HTTP request for a PHP script *addcart.php* is sent to the server. At the server, the script *addcart.php* is interpreted by the PHP script engine and, after carrying out the database actions in the script, no output is produced. Instead—and this is the key to one-component querying—an HTTP Location: header is sent as a response to the web browser, and this header causes the browser to request the original calling page, *browse.php*. The result is that the calling page is redisplayed, and the user has the impression that he remained on the query input component page.

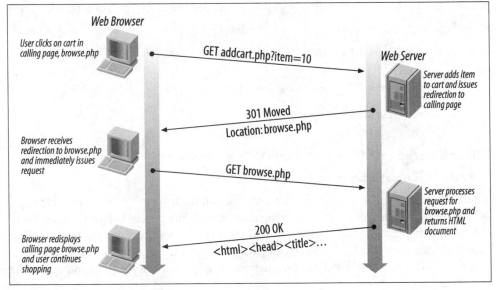

Figure 5-7. The principle of one-component querying

A good example of an application of one-component queryING was illustrated in the last section, where we showed how Add to Cart functionality can be incorporated in the winestore panel. One excellent way to support Add to Cart is to author a script that adds the wine to the user's cart and then redirects the user back to the panel. The cart is updated after a click, and the user can continue reading about and, hopefully, purchasing wines.

Example 5-8 shows a one-component script. In practice, the script adds a quantity of a specific wine to a shopping cart, using the parameters embedded in the links in the page generated by the script in Example 5-7. However, for simplicity we have not included the database queries here; modifying the database is the subject of the next chapter, and the full code for this example is presented in Chapter 11.

Example 5-8. Implementing one-component querying for the Add to Cart functionality

```
<?
    if (!empty($wineId) && !empty($qty))
    {
      // Database functionality goes here

      // This is the key to one-component querying:
      // Redirect the browser back to the calling page,
      // using the HTTP response header "Location:"
      // and the PHP environment variable $HTTP_REFERER
      header("Location: $HTTP_REFERER");
      exit;
    } else
      echo "Incorrectly called.";
?>
```

The key to Example 5-8 is the final two lines of a successful execution of the script:

```
header("Location: $HTTP_REFERER");
exit;
```

The header( ) function sends an additional HTTP response header. In one-component querying, the response includes the Location header that redirects a browser to another URL, in this case the URL of the calling page. The URL of the calling page is automatically initialized into the PHP web server environment variable $HTTP_REFERER. The exit statement causes the script to abort after sending the header.

Consider an example where the calling page is the resource *example.5-7.php* that is output by the script in Example 5-7. This is the page that shows the user the Hot New Wines panel and allows the user to click on a link to add an item to her shopping basket. The user then clicks on a link on this page and requests this URL:

```
http://localhost/example.5-8.php?qty=1&wineId=801
```

After successfully completing the request by running the script in Example 5-8 and adding the item to the shopping cart, the following header is sent back to the browser as a response:

```
Location: http://localhost/example.5-7.php
```

This header redirects the browser back to the calling page, completing the one-component query.

The header( ) command can be issued only before data is sent. In one-component querying, the script that carries out the database actions shouldn't produce any output, so this usually isn't a problem. A call to the header( ) function should also be followed by an exit statement if no further processing of statements after the header( ) function call is desired. We discussed the symptoms of header( ) function problems and how to solve them in Chapter 2.

One-component querying is useful in situations where only the query screen is required or the results page and the query page are the same page. For example, in the winestore, one-component querying is used to update quantities in the shopping cart when the user alters the quantities of wine in his shopping cart. In general, one-component querying works well for simple update operations; these are the subject of Chapter 6.

Case Study: Previous and Next Browsing

The subject of this section is a case study that uses the concepts we have discussed so far in this chapter. We show how to develop page browsing tools to display results over several pages and permit users to move between these pages. We develop this code as a generic, reusable module. A modified version of the code is used in the winestore, and the winestore browsing code is included in Chapter 13.

The aim of our case study is to show how to display large result sets in pages. Each page should be able to be displayed efficiently and viewed without using the web browser's vertical scroll bar. We also aim to make the component intuitive to use, allow direct access to any page in the results, and allow pages to be navigated using previous and next hypertext links.

We develop the module step-by-step. We begin by developing support for multiple results pages, and the previous and next links. Later in this section, we add functionality to display page numbers as links that permit direct access to a chosen page. The output of the final version of the module when it is used to browse winestore regions is shown in Figure 5-8.

In this section, as a generic page-based browser is developed, we retire the special-purpose displayWinesList( ) function completed in Example 5-6. It's replaced with a new, generic, multipurpose function browse( ). However, before we discuss how this is done, we describe what we need to achieve.

The following features are required when a user browses the wines in a region:

- Only one page of wineries is shown at a time. When the user runs the query, only the first 20 rows of results are shown.
- As in Figure 5-8, an embedded Next link displays that allows the user to move to the next page of rows. If the user is accessing the first page, the Next link runs a query that shows the second page of results; that is, rows 21 to 40.
- When the user reaches the last page of results—which usually has less than 20 rows—the Next link is hidden.
- An embedded Previous link is shown that moves backward through the pages.
- The Previous link is hidden when the first page is displayed.

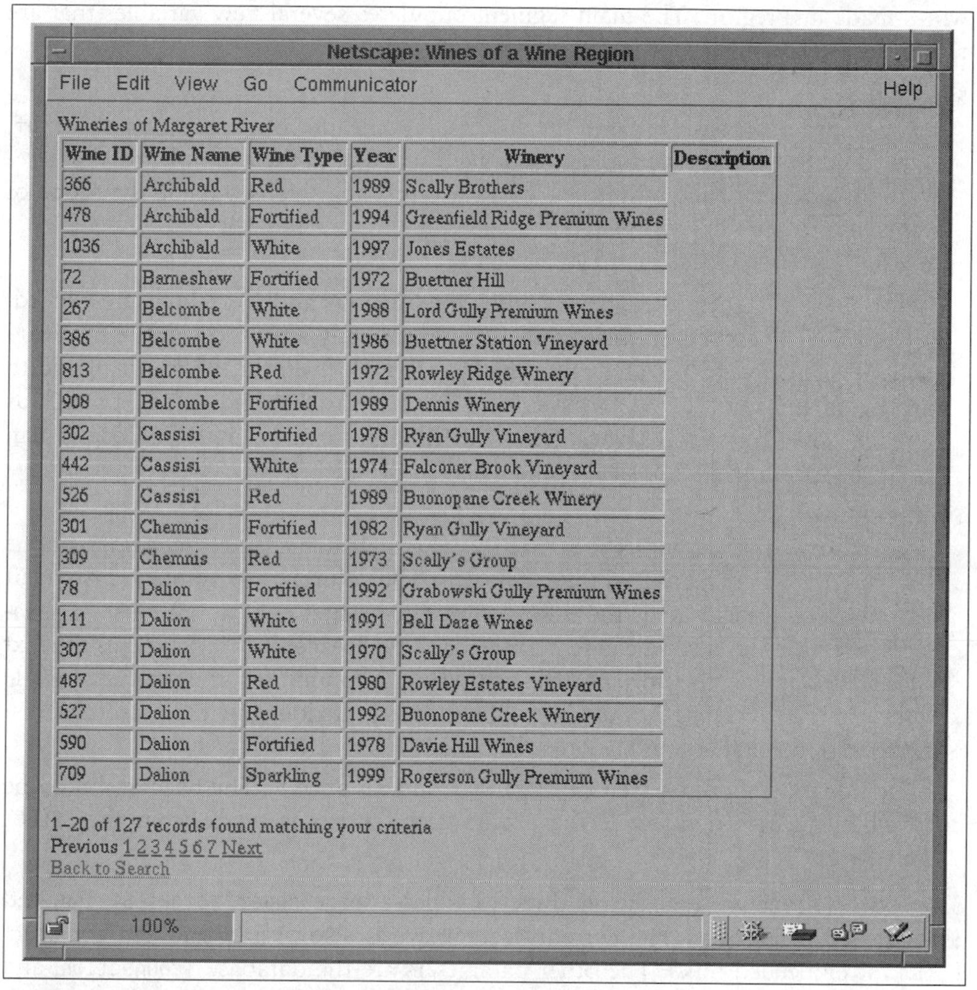

Wine ID	Wine Name	Wine Type	Year	Winery	Description
366	Archibald	Red	1989	Scally Brothers	
478	Archibald	Fortified	1994	Greenfield Ridge Premium Wines	
1036	Archibald	White	1997	Jones Estates	
72	Barneshaw	Fortified	1972	Buettner Hill	
267	Belcombe	White	1988	Lord Gully Premium Wines	
386	Belcombe	White	1986	Buettner Station Vineyard	
813	Belcombe	Red	1972	Rowley Ridge Winery	
908	Belcombe	Fortified	1989	Dennis Winery	
302	Cassisi	Fortified	1978	Ryan Gully Vineyard	
442	Cassisi	White	1974	Falconer Brook Vineyard	
526	Cassisi	Red	1989	Buonopane Creek Winery	
301	Chemnis	Fortified	1982	Ryan Gully Vineyard	
309	Chemnis	Red	1973	Scally's Group	
78	Dalion	Fortified	1992	Grabowski Gully Premium Wines	
111	Dalion	White	1991	Bell Daze Wines	
307	Dalion	White	1970	Scally's Group	
487	Dalion	Red	1980	Rowley Estates Vineyard	
527	Dalion	Red	1992	Buonopane Creek Winery	
590	Dalion	Fortified	1978	Davie Hill Wines	
709	Dalion	Sparkling	1999	Rogerson Gully Premium Wines	

Figure 5-8. A generic page browsing tool with previous and next links

This can be further improved by adding page numbers to each page that allow direct access to other pages without repeatedly clicking on the previous or next links. We discuss this functionality later in this section.

Step 1: Using the Generic browse Function

We show how the Previous and Next links are created with PHP in the `browse( )` function later, but let's return for a moment to the main body of the browsing script. Example 5-9 shows a script that uses the new generic `browse( )` function to show the wines made in a region. The main segment populates several new variables that are parameters to the browse( ) function:

$pageHeader

A header for the results pages. In this case, the header is a text string Wines of, followed by the name of the region being displayed; in the example, this can create the grammatically odd Wines of All, but fixing this is outside the scope of this discussion.

$browseString

Part of the URL that is requested when the Previous and Next links are clicked. The value of $browseString is appended immediately after the ? in the URL and duplicates the variables and values passed through from the <form> displayed to the user. In Example 5-9, $browseString forms a variable and value pair such as regionName=Margaret%20River. The PHP library function rawurlencode( ) can encode spaces and other special characters in the URL.

$header

A 2D array that contains the HTML column headers and the names of the attributes to be displayed in these columns. The columns are numbered from left to right, so $header[0] is the information for the first column. We use associative access to the second element for readability: $header[0]["header"] is the text that displays at the top of the first HTML column in the <table>, while $header[0]["attrib"] is the name of the query attribute in the result set displayed in the first column.

Each column should have both a header and an attrib. The header should be human-readable text, while the attrib is the attribute name from the SELECT clause of the SQL query.

The browse() function takes these three variables—$pageHeader, $browseString, and $header—as parameters. The current $scriptName is also passed and can construct URLs for embedded links. The other parameters are the database $connection, and the $offset in the result set of the first row on the page that is displayed. The value of $offset is initially zero after running a query and, because it isn't part of the <form>, it's initialized in Example 5-9 to zero when not set. In this example, we show only the modified section of the main component of the script for preparing a query. The function browse( ), shown in Example 5-10, is called in this fragment to provide generic browsing.

Example 5-9. Adding browsing functionality to the winestore database

```
// Untaint the user data
$regionName = clean($regionName, 30);

$scriptName = "example.5-9.php";
```

```
// Is there any user data?
if (empty($regionName))
{
    // No, so show the <form>
?>
<form action="<?=$scriptName;?>" method="GET">
  <br>Enter a region to browse :
  <input type="text" name="regionName" value="All">
  (type All to see all regions)
  <br>
  <input type="submit" value="Show wines">
</form>
<br><a href="index.html">Home</a>
<?php
  } // if user data
  else
  {
    // Yes, there is user data so show the results

    // Connect to the DBMS
    if (!($connection = @ mysql_connect($hostName,
                                         $username,
                                         $password)))
        showerror();

    if (!mysql_select_db($databaseName, $connection))
        showerror();

    // Set $offset to zero if not previously set
    if (empty($offset))
        $offset = 0;

    // Build the query
    $query = "SELECT w.wine_id,
                     w.wine_name,
                     w.description,
                     w.type,
                     w.year,
                     wry.winery_name
              FROM winery wry, region r, wine w
              WHERE wry.region_id = r.region_id
              AND w.winery_id = wry.winery_id";

    // Add the regionName if the user has provided it
    if ($regionName != "All")
        $query .= " AND r.region_name = \"$regionName\"";

    // Add a sort on the end of the query
    $query .= " ORDER by w.wine_name";
```

```
        // Initialize the browse() function parameters

        // Query prefix for the next/previous links
        $browseString = "regionName=" .
                        rawurlencode($regionName);

        // Page header for the browse screen
        $pageHeader = "Wines of " . $regionName;

        // HTML <TABLE> column headers
        $header[0]["header"] = "Wine ID";
        $header[1]["header"] = "Wine Name";
        $header[2]["header"] = "Wine Type";
        $header[3]["header"] = "Year";
        $header[4]["header"] = "Winery";
        $header[5]["header"] = "Description";

        // Query attributes to display in <TABLE> columns
        $header[0]["attrib"] = "wine_id";
        $header[1]["attrib"] = "wine_name";
        $header[2]["attrib"] = "type";
        $header[3]["attrib"] = "year";
        $header[4]["attrib"] = "winery_name";
        $header[5]["attrib"] = "description";

        // Call generic browsing code to browse query
        browse($scriptName, $connection,
               $browseString, $offset, $query,
               $pageHeader, $header);

    } // end if else user data
?>
</body>
</html>
```

Step 2: Implementing the Generic browse Function

The initial implementation of the browse( ) function is shown in Example 5-10. The structure is similar to that of the hardcoded displayWinesList( ), with the additional features to display the result set page-by-page with the embedded Previous and Next links.

Example 5-10. Generic browsing code for any query

```
define(ROWS, 20);

// Browse through the $connection by the running $query.

// Begin the display of data with row $rowOffset.
// Put a header on the page, $pageHeader
```

Example 5-10. Generic browsing code for any query (continued)

```php
// Use the array $header[]["header"] for headers on
// each <table> column
// Use the array $header[]["attrib"] for the names
// of the database attributes to show in each column

// Use $browseString to prefix an embedded link
// to the previous, next, and other pages

function browse($scriptName,
                $connection,
                $browseString,
                $rowOffset,
                $query,
                $pageHeader,
                $header)
{

   // (1) Run the query on the database through the
   // connection
   if (!($result = @ mysql_query ($query, $connection)))
      showerror();

   // Find out how many rows there are
   $rowsFound = @ mysql_num_rows($result);

   // Is there any data?
   if ($rowsFound != 0)
   {
      // Yes, there is data.

      // (2a) The "Previous" page begins at the current
      // offset LESS the number of ROWS per page
      $previousOffset = $rowOffset - ROWS;

      // (2b) The "Next" page begins at the current offset
      // PLUS the number of ROWS per page
      $nextOffset = $rowOffset + ROWS;

      // (3) Seek to the current offset
      if (!mysql_data_seek($result, $rowOffset))
         showerror();

      // (4a) Output the header and start a table
      echo $pageHeader;
      echo "<table border=\"1\">\n<tr>";

      // (4b) Print out the column headers from $header
      foreach ($header as $element)
         echo "\n\t<th>" . $element["header"] . "</th>";

      echo "\n</tr>";
```

Example 5-10. Generic browsing code for any query (continued)

```php
    // (5a) Fetch one page of results (or less if on the
    // last page)
    for ( $rowCounter = 0;
          (($rowCounter < ROWS) &&
           ($row = @ mysql_fetch_array($result)) );
          $rowCounter++)
    {
        // Print out a row
        echo "\n<tr>";

        // (5b) For each of the attributes in a row
        foreach($header as $element)
        {
            echo "\n\t<td>";

            // Get the database attribute name for the
            // current attribute
            $temp = $element["attrib"];

            // Print out the value of the current
            // attribute
            echo $row["$temp"];

            echo "</td>";
        } // end foreach attribute

        echo "\n</tr>\n";
    } // end for rows in the page

    // Finish the results table, and start a footer
    echo "\n</table>\n<br>";

    // (6) Show the row numbers that are being viewed
    echo ($rowOffset + 1) . "-" .
        ($rowCounter + $rowOffset) . " of ";
    echo "$rowsFound records found matching " .
        "your criteria\n<br>";

    // (7a) Are there any previous pages?
    if ($rowOffset > 0)
        // Yes, so create a previous link
        echo "\n\t<a href=\"" . $scriptName .
            "?offset=" . rawurlencode($previousOffset) .
            "&amp;" . $browseString .
            "\">Previous</a> ";
    else
        // No, there is no previous page so don't
        // print a link
        echo "Previous ";

    // (7b) Are there any Next pages?
    if (($row != false) && ($rowsFound > $nextOffset))
```

Example 5-10. Generic browsing code for any query (continued)

```
                // Yes, so create a next link
                echo "\n\t<a href=\"" . $scriptName .
                    "?offset=" . rawurlencode($nextOffset) .
                    "&amp;" . $browseString .
                    "\">Next</a> ";
        else
                // No, there is no next page so don't
                // print a link
                echo "Next ";

    } // end if rowsFound != 0
    else
    {
      echo "<br>No rows found matching your criteria.\n";
    }
    // (7c) Create a link back to the query input page
    echo "<br><a href=\"" . $scriptName .
        "\">Back to Search</a><br>";
}
```

The browse() function performs the following steps that are numbered in the comments in Example 5-10:

1. It runs the $query through the $connection. If there are rows returned from the query, the remaining steps are followed. If not, a message is printed.

2. It calculates where in the result set a Previous and Next link should be relative to the current offset, $rowOffset, that was passed in as a parameter:

   ```
   // (2a) The "Previous" page begins at the current
   // offset LESS the number of ROWS per page
   $previousOffset = $rowOffset - ROWS;
   ```

   ```
   // (2b) The "Next" page begins at the current offset
   // PLUS the number of ROWS per page
   $nextOffset = $rowOffset + ROWS;
   ```

   The offsets are used later to construct the Previous and Next links. ROWS is the numbers of rows per HTML page, and is defined as 20 at the beginning of Example 5-10.

3. It then uses mysql_data_seek( ) to seek in the result set, so that a subsequent call to mysql_fetch_array( ) retrieves row number $rowOffset.

4. The code then prints out the page header and iterates through the $header array printing out the associatively accessed "header" elements as <table> headings in the first <table> row.

5. The script then retrieves and prints one page of rows from the result set (or, if there is less than a page of rows left to process, as many rows as are available).

   A for loop retrieves each row, and then a foreach loop prints out each attribute value in the row according to how it's listed in the $header associative array element `attrib`. To allow attributes to be referenced associatively by name, `mysql_fetch_array()` is used.

6. Having printed the data in a `<table>`, the script prints out the range of rows displayed (from `$rowOffset` + 1 through `$rowOffset` + `$rowCounter`) and the total number of rows that are retrieved with the query.

7. To conclude the function, the script produces the Previous and Next embedded links if they are required, and a Back to Search link. The previous link is created with the following code fragment:

```
// Are there any previous pages?
if ($rowOffset > 0)
    // Yes, so create a previous link
    echo "<a href=\"" . $scriptName .
        "?offset=" . rawurlencode($previousOffset) .
        "&amp;" . $browseString .
        "\">Previous</a> ";
    else
        // No, there is no previous page so don't
        // print a link
        echo "Previous ";
```

A Previous link is produced only if the first row displayed—`$rowOffset`—isn't row zero; that is, we have just produced a second or later page. The code is a little cryptic, but it produces an embedded hypertext link to `$scriptName`, with the parameter `$browseString` that provides parameters to another query, and the offset variable set to the value of `$previousOffset` calculated earlier.

The `rawurlencode()` function isn't strictly needed here—we are only coding a number—but consistently using it to create URLs with correctly encoded characters is good practice. The Next link is created with similar logic, and the Back to Search link is a static link to `$scriptName` without any parameters.

We have now developed a generic browser and applied it to browsing the wines of a region. A similar skeleton to Example 5-9 can be developed to browse customers, inventories, or orders, and all can use the generic `browse()` function.

Step 3: Adding Page Numbers

In this section, we extend the `browse()` function to produce page numbers to permit direct access to the pages, removing the need for the user to repeatedly click the Previous or Next links to find a particular page or row. The extended fragment of `browse()` that produces the page links is shown in Example 5-11.

Example 5-11. Adding direct page access to browse()

```
// (7a) Previous link code goes here

// Output the page numbers as links
// Count through the number of pages in the results
```

Example 5-11. Adding direct page access to browse() (continued)

```
for($x=0, $page=1;
    $x<$rowsFound;
    $x+=ROWS, $page++)
    // Is this the current page?
    if ($x < $rowOffset ||
        $x > ($rowOffset + $numRowsToFetch - 1))
        // No, so print out a link
        echo "<a href=\"" . $scriptName .
            "?offset=" . rawurlencode($x) .
            "&amp;" . $browseString .
            "\">" . $page   . "</a> ";
    else
        // Yes, so don't print a link
        echo $page   . " ";

// (7b) Next link code goes here
```

The page number code consists of a `for` loop that works as follows:

- The loop begins counting rows using the variable `$x`—starting at row zero—and pages using `$page`, starting on page one. The loop finishes when `$x` is equal to the number of rows in the query result set.

- In the body of the loop, if the row `$x` isn't on the current page displayed in the HTML `<table>`, an embedded link is output that is marked with the page number `$page`. The link is to the script resource `$scriptName`, with the parameters in `$browseString` and an offset of the current value of `$x`. The current value of `$x` is the first row on the page numbered `$page`. Clicking on the link requests the script again and produces the results for `$page` that begin with the row with an offset of `$x`.

  For example, if `$x` is row 220, and the `$page` is 11, the embedded link output by the code fragment is:

  ```
  <a href= "example.5-11.php? offset=220&amp;regionName=Margaret%20River">11</a>
  ```

- If `$x` is a row on the currently displayed page, the code outputs the page number without the embedded hypertext link.

The case study of a generic `browse()` function is now complete. Additional features can be added, as discussed briefly in the next section.

What's Missing from the Previous and Next Browser

Features that aren't described here but could be incorporated in the `browse()` function include:

- Configurable colors for columns, headers, and links.
- Configurable column alignment and fonts.

- Other layouts, such as horizontal table-based layouts. See the winestore Hot New Wines panel as an example. A horizontal layout is used in the online winestore and is accessible from the book's web site.

- Embedding of links in the body of the `<table>` so that other queries can be run by clicking on data in the `<table>`. Our customized version for the winestore that is described in Chapter 13 supports this feature.

- Spreadsheet-like features, such as the ability to click on a column heading to sort the data by that column.

Case Study: Producing a select List

To conclude this chapter, we present a short case study of dynamically producing `<form>` components from a database. The techniques used are an application of the five-step querying process from Chapter 4.

We have already identified that the scripts in most of this chapter's examples require that the user remember and reproduce the names of the wine regions. A far better approach—and one that works well for small numbers of items—is to present values using the HTML `<select>` input type. For the wine regions, the `<select>` input has the following structure:

```
<select name="regionName">
<option selected> All
<option> Barossa Valley
<option> Coonawarra
<option> Goulburn Valley
<option> Lower Hunter Valley
<option> Margaret River
<option> Riverland
<option> Rutherglen
<option> Swan Valley
<option> Upper Hunter Valley
</select>
```

With only a small number of wine regions, it is tempting to develop a static HTML page with an embedded list of region names. However, this is poor and inflexible. If the *region* database table changes—that is, new regions are added or deleted or you want to change a region_name value—you have to remember to update the HTML page. Moreover, a spelling mistake or an extra space when creating the HTML page renders a `<select>` option useless, because it no longer matches the values in the database when used for querying. A better approach is to use the techniques from Chapter 4 to dynamically query the database and produce a `<select>` element using the region_name values stored in the *region* table.

Consider the approach of dynamically producing HTML. First, you retrieve the set of different values of the region_name attribute in the *region* table. Then, you format the values as HTML `<option>` elements and present a HTML `<form>` to the user.

When the user chooses a region and submits the <form>, you should run a query that uses the region name the user selected as one of the query parameters to match against data in the database and to produce a result set. Because the values chosen by the user in the <form> are compared against database values, it makes sense that the list values should originate from the database.

In this section, we develop a component that can be reused to produce select lists in different modules of a web database application. An example that uses this new component is shown in Example 5-12.

Example 5-12. Producing an HTML <form> that contains a database-driven select list

```
// Connect to the DBMS
if (!($connection = @ mysql_connect($hostName,
                                     $username,
                                     $password)))
   showerror();

if (!mysql_select_db($databaseName, $connection))
   showerror();

echo "\nRegion: ";

// Produce the select list
// Parameters:
// 1: Database connection
// 2. Table that contains values
// 3. Attribute that contains values
// 4. <SELECT> element name
// 5. An additional non-database value
// 6. Optional <OPTION SELECTED>
selectDistinct($connection,
               "region",
               "region_name",
               "regionName",
               "All",
               "All");

echo "\n<br><input type=\"submit\"" .
     "value=\"Show wines\">" .
     "\n</form>\n<br>";
echo "<a href=\"index.html\">Home</a>";
```

The component itself is discussed later but is encapsulated in the function selectDistinct( ), which takes the following parameters:

- A database connection handle, in this case, a connection opened with mysql_ connect and stored in $connection.
- A database name, $database, which is a variable that is set to winestore in the include file *db.inc*, as discussed in Chapter 4.

- The database table from which to produce the list. In this case, the table *region* contains the region name data.
- The database table attribute with the values to be used as the text for each `<option>` element shown to the user in the list. In this example, it's `region_name` from the *region* table.
- The name of the HTML `<select>` element. We use `regionName`, but this can be anything and isn't dependent on the underlying database.
- An additional option to add to the list if required; the value `All` doesn't occur in the *region* database table but is an extra value added to the list.
- An optional default value to output as the `<option selected>` in the list; this option is shown as selected when the user accesses the page. `All` is used as a default here.

The output of the function for the parameters used in Example 5-12 is shown in Figure 5-9.

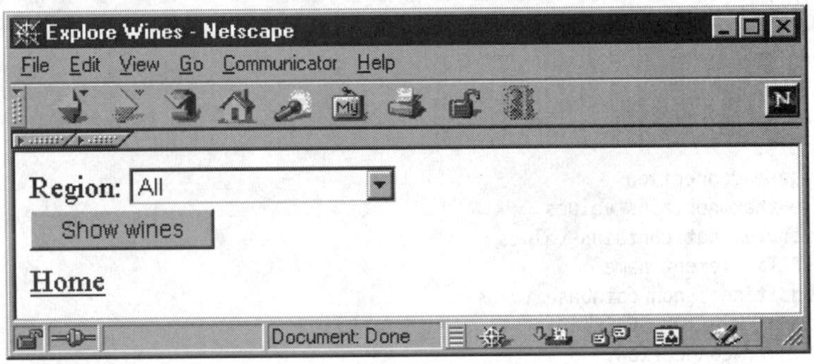

Figure 5-9. The selectDistinct() function in action

The remainder of the script fragment in Example 5-12 produces the other required tags in the HTML document.

Implementing the selectDistinct Function

This section details the implementation of the generic `selectDistinct()` function. The function produces a `<select>` list with an optional `<option selected>` element using attribute values retrieved from a database table. One additional non-database item can be added to the list. The body of the function is shown in Example 5-13.

Example 5-13. The body of the selectDistinct() function for producing select lists

```
function selectDistinct ($connection,
                         $tableName,
                         $columnName,
                         $pulldownName,
```

Example 5-13. The body of the selectDistinct() function for producing select lists (continued)

```
                        $additionalOption,
                        $defaultValue)
{
    $defaultWithinResultSet = FALSE;

    // Query to find distinct values of $columnName
    // in $tableName
    $distinctQuery = "SELECT DISTINCT $columnName
                      FROM $tableName";

    // Run the distinctQuery on the databaseName
    if (!($resultId = @ mysql_query ($distinctQuery,
                                    $connection)))
        showerror();

    // Retrieve all distinct values
    $i = 0;
    while ($row = @ mysql_fetch_array($resultId))
        $resultBuffer[$i++] = $row[$columnName];

    // Start the select widget
    echo "\n<select name=\"$pulldownName\">";

    // Is there an additional option?
    if (isset($additionalOption))
        // Yes, but is it the default option?
        if ($defaultValue == $additionalOption)
            // Show the additional option as selected
            echo "\n\t<option selected>$additionalOption";
        else
            // Just show the additional option
            echo "\n\t<option>$additionalOption";

    // check for a default value
    if (isset($defaultValue))
    {
        // Yes, there's a default value specified

        // Check if the defaultValue is in the
        // database values
        foreach ($resultBuffer as $result)
            if ($result == $defaultValue)
                // Yes, show as selected
                echo "\n\t<option selected>$result";
            else
                // No, just show as an option
                echo "\n\t<option>$result";
    } // end if defaultValue
    else
    {
        // No defaultValue
```

Example 5-13. The body of the selectDistinct() function for producing select lists (continued)

```
        // Show database values as options
        foreach ($resultBuffer as $result)
            echo "\n\t<option>$result";
    }
    echo "\n</select>";
} // end of function
```

The implementation of selectDistinct( ) is useful for most cases in which a <select> list needs to be produced. The first section of the code queries the table $tableName passed as a parameter, extracts the values of the attribute $columnName—also passed as a parameter—into an array $resultBuffer, and produces a <select> element with the name attribute $pulldownName. The code is a five-step querying module.

The remainder of the code deals with the possible cases for a default value passed though as $defaultValue:

- If there is an $additionalOption, it is output as an <option>. If it is also the default option, it is output as the <option selected>.

- If there is no $defaultValue passed through as a parameter, the code produces an option for each value in $resultBuffer with no <option selected>.

- If there is a $defaultValue, the code iterates through the $resultBuffer to see if this value is in the result set. If the value does occur in the $resultBuffer, it is output as the <option selected>.

The regionName select list for the online winestore has the default option of All—which isn't a region in the *region* table—and this is added manually to the list of options the user can choose from.

Generic, database-independent—or at least table-independent—code is a useful addition to a web database application. Similar functions to selectDistinct( ) can be developed using the same five-step process to produce radio buttons, checkboxes, multiple-select lists, or even generic complete <form> pages based on a database table.

Writing to Web Databases

Many web database systems aren't only information resources for users but are also tools for storing new information. In our online winestore, users and administrators write data to the database in several situations. Users can purchase wines by creating an order, they can become members, they can manage a shopping cart, and the winestore administrator can manage the stock.

Writing data in web database applications requires different techniques than reading data. Issues of transactions and concurrency become important, and we introduce these issues and the principles of dealing with them in this chapter. The introduction is practical: we focus on the basic management techniques of locking and unlocking tables, and how to safely implement simple database writes in MySQL when there is more than one user simultaneously accessing a database. Most importantly, we identify when special approaches are required, and when these can be safely omitted from a web database application.

We begin by discussing a <form> designed to capture input for database writes. We also include more simple example scripts that illustrate more about PHP and its use in processing <form> input. We discuss some of the problems of <form> submission and validation further in the next chapter.

We also include in this chapter an example illustrating the reload problem, where variables and values are resubmitted when a web page in a browser is, for example, resized. This has practical problems—such as inadvertently buying two bottles of wine—and we discuss a solution that uses HTTP headers.

We then discuss how files can be uploaded from a web browser to a web server and the data then inserted into a MySQL table. We use as an example the uploading of GIF images of maps of wine regions. We also show how these images can be displayed using SQL queries.

By the conclusion of this chapter, we will have covered the skills to build a simple but complete web database application. Several advanced topics remain, including validation of user-supplied data, adding state to a web database application, and authenticating users. We cover these three topics in the next three chapters.

Database Inserts, Updates, and Deletes

Simple database insertions and updates are much the same as queries. We begin this section with a simple case study example that is similar to the querying examples we presented in the last two chapters. However, inserting, updating, and deleting data does require some additional care. After presenting this first example of inserting data, we show a common problem that our first example suffers from—the reload problem—and discuss a solution. After that, we return to further, richer examples of writing to a database and discuss more complex problems and solutions.

Example 6-1 shows a script that presents a <form> for adding a new region to the *winestore* database and requires the user to provide a new region name and description. The script is similar to the user-driven combined scripts of Chapter 5. If the region name and description are both not empty, an INSERT SQL statement is prepared to insert the new region, using a NULL value for the region_id. As we discussed in Chapter 3, inserting NULL into an auto_increment PRIMARY KEY attribute allocates the next available key value.

If the query is successful—and one row is affected as expected—a success message is printed. If an error occurs, error handling using the method described in Chapter 4 is used. We discuss the function mysql_affected_rows( ) later in the "Inserting, Updating, and Deleting Data" section.

Example 6-1. A combined script to insert a new region in the winestore database

```
<!DOCTYPE HTML PUBLIC
            "-//W3C//DTD HTML 4.0 Transitional//EN"
            "http://www.w3.org/TR/html4/loose.dtd">
<html>
<head>
  <title>Insert a Region</title>
</head>
<body>
<?php
  include 'db.inc';
  include 'error.inc';

  // Test for user input
  if (empty($regionName) || empty($description))
  {
?>
  <form method="GET" action="example.6-1.php">
    Region_name:
    <br>
    <input type="text" name="regionName" size=80>
    <br>Description:
```

```
    <br>
    <textarea name="description" rows=4 cols=80></textarea>
    <br>
      <input type="submit">
   </form>
<?php
   }
   else
   {
      if (!($connection = @ mysql_connect($hostName,
                                          $username,
                                          $password)))
         die("Could not connect to database");

      if (!mysql_select_db($databaseName, $connection))
         showerror();

      $insertQuery = "INSERT INTO region VALUES
                  (NULL, " .
                  "\"" . $regionName . "\", " .
                  "\"" . $description . "\", " .
                  "NULL)";

      if ((@ mysql_query ($insertQuery,
                          $connection))
             && @ mysql_affected_rows() == 1)
         echo "<h3>Region successfully inserted</h3>";
      else
         showerror();
   } // if else empty()
?>
</body>
</html>
```

Most write operations can use a format similar to that of Example 6-1. In particular, where database changes are reasonably infrequent and can be performed in one step, most of the more complex issues we describe later in the "Issues in Writing Data to Databases" section can be ignored. For the winestore, adding or updating customer details, regions, wineries, and inventory requires almost no more sophistication.

However, as noted earlier, Example 6-1 does have one undesirable side effect that is common in web database applications. The problem isn't really related to modifying the database but rather to the statelessness of the HTTP protocol. We discuss this side effect—the reload problem—and an effective solution in the next section.

Reloading Data and Relocation Techniques

Simple updates using the approach shown in Example 6-1 are susceptible to a common problem of the stateless HTTP protocol that we call the *reload problem*.

Consider what happens when a user successfully enters a new region name and description, and clicks the Submit button. Since the script is a combined script, the same code is executed for a second time, the HTTP encoded variables and values are passed through with the GET method request, a new row is inserted in the *region* table, and a success message is displayed. So far, everything is going according to plan.

Consider now what happens if the user reloads the success message page with the Reload or Refresh button in the browser. Unfortunately, the variables and values are resubmitted to the same script, and another *region* row—with the same name and description—is added to the *region* table. There is no way in this example that the first click of the Submit button to add the first row can be distinguished from a second action that sends the same variables and values to the script. A representation of the reload problem is shown in Figure 6-1.

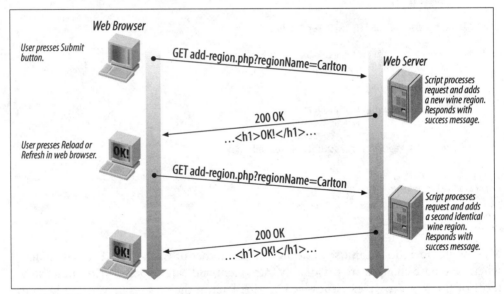

Figure 6-1. The reload problem

The same reload problem occurs when the user stores the URL as a bookmark or favorite location in her browser and then later requests the URL. Other actions that return to the success page, such as using the Back button, have the same undesirable effect. Perhaps surprisingly, resizing the browser window or printing the page also creates a new HTTP request and causes the reload problem. In our case, each request for the URL adds another identical region to the winestore!

The reload problem occurs in many situations. Actions that rerequest a document from the server include pressing the Reload or Refresh buttons, printing, saving the URL in the browser and returning to the page using a bookmark or favorite, using the Back or Forward buttons, pressing the Enter key in the URL Location entry box, and resizing the browser window.

The reload problem isn't always a significant problem. For example, if you use the SQL UPDATE statement to update customer details, and the values are amended with the same correct values repeatedly, there is no data duplication. Indeed, if a row is deleted and the user repeats the operation, the user, at worst, sees a MySQL DBMS error message. However, while some UPDATE and DELETE operations are less susceptible to the reload problem, a well-designed system avoids the problem altogether. Avoidance prevents user confusion and unnecessary DBMS activity. We discuss a solution in a moment.

The HTTP POST method is a little less susceptible to the reload problem than the GET method. If a user reretrieves the script after the first database change, the browser should ask the user whether or not to repost form data as per the HTTP specification. If the user answers OK, the database operation is repeated causing the problem. However, if the user bookmarks the page or reenters the URL at a later time, the <form> is redisplayed because the POST variables and values aren't part of the URL and are lost.

A solution to the reload problem is shown in Figure 6-2, based on the HTTP Location: header, the same header used for one-component querying in Chapter 5. The reload solution works as follows:

1. The user submits the <form> with the variables and values for a database write operation (an SQL INSERT, UPDATE, or DELETE).
2. The SQL write operation is attempted.
3. Whether or not the modification is successful, an HTTP Location: header is sent to the browser to redirect the browser to a new, receipt page.

   HTTP GET encoded variables and values are usually included with the Location: header to indicate whether the action was successful or not. Additionally, text to display might be sent as part of the redirection URL.
4. An informative—but harmless—receipt page is displayed to the user, including a success or failure message, and other appropriate text.

The HTTP redirection solves the reload problem. If the user reloads the receipt page the browser has been redirected to, he sees the receipt again, and no database write operations occur. Moreover, since the receipt page receives information about the success or failure of the operation—and any other information identifying the action—encoded in the URL, the receipt page URL can be saved and reloaded in the future without any undesirable effect.

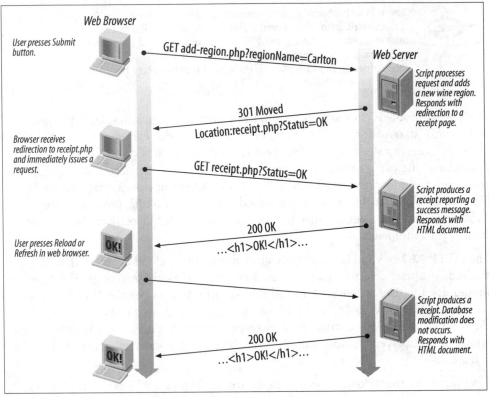

Figure 6-2. Solving the reload problem with a redirection to a receipt page

Solving the reload problem in practice

A modified version of Example 6-1 with the redirect functionality is shown in Example 6-2. The code is almost identical to that of Example 6-1, with two exceptions.

The first difference in the script in Example 6-2 is that regardless of whether the database insert succeeds or fails, the header( ) function is called. This redirects the browser to the script shown in Example 6-3 by sending a Location: example.6-3.php HTTP header. The difference between the success and failure cases is what is appended to the URL as a query string. In the case of success, status=T and the value of the added region_id attribute are sent. A value of status=F is sent on failure.

The second difference is that the script allows the user to upload a map of the wine region in GIF format for storage in the database. We discuss this functionality in the next section. The script also uses the function mysql_insert_id( ); look for this function in the later section "Inserting, Updating, and Deleting Data."

Example 6-2. An insertion script

```php
<?php
  include 'db.inc';
  include 'error.inc';

  if (empty($regionName) || empty($description))
  {
?>
    <!DOCTYPE HTML PUBLIC
              "-//W3C//DTD HTML 4.0 Transitional//EN"
              "http://www.w3.org/TR/html4/loose.dtd">
    <html>
    <head>
      <title>Insert a Region</title>
    </head>
    <body>
    <form enctype="multipart/form-data"
     action="example.6-2.php" method="post">
    Region_name:
    <br><input type="text" name="regionName" size=80>
    <br>Description:
    <br><textarea name="description" rows=4 cols=80>
    </textarea>
    <input type="hidden"
      name="MAX_FILE_SIZE" value="100000">
    <br>Region map (GIF format):
    <input name="userfile" type="file">
    <br><input type="submit">
    </form>
    </body>
    </html>
<?php
  }
  else
  {
    $regionName = clean($regionName, 50);
    $description = clean($description, 2048);

    if (!($connection = @ mysql_connect($hostName,
                                        $username,
                                        $password)))
      die("Could not connect to database");

    if (!mysql_select_db($databaseName, $connection))
      showerror();

    // Was an image file uploaded?
    if (is_uploaded_file($userfile))
    {
      // Open the uploaded file
      $file = fopen($userfile, "r");
```

Example 6-2. An insertion script (continued)

```
        // Read in the uploaded file
        $fileContents =
          fread($file, filesize($userfile));

        // Escape special characters in the file
        $fileContents = AddSlashes($fileContents);
    }
    else
      $fileContents = NULL;

    // Insert region data, including the image file
    $insertQuery = "INSERT INTO region VALUES
                 (NULL, " .
                 "\"" . $regionName . "\", " .
                 "\"" . $description . "\", " .
                 "\"" . $fileContents . "\")";

    if ((@ mysql_query ($insertQuery,
                    $connection))
       && @ mysql_affected_rows( ) == 1)
        header("Location: example.6-3.php?" .
               "regionId=". mysql_insert_id($connection) .
               "&status=T");
      else
        header("Location: example.6-3.php?" .
               "status=F");
    }
?>
```

The script in Example 6-3 is a receipt page. When requested with a parameter status=T, it queries the database and displays the details of the newly inserted region. The region is identified by the value of the query string variable regionId. The script also uses another script to display the image of the map inserted by the user; this approach is discussed next. On failure, where status=F, the script displays a database insertion failure message. If the script is unexpectedly called without a status parameter, an error message is displayed.

Example 6-3. The redirection receipt page

```
<!DOCTYPE HTML PUBLIC
             "-//W3C//DTD HTML 4.0 Transitional//EN"
             "http://www.w3.org/TR/html4/loose.dtd">
<html>
<head>
  <title>Region Receipt</title>
</head>

<body bgcolor="white">
<?php
  include 'db.inc';
  include 'error.inc';
```

Example 6-3. The redirection receipt page (continued)

```php
$regionId = clean($regionId, 3);
$status = clean($status, 1);

// did the insert operation succeed?
switch ($status)
{
case "T":
   // Yes, insert operation succeeded.
   // Show details of the new region as
   // a receipt page. The new region_id
   // is in the variable $regionId

   $query = "SELECT * FROM region WHERE " .
          "region_id = $regionId";

   // Connect to the MySQL DBMS
   if (!($connection = @ mysql_connect($hostName,
                                 $username,
                                 $password)))
      die("Could not connect to database");

   if (!mysql_select_db($databaseName, $connection))
      showerror( );

   // Run the query on the DBMS
   if (!($result = @ mysql_query ($query, $connection)))
      showerror( );

   if ($row = @ mysql_fetch_array($result))
   {
      echo "The following region was added";
      echo "\n<br>Region number: " . $row["region_id"];
      echo "\n<br>Region name: " . $row["region_name"];
      echo "\n<br>Region description: " .
           $row["description"];
      // Use the script example.6-4.php to display
      // the map GIF
      echo "\n<br>Region map : " .
           "\n<br><img src=\"example.6-4.php?region_id=" .
           $regionId . "\">";
   } // if mysql_fetch_array( )

   // leave the switch statement
   break;

case "F":
   // No, insert operation failed
   // Show an error message
   echo "The region insert operation failed.";
   echo "<br>Contact the winestore administrator.";
```

Example 6-3. The redirection receipt page (continued)

```
        // leave the switch statement
        break;

    default:
        // User did not provide a status parameter
        echo "You arrived unexpectedly at this page.";
    } // end of switch
?>
</body>
</html>
```

Several different receipt pages would be developed for an application to informatively display enough information for each different insert, update, and delete operation.

Uploading and Inserting Files into Databases

Examples 6-2 and 6-3 also show how files can be uploaded from a web browser to a web server, the file data inserted into a database, and the data then retrieved and displayed as part of a web page. In the examples, the file uploaded is a GIF image, but the techniques can be applied to any file or content type.

Files are transferred using the <form> encoding type multipart/form-data and the POST method. Most modern browsers—such as Netscape and Internet Explorer—support this encoding type and the <input> of type file. The <input> of type file displays a widget into which the user can enter a filename; it also displays a Browse button that displays a file dialog for finding files. Therefore, the following fragment from Example 6-2 is all that is needed for a user to select a file and for it to be transferred from a browser to a server:

```
<form enctype="multipart/form-data" action="example.6-2.php" method="post">
<br>Region map (GIF format):
<input name="userfile" type="file">
<br><input type="submit">
</form>
```

The uploaded file and information about it can be accessed directly at the web server using PHP. Assuming the <input> widget of type file has a name=userfile, the name of the file on the web server can be accessed as $userfile. The original name of the file on the browser can also be accessed as $userfile_name, the file size as $userfile_size, and the type of the file as $userfile_type.

The following fragment from Example 6-3 checks if a file has been uploaded and, if so, reads the contents of the file into the variable $fileContents:

```
        // Was an image file uploaded?
        if (is_uploaded_file($userfile))
        {
```

```
    // Open the uploaded file
    $file = fopen($userfile, "r");

    // Read in the uploaded file
    $fileContents =
        fread($file, filesize($userfile));

    // Escape special charcters in the file
    $fileContents = AddSlashes($fileContents);
}
else
    $fileContents = NULL;
```

 The library function is_uploaded_file() should always be used to make sure the file being processed was actually uploaded to the web server. Without the check, a security problem can arise if the user supplies the filename of a file on the web server as a value for userfile using a GET or POST request.

The function fopen() opens a file on disk; in this example, it opens the file in read mode by supplying the r flag as the second parameter. The function fread() reads the contents of a file, in this case into the variable $fileContents. In this example, the number of bytes read from the file is the file size, determined by using the function filesize(). After reading the file, any special characters are escaped by adding slashes using the AddSlashes() function. It's necessary to do this before the content of the file can be added to the database.

The file data in $fileContents is then inserted in the same way as any other data into the *region* table:

```
// Insert region data, including the image file
$insertQuery = "INSERT INTO region VALUES
                (NULL, " .
                "\"" . $regionName . "\", " .
                "\"" . $description . "\", " .
                "\"" . $fileContents . "\")";
```

The end result is that a new region has a name, a textual description, and an associated GIF image stored as the map attribute.

Displaying images from a database is straightforward. The script shown in Example 6-4 retrieves a map image from the *region* table and outputs the image using the echo statement. The region_id of the required image is supplied as a parameter using the GET method. A header is output to the browser that defines the MIME type of the image, in this case image/gif, and the data follows.

Example 6-4. A script to retrieve GIF images from the region table map attribute
```
<?
  include 'db.inc';
  include 'error.inc';
```

Example 6-4. A script to retrieve GIF images from the region table map attribute (continued)

```
$region_id = clean($region_id, 2);

if (empty($region_id))
   exit;

// Connect to the MySQL DBMS
if (!($connection = @ mysql_pconnect($hostName,
                                     $username,
                                     $password)))
   die("Could not connect to database");

if (!mysql_select_db($databaseName, $connection))
   showerror();

$query = "SELECT map FROM region
          WHERE region_id = $region_id";

// Run the query on the DBMS
if (!($result = @ mysql_query ($query,$connection)))
   showerror;

$data = @ mysql_fetch_array($result);

if (!empty($data["map"]))
{
   // Output the GIF MIME header
   header("Content-Type: image/gif");
   // Output the image
   echo $data["map"];
}
?>
```

The script in Example 6-4 is requested by an embedded `<img>` tag in Example 6-3:

```
echo "\n<br>Region map : " .
     "<img src=\"example.6-4.php?region_id=" .
     $regionId . "\">";
```

The result is that when the user views the receipt page in Example 6-3, the uploaded image from the database is displayed.

The techniques we have described work for small files such as most GIF images. Several additional configuration steps are required if files larger than a few megabytes are to be uploaded:

- As in Example 6-2, an additional hidden `<form>` field must be added to specify the maximum allowed upload file size, such as:
  ```
  <input type="hidden" name="MAX_FILE_SIZE" value="100000">
  ```
- The memory limit of a PHP script should be greater than the maximum file size. This can be set by adjusting the memory_limit parameter in the *php.ini* file, which was copied to */usr/local/lib/* in the installation instructions in Appendix A.

- The maximum file upload size should be set by modifying the `upload_max_filesize` parameter in the *php.ini* file.

- The maximum `POST` size should be set to be greater than the maximum file size by modifying the `post_max_size` parameter in the *php.ini* file.

- The maximum execution time for a PHP script should set to an appropriate value to allow the upload to complete. The default value is 30 seconds. The parameter can be changed by modifying the `max_execution_time` parameter in the *php.ini* file.

- The web server must be restarted after any changes, so that the *php.ini* configuration file is reread. This can be done by executing the command `apachectl restart` in the directory */usr/local/apache/bin/*, assuming the installation instructions in Appendix A were followed.

Inserting, Updating, and Deleting Data

In this section, we complete our discussion of the basics of modifying data by individually considering inserting, updating, and deleting data. We illustrate the principles of each technique in PHP through introductory case study examples; complete examples are presented in Chapters 10 to 13. Let's begin by looking at two useful PHP functions, both of which have already been used in Examples 6-1 and 6-2.

PHP DML functions for database modifications

The following two functions are used with the MySQL functions described in Chapter 4. The first, `mysql_affected_rows()`, is used to insert, delete, and update data. The second, `mysql_insert_id()`, is used only for insert operations.

`int mysql_affected_rows([resource connection])`

Reports the number of rows affected by the last `UPDATE`, `DELETE`, or `INSERT` SQL statement. The function takes as an optional parameter a DBMS connection resource handle. If no parameter is passed, the most recently opened connection is assumed. The function should not be used with `SELECT` statements; `mysql_num_rows()` should be used instead.

For example, if a customer is deleted with the SQL statement:

```
DELETE FROM customer WHERE CUST_ID=1
```

then `mysql_affected_rows()` returns a value of 1 if that customer has been successfully deleted. If the query:

```
INSERT INTO customer SET cust_id = 700
```

is executed successfully, the function also returns 1.

However, the function may report that zero rows were affected, even if a statement works successfully, because it is possible that an operation may not modify the database. For example, the statement:

```
UPDATE customer SET zipcode='3053' WHERE city = 'Carlton'
```

always executes but `mysql_affected_rows( )` returns 0 if there are no customers who live in Carlton. Similarly, if a *customer* row has already been deleted, the function returns 0.

int mysql_insert_id([resource *connection*])

Returns the `AUTO_INCREMENT` identifier value associated with the most recently executed SQL INSERT statement. The function is used, for example, to find the `cust_id` of a new customer when relying on `AUTO_INCREMENT` to allocate the next available `cust_id` primary key value after an `INSERT INTO customer` operation.

The last connection opened is assumed if the connection resource handle parameter is omitted.

This function should be called immediately after the insertion of a row and the result saved in a variable, since the function works for a connection and not on a per-query basis. Subsequent insertions through the same connection make it impossible to retrieve previous key values using this function.

Inserting data

We have already illustrated several examples of insertion of data. Let's consider the principles of insertion and a more complex example.

Phase one of the insertion process is data entry. Example 6-5 shows an HTML `<form>` for capturing data to be inserted into the winestore *customer* table. The `<form>` allows entry of customer details into `<input type="text">` controls. Only mandatory customer details are entered through this example; the completed customer `<form>` is presented in Chapter 10.

The date of birth entry—as noted in the instruction before the control—is required in the format DD/MM/YYYY. This requires later conversion to the native MySQL YYYY-MM-DD database format before storing in the database. This conversion is a validation step and, as such, is part of the second phase of insertion that is discussed in detail in Chapter 7. The HTML `<form>` rendered in a Netscape browser is shown in Figure 6-3.

Example 6-5. An HTML <form> that collects customer data

```
<!DOCTYPE HTML PUBLIC
   "-//W3C//DTD HTML 4.0 Transitional//EN"
   "http://www.w3.org/TR/html4/loose.dtd">
<html>
<head><title>Customer Details</title></head>
<body bgcolor="white">
<form method="POST" action="example.6-6.php">
```

Example 6-5. An HTML <form> that collects customer data (continued)

```
<h1>Customer Details</h1>
<h3>Please fill in the details below to join.
Fields shown in <font color="red">red</font> are
mandatory.</h3>

<table>
<col span="1" align="right">

<tr>
   <td><font color="red">Surname:</font></td>
   <td><input type="text" name="surname" size=50></td>
</tr>

<tr>
   <td><font color="red">First Name:</font></td>
   <td><input type="text" name="firstName" size=50></td>
</tr>

<tr>
   <td><font color="red">Address:</font></td>
   <td><input type="text" name="address1" size=50></td>
</tr>

<tr>
   <td><font color="red">City:</font></td>
   <td><input type="text" name="city" size=50></td>
</tr>

<tr>
   <td><font color="red">Date of birth (dd/mm/yyyy):</font> </td>
   <td><input type="text" name="dob" size=10></td>
</tr>

<tr>
   <td><font color="red">Email/username:</font></td>
   <td><input type="text" name="email" size=50></td>
</tr>

<tr>
   <td><input type="submit" value="Submit"></td>
</tr>

</table>
</form>
</body>
</html>
```

The second phase of insertion is data validation and then the database operation itself. Example 6-6 shows the PHP script to insert a new customer. The script has a simple structure, with naive validation that tests only whether values have been supplied for the mandatory fields.

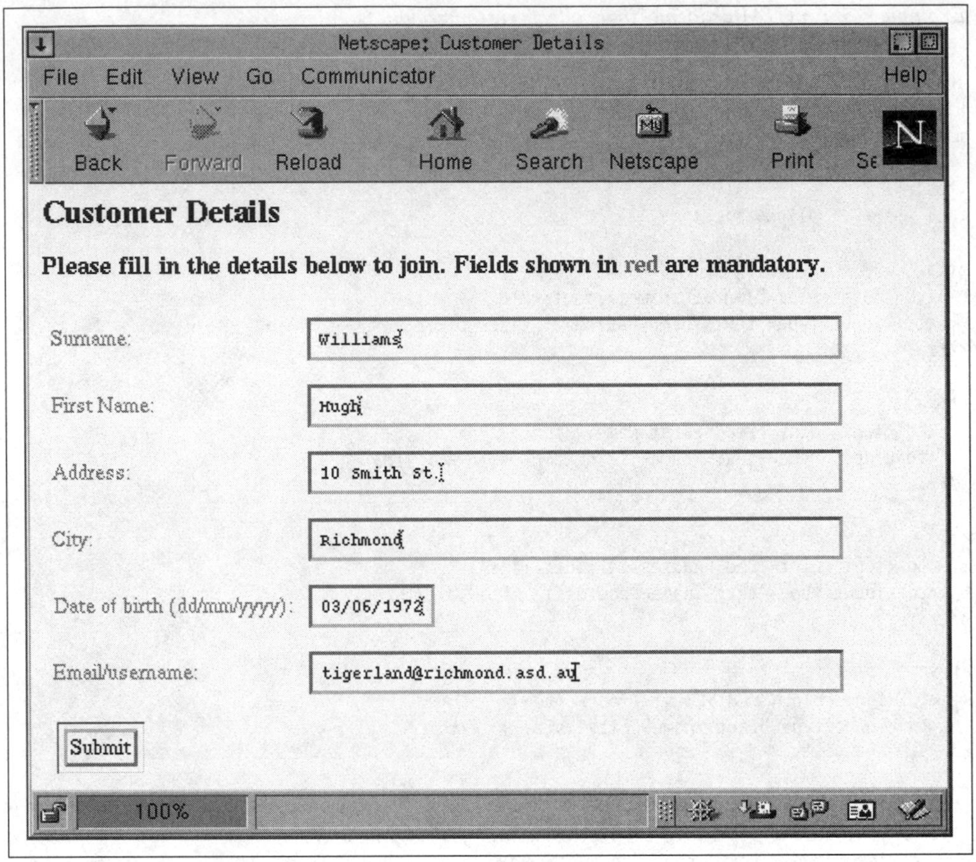

Figure 6-3. The customer entry <form> from Example 6-5 rendered in a Netscape browser

Example 6-6. A validation example that tests for mandatory fields

```php
<?php
  include 'error.inc';
  include 'db.inc';

  // Initialise an error string
  $errorString = "";

  // Clean and trim the POSTed values
  foreach($HTTP_POST_VARS as $varname => $value)
      $formVars[$varname] = trim(clean($value, 50));

  // Validate the firstname
  if (empty($formVars["firstName"]))
      // First name cannot be a null string
      $errorString .=
          "\n<br>The first name field cannot be blank.";
```

Example 6-6. A validation example that tests for mandatory fields (continued)

```php
// Validate the Surname
if (empty($formVars["surname"]))
    // the user's surname cannot be a null string
    $errorString .=
        "\n<br>The surname field cannot be blank.";

// Validate the Address
if (empty($formVars["address1"]))
    // the user's address cannot be a null string
    $errorString .=
        "\n<br>You must supply at least one address line.";

// Validate the City
if (empty($formVars["city"]))
    // the user's city cannot be a null string
    $errorString .= "\n<br>You must supply a city.";

// Validate Date of Birth
if (empty($formVars["dob"]))
    // the user's date of birth cannot be a null string
    $errorString .= "\n<br>You must supply a date of birth.";

elseif (!ereg("^([0-9]{2})/([0-9]{2})/([0-9]{4})$",
        $formVars["dob"], $parts))
    // Check the format
    $errorString .=
        "\n<br>The date of birth is not a valid date " .
        "in the format DD/MM/YYYY";

if (empty($formVars["email"]))
    // the user's email cannot be a null string
    $errorString .= "\n<br>You must supply an " .
                    "email address.";

// Now the script has finished the validation,
// check if there were any errors
if (!empty($errorString))
{
    // There are errors.  Show them and exit.
?>
<!DOCTYPE HTML PUBLIC
    "-//W3C//DTD HTML 4.0 Transitional//EN"
    "http://www.w3.org/TR/html4/loose.dtd" >
<html>
<head><title>Customer Details Error</title></head>
<body bgcolor="white">
<h1>Customer Details Error</h1>
<?=$errorString?>
<br>
<a href="example.6-5.php">Return to the customer form</a>
</body>
</html>
```

Example 6-6. A validation example that tests for mandatory fields (continued)

```php
<?php
    exit;
  }

  // If we made it here, then the data is valid

  if (!($connection = @ mysql_pconnect($hostName,
                                       $username,
                                       $password)))
    die("Could not connect to database");

  if (!mysql_select_db($databaseName, $connection))
    showerror( );

  // Reassemble the date of birth into database format
  $dob = " \"$parts[3]-$parts[2]-$parts[1]\"";

  // Create a query to insert the customer
  $query = "INSERT INTO customer
     set cust_id = NULL, " .
     "surname = \"" . $formVars["surname"] . "\", " .
     "firstname = \"" . $formVars["firstName"] . "\", " .
     "addressline1 = \"" . $formVars["address1"] . "\", " .
     "city = \"" . $formVars["city"] . "\", " .
     "email = \"" . $formVars["email"] . "\", " .
     "birth_date = $dob";

  // Run the query on the customer table
  if (!(@ mysql_query ($query, $connection)))
    showerror( );

  // Find out the cust_id of the new customer
  $custID = mysql_insert_id( );

  // Now show the customer receipt
  header("Location: customer_receipt.php?custID=$custID");
?>
```

If an error occurs in the validation process in Example 6-6, the script appends an error description to the string $errorString. The validation of the $dob variable is more complex than that of other fields because the data entry format and database storage format of the field are different, and there are specific requirements for the structure of a date field in a MySQL database table; the techniques used for this reformatting step are discussed in the next chapter.

If an error has occurred, the descriptive string $errorString is output to the browser, followed by an embedded link to allow the user to return to the <form> in Example 6-5. Unfortunately, if the user does click on this link—instead of pressing the Back button—she is returned to an empty <form>. A solution to this problem is presented in Chapter 8.

If the validation succeeds, the final step of the insertion process is completed. Any data that must be reformatted for insertion is modified, and the INSERT query executed. In this implementation, NULL is inserted as the cust_id attribute to use the auto_increment feature and avoid any of the problems discussed in the later section "Issues in Writing Data to Databases." If the query succeeds, the script redirects to a receipt page that reports the results; we don't discuss the receipt page here, but the complete code is presented in Chapter 10.

Updating data

Updating data is usually a more complex process than inserting it. A three-step process for updates is used in most web database applications:

1. Using a key value, matching data is read from the database.
2. The data is presented to the user for modification.
3. The data is updated by writing the modified data to the database, using the key value from the first step.

The first step of this process is usually user-driven: the user provides information that identifies the data to be updated. The information to identify the data—for example, a primary key value such as a cust_id—might be gathered in one of several ways:

- It may be entered into a <form> by the user. For example, the user may be asked to type in or select from a list the customer identifier of the customer he wishes to modify.

- It may be determined from another user-driven query. For example, the user might provide a surname and a first name through a <form>, and a SELECT query can then retrieve the unique customer identifier cust_id of that customer from the database (assuming the surname and first name combination is unique).

- It may be formatted into an embedded link by a script. For example, you can produce a list of descriptions of regions from the winestore, where each entry in the list is a hypertext link that has the unique region identifier encoded as a query string.

These methods of gathering data from the user are discussed in Chapter 5. Here, let's assume that a primary key is provided through one of these techniques, and the value of the primary key has been encoded in an HTTP request that can be processed by the update script.

Step 1 is completed by retrieving the data that matches the primary key value provided by the user. Step 2 is to present the data to the user. To achieve this, a <form> is usually created that contains the values of each attribute that can be modified. In some cases, some attributes may not be presented to the user, and other values may require reformatting from their database representation for presentation. Reformatting is discussed in detail in Chapter 7.

In addition to presenting the data to the user, a method is required to store the primary key value associated with the data, because it is needed in Step 3 as a key to update the data. There are several approaches to maintaining this key across the three-step process, and one simple approach is presented in the next section.

Step 2 is complete when the user submits the <form> containing the modified data. Step 3 updates the database; this uses the same process as inserting new data.

Case study: Inserts and updates in practice

Example 6-7 shows a modified version of Example 6-5 that supports database updates. The script implements the first two steps of the three-step update process from the previous section. We discuss the third step later in this section.

Example 6-7. Allowing entry of new customer details and displaying customer details

```php
<?php
  include 'db.inc';
  include 'error.inc';

  $custID = clean($custID, 5);

  // Has a custID been provided?
  // If so, retrieve the customer details for editing.
  if (!empty($custID))
  {
    if (!($connection = @ mysql_pconnect($hostName,
                                         $username,
                                         $password)))
      die("Could not connect to database");

    if (!mysql_select_db($databaseName, $connection))
      showerror();

    $query = "SELECT * FROM customer
              WHERE cust_id = " . $custID;

    if (!($result = @ mysql_query($query, $connection)))
      showerror();

    $row = mysql_fetch_array($result);

    // Reset $formVars, since we're loading from
    // the customer table
    $formVars = array();

    // Load all the form variables with customer data
    $formVars["surname"] = $row["surname"];
    $formVars["firstName"] = $row["firstname"];
    $formVars["address1"] = $row["addressline1"];
    $formVars["city"] = $row["city"];
    $formVars["email"] = $row["email"];
```

```
        $formVars["dob"] = $row["birth_date"];
        $formVars["dob"] = substr($formVars["dob"], 8, 2) .
                           "/" .
                           substr($formVars["dob"], 5, 2) .
                           "/" .
                           substr($formVars["dob"], 0, 4);
    }
?>
<!DOCTYPE HTML PUBLIC
    "-//W3C//DTD HTML 4.0 Transitional//EN"
    "http://www.w3.org/TR/html4/loose.dtd" >
<html>
<head><title>Customer Details</title></head>
<body bgcolor="white">
<form method="post" action="example.6-8.php">
<h1>Customer Details</h1>
<h3>Please fill in the details below to join.
    Fields shown in <font color="red">red</font> are
    mandatory.</h3>
<table>
<col span="1" align="right">

<tr>
   <td><input type="hidden" name="custID"
   value="<? echo $custID;?>"></td>
</tr>

<tr>
   <td><font color="red">First name:</font></td>
   <td><input type="text" name="firstName"
   value="<? echo $formVars["firstName"]; ?>" size=50></td>
</tr>

<tr>
   <td><font color="red">Surname:</font></td>
   <td><input type="text" name="surname"
   value="<? echo $formVars["surname"]; ?>" size=50></td>
</tr>

<tr>
   <td><font color="red">Address:</font></td>
   <td><input type="text" name="address1"
   value="<? echo $formVars["address1"]; ?>" size=50></td>
</tr>

<tr>
   <td><font color="red">City:</font></td>
   <td><input type="text" name="city"
   value="<? echo $formVars["city"]; ?>" size=20></td>
</tr>
```

Example 6-7. Allowing entry of new customer details and displaying customer details (continued)

```
<tr>
   <td><font color="red">Date of birth (dd/mm/yyyy):</font> </td>
   <td><input type="text" name="dob"
   value="<? echo $formVars["dob"]; ?>" size=10></td>
</tr>

<tr>
   <td><font color="red">Email/username:</font></td>
   <td><input type="text" name="email"
   value="<? echo $formVars["email"]; ?>" size=50></td>
</tr>

<tr>
   <td><input type="submit" value="Submit"></td>
</tr>

</table>
</form>
</body>
</html>
```

Step 1 of the update process works as follows. The script in Example 6-7 can process a custID passed through with an HTTP request. If the variable is set—for example, custID=1—this is an update operation. For an update, the script queries the database for the matching customer row and initializes variables with the results of the query. For example, when a surname is retrieved for a customer, the variable $formVars["surname"] is initialized with data from the database using:

```
$formVars["surname"] = $row["surname"]
```

This initialization of variables completes the first step of the update process.

The second step of the process—displaying the retrieved data for modification by the user—is achieved by modifying the <form>. We include throughout the <form> code in Example 6-7 short PHP scripts that initialize each <input> widget by setting the value attribute. For example, consider the HTML and PHP code fragment:

```
<tr>
   <td><font color="red">Surname:</font></td>
   <td><input type="text" name="surname"
   value="<? echo $formVars["surname"]; ?>" size=50></td>
</tr>
```

This fragment creates a text input widget to enter a surname and uses a short PHP fragment to prefill the widget with the value of the variable $formVars["surname"]. If the variable was initialized and isn't empty, the database value is displayed for editing by the user.

The second step of the process is completed by embedding the value of $custID in the <form> as a hidden input element. The $custID is embedded so it can be passed to the next script, where it then constructs the SQL query to perform the update

---

operation. There are other ways this value can be passed through the three steps; these techniques are the subject of Chapter 8.

Example 6-8 implements the third step. The process is the same as inserting new data, with the exception of the SQL query that uses the $custID from the customer <form> to identify the row to be updated. The script not only supports updates but also supports the insert functionality of Example 6-6; if $custID isn't set, the data is inserted as a new row. As previously, after the database operation, the browser is redirected to a receipt page to avoid the reload problem. However, the update process is now susceptible to other problems that are described in the later section "Issues in Writing Data to Databases."

Example 6-8. Updating existing and inserting new customer rows

```php
<?php
  include 'error.inc';
  include 'db.inc';

  $custID = clean($custID, 5);

  // Initialise an error string
  $errorString = "";

  // Clean and trim the POSTed values
  foreach($HTTP_POST_VARS as $varname => $value)
      $formVars[$varname] = trim(clean($value, 50));

  // Validate the firstname
  if (empty($formVars["firstName"]))
      // First name cannot be a null string
      $errorString .=
          "\n<br>The first name field cannot be blank.";

  // Validate the Surname
  if (empty($formVars["surname"]))
      // the user's surname cannot be a null string
      $errorString .=
          "\n<br>The surname field cannot be blank.";

  // Validate the Address
  if (empty($formVars["address1"]))
      // the user's address cannot be a null string
      $errorString .=
        "\n<br>You must supply at least one address line.";

  // Validate the City
  if (empty($formVars["city"]))
      // the user's city cannot be a null string
      $errorString .= "\n<br>You must supply a city.";

  // Validate Date of Birth
  if (empty($formVars["dob"]))
```

```
      // the user's date of birth cannot be a null string
    $errorString .= "\n<br>You must supply a date of birth.";

  elseif (!ereg("^([0-9]{2})/([0-9]{2})/([0-9]{4})$",
               $formVars["dob"], $parts))
      // Check the format
      $errorString .=
        "\n<br>The date of birth is not a valid date " .
        " in the format DD/MM/YYYY";

  if (empty($formVars["email"]))
      // the user's email cannot be a null string
      $errorString .=
        "\n<br>You must supply an email address.";

  // Now the script has finished the validation,
  // check if there were any errors
  if (!empty($errorString))
  {
      // There are errors.  Show them and exit.
?>
<!DOCTYPE HTML PUBLIC
   "-//W3C//DTD HTML 4.0 Transitional//EN"
   "http://www.w3.org/TR/html4/loose.dtd" >
<html>
<head><title>Customer Details Error</title></head>
<body bgcolor="white">
<h1>Customer Details Error</h1>
<?=$errorString?>
<br>
<a href="example.6-7.php">Return to the customer form</a>
</body>
</html>
<?php
      exit;
  }

  // If we made it here, then the data is valid

  if (!($connection = @ mysql_pconnect($hostName,
                                       $username,
                                       $password)))
    die("Could not connect to database");

  if (!mysql_select_db($databaseName, $connection))
    showerror( );

  // Reassemble the date of birth into database format
  $dob = " \"$parts[3]-$parts[2]-$parts[1]\"";

  // Is this an update?
  if (!empty($custID))
```

Example 6-8. Updating existing and inserting new customer rows (continued)

```
{
    // Create a query to update the customer
    $query = "UPDATE customer SET ".
     "surname = \"" . $formVars["surname"] . "\", " .
     "firstname = \"" . $formVars["firstName"] . "\", " .
     "addressline1 = \"" . $formVars["address1"] . "\", " .
     "city = \"" . $formVars["city"] . "\", " .
     "email = \"" . $formVars["email"] . "\", " .
     "birth_date = " . $dob .
     " WHERE cust_id = $custID";
}
else
    // Create a query to insert the customer
    $query = "INSERT INTO customer
      set cust_id = NULL, " .
     "surname = \"" . $formVars["surname"] . "\", " .
     "firstname = \"" . $formVars["firstName"] . "\", " .
     "addressline1 = \"" . $formVars["address1"] . "\", " .
     "city = \"" . $formVars["city"] . "\", " .
     "email = \"" . $formVars["email"] . "\", " .
     "birth_date = $dob";

// Run the query on the customer table
if (!(@ mysql_query ($query, $connection)))
    showerror();

// Is this an insert?
if (empty($custID))
    // Find out the cust_id of the new customer
    $custID = mysql_insert_id();

// Now show the customer receipt
header("Location: customer_receipt.php?custID=$custID");
?>
```

Deleting data

The basic principle of deletion is a two-step process: first, identify the row or rows to be deleted; and second, remove the data with an SQL DELETE statement.As in an update, the first step requires a key value be provided, and any technique described for capturing keys in updates can be used. We assume here that a unique, primary key value for the row to be deleted is available.

Deleting rows using a primary key value is a minor modification to the update functionality of the script in Example 6-8. For example, the following fragment creates and runs a query to delete a specified customer identified by the value of $custID:

```
// Connect to the database, clean, and validate data

// We have a custID. Set up a delete query
$query = "DELETE FROM customer
```

```
              WHERE cust_id = $custID";

    if ( (@ mysql_query ($query, $connection))
         && @ mysql_affected_rows() == 1)
    {
      // Query ran ok

      // Relocate to the receipt page with status=T
      header("Location: " .
             "delete_receipt.php?" .
             "cust_id=$custID" .
             "&status=T");
    }
    else
    {
      // Failed to delete customer row.
      // Relocate to the status page with status=F
      header("Location: " .
             "delete_receipt.php?" .
             "status=F");
    }
```

Issues in Writing Data to Databases

In this section, we discuss issues that emerge in database applications when multiple users access a database system; some users are inserting, updating, or deleting data, while others run queries.

To motivate the problems and solutions discussed here, consider an example. Imagine a user of the winestore wants to buy the last bottle of an expensive, rare wine that's in stock. The user browses the database and finds the wine. There is only bottle left, and the user quickly adds this to her shopping cart. The shopping cart is a row in the *order* table with only one related row in the *items* table. Now, the user decides to finalize the purchase and is presented with a summary of the shopping cart.

However, while the user fumbles about finding her password to log in, another user enters the system. This user quickly locates the same wine, sees that there is only one bottle left, adds it to his shopping cart, logs in to the system, and purchases the wine. When our first user finally logs in to finalize the order, all the details look fine, but the wine has actually been sold. Our database UPDATE operation to deduct from the inventory fails since the stock value is already zero, and we end up reporting an error to our original—now very unhappy and confused—user.

Consider another example. Imagine that one of our winestore stock managers wants to order 12 more bottles of a popular wine, but only if there are less than two dozen bottles currently in stock. The manager runs a query to sum the total stock for that wine from the inventory table. The result is that there are 15 bottles left, so the manager decides to place an order. However, he heads off to fill his coffee cup first, leaving the system displaying the query result.

A second stock manager arrives at her desk with the same intention: to order more of this popular wine if there are less than 24 bottles. The result of the query is the same: 15 bottles. The second manager orders a dozen bottles, and updates the inventory to 27, knowing the bottles will arrive in the afternoon. The problem occurs when the first manager returns: he doesn't rerun the query—why should he?—and he too orders 12 bottles and updates the inventory to 27. Now the system has record of 27 bottles, but two dozen will arrive in the afternoon to take the total to 39!

The first problem is a design issue—as well as an example of an *unrepeatable* read— and one that can be solved with more restrictive system requirements, knowledge of how the DBMS behaves, and some careful script development. The second is a classic problem—what textbooks describe as a *lost update*—and it requires more understanding of relational database problems and theory. We cover simple solutions to fundamental problems like these here, and discuss how MySQL implements locking for transactions, concurrency, and performance.

This section isn't intended as a substitute for a relational database text. Most textbooks contain extensive treatment of transaction and concurrency topics, and most of these are highly relevant to the state problems of web database applications.

Transactions and Concurrency

We have illustrated two examples of the problems users have when they access a web database at the same time (that is, concurrently). Allowing uncontrolled interleaving of SQL statements—where each of the users is reading and writing—can result in several well-known problems. The management of a group of SQL statements—we call these *transactions*—is one important area of the theory and practice of relational databases. Here are four of the more common problems of concurrent read and write transactions:

Lost update problem
> User A reads from the database, recording a value. User B reads the same value, then updates the value immediately. User A then updates the value, overwriting the update written by User B. An example of this lost update problem was described in the introduction to this section through the stock update example.

Dirty read problem
> User A reads a value from the database, changes the value, and writes it back to the database. User B then reads the value, changes the value, and writes it back to the database. User A then decides not to proceed for some reason with the rest of his actions and therefore wants to undo the changes he made. The problem is that User B has read and used the changed value, resulting in a dirty read problem.

Consider an example: a manager decides to add a 3% surcharge to a particular wine inventory, so she reads and updates the cost of that wine in the *inventory* table. Another manager decides to apply a 10% discount to all wines made by a particular winery, which happens to include the wine just surcharged. After all this, the first manager realizes she has made a mistake: the wrong wine was updated! Unfortunately, the second manager has already used this incorrect value as input into his update, and the change can't be undone correctly.

Incorrect summary problem
One user updates values while another reads and summarizes the same values. Values summarized may be read before or after each individual update, resulting in unpredictable results.

For example, consider a case in the winestore in which one user updates inventories and another produces a management stock report.

Unrepeatable read problem
A value is read in by a user, updated by another user, and subsequently reread by the first user for verification. Despite not modifying the value, the first user encounters two different values, i.e., an unrepeatable read.

Fortunately, most of these problems can be solved through *locking* or careful design of scripts that carry out database transactions. However, some problems may be deliberately unsolved in a particular system because they restrict the system requirements or add unnecessary complexity. We discuss locking in the next section.

Locking for Concurrency in MySQL

It has been shown that a simple scheme called locking—actually, *two-phase locking*—solves the four transaction problems identified in the last section.

When and how to lock tables

The first and most important point is that the primary use of locking is to solve concurrency problems. If scripts are being implemented that write to the database but aren't multistep operations susceptible to the problems described in the last section, locks aren't needed. Simple scripts that insert one row, delete one row, or update one row, and that don't use results of a previous SELECT or data entered by the user as input, don't require a lock.

Locking is required only when developing scripts that first read a value from a database and later write that value to the database. Locks are never required for self-contained insert, update, or delete operations such as updating a customer's details, adding a region to the *region* table, or unconditionally deleting an inventory. Locking may not be required for all parts of a web database application: parts of the application can still be safely used without violating any locking conditions.

Locks are variables with a special property. With its default settings, each MySQL table has an associated lock variable. If a user sets the lock variable for a particular table, no other user can perform particular actions on that table. The user who has set the lock variable *holds* the lock on the table. In practice, there are two kinds of locks for each table: READ LOCKs, when a user is only reading from a table, and WRITE LOCKs, when a user is both reading and writing to a table.

Having locks in a DBMS leads to four rules of use:

- If a user wants to write to a table, and she is performing a transaction susceptible to a concurrency problem, she must obtain a WRITE LOCK on that table.

- If a user only wants to read from a table, and he is performing a transaction susceptible to a concurrency problem, he must obtain a READ LOCK on that table.

- If a user requires a lock, she must lock all tables used in the transaction.

- A user must release all locks when a database transaction is complete.

When a user holds a WRITE LOCK on a table, no other users can read or write to that table. When a user holds a READ LOCK on a table, other users can also read or hold a READ LOCK, but no user can write or hold a WRITE LOCK on that table.

> SELECT, UPDATE, INSERT, or DELETE operations that don't use LOCK TABLES don't proceed if locks are held that would logically prevent their operation. For example, if a user holds a WRITE LOCK on a table, no other user can issue a SELECT, UPDATE, INSERT, DELETE, or LOCK operation on that table.

The following segment of an interaction with the MySQL command interpreter illustrates the use of locks in a summarization task that requires locking:

```
mysql> LOCK TABLES items READ, temp_report WRITE;
mysql> SELECT sum(price) FROM items WHERE cust_id=1;
+------------+
| sum(price) |
+------------+
|     438.65 |
+------------+
1 row in set (0.04 sec)

mysql> UPDATE temp_report SET purchases=438.65
       WHERE cust_id=1;
mysql> UNLOCK TABLES;
```

In this example, a temporary table called *temp_report* is updated with the result of a SELECT operation on the *items* table. If locks aren't used, the *items* table can be modified by another user, possibly altering the summary value of $438.65 used as input to the UPDATE operation. There are two locks obtained for this transaction: first, a READ LOCK on *items*, since we don't need to change *items* but we don't want another user to make a change to it; and, second, a WRITE LOCK on *temp_report*, because we want to change the table, and we don't want other users to read or write to the report while we make changes. The UNLOCK TABLES operation releases all locks held; locks can't be progressively released.

It isn't permitted by MySQL to lock only one of the two tables used in the transaction above. The following rules apply to locks:

- If a lock is held, all other tables that are to be used must also be locked. Failing to do so results in a MySQL error.
- If aliases are used in queries—for example:

  ```
  SELECT * from customer c where c.custid=1
  ```

  the alias must be locked with:

  ```
  LOCK TABLES customer c READ
  ```

  or:

  ```
  LOCK TABLES customer c WRITE
  ```

  (depending on the transaction requirements).
- If different aliases for the same table are used, each different alias must be locked.

In many cases—including those in which locking is required if the tasks are implemented intuitively—locking can be avoided. When designing transactions, careful use of mysql_insert_id( ) (as opposed to using max( ) to find the next available identifier), use of temporary summary tables, and updates that are relative (such as UPDATE customer SET discount=discount*1.1) are practical techniques to avoid using the output of previous SELECT statements.

The LOCK TABLES and UNLOCK TABLES statements in MySQL

The LOCK TABLES statement is used to lock the listed tables in either READ or WRITE mode. As discussed earlier, all tables that are accessed in the transaction must be locked in either READ or WRITE mode and must be listed in a single LOCK TABLES statement.

A script that issues a LOCK TABLES statement is suspended until all locks listed are successfully obtained. There is no time limit in waiting for locks. For locks that can't be immediately obtained—because the lock is held by another user or an operation is running on the table already—the request is placed at the back of either the *write-* or *read-lock queue* for the table, depending on the lock required. The write-lock queue has priority over the read-lock queue, so a user who wants a write lock obtains it when it becomes available, regardless of how long another user has been waiting in the read-lock queue. This is a design decision in MySQL that gives priority to database modifications over database queries.

MySQL is designed to give writing priority over reading. Regardless of how long a user has been queued in the READ LOCK queue, any request in the WRITE LOCK queue receives priority. This can lead to a problem called *starvation*, where a transaction never completes because it can't obtain the required locks. However, since most web database applications read from databases much more than they write, and locks are required in only a few situations, starvation is very uncommon in practice.

If low-priority writing is essential to an application, a LOW_PRIORITY option can be prefixed before the WRITE clause. If a transaction is queued for a LOW_PRIORITY WRITE, it receives the lock only when the READ LOCK queue is empty and no other users are reading from the table. Again, consideration of possible starvation is important.

Locks can't be progressively obtained through several LOCK TABLES statements. Indeed, issuing a second LOCK TABLES is the same as issuing an UNLOCK TABLES to release all locks and then issuing the second LOCK TABLES. There are good reasons for the strictness of this related to a well-known locking problem called *deadlock*, which we don't discuss here. However, MySQL is deadlock-free because of the strictness and functionality of the LOCK TABLES and UNLOCK TABLES statements.[*]

MySQL has a feature called INSERT DELAYED for insertion that is described in the MySQL manual.

Don't mix locking with INSERT DELAYED for insertion operations. The INSERT DELAYED process is carried out by the MySQL DBMS at a later time—under its own control—and the locks held by the user can't be used by the DBMS. INSERT DELAYED should be used only in situations in which locking isn't required.

Locking for performance

Locking is primarily designed to ensure that concurrent transactions can execute safely. However, locking is also a useful performance tool to optimize the performance of a particular transaction.

Consider, for example, a situation where we urgently require a complex report on the stock in the winestore that uses a slow SELECT statement with a GROUP BY, ORDER BY, and HAVING clause, and that joins together many tables. With other users running queries and using system resources, this query may run even slower. A solution is to use LOCK TABLES with the WRITE option to stop other users running queries or database updates, and to have exclusive access to the database for the query duration.

---

[*] Deadlock is a difficult problem. As recently as Version 3.22.23 of MySQL, there were bug fixes to MySQL to avoid deadlocking problems in the DBMS.

This permits better optimization of the query processing by the DBMS, dedication of all the system resources to the query, and faster disk access.

The downside of locking for performance is the reduction in concurrent access to the database. Users may be inconvenienced by slow responses or timeouts from the web database application. Locking for performance should be used sparingly.

Locking Tables in Web Database Applications

Example 6-9 shows a PHP function, updateDiscount( ), that requires locking to ensure that the value returned from the SELECT query can't change before the UPDATE operation. The script is designed to be run either by the winestore system administrator—it would then require a <form> for user input—or as the final module in the ordering process for users. Another example that requires locking for winestore ordering is included in Chapter 12.

The script in Example 6-9 is designed to reward loyal customers. If the customer has spent a significant amount on an order at the winestore, a percentage discount is applied to her order. The function updateDiscount( ) forms the body of the script. It takes as parameters a cust_id, an order_id for that customer, a discount to apply to that order, and a threshold total. If the total amount spent by the user exceeds the threshold total, the discount is applied to the order.

Example 6-9. The updateDiscount function in which locking is required

```
function updateDiscount($custId, $orderId,
                        $discount, $minimum,
                        $connection)
{
    $ok = false;

    // Lock all tables required in this transaction
    $query = "LOCK TABLES items READ,
            orders WRITE, customer READ";

    if (!mysql_query($query, $connection))
        showerror( );

    // Run query to find out how much a user
    // has spent in this purchase
    $query = "SELECT SUM(price*qty)
            FROM items, orders, customer
            WHERE customer.cust_id =
                    orders.cust_id
            AND orders.order_id = items.order_id
            AND items.cust_id = orders.cust_id
            AND orders.order_id = $orderId
            AND customer.cust_id = $custId";
```

Example 6-9. The updateDiscount function in which locking is required (continued)

```
    if (!($result = mysql_query($query, $connection)))
        showerror( );

    // Get the $row with the total spent
    $row = mysql_fetch_array($result);

    // Is the amount spent more than the threshold?
    if ($row["SUM(price*qty)"] > $minimum)
    {
        // Yes, so give the customer a discount
        // for this order
        $query = "UPDATE orders
                SET discount = $discount
                WHERE cust_id = $custId
                AND order_id = $orderId";

        if (!mysql_query($query, $connection))
            showerror( );

        $ok = true;
    }

    // Unlock the tables
    $query = "UNLOCK TABLES";

    if (!mysql_query($query, $connection))
        showerror( );

    // Return whether the discount was given or not
    return $ok;
}
```

The locking of *items*, *orders*, and *customer* is performed before the query, and the
UNLOCK TABLES statement is issued after the database update of the discount. As discussed in the last section, all tables and aliases that are used must be locked for either
READ or WRITE. MySQL reports an error if, for example, *items* is accessed but not
locked while *orders* and *customer* were locked. If an unlocked table needs to be
accessed—or locking must be avoided for a particular table—a second DBMS connection can be opened and used.

Locking methods that don't work in web database applications

There are several locking paradigms that don't work in a web database application
because of the statelessness of HTTP. Each approach fails, because there is either no
guarantee or no possibility that the locked tables will be unlocked. If tables are
locked indefinitely, other transactions can't proceed, and the DBMS will most likely
need to be shut down and restarted.

Be careful with locking in web database applications. Remember the basic rule that all locks should be unlocked by the same script during the same execution of the script.

All web scripts that require locking should have the structure lock, query, update, and unlock. There must be no user interaction or intervening calls to other scripts that require input.

The following approaches to transactions and locking in a web database application should be avoided:

- Failing to issue an UNLOCK TABLES on a locked persistent database connection opened with mysql_pconnect( ). The locks aren't released when the script terminates, and there is no guarantee that the script will be run in the future or that the same persistent connection will be used again.

  It isn't necessary to issue an UNLOCK TABLES if a nonpersistent connection opened with mysql_connect( ) is used. Locks are automatically released when the script finishes. However, it is good practice to include the UNLOCK TABLES statement.

- Locking one or more tables during the first execution of a script, then querying or updating during a second or subsequent execution of the script. Remember that each database connection in a script is independent and is treated as a different user by MySQL. Such an approach queries and updates without locks unless, by chance, the same persistent connection that issued the locks is reused. A subsequent UNLOCK TABLES may fail.

- Retrieving a value such as the next available primary key value, presenting this to the user, waiting for the user to enter further details, and then adding a row to the database with that identifier. Remember that another user may add a row while the first user is entering the required details, and locks should never be carried across several scripts or different executions of the same script.

Locking with an auxiliary table

If values must be shown to a user, consider adding a summary table for identifiers, or copying rows to a temporary table. For example, an identifier table can store the next available identifier for each other table, this can then be incremented by the script and the value can be used in subsequent scripts without locking problems and without any clashes in numbering.

This solution is shown in Example 6-10, using an auxiliary table named *ids* that manages the next available region_id attribute. The use of the additional table prevents duplicate rows being inserted, and avoids any problems with locking or updates.

Example 6-10. An auxiliary table manages the next region_id attribute

```php
<?php
    // This code needs an auxiliary table called "ids"
    // that might be created with:
```

Example 6-10. An auxiliary table manages the next region_id attribute (continued)

```
// CREATE TABLE ids (
// region_id int default 0,
// other_id int default 0,
// another_id int default 0
// );
// It has one row, and no primary key is required.
// After creating the table, a row is needed,
// so issue an: INSERT INTO ids (NULL, NULL, NULL);
// (if it's being added later, use MAX( ) to get the
//  correct ID values!)

include 'db.inc';
include 'error.inc';

function getNextRegion ($connection)
{
    // A nice way to do it... use an auxiliary table
    // Lock the auxiliary table
    $query = "LOCK TABLES ids WRITE";

    if (!mysql_query($query, $connection))
       showerror( );

    // Add one to the region_id attribute
    $query = "UPDATE ids SET region_id = region_id + 1";

    if (!mysql_query($query, $connection))
       showerror( );

    // Find out the new value of region_id
    $query = "SELECT * FROM ids";

    if (!($result = mysql_query($query, $connection)))
       showerror( );

    // Get the row that is returned
    $row = mysql_fetch_array($result);

    // Unlock the table
    $query = "UNLOCK TABLES";

    if (!mysql_query($query, $connection))
       showerror( );

    // Return the region_id
    return ($row["region_id"]);
}
// MAIN -----
if (!($connection = @ mysql_connect($hostName,
                                    $username,
                                    $password)))
    die("Could not connect to database");
```

Example 6-10. An auxiliary table manages the next region_id attribute (continued)

```php
  if (!mysql_select_db($databaseName))
      showerror();

  if (empty($regionId))
  {
      $regionId =
          getNextRegion($connection, $databaseName);
?>
<!DOCTYPE HTML PUBLIC
  "-//W3C//DTD HTML 4.0 Transitional//EN"
  "http://www.w3.org/TR/html4/loose.dtd">
<html>
<head>
  <title>Insert a region</title>
</head>
<body bgcolor="white">
region_id: <?= $regionId ?>
<br>
<form method="post" action="example.6-10.php">
  <input type="hidden"
   name="regionId" value="<?=$regionId;?>">

  <br>region_name:
  <br><input type="text" name="regionName" size=80>
  <br>description:
  <br><textarea name="description" rows=4 cols=80>
      </textarea>
  <br><input type="submit">
</form>
</body>
</html>
<?php
  }
  else
  {
      $regionId = clean($regionId, 3);
      $regionName = clean($regionName, 20);
      $description = clean($description, 255);

      $query = "INSERT INTO region SET " .
        "region_id = " . $regionId . ", " .
        "region_name = \"" . $regionName . "\", " .
        "description = \"" . $description . "\"";

      if ((@ mysql_query ($query, $connection))
            && @ mysql_affected_rows() == 1)
        header("Location:insert_receipt.php?" .
               "values=$regionId&status=T");
      else
        header("Location: insert_receipt.php?status=F");
  }
?>
```

The table-level locking paradigm in MySQL

Until recently, MySQL supported only table locking. Other DBMSs support locking at other levels, including locking rows, groups of rows, attributes across all rows in a table, and disk pages.

A common argument against using MySQL has been that table locking is too heavy-handed and that it limits concurrency in web database applications. This isn't really true, except when there are specific requirements that are uncharacteristic of web database applications.

Table locking works particularly well in web database applications, where typically:

- DELETE and UPDATE operations are on specific rows—most often accessed by the primary key value—and the rows are accessed through an index.
- There are many more read operations than write operations.
- Operations require locks on whole tables. Examples include GROUP BY operations, updates of sets of rows, and reading in most rows in a table.

By default, MySQL uses a type of table called *MyISAM*. Up to now, the *MyISAM* and *heap* have supported only table locking. However, three new database types have recently become supported by MySQL, and these have different locking paradigms:

- The *Berkeley Database* (BDB) tables have disk page-level locking; the LOCK TABLES statement can still be used in *BDB*.
- The *InnoDB* tables have row-level locking. They are designed to support very large volumes of data efficiently, and the locking mechanisms are designed to have low overheads.
- The *Gemini* tables have both row- and table-level locking; unlike the other table types that can be used with MySQL, the *Gemini* table is covered by a commercial license and isn't free software.

Support for *BDB* and *InnoDB* tables must be compiled into MySQL during the installation process, and each requires MySQL 3.23.34 or a later version. The *Gemini* table type is a component of the commercially available NuSphere product range. Configuration of these table types is outside the scope of this book.

Interestingly, the *MyISAM* tables permit a limited form of concurrency that isn't immediately obvious with the table-locking paradigm. When a mix of select and write operations occur on a *MyISAM* table, MySQL automatically allows write operations to change copies of the data. Other SELECT statements being run by other users read the unchanged data and, when they are completed, the modified copies are written back to the database. This approach is known as *data versioning*.

Other locking paradigms

The row-locking paradigm is used in the *InnoDB* and *Gemini* table types, and is the dominant paradigm in other DBMSs. The *BDB* table type offers page locking, which is similar to locking selected rows.

Row or page locking works well in situations that are infrequently seen in web database applications, such as:

- Transaction environments where a number of steps need to be undone or rolled back.
- Many users are writing to the same tables concurrently.
- Locks need to be maintained for long periods of time.

The drawbacks of row and page locking include:

- Higher memory requirements to manage an increased number of locks
- Poor performance, since there is much more locking and unlocking activity
- Slow locking for operations that require locks on a whole table, such as GROUP BY operations

What isn't covered here

There are two significant topics related to transactions and concurrency that aren't covered in this chapter. We have omitted these topics because they are less important in web database applications than in traditional relational systems, and because this book isn't intended as a substitute for a good relational database text or the documentation of the MySQL DBMS.

The first is a more traditional treatment of transactions from a commit and rollback perspective. The *InnoDB*, *BDB*, and *Gemini* table types support a model where a statement can be issued to begin a transaction that consists of several database operations. On completion of the operations, a commit statement can be issued to write the changes to the database and verify that these changes have occurred. If, for some reason, the operations need to be undone—for example, when a user presses Cancel—a rollback command can be issued to return the database to its original state.

Commit and rollback processing is useful, but it can be argued that it is less interesting in the stateless HTTP environment, in which operations need to be as independent as possible. For most practical purposes in web database applications, complex transactional processing isn't required.

The second topic we have not covered is recovery. Database recovery techniques are based on logging, in which database changes are written to a file that can be used for transaction rollback and for DBMS system recovery. MySQL does support logging for recovery, and more details can be found in the MySQL manual.

CHAPTER 7

Validation on the Server and Client

Validation is essential to web database applications. Ensuring that data meets user and system requirements is important, but ensuring that the database constraints are met by the data is critical. There are three possible data environments in which validation can occur in a three-tiered web database application: in the DBMS, in server-side scripts, and on the client. We discuss the merits and possibilities of these approaches to validation in this chapter.

As the name suggests, client-tier validation occurs at the client browser before a request is sent to the server and is usually validation of <form> data. The most common way to implement client-tier validation is using the scripting language best known as *JavaScript*. JavaScript isn't a fully fledged programming language, but it's one that can be effectively used for simple tasks such as validation. The drawback of validation at the client is that it depends on the user and his environment: the user can disable JavaScript, and can willfully or passively circumvent the validation, and the client environment isn't usually managed or standardized by the developer of the web database application.

Server-side validation is usually performed in a middle-tier script and is the essential validation tool. When data is inserted, updated, or deleted at the DBMS, it's undesirable to rely on the constraint-checking validation implicitly performed by the DBMS in the database tier. Trapping errors using the PHP MySQL error functions is difficult, has unnecessary network and DBMS overhead, and is hard to present to the user in a meaningful way. A much better approach is to use the middle-tier PHP scripts to validate data and ensure that all constraints of the database are met before modifying the database.

In this chapter, we extend our discussion of validation in PHP. We have already introduced basic validation principles in Chapter 5 with the clean() function for security and in Chapter 6 with the field empty() checks used before modifying the *customer* table. We extend those discussions here by introducing the principles of validation and the practice of validating <form> variables and values with PHP. We use the customer <form> we developed in Chapter 6 as our case study. We then consider in more detail the variables and values that are sent from a browser to a server, their variations, and the traps to watch for.

After discussing server-side validation, we discuss client-side JavaScript and how simple validation can be performed at the client to save network costs and improve responsiveness of an application to the user. We also introduce other simple tasks that can be effectively accomplished with JavaScript.

Validation and Error Reporting for Web Database Applications

There is nothing worse for a user than annoying, overly persistent, inaccurate, or uninformative validation. For example, error messages that describe an error but don't specify which field contains the error are difficult to correct. However, there is no correct recipe for balancing validation with system requirements: what is pleasing or mandated by requirements in one application might be annoying or useless in another. In this section, we consider practical validation models for web database applications.

Validation is actually two processes: finding errors and presenting error messages. Finding errors can be *interactive*—where data is checked as it's entered—or it can be *post-validation*, where the data is checked after entry. Presenting errors can be *field-by-field*—where a new error message is presented to the user for each error found—or it can be *batched*, where all errors are presented as a single message. There are other dimensions to validation and error processing, such as the *degree of error* that is tolerated and the *experience level* of the user. However, considering only the basic processes, the choice of when to error-check and when to notify the user, leads to four common approaches:

Interactive validation with field-by-field errors
> The data in each field is validated when the user exits or changes the field. If there is an error, the user is alerted to that error and may be required to fix the error before proceeding.

Interactive validation with batch errors
> The data in all fields is validated when the user leaves one field. If there are one or more errors, the user is alerted to these, and normally the user can't proceed beyond the current page without fixing all errors.

Post-validation with field-by-field errors
> The user first enters all data with no validation. The data is then checked and errors are reported field-by-field in separate error messages to the user. Usually, for each error, the cursor is placed in the field requiring amendment.

Post-validation with batch errors
The user first enters all data with no validation. The data is then checked, and all errors in the data are reported in one message to the user. The user then fixes all errors and resubmits the data for revalidation.

In Chapter 6—without discussing the details—we covered several simple post-validation techniques to check whether mandatory <form> data was entered before inserting or updating data in the database. In addition, we used a batch reporting method, where errors were reported as a list by constructing an error string. In the case study example in this chapter, we discuss additional validation for the customer <form> data to more carefully inspect both mandatory and optional fields. The completed validation code is listed in Chapter 10.

Models That Don't Work

Interactive models are difficult to implement in the web environment. Server-side scripts are impractical for this task, since an HTTP request and response is required to validate each field that's entered. This is usually unacceptable, because the user is required to submit the data after entering each field, response times are likely to be slow, and the server load high.

Client-side scripts can implement an interactive model. However, validation on the client should not be the only method of validation because—as we emphasized in Chapter 5—the user can passively or actively avoid the client-side processes. We discuss the partially interactive solution of including client-side scripts with an HTML <form> later in this chapter.

Models That Do Work

Post-validation models are practical in web database applications. Both client- and server-side scripts can validate all <form> data during the submission process. In many applications, reasonably comprehensive validation is performed on the client side when the user clicks the <form> submit button. If this validation succeeds, data is submitted to the server and the same—or more comprehensive—validation is performed. Duplicating client validation on the server is essential because of the unreliability of client-side scripts and lack of control over the client environment.

Client-side validation reduces server and network load, because the user's browser ensures the data is valid prior to the HTTP request. Client-side validation is also usually faster for the user.

The post-validation model can be combined with either field-by-field or batch error reporting. For server-side validation, the batch model is preferable to a field-by-field implementation, as the latter approach has more overhead and is usually slower because each <form> error requires an additional HTTP request and response.

For client-side post-validation, either error-reporting model can be used. The advantage of the field-by-field model is that the cursor can be directed to the field containing the error, making error correction easier. The disadvantage is that several errors require several error messages, and this can be frustrating for the user. The advantage of the batch approach is that all errors are presented in one message. The disadvantage is that the cursor can't easily be directed to the field requiring correction.

Server-side validation is essential to secure a web database and to ensure that system and DBMS constraints are met.

Client-side validation may be implemented in addition to server-side validation, but all client-side functionality should be duplicated at the server side. Never trust the user or the client browser.

The choice of which reporting model to use depends on the size and complexity of the <form> and on the system requirements.

In the next section, we introduce the practice of server-side post-validation using the batch error reporting method. We introduce client-side scripting as a tool for validation and error reporting in the "Client-Side Validation with JavaScript" section.

Server-Side Validation

In this section, we introduce validation on the server. The techniques described here are typical of those that validate a <form> after the user has submitted data to the server. We show how to extend and integrate this approach further in Chapter 8 so that the batch errors are reported as part of the customer <form>, and we show the completed customer entry <form> and validation in Chapter 10.

Case Study: Customer Validation in the Winestore

In this section, we show how to validate selected winestore customer <form> data, including examples of the validation checks required for mandatory fields, field lengths, and data types. Many functions—including the regular expression and string functions—are discussed in detail in Chapter 2.

Our system requirements in Chapter 1 note the following validation requirements:

- A user must provide a surname, first name, one address line, a city, a state, a zip code, a country, a birth date, an email address, and a password.

- The user may also optionally provide a middle initial, a title, two additional address lines, a state, a telephone number, and a fax number.

Testing whether mandatory fields have been entered is straightforward, and we have implemented this in our examples in Chapter 6. For example, to test if the user's surname has been entered, use the following approach:

```
// Validate the Surname
if (empty($formVars["surname"]))
    // the user's surname cannot be a null string
    $errorString .=
        "\n<br>The surname field cannot be blank.";
```

For optional fields, omit this check.

While it isn't specified in the brief system requirements, it's reasonable to assume that the fields provided by the user should be validated using additional checks. For example, telephone and fax numbers should be numeric and conform to a well-known template. Email addresses should meet the requirements of the RFC-2822 document available from *http://www.ietf.org* or at least a reasonable approximation; moreover, the domain part of the email address—such as *webdatabasebook.com*—should be an actual, existing domain. We describe additional validation steps in this section; the complete code for the customer <form> validation is listed in Chapter 10.

Validating dates

Dates of birth, expiry dates, order dates, and other dates are commonly entered by users. Most dates require checks to see if the date is valid and also if it's in a required range. In the customer <form>, the user is required to provide a date of birth. We validate this date of birth to check it has been entered, and to check its format, its validity, and whether it's within a range; the range of valid dates in the example begins with the user being alive—we assume alive users are born after 1890—and ends with the user being at least 18 years of age.

Date-of-birth checking is implemented with the following code fragment:

```
// Validate Date of Birth
if (empty($formVars["dob"]))
    // the user's date of birth cannot be a null string
    $errorString .= "You must supply a date of birth.";

elseif (!ereg("^([0-9]{2})/([0-9]{2})/([0-9]{4})$",
        $formVars["dob"], $parts))
    // Check the format
    $errorString .=
        "The date of birth is not a valid date in the " .
        "format DD/MM/YYYY";

elseif (!checkdate($parts[2],$parts[1],$parts[3]))
    $errorString .= "The date of birth is invalid. " .
    "Please check that the month is between 1 and 12, " .
    "and the day is valid for that month.";
```

```
    elseif (intval($parts[3]) < 1890)
        // Make sure that the user has a reasonable birth year
        $errorString .=
           "You must be alive to use this service.";

    // Check whether the user is 18 years old.
    // If all the following are NOT true,
    // then report an error.
    elseif
            // Were they born more than 19 years ago?
            (!((intval($parts[3]) < (intval(date("Y") - 19))) ||

            // No, so were they born exactly 18 years ago, and
            // has the month they were born in passed?
            (intval($parts[3]) == (intval(date("Y")) - 18) &&
            (intval($parts[2]) < intval(date("m")))) ||

            // No, so were they born exactly 18 years ago
            // in this month, and was the day today or earlier
            // in the month?
            (intval($parts[3]) == (intval(date("Y")) - 18) &&
            (intval($parts[2]) ==  intval(date("m"))) &&
            (intval($parts[1]) <= intval(date("d"))))))))

        $errorString .=
           "You must be 18+ years of age to use this service.";
```

If any date test fails, an error string is appended to the $errorString, and no further checks of the date are made. A valid date passes all the tests.

The first check tests if a date has been entered. The second check uses a regular expression to check whether the date consists of numbers and if it matches the template DD/MM/YYYY:

```
(!ereg("^([0-9]{2})/([0-9]{2})/([0-9]{4})$",
$formVars["dob"], $parts))
```

Whatever the result of this check, the expression also explodes the date into the array $parts so that the component that matches the first grouped expression ([0-9{2}) is found in $parts[1], the second grouped expression in $parts[2], and the third grouped expression in $parts[3]. The ereg( ) function stores the string matching the complete expression in $parts[0]. The overall result of processing a date that matches the template is that the day of the month is accessible as $parts[1], the month as $parts[2], and the year as $parts[3].

The third check uses the exploded data stored in the array $parts and the function checkdate( ) to test if the date is a valid calendar date. For example, the date 31/02/1970 would fail this test.

The fourth check tests if the year is greater than 1890. The function intval( ) converts a string to an integer. A test such as if ($parts[3] < 1890) may not work as desired, because $parts[3] is a string—which can be unreliably converted to an integer, as discussed in Chapter 2—and 1890 is an integer. Both the PHP functions intval( )—to convert strings to integers for comparisons—and strval( )—to convert integers to strings—are useful tools in range-checking <form> fields.

The fifth and final check tests if the user is 18 years of age or older. There are many ways to do this, with perhaps the most obvious being finding the difference between the date of birth and the current date using library functions, and checking that this difference is more than 18 years. The strtotime( ) function converts a date string in the format MM/DD/YYYY to a large numeric Unix timestamp value that represents the number of seconds since January 1, 1970. This can be cast to a float to ensure reliable comparison as discussed in Chapter 2.

However, our approach here to validating if a user is over 18 years of age uses only logic, and the intval( ) and date( ) functions:

```
// Check whether the user is 18 years old.

// If all the following are NOT true,
// then report an error.
elseif
      // Were they born more than 19 years ago?
      (!((intval($parts[3]) < (intval(date("Y") - 19))) ||

      // No, so were they born exactly 18 years ago, and
      // has the month they were born in passed?
      (intval($parts[3]) == (intval(date("Y")) - 18) &&
      (intval($parts[2]) < intval(date("m")))) ||

      // No, so were they born exactly 18 years ago
      // in this month, and was the day today or earlier
      // in the month?
      (intval($parts[3]) == (intval(date("Y")) - 18) &&
      (intval($parts[2]) ==  intval(date("m"))) &&
      (intval($parts[1]) <= intval(date("d"))))))
$errorString .=
      "You must be 18+ years of age to use this service.";
```

First, we check if the user's date of birth is 19 or more years ago; if this is the case, there is no error. Second, we check if the user was born exactly 18 years ago in a month earlier than the current month; if this is the case, again there is no error. Last, we check if the user was born exactly 18 years ago, in the current month, and on a day less than or equal to the current day; yet again, if this is true, there is no error. The parameters to the function date( ) are discussed in Chapter 2.

There are other approaches to checking differences between dates. For example, one approach is to use the MySQL functions described in Chapter 3 through an SQL query. The query need not use a database; that is, SQL can be used as a simple calculator. This approach is perhaps less desirable than the approach we have described, because there is no database activity involved in our example, and database activity adds unnecessary overhead. However, if one or more dates are extracted in the script from a database, MySQL date and time functions are a useful alternative.

Validating numeric fields

Checking that values are numeric, are within a range, or have the correct format is another common validation task. For winestore customers, there are three numeric fields: the zip code, and the fax and telephone numbers.

We validate zip codes using a regular expression:

```
// Validate Zipcode
if (!ereg("^([0-9]{4,5})$", $formVars["zipcode"]))
    $errorString .=
        "The zipcode must be 4 or 5 digits in length";
```

This permits a zip code of either four or five digits in length; this works for both U.S. zip codes and Australian postcodes, but it's unsuitable for many other countries. Another common validation check with zip codes is to check that they match the city or state using a database table, but we don't consider this approach here.

The optional phone and fax numbers are also validated using regular expressions:

```
// Phone is optional, but if it is entered it must have
// correct format
$validPhoneExpr = "^([0-9]{2,3}[ ]?)?[0-9]{4}[ ]?[0-9]{4}$";

if (!empty($formVars["phone"]) &&
    !ereg($validPhoneExpr, $formVars["phone"]))
    $errorString .=
        "The phone number must be 8 digits in length, " .
        "with an optional 2 or 3 digit area code";
```

The if statement contains two clauses: a check as to whether the field contains data and, if that is true, a check of the contents of the field using ereg( ). As discussed in Chapter 2—as in many other programming languages—the second clause is checked only if the first clause is true when an AND (&&) expression is evaluated. If the variable is empty, the ereg( ) expression isn't evaluated.

The ereg( ) expression works as follows:

- The expression ^([0-9]{2,3}[ ]?)? matches either zero or one occurrence of the bracketed expression at the beginning of the value. Inside the brackets, the expression that is matched is either two or three digits and an optional single space character (represented as [ ]?). For example, a string "03 " matches, as does "013 ", "03", and "013".

- The rest of the expression [0-9]{4}[ ]?[0-9]{4}$ matches exactly four digits, followed by an optional space, followed by another four digits, and then the end of the string is expected. For example, the strings 1234 1234 and 12341234 both match the expression.

- The entire expression matches the following classes of strings: 03 1234 1234, 013 1234 1234, 1234 1234, 0312341234, 01312341234, 03 12341234, 013 12341234, 12341234, 0131234 1234, and 031234 1234.

Validating email addresses

Email addresses are another common data entry item that requires field organization checking. There is a standard maintained by the Internet Engineering Task Force (IETF) called RFC-2822 that defines what a valid email address can be, and it's much more complex than might be expected. For example, an address such as the following is valid:

```
" <test> "@webdatabasebook.com
```

We use the following complex regular expression and network functions to validate an email address:

```
$validEmailExpr =
   "^[0-9a-z~!#$%&_-]([.]?[0-9a-z~!#$%&_-])*" .
   "@[0-9a-z~!#$%&_-]([.]?[0-9a-z~!#$%&_-])*$";

if (empty($formVars["email"]))
   // the user's email cannot be a null string
   $errorString .= "You must supply an email address.";

elseif (!eregi($validEmailExpr, $formVars["email"]))
   // The email must match the above regular expression
   $errorString .=
   "The email address must be in the name@domain format.";

elseif (strlen($formVars["email"]) > 50)
   // The length cannot exceed 50 characters
   $errorString . =
   "The email address can be no longer than 50 characters.";

elseif (!(getmxrr(substr(strstr($formVars["email"], '@'), 1), $temp)) ||
   checkdnsrr(gethostbyname(substr(strstr($formVars["email"], '@'), 1)),"ANY"))
   // There must be a Domain Name Server (DNS) record
   // for the domain name
   $errorString .= "The domain does not exist.";
```

If any email test fails, an error string is appended to the $errorString, and no further checks of the email value are made. A valid email passes all tests.

The first check tests to make sure that an email address has been entered. If it's omitted, an error is generated. It then uses a regular expression to check if the email address matches a template. It isn't RFC-2822-compliant but works reasonably for most email addresses:

- It uses eregi( ), so either upper- or lowercase are matched by the use of a-z.
- It expects the string to begin with a character from the set 0-9, a-z, and ~!#$%&_-. There has to be at least one character from this set at the beginning of the email address for it to be valid.
- After the first character matches, there is an optional bracketed expression:

    ([.]?[0-9a-z~!#$%&_-])*

    This expression is optional since it's suffixed with the * operator. However, if it does match, it matches any number of the characters specified. There can only be one consecutive full-stop if a full-stop occurs, as determined by the expression [.]?. The expression, for example, matches the string fred.williams.test% but not fred..williams.
- After the initial part of the email address, an @ character is expected. The @ has to occur after the first word for the string to be valid; our regular expression rejects email addresses that have only the initial or local component such as fred.
- Our validation expects there to be another word of at least length 1 after the @ symbol, and this can be followed by any combination of the permitted characters. Strings of permitted characters can be separated by a single full-stop.
- The function is imperfect. It allows several illegal email addresses and doesn't allow many that are legal but unusual.

The third step is to check the length of the email address. If it exceeds 50 characters, an error is generated. The fourth and final step is to check whether the domain of the email address actually exists:

```
elseif (!(getmxrr(substr(strstr($formVars["email"], '@'), 1), $temp)) ||
    checkdnsrr(gethostbyname(substr(strstr($formVars["email"], '@'), 1)),"ANY"))
    // There must be a Domain Name Server (DNS) record
    // for the domain name
    $errorString .= "The domain does not exist.";
```

The function getmxrr( ) queries an Internet domain name server (DNS) to check if there is a record of the email domain as a mail exchanger (MX). If the domain isn't an MX, the domain is checked with the DNS using the checkdnsrr( ) function, after converting the domain name to a numeric IP address with the gethostbyname( ) function. The second parameter to checkdnsrr( ) is the type of records to check, and ANY record is specified valid. If both tests fail, the domain of the email address isn't valid and we reject the email address.

Processing <form> Data on the Server Side

In this section, we discuss the validation peculiarities of the HTML <form> environment and what is actually submitted from a <form> in an HTTP request.

Processing <form> controls with the MULTIPLE attribute

Simple <form> elements, such as the <input> element, allow only one value to be associated with them. For example, an <input> element with the name attribute surname may have an associated value of Smith; in a URL query string, this association is represented as surname=Smith. Indeed, all the controls included in <form> examples in previous chapters have only one associated value. However, the <select multiple> element allows the association of more than one value with a variable in a <form>.

The <select multiple> element allows users to select zero or more items from a list. When the selected values are sent through using the GET or POST methods, each selected item has the same variable name but a different value. For example, consider what happens when the user selects options b and c in the following HTML <form>:

```
<form method="GET" action="click.php">
<select multiple name="choice">
<option>a</option>
<option>b</option>
<option>c</option>
<option>d</option>
</select>
<br><input type="submit">
</form>
```

When the user clicks Submit, the following URL is requested:

```
http://localhost/click.php?choice=b&choice=c
```

From a PHP perspective, this means that the variable $choice—which has the same name as that of the <select multiple>—is overwritten as the request is decoded, and an echo $choice prints the last value that was selected. In this case, echo $choice outputs c.

There are at least two solutions to this problem in PHP. First, it's possible to add more complex processing of the two automatically initialized arrays, HTTP_GET_VARS or HTTP_POST_VARS, to detect duplicate variable names and handle these for generic processing. Second, more elegantly and simply, you can use a PHP feature, which is described next.

The second approach works as follows. You modify the <form> and replace the name of the <select multiple> with an array-like structure, name="choice[]". The PHP interpreter then treats the variable as an array and stores the multiple values into $choice[0], $choice[1], etc. In the previous example, the <select multiple> element is renamed as choice[]:

```
<html><form method="GET">
<select multiple name="choice[]">
<option>a</option>
<option>b</option>
```

```
<option>c</option>
<option>d</option>
</select>
<br><input type="submit">
</select></form></html>
```

If the user selects options b and c, the following PHP fragment prints out all selected values, in this case both b and c:

```
foreach($choice as $value)
   echo $value;
```

The bracket array notation in a `<form>` can cause some problems with client-side scripts—such as those written in JavaScript—and such `<form>` elements should be referenced wrapped in single quotes in a JavaScript script. Client-side JavaScript for validation is discussed later in this chapter.

Interestingly, `<textarea>` and `<input>` elements can also be suffixed with brackets to put values into an array, should the need arise.

Other `<form>` issues

Checkbox elements in a `<form>` have the following format:

```
<form method="GET" action="click.php">
<input type="checkbox" name="check">
<input type="submit">
</form>
```

A checkbox has two states, on and off, and is usually rendered as a small clickable square in a graphical web browser. If the checkbox in the example is clicked, and the `<form>` submitted, the following URL is requested:

```
http://localhost/click.php?check=on
```

However, if the checkbox isn't clicked, the URL requested is as follows:

```
http://localhost/click.php
```

The important difference is that a checkbox is never off from the server perspective. If the checkbox isn't clicked, no variable or value is submitted to the server. Therefore, in a PHP script, a checkbox should be tested with the following fragment:

```
if ($check == "on")
   echo "Checkbox is on";
else
   echo "Checkbox is off";
```

Additionally, in the previous example, if the checkbox isn't clicked, it isn't possible to determine whether the `<form>` has been submitted or has never been displayed. An easy solution is to add a name attribute to the submit `<input>` element as follows:

```
<form method="GET" action="click.php">
<input type="checkbox" name="check">
<input type="submit" name="submit" value="Submit Query">
</form>
```

If this `<form>` is submitted with the checkbox in the off state, the following URL is requested:

```
http://localhost/click.php?submit=Submit+Query
```

Testing whether the variable `$submit` is `empty( )` can then distinguish between the initial display of the `<form>` and a subsequent submission of the `<form>` with the checkbox in the off state. The following script skeleton performs this check:

```
if (!empty(submit))
    // carry out processing
else
    // display the <form>
```

In addition, the naming of submit `<input>` elements permits more than one submit button to be added to a `<form>`. This allows two or more different types of submission that may have different validation or other behavior. For example, both Save and Cancel buttons may be present in the `<form>` as two different types of submission process. We use this approach in the winestore and discuss it further in Chapter 11.

Multiple `<select>` elements have the same property as checkboxes; if no item in the list is selected, no variable or value is submitted to the server.

Client-Side Validation with JavaScript

In this section, we briefly introduce the JavaScript scripting language as a client-side method for validation and other simple tasks. JavaScript isn't a fully fledged programming language like PHP: it can't connect to databases, it's limited as to which system resources it can interact with, and it can't do most tasks a web database application requires. However, JavaScript is good for interacting with a `<form>` and for controlling the display of data to the user.

The client-side scripting language we use here is best known as Java-Script. However, in June 1998, the European Computer Manufacturers Association (ECMA) agreed to be responsible for the standard implementations of the scripting language by Microsoft, Netscape, and Sun. Accordingly, the real name of the language is now ECMA-Script, based on the standard ECMA-262. The most recent version of ECMA-262 is the third edition, dated December 1999.

Common uses of JavaScript in web database applications include:

- Validation of `<form>` data, the main topic of this section.
- Simple interaction with `<form>` data; e.g., JavaScript is often used to calculate values and display these in a data-entry widget.

- Enhancing user interactions by adding dynamic elements to a web page. Common features include pull-down menus, mouseover changes to the presentation (*rollovers*), and dialog boxes.

- Customizing the browser and using information from the browser to enhance presentation.

Most of these techniques are oriented around events. An *event* is an action that occurs—such as a mouse passing over an object or a user clicking on a button—and that can be trapped through JavaScript code.

Validating <form> Data with JavaScript

 In a web database application, client-side validation should implement the same or less validation than a server-side script.

Never rely on client-side validation as the only method to ensure that system requirements, security policies, or DBMS constraints are met.

Client-side validation is optional but has benefits, including faster response to the user than server-side validation, a reduction in web-server load, and a reduction in network traffic. Moreover, client-side validation can be implemented as interactive validation, not only as post-validation, as on the server side. However, validation in the client tier is unreliable: the user can bypass the validation through design, error, or configuration. For that reason, client-side validation is a tool that should be used only to improve speed, reduce load, and add features, and never to replace server-side validation.

Consider the short JavaScript validation example in Example 7-1.

Example 7-1. A simple JavaScript example to check if a <form> field is empty

```
<!DOCTYPE HTML PUBLIC
            "-//W3C//DTD HTML 4.0 Transitional//EN"
            "http://www.w3.org/TR/html4/loose.dtd">
<html>
<head>
  <title>Simple JavaScript Example</title>

<script type="text/javascript">
<!-- Hide the script from old browsers
function containsblanks(s)
{
  for(var i = 0; i < s.value.length; i++)
  {
     var c = s.value.charAt(i);
     if ((c == ' ') || (c == '\n') || (c == '\t'))
     {
        alert('The field must not contain whitespace');
        return false;
```

```
        }
    }
    return true;
}
// end hiding -->
</script>
</head>

<body>
    <h2>Username Form</h2>
    <form onSubmit="return(containsblanks(this.userName));"
     method="post" action="test.php">
    <input type="text" name="userName" size=10>
    <input type="submit" value="SUBMIT">
    </form>
</body>
</html>
```

This example is designed to check if a userName field contains whitespace and, if so, to show a dialog box containing an error message to the user. The dialog box is shown in Figure 7-1.

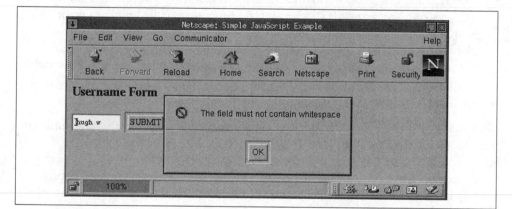

Figure 7-1. The dialog box produced when whitespace is entered in the userName field

The example contains no PHP but only a mixture of HTML and JavaScript. Almost all the JavaScript is encapsulated between the <script> and </script> tags in the first 17 lines of the example. The JavaScript function contained in the tags, containsblanks( ), is executed when the user submits the <form>.

The function call is part of the <form> element:

```
<form onSubmit="return(containsblanks(this.userName));"
    method="post" action="test.php">
```

When the submission event occurs—the user presses the Submit button—the onSubmit action handler is triggered. In this case, the function containsblanks( ) is called with one parameter, this.userName. The object this refers to the <form> itself and the expression this.userName refers to the input widget within the <form>. The function call itself is wrapped in a return( ) expression. The overall result of executing containsblanks( ) is that if the function returns false, the <form> isn't submitted to the server; if the function returns true, the HTTP request proceeds as usual.

The syntax of the JavaScript code is similar to PHP, and to other languages such as C and Java. The function containsblanks( ) works as follows:

- A for loop repeatedly performs actions on the characters entered by the user. The expression s.value.length refers to the length of the string value entered by the user into the userName widget. The length property is one of the predefined properties of the value attribute of the <input> widget.

- Each character in the string entered by the user is stored in a character variable c. s.value.charAt(i) is again an expression related to the value entered by the user in the <form>. The value attribute of the widget has an associated function (or, more correctly, a method) called charAt( ) that returns the value of the character at the position passed as a parameter. For example, if the user enters test in the widget, s.value.charAt(0) returns t, and s.value.charAt(1) returns e.

- The if statement checks whether the current character is a space, a tab character, or a carriage return. If so, the alert( ) function is called with an error string as a parameter. The alert( ) function presents a dialog box in the browser that shows the error message and has an OK button, as shown in Figure 7-1. When the user clicks OK, the function returns false, and the submission process stops.

- If the string doesn't contain any whitespace, the function containsblanks( ) returns true, and the <form> submits as usual.

Note that the HTML comment tags are included inside the <script> tags and surround the actual body of the JavaScript script. This is good practice, because if Java-Script is disabled or the user has an old browser that knows nothing about scripts, the comments hide the script from a potentially confused browser. An old browser happily displays the HTML page as usual, and most also ignore the onSubmit event handler in the <form> element.

Case study: A generic JavaScript validation function

The example in this section shows more features of JavaScript as a validation tool. An example of errors produced by applying the techniques described in this section to customer validation is shown in Figure 7-2.

A sophisticated and general-purpose data entry function for post-validation and batch error reporting is shown in Example 7-2. Only part of the script is shown; the remainder of the script includes the same PHP code to retrieve data and the HTML to display the customer <form> as in Example 6-7 in Chapter 6.

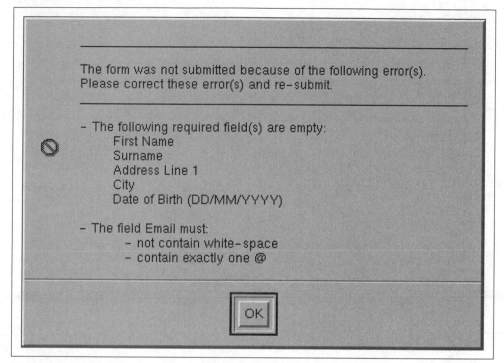

Figure 7-2. A dialog box showing errors produced by the JavaScript validation function

Example 7-2. A general-purpose JavaScript <form> validation function

```
<!-- The following code is a modified version of that
     described below -->

<!-- This example is from the book _JavaScript:
     The Definitive Guide_.  -->
<!-- Written by David Flanagan.  Copyright (c) 1996
     O'Reilly & Associates. -->
<!-- This example is provided WITHOUT WARRANTY either
     expressed or implied.-->
<!-- You may study, use, modify, and distribute it for
     any purpose.  -->

<!DOCTYPE HTML PUBLIC
          "-//W3C//DTD HTML 4.0 Transitional//EN"
          "http://www.w3.org/TR/html4/loose.dtd">
<html>
<head>
  <title>Customer Entry Form</title>

<script type="text/javascript">
<!-- Hide the script from old browsers
```

```
// A utility function that returns true if a string
// contains only whitespace characters.
function isblank(s)
{
  for(var i = 0; i < s.length; i++)
  {
    var c = s.charAt(i);
    if ((c != ' ') &&
        (c != '\n') &&
        (c != '\t'))
      return false;
  }
  return true;
}


// This is the function that performs <form> validation.
// It will be invoked from the onSubmit() event handler.
// The handler should return whatever value this function
// returns.
function verify(f)
{
  var msg;
  var empty_fields = "";
  var errors = "";

  // Loop through the elements of the form, looking for all
  // text and textarea elements that don't have an
  //  "optional" property defined.  Then, check for fields
  // that are empty and make a list of them.
  // Also, if any of these elements have a "min" or a "max"
  // property defined, then verify that they are numbers
  // and that they are in the right range.
  // Put together error messages for fields that are wrong.
  for(var i = 0; i < f.length; i++)
  {
    var e = f.elements[i];

    if (((e.type == "text") ||
         (e.type == "textarea")) &&
        !e.optional)
    {
      // first check if the field is empty
      if ((e.value == null) ||
          (e.value == "") ||
          isblank(e.value))
      {
        empty_fields += "\n          " +
                        e.description;
        continue;
      }
    }
```

Example 7-2. A general-purpose JavaScript <form> validation function (continued)

```
    // Now check for fields that are supposed
    // to be numeric.
    if (e.numeric ||
        (e.min != null) ||
        (e.max != null))
    {
        var v = parseFloat(e.value);
        if (isNaN(v) ||
            ((e.min != null) && (v < e.min)) ||
            ((e.max != null) && (v > e.max)))
        {
            errors += "\n- The field " +
                        e.description +
                        " must be a number";
            if (e.min != null)
                errors += " that is greater than " +
                        e.min;

            if (e.max != null &&
                e.min != null)
                errors += " and less than " +
                        e.max;

            else if (e.max != null)
                errors += " that is less than " +
                        e.max;

            errors += ".\n";
        }
    }


    // Now check for fields that are supposed
    // to be emails.
    // Not exactly as described in RFC 2822, but
    // a rough attempt
    // of the form "local-bit@domain-bit"
    if (e.email && !isblank(e.value))
    {
        var seenAt = false;
        var append = "";
        for(var j = 0; j < e.value.length; j++)
        {
            var c = e.value.charAt(j);
            if ((c == ' ') ||
                (c == '\n') ||
                (c == '\t'))
                append +=
"\n         - not contain white-space";
            if ((c == '@') && (seenAt == true))
                append +=
"\n         - contain only one @";
            if ((c == '@'))
```

```
                seenAt = true;
        }

        if (seenAt == false)
            append +=
"\n            - contain exactly one @";
        if (append)
            errors += "- The field " +
                    e.description +
                    " must: " + append;
    }


    // Now check for fields that are supposed
    // to be DOBs.
    if (e.dob && !isblank(e.value))
    {
        var slashCount = 0;
        var append = "";
        var addedError1 = false;
        var addedError2 = false;

        for(var j = 0; j < e.value.length; j++)
        {
            var c = e.value.charAt(j);

            if ((c == '/'))
                slashCount++;

            if (c != '/' &&
                (c < '0' || c > '9') &&
                addedError1 == false)
            {
                addedError1 = true;
                append +=
"\n            - must contain only numbers " +
"and forward-slashes";
            }
        }

        if (j != 10 || slashCount != 2)
            append +=
"\n            - must have the format DD/MM/YYYY";
        if (slashCount != 2)
            append +=
"\n            - must contain two slashes";
        if (append)
            errors +=  "- The field " +
                    e.description +
                    " must: " + append;
    }
```

```
                // Now check for fields that are supposed
                // not to have spaces
                if (e.nospaces)
                {
                    var seenAt = false;
                    var append = "";

                    for(var j = 0; j < e.value.length; j++)
                    {
                        var c = e.value.charAt(j);

                        if ((c == ' ') ||
                            (c == '\n') ||
                            (c == '\t'))
                            errors += "- The field " + e.description +
                                    " must not contains white-space";
                    }
                }

            } // if (type is text or textarea) and !optional
        } // for each character in field

        // Now, if there were any errors, then display the
        // messages, and return true to prevent the form from
        // being submitted.  Otherwise return false
        if (!empty_fields && !errors)
            return true;

        msg  = "_____ _ _\n\n"
        msg += "The form was not submitted because of the " +
                "following error(s).\n";
        msg += "Please correct these error(s) and re-submit.\n";
        msg += "_____ _ _\n\n"

        if (empty_fields)
        {
            msg += "- The following required field(s) are empty:"
                    + empty_fields + "\n";
            if (errors)
                msg += "\n";
        }
        msg += errors;
        alert(msg);
        return false;
    }
    // end hiding -->
    </script>

</head>
<body>
<h2>Customer Details</h2>
<hr>
```

Example 7-2. A general-purpose JavaScript <form> validation function (continued)

```
<form onSubmit="this.firstName.nospaces = true;
  this.firstName.description = 'First Name';
  this.surname.description = 'Surname';
  this.address1.description = 'Address Line 1';
  this.city.description = 'City';
  this.email.description = 'Email';
  this.email.email = true;
  this.dob.dob = true;
  this.dob.description = 'Date of Birth (DD/MM/YYYY)';
  return verify(this);"
  method="post" action="example.6-8.php">
```

In the example, the `<form>` tag contains a long script for the `onSubmit` event that is called when the user clicks the Submit button. The code creates and sets properties for each data entry widget. As all widgets are mandatory, a `description` property is created and set (e.g., `this.email.description = 'Email'`). This description is later displayed in an error dialog box if data isn't entered. For widgets that are optional—there are none in this example, but the full customer `<form>` in Chapter 10 has them—an `optional = true` property can be set.

For widgets that require specific validation, a property that describes the data type is set. For example, the `email` widget has a property of `this.email.email = true` to ensure that validation appropriate to an `email` field is performed. After setting all properties for all fields, the `verify( )` function is called with the `<form>` (`this` refers to the `<form>`) object as a parameter; the `<form>` object includes all widgets and their properties.

For compactness, we don't describe in detail how the `verify( )` function works. However, it has the following features:

- The function progressively creates a message to display to the user—much like `$errorString` in the PHP validation—as errors are detected. After collecting all errors, an error dialog box is shown listing all errors the user needs to correct before the `<form>` will submit. An example of the error dialog box is shown in Figure 7-2.
- All widgets that are inputs of type `text` or `textarea` and aren't optional are checked to ensure they contain data.
- Numeric fields are checked to ensure they are actually numeric and, if the value must fall in a range, the value is checked to ensure it's within the range.
- Emails are checked in a simplistic way. The email must contain exactly one @ symbol and must not contain whitespace.
- Dates are checked to ensure they are in the DD/MM/YYYY format used in most countries.
- Fields that should not contain whitespace are checked to ensure they don't contain spaces, tabs, or carriage returns.

The verify( ) function isn't comprehensive and certainly doesn't do all the validation proposed for the winestore customer <form>. However, in most cases, the customer <form> can't be submitted without a good chance of it passing the server-side validation checks.

JavaScript code can be reused across multiple HTML pages without adding the code to each page. For example, the code surrounded by the <script> and </script> tags in Example 7-2 can be saved in the file *valid.js* and then included into several HTML pages using the src attribute of the <script> element:

```
<script type="text/javascript" src="valid.js">
</script>
```

This approach has the advantage of reducing network traffic if the user has a web browser cache, because a copy of the script can be reused in multiple HTML pages.

Case study: A password <form> validation function

Example 7-3 gives a final example of JavaScript validation. In this example, the validation is interactive; that is, the fields are validated as data is entered. Instead of the onSubmit event, an onChange event is trapped for the two password widgets, formPassword1 and formPassword2; the function thesame( ) is called whenever the user changes the data in a widget and then leaves it. The reporting is field-by-field, and a sample dialog box output by the script is shown in Figure 7-3.

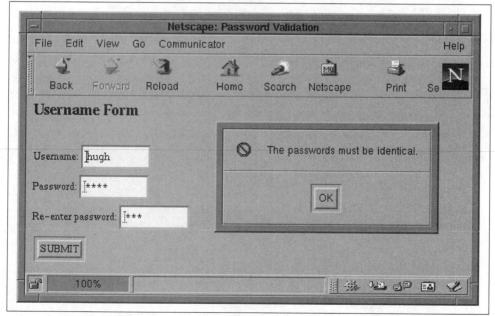

Figure 7-3. A dialog box produced by the script in Example 7-3

The function thesame( ) checks if the current widget contains data. If it does, the data in the widget is compared to the data in the other password widget. If the data in the widgets is different, an error message is shown to the user. It's necessary to test whether both widgets actually contain data in interactive validation; without this check, the function annoyingly displays an error before the user has the opportunity to enter data into both widgets.

Example 7-3. Using JavaScript for interactive validation of password fields

```
<!DOCTYPE HTML PUBLIC
            "-//W3C//DTD HTML 4.0 Transitional//EN"
            "http://www.w3.org/TR/html4/loose.dtd">
<html>
<head>
  <title>Password Validation</title>

<script type="text/javascript">
<!-- Hide the script
function thesame(value1, value2, description)
{
  if (((value1 != null) ||
      (value1 != "")) &&
      value2 != "" &&
      value1 != value2)
  {
      alert("The " + description + " must be identical.");
      return (false);
  }
  return (true);
}
// end hiding -->
</script>
</head>

<body>
  <h2>Username Form</h2>
  <form
 method="post" action="test.php">
  <br>Username:
  <input type="text" name="userName" size=10>
  <br>Password:
  <input type="password" name="formPassword1" onChange="
    thesame(formPassword1.value, formPassword2.value,
            'passwords');"
    size=10>
  <br>Re-enter password:
  <input type="password" name="formPassword2" onChange="
    thesame(formPassword2.value, formPassword1.value,
            'passwords');"
    size=10>
  <br><input type="submit" value="SUBMIT">
```

Example 7-3. Using JavaScript for interactive validation of password fields (continued)

```
    </form>
  </body>
</html>
```

There are several other events that are commonly trapped and handled in validation:

onBlur
> When a user removes focus from a `<form>`, `<frame>`, or window

onClick
> Left mouse button click on a `<form>` element

onFocus
> When a user brings focus to a `<form>`, `<frame>`, or window

onUnload
> When the user exits a page

JavaScript Tips and Tricks

In this section we present other common tools implemented with JavaScript that aren't particular to web database applications. Examples include:

- Mouse rollovers, where an image is changed to highlight an option as the mouse cursor passes over it
- Calculating and updating `<form>` fields based on user changes to data
- Interacting with the web browser and windows to trigger events and manipulate presentation
- Detecting which browser application and version the user is using

Rollover presentation with mouseOver events

Example 7-4 shows a basic implementation of the common rollover feature used in many web applications.

Example 7-4. mouseOver example with JavaScript

```
<!DOCTYPE HTML PUBLIC
            "-//W3C//DTD HTML 4.01 Transitional//EN"
            "http://www.w3.org/TR/html401/loose.dtd">
<html>
<head>
<title>MouseOver Example</title>
</head>

<body bgcolor="#ffffff">
<a href="add_to_cart.php"
  onMouseOut="cart.src='cart_off.jpg'"
  onMouseOver="cart.src='cart_on.jpg'">
```

Example 7-4. mouseOver example with JavaScript (continued)

```
<img src="cart_off.jpg" border=0 name="cart"
    alt="cart picture"></a>
</body>
</html>
```

When the page is first loaded, an image of a shopping cart in plain gray off-mode is shown; the image is used in the front page of the winestore. As usual, the image is loaded with the HTML fragment:

```
<img src="cart_off.jpg" border=0 name="cart">
```

The only difference to the usual approach of loading images is that the <img> tag has a name attribute, in this case name="cart".

If the mouse passes over the cart image, an onMouseOver event is generated, and the JavaScript action carried out is:

```
onMouseOver="cart.src='cart_on.jpg'"
```

The event handler changes the value of the src attribute of the <img> tag with the name="cart". The result is that a new image is loaded to replace the off-mode image with an on-mode image. In this case, a shopping cart with a blue foreground is shown.

When the mouse leaves the image region, the onMouseOut event is generated and handled with the following JavaScript fragment:

```
onMouseOut="cart.src='cart_off.jpg'"
```

This restores the original gray off-mode image. The impression to the user is that the cart element is highlighted as the user focuses on the element; the same technique is used to highlight menu options and to produce pop-up and pull-down menus.

Prefilling <form> data with JavaScript calculations

Another common use of JavaScript is to prefill a <form> with data from a calculation. Example 7-5 shows how data can be managed and updated in the winestore shopping cart (this approach isn't actually used in the online winestore).

When the user changes the quantity of wine he intends to purchase, an onChange event is generated. This change event is handled by the update( ) function, which modifies the value attribute of the total widget, showing the new total cost to the user. The new value shown to the user is calculated by multiplying together the quantity.value and the unit.value. Of course, as in all web database applications, the values and mathematics should be rechecked at the server when the <form> is submitted to the server.

Example 7-5. Using JavaScript to dynamically update values of <form> widgets

```
<!DOCTYPE HTML PUBLIC
            "-//W3C//DTD HTML 4.01 Transitional//EN"
            "http://www.w3.org/TR/html401/loose.dtd">
<html>
<head>
   <title>Dynamic Form Update Example</title>

<script type="text/javascript">
<!-- Hide the script from old browsers
function update(quantity, unit, total)
{

    total.value = unit.value * quantity.value;
}
// end the hiding -->
</script>
</head>

<body>
<h1>Your Shopping Cart</h1>
<form method="get" action="test.php">
<table border="0" width="100%" cellpadding="0" cellspacing="5">
<tr>
   <td>Quantity </td>
   <td>Wine</td>
   <td>Unit Price</td>
   <td>Total</td>
</tr>

<tr>
   <td><input type="text" name="quantity" value="1"
       size=3 onChange="update(quantity,unit,total);">
   <td>1997 Anderson and Sons Wines Belcombe Grenache</td>
   <td>$<input type="text" value="17.29" name="unit"
       readonly></td>
   <td>$<input type="text" value="17.29" name="total"
       align="right" readonly></td>
</tr>
</table>
<input type="submit" value="Purchase Wines">
</form>
</body>
</html>
```

Interacting with the web browser

Unfortunately, JavaScript can be used to annoy. We have all suffered the continual popping-up of new windows without the usual toolbars (these are known as *consoles*), changes in the browser appearance, and resizing of the browser.

Having said that, adding features that are helpful is desirable. Example 7-6 shows four examples of handlers for buttons that use methods or functions defined for the browser window object. The function `window.close( )` closes the focused window, `window.print( )` shows the print dialog window, `windows.history.go(-1)` goes back one page, and `window.open( )` opens a new browser window.

Example 7-6. Closing and opening windows with JavaScript, printing the current page, and adding a Back button to a <form>

```
<!DOCTYPE HTML PUBLIC
                "-//W3C//DTD HTML 4.01 Transitional//EN"
                "http://www.w3.org/TR/html401/loose.dtd">
<html>
<head>
  <title>Playing with the Browser and Windows</title>
</head>
<body>
<h1>Playing with the Browser and Windows</h1>
<form action="example.7-6.php">
  <input type="button" value="Close Window"
      onClick="window.close( );">
  <br><input type="button" value="Print Window"
      onClick="window.print( );">
  <br><input type="button" value="Go Back"
      onclick="javascript:window.history.go(-1);">
  <br><input type="button" value="Visit the book site"
      onClick="
          window.open('http://www.webdatabasebook.com/',
          'BookSite',
          'toolbar=yes,location=yes,menubar=yes,
          directories=yes,scrollbar=yes,resizable=yes');">
</form>
</body></html>
```

The page rendered in a Netscape browser is shown in Figure 7-4.

Only `window.open( )` has any complexity. The first parameter is the URL to request in the new window, the second is a title, and the third is a set of properties the new window has. Without the list of properties that are included, the default new window has no Location box, no toolbars, no scrollbars, and can't be resized: it's an evil console!

Which browser is the user using?

More advanced JavaScript highlights annoying differences in support of standard features by different browsers. Even different versions of Netscape or Internet Explorer support different JavaScript features.

Example 7-7 shows how the browser application name and version can be detected with both JavaScript and PHP. The output of the script rendered in a Netscape browser is shown in Figure 7-5. If a JavaScript script requires customization for a

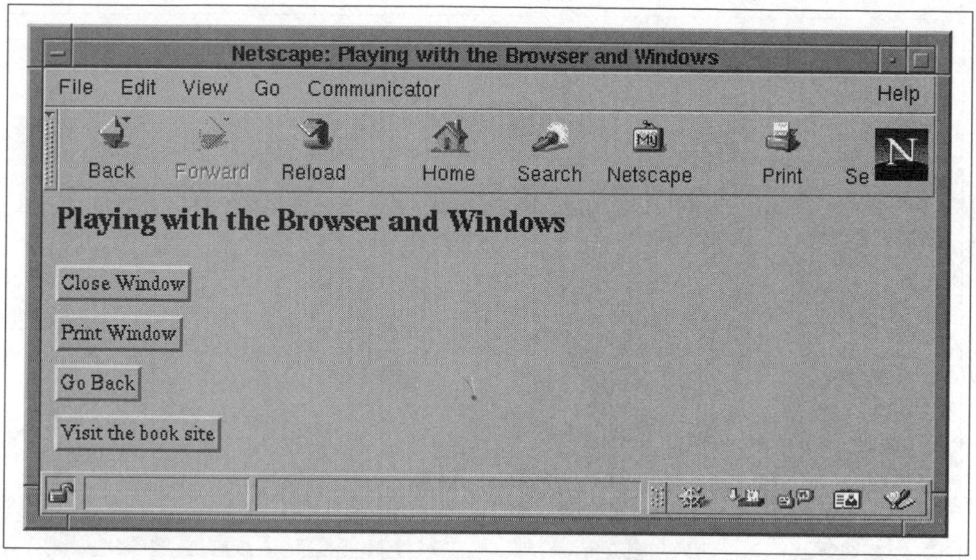

Figure 7-4. Controlling the browser behavior through buttons

particular product, if statements can carry out actions in different ways. Another common approach in JavaScript-intensive web database applications is to write two sites: one that uses Internet Explorer JavaScript and another that uses Netscape Navigator JavaScript.

Example 7-7. Which browser is the user using?

```
<!DOCTYPE HTML PUBLIC
            "-//W3C//DTD HTML 4.01 Transitional//EN"
            "http://www.w3.org/TR/html401/loose.dtd">
<html>
<head>
  <title>Playing with the Browser and Windows</title>
</head>
<body>
<script type="text/javascript">
<!-- Hide the script from old browsers
  var version = navigator.appName
  var number = parseInt(navigator.appVersion)
  alert("You are using the " + version +
        " browser, version " + number);
// end the hiding -->
</script>

This page should pop up a box if you have a JavaScript-capable and enabled
browser.
<br>But, using PHP, we can tell you that you're using the
<? printf("%s", $HTTP_USER_AGENT); ?> browser.
</body></html>
```

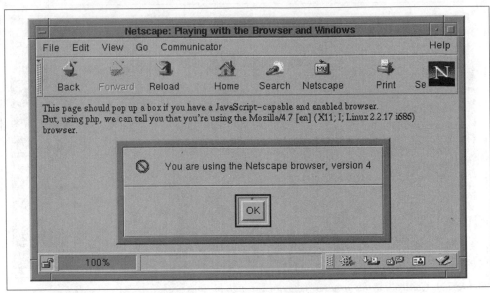

Figure 7-5. Detecting the browser application details using the script in Example 7-7

Comments

The short examples in this section implement common JavaScript web database features, and we recommend that JavaScript be used only for these simple manipulations and the basic validation tasks. Using JavaScript for more complex tasks may reveal annoying differences between browser applications, browser versions, and different platforms. These differences can be compounded by the fact that the web database application developer usually has little control over the standardization of the client JavaScript environment.

Pointers to books and other resources on JavaScript are included in Appendix E.

Building complex JavaScript adds a thicker client to a web database application.

This book is focused on thin clients, where the majority of the application logic resides in the middle tier. We recommend that JavaScript be kept simple: complex tasks should be left to the middle-tier scripts, and interfaces should still function correctly even if JavaScript is faulty or disabled.

If complex JavaScript is required or desired, make sure it's tested on all the popular platforms with the popular browser products and versions.

CHAPTER 8

Sessions

A fundamental characteristic of the Web is the stateless interaction between browsers and web servers. As discussed in Chapter 1, HTTP is a stateless protocol. Each HTTP request a browser sends to a web server is independent of any other request. The stateless nature of HTTP allows users to browse the Web by following hypertext links and visiting pages in any order. HTTP also allows applications to distribute or even replicate content across multiple servers to balance the load generated by a high number of requests. These features are possible because of the stateless nature of HTTP.

This stateless nature suits applications that allow users to browse or search collections of documents. However, applications that require complex user interaction can't be implemented as a series of unrelated, stateless web pages. An often-cited example is a shopping cart in which items are added to the cart while searching or browsing a catalog. The state of the shopping cart—the selected items—needs to be stored somewhere. When the user requests the order page, the items for that user need to be displayed.

Stateful web database applications can be built using *sessions*, and session management is the topic of this chapter. In this chapter we:

- Discuss how sessions are managed in the stateless environment of the Web and introduce the three characteristics of server-side session management
- Introduce cookies for storing state
- Show how to use and configure the PHP session management library
- Use PHP session management to improve the client entry <form> in the winestore case study
- Provide a brief list of reasons for using, or avoiding, session management over the Web

The focus of this chapter is on the session management provided by PHP. However, other techniques to keep state are briefly discussed, including the use of cookies.

Building Applications That Keep State

Applications sometimes need to use the result of one request when processing another. For example, a request that adds an item to a shopping cart needs to be remembered when the request is made to create the order. In other words, the state of the application needs to be stored between HTTP requests. There are two ways to achieve this: variables that hold the state can be stored in the browser and included with each request or variables can be stored on the server.

Most of this chapter is devoted to the second alternative, where the middle tier stores and manages the application state using sessions. However, in this section we briefly discuss solutions that store state in the client tier. One technique described in this section is the use of cookies. While cookies can store state in the client tier, they are also used in middle-tier session management, as described later in this chapter.

Managing State in the Client Tier

Data sent with the GET or POST methods can include the application state with each HTTP request. An illustration of this approach can be seen in the previous and next browsing features developed in Chapter 5. In this example, there are two pieces, or *states*, that need to be considered when a page is browsed: the query parameters the user provided and which page should be displayed.

The solution developed in Chapter 5 encodes the query and an offset as an embedded link. An example URL that displays the fourth page of results may be as follows:

    http://localhost/example.5-10.php?regionName=All&offset=40

This solution allows navigation through large search result sets. Similar solutions are used in the URLs generated to jump between the results pages of web search engines such as Google or Altavista. Cookies can be used for the same purpose.

Encoding the variables that hold state with each HTTP request increases the amount of data that has to be transmitted over the Web, and when data is encoded using the GET method, applications can generate long URLs. While HTTP doesn't restrict the length of URLs, some older browsers and proxy servers do enforce limits.

When state variables are encoded as part of the URL, or even when they are included as cookies, it is possible for the user to change the values that are sent with the request. For example, a user can enter the following URL manually if she wants to see the records starting from row #7 in the result set:

    http://localhost/example.5-10.php?regionName=All&offset=7

Changing the offset in a results page is harmless, but changing the item price of a bottle of wine is more serious. As discussed in Chapters 6 and 7, an application can't rely on data that is sent from the browser.

Cookies

Cookies are often used to store application state in a web browser. As with data sent with the GET or POST methods, cookies are sent with HTTP requests made by a browser. A *cookie* is a named piece of information that is stored in a web browser. A browser can create a cookie using JavaScript, but a cookie is usually sent from the web server to the client in the Set-Cookie header field as part of an HTTP response. Consider an example HTTP response:

```
HTTP/1.0 200
Content-Length: 1276
Content-Type: text/html
Date: Tue, 06 Nov 2001 04:12:49 GMT
Expires: Tue, 06 Nov 2001 04:12:59 GMT
Server: simwebs/3.1.6
Set-Cookie: animal=egg-laying-mammal

<html>...</html>
```

The web browser that receives this response remembers the cookie and includes it as the header field Cookie in subsequent HTTP requests to the same web server. For example, if a browser receives the response just shown, a subsequent request has the following format:

```
GET /duck/bill.php HTTP/1.0
Connection: Keep-Alive
Cookie: animal=egg-laying-mammal
Host: www.webdatabasebook.com
Referer: http://www.webdatabasebook.com/
```

There are several additional parameters used with the Set-Cookie header that define when a cookie can be included in a request:

- A cookie can have a date and time at which it expires. The browser includes the cookie in requests up until that date and time. If no expiry date is given, the cookie is remembered only while the browser is running. Cookies that are kept only while the browser is running are known as *session cookies*.

- A domain limits the sites to which a browser can send the cookie. If no domain is set, the browser includes the cookie only in requests sent to the server that set the cookie.

- Browsers don't include the cookie in requests for resources that aren't in the specified path. This is useful if only part of a web site requires that a cookie be sent. For example, if the path is set to */admin*, requests for resources in that path, such as *http://localhost/admin/home.php* include the cookie, while requests for resources in other paths, such as *http://localhost/winestore/home.php*, do not.

- A cookie can also be marked as secure, instructing the browser to send the cookie only when using a secure connection through the Secure Sockets Layer protocol. This prevents sensitive data stored in a cookie from being transmitted in an insecure form. Encryption using the SSL software is discussed in Chapter 9.

Cookies can be included in an HTTP response using the header() function; however, the developer needs to know how to encode the cookie name, value, and the other parameters described earlier in the Set-Cookie header field. To simplify cookie creation, PHP provides the setcookie() function that generates a correct header field.

When an HTTP request that contains cookies is processed, PHP makes the values of the cookies available to the script in the global associative array $HTTP_COOKIE_VARS. If register_globals is enabled, a variable with the name of the cookie is also initialized by PHP; the register_globals feature in the *php.ini* file is discussed in Chapter 5. Example 8-1 tests to see if the variable $count has been set from a cookie, and either sets the value to 0 or increments $count accordingly. The script also creates a cookie named start, with the value set to the current time, when the $count is set to 0. The cookie start is set only at the beginning of this stateful interaction.

Example 8-1. Setting a cookie using PHP

```
<?php

// See if the HTTP request has set $count as the
// result of a Cookie called "count"
if(!isset($count)) {
  // No cookie called count, set the counter to zero
  $count = 0;

  // .. and set a cookie with the "start" time
  // of this stateful interaction
  $start = time();
  setcookie("start", $start, time()+600, "/", "", 0);

} else {
    $count++;
}

// Set a cookie "count" with the current value
setcookie("count", $count, time()+600, "/", "", 0);

?>
<!DOCTYPE HTML PUBLIC
    "-//W3C//DTD HTML 4.0 Transitional//EN"
    "http://www.w3.org/TR/html4/loose.dtd" >
<html>
  <head><title>Cookies</title></head>
  <body>
    <p>This page comes with cookies: Enjoy!
    <br>count = <?=$count ?>.
    <br>start = <?=$start ?>.
    <p>This session has lasted
```

Example 8-1. Setting a cookie using PHP (continued)

```
   <?php
      $duration = time( ) - $start;
   echo "$duration";
    ?>
    seconds.
  </body>
</html>
```

The setcookie( ) function is called with six arguments, although only the first—the name—is required:

```
int setcookie(string name, [string value], [int expire], [string path], string
domain, [int secure])
```

The two calls to setcookie( ) in Example 8-1 add the Set-Cookie header field to the HTTP response. The first encodes the start cookie with the value of the current time as an integer returned from the time( ) function. The second encodes the count cookie with the value of the variable $count. Both cookies are set with the expiry date of the current time plus 600 seconds; that is, 10 minutes. With the *path* parameter set to /, the browser includes the cookies with all requests to the site. By passing an empty string for the domain, the browser includes the cookies only with requests to the domain of the machine serving this page. The final parameter 0 allows the browser to transmit the cookies over both secure and insecure connections.

Cookies can be used for simple applications that don't require complex data to be kept between requests. However, there is a limit on the number and size of cookies that can be set: a browser can keep only the last 20 cookies sent from a particular domain, and the values that a cookie can hold are limited to 4 KB in size. Also, there are arguments about both the privacy and the security of applications that use cookies, and users often disable cookie support in their browsers. We discuss some of the security issues of cookies in Chapter 9.

Session Management Over the Web

Storing the state in the web server—the middle tier—can solve the problem of increased request size and protect the state of an application from accidental or intentional changes a user might make.

A *session* is a way to identify and manage the state—the *session variables*—for a particular user. When a user sends an HTTP request, the middle tier must process the current request in the context of the user's session. When a session is started, the client is given a *session identifier*—often a cookie—that is included with subsequent requests to the server. The server uses the session identifier to locate the corresponding session before processing the request.

Rather than storing all the variables needed to maintain state and include them with each request, the browser stores a single session identifier that finds and initializes the variables stored on the server. The session identifier is like the ticket given at a cloak room. The ticket is much easier to carry around and ensures that the holder gets her own hat and coat.

One implication of storing session variables in the middle tier is that data needs to be stored for each session. The question is, for how long? Because HTTP is stateless, there is no way to know when a user has finished with a session. Ideally, the user logs out of an application, and the logout script ends the session. However, because a server can never be sure if a user is still there, the server needs to clean up old sessions that have not been used for a period of time. This last point is important, because sessions consume resources on the server, and dormant sessions may present a security risk. How long the timeout should be depends on the needs of the application, and we discuss this in more detail later in this chapter.

In summary, there are three characteristics session management over the Web must exhibit:

- Information or state must be *stored*. For example, a selected bottle of wine in a shopping cart, a customer name, or a credit card number must be maintained across multiple HTTP requests.

- Each HTTP request must carry an *identifier* that allows the server to process the request in the context of the stored state. For example, when an order is submitted, it must be processed with the correct items and customer details.

- Sessions need to have a *timeout*. Otherwise, if a user leaves the web site, there is no way the server can tell when the session should end.

PHP Session Management

With the release of PHP4, session management was introduced as an extension to the PHP language. PHP provides several session-related functions, and developing applications that use PHP sessions is straightforward. The three important features of session management are mostly taken care of by the PHP scripting engine.

In this section, we present how to use PHP sessions, showing how sessions are started and ended and how session variables are used. We list the PHP functions for building session-based web applications. Because not all browsers support cookies, and some users actively disable them, we describe how to use PHP sessions without relying on cookies. Finally, we show how to configure PHP session management with a discussion on the garbage collection used to remove old sessions and other configuration parameters.

Overview

An overview of PHP session management is shown in Figure 8-1. When a user first enters the session-based application by making a request to a page that starts a session, PHP generates a session ID and creates a file that stores the session-related variables. PHP sets a cookie to hold the session ID in the response the script generates. The browser then records the cookie and includes it in subsequent requests. In the example shown in Figure 8-1, the script *welcome.php* records session variables in the session store, and a request to *next.php* then has access to those variables because of the session ID.

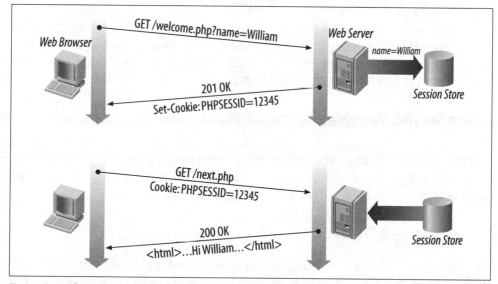

Figure 8-1. The interaction between the browser and the server when initial requests are made to a session-based application

The out-of-the-box configuration of PHP session management uses disk-based files to store session variables. Using files as the session store is adequate for most applications in which the numbers of concurrent sessions are limited. A more scalable solution that uses a MySQL database as a session store is provided in Appendix D.

Starting a Session

PHP provides a session_start( ) function that creates a new session and subsequently identifies and establishes an existing one. Either way, a call to the session_start( ) function initializes a session.

The first time a PHP script calls session_start( ), a session identifier is generated, and, by default, a Set-Cookie header field is included in the response. The response sets up a session cookie in the browser with the name PHPSESSID and the value of the session identifier. The PHP session management automatically includes the cookie without the need to call to the setcookie( ) or header( ) functions.

The session identifier (ID) is a random string of 32 hexadecimal digits, such as fcc17f071bca9bf7f85ca281094390b4. As with other cookies, the value of the session ID is made available to PHP scripts in the $HTTP_COOKIE_VARS associative array and in the $PHPSESSID variable.

When a new session is started, PHP creates a session file. With the default configuration, session files are written in the */tmp* directory using the session identifier, prefixed with *sess_*, for the filename. The filename associated with our example session ID is */tmp/sess_fcc17f071bca9bf7f85ca281094390b4*.

If a call is made to session_start( ), and the request contains the PHPSESSID cookie, PHP attempts to find the session file and initialize the associated session variables as discussed in the next section. However, if the identified session file can't be found, session_start( ) creates an empty session file.

Using Session Variables

Variables need to be registered with the session_register( ) function that's used in a session. If a session has not been initialized, the session_register( ) function calls session_start( ) to open the session file. Variables can be registered—added to the session file—with the session_register( ) call as follows:

```
// Register the variable named "foo"
session_register("foo");
$foo = "bar";
```

Note that it is the name of the variable that is passed to the session_register( ) function, not the variable itself. Once registered, session variables are made persistent and are available to scripts that initialize the session. PHP tracks the values of session variables and saves their values to the session file: there is no need to explicitly save a session variable before a script ends. In the previous example, the variable $foo is automatically saved in the session store with its value bar.

Variables can be removed from a session with the session_unregister( ) function call; again, the name of the variable is passed as the argument, not the variable itself. A variable that is unregistered is no longer available to other scripts that initialize the session. However, the variable is still available to the rest of the script immediately after the session_unregister( ) function call.

Scripts that initialize a session have access to the session variables through the associative array $HTTP_SESSION_VARS, and PHP automatically initializes the named session variables if register_globals is enabled.

Example 8-2 shows a simple script that registers two variables: an integer $count, which is incremented each time the script is called, and $start, which is set to the current time from the library function time( ) when the session is first initialized. The script tests if the variable $count has been registered to determine if a new session has been created. If the variable $count has been registered already, the script increments its value.

Do not use the existence of $PHPSESSID as indicative of a new session, or as a method to access the session ID. The first time a script is called and the session is created, the PHPSESSID cookie may not be set. Only subsequent requests are guaranteed to contain the PHPSESSID cookie. PHP provides a session_id( ) function that returns the session ID for the initialized session.

The script shown in Example 8-2 displays both variables: $count shows how many times the script has been called, and time( ) - $start shows how many seconds the session has lasted.

Example 8-2. Simple PHP script that uses a session

```php
<?php
  // Initialize a session. This call either creates
  // a new session or re-establishes an existing one.
  session_start( );

  // If this is a new session, then the variable
  // $count will not be registered
  if (!session_is_registered("count"))
  {
    session_register("count");
    session_register("start");

    $count = 0;
    $start = time( );
  }
  else
  {
    $count++;
  }

  $sessionId = session_id( );
?>
<!DOCTYPE HTML PUBLIC
    "-//W3C//DTD HTML 4.0 Transitional//EN"
    "http://www.w3.org/TR/html4/loose.dtd" >
<html>
  <head><title>Sessions</title></head>
  <body>
    <p>This page points at a session
        (<?=$sessionId?>)
    <br>count = <?=$count?>.
    <br>start = <?=$start?>.
    <p>This session has lasted
      <?php
```

Example 8-2. Simple PHP script that uses a session (continued)

```
        $duration = time( ) - $start;
    echo "$duration";
    ?>
        seconds.
  </body>
</html>
```

Session variables can be of the type Boolean, integer, double, string, object, or arrays of those variable types. Care must be taken when using object session variables, because PHP needs access to the class definitions of registered objects when initializing an existing session. If objects are to be stored as session variables, you should include class definitions for those objects in all scripts that initialize sessions, whether the scripts use the class or not. Objects and classes are described in Chapter 2.

PHP stores session variables in the session file by *serializing* the values. The serialized representation of a variable includes the name, the type, and the value as a stream of characters suitable for writing to a file. Here's an example of a file that was created when the script shown in Example 8-2 was run several times:

```
count|i:6;start|i:986096496;
```

A PHP developer need not worry how serialization occurs; PHP session management takes care of reading and writing session variables automatically.

Ending a Session

At some point in an application, sessions may need to be destroyed. For example, when a user logs out of an application, a call to the session_destroy( ) function can be made. A call to session_destroy( ) removes the session file from the system but doesn't remove the PHPSESSID cookie from the browser.

Example 8-3 shows how the session_destroy( ) function is called. A session must be initialized before the session_destroy( ) call can be made. You should also test to see if $PHPSESSID is a set variable before killing the session. This prevents the code from creating a session, then immediately destroying it if the script is called without identifying a session. However, if the user has previously held a session cookie, PHP initializes the $PHPSESSID variable, and the code redundantly creates and destroys a session.

Example 8-3. Ending a session

```
<?php
  // Only attempt to end the session if there
  // is a $PHPSESSID set by the request.
  if(isset($PHPSESSID)) {
    $message = "<p>End of session ($PHPSESSID).";
    session_start( );
```

Example 8-3. Ending a session (continued)

```
    session_destroy();
  } else {
    $message = "<p>There was no session to destroy!";
  }
?>
<!DOCTYPE HTML PUBLIC
  "-//W3C//DTD HTML 4.0 Transitional//EN"
  "http://www.w3.org/TR/html4/loose.dtd" >
<html>
  <head><title>Sessions</title></head>
  <body>
    <?=$message?>
  </body>
</html>
```

Functions for Accessing Sessions in PHP

In this section we list the key functions used to build session-based applications in PHP. Greater control over sessions can be achieved through the configuration of PHP—as we discuss in the "Configuration of PHP Session Management" section—or by using GET variables to encode the session ID, as discussed in the next section.

Boolean session_start()

Initializes a session by either creating a new session or using an identified one. Checks for the variable $PHPSESSID in the HTTP request. If a session identifier isn't included in the request, or an identified session isn't found, a new session is created. If a session ID is included in the request, and a session isn't found, a new session is created with the PHPSESSID encoded in the request. When an existing session is found, the session variables are read from the session store and initialized. Using PHP's default settings, a new session is created as a file in the */tmp* directory. This function always returns true.

string session_id([string *id*])

Can be used in two ways: to return the ID of an initialized session and to set the value of a session ID before a session is created. When used to return the session ID, the function must be called without arguments after a session has been initialized. When used to set the value of the session ID, the function must be called with the ID as the parameter before the session has been initialized.

Boolean session_register(mixed *name* [, mixed ...])

Registers one or more variables in the session store. Each argument is the name of a variable, or an array of variable names, not the variable itself. Once a variable is registered, it becomes available to any script that identifies that session. This function calls the session_start() code internally if a session has not been initialized. The session_unregister() function is called to remove a variable from the session. Returns true when the variables are successfully registered.

Boolean session_is_registered(string *variable_name*)

> Returns true if the named variable has been registered with the current session and false otherwise. Using this function to test if a variable is registered is a useful way to determine if a script has created a new session or initialized an existing one.

session_unregister(string *variable_name*)

> Unregisters a variable with the initialized session. Like the session_register() function, the argument is the name of the variable, not the variable itself. Unlike the session_register() function, the session needs to be initialized before calling this function. Once a variable has been removed from a session with this call, it is no longer available to other scripts that initialize the session. However, the variable is still available to the rest of the script that calls session_unregister().

session_unset()

> Unsets the values of all session variables. This function doesn't unregister the actual session variables. A call to session_is_registered() still returns true for the session variables that have been unset.

Boolean session_destroy()

> Removes the session from the PHP session management. With PHP's default settings, a call to this function removes the session file from the /tmp directory. Returns true if the session is successfully destroyed and false otherwise.

Session Management Without Cookies

A change that can be made to the default PHP session management is to encode the $PHPSESSID value as an attribute in a GET or POST method request and avoid the need to set a cookie.

A simple experiment that illustrates what happens when users disable cookies is to request the script shown in Example 8-2 from a browser that has cookie support turned off. When repeated requests are made, the counter doesn't increment, and the session duration remains at zero seconds. Because a cookie isn't sent from the browser, the variable $PHPSESSID is never set. The other side effect is that each time the page is requested, a session file is created in the /tmp directory. Many users configure their browsers to not accept cookies, and session-based applications won't work unless they are written to handle the missing cookie.

The session identifier that would have been sent as a cookie in this experiment can be transmitted in a GET or POST method request. While the session_start() function can use $PHPSESSID set by either a GET or POST method request, it is more practical to use the GET variable. Using the POST variable leads to the reload problem described in Chapter 6. Continuing the experiment, requests that don't contain the cookie can identify an existing session by setting an attribute in a GET method request with the name PHPSESSID and the value of the session ID. For example, an initial request can be made to Example 8-1 with the URL:

```
http://localhost/example.8-1.php
```

This creates a session and an associated file such as:

```
/tmp/sess_be20081806199800da22e24081964000
```

Subsequent requests can be made that include the PHPSESSID:

```
http://localhost/example.8-1.php?PHPSESSID=be20081806199800da22e24081964000
```

The response shows the counter set to 1 and the correct session duration. Repeated requests to this URL behave as expected: the counter increments, and the calculated duration increases.

If you write session-based applications to use the URL to identify sessions, the application doesn't fail for users who don't allow cookies. Applications can use a test cookie to see if cookies are supported by the browser or just not use cookies at all.

When register_globals is enabled, and both a cookie and GET or POST are used to set the $PHPSESSID, the cookie wins. A GET or POST attribute value is overwritten by the value associated with the cookie because of the default order in which PHP initializes those variables.

The safe way to read cookies and GET and POST attributes that have name conflicts is to use the $HTTP_COOKIE_VARS, $HTTP_GET_VARS, and $HTTP_POST_VARS arrays.

Another advantage of avoiding cookies is that some browsers, such as Netscape and Internet Explorer, share cookies across all instances of the program running for a particular user on the same machine. This behavior prevents a user from having multiple sessions with a web database application.

Encoding the session ID as a GET variable

Scripts that generate embedded links to pages that use session variables need to include a GET attribute named PHPSESSID in the URL. This can be done using the basic PHP string support and calls to session_id( ). For example:

```php
<?php
  // Initialize the session
  session_start( );

  // Generate the embedded URL to link to
  // a page that processes an order
  $orderUrl = "/order.php?PHPSESSID=" . session_id( );
?>

<a href="<?=$orderUrl ?>">Create Order</a>
```

To aid the creation of URLs that link to session-based scripts, PHP sets the constant SID that contains the session ID in the form suitable to use as a URL query string. If there is no session initialized, PHP sets the value of SID to be a blank string. If a session is initialized, it sets the SID to a string containing the session ID in the form:

```
PHPSESSID=be20081806199800da22e24081964000
```

By including the value of SID when URLs are constructed, the hypertext links correctly identify the session. A link that points to a script that expects a session ID can be encoded like this:

```
<?php
  // Initialize the session
  session_start();
?>

<a href="/order.php?<?=SID?>">Create Order</a>
```

As an alternative to writing code to formulate the session ID into the URL, PHP includes a URL *rewrite* feature that automatically modifies reference URLs to include the session ID as a GET attribute. To activate this feature, PHP needs to be configured with --enable-trans-id and then recompiled. Once URL rewrite is activated, PHP parses the HTML generated by scripts and automatically alters the embedded URLs to include the PHPSESSID query string. The URL rewrite feature has the disadvantage that extra processing is required to parse every generated page.

Turning off cookies

PHP session management can be instructed not to set the PHPSESSID cookie by changing the session.use_cookies parameter to 0 in the *php.ini* file. The session configuration parameters in the *php.ini* file are described in the later section "Configuration of PHP Session Management."

Garbage Collection

While it is good practice to build applications that provide a way to end a session—with a script that makes a call to session_destroy( )—there is no guarantee that a user will log out by requesting the appropriate PHP script. PHP session management has a built-in garbage collection mechanism that ensures unused session files are eventually cleaned up. This is important for two reasons: it prevents the directory from filling up with session files that can cause performance to degrade and, more importantly, it reduces the risk of someone guessing session IDs and hijacking an old unused session.

There are two parameters that control garbage collection: session.gc_maxlifetime and session.gc_probability, both defined in the *php.ini* file. A garbage collection process is run when a session is initialized, for example, when session_start( ) is called. Each session is examined by the garbage collection process, and any sessions that have not been accessed for a specified period of time are removed. This period is specified as seconds of inactivity in the gc_maxlifetime parameter—the default value being 1,440 seconds. The file-based session management uses the update time of the file to determine the last access. To prevent the garbage collection process from removing active session files, PHP must modify the update time of the file when session variables are read, not just when they are written.

The garbage collection process can become expensive to run, especially in sites with high numbers of users, because the last-modified date of every session file must be examined. The second parameter gc_probability sets the percentage probability that the garbage collection process will be activated. A setting of 100% ensures that sessions are examined for garbage collection with every session initialization. The default value of 1% means that garbage collection occurs with a probability of 1 in 100.* Depending on the requirements, some figure between these two extremes balances the needs of the application and performance. Unless a site is receiving less that 1,000 hits per day, the probability should be set quite low. For example, an application that receives 1,000 hits in a 10-hour period with a gc_probability setting of 10% runs the garbage collection function, on average, once every 6 minutes. Setting the gc_probability too high adds unnecessary processing load on the server.

When it is important to prevent users from accessing old sessions, the gc_probability should be increased. For example, the default session configuration sets up a cookie in the browser to be deleted when the browser program is terminated. This prevents a user from accidentally reconnecting to an old session. However, if the session ID is encoded into a URL, a bookmarked page can find an old session if it still exists. If session IDs are passed using the GET method, you should increase the probability of running garbage collection.

Configuration of PHP Session Management

There are several parameters that can be manipulated to change the behavior of the PHP session management. These parameters are set in the *php.ini* file in the section headed [Session].

session.save_handler

>   This parameter specifies the method used by PHP to store and retrieve session variables. The default value is files, to indicate the use of session files, as described in the previous sections. The other values that this parameter can have are: mm to store and retrieve variables from shared memory, and user to store and

---

* Perhaps the gc_maxlifetime parameter should have been called gc_minlifetime, because the value represents the minimum time garbage collection permits an inactive session to exist. Remember that garbage collection is performed only when a request that initializes a session is made, and then only with the probability set by gc_probability.

retrieve variables with user-defined handlers. In Appendix D we describe how to create user-defined handlers to store session variables in a MySQL database.

session.save_path

This parameter specifies the directory in which session files are saved when the session.save_handler is set to files. The default value is /tmp. When implementing user-defined save_handler methods, the value of this parameter is passed as an argument to the function that opens a session. User-defined handlers are discussed in Appendix D.

session.use_cookies

This parameter determines if PHP sets a cookie to hold the session ID. Setting this parameter to 0 stops PHP from setting cookies and may be considered for the reasons discussed in the previous section. The default value is 1, meaning that a cookie stores the session ID.

session.name

This parameter controls the name of the cookie, GET attribute, or POST attribute that is used to hold the session ID. The default is PHPSESSID, and there is no reason to change this setting unless there is a name collision with another variable.

session.auto_start

With the default value of 0 for this setting, PHP initializes a session only when a session call such as session_start() or session_register() is made. If this parameter is set to 1, sessions are automatically initialized if a session ID is found in the request. Allowing sessions to autostart adds unnecessary overhead if session values aren't required for all scripts.

session.cookie_lifetime

This parameter holds the life of a session cookie in seconds and is used by PHP when setting the expiry date and time of a cookie. The default value of 0 sets up a session cookie that lasts only while the browser program is running. Setting this value to a number of seconds other than 0 sets up the cookie with an expiry date and time. The expiry date and time of the cookie is set as an absolute date and time, calculated by adding the cookie_lifetime value to the current date and time on the server machine.*

session.cookie_path

This parameter sets the valid path for a cookie. The default value is /, which means that browsers include the session cookie in requests for resources in all paths for the cookie's domain. Setting this value to the path of the session-based scripts can reduce the number of requests that need to include the cookie. For example, setting the parameter to /winestore instructs the browser to include

---

* The actual expiry of the cookie is performed by the browser, which compares the expiry date and time of the cookie with the client machine's date and time. If the date and time are incorrectly set on the client, a cookie might expire immediately or persist longer than expected.

the session cookie only with requests that start with *http://www.webdatabasebook.com/winestore/*.

session.cookie_domain

This parameter can override the domain for which the cookie is valid. The default is a blank string, meaning that the cookie is set with the domain of the machine running the web server, and the browser includes the cookie only in requests sent to that domain.

session.cookie_secure

This parameter sets the secure flag of a cookie, which prevents a browser from sending the session cookie over nonencrypted connections. When this setting is 1, the browser sends the session cookie over a network connection that is protected using the Secure Sockets Layer, SSL. We discuss SSL in the next chapter and provide installation instructions in Appendix A. The default value of 0 allows a browser to send the session cookie over encrypted and nonencrypted services.

session.serialize_handler

This parameter sets up the method by which variables are serialized, that is, how they are converted into a stream of bytes suitable for the chosen session store. The default value is php, which indicates use of the standard PHP serialization functions. An alternative is wddx, which uses the WDDX libraries that encode variables as XML.

session.gc_probability

This parameter determines the probability that the garbage collection process will be performed when a session is initialized. The default value of 1 sets a 1% chance of garbage collection. See the discussion in the previous section for a full explanation of garbage collection.

session.gc_maxlifetime

This parameter sets the life of a session in number of seconds. The default value is 1440, or 24 minutes. Garbage collection destroys a session that has been inactive for this period. See the discussion in the previous section for a full explanation of garbage collection.

session.referer_check

This parameter can restrict the creation of sessions to requests that have the HTTP Referer: header field set. This is a useful feature if access to an application is allowed only by following a hypertext link from a particular page such as a welcome page. If the HTTP Referer header field doesn't match the value of this parameter, PHP creates a session, but the session is marked as invalid and unusable. The default value of a blank string applies no restriction.

session.entropy_file

PHP generates the session IDs from a random number seeded by the system date and time. Because the algorithm is known—it can be looked up in the PHP source code—it makes guessing session IDs a little easier. If this parameter is set to the name of a file, the first *n* bytes from that file (where *n* is specified by the session.entropy_length parameter) make the ID less predictable. The default value is left blank, meaning the default seeding method is used. One alternative is to use /dev/urandom, a special Unix device that produces a pseudorandom number.

session.entropy_length

This parameter is the number of bytes to use when generating a session ID from the file specified by session.entropy_file. The default value is 0, the required value when no entropy file is set.

session.cache_limiter

This parameter controls how responses can be cached by the browser. The default is nocache, meaning that PHP sets up the HTTP response to avoid browser caching. PHP sets the HTTP/1.1-defined header field Cache-Control to no-cache, the HTTP/1.0 header field Pragma to no-cache, and—for good measure—the Expires header field to Thu, 19 Nov 1981 08:52:00 GMT. Applications that use sessions—and even stateless web database applications—can be adversely affected when browsers cache pages. The other values allowed, private and public, allow responses to be cached. The distinction between private and public is apparent when a proxy server caches responses. See Appendix B for more details about HTTP caching.

session.cache_expire

This parameter is used when caching is allowed; it sets the expiry date and time of the response to be the current system time plus the parameter value in minutes. The default value is 180.

Case Study: Adding Sessions to the Winestore

In this section we use sessions to improve the user interaction with the client entry <form> developed in Chapter 6. The improvements focus on the interaction when the <form> is submitted and fields don't validate. We modify the scripts to:

- Display error messages on the client entry <form>
- Use session variables to pass back the submitted fields to the <form> generation script, saving the user rekeying all the data to correct the errors

Improving the Client Entry <form>

The client entry <form>, generated by the script shown in Example 6-7, collects client fields to either create a new client or edit the details of an existing client. The script shown in Example 6-8 performs the server-side validation of the client <form> data, and updates or inserts a row in the *customer* table if there are no errors.

If the validation fails, the script shown in Example 6-8 generates a page to display the errors to the user, and the user then follows a hypertext link back to the client entry <form> to reenter the fields. The solution provided by Examples 6-7 and 6-8 suffers three problems:

- The user is forced to reenter the entire client entry <form> from scratch when an error is encountered during validation
- The errors that are encountered during validation are displayed by Example 6-8 and not the entry <form> where they would be useful
- The error page generated by Example 6-8 isn't safe from the reload problem described in Chapter 6

In this section we develop the scripts to make use of session variables to solve these problems. Rather than displaying the error messages on a page generated by the validation script, we make the necessary changes to display the errors in red above the appropriate fields on the client entry <form>, as shown in Figure 8-2.

Both the script that generates the client entry <form> and the script that validates the data need to be modified to use sessions and the session variables. Because the validation script processes the fields collected in the client <form> and generates any associated errors, we look at the changes required for that script first.

The Validation Script

We begin the improvements to the validation script with the changes required to support an error message session variable and then discuss how to record the values to pass back to the client entry <form> generation code. We then present the complete structure of the modified validation script.

Improving error messages

We examine the changes required for error messages first. The validation script checks each variable submitted from the client <form>. Each field is checked with more or less rigor, depending on the purpose of the field. The script shown in Example 6-8 builds up a long formatted error message by concatenating error messages together as they are found. In the modified script, an associative array is registered to hold error messages associated with each field. This allows more flexibility when displaying the error messages.

First, we need to initialize a session and register a variable to hold an array of errors. This is achieved by adding the following lines to the start of the script:

```
// Initialize a session
session_start();
```

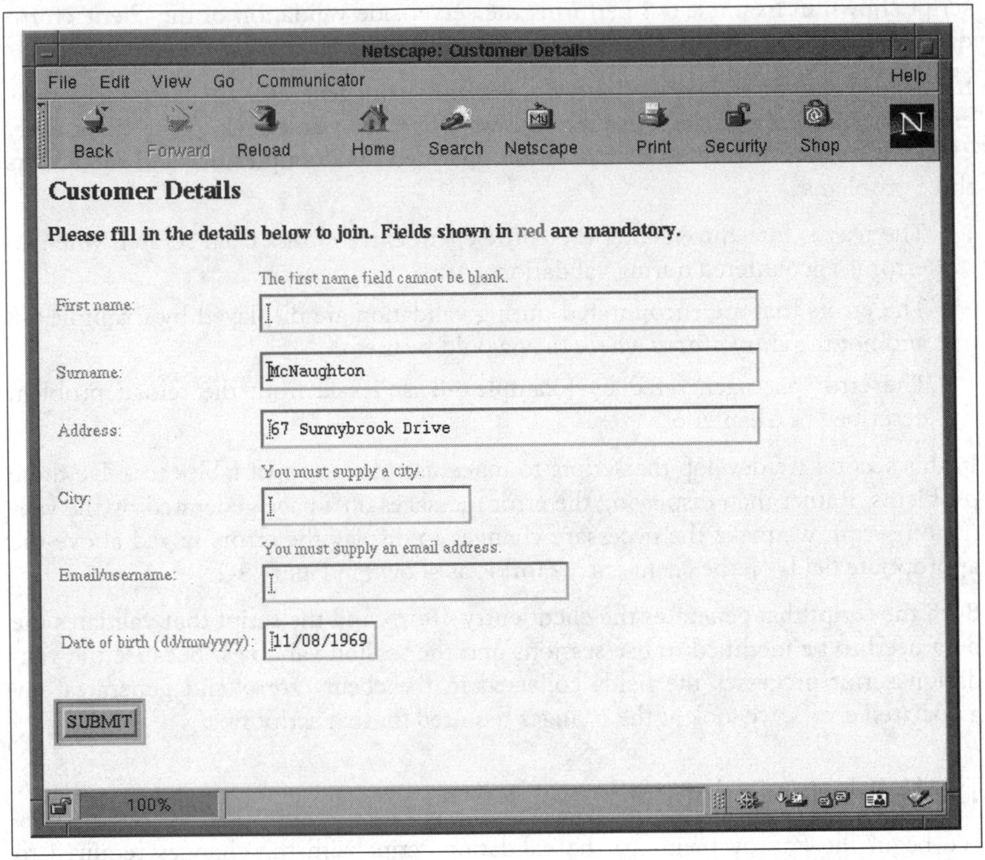

Figure 8-2. Client entry <form> showing error messages placed above the appropriate fields

```
// Register an error array - just in case!
if (!session_is_registered("errors"))
    session_register("errors");

// Clear any errors that might have been
// found previously
$errors = array();
```

Because this validation script may be called several times in a session, any errors that may have been recorded previously need to be cleared. This is the reason for setting the $errors value to a new, empty array.

The script checks each variable and adds an error message to the associative array $errors if an error is encountered. The error message is indexed by the name of the field being checked. For example, the validation of the surname is coded as:

```
// Validate the Surname
if (empty($formVars["surname"]))
    // the user's surname cannot be a null string
```

```
        $errors["surname"] =
          "The surname field cannot be blank.";
```

Once all the fields have been validated, you can test the size of the array $errors to determine if any errors were encountered. If the size of the $errors array is 0, you create or update the row as before. If there are any error messages in the array, you need to display them.

```
// Now the script has finished the validation,
// check if there were any errors
if (count($errors))
{
    // There are errors. Relocate back to the
    // client form
    header("Location: example.8-5.php");
    exit;
}
```

In Example 6-8, the script itself displays any errors, and because the request contains variables in a POST method request, the resulting page suffers from the reload problem discussed in Chapter 6. In a nonsession-based environment, this problem can't be solved with a Location: header field, as the error messages are lost. In the validation script developed here, we relocate back to the client entry <form>—shown later, in Example 8-5—and let it display the errors held in the session variable $errors. We show the changes that allow the client entry <form> to display error messages in the next section.

Saving last-entered values as a session variable

We now develop the script to pass the field data from the validation script back to the client entry <form> to avoid rekeying when an error occurs. The script is modified by saving the user-entered data in another session variable, the associative array $formVars. The client details <form> already uses an array, $formVars, to populate the entry fields from a *customer* record when editing an existing client. By setting the $formVars session variable in the validation script, the client entry <form> populates the <input> fields with the values that were last entered.

The following code—inserted just after $errors is registered as a session variable—registers the array $formVars and then loops through each user-entered variable, setting a value in the array, indexed by the name of the variable. Note that the clean( ) function described in Chapter 5 is used to secure the user data.

```
// Set up a $formVars array with the POST variables
// and register with the session.
if (!session_is_registered("formVars"))
    session_register("formVars");

foreach($HTTP_POST_VARS as $varname => $value)
    $formVars[$varname] = trim(clean($value, 50));
```

When the modified client entry `<form>` is run, the most recent values entered from the session variable $formVars are shown.

While the $HTTP_POST_VARS associative array can be stored in a session and accessed like any other session variable, there is a catch. The value of $HTTP_POST_VARS is determined by PHP before scripts are run. If a session has registered a variable with the name $HTTP_POST_VARS, the values held in $HTTP_POST_VARS that were set up by PHP—as a result of processing a POST request—are overwritten by the session variable.

If register_globals is enabled in *php.ini*, the GET or POST variables PHP sets up can also be overwritten by session variables with the same name.

The safe way to read cookies, GET, and POST variables that have name conflicts is to use the $HTTP_COOKIE_VARS, $HTTP_GET_VARS, and $HTTP_POST_VARS associative arrays, as discussed in Chapter 6.

The final change needed in Example 6-8 is to destroy the session when the script successfully saved a row in the *customer* table:

```
// Clear the session
session_destroy();
```

The final validation script

Example 8-4 shows the final validation script derived from Example 6-8.

Example 8-4. The complete validation script derived from Example 6-8

```php
<?php
  include 'db.inc';
  include 'error.inc';

  // Initialize a session
  session_start();

  // Register an error array - just in case!
  if (!session_is_registered("errors"))
    session_register("errors");

  // Clear any errors that might have been
  // found previously
  $errors = array();

  // Set up a $formVars array with the POST variables
  // and register with the session.
  if (!session_is_registered("formVars"))
    session_register("formVars");

  foreach($HTTP_POST_VARS as $varname => $value)
    $formVars[$varname] = trim(clean($value, 50));
```

```
// Vaildate the firstName
if (empty($formVars["firstName"]))
    // First name cannot be a null string
    $errors["firstName"] =
        "The first name field cannot be blank.";

// Validate the Surname
if (empty($formVars["surname"]))
    // the user's surname cannot be a null string
    $errors["surname"] =
        "The surname field cannot be blank.";

// Validate the Address
if (empty($formVars["address1"]))
    // all the fields of the address cannot be null
    $errors["address"] =
        "You must supply at least one address line.";

// Validate the City
if (empty($formVars["city"]))
    // the user's city cannot be a null string
    $errors["city"] = "You must supply a city.";

// Validate Date of Birth
if (empty($formVars["dob"]))
    // the user's date of birth cannot be a
    // null string
    $errors["dob"] =
        "You must supply a date of birth.";

elseif (!ereg("^([0-9]{2})/([0-9]{2})/([0-9]{4})$",
        $formVars["dob"],
        $parts))
    // Check the format
    $errors["dob"] =
        "The date of birth is not a valid date " .
        "in the format DD/MM/YYYY";

if (empty($formVars["email"]))
    // the user's email cannot be a null string
    $errors["email"] =
        "You must supply an email address.";

// Now the script has finished the validation,
// check if there were any errors
if (count($errors))
{
    // There are errors.  Relocate back to the
    // client form
    header("Location: example.8-5.php");
    exit;
}
```

```php
// If we made it here, then the data is valid

if (!($connection = @ mysql_pconnect($hostName,
                                      $username,
                                      $password)))
   showerror();

if (!mysql_select_db($databaseName, $connection))
   showerror();

// Reassemble the date of birth into database format
$dob = " \"$parts[3]-$parts[2]-$parts[1]\"";

// Is this an update?
if (!empty($custID))
{
  $query = "UPDATE customer SET " .
    "surname = \"" . $formVars["surname"] . "\", " .
    "firstname = \"" . $formVars["firstName"] . "\", " .
    "addressline1 = \"" .
               $formVars["address1"] . "\", " .
    "city = \"" . $formVars["city"] . "\", " .
    "email = \"" . $formVars["email"] . "\", " .
    "birth_date = " . $dob .
    " WHERE cust_id = $custID";
}
else
   // Create a query to insert the customer
   $query = "INSERT INTO customer SET" .
     "cust_id = NULL, " .
     "surname = \"" . $formVars["surname"] . "\", " .
     "firstname = \"" .
                $formVars["firstName"] . "\", " .
     "addressline1 = \"" .
                $formVars["address1"] . "\", " .
     "city = \"" . $formVars["city"] . "\", " .
     "email = \"" . $formVars["email"] . "\", " .
     "birth_date = $dob";

// Run the query on the customer table
if (!(@ mysql_query ($query, $connection)))
   showerror();

// Is this an insert?
if (empty($custID))
// Find out the cust_id of the new customer
$custID = mysql_insert_id();

// Clear the session
session_destroy();
```

```
 // Now show the customer receipt
 header("Location: customer_receipt.php?custID=$custID");
?>
```

The Client Entry <form> Script

Now let's turn to the changes required for the script that generates the client entry
<form> shown in Example 6-7. In the last section, we set up two session variables:
the associative array $errors used to hold a list of error messages found in the vali-
dation script and the associative array $formVars used to hold the POST variables
you processed.

Displaying previously entered values

As Example 6-7 already sets the value attribute of the <input> elements from the
array $formVars, there are no changes needed to display previously entered values;
Example 6-7 uses $formVars when displaying the current values of clients from the
customer table. By setting $formVars as a session variable, Example 6-7 displays the
values passed back from the validation script with each <input> field.

Displaying error messages

Changes are required to display the errors that are saved in the session variable
$errors in the validation script. We have added the function fieldError() to help
display the error messages above the <input> fields. The function takes two parameters: $errors, which is the associative array of error messages, and $fieldName, which
is the index into the array.

```
 function fieldError($fieldName, $errors)
 {
   if (isset($errors[$fieldName]))
     echo
      "<font color=RED>$errors[$fieldName]</font><br>";
 }
```

This function tests if the indexed error message exists and, if so, echoes an appropriately formatted error message. When each <input> element is displayed, a call is
made to the fieldError() function, as shown for the firstName and surname fields:

```
 <tr>
   <td><font color="red">First name:</font></td>
   <td><? echo fieldError("firstName", $errors); ?>
      <input type="text" name="firstName"
         value="<? echo $formVars["firstName"]; ?>"
         size=50></td>
 </tr>
 <tr>
   <td><font color="red">Surname:</font></td>
   <td><? echo fieldError("surname", $errors); ?>
```

```
<input type="text" name="surname"
    value="<? echo $formVars["surname"]; ?>"
    size=50></td>
</tr>
```

Figure 8-2 shows the final results: a client entry <form> with error messages placed over the corresponding fields.

The final client entry script

Example 8-5 shows the complete client entry script, derived from Example 6-7, that displays the previous <form> values and the error messages held in session variables.

Example 8-5. Client entry form derived from Example 6-7

```php
<?php
  include 'db.inc';
  include 'error.inc';

  function fieldError($fieldName, $errors)
  {
    if (isset($errors[$fieldName]))
      echo
        "<font color=RED>$errors[$fieldName]</font><br>";
  }

  // Connect to a session.
  // Up to three session variables can be registered:
  // (1) $formVars - previously entered data that has
  //     failed validation
  // (2) $errors - an array of error messages, up to
  //     one per widget
  // (3) $custID - the customer ID of a customer
  //     to edit
  session_start();

  // $custID can also be passed as a GET parameter
  // If it is, override any session variable
  if (!empty($HTTP_GET_VARS["custID"]))
    $custID = clean($HTTP_GET_VARS["custID"], 5);

  // Has a custID been provided and are there no errors?
  // If so, retrieve the customer details for editing.
  if (!empty($custID) && empty($errors))
  {
    // Register the custID as a session variable
    if (!session_is_registered("custID"))
      session_register("custID");

    if (!($connection = @ mysql_pconnect($hostName,
                                         $username,
                                         $password)))
      die("Could not connect to database");
```

Example 8-5. Client entry form derived from Example 6-7 (continued)

```php
        if (!mysql_select_db($databaseName, $connection))
            showerror();

        $query = "SELECT * FROM customer
                    WHERE cust_id = " . $custID;

        if (!($result = @ mysql_query($query, $connection)))
            showerror();

        $row = mysql_fetch_array($result);

        // Reset $formVars, since we're loading from
        // the customer table
        $formVars = array();

        // Load all the form variables with customer data
        $formVars["surname"] = $row["surname"];
        $formVars["firstName"] = $row["firstname"];
        $formVars["address1"] = $row["addressline1"];
        $formVars["city"] = $row["city"];
        $formVars["email"] = $row["email"];
        $formVars["dob"] = $row["birth_date"];
        $formVars["dob"] =
                substr($formVars["dob"], 8, 2) . "/" .
                substr($formVars["dob"], 5, 2) . "/" .
                substr($formVars["dob"], 0, 4);
    }
?>
<!DOCTYPE HTML PUBLIC
    "-//W3C//DTD HTML 4.0 Transitional//EN"
    "http://www.w3.org/TR/html4/loose.dtd" >
<html>
<head><title>Customer Details</title></head>
<body bgcolor="white">
<form method="post" action="example.8-4.php">
<h1>Customer Details</h1>
<?php
    // Show meaningful instructions for UPDATE or INSERT
    if (!empty($custID))
        echo "<h3>Please amend your details below as
                required. Fields shown in
                <font color=\"red\">red</font> are
                mandatory.</h3>";
    else
        echo "<h3>Please fill in the details below to
                join. Fields shown in
                <font color=\"red\">red</font> are
                mandatory.</h3>";
?>
<table>
<col span="1" align="right">
```

Example 8-5. Client entry form derived from Example 6-7 (continued)

```
<tr><td><font color="red">First name:</font></td>
    <td><? echo fieldError("firstName", $errors); ?>
        <input type="text" name="firstName"
            value="<? echo $formVars["firstName"]; ?>"
            size=50></td>
</tr>
<tr><td><font color="red">Surname:</font></td>
    <td><? echo fieldError("surname", $errors); ?>
        <input type="text" name="surname"
            value="<? echo $formVars["surname"]; ?>"
            size=50></td>
</tr>
<tr><td><font color="red">Address:</font></td>
    <td><? echo fieldError("address", $errors); ?>
        <input type="text" name="address1"
            value="<? echo $formVars["address1"]; ?>"
            size=50><td>
</tr>
<tr><td><font color="red">City:</font></td>
    <td><? echo fieldError("city", $errors); ?>
        <input type="text" name="city"
            value="<? echo $formVars["city"]; ?>"
            size=20><td>
</tr>
<tr><td><font color="red">Email/username:</font></td>
    <td><? echo fieldError("email", $errors); ?>
        <input type="text" name="email"
            value="<? echo $formVars["email"]; ?>"
            size=30><td>
</tr>
<tr><td>
    <font color="red">Date of birth (dd/mm/yyyy):</font>
    </td>
    <td><? echo fieldError("dob", $errors); ?>
        <input type="text" name="dob"
            value="<? echo $formVars["dob"]; ?>"
            size=10><td>
</tr>
</table><br>
<input type="submit" value="SUBMIT">
</form>
</body>
</html>
```

When to Use Sessions

So far in this chapter we have described how to implement stateful applications using sessions, but we have not discussed when they should or should not be used. Sessions allow some kinds of applications to be developed that otherwise would be difficult to implement on the Web. However, because HTTP is a stateless protocol, building a stateful application can present problems and restrictions. Avoiding the need to maintain state information is often a desirable goal. In this section we list some reasons sessions are used and some reasons to avoid them.

Reasons to Use Sessions

Sessions can be used in web database applications for several reasons. Many traditional database applications use sessions to help control user interaction, while other applications use sessions to reduce server processing.

Performance

In a stateless environment, an application may need to repeat an expensive operation. An example might be a financial calculation that requires many SQL statements and calls to mathematics libraries before displaying the results on several web pages. An application that uses a session variable to remember the result exposes the user, and the server, to the cost of the calculation only once.

Sequence of interaction

Often a database application—or indeed any application—needs to present a series of screens in a controlled order. One style of application—known as a *wizard*—guides a user through what would otherwise be a complex task with a series of screens. Wizards are sometimes used for complex configurations, such as some software installations, and often alter the flow of screens based on user input. Some applications require that a user enter via a known page. Applications, such as online banking, often force a user to enter via a login page rather than allow access directly to a function such as funds transfer.

Intermediate results

Many database applications validate data before creating or updating a record in the database, preventing erroneous data from being saved. Sessions can keep the intermediate data, so that incomplete data can be edited—rather that rekeyed—when errors are detected. Earlier in this chapter we used sessions to improve the interaction between the client entry <form> and validation scripts of the winestore application. In the case study, the fields entered by the user are held in an array as a session variable until the validation is successful. Another example where intermediate results can be used is when a database application collects and validates data for a single record over a number of fill-in forms. A shopping cart is an example where complete data may not be created until a user requests a purchase. The winestore application doesn't implement the shopping cart this way; rather, a shopping cart is implemented by creating a row in the *orders* table and adding rows to the *items* table as items are selected. The winestore application then needs to store only the cust_id and the order_no—the combination is the primary key of the *orders* table—as session variables while a shopping cart is being used. We develop the shopping cart in Chapter 11.

Personalization

Sessions can personalize a web site. Personalization not only includes background color or layout alternatives, but can include recording a user's interests and modifying searches. The winestore application can record favorite regions or a buyer's price range as session variables; each query could then be modified to reflect these settings. A result screen displays "wines from your favorite regions within your budget" before displaying other wines.

Reasons to Avoid Sessions

The reasons to avoid sessions focus mainly on the stateless nature of HTTP. The features of HTTP that support browsing access to a disparate collection of resources don't support stateful applications. Stateful applications work over the Web often at the expense of HTTP features.

Need for centralized session store

In an application that uses sessions, each HTTP request needs to be processed in the context of the session variables to which that request belongs. The state information recorded as the result of one request needs to be available to subsequent requests. Most applications that implement sessions store session variables in the middle tier. Once a session is created, all subsequent requests must be processed on the web server that holds the session variables. This requirement prevents such applications from using HTTP to distribute requests across multiple servers and therefore can't easily scale horizontally to handle large numbers of requests.* One way for a web database application to allow multiple web servers is to store session variables in the database tier. This approach is described in Appendix D, where we provide a PHP and MySQL implementation of a database-tier session store.

Performance

When a server that offers session management processes a request, there is the unavoidable overhead of identifying and accessing session variables. The session overhead results in longer processing times for requests, which affects the performance and capacity of a site. While sessions can improve application performance—for example, a session can keep the result of an expensive operation—the gains may

---

* Scaling up an application—increasing the number of requests an application can respond to in a given period—can be achieved horizontally by providing more machines, and vertically by providing a single bigger, faster, or more efficient machine.

be limited and outweighed by the extra processing required. Servers that manage session variables in memory require more memory. As the amount of memory used by the web server grows, a system may need to move portions of memory to disk—an operation known as *swapping*. Swapping memory in and out of disk storage is slow and can severely degrade the performance of a server. Servers that use files—such as the default PHP session management—incur the cost of reading and writing a file on disk each time a session is accessed.

Timeouts

Sessions can also cause synchronization problems. Because HTTP is stateless, there is no way of knowing when a user has really finished with an application. Other network applications can catch the fact that a connection has been dropped and clean up the state that was held on behalf of that user, even if the user did not use a logout procedure (such as typing exit or clicking on a logout button). The Telnet application is such an example where a user makes a connection to a system over the Internet. However, unlike HTTP, the TCP/IP connection for Telnet is kept for the length of the session, and if the connection is lost—say, if the client's PC crashes or the power is lost—the user is logged out of the remote system. With a session over the Web, the server doesn't know about these events and has to make a decision as to how long to keep the session information. In the case of PHP session management, a garbage collection scheme is used, as we discussed earlier in this chapter.

Bookmark restrictions

Because HTTP is stateless, browsers allow users to save URLs as a list of bookmarks or favorite sites. The user can return to a web site at a later date by simply selecting a bookmarked URL. Web sites that provide weather forecasts, stock prices, and even search results from a web search engine are examples of the sites a user might want to bookmark. Consider the URL for a fictional site that provides stock prices:

```
http://www.someexchange.com/stockprice.php?code=SIMCO
```

The URL encodes a query that identifies a particular stock, and presumably, the script *stockprice.php* uses the query to display the current stock price of the company. The URL can be bookmarked because it contains all that is needed to generate the stock price page for the given company code. An alternative site may collect the company code using a <form> and, when the form is submitted, use a session variable to hold the company code as a query. The script that generates the stock price page reads the session variable, looks up the current price, and generates the result for the entered company code. If a user bookmarks the session-based stock price page and comes back in a week, the session that stored the company code is unlikely to still exist, and the script fails to display the desired company's stock price.

Sometimes bookmarking a page makes no sense. Consider an online banking application that allows transfer of funds between two accounts. A user would log in to the application, then request the transfer page that collects the source and target account details in a <form>. When that <form> is submitted, a confirmation page is shown without actually performing the transaction. Revisiting this page through a bookmark has no meaning if the transaction was subsequently confirmed or canceled. Generally, the pages generated from applications such as online banking can't be bookmarked because of the reliance on session variables. Session management in such applications is often tied closely to authentication, a topic explored further in Chapter 9.

Security

Sessions can provide a way for a hacker to break into a system. Sessions can be open to hijacking; a hacker can take over after a legitimate user has logged into an application. There is much debate about the security of session-based applications on the Web, and we discuss some issues of session security in the next chapter.

CHAPTER 9

Authentication and Security

There are many database applications in which restrictions need to be applied to control user access. Some applications deal with sensitive information such as bank account details, while others provide information or services only to paying customers. These applications need to authenticate and authorize user requests, typically by collecting a username and password, and checking these against a list of valid users. As well as authenticating those who have access to a service, web applications often need to protect the data that is transmitted over the Internet from those who shouldn't see it.

In this chapter we discuss the techniques used to build web database applications that authenticate, authorize, and protect the data that is transmitted over the Web. The topics covered in this chapter include:

- How HTTP authentication works and how it can be used with Apache and PHP
- Writing PHP scripts to manage user authentication and authorization
- Writing PHP scripts that authenticate users against a table in a database
- The practical aspects of building session-based web database applications to authenticate users, including techniques that don't use HTTP authentication
- A case study example that develops an authentication framework, demonstrating many of the techniques presented in this chapter
- The features of the encryption services provided by the Secure Sockets Layer

HTTP Authentication

The HTTP standard provides support to authenticate and authorize user access. When a browser sends an HTTP request for a resource that requires authentication, a server can challenge the request by sending a response with the status code of 401 Unauthorized. When an unauthorized response is received, the browser presents a dialog box that collects a username and password; a dialog box presented by

Netscape is shown in Figure 9-1. After the username and password have been entered, the browser then resends the request containing an extra header field that encodes the user credentials.

Figure 9-1. Netscape requests a username and password

This support doesn't authenticate a user or provide authorization to access a resource or service. The server needs the encoded username and password to establish the user's credentials and then decide if the user is authorized to receive the requested resource. How the server performs the authentication depends on the application. An Apache server, configured to protect resources with authentication, uses a file that contains a list of usernames and encrypted passwords, while other applications might use a table of users in a database.

How HTTP Authentication Works

Figure 9-2 shows the interaction between a web browser and a web server when a request is challenged The browser sends a request for a resource stored on the server. The server sends back a challenge response with the status code set to 401 Unauthorized, and the header field WWW-Authenticate. The WWW-Authenticate field contains parameters that instruct the browser on how to meet the challenge. The browser may need to prompt for a username and password to meet the challenge. The browser then resends the request, including the Authorization header field that contains the credentials the server requires.

Example 9-1 shows the HTTP response sent from an Apache server when a request is made for a resource that requires authentication.

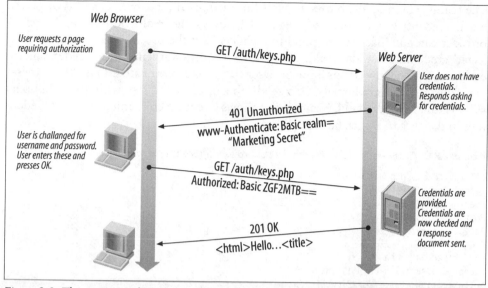

Figure 9-2. The sequence of HTTP requests and responses when an unauthorized page is requested

Example 9-1. An unauthorized response sent by Apache

```
HTTP/1.1 401 Authorization Required
Date: Mon, 21 May 2001 23:40:54 GMT
Server: Apache/1.3.19 (Unix) PHP/4.0.5
WWW-Authenticate: Basic realm="Marketing Secret"
Connection: close
Content-Type: text/html; charset=iso-8859-1

<!DOCTYPE HTML PUBLIC "-//IETF//DTD HTML 2.0//EN">
<HTML><HEAD>
<TITLE>401 Authorization Required</TITLE>
</HEAD><BODY>
<H1>Authorization Required</H1>
This server could not verify that you
are authorized to access the document
requested. Either you supplied the wrong
credentials (e.g., bad password), or your
browser doesn't understand how to supply
the credentials required.<P>
<HR>
<ADDRESS>Apache/1.3.19 Server at dexter Port 80</ADDRESS>
</BODY></HTML>
```

The WWW-Authenticate header field contains the *challenge method*, the method by which the browser collects and encodes the user credentials. In the example the method is set to Basic. The header field also contains the name of the realm the authentication applies to.

The realm is used by the browser to label usernames and passwords and is displayed when credentials are collected; Figure 9-1 shows the realm *Marketing Secret*. A browser can automatically respond to a challenge if the browser has previously collected credentials for the realm. The browser stores authentication credentials for each realm it encounters until the browser program is terminated. Once the browser has collected the credentials, it resends the original request with the additional `Authorization` header field. Example 9-2 shows a request containing encoded credentials in the `Authorization` header field.

Example 9-2. An authorized request sent by the browser after the credentials have been collected

```
GET /auth/keys.php HTTP/1.0
Connection: Keep-Alive
User-Agent: Mozilla/4.51 [en] (WinNT; I)
Host: localhost
Accept: image/gif, image/jpeg, image/pjpeg, image/png, */*
Accept-Encoding: gzip
Accept-Language: en
Accept-Charset: iso-8859-1,*,utf-8
Authorization: Basic ZGF2ZTpwbGF0eXB1cw==
```

The `Basic` encoding is just that: basic! The string that is encoded into the `Authorization` header field is simply the username and the password separated by a colon character and then base-64 encoded. Base-64 encoding isn't designed to protect data; rather it allows binary data to be transmitted over a network, and therefore provides no real protection of the username and password. The `Basic` encoding of the credentials provides protection from casual inspection only.

Some web servers, including Apache, support the `Digest` encoding method. The `Digest` method is more secure than the `Basic` method because the password isn't sent over the network. When the `Digest` method is used, the server generates a random string to send with the authorization challenge. The browser then encrypts the random string using the password provided by the user as an encryption key. The encrypted string is sent back to the server in the `Authorization` header field, as the resource is rerequested. The server uses a copy of the password stored at the server to encrypt the same random string and compares it to the encrypted string that has just arrived. If they match, the server has authenticated the user. The advantage is that only the encrypted random string is exchanged, not the user password.

Both the web server and the browser need to support the `Digest` encoding method. Unfortunately, most browsers support only `Basic`. Microsoft has developed a proprietary method for use with HTTP authentication called `NTLM` that is supported only by Internet Explorer and Microsoft's IIS web server.

While the `Basic` encoding method provides no real security, the Secure Sockets Layer (SSL) protocol can protect the HTTP requests and responses sent between browsers and servers. Because of SSL, there is little pressure on browser builders to implement more secure schemes. For web database applications that transmit sensitive information, such as passwords, we recommend SSL be used. We discuss SSL later in this chapter.

Using Apache to Authenticate

The simplest method to restrict access to an application is to use the Apache authentication support. The Apache server can easily be configured to use HTTP authentication to protect the resources it serves. Apache allows authentication to be set up on a directory-by-directory basis by adding parameters to the Directory setting in the *httpd.conf* configuration file. The following example shows part of an *httpd.conf* file that protects the resources—HTML files, PHP scripts, images, and so on—stored in the */usr/local/apache/htdocs/auth* directory:

```
# Set up an authenticated directory
<Directory "/usr/local/apache/htdocs/auth">
   AuthType Basic
   AuthName "Secret Mens Business"
   AuthUserFile /usr/local/apache/allow.users
   require hugh, dave, jim
</Directory>
```

If PHP scripts and other sensitive resources are placed within a protected directory, a user can access the application only by first passing the Apache authentication. The Apache server responds with a challenge to unauthorized requests for any resources in the protected directory. The AuthType is set to Basic to indicate the method that encodes the username and password collected from the browser, and the AuthName is set to the name of the realm. Apache authorizes users who are listed in the require setting by checking the username and password against those held in the AuthUserFile. There are other parameters that aren't discussed here; you should refer to the Apache references listed in Appendix E for full configuration details.

For simple web database applications, Apache authentication provides a suitable solution. When usernames and passwords need to be checked against a database or some other source, or when HTTP authentication can't meet the needs of the application, authentication can be managed by PHP. The next section describes how PHP can manage HTTP authentication directly without configuring Apache. Later, in the "Web Database Applications and Authentication" section, we describe how to provide authentication without using HTTP authentication support.

HTTP Authentication with PHP

PHP can access the credentials collected using the HTTP mechanisms introduced in the last section, and can actually manage the HTTP authentication without relying on Apache's configuration.

Access to User Credentials from PHP

PHP provides access to the encoded credentials from the HTTP Authorized header field through the global variables $PHP_AUTH_USER, $PHP_AUTH_PW, and $PHP_AUTH_TYPE. PHP initializes the variable $PHP_AUTH_USER with the username and $PHP_AUTH_PW with the password entered into the browser authentication dialog box. The global variable $PHP_AUTH_TYPE is initialized with the encoding type used by the browser; typically this value is set to Basic.

The script shown in Example 9-3 reads the authentication global variables and displays them in the body of the response. For the PHP code in Example 9-3 to display the authentication credentials, the script needs to be requested after a user has been challenged for a username and password. This happens if the file containing the script is placed within a directory configured by Apache to require authentication.

Example 9-3. PHP access to authentication

```
<!DOCTYPE HTML PUBLIC
    "-//W3C//DTD HTML 4.0 Transitional//EN"
    "http://www.w3.org/TR/html4/loose.dtd" >
<html>
  <head><title>Authentication</title></head>
  <body>
    <h2>Hi there <?=$PHP_AUTH_USER?></h2>

    <p>Thank you for your password
             '<?=$PHP_AUTH_PW?>'!

  </body>
</html>
```

Applications can use the encoded credentials to support features that rely on identifying the user. For example, an application that charges on a per-page view basis might use the $PHP_AUTH_USER variable when recording an access to a particular page. In this way, Apache can provide the authentication, and the application records the users' usage. While this approach removes the need to write any PHP code to implement authentication, users and passwords need to be maintained in an Apache password file. In the next section we describe how to manage HTTP authentication from within a PHP script, thus relieving Apache of authentication responsibilities and allowing different logic to be applied to the authorization of requests.

Managing HTTP Authentication with PHP

Rather than configuring Apache to authenticate requests, PHP scripts can manage the HTTP authentication challenge directly. Scripts can be written to test the $PHP_AUTH_USER and $PHP_AUTH_PW variables and send a response containing the WWW-Authenticate header to challenge the browser. When a request contains a username and password, the script can authenticate and authorize the request using any logic

that is required. In Example 9-4 the user credentials set in the $PHP_AUTH_USER and
$PHP_AUTH_PW variables are passed to the function authenticated( ). This function
uses the unsophisticated authentication scheme of checking that the password is the
same as the username. In the next section we show how to implement a secure
scheme that stores passwords in a database.

Example 9-4. Script generates an unauthorized response if credentials aren't in request

```php
<?php
function authenticated($username, $password)
{
  // If either the username or the password are
  // not set, the user is not authenticated
  if (!isset($username) || !isset($password))
    return false;

  // If the username is the same as the password
  // then the user is authenticated
  if ($username == $password)
    return true;
  else
    return false;
}

//Main --------

if(!authenticated($PHP_AUTH_USER, $PHP_AUTH_PW))
{
  // No credentials found - send an unauthorized
  // challenge response
  header("WWW-Authenticate: Basic realm=\"Flat Foot\"");
  header("HTTP/1.0 401 Unauthorized");

  // Set up the body of the response that is
  // displayed if the user cancels the challenge
?>
<!DOCTYPE HTML PUBLIC
  "-//W3C//DTD HTML 4.0 Transitional//EN"
  "http://www.w3.org/TR/html4/loose.dtd" >
 <html>
   <head>
     <title>Web Database Applications</title>
   </head>
   <body>
     <h2>You need a username and password to
             access this service</h2>
     <p>If you have lost or forgotten your
             password, tough!
   </body>
 </html>
 <?php

  exit;
```

```
}

// The response to authorized users
?>
<!DOCTYPE HTML PUBLIC
   "-//W3C//DTD HTML 4.0 Transitional//EN"
   "http://www.w3.org/TR/html4/loose.dtd" >
<html>
  <head>
    <title>Web Database Applications</title>
  </head>
  <body>
    <h2>Welcome!</h2>
  </body>
</html>
```

The authenticated( ) function returns false if either the $username or $password hasn't been set, or if the two values aren't the same. If the user credentials fail the test, you respond with the header field WWW-Authenticate with the encoding scheme Basic and the realm name Flat Foot. You can also set the response line to include the status code 401 Unauthorized. The PHP manual suggests sending the WWW-Authenticate header before the HTTP/1.0 401 Unauthorized header to avoid problems with some versions of Internet Explorer browsers.

The first time a browser requests this page, the script sends a challenge response containing the 401 Unauthorized header field. If the user cancels the authentication challenge, usually by clicking the cancel button in a dialog box that collects the credentials, the HTML encoded in the challenge response is displayed.

While the script shown in Example 9-4 duplicates much of the HTML used for the authorized response and the challenge response, you can't simplify the script by putting the common HTML at the start of the file. Because the script calls the header( ) function when credentials aren't included in the request or the supplied credentials don't authenticate, you can't output any of the response body until you know if the user has authenticated.

Authorizing User Access

Writing PHP scripts to manage the authentication process allows for flexible authorization logic to be applied when processing a request. Authenticating a user successfully against a list or table of known users doesn't automatically authorize that user to access an application. For example, an application might apply restrictions based on group membership: a user belonging to the DIRECTORS group gets to see the reports from the budget database, while others can't. The number of schemes for restricting access is limited only by a developer's imagination or more often by that of the marketing department. A user of a subscription-based service might supply a correct username and password, but be denied access when a fee is 14 days overdue. Access might be denied on Thursday evenings when system maintenance is performed. Implementing such authorization schemes requires designing the appropriate user table or tables.

There are several HTTP status codes that are appropriate to use when denying access to a user. Earlier, we used the response code of 401 Unauthorized to control HTTP authentication. The response status code of 403 Forbidden is appropriate if an explanation as to why access has been denied is required. Example 9-5 uses the code of 403 Forbidden. The HTTP/1.1 standard describes 17 4xx status codes that have various meanings. The infamous 404 Not Found is returned by Apache if the requested resource doesn't exist, and a PHP script can return this code if the exact reason for the refusal needs to be hidden. The code 402 Payment Required has been included, but the HTTP standard has not provided an interpretation of how it should be used.

Limits placed on IP addresses

A PHP script can access the IP address from which a request was sent by inspecting the server variable $REMOTE_ADDR. This remote address can restrict access. A simple example allows access only from a specific IP address. This can be used to implement administration scripts that allow access only from a specific computer. A variation, shown in Example 9-5, is to allow access to users on a particular network subnet. Example 9-5 limits access to the main content of the script to requests sent from clients with a range of IP addresses that begin with 141.190.17.

Example 9-5. PHP script that forbids access from browsers outside an IP subnet

```php
<?php
if(strncmp("141.190.17", $REMOTE_ADDR, 10) != 0)
{
    header("HTTP/1.0 403 Forbidden");
  ?>
  <!DOCTYPE HTML PUBLIC
      "-//W3C//DTD HTML 4.0 Transitional//EN"
      "http://www.w3.org/TR/html4/loose.dtd" >
  <html>
    <head><title>Marketing Department</title></head>
    <body>
      <h2>403 Forbidden</h2>
      <p>You cannot access this page from outside
         the Marketing Department.
    </body>
  </html>
  <?
  exit;
}
?>
<!DOCTYPE HTML PUBLIC
    "-//W3C//DTD HTML 4.0 Transitional//EN"
```

```
    "http://www.w3.org/TR/html4/loose.dtd" >
<html>
  <head><title>Marketing Department</title></head>
  <body>
    <h2>Marketing secrets!</h2>
    <p>Need new development team - the old one
      says <em>No</em> far too often.
  </body>
</html>
```

Another limit that can be applied using the IP address is to help prevent session hijacking—a problem discussed later in this chapter.

Authentication Using a Database

In a web database application, usernames and passwords can be stored in a table rather than a file. This moves the data stored about users into a database and can simplify the management of an application. In this section we develop techniques to store usernames and passwords securely in a table.

Later in this chapter we continue the development of the winestore application using the *customer* table as a source of authentication details. To demonstrate the principles, consider the following simple table:

```
CREATE TABLE users (
  user_name varchar(10) not null,
  password varchar(15) not null,
  PRIMARY KEY (user_name),
  KEY password (password)
);
```

This table defines two attributes: user_name and password. The user_name must be unique, and in the *users* table, it is defined as the primary key. The password attribute needs to be indexed as you formulate queries on the password in the authentication script developed later in this section. It's unwise to store user passwords as plain text in this table. There are many ways to retrieve passwords from a database, and even with good web site practices and policies, storing plain-text passwords is a security risk.

PHP provides the crypt( ) function that can protect passwords stored in a database:

string crypt(string *plainText* [, string *salt*])
> Returns an encrypted string using the Unix *DES encryption* method. The plain text to be encrypted is passed as the first argument, with an optional second argument used to salt the DES encryption algorithm. By default, the *salt* is a two-character string used by DES to make the encrypted string harder to crack; PHP generates a random salt if one isn't provided. The first two characters of the returned value is the salt used in the encryption process. This function is

one-way: the returned value can't be decrypted back into the original string. There are several PHP constants that control the encryption process, and the default behavior is assumed in the examples. You should consult the PHP manual for more details.

Rather than encrypt the password directly, the crypt( ) function encrypts a *digest* of the password, and the result is a constant length irrespective of the password length. A two-character seed or *salt* is used by the crypt( ) function to effectively provide an encryption key. If a salt isn't passed to the function, crypt( ) generates its own random string.

A common strategy for storing passwords uses the first two characters of the username as the salt to the crypt( ) function. This method of salting the encryption process helps to hide the cases where two or more users happen to choose the same password. Example 9-6 shows how a password is encrypted using the username to salt the crypt( ) function and updated in a user row. The updatePassword( ) function takes a MySQL connection handle, a username, and a password as parameters. The function creates the encrypted password and executes an UPDATE statement to update the password for the selected user row.

Example 9-6. A function to update a password in the users table

```php
<?php
include "db.inc";

// Update a password in a users table
function updatePassword($connection,
                        $username,
                        $password)
{
  // Use the first two characters of the
  // username as a salt
  $salt = substr($username, 0, 2);

  // Create the encrypted password
  $stored_password = crypt($password, $salt);

  // Update the user row
  $update_query =
    "UPDATE users
     SET password = '$stored_password'
     WHERE user_name = '$username'";

  // Execute the UPDATE
  $result = @ mysql_query ($update_query,
                           $connection)
  or showerror();
}

?>
```

The following SELECT statement shows how rows in the *users* table might look:

```
mysql> SELECT * FROM users;
+-----------+---------------+
| user_name | password      |
+-----------+---------------+
| robin     | roGNvdAjJ1BDw |
| sue       | suRQON4.ZOhO. |
| jill      | jiDKFQigcAGTc |
| margaret  | maNLEWbP2wdY. |
| sally     | saHXb3nOaykJM |
| penny     | pekh5W4yLAyd. |
+-----------+---------------+
6 rows in set (0.00 sec)
```

Because crypt() is one way, once a password is stored, there is no way to read back the original. This prevents desirable features such as reminding a user of his forgotten password. However, importantly, it prevents all but the most determined attempts to get access to the passwords.

When a script needs to authenticate a username and password collected from an authentication challenge, a query is executed to find a user row in the *users* table. Example 9-7 shows the authenticateUser() function that constructs and executes this query. The function is called by passing in a handle to a connected MySQL server and the username and password collected from the authentication challenge. The script begins by testing $username and $password. If neither is set, the function returns false. The $password is then encrypted using the crypt() function with the first two characters from the $username as the salt. A SELECT query is constructed to search the *users* table. A query is then executed that searches for a user row in which the user_name and password attributes have the respective values of $username and the encrypted password. If a row is found, the $username and $password have been authenticated, and the function returns true.

Example 9-7. Authenticating a user against an encrypted password in the users table

```php
<?php
include 'db.inc';

function authenticateUser($connection,
                          $username,
                          $password)
{
  // Test the username and password parameters
  if (!isset($username) || !isset($password))
    return false;

  // Get the two character salt from the
  // username collected from the challenge
  $salt = substr($username, 0, 2);
```

```
// Encrypt the password collected from
// the challenge
$crypted_password = crypt($password, $salt);

// Formulate the SQL find the user
$query = "SELECT password FROM users
             WHERE user_name = '$username'
             AND password = '$crypted_password'";

// Execute the query
$result = @ mysql_query ($query,
                          $connection)
or showerror();

// exactly one row? then we have found the user
if (mysql_num_rows($result) != 1)
  return false;
else
  return true;

}
?>
```

The `authenticateUser( )` function developed in Example 9-7 is likely to be used in many scripts and writing the code to a *authentication.inc* file allows the function to be included in the scripts that require authentication. We could rewrite Example 9-4 to use the database authentication function by including the *authentication.inc* file:

```
<?php
include("authentication.inc");
include("db.inc");
include("error.inc");

// Connect to the MySQL server
// Connect to the Server
if (!($connection = mysql_connect($hostName,
                          $username, $password)))

     die("Could not connect to database");
if (!mysql_selectdb("$databaseName, $connection)
   showerror();

if !authenticateUser($connection,
                     $PHP_AUTH_USER,
                     $PHP_AUTH_PW)))
{
  // No credentials found - send an unauthorized
  // challenge response ...
  header("WWW-Authenticate: Basic realm=\"Flat Foot\"");
  header("HTTP/1.0 401 Unauthorized");
```

```
// ...

  exit;
}

// The HTML response to authorized users ...

?>
```

MySQL encryption

MySQL provides the encryption function password( ) that can be used instead of the crypt( ) function; we introduced this function in Chapter 3. The MySQL password( ) function can be incorporated into the SQL update or insert queries:

```
$update_query =
  "UPDATE users
     SET password = password($password)
     WHERE user_name = '$username'";
```

Like crypt( ), the MySQL password( ) function is a one-way function, but it is simpler to use because it doesn't require a salt string. However, when identical passwords are used, they are stored as identical encrypted strings. Another disadvantage to using the MySQL password( ) function is that the password is transmitted between the web server and the MySQL DBMS in its unencrypted form. We recommend that crypt( ) be used rather than the MySQL password( ) function when building web database applications.

Encrypting other data in a database

The PHP crypt( ) and MySQL password( ) functions can be used only to store passwords, personal identification numbers (PINs), and so on. These functions are one-way: once the original password is encrypted and stored, you can't get it back because there are no corresponding decode functions. These functions can't be used to store sensitive information an application needs to retrieve. For example, when a customer submits an order, the customer's credit-card number needs to be decrypted and used by the application to complete the transaction.

To store sensitive information the application needs to use, you need two-way functions that use a secret key to encrypt and decrypt the data. We discuss encryption briefly later, in the "Protecting Data on the Web" section. One significant problem when using a key to encrypt and decrypt data is the need to securely manage the key. The issue of key management is beyond the scope of this book.

PHP provides a set of functions that access the mcrypt library, which provides encryption and decryption support using a variety of encryption standards. To use mcrypt functions, you must install the libmcrypt library and then compile PHP with the --with-mcrypt parameter.

MySQL also has the reversible encode( ) and decode( ) functions described in Chapter 3.

Web Database Applications and Authentication

So far in this chapter we have presented techniques that control access to resources—in particular, PHP scripts—based around HTTP authentication. The simplest technique discussed so far is to configure Apache to perform the authentication and authorization. For greater flexibility, we have described how PHP can manage the authentication process, allowing scripts to apply whatever logic is required to meet the authorization needs.

In this section we discuss issues of building web database applications:

- Examining why HTTP authentication works well with stateless applications
- Showing how a stateful application might manage HTTP authentication and the issues that are faced when building session-based web database applications
- Discussing some reasons why HTTP authentication may not be suitable for all applications
- Developing an authentication framework that can be used in a web database application illustrating the techniques presented in this section and earlier in this chapter

Building Stateless Applications

HTTP authentication is particularly well suited to stateless applications. HTTP authentication protects sets of resources, or realms, by challenging requests that don't contain authenticated credentials. We described the HTTP authentication process at the beginning of this chapter. Once an authenticated set of credentials has been collected for a realm, the user can browse the resources protected by that realm. For example, a web site may contain a set of browsable files—resources—on a web server. It doesn't matter which resource is requested; the first time a user accesses the site, she is challenged. Once the credentials are established, the user can browse the resources unchallenged.

HTTP authentication also supports bookmarking—the ability to add URLs to a list of bookmarks or favorite sites. The user can request the protected resource from the web site at a later date by selecting a bookmarked URL. If the user has not visited that site for some time, the request is challenged and the user is prompted for a username and password.

The techniques we have presented so far in this chapter can authenticate stateless applications. If you configure Apache to authenticate requests to an application's

PHP scripts, no extra code needs to be written. If more authorization control is required, a function similar to the `authenticateUser()` function, shown in Example 9-7, can be included at the start of each script.

Building Session-Based Applications

Building stateful web applications requires special care because of the stateless nature of HTTP. In Chapter 8 we presented session management as a technique for building stateful applications. Many web database applications—such as on-line banking—require both authentication and session management. We now look at some of the issues that arise when building session-based applications that require user authentication.

Forcing users to a login page

Many traditional database applications require users to log in before they can perform any operations. For example, an online banking application may allow access only after a user has entered credentials from a login page. In session-based applications, forcing users to always authenticate themselves via a login script allows session variables to be registered so that the rest of the application pages operate correctly. A single point of entry can also record when users access an application or force users to view advertising.

Using HTTP authentication, if a user makes a request for a script other than the login page of the application, and the request doesn't contain the `Authorization` header field, the response should redirect the user to the login page. This fragment of code sets the `Location` header field, which instructs the browser to relocate to the login page if either the `$PHP_AUTH_USER` or `$PHP_AUTH_PW` variables aren't set:

```php
<?php
// If this is an unauthorized request, just
// re-locate to the login page of the application
if (!isset($PHP_AUTH_USER) || !isset($PHP_AUTH_PW))
  header("Location: login.php")
  exit();

  // ... perform authentication and authorization ...
?>

... rest of script ...
```

Authenticating without HTTP

HTTP authentication provides a simple mechanism for building applications that need to control user access. HTTP authentication supports stateless applications well and, with additional coding, can support stateful, session-based applications. However, HTTP authentication may not meet the requirements of some web database applications. Consider the following problems of HTTP authentication:

Browsers remember passwords

When a user enters his username and password into a browser authentication dialog box—such as that shown in Figure 9-1—the browser remembers the credentials until the browser program is terminated or a new set of credentials are collected. When the user finishes with a web application—even if the application includes a logout page—the browser remembers the user credentials and allows access back to the same pages without challenge. Users may think they have logged off from an application correctly, only to leave an unattended browser as a security risk. By typing in a URL or simply using the Back button, another user can access the application unchallenged. The only sure way to protect against this kind of access is to terminate the browser.

Applications can be written to minimize this risk. By writing scripts that deliberately respond as unauthorized to a request that contains authenticated credentials, an application can enforce the intention of a logout. However, the application has to remember that the user logged out—or timed out—and respond accordingly. Such schemes lead to clumsy interactions with the user

Limited to the browser authentication dialog

When an application uses HTTP authentication, the method for collecting user credentials is limited to the authentication dialog box provided by the browser. An online application might want to present the login page with some site advertising. For example, the login page of an online store, such as our winestore, can include new arrivals of stock as advertisements.

Another feature that isn't supported using the basic HTTP authentication is allowing users to authenticate themselves with credentials other than a username and a password. You can allow a user who has forgotten his password, to go to an alternate login page that asks for his date of birth, his mother's maiden name, or other personal details to authenticate. For this kind of application you should collect a new password and restrict the number of attempts to the alternate login screen; otherwise, there could be a security risk.

Some applications require multiple logins. For example, an application might be a corporate information system that requires all users to log in for basic access but then requires an additional username and password to access a restricted part of the site. HTTP doesn't allow for multiple Authorization header fields in the one request

Authentication can be built into session-based applications by collecting user credentials in a `<form>`. When the `<form>` is submitted, the username and password are authenticated, and the authenticated state is recorded as a session variable. The authentication and authorization techniques developed earlier in this chapter—for example the authenticateUser( ) function shown in Example 9-7—can easily be modified to work with `<form>` data rather than $PHP_AUTH_USER and $PHP_AUTH_PW.

Collecting user credentials in a `<form>` and storing the authenticated state in a session has disadvantages. First, the username and password aren't encoded—not even in a basic form—when passed from the browser to the web server. This problem is solved by using the Secure Sockets Layer protocol as discussed later in this chapter. Second, session hijacking may arise because the state of the session is used to control access to the application.

Session hijacking

By using the authenticated state stored as a session variable, a session-based application can be open to hijacking. When a request is sent to a session-based application, the browser includes the session identifier, usually as a cookie, to access the authenticated session. Rather than snoop for usernames and passwords, a hacker can use a session ID to hijack an existing session. Consider an online banking application in which a hacker waits for a real user to log in and then takes over the session, by including the session ID in a request, and transfers funds into his own account. If the session isn't encrypted, it is easy to read the session ID or, for that matter, the username and password. We recommend that any application that transmits usernames, passwords, cookies that identify sessions, or personal details should be protected using encryption.

Even if the connection is encrypted, the session ID may still be vulnerable. If the session ID is stored in a cookie on the client, it is possible to trick the browser into sending the cookie unencrypted. This can happen if the cookie was set up by the server without the secure parameter that prevents cookie transmission over an insecure connection. Cookie parameters and how to set up PHP session management to secure cookies are discussed in Chapter 8.

Hijack attempts can also be less sophisticated. A hacker can hijack a session by randomly trying session IDs in the hope that an existing session might be found. On a busy site many hundreds of sessions might exist at any one time, increasing the chance of the success of such an attack. One precaution is to reduce the number of idle sessions by setting short maximum lifetimes for dormant sessions, as discussed in Chapter 8.

Another precaution is to use session IDs that are hard to guess. The default PHP session management uses a random number—that can be configured with a random seed—passed through an MD5 hashing algorithm, which generates a 32-character ID. The randomness and use of MD5 hashing in PHP session IDs make them much harder to guess than an ID based on other parameters, such as the system time, the client IP address, or the username.

Recording IP addresses to detect session hijack attempts

Earlier in this chapter we showed how to access the IP address of the browser when processing a request. The script shown in Example 9-5 checked the IP address set in the $REMOTE_ADDR variable against a hardcoded value to limit access to users on a particular subnet.

The IP address of the client that sent a request can be used to help prevent session hijacking. If the IP address set in $REMOTE_ADDR variable is recorded as a session variable when a user initially connects to an application, subsequent requests can be checked and allowed only if they are sent from the same IP address.

 Using the IP address as recorded from the HTTP request has limitations. Network administrators often configure proxy servers to hide the originating IP address by replacing it with the address of the proxy server. All users who connect to an application via such a proxy server appear to be located on the one machine. Some large sites—such as a large university campus—might even have several proxy servers to balance load, so successive requests coming from a single user might appear to change address.

Case Study: Customer Authentication

The case study example in this chapter is an authentication framework that doesn't rely on HTTP authentication to collect the username and password. The scripts developed in the case study illustrate how several techniques are applied and how the issues raised relating to session-based applications are solved. In this case study, we:

- Develop a login <form> to collect user credentials
- Authenticate the user credentials against encrypted passwords stored in the *customer* table
- Use the IP address of the login request to deny access to requests from other machines
- Develop a function that is included on each page to deny access without a successful login
- Develop a logout function

Case study overview

Each customer of the winestore has an entry in the *customer* table that records confidential account details, including delivery address and credit-card details. Given such information, there is a good reason to restrict access to the application and protect confidential data.

We design the login page as a <form>, and the authentication is handled by the script that processes POST variables. The POST method is used rather than GET method to prevent the username and password from appearing in the URL. The authentication uses a query on the *customer* table to check the credentials; we use the approach described in the "Authentication Using a Database" section.

We create a session to record the username that is authenticated and the IP address of the machine from which the login request originated. Each protected script then tests for the existence of the session variables that hold the authenticated name and the originating IP address and checks these against the originating IP address of the request for that script.

While the pages we have developed on the online winestore site are more attractive than the examples in this section, the structure of the code is the same.

Login page

The login page displays a <form> that collects a username and password and is used as the entry point for winestore customers. The login page is also used when a login attempt fails, as the destination page when a member logs out, and as a warning page when an unauthorized request is made to a script that requires a user to log in. Also, if a user that is already authorized requests the login page, we display a message to indicate that the user is already logged on. Figure 9-3 shows the rendered login <form> with a message showing a failed login attempt.

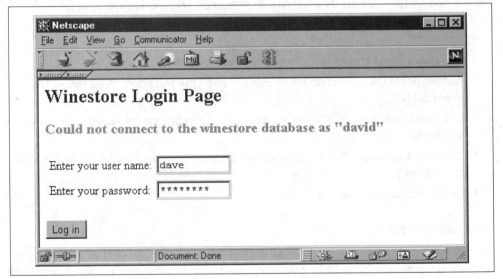

Figure 9-3. The login page shows a failed login attempt

Example 9-8 shows the login script with two helper functions that generate the HTML. The function login_page() generates the HTML <form> that collects two named <input> fields: formUsername and formPassword. The argument $loginMessage passes any error or warning messages the login page needs to display. If the $loginMessage is set, a formatted message is generated and included in the page.

When the <form> is submitted, the formUsername and formPassword fields are encoded as POST variables and are processed by the script that performs the authentication.

The function logged_on_page( ) in Example 9-8 generates the HTML that is used when the script detects that a user has already logged in to the application. The main part of the script initializes a session and checks if the user has already been authorized. If the session variable authenticatedUser is registered, the user has already been authorized and the function logged_on_page( ) is called. If not, the entry <form> is displayed by calling the function login_page( ), and the session is destroyed.

Example 9-8. The PHP script that generates the login <form>

```php
<?php
// Function that returns the HTML FORM that is
// used to collect the username and password

function login_page($errorMessage)
{
  // Generate the Login-in page
  ?>

<!DOCTYPE HTML PUBLIC
    "-//W3C//DTD HTML 4.0 Transitional//EN"
    "http://www.w3.org/TR/html4/loose.dtd" >
  <html>
    <head><title>Login</title></head>
    <body>
    <h2>Winestore Login Page</h2>
    <form method="POST" action="example.9-9.php">

  <?
  // Include the formatted error message

  if (isset($errorMessage))
    echo
      "<h3><font color=red>$errorMessage</font></h3>";

  // Generate the login <form> layout
  ?>
    <table>
      <tr><td>Enter your username:</td>
          <td><input type="text" size=10
                  maxlength=10
                  name="formUsername"></td></tr>
      <tr><td>Enter your password:</td>
          <td><input type="password" size=10
                  maxlength=10
                  name="formPassword"></td></tr>
    </table>
    <p><input type="submit" value="Log in">
    </form>
    </body>
```

Example 9-8. The PHP script that generates the login <form> (continued)

```
  </html>
  <?
}


//
// Function that returns HTML page showing that
// the user with the $currentLoginName is logged on

function logged_on_page($currentLoginName)
{

  // Generate the page that shows the user
  // is already authenticated and authorized
  ?>

<!DOCTYPE HTML PUBLIC
      "-//W3C//DTD HTML 4.0 Transitional//EN"
      "http://www.w3.org/TR/html4/loose.dtd" >
  <html>
  <head><title>Login</title></head>
  <body>
    <h2>Winestore</h2>
    <h2>You are currently logged in as
        <?=$currentLoginName ?></h2>
    <a href="example.9-10.php">Logout</a>
  </body>
  </html>
  <?
}

// Main
session_start();

// Check if we have established a session
if (isset($HTTP_SESSION_VARS["authenticatedUser"]))
{
  // There is a user logged on
  logged_on_page(
          $HTTP_SESSION_VARS["authenticatedUser"]);
}
else
{
  // No session established, no POST variables
  // display the login form + any error message
  login_page($HTTP_SESSION_VARS["loginMessage"]);

  session_destroy();
}
?>
```

It is important that the script test the associative array holding the session variable $HTTP_SESSION_VARS["authenticatedUser"] rather than the global variable

$authenticatedUser. Because of the default order in which PHP initializes global variables from GET, POST, and session variables, a user can override the value of $authenticatedUser simply by defining a GET or POST variable in the request. We discussed security problems with PHP variable initialization in Chapter 5.

Authentication script

When the login <form> is submitted, the POST variables are processed by the authentication script shown in Example 9-9. The authentication is performed by passing a handle to a connected MySQL server, the username, and the password to the function authenticateUser( ). The function executes a query to find the *user* row with the same username and encrypted password. As with the code in Example 9-7, we use the first two characters from the username as the salt string to the crypt( ) function.

The Boolean control variable $authenticated is set to the return value of the authenticateUser( ) function. If $authenticated is true, the username is registered as the $authenticatedUser session variable and the IP address of the client machine from which the request originated as the $loginIpAddress session variable.

If the authentication fails and $authenticated is set to false, the $loginMessage session variable is registered containing the appropriate message to display on the login <form> as shown in Figure 9-3. In Example 9-9 we always relocate back to the login page, keeping the code reasonably simple. An alternative would be to relocate back to a customer welcome page when authentication succeeds and relocate back to the login page only when authentication fails.

Example 9-9. Authentication script

```php
<?php
include 'db.inc';
include 'error.inc';

function authenticateUser($connection,
                          $username,
                          $password)
{
  // Test that the username and password
  // are both set and return false if not
  if (!isset($username) || !isset($password))
    return false;

  // Get the two character salt from the username
  $salt = substr($username, 0, 2);

  // Encrypt the password
  $crypted_password = crypt($password, $salt);

  // Formulate the SQL query find the user
  $query = "SELECT password FROM users
```

Example 9-9. Authentication script (continued)

```
                WHERE user_name = '$username'
                AND password = '$crypted_password'";

  // Execute the query
  $result = @ mysql_query ($query,
                           $connection)
  or showerror();

  // exactly one row? then we have found the user
  if (mysql_num_rows($result) != 1)
    return false;
  else
    return true;

}


// Main ----------

  session_start();

  $authenticated = false;

  // Clean the data collected from the user
  $appUsername =
    clean($HTTP_POST_VARS["formUsername"], 10);
  $appPassword =
    clean($HTTP_POST_VARS["formPassword"], 15);

  // Connect to the MySQL server
  $connection = @ mysql_connect($hostname,
                                $username,
                                $password)
  or die("Cannot connect");
  if (!mysql_selectdb($databaseName,
                      $connection))
      showerror()

  $authenticated = authenticateUser($connection,
                                    $appUsername,
                                    $appPassword);

  if ($authenticated == true)
  {
    // Register the customer id
    session_register("authenticatedUser");
    $authenticatedUser = $appUsername;

    // Register the remote IP address
    session_register("loginIpAddress");
    $loginIpAddress = $REMOTE_ADDR;
  }
```

Example 9-9. Authentication script (continued)

```
else
{
  // The authentication failed
  session_register("loginMessage");
  $loginMessage =
    "Could not connect to the winestore " .
    "database as \"$appUsername\"";
}

// Relocate back to the login page
header("Location: example.9-8.php");
?>
```

Logout script

A separate script is called when a user logs out of the application. Example 9-10 shows the script that unregisters the $authenticatedUser session variable, registers the $loginMessage variable containing the appropriate message, and relocates back to the login script. The login script checks if the $loginMessage session variable is registered and displays the message that the user has logged out.

Example 9-10. Logout script

```
<?php
  session_start();

  $appUsername =
    $HTTP_SESSION_VARS["authenticatedUser"];

  $loginMessage =
    "User \"$appUsername\" has logged out";

  session_register("loginMessage");

  session_unregister("authenticatedUser");

  // Relocate back to the login page
  header("Location: example.9-8.php");
?>
```

Authorizing other requests

The scripts shown in Examples 9-8, 9-9, and 9-10 form a framework that manages the login and logout functions and sets up the authentication control session variables. Scripts that require authorization need to check the session variables before they generate any output.

The authorization code that checks the authentication control session variables, shown in Example 9-11, can be written to a separate file and included with each protected page using the `include` directive. This saves having to rewrite the code for each page that requires authorization.

Example 9-11 begins by initializing the session and calculating two Boolean flags. The first flag `$notAuthenticated` is set to `true` if the session variable `$authenticatedUser` isn't set. The second flag `$notLoginIp` is set to `true` only if the session variable `$loginIpAddress` is set and has the same value as the IP address of the client that sent this request. The IP address of the client that sent the request is available to scripts in the server environment variable `$REMOTE_ADDR`. Unlike with environment variables, PHP doesn't overwrite `$REMOTE_ADDR` by a `GET` or `POST` variable with the same name.

Both the `$notAuthenticated` flag and the `$notLoginIp` flag are tested, and if either is true, an appropriate `$loginMessage` is set and registered with the session, and then the `Location:` header field is sent with the HTTP response to relocate the browser back to the login script. The two cases are separated, because the script might be enhanced to record more information about the possible hijack attempt and even to destroy the session.

Example 9-11. Code that checks the authenticated state from the session variables

```
<?php
  session_start();

  $loginScript = "example.9-8.php";

  // Set a boolean flag to check if
  // a user has authenticated
  $notAuthenticated =
    !isset($HTTP_SESSION_VARS["authenticatedUser"]);

  // Set a boolean flag to true if this request
  // originated from the same IP address
  // as the one that created this session
  $notLoginIp =
    isset($HTTP_SESSION_VARS["loginIpAddress"])
    && ($HTTP_SESSION_VARS["loginIpAddress"] !=
        $REMOTE_ADDR);

  // Check that the two flags are false
  if($notAuthenticated)
  {
    // The request does not identify a session
    session_register("loginMessage");
    $loginMessage =
      "You have not been authorized to access the " .
      "URL $REQUEST_URI";

    // Re-locate back to the Login page
    header("Location: " . $loginScript);
    exit;
```

```
}
else if($notLoginIp)
{
  // The request did not originate from the machine
  // that was used to create the session.
  // THIS IS POSSIBLY A SESSION HIJACK ATTEMPT

  session_register("loginMessage");
  $loginMessage =
    "You have not been authorized to access the " .
    "URL $REQUEST_URI from the address $REMOTE_ADDR";

  // Re-locate back to the Login page
  header("Location: " . $loginScript);
  exit;
}

?>
```

To use the code developed in Example 9-11 to protect a page, we only need to include the file containing the code. If we saved Example 9-11 to *auth.inc*, protecting a page is easy:

```
<?php include("auth.inc"); ?>
<!DOCTYPE HTML PUBLIC
    "-//W3C//DTD HTML 4.0 Transitional//EN"
    "http://www.w3.org/TR/html4/loose.dtd" >
<html>
    ...
    <h2>Your Credit Card details</h2>
    ...
    <p><a href="example.9-10.php">Logout</a>
    ...
</html>
```

As discussed in Chapter 4, including files with the *.inc* extension presents a security problem. If the user requests the include file, the source of the include file is shown in the browser.

There are three ways to address this problem:

- Store the include files outside the document tree of the Apache web server installation. For example, store the include files in the directory */usr/local/include/php* and use the complete path in the include directive.

- Use the extension *.php* instead of *.inc*. In this case, the include file is interpreted by the PHP script engine and produces no output because it contains no main body.

- Configure Apache so that files with the extension *.inc* can't be retrieved.

Protecting Data on the Web

The Web isn't a secure environment. The open nature of the networking and web protocols—TCP, IP, and HTTP—has allowed the development of many tools that can listen in on data transmitted between browsers and web servers. It is easy to snoop on passing traffic and read the contents of HTTP requests and responses. With a little extra effort, a hacker can manipulate traffic and even masquerade as another user.

If an application transmits sensitive information over the Web, an encrypted connection should be provided between the browser and the web server. The information that would warrant an encrypted connection includes:

- Sensitive information held on the server; e.g., commercial-in-confidence documents and bank account balances
- User credentials—usernames and passwords—used to gain access to sensitive services such as online banking or the administration of the winestore
- Personal details collected from the user, such as credit card numbers
- Session IDs—used by the server to link HTTP requests to session variables

In this section we focus on the common method of encrypting data sent over the Web using the Secure Sockets Layer. We discuss the basic mechanics of SSL in this section, and provide an installation and configuration guide for SSL and Apache as part of Appendix A.

This section isn't designed to cover the enormous topic of encryption. We limit our brief discussion to the features of SSL, and how SSL can protect web traffic. More details about cryptographic systems can be found in the references listed in Appendix E.

The Secure Sockets Layer Protocol

The data that is sent between web servers and browsers can be protected using the encryption services of the Secure Sockets Layer protocol, SSL. The SSL protocol addresses three goals:

Privacy
> The content of a message transmitted over the Internet can't be understood by a casual (or determined) observer.

Integrity
> The contents of a message received are correct and has not been tampered with.

Authentication
> Both the sender and receiver of a message can be sure of each other's identity.

SSL was originally developed by Netscape, and there are two versions: SSL v2.0 and SSL v3.0. We don't detail the differences here, but Version 3.0 supports more security features than 2.0. The SSL protocol isn't a standard as such, and the Transport Layer Security 1.0 (TLS) protocol has been proposed by the Internet Engineering Task Force (IETF) as an SSL v3.0 replacement.

SSL architecture

To understand how SSL works, you need to consider how browsers and web servers actually send and receive HTTP messages. Browsers send HTTP requests by calling on the host systems' TCP/IP networking software, the software that does the work of sending and receiving data over the Internet. When a request is to be sent—for example when a user clicks on a hypertext link—the browser formulates the HTTP request in memory and uses the host's TCP/IP network service to send the request to the server. TCP/IP doesn't care that the message is HTTP; it is only responsible for getting the complete message to the destination. When a web server receives a message, data is read from its host's TCP/IP service and then interpreted as HTTP. We discuss the relationship between HTTP and TCP/IP in more detail in Appendix B.

As shown in Figure 9-4, The SSL protocol operates as a layer between the browser and the TCP/IP services provided by the host. A browser passes the HTTP message to the SSL layer to be encrypted before the message is passed to the host's TCP/IP service. The SSL layer, configured into the web server, decrypts the message from the TCP/IP service and then passes it to the web server. Once SSL is installed and the web server is configured correctly, the HTTP requests and responses are automatically encrypted. There is no scripting required to use the SSL services.

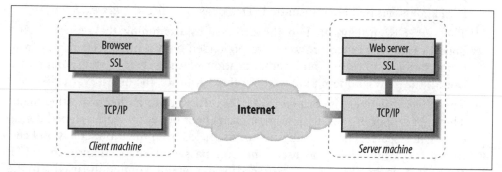

Figure 9-4. HTTP clients and servers, SSL, and the network layer that implements TCP/IP

Because SSL sits between HTTP and TCP/IP, secure web sites technically don't serve HTTP, at least not directly over TCP. URLs that locate resources on a secure server begin with *https://*, which means HTTP over SSL. The default port for an SSL service is 443, not port 80 as with HTTP; for example, when a browser connects to *https://secure.example.com*, it makes a TCP/IP connection to port 443 on *secure.example.com*. Most browsers and web servers can support SSL, but keys and certificates need to be included in the configuration of the server (and possibly the browser, if client certification is required).

Cipher suites

To provide a service that addresses the goals of privacy, integrity, and authentication, SSL uses a combination of cryptographic techniques and functions, such as message digests, digital certificates, and, of course, encryption. There are many different standard algorithms that implement these functions, and SSL can use different combinations to meet particular requirements, such as being legal to use in a particular country! When an SSL connection is established, clients and servers negotiate the best combination of techniques—based on common capabilities—to ensure the highest level of protection. The combinations of techniques that can be negotiated are known as *cipher suites*.

SSL sessions

When a browser connects to a secure site, the SSL protocol performs the following four steps:

1. A cipher suite is negotiated. The browser and the server identify the major SSL version supported, and then the configured capabilities. The strongest cipher suit that can be supported by both systems is chosen.

2. A secret key is shared between the server and the browser. Normally the browser generates a secret key that is asymmetrically encrypted using the server's public key. Only the server can learn the secret by decrypting it with the corresponding private key. The shared secret is used as the key to encrypt and decrypt the HTTP messages that are transmitted. This phase is called the *key exchange*.

3. The server is authenticated to the browser by examining the server's X.509 digital certificate. Often browsers are preloaded with a list of certificates from Certification Authorities, and authentication of the server is transparent to a user. If the browser doesn't know about the certificate, the user is warned.

4. The server examines the browser's X.509 certificate to authenticate the client. This step is optional and requires that each client be set up with a signed digital certificate. Apache can be configured to use fields from the browser's X.509 certificate as if they were the username and password encoded into an HTTP `Authorization` header field. Client certificates aren't commonly used on the Web.

These four steps briefly summarize the network handshaking between the browser and server when SSL is used. Once the browser and server have completed these steps, the HTTP request can be encrypted by SSL and sent to the web server.

The SSL handshaking is slow, and if this was to occur with every HTTP request, the performance of a secure web site would be poor. To improve performance, SSL uses the concept of sessions to allow multiple requests to share the negotiated cipher suite, the shared secret key, and the certificates. An SSL session is managed by the SSL software and isn't the same as a PHP session.

Certificates and Certification Authorities

A signed *digital certificate* encodes information so that the integrity of the information and the signature can be tested. The information contained in a certificate that is used by SSL includes details about the organization and the organization's public key. The public key that is contained in a certificate matches a private key held by the organization that is configured into the organization's web server. The browser uses the public key when an SSL session is established to encrypt a secret. The secret can only be decrypted using the private key configured into the organization's server. Encryption techniques that use a public and private key are known as *asymmetric*, and SSL uses asymmetric encryption to exchange a secret key. The secret key can then be used to encrypt the messages transmitted over the Internet.

A signed certificate also contains details about the *Certification Authority* (CA). The CA digitally signs a certificate by adding its own organization details, an encrypted digest of the certificate, and its own public key. With this information encoded, the complete signed certificate can be verified as being correct.

There are dozens, perhaps hundreds, of CAs. A browser—or the user confronted by a browser warning—can't be expected to recognize the digital signatures from all these authorities. The X.509 certificate standard solves this problem by allowing issuing CAs to have their signatures digitally signed by a more authoritative CA, who can in turn have its signature signed by yet another, more trusted CA. Eventually the chain of signatures ends with that of a root Certification Authority. It is the certificates from the root CAs that are often preinstalled in a browser. Some browsers allow users to add their own trusted certificates.

Self-signed certificates can be created and used to configure a web server with SSL. We show how to create self-signed certificates in Appendix A. But will they be trusted? The answer is probably not for secure applications.

CHAPTER 10
Winestore Customer Management

This chapter is the first of four that outline the case study winestore application. It contains an overview of the complete application, as well as the customer management scripts for the winestore. We also introduce the include files that store common functionality used throughout the application.

The material presented here doesn't fully explain the scripts from the online winestore. The descriptions are outlines, and careful reading of the scripts is required to fully understand the functionality. Also, we avoid duplicating our discussions of the principles and basic techniques for building web database applications. Chapters 2 through 9 are required background reading to fully understand the implementations outlined here.

The online winestore illustrates the practice of developing web database applications and isn't a production e-commerce application. It is a complete application but doesn't have all the features of a full production system. Such a system would include features such as credit-card processing, a password change facility, prompts that confirm whether a user wishes to proceed with updates or orders, more comprehensive search features, and an administrative interface. However, we plan to add additional features to the online examples, and updates are available from the book's web site at *http://www.oreilly.com/catalog/webdbapps/* or at the authors' site, *http://www.webdatabasebook.com*.

We recommend downloading and installing the online winestore on a local machine by following the instructions in Appendix A and Chapter 3. The best way to understand the code is to have a local copy of the application, to open the scripts in an editor, and to walk through the scripts while using the application with a browser. Modifications of the scripts are encouraged. Suggestions are welcome by email to *hugh@computer.org*.

The scripts outlined in this chapter perform the following functions:

Becoming a member
> The complete customer `<form>` based on the simplified version presented in Chapter 6 and 8.

Updating customer details
> This functionality is integrated into the script used for becoming a member, and is again an extension of the customer `<form>` from Chapters 6 and 8.

Checking customer details
> The complete validation and database management processes for updating and creating new customers. These processes extend the customer `<form>` introduced in Chapter 6 by applying the validation techniques from Chapter 7. The process includes creating and storing passwords using the encryption techniques discussed in Chapter 9.

Providing a customer receipt
> A receipt page that presents the results of the customer membership processing and avoids the reload problem discussed in Chapter 6.

Logging in
> Authenticating a user and using sessions to track the user login status. This is an application of the techniques discussed in Chapters 8 and 9.

Miscellaneous database functions and common functions
> An introduction to the *include.inc* file used throughout the winestore application, as well as the customer error handler implemented using the PHP error library.

Overview of the Winestore Application

The winestore application was developed to meet the requirements outlined in Chapter 1. It has four separate modules that we discuss in this and the next three chapters:

Customer management
> Becoming a member, amending membership details, logging in, and logging out. The scripts that implement this functionality are in this chapter. The web database application techniques illustrated include querying and writing data, sessions, post validation, batch error reporting, encryption of passwords, receipt pages to avoid the reload problem, and managing user authentication.

Shopping cart
> Adding wines to a shopping cart, deleting items from the cart, adjusting quantities, and emptying the cart. The shopping cart is discussed in Chapter 11.

Ordering and shipping

Processing the cart so that it becomes an order, confirming shipping details by email, and confirming shipping details with an HTML receipt. These scripts are the subject of Chapter 12.

Browsing and searching

Searching and browsing the wines. The searching and browsing module is briefly outlined in Chapter 13, along with related topics.

Winestore Scripts

Figures 10-1 and 10-2 show the scripts developed for the winestore application and how they interact. The three key user interface scripts, *cart.1*, *search.1*, and *cart.2*, are shown in both figures. *cart.5,* the key script that manages browser redirection using the header( ) function, is omitted from the figures; we discuss why later in this section. Figure 10-1 shows the cart, customer, searching, ordering, and shipping scripts. Scripts are shown as boxes. Solid boxes indicate scripts that interact with the user, while dashed boxes don't produce output but instead redirect to the script shown.

The main or home page of the online winestore is shown in Figures 10-1 and 10-2 and is labeled *cart.1*. This page allows the user to add bottles and cases of the three selected "hot new wines" to his shopping cart; this functionality is shown by the double-ended arrow to the add to cart script labeled *cart.3*. The *cart.3* script is shown as a dashed rectangle in Figure 10-1, indicating that it's a one-component query module that has no output and instead redirects to the calling page.

The front page also allows the user to view his shopping cart by clicking on the cart icon or the View Cart button at the base of the page. View-the-cart functionality is provided by the *cart.2* script introduced later in this section. Four other actions are also possible from the front page:

- Searching the wines using the script *search.1*
- Becoming a member or changing customer details using the *customer.2* script
- Emptying the cart using the *cart.4* script
- Logging in or logging out using the scripts *order.1* and *order.2*, respectively

The customer management process is provided by five scripts. The *customer.1*, *customer.2*, and *customer.3* scripts provide the become-a-member and change details features. The script *customer.2* presents an empty customer <form> to new customers. The <form> allows entry of all customer details, including an email address that is used as the login name of the user and a password for future visits to the site. The *customer.1* script validates customer data and, on success, writes to the database and redirects to the customer receipt script *customer.3*. On validation failure, *customer.1*

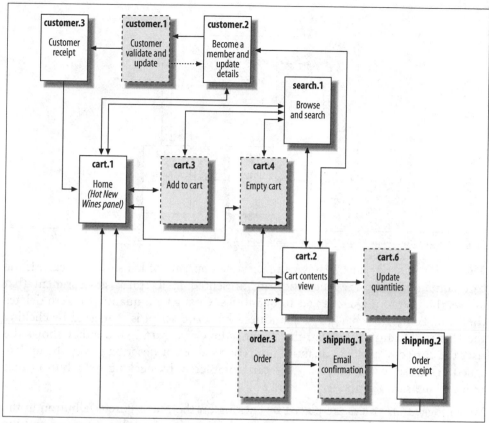

Figure 10-1. The winestore application architecture

redirects to *customer.2*, where the validation errors are reported interleaved with the `<form>` widgets.

For customers who are amending their details, the password and email `<input>` widgets are omitted from the customer `<form>`. For compactness, we have omitted password-change functionality from the online site. Other possible extensions to the password module include emailing password reminders to the user and emailing account activation details.

The remaining two customer scripts are shown in Figure 10-2. The login and logout scripts are shown, along with the three scripts from Figure 10-1 that interact with these scripts. The login script interacts with the user, while the logout script doesn't produce output but instead redirects to the home page.

The script *order.1* allows a user to provide his username and password credentials. On successful processing of credentials, the user is logged in. A logged-in user can then log out using the *order.2* script. The *order.2* logout script is a one-component script that always redirects the browser to the front page after the logout action.

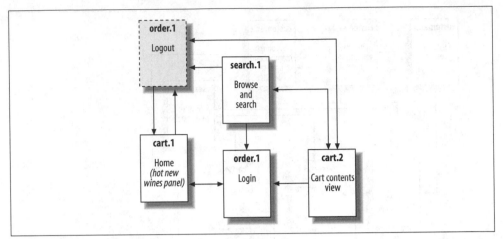

Figure 10-2. More winestore application architecture

The view cart script *cart.2* shows the user the contents of his shopping cart. If the cart contains items, the quantities are presented in a <form> environment that allows the user to make changes to quantities. Changing a quantity to zero deletes the item. To update changes in quantities, the *cart.6* script is requested by clicking the Update Quantities button; this script redirects to *cart.2*, and either shows the user the correctly updated quantities or reports an error describing why the update failed. The user can also empty his cart completely by clicking on a button that requests the *cart.4* script.

When logged in, orders are placed by clicking on the Make Purchase button in the view cart screen. When the button is clicked, the script *order.3* is requested and the complex database processing used to finalize an order is performed; an overview of the purchasing process is presented in Chapter 3, and we outline the script in Chapter 12. If the ordering process fails, *order.3* redirects to *cart.2,* where errors are reported. If the ordering process succeeds, *order.3* redirects to *shipping.1*. The *shipping.1* script sends the user an email confirmation of his order and redirects to *shipping.2* which shows the user the same receipt as an HTML page. From *shipping.2,* the user can return to the home page.

The view cart script *cart.2* also allows the user to return to the home page, search, log in, log out, or use the customer module.

The *search.1* script allows the user to browse wines that are in stock. The user can also choose to browse a specific wine type—such as Red or White—and a specific region such as Margaret River. Bottles or cases of wine can be added to the shopping cart by clicking on a link that requests and passes parameters to the *cart.3* script. As on the other main pages, the user can also click on buttons to view his cart, empty his cart, return to the home page, become a member, log in, log out, or update his membership details.

At the beginning of this section we stated that one important script was omitted from Figures 10-1 and 10-2. This script is *cart.5*. This script is requested when a button is pressed on all pages that have more than one button, and it's responsible for redirecting the browser to the correct script. Each button is an `<input>` element of type `submit`, and all are elements of one `<form>`. As there is only one `<form>`, only one script can be specified as the `action` attribute, and this script is *cart.5*. The script processes requests, identifies which button was clicked by inspecting the `name` attribute of the `<input>` element, and then redirects the browser to the appropriate script. Therefore, in practice, many arrows shown in Figures 10-1 and 10-2 should actually pass via *cart.5*.

An alternative approach to redirection via *cart.5* is to include multiple `<form>` elements in a script or use embedded links instead of buttons. Both alternatives work well, but all approaches have drawbacks. The advantage of our approach is that buttons are intuitive for the user and the HTML is kept simple. The disadvantage is the extra HTTP response and request required for each redirection.

The winestore application can be used at either the book's web site or on your local server, if you have followed the instructions to install the examples in Appendix A. The source code described can also be viewed at the book's web site and—if the installation instructions have been followed—can be edited and viewed in the directory */usr/local/apache/htdocs/wda/* on your local server. A summary of the winestore scripts, their filenames, and functions is shown in Table 10-1.

Table 10-1. The winestore scripts, filenames, and functions

Script	Filename	Function
cart.1	example.cart.1.php	Home page and Hot New Wines panel
cart.2	example.cart.2.php	Cart contents view
cart.3	example.cart.3.php	Add to cart
cart.4	example.cart.4.php	Empty cart
cart.5	example.cart.5.php	Manage redirection
cart.6	example.cart.6.php	Update cart quantities
customer.1	example.customer.1.php	Validate and update customer
customer.2	example.customer.2php	Customer entry <form>
customer.3	example.customer.3.php	Customer receipt
order.1	example.order.1.php	Log in
order.2	example.order.2.php	Log out
order.3	example.order.3.php	Finalize order
shipping.1	example.shipping.1.php	Email order confirmation
shipping.2	example.shipping.2.php	Order receipt
search.1	example.search.1.php	Browse and search wines
include.inc	include.inc	Common functionality

Table 10-1. *The winestore scripts, filenames, and functions (continued)*

Script	Filename	Function
db.inc	db.inc	DBMS parameters
error.inc	error.inc	Custom error handler

Customer Management

In this section, we outline the customer management scripts *customer.1*, *customer.2*, and *customer.3*. The *customer.2* script is for data entry of customer details and reporting errors and is based on the customer <form> case study from Chapters 6 and 8. The *customer.1* script performs data validation and writes the customer details to the winestore database. It is also based on the case study examples from Chapters 6 and 8. The *customer.3* receipt is designed to avoid the reload problem after writing to the database.

Customer Validation

Example 10-1 lists the *customer.1* script. It is based on Example 8-4 and has the same structure with two exceptions:

- It validates a superset of customer fields, that is, all the fields listed in Chapter 1.
- It manages the encryption of passwords and user account allocation.

The validation techniques used for the additional fields—such as the telephone and fax numbers, email address, zip code, and so on—are discussed in Chapter 7.

Example 10-1. The complete winestore customer validation script, customer.2

```
<?php
   // This script validates customer data entered into
   // example.customer.2.php.
   // If validation succeeds, it INSERTs or UPDATEs
   // a customer and redirect to a receipt page; if it
   // fails, it creates error messages and these are later
   // displayed by example.customer.2.php.

   include 'include.inc';

   set_error_handler("errorHandler");

   // Initialize a session
   session_start();

   // Register an error array - just in case!
   if (!session_is_registered("errors"))
      session_register("errors");
```

Example 10-1. The complete winestore customer validation script, customer.2 (continued)

```
// Clear any errors that might have been
// found previously
$errors = array();

// Set up a $formVars array with the POST variables
// and register with the session.
if (!session_is_registered("formVars"))
   session_register("formVars");

foreach($HTTP_POST_VARS as $varname => $value)
   $formVars[$varname] = trim(clean($value, 50));

// Validate the firstName
if (empty($formVars["firstName"]))
   // First name cannot be a null string
   $errors["firstName"] =
      "The first name field cannot be blank.";

elseif (!eregi("^[a-z'-]*$", $formVars["firstName"]))
   // First name cannot contain white space
   $errors["firstName"] =
   "The first name can only contain alphabetic " .
      "characters or \"-\" or \"'\"";

elseif (strlen($formVars["firstName"]) > 50)
   $errors["firstName"] =
   "The first name can be no longer than 50 " .
      "characters";

// Validate the Surname
if (empty($formVars["surname"]))
   // the user's surname cannot be a null string
   $errors["surname"] =
      "The surname field cannot be blank.";

elseif (strlen($formVars["surname"]) > 50)
   $errors["surname"] =
      "The surname can be no longer than 50 " .
      "characters";

// Validate the Address
if (empty($formVars["address1"]) &&
   empty($formVars["address2"]) &&
   empty($formVars["address3"]))
   // all the fields of the address cannot be null
   $errors["address"] =
      "You must supply at least one address line.";
else
{
   if (strlen($formVars["address1"]) > 50)
     $errors["address1"] =
      "The address line 1 can be no longer " .
```

Example 10-1. The complete winestore customer validation script, customer.2 (continued)

```
          "than 50 characters";
    if (strlen($formVars["address2"]) > 50)
      $errors["address2"] =
        "The address line 2 can be no longer " .
        "than 50 characters";
    if (strlen($formVars["address3"]) > 50)
      $errors["address3"] =
        "The address line 3 can be no longer " .
        "than 50 characters";
}

// Validate the user's Initial
if (!empty($formVars["initial"]) &&
    !eregi("^[a-z]{1}$", $formVars["initial"]))
    // If there is a middle initial, it must be
    // one character in length
    $errors["initial"] =
        "The initial field must be empty or one " .
        "character in length.";

// Validate the City
if (empty($formVars["city"]))
    // the user's city cannot be a null string
    $errors["city"] = "You must supply a city.";

elseif (strlen($formVars["city"]) > 20)
    $errors["city"] =
      "The city can be no longer than 20 characters";

// Validate State - any string less than 21 characters
if (strlen($formVars["state"]) > 20)
    $errors["state"] =
        "The state can be no longer than 20 characters";

// Validate Zipcode
if (!ereg("^([0-9]{4,5})$", $formVars["zipcode"]))
    $errors["zipcode"] =
        "The zipcode must be 4 or 5 digits in length";

  // Validate Country
if (strlen($formVars["country"]) > 20)
    $errors["country"] =
        "The country can be no longer than 20 characters";

// Phone is optional, but if it is entered it must have
//  correct format
$validPhoneExpr =
    "^([0-9]{2,3}[ ]?)?[0-9]{4}[ ]?[0-9]{4}$";

if (!empty($formVars["phone"]) &&
    !ereg($validPhoneExpr, $formVars["phone"]))
    $errors["phone"] =
```

Example 10-1. The complete winestore customer validation script, customer.2 (continued)

```
            "The phone number must be 8 digits in length, " .
            "with an optional 2 or 3 digit area code";

    // Fax is optional, but if it is entered it must
    // have correct format
    if (!empty($formVars["fax"]) &&
        !ereg($validPhoneExpr, $formVars["fax"]))
        $errors["fax"] =
            "The fax number must be 8 digits in length, with " .
            "an optional 2 or 3 digit area code";

    // Validate Date of Birth
    if (empty($formVars["dob"]))
        // the user's date of birth cannot be a null string
        $errors["dob"] = "You must supply a date of birth.";

    elseif (!ereg("^([0-9]{2})/([0-9]{2})/([0-9]{4})$",
            $formVars["dob"], $parts))
        // Check the format
        $errors["dob"] =
            "The date of birth is not a valid date in the " .
            "format DD/MM/YYYY";

    elseif (!checkdate($parts[2],$parts[1],$parts[3]))
        $errors["dob"] =
            "The date of birth is invalid. Please check " .
            "that the month is between 1 and 12, and the " .
            "day is valid for that month.";

    elseif (intval($parts[3]) < 1890)
        // Make sure that the user has a reasonable birth year
        $errors["dob"] =
            "You must be alive to use this service!";

    elseif
        // Check whether the user is 18 years old.
        // If all the following are NOT true, then report
        // an error.
        // Were they born more than 19 years ago?
        (!((intval($parts[3]) < (intval(date("Y") - 19))) ||

        // No, so were they born exactly 18 years ago, and
        // has the month they were born in passed?
        (intval($parts[3]) == (intval(date("Y")) - 18) &&
         intval($parts[2]) < intval(date("m")))) ||

        // No, so were they born exactly 18 years ago in this
        // month, and was the day today or earlier in the month?
        (intval($parts[3]) == (intval(date("Y")) - 18) &&
         intval($parts[2]) ==  intval(date("m"))) &&
         intval($parts[1]) <= intval(date("d")))))))
        $errors["dob"] =
```

```
            "You must be 18+ years of age to use this ".
            "service.";

// Only validate email if this is an INSERT
if (!session_is_registered("loginUsername"))
{
  // Check syntax
  $validEmailExpr =
      "^[0-9a-z~`!#$%&_-]([.]?[0-9a-z~!#$%&_-])*" .
      "@[0-9a-z~!#$%&_-]([.]?[0-9a-z~!#$%&_-])*$";

  if (empty($formVars["email"]))
      // the user's email cannot be a null string
      $errors["email"] =
          "You must supply an email address.";

  elseif (!eregi($validEmailExpr, $formVars["email"]))
      // The email must match the above regular
      // expression
      $errors["email"] =
          "The email address must be in the " .
          "name@domain format.";

  elseif (strlen($formVars["email"]) > 50)
      // The length cannot exceed 50 characters
      $errors["email"] =
          "The email address can be no longer than " .
          "50 characters.";

  elseif (!(getmxrr(substr(strstr($formVars["email"],
          '@'), 1), $temp)) ||
          checkdnsrr(gethostbyname(
                  substr(strstr($formVars["email"],
                      '@'), 1)),"ANY"))
      // There must be a Domain Name Server (DNS)
      // record for the domain name
      $errors["email"] =
          "The domain does not exist.";

  else
  {
    // Check if the email address is already in use in
    //  the winestore
    if (!($connection = @ mysql_pconnect($hostName,
                                         $username,
                                         $password)))

        showerror();

    if (!mysql_select_db($databaseName, $connection))
        showerror();
```

```
        $query = "SELECT * FROM users
                  WHERE user_name = '" .
                  $formVars["email"] . "'";

        if (!($result = @ mysql_query ($query,
                                       $connection)))
            showerror();

        // Is it taken?
        if (mysql_num_rows($result) == 1)
            $errors["email"] =
                "A customer already exists with this " .
                "login name.";
    }
}

// Only validate password if this is an INSERT
// Validate password - between 6 and 8 characters
if (!session_is_registered("loginUsername") &&
    (strlen($formVars["loginPassword"]) < 6 ||
    strlen($formVars["loginPassword"] > 8)))
    $errors["loginPassword"] =
        "The password must be between 6 and 8 " .
        "characters in length";

// Now the script has finished the validation,
// check if there were any errors
if (count($errors) > 0)
{
    // There are errors.  Relocate back to the
    // customer <form>
    header("Location: example.customer.2.php");
    exit;
}

// If we made it here, then the data is valid

if (!isset($connection))
{
    if (!($connection = @ mysql_pconnect($hostName,
                                          $username,
                                          $password)))
        showerror();

    if (!mysql_select_db($databaseName, $connection))
        showerror();
}

// Reassemble the date of birth into database format
$dob = "\"$parts[3]-$parts[2]-$parts[1]\"";
```

```
// Is this an update?
if (session_is_registered("loginUsername"))
{
    $custID = getCustomerID($loginUsername, $connection);

    $query = "UPDATE customer SET ".
    "title = \"" . $formVars["title"] . "\", " .
    "surname = \"" . $formVars["surname"] . "\", " .
    "firstname = \"" . $formVars["firstName"] . "\", " .
    "initial = \"" . $formVars["initial"] . "\", " .
    "addressline1 = \"" . $formVars["address1"] . "\", " .
    "addressline2 = \"" . $formVars["address2"] . "\", " .
    "addressline3 = \"" . $formVars["address3"] . "\", " .
    "city = \"" . $formVars["city"] . "\", " .
    "state = \"" . $formVars["state"] . "\", " .
    "zipcode = \"" . $formVars["zipcode"] . "\", " .
    "country = \"" . $formVars["country"]. "\", " .
    "phone = \"" . $formVars["phone"] . "\", " .
    "fax = \"" . $formVars["fax"] . "\", " .
    "birth_date = " . $dob .
    " WHERE cust_id = $custID";
}
else
    $query = "INSERT INTO customer VALUES (NULL, " .
            "\"" . $formVars["surname"] . "\", " .
            "\"" . $formVars["firstName"] . "\", " .
            "\"" . $formVars["initial"] . "\", " .
            "\"" . $formVars["title"] . "\", " .
            "\"" . $formVars["address1"] . "\", " .
            "\"" . $formVars["address2"] . "\", " .
            "\"" . $formVars["address3"] . "\", " .
            "\"" . $formVars["city"] . "\", " .
            "\"" . $formVars["state"] . "\", " .
            "\"" . $formVars["zipcode"] . "\", " .
            "\"" . $formVars["country"] . "\", " .
            "\"" . $formVars["phone"] . "\", " .
            "\"" . $formVars["fax"] . "\", " .
            "\"" . $formVars["email"] . "\", " .
            $dob . ", " .
            0 . ")";

// Run the query on the customer table
if (!(@ mysql_query ($query, $connection)))
    showerror();

// If this was an INSERT, we need to INSERT
// also into the users table
if (!session_is_registered("loginUsername"))
{
    // Get the customer id that was created
    $custID = @ mysql_insert_id($connection);
```

```
        // Use the first two characters of the
        // email as a salt for the password
        $salt = substr($formVars["email"], 0, 2);

        // Create the encrypted password
        $stored_password =
            crypt($formVars["loginPassword"], $salt);

        // Insert a new user into the user table
        $query = "INSERT INTO users
                SET cust_id = $custID,
                    password = '$stored_password',
                    user_name = '" . $formVars["email"] . "'";

        if (!($result = @ mysql_query ($query, $connection)))
            showerror();

        // Log the user into their new account
        session_register("loginUsername");

        $loginUsername = $formVars["email"];
    }

    // Clear the formVars so a future <form> is blank
    session_unregister("formVars");
    session_unregister("errors");

    // Now show the customer receipt
    header("Location: example.customer.3.php?custID=$custID");
?>
```

The following fragment of Example 10-1 manages the creation of a new user account but only if this is a new customer:

```
        if (!session_is_registered("loginUsername"))
        {
            // Get the customer id that was created
            $custID = @ mysql_insert_id($connection);

            // Use the first two characters of the
            // email as a salt for the password
            $salt = substr($formVars["email"], 0, 2);

            // Create the encrypted password
            $stored_password =
                crypt($formVars["loginPassword"], $salt);

            // Insert a new user into the user table
            $query = "INSERT INTO users
                    SET cust_id = $custID,
                        password = '$stored_password',
                        user_name = '" . $formVars["email"] . "'";
```

```
        if (!($result = @ mysql_query ($query, $connection)))
            showerror();

        // Log the user into their new account
        session_register("loginUsername");

        $loginUsername = $formVars["email"];
    }
```

The session variable `loginUsername` indicates whether or not the user is logged in. Therefore, the fragment adds a new row to the *users* table only if the user isn't logged in. To store the password, the techniques from Chapter 9 are applied, and the password is encrypted using `crypt()` with the first two characters of the email address as the seed. After adding the row, the user is logged in by registering the session variable `loginUsername` and assigning the email address value to it.

For updates of customer details, the external function `getCustomerID()` is called prior to updating the row. The function returns the customer `cust_id` associated with the `loginUsername` session variable passed as a parameter. The function is defined in the *include.inc* file.

If validation fails in Example 10-1, the script redirects to the *customer.2* script shown in Example 10-2. Any validation error messages are recorded in the array `errors` and this array is used to display the messages interleaved with the customer `<form>` widgets. If validation and the database write succeed, the script redirects to the *customer.3* script shown in Example 10-3.

The Customer <form>

The script *customer.2* is shown in Example 10-2. The script displays a `<form>` for customer data entry. If the user is logged in and validation has not previously failed, the customer data is retrieved from the *customer* table and used to populate the `<form>` widgets. If the user isn't logged in, and validation has not previously failed, a blank `<form>` is shown to collect new member details. If data has failed validation, the `formVars` array that is registered as a session variable is used to repopulate the `<form>`, and the error messages from the `errors` array are displayed.

Two external functions from *include.inc* are used in Example 10-2:

`void showMessage()`
> This function outputs any errors or notices created by other scripts. These messages include login errors, cart update problems, ordering problems, etc.

`void showLogin()`
> This function outputs in the top-right corner of the browser whether the user is logged in or not. If the user is logged in, it outputs his email address.

The country widget has only three possible values: Australia, United States, and Zimbabwe, In a full implementation of our case study, a database table of country names would be maintained, and the function selectDistinct( ) would present the <select> list. The function selectDistinct( ) is discussed in Chapter 5.

Example 10-2. The customer <form> script customer.1

```php
<?php
  // This script shows the user a customer <form>.
  // It can be used both for INSERTing a new customer and
  // for UPDATE-ing an existing customer. If the customer
  // is logged in, then it is an UPDATE; otherwise, an
  // INSERT.
  // The script also shows error messages above widgets
  // that contain erroneous data; errors are generated
  // by example.customer.1.php

  include 'include.inc';

  set_error_handler("errorHandler");

  // Show an error in a red font
  function fieldError($fieldName, $errors)
  {
    if (isset($errors[$fieldName]))
      echo "<font color=\"red\">" .
           $errors[$fieldName] .
           "</font><br>";
  }

  // Connect to a session
  session_start();

  // Is the user logged in and were there no errors from
  // a previous validation?
  // If so, look up the customer for editing
  if (session_is_registered("loginUsername") &&
      empty($errors))
  {
    if (!($connection = @ mysql_pconnect($hostName,
                                         $username,
                                         $password)))
      showerror();

    if (!mysql_select_db($databaseName, $connection))
      showerror();

    $custID = getCustomerID($loginUsername, $connection);

    $query = "SELECT * FROM customer
             WHERE cust_id = " . $custID;

    if (!($result = @ mysql_query($query, $connection)))
      showerror();
```

Example 10-2. The customer <form> script customer.1 (continued)

```php
    $row = mysql_fetch_array($result);

    // Reset $formVars, since we're loading from
    // the customer table
    $formVars = array( );

    // Reset the errors
    $errors = array( );

    // Load all the form variables with customer data
    $formVars["title"] = $row["title"];
    $formVars["surname"] = $row["surname"];
    $formVars["firstName"] = $row["firstname"];
    $formVars["initial"] = $row["initial"];
    $formVars["address1"] = $row["addressline1"];
    $formVars["address2"] = $row["addressline2"];
    $formVars["address3"] = $row["addressline3"];
    $formVars["city"] = $row["city"];
    $formVars["state"] = $row["state"];
    $formVars["zipcode"] = $row["zipcode"];
    $formVars["country"] = $row["country"];
    $formVars["phone"] = $row["phone"];
    $formVars["fax"] = $row["fax"];
    $formVars["email"] = $row["email"];
    $formVars["dob"] = $row["birth_date"];
    $formVars["dob"] = substr($formVars["dob"], 8, 2) .
                       "/" .
                       substr($formVars["dob"], 5, 2) .
                       "/" .
                       substr($formVars["dob"], 0, 4);
  }

?>
<!DOCTYPE HTML PUBLIC
   "-//W3C//DTD HTML 4.0 Transitional//EN"
   "http://www.w3.org/TR/html4/loose.dtd" >
<html>
<head><title>Customer Details</title></head>
<body bgcolor="white">
<?php
  // Show the user login status
  showLogin( );
?>
<form method="post" action="example.customer.1.php">
<h1>Customer Details</h1>
<?php
  // Display any messages to the user
  showMessage( );

  // Show meaningful instructions for UPDATE or INSERT
  if (session_is_registered("loginUsername"))
      echo "<h3>Please amend your details below as " .
```

Example 10-2. The customer <form> script customer.1 (continued)

```
            "required. Fields shown in " .
            "<font color=\"red\">red</font> are " .
            "mandatory.</h3>";
    else
        echo "<h3>Please fill in the details below to " .
            "join. Fields shown in " .
            "<font color=\"red\">red</font> are ".
            "mandatory.</h3>";
?>
<table>
<col span="1" align="right">

    <tr><td><font color="red">Title:</font></td>
    <td><select name="title">
        <option <?php if ($formVars["title"]=="Mr")
                echo "selected";?>>Mr
        <option <?php if ($formVars["title"]=="Mrs")
                echo "selected";?>>Mrs
        <option <?php if ($formVars["title"]=="Ms")
                echo "selected";?>>Ms
        <option <?php if ($formVars["title"]=="Dr")
                echo "selected";?>>Dr
        </select><br></td>
    </tr>

    <tr><td><font color="red">First name:</font></td>
    <td><? echo fieldError("firstName", $errors); ?>
        <input type="text" name="firstName"
        value="<? echo $formVars["firstName"]; ?>"
        size=50></td>
    </tr>

    <tr><td><font color="red">Surname:</font></td>
    <td><? echo fieldError("surname", $errors); ?>
        <input type="text" name="surname"
        value="<? echo $formVars["surname"]; ?>"
        size=50></td>
    </tr>

    <tr><td>Initial: </td>
    <td><? echo fieldError("initial", $errors); ?>
        <input type="text" name="initial"
        value="<? echo $formVars["initial"]; ?>"
        size=1></td>
    </tr>

    <tr><td><font color="red">Address:</font></td>
    <td><? echo fieldError("address", $errors); ?>
        <? echo fieldError("address1", $errors); ?>
        <input type="text" name="address1"
        value="<? echo $formVars["address1"]; ?>"
```

Example 10-2. The customer <form> script customer.1 (continued)

```
      size=50></td>
   </tr>

   <tr><td></td>
   <td><? echo fieldError("address2", $errors); ?>
      <input type="text" name="address2"
      value="<? echo $formVars["address2"]; ?>"
      size=50></td>
   </tr>

   <tr><td></td>
   <td><? echo fieldError("address3", $errors); ?>
      <input type="text" name="address3"
      value="<? echo $formVars["address3"]; ?>"
      size=50></td>
   </tr>

   <tr><td><font color="red">City:</font></td>
   <td><? echo fieldError("city", $errors); ?>
      <input type="text" name="city"
      value="<? echo $formVars["city"]; ?>"
      size=20></td>
   </tr>

   <tr><td>State: </td>
   <td><? echo fieldError("state", $errors); ?>
   <input type="text" name="state"
      value="<? echo $formVars["state"]; ?>"
      size=20></td>
   </tr>

   <tr><td><font color="red">Zipcode:</font></td>
   <td><? echo fieldError("zipcode", $errors); ?>
   <input type="text" name="zipcode"
      value="<? echo $formVars["zipcode"]; ?>"
      size=5></td>
   </tr>

   <tr><td>Country: </td>
   <td><? echo fieldError("country", $errors); ?>
      <select name="country">
      <option <?php
         if ($formVars["country"]=="Australia")
            echo "selected";?>>Australia
      <option <?php
         if ($formVars["country"]=="United States")
            echo "selected";?>>United States
      <option <?php
         if ($formVars["country"]=="Zimbabwe")
            echo "selected";?>>Zimbabwe
      </select></td>
   </tr>
```

Example 10-2. The customer <form> script customer.1 (continued)

```
    <tr><td>Telephone: </td>
    <td><? echo fieldError("phone", $errors); ?>
    <input type="text" name="phone"
        value="<? echo $formVars["phone"]; ?>"
        size=15></td>
     </tr>

     <tr><td>Fax: </td>
    <td><? echo fieldError("fax", $errors); ?>
        <input type="text" name="fax"
      value="<? echo $formVars["fax"]; ?>"
        size=15></td>
     </tr>

     <tr><td><font color="red">Date of birth
                          (dd/mm/yyyy):</font> </td>
    <td><? echo fieldError("dob", $errors); ?>
        <input type="text" name="dob"
      value="<? echo $formVars["dob"]; ?>"
        size=10></td>
     </tr>

<?php
  // Only show the username/email and password
  // <input> widgets to new users
  if (!session_is_registered("loginUsername"))
  {
?>    <tr><td><font color="red">Email/username:</font></td>
   <td><? echo fieldError("email", $errors); ?>
       <input type="text" name="email"
       value="<? echo $formVars["email"]; ?>"
       size=50></td>
    </tr>

    <tr><td><font color="red">Password:</font></td>
    <td><? echo fieldError("loginPassword", $errors); ?>
        <input type="password" name="loginPassword"
      value="<? echo $formVars["loginPassword"]; ?>"
        size=8></td>
     </tr>
<?php
  }
?>
<tr>
    <td><input type="submit" value="Submit"></td>
</tr>
</table>
</form>
<br><a href="http://validator.w3.org/check/referer">
    <img src="http://www.w3.org/Icons/valid-html401"
```

Example 10-2. The customer <form> script customer.1 (continued)

```
      height="31" width="88" align="right" border="0"
      alt="Valid HTML 4.01!"></a>
</body>
</html>
```

The Customer Receipt Page

Example 10-3 shows the customer receipt script, *customer.3*, that is called after a database write to insert or update a customer. The script is a receipt page that can be bookmarked—it expects a cust_id as a GET method parameter—and the script does nothing but read details from the database. Reloading of the page therefore has no undesirable side effects. Customer receipts can be viewed only when logged in, and a user is permitted to view only her own customer receipts; if the user attempts to retrieve another user's details, a warning message is shown to the user, and the cust_ id is updated to be her own.

Example 10-3. The customer.3 customer receipt page

```php
<?php
  // This script shows the user a receipt for their customer
  // UPDATE or INSERT.
  // It carries out no database actions and can be
  // bookmarked. The user must be logged in to view it.

  include 'include.inc';

  set_error_handler("errorHandler");

  // Show the user a customer INSERT or UPDATE receipt
  function show_HTML_receipt($custID, $connection)
  {
    $query = "SELECT * FROM customer
           WHERE cust_id = $custID";

    if (!($result = @ mysql_query ($query, $connection)))
       showerror();

    // There is only one matching row
    $row = @ mysql_fetch_array($result);

    echo "\n<h1>Account details for " .
        "<font color=\"red\">" . $row["email"] .
        "</font></h1>\n";

    echo "<p><i>Please record your password " .
        "somewhere safe for future use</i>\n";

    echo "<p>Your shipping and billing details are " .
        "as follows:\n<br><b> " .
        $row["title"] . " " .
```

Example 10-3. The customer.3 customer receipt page (continued)

```
            $row["firstname"] . " " .
            $row["initial"] . " " .
            $row["surname"] . "\n<br>" .
            $row["addressline1"] . "\n";

     if ($row["addressline2"] != "")
        echo "\n<br>" .
             $row["addressline2"];

     if ($row["addressline3"] != "")
        echo "\n<br>" .
             $row["addressline3"];

     echo "\n<br>" .
          $row["city"] . " " .
          $row["state"] . " " .
          $row["zipcode"] . "\n<br>" .
          $row["country"] . "</b><br>\n";

     if ($row["phone"] != "")
        echo "\n<br><b>Telephone: " .
             $row["phone"] . "</b>";

     if ($row["fax"] != "")
        echo "\n<br><b>Fax: " .
             $row["fax"] . "</b>";

     $row["dob"] = substr($row["birth_date"], 8, 2) . "/" .
                   substr($row["birth_date"], 5, 2) . "/" .
                   substr($row["birth_date"], 0, 4);

     echo "\n<br><b>Date of Birth: " .
          $row["dob"] . "</b>\n<br>";

}

// Main ----------

// Re-establish the existing session
session_start();

// Check if the user is logged in - this should never
// fail unless the script is run incorrectly
if (!session_is_registered("loginUsername"))
{
   session_register("message");
   $message = "You must login to view your " .
              "customer receipt.";

   header("Location: example.cart.1.php");
   exit;
}
```

Example 10-3. The customer.3 customer receipt page (continued)

```php
   // Check the correct parameters have been passed
   if (!isset($custID))
   {
      session_register("message");

      $message = "Incorrect parameters to " .
                 "example.customer.3.php";

      // Redirect the browser back to the calling page,
      // using the HTTP response header "Location:"
      // and the PHP environment variable $HTTP_REFERER
      header("Location: $HTTP_REFERER");
      exit;
   }

   // Check this customer matches the custID
   if ($custID != getCustomerID($loginUsername, NULL))
   {
      session_register("message");

      $message = "You can only view your own " .
                 "customer receipt!";

      $custID = getCustomerID($loginUsername, NULL);
   }

   // Open a connection to the DBMS
   if (!($connection = @ mysql_pconnect($hostName,
                                        $username,
                                        $password)))
      showerror();

   if (!mysql_select_db($databaseName, $connection))
      showerror();

?>
<!DOCTYPE HTML PUBLIC
   "-//W3C//DTD HTML 4.01 Transitional//EN"
   "http://www.w3.org/TR/html401/loose.dtd">
<html>
<head>
  <title>Hugh and Dave's Online Wines</title>
</head>
<body bgcolor="white">
<?php
   // Show the user login status
   showLogin();

   // Show the user any messages
   showMessage();
```

Example 10-3. The customer.3 customer receipt page (continued)

```
    // Show the customer confirmation
    show_HTML_receipt($custID, $connection);

    // Show buttons
    echo "<form action=\"example.cart.5.php\"" .
        " method=\"GET\">";
    echo "<table>";

    echo "<td><input type=\"submit\" name=\"home\"" .
        " value=\"Home\"></td>";

?>
</table>
</form>
<br><a href="http://validator.w3.org/check/referer"><img
    src="http://www.w3.org/Icons/valid-html401"
    height="31" width="88" align="right" border="0"
    alt="Valid HTML 4.01!"></a>
</body>
</html>
```

Authenticating Users

Example 10-4 shows the *order.1* script that is used for logging into the winestore application. The script is based on Examples 9-8 and 9-9 from Chapter 9. If the user isn't logged in—which should always be the case unless the script is unexpectedly called—and no credentials have been provided from a previous login attempt, the script displays a login <form> to the user. When the user successfully logs in, the script redirects to the calling page that's stored in the session variable referer; if referer isn't set, it redirects to the home page.

When the user provides credentials—a username and a password—the script is re-requested through the <form> submission process. The script encrypts the password provided by the user and checks if this matches the password stored in the *users* table. If it matches, the user is logged in by registering the session variable loginUsername and unregistering any session variables associated with failed attempts to update customer details. The session variable loginUsername stores the user's email address, which, as discussed earlier, is the same as his username. If the password is incorrect, an error is generated, and the login <form> is redisplayed so the user can try again.

The framework used here is typical of authentication in a web database application. However, possible improvements to the process can include limiting the number of failed login attempts, a password changing feature, a password reminder module—where the user is sent a password hint such as "What is your mother's maiden name?"—and security restrictions such as requiring that a password contain a mixture of uppercase, lowercase, numeric, and special characters.

Example 10-4. The order.1 login script for logging into the winestore application

```php
<?php
// This script manages the login process.
// It should only be called when the user is not
// logged in.
// If the user is logged in, it will redirect back
// to the calling page.
// If the user is not logged in, it will show a login
// <form>

include 'include.inc';

set_error_handler("errorHandler");

function check_login($loginUsername, $loginPassword)
{
  global $referer;
  global $username;
  global $password;
  global $hostName;
  global $databaseName;
  global $message;

  // Get the two character salt from the
  // user-name collected from the challenge
  $salt = substr($loginUsername, 0, 2);

  // Encrypt the loginPassword collected from
  // the challenge
  $crypted_password = crypt($loginPassword, $salt);

  // Formulate the SQL find the user
  $query = "SELECT password FROM users
              WHERE user_name = '$loginUsername'
              AND password = '$crypted_password'";

  // Open a connection to the DBMS
  if (!($connection = @ mysql_pconnect($hostName,
                                       $username,
                                       $password)))
    showerror();

  if (!mysql_select_db($databaseName, $connection))
    showerror();

  // Execute the query
  if (!($result = @ mysql_query($query, $connection)))
    showerror();

  // exactly one row? then we have found the user
  if (mysql_num_rows($result) == 1)
  {
```

Example 10-4. The order.1 login script for logging into the winestore application (continued)

```
        // Register the loginUsername to show the user
        // is logged in
        session_register("loginUsername");

        // Clear any other session variables
        if (session_is_registered("errors"))
            // Delete the form errors session variable
            session_unregister("errors");

        if (session_is_registered("formVars"))
            // Delete the formVars session variable
            session_unregister("formVars");

        // Do we need to redirect to a calling page?
        if (session_is_registered("referer"))
        {
            // Delete the referer session variable
            session_unregister("referer");

            // Then, use it to redirect
            header("Location: $referer");
            exit;
        }
        else
        {
            header("Location: example.cart.1.php");
            exit;
        }
    }
    else
    {
        // Ensure loginUsername is not registered, so
        // the user is not logged in
        if (session_is_registered("loginUsername"))
            session_unregister("loginUsername");

        // Register an error message
        session_register("message");
        $message = "Username or password incorrect. " .
                    "Login failed.";

        // Show the login page
        // so the user can have another go!
        login_page();
        exit;
    }
}

// Function that shows the HTML <form> that is
// used to collect the username and password
function login_page()
{
```

```php
   global $message;

   ?>
<!DOCTYPE HTML PUBLIC
    "-//W3C//DTD HTML 4.0 Transitional//EN"
    "http://www.w3.org/TR/html4/loose.dtd" >
<html>
  <head>
     <title>Winestore Login Page</title>
  </head>
<body bgcolor="white">
<?php
  // Show login status (should be logged out!)
  showLogin();
?>
     <h2>Winestore Login Page</h2>
     <form method="POST" action="example.order.1.php">
<?php
  // Show messages
  showMessage();
  ?>
<table>
<tr>
     <td>Enter your username:</td>
     <td><input type="text" size=15
        maxlength=30
        name="loginUsername"></td>
</tr>
<tr><td>Enter your password:</td>
     <td><input type="password" size=15
        maxlength=8
        name="loginPassword"></td>
</tr>
<tr>
     <td><input type="submit" value="Log in"></td>
</tr>
</table>
<br><a href="http://validator.w3.org/check/referer">
     <img src="http://www.w3.org/Icons/valid-html401"
      height="31" width="88" align="right" border="0"
      alt="Valid HTML 4.01!"></a>
</form>
</body>
</html>
<?php
}

// ------------------

// Initialise the session
session_start();
```

Example 10-4. The order.1 login script for logging into the winestore application (continued)

```php
if (isset($HTTP_POST_VARS["loginUsername"]))
  $loginUsername =
      clean($HTTP_POST_VARS["loginUsername"], 30);

if (isset($HTTP_POST_VARS["loginPassword"]))
  $loginPassword =
      clean($HTTP_POST_VARS["loginPassword"], 8);

// Check if the user is already logged in
if (session_is_registered("loginUsername"))
{
  // If they are, then just bounce them back where
  // they came from
  if (session_is_registered("referer"))
  {
    session_unregister("referer");
    header("Location: $referer");
    exit;
  }
  else
  {
    header("Location: example.cart.1.php");
    exit;
  }
}

// Have they provided only one of a username and
// password?
if ((empty($HTTP_POST_VARS["loginUsername"]) &&
    !empty($HTTP_POST_VARS["loginPassword"])) ||
    (!empty($HTTP_POST_VARS["loginUsername"]) &&
    empty($HTTP_POST_VARS["loginPassword"])))
{
  // Register an error message
  session_register("message");
  $message = "Both a username and password must " .
             "be supplied.";
}

// Have they not provided a username/password,
// or was there an error?
if (!isset($loginUsername) ||
    !isset($loginPassword) ||
    session_is_registered("message"))
  login_page( );
else
  // They have provided a login. Is it valid?
  check_login($loginUsername, $loginPassword);
?>
```

Example 10-5 lists the winestore *order.2* logout script. The script is simple: if the session variable loginUsername is registered—this variable indicates the user is logged in—it's unregistered; if it isn't registered, the script has been unexpectedly called, and an error message is generated. In either case, the script then redirects back to the calling page stored in the session variable referer, or to the home page if referer isn't set. The script is a one-component script; that is, it carries out a function, produces no output, and redirects back to the calling page.

Example 10-5. The order.2 logout script for logging out of the winestore application

```php
<?php
  // This script logs a user out and redirects
  // to the calling page.

  include 'include.inc';

  set_error_handler("errorHandler");

  // Restore the session
  session_start();

  // Is the user logged in?
  if (session_is_registered("loginUsername"))
     session_unregister("loginUsername");
  else
  {
     // Register a message to show the user
     session_register("message");
     $message = "Error: you are not logged in!";
  }

  // Redirect the browser back to the calling page
  if (session_is_registered("referer"))
  {
     // Delete the redirection session variable
     session_unregister("referer");

     // Then, use it to redirect to the calling page
     header("Location: $referer");
     exit;
  }
  else
     header("Location: example.cart.1.php");
?>
```

The Winestore Include Files

The winestore include files are shown in Examples 10-6, 10-7, and 10-8. The *db.inc* include file in Example 10-6 and the *error.inc* include file in Example 10-8 are both included in the *include.inc* file in Example 10-7.

Example 10-6 shows the *db.inc* file that lists the DBMS credentials for connecting to the winestore database. The settings must be changed for a local installation of the winestore application.

Example 10-6. The db.inc include file

```php
<?php
  $hostName = "localhost";
  $databaseName = "winestore";
  $username = "fred";
  $password = "shhh";
?>
```

The *db.inc* include file stores the DBMS and database credentials to access the online winestore. The hostName setting is the server name of the DBMS, the databaseName setting is the winestore database name, and the username and password are those used to access the MySQL DBMS. This file is identical to Example 4-7 and is discussed in Chapter 4.

The *include.inc* file shown in Example 10-7 stores the common function used throughout the winestore application.

Example 10-7. The include.inc file

```php
<?php
    // This file contains functions used in more than
    // one script in the cart module

    include 'db.inc';
    include 'error.inc';

    // Untaint user data
    function clean($input, $maxlength)
    {
      $input = substr($input, 0, $maxlength);
      $input = EscapeShellCmd($input);
      return ($input);
    }

    // Print out the varieties for a wineID
    function showVarieties($connection, $wineID)
    {
      // Find the varieties of the current wine,
      // and order them by id
      $query = "SELECT gv.variety
              FROM grape_variety gv,
                   wine_variety wv, wine w
              WHERE w.wine_id = wv.wine_id
              AND wv.variety_id = gv.variety_id
              AND w.wine_id = $wineID
              ORDER BY wv.id";
```

Example 10-7. The include.inc file (continued)

```
    // Run the query
    if (!($result = @ mysql_query($query, $connection)))
        showerror( );

    $varieties = "";

    // Retrieve and print the varieties
    while ($row = @ mysql_fetch_array($result))
        $varieties .= " " . $row["variety"];

    return $varieties;
}

// Show the user the details of one wine in their
// cart
function showWine($wineId, $connection)
{
    global $username;
    global $password;
    global $databaseName;

    $wineQuery = "SELECT year, winery_name, wine_name
                FROM winery, wine
                WHERE wine.winery_id = winery.winery_id
                AND wine.wine_id = $wineId";

    $open = false;

    // If a connection parameter is not passed, then
    // use our own connection to avoid any
    // locking problems
    if (!isset($connection))
    {
        if (!($connection = @ mysql_connect($hostName,
                                            $username,
                                            $password)))
            showerror( );

        if (!mysql_select_db($databaseName, $connection))
            showerror( );

        $open = true;
    }

    // Run the query created above on the database
    // through the connection
    if (!($result = @ mysql_query ($wineQuery,
                                    $connection)))
        showerror( );

    $row = @ mysql_fetch_array($result);
```

Example 10-7. The include.inc file (continued)

```
      // Print the wine details
      $result = $row["year"] . " " .
               $row["winery_name"] . " " .
               $row["wine_name"];

      // Print the varieties for this wine
      $result .= showVarieties($connection, $wineId);

      if ($open == true)
        @ mysql_close($connection);

      return $result;
}

// Print out the pricing information for a wineID
function showPricing($connection, $wineID)
{
   // Find the price of the cheapest inventory
   $query = "SELECT min(cost)
             FROM inventory
             WHERE wine_id = $wineID";

   // Run the query
   if (!($result = @ mysql_query($query,
                                 $connection)))
      showerror();

   // Retrieve the cheapest price
   $row = @ mysql_fetch_array($result);

   printf("<b>Our price: </b>$%.2f",
          $row["min(cost)"]);
   printf(" ($%.2f a dozen)",
          ($row["min(cost)"] * 12));
}

// Show the total number of items and dollar value of
// the shopping cart, as well as a clickable cart icon
function showCart($connection)
{
   global $order_no;

   // Initialise an empty cart
   $cartAmount = 0;
   $cartCount = 0;

   // If the user has added items to their cart,
   // then the variable order_no will be registered
   if (session_is_registered("order_no"))
   {
      $cartQuery = "SELECT qty, price " .
                   "FROM items " .
```

Example 10-7. The include.inc file (continued)

```
                    "WHERE cust_id = -1 " .
                    "AND order_id = " . $order_no;

        // Find out the number and the dollar value of
        // the items in the cart. To do this, we run
        // the cartQuery through the connection on
        // the database
        if (!($result = @ mysql_query ($cartQuery,
                                        $connection)))

            showerror();

        while ($row = @ mysql_fetch_array($result))
        {
            $cartAmount += $row["price"] * $row["qty"];
            $cartCount += $row["qty"];
        }
    }

    // This sets up the cart picture.
    // The user can click on it to see the contents of
    // their cart. It also contains JavaScript, so that
    // the cart highlights
    // when the mouse is over it (a "roll-over")
    echo "<table>\n<tr>\n\t<td>";
    echo "<a href=\"example.cart.2.php\" " .
        "onMouseOut=\"cart.src='cart_off.jpg'\" " .
        "onMouseOver=\"cart.src='cart_on.jpg'\"> " .
        "<img src=\"cart_off.jpg\" vspace=0 border=0 " .
        "alt=\"cart picture\" name=\"cart\"></a>\n";
    echo "\t</td>\n";
    printf("\t<td>Total in cart: $%.2f (%d items)</td>\n",
            $cartAmount, $cartCount);
    echo "</tr>\n</table>";
}

// Display any messages that are set, and then
// clear the message
function showMessage()
{
    global $message;

    // Is there an error message to show the user?
    if (session_is_registered("message"))
    {
        echo "<h3>";
        echo "<font color=\"red\">$message</font></h3>";
        // Clear the error message
        session_unregister("message");
        $message = "";
    }
}
```

Example 10-7. The include.inc file (continued)

```
// Show whether the user is logged in or not
function showLogin()
{
    global $loginUsername;

    // Is the user logged in?
    if (session_is_registered("loginUsername"))
        echo "<p align=\"right\">You are currently " .
            "logged in as <b>$loginUsername</b></p>\n";
    else
        echo "<p align=\"right\">You are currently " .
            "not logged in</p>\n";
}

// Show the user a login or logout button.
// Also, show them membership buttons as appropriate.
function loginButtons()
{
    if (session_is_registered("loginUsername"))
    {
        echo "\n\t<td><input type=\"submit\"" .
            " name=\"logout\" value=\"Logout\"></td>\n";
        echo "\n\t<td><input type=\"submit\"" .
            "name=\"account\" value=\"Change " .
            "Details\"></td>\n";
    }
    else
    {
        echo "\t<td><input type=\"submit\" " .
            "name=\"login\" value=\"Login\"></td>\n";
        echo "\n\t<td><input type=\"submit\" " .
            "name=\"account\" value=\"Become " .
            "a Member\"></td>\n";
    }
}

// Get the cust_id using loginUsername
function getCustomerID($loginUsername, $connection)
{
    global $databaseName;
    global $username;
    global $password;
    global $hostName;

    $open = false;

    // If a connection parameter is not passed, then
    // use our own connection to avoid any locking
    // problems
    if (!isset($connection))
    {
```

Example 10-7. The include.inc file (continued)

```
        if (!($connection = @ mysql_connect($hostName,
                                             $username,
                                             $password)))
        showerror();

        if (!mysql_select_db($databaseName,
                             $connection))
        showerror();

        $open = true;
    }

    // We find the cust_id through the users table,
    // using the session variable holding their
    // loginUsername.
    $query = "SELECT cust_id
              FROM users
              WHERE user_name = \"$loginUsername\"";

    if (($result = @ mysql_query ($query, $connection)))
        $row = mysql_fetch_array($result);
    else
        showerror();

    if ($open == true)
        @ mysql_close($connection);

  return($row["cust_id"]);
}

// Produce a <select> list containing database
// elements
function selectDistinct ($connection,
                         $tableName,
                         $columnName,
                         $pulldownName,
                         $additionalOption,
                         $defaultValue)
{
    $defaultWithinResultSet = FALSE;

    // Query to find distinct values of $columnName
    // in $tableName
    $distinctQuery = "SELECT DISTINCT $columnName
                      FROM $tableName";

    // Run the distinctQuery on the databaseName
    if (!($resultId = @ mysql_query ($distinctQuery,
                                     $connection)))
        showerror();
```

Example 10-7. The include.inc file (continued)

```
    // Retrieve all distinct values
    $i = 0;
    while ($row = @ mysql_fetch_array($resultId))
        $resultBuffer[$i++] = $row[$columnName];

    // Start the select widget
    echo "\n<select name=\"$pulldownName\">";

    // Is there an additional option?
    if (isset($additionalOption))
        // Yes, but is it the default option?
        if ($defaultValue == $additionalOption)
            // Show the additional option as selected
            echo "\n\t<option selected>$additionalOption";
        else
            // Just show the additional option
            echo "\n\t<option>$additionalOption";

    // check for a default value
    if (isset($defaultValue))
    {
        // Yes, there's a default value specified

        // Check if the defaultValue is in the
        // database values
        foreach ($resultBuffer as $result)
            if ($result == $defaultValue)
                // Yes, show as selected
                echo "\n\t<option selected>$result";
            else
                // No, just show as an option
                echo "\n\t<option>$result";
    } // end if defaultValue
    else
    {
        // No defaultValue

        // Show database values as options
        foreach ($resultBuffer as $result)
            echo "\n\t<option>$result";
    }
    echo "\n</select>";
} // end of function
?>
```

The *include.inc* file shown in Example 10-7 contains the following functions that are used throughout the winestore application:

string clean(string *input*, integer *maxlength*)

Untaints a user-supplied *input* string by processing it with `EscapeShellCmd( )` and takes a substring of length *maxlength*. Returns the untainted string. This function is discussed in Chapter 5.

void showVarieties(resource *connection*, int *wineID*)

Queries the *winestore* database through the DBMS connection resource. Prints the wine varieties associated with the wine identified by the `wine_id` *wineID*.

string showWine(int *wineID*, resource *connection*)

Queries the *winestore* database through the DBMS connection resource. Returns the year, winery name, wine details, and varieties of the wine identified by *wineID*. The function `showVarieties( )` is called to output the varieties. If the connection resource is NULL, a new nonpersistent connection to the DBMS is opened and closed; this can be used to avoid having to lock the tables associated with a wine if the calling function requires locks for other operations.

void showPricing(resource *connection*, int *wineID*)

Queries the *winestore* database through the DBMS connection resource. Prints the price of the wine identified by *wineID* and the cost of a case of that wine where—for simplicity—a case of 12 bottles costs 12 times as much as 1 bottle.

void showCart(resource *connection*)

Produces a shopping cart icon that is an embedded link to the script *cart.2*. The icon is a rollover, in which JavaScript loads a highlighted cart image when the mouse is over the image. The script also queries the *winestore* database through the DBMS connection resource and sums the total number of items and the dollar value of the items in the user's shopping cart. These total values are reported next to the cart.

void showMessage( )

Reports any messages registered in the session variable `message`. If a message is displayed, the session variable `message` is unregistered so that a message appears only once.

void showLogin( )

Reports whether the user is logged in or not based on whether the `loginUsername` session variable is registered. If the user is logged in, the message includes the user's login name.

void loginButtons( )

Displays <form> buttons. If the user is logged in, the "logout" and "customer change details" buttons are shown. If the user isn't logged in, the "login" and "become a member" buttons are shown.

string getCustomerID(string *loginUsername*, resource *connection*)

Returns the `cust_id` associated with the user's email address or login name *loginUsername*. Queries the *winestore* database through the DBMS *connection* resource. If the *connection* resource is NULL, a new, nonpersistent connection to

---

the DBMS is opened and closed; this can be used to avoid having to lock the tables associated with a wine if the calling function requires locks for other operations.

void selectDistinct (resource *connection*, string *tableName*, string *columnName*, string *pulldownName*, string *additionalOption*, string *defaultValue*)

Produces a drop-down list using the HTML <select> element. Values from the *columnName* attribute of the table *tableName* are used to populate the <select> element with the name *pulldownName*. The <option> *defaultValue* is shown selected, and an additional nondatabase value—such as All—can be added with the *additionalOption* parameter. This function is described in detail in Chapter 5.

Custom Error Handlers

A custom error handler is used in the winestore in preference to the built-in PHP error handler. Example 10-8 shows this handler incorporated in the include file *error.inc*.

Example 10-8. The error.inc custom error handler

```
<?
  // Trigger an error condition
  function showerror()
  {
    if (mysql_errno() || mysql_error())
      trigger_error("MySQL error: " .
                    mysql_errno() .
                    " : " . mysql_error(),
                    E_USER_ERROR);
    else
      trigger_error("Could not connect to DBMS",
                    E_USER_ERROR);
  }

  // Abort on error. Deletes session variables to leave
  // us in a clean state
  function errorHandler($errno, $errstr,
                        $errfile, $errline)
  {
    switch ($errno)
    {
      case E_USER_NOTICE:
      case E_USER_WARNING:
      case E_WARNING:
      case E_NOTICE:
      case E_CORE_WARNING:
      case E_CORE_NOTICE:
      case E_COMPILE_WARNING:
        break;
      case E_USER_ERROR:
      case E_ERROR:
```

Example 10-8. The error.inc custom error handler (continued)

```
          case E_PARSE:
          case E_CORE_ERROR:
          case E_COMPILE_ERROR:
              session_start();

              if (session_is_registered("message"))
                  session_unregister("message");

              if (session_is_registered("order_no"))
                  session_unregister("order_no");

              $errorString =
  "Winestore system error: $errstr (# $errno).<br>\n" .
  "Please report the following to the administrator:<br>\n" . "Error in line $errline of
file $errfile.<br>\n";

              // Send the error to the administrator by email
              error_log($errorString, 1, "hugh");
?>
<h2>Hugh and Dave's Online wines is temporarily unavailable</h2>
The following has been reported to the administrator:
<br><b><font color="red"><?=$errorString;?></b></font>
<?php
              // Stop the system
              die();

          default:
              break;
      }
   }
?>
```

At the beginning of each script in the winestore application, the handler is registered:

```
      set_error_handler("errorHandler");
```

After this registration, any error, warning, or notice encountered in the script will cause the function errorHandler( ) to be called.

The function set_error_handler( ) has the following prototype:

```
      string set_error_handler(string error_handler)
```

On success, the function returns the previously defined error handler function name as a string. The parameter *error_handler* is the name of the user-defined handler function, in our example errorHandler. The returned value can be used later to restore the previous error handler with set_error_handler( ).

PHP requires that the user-defined errorHandler( ) function have at least two parameters: an error number and an error string. Three additional optional parameters can be included in a custom error handler: the script file that caused the error, the line number with the error, and additional variable context information. Our handler supports the first two of the three optional parameters.

Eight different errors, warnings, and notices can be generated by PHP during script processing or during the precompilation process, generated by the PHP script engine itself, or triggered manually by the developer. Our errorHandler( ) function ignores all notices and warnings by returning if the error number errno parameter falls into the WARNING or NOTICE classes. However, for all errors in the ERROR class and for PARSE errors, our custom error handler carries out several actions:

1. It logs out the user and deletes any registered session messages.
2. It creates a string that incorporates details of the error.
3. It emails the error message to the system administrator—in this case to the email account hugh—using the PHP library error_log( ) function.
4. It outputs the error message to the browser.

The advantage of a custom error handler is that additional features, such as deleting session variables, closing database connections, and sending email messages, can be incorporated in the error process.

The error_log( ) function has the following prototype:

```
int error_log (string message, int message_type [, string destination [, string
extra_headers]])
```

The string message is the error message to be logged. The message_type can be 0, 1, or 3. A setting of 0 sends the message to the PHP system error logger, which is configured using the error_log directive in the *php.ini* file. A setting of 1 sends an email to the *destination* email address using the mail( ) function with any additional email *extra_headers* that are provided; the mail( ) function and the use of extra headers is discussed in Chapter 12. A setting of 3 appends the message to the file *destination*. A setting of 2 isn't available in PHP4.

The showerror( ) function is also part of *error.inc*. This function is called whenever a MySQL function fails throughout the winestore scripts. The function tests if mysql_error( ) or mysql_errno( ) return nonzero values and, if so, it triggers a user-generated error using the trigger_error( ) PHP library function:

```
void trigger_error (string error_message [, int error_type])
```

The trigger_error( ) function has two parameters: an *error_message*—which is created using the return values of the MySQL error functions—and an optional *error_type* that's set to E_USER_ERROR. If MySQL hasn't reported an error, the mysql_connect( ) or mysql_pconnect( ) functions have failed, and a message indicating this is manually created. The result of calling trigger_error( ) is that the PHP script engine calls our custom registered handler, errorHandler( ).

CHAPTER 11

The Winestore Shopping Cart

In this chapter, we introduce the shopping cart developed for the online winestore. The shopping cart is typical of those used in online stores: the user can add items to the cart and manage the quantities of the different items. The solution we outline is scalable and practical. The cart data is stored in the *winestore* database tables, and only one session variable per user is required to track the cart's identity.

This chapter is the second of four that outline the complete winestore application. As discussed in Chapter 10, the descriptions of the scripts aren't comprehensive, and we assume you've read Chapters 2 to 9 as background. Also, we encourage you to install a local copy of the application and to view, edit, and use the scripts while reading this chapter.

We present here the four scripts that manage the shopping cart, a fifth script that produces the home page that includes the Hot New Wines panel, and a sixth script that manages redirection to other pages when the user clicks on buttons.

The scripts in this chapter perform the following functions:

Present the home page
    Display the Hot New Wines panel based on the examples developed in Chapters 4 and 5

View the shopping cart
    Query the database and display the contents of the user's shopping cart

Add items to the cart
    Add a quantity of a specific wine to the user's shopping cart

Empty the cart
    Delete all the items in the cart and remove the cart

Update quantities
    Manage changes to the number of bottles of wines in the cart, including deletion of one or more wines

Process button clicks and redirect the browser
> Manage the redirections required when the user presses the different buttons on each of the winestore pages

As with the other modules in the winestore, the shopping cart isn't a production system. The scripts presented here illustrate the practice of developing a web database application. Techniques shown include database interactivity, concurrency management, using sessions, and one- and two-component querying.

The Winestore Home Page

Example 11-1 shows the final implementation of the winestore home page containing the Hot New Wines panel. The Hot New Wines panel is discussed in more detail in Chapter 4, and the one-component functionality for adding one or a dozen bottles of wine to the cart is discussed in Chapter 5. We discuss how clicks on the add-to-cart links are managed later in the "The Shopping Cart Architecture" section.

The Hot New Wines panel is based on scripts presented in Chapter 4 and is encapsulated in the function showPanel( ) in Example 11-1. The functions showVarieties( ), which displays the varieties of a specific wine, and showPricing( ), which shows the per-bottle and the per-case price of a wine, are part of the *include.inc* file discussed in Chapter 10.

The main body of the script presents the front page using a mixture of HTML and calls to functions. The function showCart( ) displays an embedded link cart icon and the dollar total and number of items in the cart. The function showMessage( ) displays any message registered in the session variable message, and the showLogin( ) function displays the user's login status. The function loginButtons( ) shows the user different buttons depending on whether or not she is currently logged in. All these functions are part of *include.inc* and discussed in Chapter 10.

The following code fragment inserts the file *disclaimer* into the body of the HTML:

```
require 'disclaimer';
```

The file is a text message that alerts the user that our system doesn't really sell wines and that the scripts are covered by the GNU public license.

Example 11-1. cart.1 displays the winestore home page

```
<?php
    // This is the script that shows the user a list of
    // wines, and allows them to select wines to add to
    // their shopping cart

    include 'include.inc';

    set_error_handler("errorHandler");
```

Example 11-1. cart.1 displays the winestore home page (continued)

```php
function showPanel($query, $connection)
{
    // Run the query on the database through
    // the connection
    if (!($result = @ mysql_query ($query, $connection)))
        showerror();

    echo "<table border=0>\n";

    // Process the three new wines
    while ($row = @ mysql_fetch_array($result))
    {
        // Begin a heading for the wine
        echo "<tr>\n\t<td bgcolor=\"maroon\">" .
            "<b><font color=\"white\">" .
            $row["year"] . " " .
            $row["winery_name"] . " " .
            $row["wine_name"] . " ";

        // Print the varieties for this wine
        echo showVarieties($connection, $row["wine_id"]);

        // Finish the first row heading
        echo "</font></b></td>\n</tr>\n";

        // Print the wine review
        if (!empty($row["description"]))
            echo "<tr>\n\t<td bgcolor=\"silver\">" .
                "<b>Review: </b>" .
                $row["description"];
                "</td>\n</tr>\n";

        // Print the pricing information
        echo "<tr>\n\t<td bgcolor=\"gray\">";

        // Print out the pricing information
        showPricing($connection, $row["wine_id"]);

        echo "</td>\n</tr>\n";

        // Show the single-bottle add to cart link
        echo "<tr>\n\t<td align=\"right\">" .
            "<a href=\"example.cart.3.php?" .
            "qty=1&amp;wineId=" .
            $row["wine_id"] .
            "\">Add a bottle to the cart</a>";

        // Show the dozen add to cart link
        echo "   " .
    "<a href=\"example.cart.3.php?qty=12&amp;wineId=" .
    $row["wine_id"] . "\">Add a dozen</a></td>\n";
```

Example 11-1. cart.1 displays the winestore home page (continued)

```
        echo "</tr>\n";

        // Blank row for presentation
        echo "\n<tr>\n\t<td></td>\n</tr>\n";
    }

    echo "</table>\n";
}

// ---------

// Initialize a session. This call either creates
// a new session or re-establishes an existing one.
session_start();

// Open a connection to the DBMS
if (!($connection = @ mysql_connect($hostName,
                                    $username,
                                    $password)))
    showerror();

if (!mysql_select_db($databaseName, $connection))
    showerror();
?>
<!DOCTYPE HTML PUBLIC
  "-//W3C//DTD HTML 4.01 Transitional//EN"
  "http://www.w3.org/TR/html401/loose.dtd">
<html>
  <head>
    <title>Hugh and Dave's Online Wines</title>
  </head>
<body bgcolor="white">
<?php
  // Show the user login status
  showLogin();

  // Show the dollar and item total of the cart
  showCart($connection);
?>
  <h1>Here are some Hot New Wines!</h1>
<?php
  // Display any messages to the user
  showMessage();

  // Show the "Hot New Wines"
  $query = "SELECT wi.winery_name,
                   w.year,
                   w.wine_name,
                   w.wine_id,
                   w.description
            FROM wine w, winery wi, inventory i
            WHERE w.winery_id = wi.winery_id
```

Example 11-1. cart.1 displays the winestore home page (continued)

```
                    AND w.wine_id = i.wine_id
                    AND w.description IS NOT NULL
                    GROUP BY w.wine_id
                    ORDER BY i.date_added DESC LIMIT 3";

    // Include our disclaimer
    require 'disclaimer';

    // Show the user the "Hot New Wines" panel
    showPanel($query, $connection);

    echo "<form action=\"example.cart.5.php\"" .
         " method=\"GET\">\n";
    echo "<table>\n<tr>\n";

    // If the cart has contents, offer the opportunity
    // to view the cart or empty the cart.
    if (session_is_registered("order_no"))
    {
       echo "\t<td><input type=\"submit\" " .
            "name=\"empty\" value=\"Empty Cart\"></td>\n";
       echo "\t<td><input type=\"submit\" " .
            "name=\"view\" value=\"View Cart\"></td>\n";
    }

    // Show the user the search screen button
    echo "\t<td><input type=\"submit\" " .
         "name=\"search\" value=\"Search\"></td>\n";

    // Show the user either a login or logout button
    loginButtons( );

    echo "\n</tr>\n</table>\n";
    echo "</form>\n";

?>
<br><a href="http://validator.w3.org/check/referer">
    <img src="http://www.w3.org/Icons/valid-html401"
    height="31" width="88"
    align="right" border="0" alt="Valid HTML 4.01!"></a>
</body>
</html>
```

The Shopping Cart Architecture

In Chapter 1, we introduced the requirements of the winestore shopping cart. A shopping cart is analogous to an incomplete order, in which each item in the cart is one or more bottles of a particular wine. Users can select any wine that is in stock to add to the cart, and wines in the cart can be purchased for up to one day after they have been added. The quantities of the wines can be updated by the user, and items in the cart can be deleted. In addition, the entire cart can be emptied.

We use the *orders* and *items* tables to manage the shopping cart. Alternative approaches include using only PHP sessions, JavaScript on the client, and database tables designed specifically for shopping cart management. The JavaScript approach is the least desirable because—as discussed in Chapter 7—JavaScript and the client are unreliable. PHP sessions are a practical, simple solution, but storing data in disk files results in unnecessary disk activity and relies on the operating system to manage I/O efficiently. The default disk file session store can be replaced with a MySQL session store, as discussed in Appendix D, but the approach is still likely to be less efficient than purpose-built database tables. Designing database tables specifically for shopping-cart management is a good solution, but—as we discuss next—it is unnecessary in the winestore application.

We use the *orders* and *items* tables as follows. When a user adds an item to his initially empty shopping cart, a new row is inserted into the *orders* table with a cust_id of -1 and the next available order_id for this customer. A cust_id of -1 distinguishes between the shopping carts in the winestore and the actual customers: actual customers have cust_id values of 1 or greater, while all shopping carts share the cust_id of -1.

The order_id allocated to the user's cart is then stored as a session variable. The existence of the session variable is used throughout the cart scripts to indicate that the shopping cart has contents, and the value of the variable is used as a key to retrieve the contents. The only practical difference between a completed order and a shopping cart is that in the latter, the customer number is -1, signifying that the items are in a shopping cart and not yet part of an actual order.

Shopping carts can be inspected using the MySQL command interpreter. First, you can inspect how many active shopping carts there are by checking the *orders* tables:

```
mysql> SELECT order_id, date
       FROM orders WHERE cust_id = -1;
+----------+--------------+
| order_id | date         |
+----------+--------------+
|        1 | 011210060918 |
|        2 | 011210061534 |
|        3 | 011210061817 |
|        4 | 011210063249 |
+----------+--------------+
4 rows in set (0.00 sec)
```

Having found that there are four shopping carts active in the system, you can inspect any cart to check their contents. Consider, for example, the contents of the fourth shopping cart:

```
mysql> SELECT item_id, wine_id, qty, price
       FROM items
```

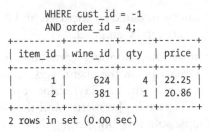

```
        WHERE cust_id = -1
        AND order_id = 4;
+---------+---------+------+-------+
| item_id | wine_id | qty  | price |
+---------+---------+------+-------+
|       1 |     624 |    4 | 22.25 |
|       2 |     381 |    1 | 20.86 |
+---------+---------+------+-------+
2 rows in set (0.00 sec)
```

From this simple inspection, we know there are four shopping carts, and the owner of the fourth cart has a total of five bottles of two different wines in her cart.

Throughout the rest of this section, we outline how the cart is implemented in PHP and how the cart is updated and emptied. We discuss converting a cart to an order in Chapter 12. Chapter 13 discusses other related topics including how the cart can be automatically emptied if the user doesn't proceed with the order within 24 hours.

Viewing the Shopping Cart

Example 11-2 shows the *cart.2* script, which displays the contents of the shopping cart. Using the same approach as in Example 11-1, the script displays the user login status, any errors or notices for the user, and a set of buttons to allow the user to request other scripts in the winestore. The body of the script is the displayCart( ) function, which queries and displays the contents of the shopping cart.

displayCart( ) checks if the cart has contents by testing for the presence of the session variable order_no. If order_no is registered, its value is the order_id associated with the shopping cart, and the following query is executed:

```
$cartQuery = "SELECT qty, price, wine_id, item_id
              FROM items
              WHERE cust_id = -1
              AND order_id = $order_no";
```

The query retrieves the items in the user's cart, and the items are then displayed in an HTML <table> environment. The quantities of each item are displayed within the <table> as <input> elements of a <form>. Each element has an associated name attribute that is set to the item_id of the item, and the value of the attribute is set to the quantity of wine in the cart. For example, consider the following HTML fragment that represents the second item in a user's cart:

```
<tr>
  <td><input type="text" size=3 name="2" value="13"></td>
  <td>1982 Grehan's Vineyard Galti Cabernet Sauvignon</td>
  <td>$20.86</td>
  <td>$271.18</td>
</tr>
```

When rendered in a browser, this item displays a quantity of 13 bottles that can be edited by the user. If the user changes the quantity and clicks on the Update

Quantities button, a request is made for the *cart.6* script to update the quantities. The request includes the item_id of 2 as the GET method attribute and the new quantity as its value. We discuss the *cart.6* script later in this section.

Example 11-2. cart.2 displays the contents of the user's shopping cart

```php
<?php
    // This script shows the user the contents of
    // their shopping cart

    include 'include.inc';

    set_error_handler("errorHandler");

    // Show the user the contents of their cart
    function displayCart($connection)
    {
        global $order_no;

        // If the user has added items to their cart, then
        // the variable order_no will be registered
        if (session_is_registered("order_no"))
        {
            $cartQuery - "SELECT qty, price, wine_id, item_id
                        FROM items
                        WHERE cust_id = -1
                        AND order_id = $order_no";

            // Retrieve the item details of the cart items
            if (!($result = @ mysql_query($cartQuery,
                                        $connection)))
                showerror();

            $cartAmount = 0;
            $cartCount = 0;

            // Create some headings for the cart
            echo "<table border=\"0\" " .
                "cellpadding=\"0\" cellspacing=\"5\">";
            echo "\n<tr>";
            echo "\n\t<th>Quantity </th>";
            echo "\n\t<th>Wine</th>";
            echo "\n\t<th>Unit Price</th>";
            echo "\n\t<th>Total</th>";
            echo "\n</tr>";

            // Go through each of the wines in the cart
            while ($row = @ mysql_fetch_array($result))
            {
                // Keep a running total of the number of items
                // and dollar-value of the items in the cart
                $cartCount += $row["qty"];
```

```
        $lineTotal = $row["price"] * $row["qty"];
        $cartAmount += $lineTotal;

        // Show the quantity of this item in a text
        // input widget. The user can alter the quantity
        // and update it
        echo "\n<tr>";
        echo "\n\t<td>" .
            "<input type=\"text\" size=3 name=\"" .
            $row["item_id"] .
            "\" value = \"" .
            $row["qty"] .
            "\"></td>";

        // Show the wine details of the item
        echo "\n\t<td>";
        echo showWine($row["wine_id"], $connection);
        echo "</td>";

        // Show the per-bottle price
        printf("\n\t<td>$%.2f</td>", $row["price"]);

        // Show the total price of this item
        printf("\n\t<td>$%.2f</td>", $lineTotal);
        echo "\n</tr>";
    }

    echo "\n<tr></tr>";

    // Show the user the total number of bottles
    // and the total cost of the items in the cart
    printf("\n<tr>\n\t<td><b>%d items</b></td>",
            $cartCount);
    echo "\n\t<td></td>\n\t<td></td>";
    printf("\n\t<td><b>$%.2f</b></td>\n</tr>",
            $cartAmount);
    echo "\n</table>";
    }
    else
    {
        // The session variable $order_no is not
        // registered. Therefore, the user has not
        // put anything in the cart
        echo "<h3><font color=\"red\">" .
            "Your cart is empty</font></h3>";
    }
}

// ---------

// Open a connection to the DBMS
if (!($connection = @ mysql_pconnect($hostName,
```

Example 11-2. cart.2 displays the contents of the user's shopping cart (continued)

```
                                      $username,
                                      $password)))
      showerror();

   if (!mysql_select_db($databaseName, $connection))
      showerror();

   // Initialize a session. This call either creates
   // a new session or re-establishes an existing one.
   session_start();

?>
<!DOCTYPE HTML PUBLIC
   "-//W3C//DTD HTML 4.01 Transitional//EN"
   "http://www.w3.org/TR/html401/loose.dtd">
<html>
<head>
   <title>Hugh and Dave's Online Wines</title>
</head>
<body bgcolor="white">
<?php
   // Show the user login status
   showLogin();
?>
<h1>Your Shopping Cart</h1>
<?php
   // Show the user any messages
   showMessage();
?>
<form action="example.cart.5.php" method="GET">
<?php
   // Show the contents of the shopping cart
   displayCart($connection);
?>

<table>
<tr>
   <td><input type="submit" name="home" value="Home"></td>
<?php
   // If the user has items in their cart, offer the
   // chance to update quantities or empty the cart or
   // finalize the purchase (if they're logged in)
   if (session_is_registered("order_no"))
   {
      echo "\n\t<td><input type=\"submit\" " .
      "name=\"update\" value=\"Update Quantities\"></td>";
      echo "\n\t<td><input type=\"submit\" " .
      "name=\"empty\" value=\"Empty Cart\"></td>";
      if (session_is_registered("loginUsername"))
         echo "\n\t<td><input type=\"submit\" " .
      "name=\"buy\" value=\"Make Purchase\"></td>";
   }
```

```
    // Show the user the search screen button
    echo "\t<td><input type=\"submit\" " .
         "name=\"search\" value=\"Search\"></td>\n";

    // Show login or logout button
    loginButtons();
?>
</tr>
</table>
</form>
<br><a href="http://validator.w3.org/check/referer">
    <img src-"http://www.w3.org/Icons/valid-html401"
    height="31" width="88" align="right" border="0"
    alt="Valid HTML 4.01!"></a>
</body>
</html>
```

Adding Items to the Shopping Cart

Example 11-3 shows the *cart.3* script, which adds items to the shopping cart. The script expects two parameters: a wineId that matches a wine_id in the *wine* table and a qty (quantity) of the wine to add to the cart. These parameters are supplied by clicking on embedded links on the home or search pages. For example, the home page contains links such as:

```
<a href="example.cart.3.php?qty=1&amp;wineId=624">
Add a bottle to the cart</a>
```

When the user clicks on the link, the *cart.3* script adds a bottle of the wine to the cart, database processing occurs, and the user is redirected back to the calling page. This use of one-component querying for adding wines to the cart is discussed in more detail in Chapter 5.

cart.3 has several steps:

1. It checks whether the shopping cart exists. If it does exist, it locks the *items* table for writing and the *inventory* table for reading. If the cart doesn't exist, the *orders* table is also locked for writing.

2. Locking is required since the script may suffer from the dirty read and lost update concurrency problems discussed in Chapter 6. These problems can occur if another user is simultaneously creating a shopping cart—without locking, both users may obtain the same cart number—or if an inventory is sold out while an item is being added to the cart, in which case the item price in the cart may be wrong.

3. After locking the required tables, the script tests whether a cart already exists. If it doesn't exist, it is created as a new row in the *orders* table with the next available order_id for the dummy customer. The order_id is then assigned to the

session variable order_no. If the cart does exist, the script checks if the item being added to the cart is already one of the items in the cart. If it is, the item_id is saved so that the quantity of the item can be updated. If it isn't in the cart, a new item_id is assigned to the new wine.

If this is a new item being added to the cart, the script queries to find the cheapest inventory price for the wine. An error is reported if the wine has sold out by registering a message as a session variable; messages are displayed by all scripts that interact with the user through a call to the showMessage( ) function incorporated in *include.inc*. Wines selling out is an unusual occurrence: it occurs only if another user purchases all the remaining stock of a wine before this user clicks on the embedded link.

4. After all checks of the cart and the inventory, the cart item is updated or inserted.

5. The table locks are released.

6. Finally, the script redirects to the calling page, completing the one-component add-to-cart script.

Example 11-3. cart.3 adds a quantity of a specific wine to the shopping cart

```php
<?php
// This script adds an item to the shopping cart
// It expects a WineId of the item to add and a
// quantity (qty) of the wine to be added

include 'include.inc';

set_error_handler("errorHandler");

// Have the correct parameters been provided?
if (empty($wineId) && empty($qty))
{
    session_register("message");

    $message =
      "Incorrect parameters to example.cart.3.php";

    // Redirect the browser back to the calling page
    header("Location: $HTTP_REFERER");
    exit;
}

// Re-establish the existing session
session_start();

$wineId = clean($wineId, 5);
$qty = clean($qty, 3);

$update = false;
```

Example 11-3. cart.3 adds a quantity of a specific wine to the shopping cart (continued)

```
// Open a connection to the DBMS
if (!($connection = @ mysql_pconnect($hostName,
                                      $username,
                                      $password)))
    showerror();

if (!mysql_select_db($databaseName, $connection))
    showerror();

// If the user has added items to their cart, then
// the variable order_no will be registered

// First, decide on which tables to lock
// We don't touch orders if the cart already exists
if (session_is_registered("order_no"))
    $query = "LOCK TABLES inventory READ, items WRITE";
else
    $query = "LOCK TABLES inventory READ,
                          orders WRITE,
                          items WRITE";

// LOCK the tables
if (!(@ mysql_query ($query, $connection)))
    showerror();

// Second, create a cart if we don't have one yet
// or investigate the cart if we do
if (!session_is_registered("order_no"))
{
    // Find out the maximum order_id, then
    // register a session variable for the new order_id
    // A cart is an order for the customer
    // with cust_id = -1
    $query = "SELECT max(order_id) FROM orders
              WHERE cust_id = -1";

    if (!($result = @ mysql_query ($query, $connection)))
        showerror();

    // Save the cart number as order_no
    // This is used in all cart scripts to access the cart
    session_register("order_no");

    $row = @ mysql_fetch_array($result);
    $order_no = $row["max(order_id)"] + 1;

    // Now, create the shopping cart
    $query = "INSERT INTO orders
              SET cust_id = -1,
                  order_id = $order_no";
```

Example 11-3. cart.3 adds a quantity of a specific wine to the shopping cart (continued)

```
      if (!(@ mysql_query ($query, $connection)))
         showerror();

      // Default the item_id to 1
      $item_id = 1;
   }
   else
   {
      // We already have a cart.
      // Check if the customer already has this item
      // in their cart
      $query = "SELECT item_id, qty FROM items
               WHERE cust_id = -1
               AND order_id = $order_no
               AND wine_id = $wineId";

      if (!($result = @ mysql_query ($query, $connection)))
         showerror();

      // Is the item in the cart already?
      if (mysql_num_rows($result) > 0)
      {
         $update - true;
         $row = @ mysql_fetch_array($result);

         // Save the item number
         $item_id = $row["item_id"];
      }

      // If this is not an update, find the
      // next available item_id
      if ($update == false)
      {
         // We already have a cart, find the maximum item_id
         $query = "SELECT max(item_id) FROM items
                  WHERE cust_id = -1
                  AND order_id = $order_no";

         if (!($result = @ mysql_query ($query,
                                   $connection)))
            showerror();

         $row = @ mysql_fetch_array($result);

         // Save the item number of the new item
         $item_id = $row["max(item_id)"] + 1;
      }
   }

   // Third, add the item to the cart or update the cart
   if ($update == false)
   {
```

```
    // Get the cost of the wine
    // The cost comes from the cheapest inventory
    $query = "SELECT count(*), min(cost) FROM inventory
              WHERE wine_id = $wineId";

    if (!($result = @ mysql_query ($query, $connection)))
       showerror( );

    $row = @ mysql_fetch_array($result);

    // This wine could have just sold out - check this
    // (this happens if another user buys the last bottle
    //  before this user clicks "add to cart")
    if ($row["count(*)"] == 0)
    {
       // Register the error as a session variable
       // This message will then be displayed back on
       // page where the user adds wines to their cart
       session_register("message");
       $message =
          "Sorry! We just sold out of this great wine!";
    }
    else
    {
       // We still have some of this wine, so save the
       // cheapest available price
       $cost = $row["min(cost)"];
       $query = "INSERT INTO items
                   SET cust_id = -1,
                       order_id = $order_no,
                       item_id = $item_id,
                       wine_id = $wineId,
                       qty = $qty,
                       price = $cost";
    }
}
else
   $query = "UPDATE items
               SET qty = qty + $qty
               WHERE cust_id = -1
               AND order_id = $order_no
               AND item_id = $item_id";

// Either UPDATE or INSERT the item
// (Only do this if there wasn't an error)
if (empty($message) &&
   (!(@ mysql_query ($query, $connection))))
  showerror( );

// Last, UNLOCK the tables
$query = "UNLOCK TABLES";
```

Example 11-3. cart.3 adds a quantity of a specific wine to the shopping cart (continued)

```php
  if (!(@ mysql_query ($query, $connection)))
    showerror();

  // Redirect the browser back to the calling page,
  // using the HTTP response header "Location:"
  // and the PHP environment variable $HTTP_REFERER
  header("Location: $HTTP_REFERER");
?>
```

Emptying the Shopping Cart

Example 11-4 lists the *cart.4* script that empties the shopping cart. The script is again a one-component module that carries out its actions, produces no output, and then redirects back to the calling page. The script removes the row in the *orders* table and any rows in the *items* table that have an order_id equal to the value of the session variable order_no. It then deletes the session variable itself, thus completing the emptying of the cart.

Example 11-4. cart.4 empties the cart

```php
<?php
  // This script empties the cart and deletes the session

  include 'include.inc';

  set_error_handler("errorHandler");

  // Initialise the session - this is needed before
  // a session can be destroyed
  session_start();

  // Is there a cart in the database?
  if (session_is_registered("order_no"))
  {
    // Open a connection to the DBMS
    if (!($connection = @ mysql_connect($hostName,
                                        $username,
                                        $password)))
      showerror();

    if (!mysql_select_db($databaseName, $connection))
      showerror();

    // First, delete the order
    $query = "DELETE FROM orders
              WHERE cust_id = -1
              AND order_id = $order_no";

    if (!(@ mysql_query ($query, $connection)))
      showerror();
```

Example 11-4. cart.4 empties the cart (continued)

```
    // Now, delete the items
    $query = "DELETE FROM items
            WHERE cust_id = -1
            AND order_id = $order_no";

    if (!(@ mysql_query ($query, $connection)))
        showerror();

    // Finally, destroy the session variable
    session_unregister("order_no");
}
else
{
    session_register("message");
    $message = "There is nothing in your cart.";
}

// Redirect the browser back to the calling page.
if (session_is_registered("referer"))
{
    session_unregister("referer");
    header("Location: $referer");
    exit;
}
else
    header("Location: $HTTP_REFERER");
?>
```

Updating the Shopping Cart Quantities

The *cart.6* script, which updates the quantities of items in the shopping cart, is shown in Example 11-5. The script is requested by the *cart.2* script and expects GET method parameters of item_id and update quantity pairs. For example, consider the following request for the script:

```
http://localhost/example.cart.6.php?1=12&2=13&3=6&update=Update+Quantities
```

This requests that the quantity of the first item in the cart be updated to 12 bottles, the second item to 13 bottles, and the third item to 6 bottles.

The script works as follows:

1. It untaints the user data using the clean( ) function and assigns the results into the array parameters.

2. It uses the foreach loop statement to iterate through each parameter. For each parameter that isn't the update parameter, it checks to ensure that the item_id and the quantity are both numbers of less than four or three digits in length, respectively. If this test fails, a message is registered as a session variable and displayed after the script redirects back to the *cart.2* script.

3. If the quantity of the wine is zero, the item is deleted from the cart.

4. If the quantity is non-zero, the quantity is updated to the value passed as a parameter.

5. If the cart is now empty—which happens if all items are set to zero quantities—the cart is deleted by removing the *cart* row from the *orders* table.

6. The script redirects back to the *cart.2* script.

Example 11-5. cart.6 updates the quantities of wines in the shopping cart

```php
<?php
    // This script updates quantities in the cart
    // It expects parameters of the form XXX=YYY
    // where XXX is a wine_id and YYY is the new
    // quantity of that wine that should be in the
    // cart

    include 'include.inc';

    set_error_handler("errorHandler");

    // Re-establish the existing session
    session_start();

    // Clean up the data, and save the results
    // in an array
    foreach($HTTP_GET_VARS as $varname => $value)
            $parameters[$varname] = clean($value, 4);

    // Did they want to update the quantities?
    // (this should be true except if the user arrives
    // here unexpectedly)
    if (empty($parameters["update"]))
    {
        session_register("message");

        $message = "Incorrect parameters to ".
                   "example.cart.6.php";

        // Redirect the browser back to the calling page
        header("Location: $HTTP_REFERER");
        exit;
    }

    // Open a connection to the DBMS
    if (!($connection = @ mysql_connect($hostName,
                                        $username,
                                        $password)))
        showerror();

    if (!mysql_select_db($databaseName, $connection))
        showerror();
```

Example 11-5. cart.6 updates the quantities of wines in the shopping cart (continued)

```
// If the user has added items to their cart, then
// the variable order_no will be registered

// Go through each submitted value and update the cart
foreach($parameters as $itemName => $itemValue)
{
   // Ignore the update variable
   if ($itemName != "update")
   {
      // The item's name must look like a wine_id
      if (ereg("^[0-9]{1,4}$", $itemName))
      {
         // The update value must be a number
         if (ereg("^[0-9]{1,3}$", $itemValue))
         {
            // If the number is zero, delete the item
            if ($itemValue == 0)
               $query = "DELETE FROM items
                        WHERE cust_id = -1
                        AND order_id = $order_no
                        AND item_id = $itemName";
            else
              // otherwise, update the value
              $query = "UPDATE items
                        SET qty = $itemValue
                        WHERE cust_id = -1
                        AND order_id = $order_no
                        AND item_id = $itemName";

            if (!(@ mysql_query ($query, $connection)))
               showerror( );

         } // if (ereg("^[0-9]{1,3}$", $itemValue))
         else
         {
            session_register("message");
            $message = "There was an error updating " .
                       "your quantities. Try again.";
         }
      } // if (ereg("^[0-9]{1,4}$", $itemName))
      else
      {
         session_register("message");
         $message = "There was an error updating " .
                    "quantities. Try again.";
      }
   } // if ($itemName != "update")
} // foreach($parameters as $itemName => $itemValue)

// The cart may now be empty. Check this.
$query = "SELECT count(*)
         FROM items
```

Example 11-5. cart.6 updates the quantities of wines in the shopping cart (continued)

```
                WHERE cust_id = -1
                AND order_id = $order_no";

   if (!($result = @ mysql_query ($query, $connection)))
      showerror();

   $row = mysql_fetch_array($result);

   // Are there no items left?
   if ($row["count(*)"] == 0)
   {
      // Delete the order
      $query = "DELETE FROM orders
               WHERE cust_id = -1
               AND order_id = $order_no";

      if (!(@ mysql_query ($query, $connection)))
         showerror();

      session_unregister("order_no");
   }

   // Go back to the cart
   header("Location: example.cart.2.php");
   exit;
?>
```

We have now completed our discussion of the shopping cart implementation. Converting a shopping cart to an order is discussed in Chapter 12. In the next section, we discuss how redirection is managed in the winestore application.

Managing Redirection

The *cart.5* script shown in Example 11-6 is a central point that manages redirection to other scripts in the winestore. All pages that have more than one button request this script using the action attribute of the <form> element. The script processes the requests, determines from the GET method attributes which script should be requested next, and then redirects the browser to that script.

For example, if the user clicks the Empty Cart button on any page, the following URL is requested:

```
http://localhost/example.cart.5.php?empty=Empty+Cart
```

The *cart.5* script is then processed, the following if test is found to be true, and the script redirects to the *cart.4* script:

```
// Did they want to empty the cart?
if (!empty($parameters["empty"]))
{
```

```
    // Redirect the browser to the empty page
    // using the HTTP response header "Location:"
    header("Location: example.cart.4.php");
    exit;
  }
```

When redirecting to some scripts, the redirection also passes on the entire QUERY_
STRING—the query string is stored in the PHP environment variable $QUERY_STRING—
as a GET method parameter. In addition, a session variable, referer, is registered in
selected cases so that in later processing the script can redirect to the original calling
page.

As discussed in Chapter 10, there are several other possible approaches for managing requests for different scripts throughout an application. An alternative to the
approach is to add each button to the HTML page as a separate <form> element with
its own action attribute. Other approaches include using embedded links or images
instead of buttons.

Example 11-6. cart.5 manages button clicks in the winestore

```php
<?php
    // This script redirects the browser to another script,
    // depending on what parameters are provided. It is used
    // for processing several submit buttons from an
    // HTML <form>

    include 'include.inc';

    set_error_handler("errorHandler");

    session_start();

    // Clean up the data, and save the results in
    // an array
    foreach($HTTP_GET_VARS as $varname => $value)
            $parameters[$varname] = clean($value, 10);

    // Did they want to view the cart?
    if (!empty($parameters["view"]))
    {
       // Redirect the browser to the cart page
       // using the HTTP response header "Location:"
       header("Location: example.cart.2.php");
       exit;
    }

    // Did they want to go home?
    if (!empty($parameters["home"]))
    {
       // Redirect the browser to the home page
       // using the HTTP response header "Location:"
       header("Location: example.cart.1.php");
```

Example 11-6. cart.5 manages button clicks in the winestore (continued)

```
      exit;
    }

    // Did they want to empty the cart?
    if (!empty($parameters["empty"]))
    {
      // Redirect the browser to the empty page
      // using the HTTP response header "Location:"
      header("Location: example.cart.4.php");
      exit;
    }

    // Did they want to update the quantities?
    if (!empty($parameters["update"]))
    {
      // Redirect the browser to the update page
      // using the HTTP response header "Location:"
      header("Location: example.cart.6.php?" .
            $QUERY_STRING);
      exit;
    }

    // Did they want to save the search?
    if (!empty($parameters["savesearch"]))
    {
      // Redirect the browser to the search save page
      // using the HTTP response header "Location:"
      header("Location: example.cart.8.php?" .
            $QUERY_STRING);
      exit;
    }

    // Did they want to login to the site?
    if (!empty($parameters["login"]))
    {
      // Save the referer page for later redirection
      if (session_is_registered("referer"))
         session_unregister("referer");
      session_register("referer");
      $referer = $HTTP_REFERER;

      // Redirect the browser to the login page
      // using the HTTP response header "Location:"
      header("Location: example.order.1.php?" .
            $QUERY_STRING);
      exit;
    }

    if (!empty($parameters["logout"]))
    {
      // Save the referer page for later redirection
      if (session_is_registered("referer"))
```

Example 11-6. cart.5 manages button clicks in the winestore (continued)

```
        session_unregister("referer");
    session_register("referer");
    $referer = $HTTP_REFERER;

    // Redirect the browser to the logout page
    // using the HTTP response header "Location:"
    header("Location: example.order.2.php?" .
        $QUERY_STRING");
    exit;
}

// Did they want to finalise the purchase?
if (!empty($parameters["buy"]))
{
    // Redirect the browser to the purchase page
    // using the HTTP response header "Location:"
    header("Location: example.order.3.php?" .
        $QUERY_STRING");
    exit;
}

// Did they want to edit customer details?
if (!empty($parameters["account"]))
{
    // Redirect the browser to the customer account
    // page using the HTTP response header "Location:"
    header("Location: example.customer.2.php");
    exit;
}

// They got here without providing an option, so
// there is a problem
echo "You arrived here unexpectedly.";
?>
```

CHAPTER 12

Ordering and Shipping at the Winestore

We complete our description of the shopping components of the winestore by outlining the ordering and shipping modules in this chapter. The ordering module manages the conversion of the shopping cart discussed in Chapter 11 to an order. The module manages the most complex database interactions in the winestore and includes locking to address concurrency problems. The shipping module consists of two receipts: an email receipt that shows how the PHP `mail( )` function is used in practice and an HTML receipt that is similar to the customer receipt in Chapter 10.

This chapter is the third of four that outline the complete winestore application. As in the previous two chapters, we emphasize that the scripts aren't a production system but an illustration of web database application practice. We encourage use of the scripts for any purpose and suggest that the best method to understand the scripts is to view, edit, and use them while reading the chapter. We also emphasize that the descriptions in this chapter are outlines and that a full understanding of the scripts requires reading and using the code.

The scripts discussed in this chapter perform the following functions:

Finalize orders
> Convert a shopping cart in the *items* and *orders* tables to an order and manage the sale of wine through the *inventory* table

Email receipts
> Send a confirmation email to the user

HTML order receipts
> Complete the ordering process with an HTML receipt that avoids the reload problem

Finalizing Orders

When a user finishes adding items to his cart, he usually proceeds to a purchase. Finalizing an order requires several steps that include checking that sufficient inventory is available to complete the order, converting the shopping cart to an order, and deducting the wines sold from the inventory. These tasks require locking of the database and are examples of moderately complex query processing. The script *order.3* shown in Example 12-1 performs these tasks.

The script works as follows:

1. It tests that the user is logged in and that the cart has contents. These tests should never fail, as the Make Purchase button is shown only when the user is viewing the cart, is logged in, and the cart has contents. If either test fails, an error message is registered, and the script redirects to the calling script.

2. The *inventory*, *items*, and *orders* tables are locked for writing, and the *users* and *customer* tables are locked for reading. The *inventory*, *items*, and *orders* tables are all updated in the purchasing process, and they must be locked because the inventory is first checked to ensure that sufficient quantities of wine are available and then later updated. Without locking, it is possible for another user to purchase the wine while this script is running, resulting in more wine being sold than is in stock. This is an example of the dirty read concurrency problem discussed in Chapter 6, and locking must be used to avoid the problem.

3. Each item in the cart is then processed, and the inventory is checked to ensure that enough wine is available. If no wine is available—the count( ) of the matching inventory rows is zero—an error message is registered. Similarly, if less wine is available than the user wants—the sum( ) of the on_hand quantity of the matching rows is less than the user's cart qty—an error message is also registered. On error, the script also updates the user's cart so that the quantity (qty) of wine in the user's cart matches the quantity that is on_hand. In the case of an error, the script uses the function showWine( ) to show the user the details of the wine. This function opens its own connection to the DBMS so that the *wine*, *wine_variety*, *winery*, and *grape_variety* tables don't need to be locked for reading in the *order*.

4. If the inventory checks succeed, the script proceeds to convert the user's cart to be a customer's order. This process is straightforward:

    a. Determine the cust_id from the loginUsername session variable using the function getCustomerID( ).

    b. Find the maximum order_id for this customer.

    c. Update the *orders* and *items* rows by replacing the cust_id of -1 with the customer's cust_id and the order_id with the next available order_id for this customer.

5. After the database has been updated, the cart is emptied using session_unregister( ) to remove the order_no session variable.

6. Having completed the order and checked the inventory, the script finishes the ordering process by reducing the inventory. This can never fail, since all required tables are locked, and you've checked that sufficient quantities are available. The

process is similar to checking the cart: you iterate through each item and, for each one, you update the inventory. The inventories are processed from oldest to newest. Consider an example in which the user wants to purchase 24 bottles of a wine. There are two inventories of this wine: the first has 13 bottles and was added in May 2000; the second has 25 bottles and was added in September 2001. To satisfy the order, the oldest inventory of 13 bottles is emptied and deleted, and the second inventory is reduced by 11 bottles.

7. With the process complete, the tables are unlocked. If there are no errors, the script redirects to the *shipping.1* script to confirm the order, and the cust_id and order_id are passed as GET method parameters. If there are errors, the user is returned to the cart view page.

Example 12-1. order.3 finalizes the user's purchase

```php
<?php
    // This script finalizes a purchase
    // It expects that a cart has contents and that the
    // user is logged in

    include 'include.inc';

    set_error_handler("errorHandler");

    // Re-establish the existing session
    session_start();

    // Check if a cart exists - this should never fail
    // unless the script is run directly
    if (!session_is_registered("order_no"))
    {
        session_register("message");
        $message =
            "There are no items in your shopping cart!";

        // Redirect the browser back to the calling page
        header("Location: $HTTP_REFERER");
        exit;
    }

    // Check if the user is logged in - this should
    // never fail unless the script is run directly
    if (!session_is_registered("loginUsername"))
    {
        session_register("message");
        $message =
            "You must login to finalize your purchase.";

        // Redirect the browser back to the calling page
        header("Location: $HTTP_REFERER");
        exit;
    }
```

Example 12-1. order.3 finalizes the user's purchase (continued)

```
// Open a connection to the DBMS
if (!($connection = @ mysql_pconnect($hostName,
                                      $username,
                                      $password)))
   showerror();

if (!mysql_select_db($databaseName, $connection))
   showerror();

// Several tables must be locked to finalize a purchase.
// We avoid locking four other tables by
// using another DBMS connection to produce the wine
// information
$query = "LOCK TABLES inventory WRITE,
                      orders WRITE,
                      items WRITE,
                      users READ,
                      customer READ";

// LOCK the tables
if (!(@ mysql_query ($query, $connection)))
   showerror();

// Process each wine in the cart and find out if
// there is sufficient stock available in the inventory
$query = "SELECT * FROM items
          WHERE cust_id = -1
          AND order_id = $order_no";

// Initialise an empty error message
$message = "";

if (!($result = @ mysql_query ($query, $connection)))
   showerror();

// Get the next wine in the cart
for ($winesInCart = 0;
     $winesInCart < mysql_num_rows($result);
     $winesInCart++)
{
   $cartRow[$winesInCart] = @ mysql_fetch_array($result);

   // Is there enough of this wine on hand?
   $query = "SELECT COUNT(on_hand), SUM(on_hand)
             FROM inventory
             WHERE wine_id = " .
             $cartRow[$winesInCart]["wine_id"];

   if (!($stockResult = @ mysql_query ($query,
                                       $connection)))
      showerror();
```

Example 12-1. order.3 finalizes the user's purchase (continued)

```
        $on_hand = @ mysql_fetch_array($stockResult);

        if ($on_hand["COUNT(on_hand)"] == 0)
            $available = 0;
        else
            $available = $on_hand["SUM(on_hand)"];

        // Is there more wine in the cart than is for sale?
        if ($cartRow[$winesInCart]["qty"] > $available)
        {
            if (!session_is_registered("message"))
                session_register("message");

            if ($available == 0)
                $message .= "Sorry! We just sold out of " .
                    showWine($cartRow[$winesInCart]["wine_id"],
                            NULL) .
                            "\n<br>";
            else
                $message .= "Sorry! We only have " .
                            $on_hand["SUM(on_hand)"] .
                            " bottles left of " .
                    showWine($cartRow[$winesInCart]["wine_id"],
                            NULL) .
                            "\n<br>";

            // Update the user's quantity to match the
            // available amount
            $query = "UPDATE items
                    SET qty = " . $available .
                    " WHERE cust_id = -1
                    AND order_id = $order_no
                    AND item_id = " .
                    $cartRow[$winesInCart]["item_id"];

            if (!(@ mysql_query ($query, $connection)))
                showerror();
        }
} // for $winesInCart < mysql_num_rows($result);

// We have now checked if there is enough wine
// available.
// If there is, we can proceed with the order.
// If not, we send the user back to the amended
// cart to think about purchasing the lesser
// amount.

if (empty($message))
{
    // Everything is ok - let's proceed then!
    // First of all, find out the user's cust_id and
    // the next available order_id for this customer.
```

Example 12-1. order.3 finalizes the user's purchase (continued)

```
$custID = getCustomerID($loginUsername, NULL);

$query = "SELECT max(order_id)
          FROM orders
          WHERE cust_id = $custID";

if (($result = @ mysql_query ($query, $connection)))
   $row = mysql_fetch_array($result);
else
   showerror( );

$newOrder_no = $row["max(order_id)"] + 1;

// Now, change the cust_id and order_id of their cart!
$query = "UPDATE orders
          SET cust_id = $custID , " .
          "order_id = " . $newOrder_no .
          " WHERE order_id = $order_no";

if (!(@ mysql_query ($query, $connection)))
   showerror( );

$query = "UPDATE items
          SET cust_id = $custID , " .
          "order_id = " . $newOrder_no .
          " WHERE order_id = $order_no";

if (!(@ mysql_query ($query, $connection)))
   showerror( );

// Officially empty the cart
session_unregister("order_no");

// Now we have to do the inventory.
// We do this one cart item at a time.
// For all items, we know that there *is*
// sufficient inventory, since we've checked earlier
foreach($cartRow as $currentRow)
{
   // Find the inventories for this wine, oldest first
   $query = "SELECT inventory_id, on_hand
             FROM inventory
             WHERE wine_id = " .
             $currentRow["wine_id"] .
             " ORDER BY date_added";

   if (!($result = @ mysql_query ($query,
                                   $connection)))
      showerror( );
```

Example 12-1. order.3 finalizes the user's purchase (continued)

```
        // While there are still bottles to be deducted
        while($currentRow["qty"] > 0)
        {
            // Get the next-oldest inventory
            $row = @ mysql_fetch_array($result);

            // Is there more wine in this inventory than
            // the user wants?
            if ($row["on_hand"] > $currentRow["qty"])
            {
                // Reduce the inventory by the amount the
                // user ordered
                $query = "UPDATE inventory
                    SET on_hand = on_hand - " .
                        $currentRow["qty"] .
                    " WHERE wine_id = " .
                        $currentRow["wine_id"] .
                    " AND inventory_id = " .
                        $row["inventory_id"];

                // The user doesn't need any more of this
                // wine
                $currentRow["qty"] = 0;
            }
            else
            {
                // Remove the inventory - we sold the
                // remainder to this user
                $query = "DELETE FROM inventory
                    WHERE wine_id = " .
                        $currentRow["wine_id"] .
                    " AND inventory_id = " .
                        $row["inventory_id"];

                // This inventory reduces the customer's
                // required amount by at least 1, but
                // we need to process more inventory
                $currentRow["qty"] -= $row["on_hand"];
            }

            // UPDATE or DELETE the inventory
            if (!(@ mysql_query ($query, $connection)))
                showerror();
        }
    }
}
else
    $message .= "\n<br>The quantities in your cart " .
                "have been updated\n.";

// Last, UNLOCK the tables
$query = "UNLOCK TABLES";
```

Example 12-1. order.3 finalizes the user's purchase (continued)

```
   if (!(@ mysql_query ($query, $connection)))
      showerror();

   // Redirect to the email confirmation page if
   // everything is ok
   // (supply the custID and orderID to the script)
   // otherwise go back to the cart page and show a message
   if (empty($message))
   {
      header("Location: example.shipping.1.php?" .
             "custID=$custID&orderID=$newOrder_no");
      exit;
   }
   else
      header("Location: example.cart.2.php");
?>
```

HTML and Email Receipts

Once an order has been processed, the winestore application confirms the shipping of the wines through both an email and an HTML receipt. The *order.3* script redirects to the *shipping.1* script shown in Example 12-2, which sends the user an email. In turn, the *shipping.1* script redirects to the *shipping.2* script shown in Example 12-3, which produces the HTML receipt. The HTML receipt can be visited again at a later time by bookmarking the URL and, as it carries out no database updates, it doesn't suffer from the reload problem described in Chapter 6. The receipt functionality is separated into two scripts so that returning to the HTML receipt doesn't cause an additional email receipt to be sent to the customer.

The function send_confirmation_email( ) in Example 12-2 creates the destination address, the subject, the body, and additional headers of an email message, and then sends that email message. The destination *to* address is created using the firstname, the surname, and the email address of the customer so that, for example, it has the following format:

```
    Michael Smith <mike@webdatabasebook.com>
```

The additional email headers are static and always have the following format:

```
    From: "Hugh and Dave's Online Wines" <help@webdatabasebook.com>
    X-Sender: <help@webdatabasebook.com>
    X-Mailer: PHP
    X-Priority: 1
    Return-Path: <help@webdatabasebook.com>
```

The subject of the email is always:

```
    $subject = "Hugh and Dave's Online Wines: Order
                Confirmation";
```

The body of the message is created by querying and retrieving the details of the customer, order, and items and appending data to the string $out. The following is an example of the body of a confirmation email:

```
Dear Dr Smith,

Thank you for placing an order at Hugh and Dave's
Online Wines.

Your order (reference #653-71) has been fictionally
dispatched, and should be arriving in your imagination
soon now. Please quote the reference number in any
correspondence.

If it existed, the order would be shipped to:

Dr Michael Smith
12 Hotham St.
Collingwood Victoria 3066
Australia

We have billed your fictional credit card

The order consists of:

Quantity  Wine                        Unit Price  Total
12         1999 Smith's Chardonnay     $22.25      $267.00

Total: $267.00

Thank you for shopping at Hugh and Dave's Online Wines!
```

The email itself is sent with the following fragment:

```
// Send the email!
mail($to, $subject, $out, $headers);
```

The mail( ) function is a PHP library function; it's discussed later in this section.

The body of the script also checks that the user is logged in, that the correct parameters of a cust_id and an order_id have been provided, and that the user viewing the receipt is the owner of the receipt. If any of the checks fail, the user is redirected so that an error message can be displayed.

Example 12-2. shipping.1 sends the user an order confirmation as an email

```
<?php
// This script sends the user a confirmation email
// for their order and then redirects to an HTML receipt
// version

include 'include.inc';

set_error_handler("errorHandler");
```

Example 12-2. shipping.1 sends the user an order confirmation as an email (continued)

```
// Send the user an email that summarizes their purchase
function send_confirmation_email($custID,
                                 $orderID,
                                 $connection)
{
  // Find customer information
  $query = "SELECT *
            FROM customer
            WHERE cust_id = $custID";

  if (!($result = @ mysql_query ($query,
                                 $connection)))
    showerror();

  // There is only one matching row
  $row = @ mysql_fetch_array($result);

  // Start by setting up the "to" address
  $to = $row["firstname"] . " " .
        $row["surname"] . " <" .
        $row["email"] . ">";

  // Now, set up the "subject" line
  $subject = "Hugh and Dave's Online Wines: " .
             "Order Confirmation";

  // And, last (before we build the email), set up
  // some mail headers
  $headers  = "From: Hugh and Dave's Online Wines" .
              "<help@webdatabasebook.com>\r\n";
  $headers .= "X-Sender: <help@webdatabasebook.com>\r\n";
  $headers .= "X-Mailer: PHP\r\n";
  $headers .= "X-Priority: 1\r\n";
  $headers .= "Return-Path: " .
              "<help@webdatabasebook.com>\r\n";

  // Now, put together the body of the email
  $out = "Dear " . $row["title"] .
         " " . $row["surname"] . ",\n" .
         "\nThank you for placing an order at " .
         "Hugh and Dave's Online Wines.\n";

  $out .= "\nYour order (reference #" . $custID .
          "-" . $orderID .
          ") has been fictionally dispatched,\n" .
          "and should be arriving in your imagination " .
          "soon now.\n" .
          "Please quote the reference number in any " .
          "correspondence.\n";

  $out .=  "\nIf it existed, the order would be " .
           "shipped to: \n\n" .
```

```php
                $row["title"] . " " .
                $row["firstname"] . " " .
                $row["initial"] . " " .
                $row["surname"] . "\n" .
                $row["addressline1"];

   if ($row["addressline2"] != "")
      $out .= "\n" . $row["addressline2"];

   if ($row["addressline3"] != "")
      $out .= "\n" . $row["addressline3"];

   $out .=  "\n" . $row["city"] . " " .
                   $row["state"] . " " .
                   $row["zipcode"] . "\n" .
                   $row["country"] . "\n\n";

   $out .= "We have billed your fictional " .
           "credit card \n\n";

   $out .=    "The order consists of:\n\n";

   // This is a heading for the order summary
   $out .=    str_pad("Quantity", 10) .
              str_pad("Wine", 55) .
              str_pad("Unit Price", 12) .
              str_pad("Total", 12) . "\n";

   $orderTotalPrice = 0;

   // list the particulars of each item in the order
   $query = "SELECT  i.qty, w.wine_name, i.price,
                     w.wine_id, w.year, wi.winery_name
             FROM    items i, wine w, winery wi
             WHERE   i.cust_id = $custID
             AND     i.order_id = $orderID
             AND     i.wine_id = w.wine_id
             AND     w.winery_id = wi.winery_id
             ORDER BY item_id";

   if (!($result = @ mysql_query ($query, $connection)))
      showerror();

   // Add each item to the email
   while ($row = @ mysql_fetch_array($result))
   {
      // Work out the cost of this line item
      $itemsPrice = $row["qty"] * $row["price"];

      $orderTotalPrice += $itemsPrice;
```

```
        $wineDetail = showWine($row["wine_id"], $connection);

        $out .= str_pad($row["qty"],10) .
                str_pad(substr($wineDetail, 0, 53), 55);

        $out .= str_pad(sprintf("$%-.2f" ,
                        $row["price"]), 10);
        $out .= "  ";
        $out .= str_pad(sprintf("$%-.2f", $itemsPrice), 12);
        $out .= "\n";
    }

   $out .= "\n\nTotal: ";

   $out .= sprintf("$%-.2f\n", $orderTotalPrice);

   $out .= "\n\nThank you for shopping at Hugh and " .
           "Dave's Online Wines!";

   // Send the email!
   mail($to, $subject, $out, $headers);
}

// Main ----------

 // Re-establish the existing session
 session_start();

 // Check if the user is logged in - this should
 // never fail if unless the script is run incorrectly
 if (!session_is_registered("loginUsername"))
 {
    session_register("message");
    $message = "You must login to finalise " .
               "your purchase.";
    header("Location: example.cart.2.php");
    exit;
 }

 // Check the correct parameters have been passed
 // unless the script is run correctly
 if (!isset($custID) || !isset($orderID))
 {
    session_register("message");
    $message = "Incorrect parameters to " .
               "example.shipping.1.php";
    header("Location: example.cart.2.php");
    exit;
 }
 // Check this customer matches the custID
 if ($custID != getCustomerID($loginUsername, NULL))
 {
```

Example 12-2. shipping.1 sends the user an order confirmation as an email (continued)

```
    session_register("message");

    $message = "You can only view your own receipts!";
    header("Location: example.order.1.php");
    exit;
}

// Open a connection to the DBMS
if (!($connection = @ mysql_pconnect($hostName,
                                     $username,
                                     $password)))
    showerror();

if (!mysql_select_db($databaseName, $connection))
    showerror();

// Send the user a confirmation email
send_confirmation_email($custID, $orderID, $connection);

// Redirect to a receipt page (this can't be the
// receipt page, since the reload problem would cause
// extra emails).
header("Location: example.shipping.2.php?" .
       "custID=$custID&orderID=$orderID");
?>
```

The mail( ) function is used to send the order confirmation receipt. The function is also useful for sending passwords to users and sending strings to users that confirm actions such as creating accounts and other tasks. It has the following function prototype:

Boolean mail (string *to*, string *subject*, string *body* [, string *additional_ headers*, string [*additional_parameters*]])

Sends an email. The function requires a destination *to* address, a *subject* string, and the *body* of an email message. Multiple destination addresses can be specified in the *to* address by separating each with a comma. Optional headers can also be specified and usually include the From: header specifying the address of the sender of the email. Headers must be separated with both a carriage return and a linefeed, usually specified with \r\n. The Cc: header that is used to carbon-copy an email to a recipient is case-sensitive; the header CC: is invalid. The *additional_parameters* parameter allows options to be supplied to the program that actually sends the email, which in most Linux installations, is *sendmail* or *procmail*. Additional parameters can usually be omitted.

The function returns true if the mail is successfully sent and false otherwise.

Example 12-3 shows the *shipping.2* script that confirms the shipping of an order using HTML. The script has an identical structure to *shipping.1* and executes the same queries. The only difference is that the script outputs HTML rather than creating strings to be emailed to the customer.

Example 12-3. shipping.2 confirms an order as an HTML receipt

```php
<?php
  // This script shows the user an HTMl receipt of their
  // purchase. It is bookmarkable and carries out no
  // database writes.
  // The user must be logged in to review a receipt.

  include 'include.inc';

  set_error_handler("errorHandler");

  function show_HTML_receipt($custID,
                             $orderID,
                             $connection)
  {
    // Find customer information
    $query = "SELECT *
              FROM customer
              WHERE cust_id = $custID";

    if (!($result = @ mysql_query ($query, $connection)))
        showerror();

    // There is only one matching row
    $row = @ mysql_fetch_array($result);

    echo "\n<h1>" .
      "Your order (reference # $custID - $orderID) " .
      "has been dispatched</h1>\n";

    echo "Thank you " .
      $row["title"] . " " .
      $row["surname"] . ", " .
      "your order has been completed and dispatched. " .
      "Your order reference number is " .
      $custID . "-" .
      $orderID .
      ". Please quote this number in any" .
      " correspondence.<br>\n";

    echo "<p>If it existed, the order would have ".
      "been shipped to: \n<br><b>" .
      $row["title"] . " " .
      $row["firstname"] . " " .
      $row["initial"] . " " .
      $row["surname"] . "\n<br>" .
      $row["addressline1"] . "\n";
```

Example 12-3. shipping.2 confirms an order as an HTML receipt (continued)

```php
if ($row["addressline2"] != "")
    echo "\n<br>" .
        $row["addressline2"];

if ($row["addressline3"] != "")
    echo "\n<br>" .
        $row["addressline3"];

echo "\n<br>" .
    $row["city"] . " " .
    $row["state"] . " " .
    $row["zipcode"] . "\n<br>" .
    $row["country"] . "</b>\n<br>\n<br>";

echo "\n<p>" .
    "We have billed your fictional credit card.";

echo "\n<table border=0 width=50% " .
 "cellpadding=0 cellspacing=5>\n" .
 "\n<tr>" .
 "\n\t<td><b>Quantity</b></td>\n" .
 "\n\t<td><b>Wine</b></td>\n" .
 "\n\t<td align=\"right\"><b>Unit Price</b></td>\n" .
 "\n\t<td align=\"right\"><b>Total</b></td>\n" .
 "\n</tr>";

$orderTotalPrice = 0;

// list the particulars of each item in the order
$query = "SELECT   i.qty, w.wine_name, i.price,
                   w.wine_id, w.year, wi.winery_name
          FROM     items i, wine w, winery wi
          WHERE    i.cust_id = $custID
          AND      i.order_id = $orderID
          AND      i.wine_id = w.wine_id
          AND      w.winery_id = wi.winery_id
          ORDER BY item_id";

if (!($result = @ mysql_query ($query, $connection)))
    showerror();

// Add each item to the receipt
while ($row = @ mysql_fetch_array($result))
{
    // Work out the cost of this line item
    $itemsPrice = $row["qty"] * $row["price"];

    $orderTotalPrice += $itemsPrice;

    $wineDetail = showWine($row["wine_id"],
                           $connection);
```

Example 12-3. shipping.2 confirms an order as an HTML receipt (continued)

```php
    echo "\n<tr>" .
        "\n\t<td>" . $row["qty"] . "</td>" .
        "\n\t<td>" . showWine($row["wine_id"],
                      $connection) . "</td>";

    printf("\n\t<td align=\"right\">$%-.2f</td>",
        $row["price"]);
    printf("\n\t<td align=\"right\">$%-.2f</td>",
        $itemsPrice);
    echo "\n</tr>\n";
  }

  echo "\n<tr></tr>" .
      "\n<tr>\n\t<td colspan=2 " .
      "align=\"left\"><i><b>Total of this order" .
      "</b></td>\n\t<td></td>";

  printf("\n\t<td align=\"right\">" .
      "$<b><i>%-.2f</b></td>\n", $orderTotalPrice);

  echo "\n</tr>\n</table>";

  echo "\n<p><i>An email confirmation has been sent " .
      "to you." .
      " Thank you for shopping at Hugh and Dave's " .
      "Online Wines.</i>";
}

// Main ----------

// Re-establish the existing session
session_start();

// Check if the user is logged in - this should never
// fail if unless the script is run incorrectly
if (!session_is_registered("loginUsername"))
{
  session_register("message");
  $message = "You must login to view your receipt.";

  // Redirect the browser back to the calling page
  header("Location: example.order.1.php");
  exit;
}

// Check the correct parameters have been passed
// unless the script is run correctly
if (!isset($custID) || !isset($orderID))
{
  session_register("message");
```

Example 12-3. shipping.2 confirms an order as an HTML receipt (continued)

```php
        $message = "Incorrect parameters to " .
                   "example.shipping.2.php";

        header("Location: $HTTP_REFERER");
        exit;
    }

    // Check this customer matches the custID
    if ($custID != getCustomerID($loginUsername, NULL))
    {
        session_register("message");

        $message = "You can only view your own receipts!";
        header("Location: example.order.1.php");
        exit;
    }

    // Open a connection to the DBMS
    if (!($connection = @ mysql_pconnect($hostName,
                                         $username,
                                         $password)))
        showerror();

    if (!mysql_select_db($databaseName, $connection))
        showerror();
?>
<!DOCTYPE HTML PUBLIC
    "-//W3C//DTD HTML 4.01 Transitional//EN"
    "http://www.w3.org/TR/html401/loose.dtd">
<html>
<head>
  <title>Hugh and Dave's Online Wines</title>
</head>
<body bgcolor="white">
<?php
    // Show the user login status
    showLogin();

    // Show the user any messages
    showMessage();

    // Show the confirmation HTML page
    show_HTML_receipt($custID, $orderID, $connection);
?>
<form action="example.cart.5.php" method="GET">
<table>
<tr>
  <td><input type="submit" name="home" value="Home"></td>
</tr>
</table>
</form>
```

Example 12-3. shipping.2 confirms an order as an HTML receipt (continued)

```
<br><a href="http://validator.w3.org/check/referer">
    <img src="http://www.w3.org/Icons/valid-html401"
    height="31" width="88" align="right" border="0"
    alt="Valid HTML 4.01!"></a>
</body>
</html>
```

CHAPTER 13

Related Topics

This chapter completes our outline of the online winestore. We present here the completed searching and browsing module, and two related topics in web database applications.

The searching and browsing module is briefly outlined in this chapter. A more comprehensive description is presented in Chapter 5. As in the previous three chapters, we suggest that the best method of understand the module is to load it into an editor and use and view the application locally while reading the chapter. We also reemphasize that the code presented here isn't a production system and requires modifications to be used in a production environment.

The scripts we outline in this chapter cover the following topics:

Cleaning up shopping carts
   Automated queries that empty unused carts.

Templates
   How to separate HTML structure from the code functionality. We illustrate the benefits by showing how the *shipping.2* order confirmation script can be rewritten to use a template.

Searching and browsing
   We list the completed wine searching and browsing script that is based on the `browse()` and `selectDistinct()` functions discussed in Chapter 5.

Automated Housekeeping

Queries are run by users through the web interface and by administrators through either administrative web interfaces or from the MySQL command interpreter. However, sometimes automated querying is necessary to produce periodic reports, update data, or delete temporary data. We discuss how queries can be automated in this section.

To show how queries can be automated, consider an example from the online winestore. The shopping cart in the online winestore is implemented using the *winestore* database. As discussed in Chapter 12, when an anonymous user adds a wine to their shopping basket, an order row is added to the *orders* table. The row is for a dummy customer with a cust_id=-1, and the next available order_id for this dummy customer. A related *items* row is created for each item in the shopping cart. The order_id is maintained in the session variable order_no so that orders by different anonymous customers aren't confused.

Our system requirements in Chapter 1 specify that if a customer doesn't purchase the wines in their shopping cart within one day, then the shopping cart should be emptied. This is an example of a DELETE operation that should be automated. It is impractical to require the administrator to run this query each day to remove junk data.

The following query can be run from the Linux shell to remove all *orders* rows that are more than one day old and are for the dummy customer:

```
% /usr/local/mysql/bin/mysql -uusername -psecret
    -e 'USE winestore; DELETE FROM orders WHERE
        unix_timestamp(date) <
  (unix_timestamp(date_add(now( ), interval -1 day)))
AND cust_id = -1;'
```

The MySQL time and date function unix_timestamp( ) converts a timestamp attribute to an integer that is accurate to the nearest second. In this query, we compare the value of the entry in the *orders* table with the value of exactly one day earlier from the current date and time. If the row is older than one day, then it is deleted. The same query works for the *items* table, when orders is replaced with items in the FROM clause.

cron Jobs

Having designed and tested the query, it can be inserted into a Unix *cron* table to automate the operation. The *crond* daemon is a process that runs by default in a Linux installation and continually checks the time. If any of the entries in user tables match the current time, then the commands in the entries are executed. Consider an example:

```
30 17 * * mon-fri echo 'Go home!'
```

This prints the string at 5:30 p.m. each working day. The two asterisks mean every day of the month, and every month of the year respectively. The string mon-fri means the days Monday to Friday inclusive. More details about cron can be found by running man crontab in a Linux shell.

We can add our housekeeping query to our *cron* table by running:

```
% crontab -e
```

This edits the user's *cron* table.

We have decided that the system should check for old shopping carts every 30 minutes. To do so, we add the following two lines to the file:

```
0 * * * * /usr/local/mysql/bin/mysql -uusername -psecret
  -e 'USE winestore; DELETE FROM orders WHERE
        unix_timestamp(date) <
  (unix_timestamp(date_add(now( ), interval -1 day)))
  AND cust_id = -1;'

30 * * * * /usr/local/mysql/bin/mysql -uusername -psecret
  -e 'USE winestore; DELETE FROM items WHERE
        unix_timestamp(date) <
  (unix_timestamp(date_add(now( ), interval -1 day)))
  AND cust_id = -1;'
```

The first line contains the complete query command for the *orders* table from earlier in this section, and the second line the *items* query. The shopping cart *orders* DELETE query runs exactly on each hour, while the *items* DELETE query runs at 30 minutes past each hour. Different times are used to balance the DBMS load.

Reports, updates, delete operations, and other tasks can be added to the *cron* table in a similar way. For example, we can output a simple report of the number of bottles purchased yesterday and send this to our email address each morning:

```
0 8 * * * mon-fri /usr/local/mysql/bin/mysql -uusername
 -psecret -e 'USE winestore; SELECT sum(qty) FROM
 items WHERE unix_timestamp(date) >
 (unix_timestamp(date_add(now( ), interval -1 day))) AND
 cust_id != -1;' | mail help@webdatabasebook.com
```

We could also have automatically written the information to a log file or to a table in the database.

Templates

Separating code from HTML can be difficult in PHP. As we discussed in Chapter 1 and have shown throughout this book, one of the best features of PHP is that scripts can be embedded anywhere in HTML documents. However, this can lead to maintenance problems: if we want to redesign the presentation of the web site, then we may need to rewrite code or, at the very least, understand how PHP and HTML are interleaved in the application. This also makes it difficult to maintain code when it is interleaved with presentational components.

A good solution for medium- to large-scale web database applications is to use *templates* to separate markup and code. In this section, we illustrate how templates can be used in PHP applications through a case study example from the online winestore. In our example, we use the open source *XTemplate* class library available from *http://sourceforge.net/projects/xtpl/*. The XTemplate library is object-based, and

Chapter 2 provides a brief introduction to the object-oriented features of PHP. There are other excellent template libraries, including most notably the *Smarty PHP template engine* available from *http://www.phpinsider.com/php/code/Smarty/*.

Templates in the Shipping Module

Examples 13-1 and 13-2 show a template module that displays the order receipt. This script, called *shipping.3*, is a replacement for the *shipping.2* script discussed in Chapter 12. The output of retrieving Example 13-2 with a Netscape web browser is shown in Figure 13-1. Example 13-1 is the application logic, and Example 13-2 is the template.

Example 13-1. shipping.3 provides an order receipt

```php
<?php
  include "xtpl.p";
  include "include.inc" ;

  set_error_handler("errorHandler");

  function show_HTML_receipt($custID, $orderID, $connection)
  {
    // Create a new XTemplate object called $xtpl
    $xtpl= new XTemplate ("example.shipping.3.xtpl");

    // Find customer information
    $query = "SELECT *
              FROM customer
              WHERE cust_id = $custID";

    if (!($result = @ mysql_query ($query, $connection)))
      showerror( );

    // There is only one matching row
    $row = @ mysql_fetch_array($result);

    // Assign the orderId to the template
    $xtpl->assign("ORDER_ID", $orderID);

    // Assign the customer data to the template
    $xtpl->assign("CUSTOMER", $row);

    // Parse the template data
    $xtpl->parse("main.customer");

    $orderTotalPrice = 0;

    // list the particulars of each item in the order
    $query = "SELECT  i.qty, w.wine_name, i.price,
                      w.wine_id, w.year, wi.winery_name
              FROM    items i, wine w, winery wi
```

Example 13-1. shipping.3 provides an order receipt (continued)

```
            WHERE    i.cust_id = $custID
            AND      i.order_id = $orderID
            AND      i.wine_id = w.wine_id
            AND      w.winery_id = wi.winery_id
            ORDER BY item_id";

    if (!($result = @ mysql_query ($query, $connection)))
        showerror();

    // Add each item to the email
    while ($row = @ mysql_fetch_array($result))
    {
        // Work out the cost of this line item
        $itemsPrice = $row["qty"] * $row["price"];

        $orderTotalPrice += $itemsPrice;

        $wineDetail = showWine($row["wine_id"], $connection);

        // Assign the qty, wine details, price, and
        // total item cost to the template
        $xtpl->assign("QTY", $row["qty"]);
        $xtpl->assign("WINE", $wineDetail);
        $xtpl->assign("PRICE",
                sprintf("%-.2f", $row["price"]));
        $xtpl->assign("TOTAL",
                sprintf("%-.2f", $itemsPrice));

        // Parse a template row of items
        $xtpl->parse("main.items.row");
    }

    // Assign the order total to the template
    $xtpl->assign("ORDER_TOTAL",
            sprintf("%-.2f", $orderTotalPrice));

    // parse all items
    $xtpl->parse("main.items");

    // parse the whole document
    $xtpl->parse("main");

    // output the templated data
    $xtpl->out("main");
}

// Main ----------

// Re-establish the existing session
session_start();
```

Example 13-1. shipping.3 provides an order receipt (continued)

```
    // Check if the user is logged in
    if (!session_is_registered("loginUsername"))
    {
        session_register("message");
        $message = "You must login to view your receipt.";

        // Redirect the browser back to the login page
        header("Location: example.order.1.php");
        exit;
    }

    // Check the correct parameters have been passed
    // unless the script is run correctly
    if (!isset($custID) || !isset($orderID))
    {
        session_register("message");
        $message = "Incorrect parameters to " .
                    "example.shipping.3.php";

        header("Location: $HTTP_REFERER");
        exit;
    }

    // Check this customer matches the custID
    if ($custID != getCustomerID($loginUsername, NULL))
    {
        session_register("message");

        $message = "You can only view your own receipts!";
        header("Location: example.order.1.php");
        exit;
    }

    // Open a connection to the DBMS
    if (!($connection = @ mysql_pconnect($hostName,
                                    $username,
                                    $password)))
        showerror();

    if (!mysql_select_db($databaseName, $connection))
        showerror();

    // Show the confirmation HTML page
    show_HTML_receipt($custID, $orderID, $connection);
?>
```

The application logic

Example 13-1 is the application logic that produces the order receipt. The script logic is identical to that of the *shipping.2* script discussed in Chapter 12. The different features of this script are the omission of any code to produce output, and the inclusion of the fragments of code that assign database values to presentation elements, parse these elements, and call functions in the template class library.

The script in Example 13-1 works as follows:

1. Include the `xtpl.p` template library.

2. In the function `show_HTML_receipt( )`, associate the script with the template shown in Example 13-2:

   ```
   $xtpl= new XTemplate ("example.shipping.3.xtpl");
   ```

   This creates a new template object called `$xtpl`.

3. Query the *customer* table and assign the returned `$row` to an element of the template named `CUSTOMER`. Also assign the `orderID` session variable to an element of the template named `ORDER_ID`. Uppercase strings are used to distinguish template elements from variables in the script, but this isn't essential. After assigning the data, parse the `main.customer` template data (we discuss the structure of the template later in this section).

4. Retrieve and assign each item in the order to the template elements `QTY`, `WINE`, `PRICE`, and `TOTAL`. Now check that this data is correctly formed and associated by parsing it. The following lines perform these functions:

   ```
   // Assign the qty, wine details, price, and total item
   // cost to the template
   $xtpl->assign("QTY", $row["qty"]);
   $xtpl->assign("WINE", $wineDetail);
   $xtpl->assign("PRICE", sprintf("%-.2f", $row["price"]));
   $xtpl->assign("TOTAL", sprintf("%-.2f", $itemsPrice));

   // Parse a template row of items
   $xtpl->parse("main.items.row");
   ```

   We explain how this relates to the template later.

5. Assign the overall order total to the template and check the overall structure of the data. The final check includes parsing the `items` and the overall `main` output, and then outputting the data with the following code:

   ```
   $xtpl->assign("ORDER_TOTAL",
   sprintf("%-.2f", $orderTotalPrice));

   // parse all items
   $xtpl->parse("main.items");

   // parse the whole document
   $xtpl->parse("main");

   // output the templated data
   $xtpl->out("main");
   ```

The template

Example 13-2 is the template itself. It consists mostly of HTML but also contains a Cascading Style Sheet for presentation. Cascading Style Sheets (CSS) are used to control the styles that present output; references that discuss the CSS standard are listed in Appendix E.

Interleaved throughout the template are the following HTML comments:

```
<!-- BEGIN: main -->
  <!-- BEGIN: customer -->
  <!-- END: customer -->
  <!-- BEGIN: items -->
    <!-- BEGIN: row -->
    <!-- END: row -->
  <!-- END: items -->
<!-- END: main -->
```

These comments describe the structural elements referenced in the PHP script in Example 13-1. The elements are nested, so that the element customer is a child of main, because <!-- BEGIN: customer --> occurs inside the <!-- BEGIN: main --> and <!-- END: main --> tags. The customer element can therefore be referenced in Example 13-1 as main.customer. A table row can be referenced in Example 13-1 as main.items.row, because the structural element row is inside items, and items is inside main.

Consider now how the template produces row data:

```
<!-- BEGIN: row -->
<tr>
  <td>{QTY}</td>
  <td>{WINE}</td>
  <td align="right">$ {PRICE}</td>
  <td align="right">$ {TOTAL}</td>
</tr>
  <!-- END: row -->
```

The tags {QTY}, {WINE}, {PRICE}, and {TOTAL} represent where data is inserted. The data is assigned to these tags in Example 13-1 using the assign() function. For example, {QTY} is the position where the order item quantities from the database appear. If there are two database rows assigned to main.items.row elements, two <tr> rows are produced as the body of the HTML <table>.

Example 13-2. HTML XTemplate used by Example 13-1 to output order receipts

```
<!-- BEGIN: main -->
<!DOCTYPE HTML PUBLIC
    "-//W3C//DTD HTML 4.01 Transitional//EN"
    "http://www.w3.org/TR/html401/loose.dtd">
<html>
<head>
  <title>Hugh and Dave's Online Wines</title>
```

Example 13-2. HTML XTemplate used by Example 13-1 to output order receipts (continued)

```
<style type="text/css">
  body {background: #ffffff;
        color: #000000;
        font-family: Arial, sans-serif}
  h1 {font: arial}
  h2 {font: arial;
      font-size: 22}
  a {color: #0000ff;
     font: helvetica;
     font-weight: bold;
     text-decoration: none}
</style>
</head>
<body bgcolor="white">
<!-- BEGIN: customer -->
<h1>Your order (reference # {CUSTOMER.cust_id} - {ORDER_ID})
has been dispatched</h1>
Thank you {CUSTOMER.title} {CUSTOMER.surname},
your order has been completed and dispatched.
Your order reference number is
{CUSTOMER.cust_id} - {ORDER_ID}.
Please quote this number in any correspondence.
<br>
<p>If it existed, the order would have been shipped to:
<br><b>
{CUSTOMER.title} {CUSTOMER.firstname} {CUSTOMER.initial}
{CUSTOMER.surname}
<br>
{CUSTOMER.addressline1}
{CUSTOMER.addressline2}
{CUSTOMER.addressline3}
<br>{CUSTOMER.city} {CUSTOMER.state} {CUSTOMER.zipcode}
<br>{CUSTOMER.country}
</b>
<br>
<br>
<p>We have billed your fictional credit card.
<!-- END: customer -->

<!-- BEGIN: items -->
<table border=0 width=50% cellpadding=0 cellspacing=5>
<tr>
  <td><b>Quantity</b></td>
  <td><b>Wine</b></td>
  <td align=\"right\"><b>Unit Price</b></td>
  <td align=\"right\"><b>Total</b></td>
</tr>
  <!-- BEGIN: row -->
<tr>
  <td>{QTY}</td>
  <td>{WINE}</td>
```

```
   <td align="right">$ {PRICE}</td>
   <td align="right">$ {TOTAL}</td>
</tr>
  <!-- END: row -->
<tr></tr>
<tr>
   <td colspan=2 align="left"><i>
     <b>Total of this order</b></td>
   <td></td>
   <td align="right">$<b><i>{ORDER_TOTAL}</b></td>
</tr>
</table>
<!-- END: items -->
<p><i>An email confirmation has been sent to you.
Thank you for shopping at Hugh and Dave's Online Wines.</i>

<form action="example.cart.5.php" method="GET">
<table>
<tr>
   <td><input type="submit" name="home" value="Home"></td>
</tr>
</table>
</form>
<br><a href="http://validator.w3.org/check/referer">
    <img src="http://www.w3.org/Icons/valid-html401"
    height="31" width="88" align="right" border="0"
    alt="Valid HTML 4.01!"></a>
</body>
</html>
<!-- END: main -->
```

The customer details are output by accessing the CUSTOMER element. For example, the shipping details are produced with the fragment:

```
<p>If it existed, the order would have been shipped to:
<br><b>
{CUSTOMER.title} {CUSTOMER.firstname} {CUSTOMER.initial}
{CUSTOMER.surname}
<br>
{CUSTOMER.addressline1}
{CUSTOMER.addressline2}
{CUSTOMER.addressline3}
<br>{CUSTOMER.city} {CUSTOMER.state} {CUSTOMER.zipcode}
<br>{CUSTOMER.country}
</b>
```

The overall result of running Example 13-1 and using the template in Example 13-2 is the output in Figure 13-1. The advantage of this approach is that the HTML in Example 13-2 can be altered independently of the script in Example 13-1 and vice versa. This means that application logic and presentation are as separate as possible.

The only links between the two are the structural markup components and the embedded tags.

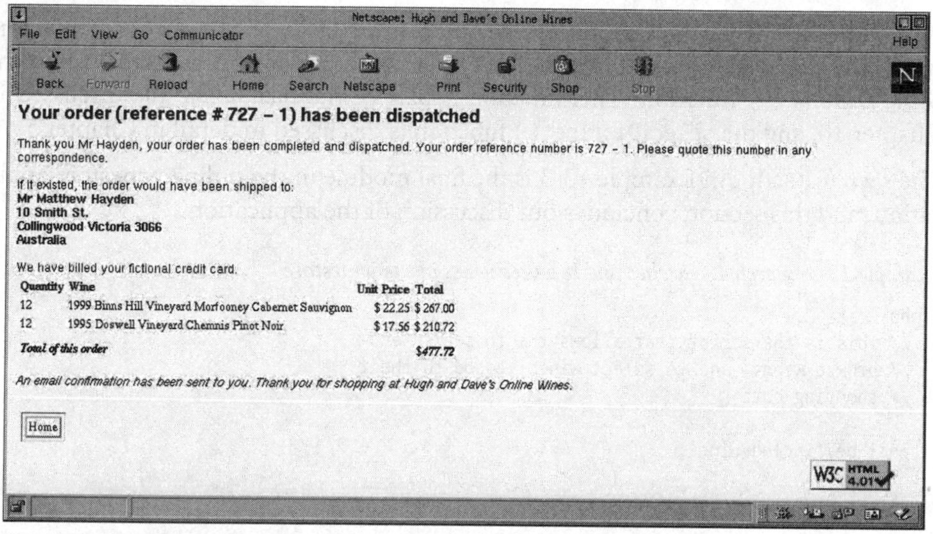

Figure 13-1. Output of Examples 13-1 and 13-2

The XTemplate library has more complex features not discussed here. More details on the use of templates can be found at the web sites listed earlier in this section.

Searching and Browsing

Example 13-3 shows the searching and browsing *search.1* script used in the winestore. The script browses wines by selecting a combination of a wine region name and a wine type. For example, the script can browse the Red wines from the Margaret River region. The user can also choose to browse All regions or All wine types. The browsing interface supports Previous and Next page functionality using embedded links, as well as direct access to any page in the results.

The script is based on the browse( ) function discussed in Chapter 5, which is included here renamed as showWines( ). The showWines( ) function is customized for presenting wine details and has calls to the functions showVarieties( ) and showPricing( ) from the *include.inc* include file. It also has embedded links to add one or a dozen bottles of the displayed wine to the shopping cart using the *cart.3* script discussed in Chapter 11.

The body of the script checks if search criteria have been provided as GET method parameters. If they have, these are used as parameters to the query that retrieves wines. If GET method parameters aren't provided, the query is configured using any previous search criteria that have been saved as the session variables sessionRegionName and sessionWineType. In either case, the current search criteria are then saved in the session variables for future use. The query string itself is created using the setupQuery( ) function.

After running the query and presenting the results with the showWines( ) function, two <select> lists containing the query parameters are presented using the selectDistinct( ) function. This function is part of the *include.inc* file discussed in Chapter 10, and the selectDistinct( ) function is discussed in detail in Chapter 5.

The *search.1* script in Example 13-3 is the final module in the online winestore application, and this section concludes our discussion of the application.

Example 13-3. search.1 searches and browses wines in the winestore

```php
<?php
    // This is the script that allows the to search and
    // browse wines, and to select wines to add to their
    // shopping cart

    include 'include.inc';

    set_error_handler("errorHandler");

    // Show the user the wines that match their query
    // This is a modified version of the browse() function
    // from Chapter 5
    function showWines($query,
                       $connection,
                       $offset,
                       $scriptName,
                       $browseString)
    {
        // Number of rows per page
        $ROWS = 12;

        // Run the query on the database through
        // the connection
        if (!($result = @ mysql_query ($query, $connection)))
            showerror();

        // Find out how many rows there are
        $rowsFound = @ mysql_num_rows($result);

        // Is there any data?
        if ($rowsFound != 0)
        {
            // Yes, there is data.

            // The "Previous" page begins at the current
            // offset LESS the number of ROWS per page
            $previousOffset = $offset - $ROWS;
```

```
// The "Next" page begins at the current offset
// PLUS the number of ROWS per page
$nextOffset = $offset + $ROWS;

// Seek to the current offset
if (!@ mysql_data_seek($result, $offset))
  showerror();

// Output the header and start a table
echo "<table border=\"0\">\n";

// Fetch one page of results (or less if on the
// last page)
for ( $rowCounter = 0;
   (($rowCounter < $ROWS) &&
    ($row = @ mysql_fetch_array($result)) );
    $rowCounter++)
{
    echo "\n<tr>\n\t<td>" . $row["year"] . " " .
       $row["winery_name"] . " " .
       $row["wine_name"];

    // Print the varieties for this wine
    echo showVarieties($connection,
                       $row["wine_id"]);

    // Print out the pricing information
    echo "\n\t<br>";
    showPricing($connection, $row["wine_id"]);

    echo "</td>";

    // Show the single-bottle add to cart link
    echo "\n\t<td><a href=\"example.cart.3.php?" .
       "qty=1&amp;wineId=" .
       $row["wine_id"] .
       "\">Add a bottle to the cart</a></td>";

    // Show the dozen add to cart link
    echo "\n\t<td><a href=\"example.cart.3.php?" .
       "qty=12&amp;wineId=" .
       $row["wine_id"] .
       "\">Add a dozen</a></td>";

    echo "\n</tr>";
} // end for rows in the page

// Finish the results table, and start a footer
echo "\n</table>\n<br>\n";

// Show the row numbers that are being viewed
echo ($offset + 1), "-",
```

```
                    ($rowCounter + $offset), " of ";
        echo "$rowsFound wines found matching " .
            "your criteria\n<br>";

        // Are there any previous pages?
        if ($offset > 0)
            // Yes, so create a previous link
            echo "<a href=\"" . $scriptName .
                "?offset=" . rawurlencode($previousOffset) .
                "&amp;" . $browseString .
                "\">Previous</a> ";
        else
            // No, there is no previous page so don't
            // print a link
            echo "Previous ";
        // Output the page numbers as links
        // Count through the number of pages in the results
        for($x=0, $page=1;
            $x<$rowsFound;
            $x+=$ROWS, $page++)
            // Is this the current page?
            if ($x < $offset || $x > ($offset + $ROWS - 1))
                // No, so print out a link
                echo "\n<a href=\"" . $scriptName .
                    "?offset=" . rawurlencode($x) .
                    "&amp;" . $browseString .
                    "\">" . $page  . "</a> ";
            else
                // Yes, so don't print a link
                echo "\n" . $page  . " ";

        // Are there any Next pages?
        if (($row != false) && ($rowsFound > $nextOffset))
            // Yes, so create a next link
            echo "\n<a href=\"" . $scriptName .
                "?offset=" . rawurlencode($nextOffset),
                "&amp;" . $browseString .
                "\">Next</a> ";
        else
            // No,  there is no next page so don't
            // print a link
            echo "\nNext ";

    } // end if rowsFound != 0
    else
    {
        echo "\n<br>No wines found matching your " .
            " criteria.\n";
    }
}
```

Example 13-3. search.1 searches and browses wines in the winestore (continued)

```
function setupQuery($regionName, $wineType)
{

    // Show the wines stocked at the winestore that match
    // the search criteria
    $query = "SELECT DISTINCT wi.winery_name,
                      w.year,
                      w.wine_name,
                      w.wine_id
             FROM wine w, winery wi,
                  inventory i, region r
             WHERE w.winery_id = wi.winery_id
             AND wi.region_id = r.region_id
             AND w.wine_id = i.wine_id";

    // Add region_name restriction if they've
    // selected a search parameter
    if ($regionName != "All")
       $query .= " AND r.region_name = \"" .
                 $regionName . "\"" .
                 " AND r.region_id = wi.region_id";

    // Add wine type restriction if they've selected
    // a search parameter
    if ($wineType != "All")
       $query .= " AND w.type = \"" .
                 $wineType . "\"";

    // Add sorting criteria
    $query .= " ORDER BY wi.winery_name, " .
              "w.wine_name, w.year";

    return ($query);
}

// ---------

// Initialize the session
session_start();

// Process the search parameters.

// If a regionName is passed as a GET parameter,
// use it. Otherwise, load the session variable
// from the last search. If there is no previous
// search and no parameter, set search to "All"
if (!empty($HTTP_GET_VARS["regionName"]))
   $regionName = clean($regionName, 30);
elseif (session_is_registered("sessionRegionName"))
   $regionName = $sessionRegionName;
else
   $regionName = "All";
```

Example 13-3. search.1 searches and browses wines in the winestore (continued)

```php
    // Load wineType, using the same approach as
    // regionName
    if (!empty($HTTP_GET_VARS["wineType"]))
        $wineType = clean($wineType, 20);
    elseif (session_is_registered("sessionWineType"))
        $wineType = $sessionWineType;
    else
        $wineType = "All";

    // Load offset
    if (!empty($HTTP_GET_VARS["offset"]))
        $offset = clean($offset, 5);
    else
        $offset = 0;

    // Save the search criteria
    $sessionRegionName = $regionName;
    $sessionWineType = $wineType;

    // Register the search criteria if needed
    if (!session_is_registered("sessionRegionName"))
    {
        session_register("sessionRegionName");
        session_register("sessionWineType");
    }

    // Open a connection to the DBMS
    if (!($connection = @ mysql_pconnect($hostName,
                                         $username,
                                         $password)))
        showerror( );

    if (!mysql_select_db($databaseName, $connection))
        showerror( );

    // Build the query using the search criteria
    $query = setupQuery($regionName, $wineType);

    // This is used to encode the search parameters
    // for embedding in links to other pages of results
    $browseString = "wineType=" .
                    urlencode($wineType) .
                    "&amp;regionName=" .
                    urlencode($regionName);

    $scriptName = "example.search.1.php";

?>
<!DOCTYPE HTML PUBLIC
  "-//W3C//DTD HTML 4.01 Transitional//EN"
  "http://www.w3.org/TR/html401/loose.dtd">
```

Example 13-3. search.1 searches and browses wines in the winestore (continued)

```
<html>
<head>
  <title>Hugh and Dave's Online Wines</title>
</head>
<body bgcolor="white">
<?php
  // Show the user login status
  showLogin( );

  // Show the dollar and item total of the cart
  showCart($connection);

  // Show a meaningful heading that describes the
  // search criteria
  echo "<h1>" . $wineType . " wines";

  if ($regionName == "All")
     echo " from all regions.";
  else
     echo " of the " . $regionName . " region.";

  echo "</h1>\n";

  // Display any messages to the user
  showMessage( );

  // Show the user their search
  showWines($query, $connection,
            $offset, $scriptName,
            $browseString);

  echo "<form action=\"example.cart.5.php\"" .
       " method=\"GET\">\n";
  echo "<table>\n<tr>\n";

  echo "\t<td>Choose a wine region:</td>\n\t<td>";
  // Produce a select list of wine regions
  selectDistinct($connection,
                 "region",
                 "region_name",
                 "regionName",
                 "All",
                 $regionName);

  echo "</td>\n</tr>\n<tr>\n";

  echo "\t<td>Choose a wine type:</td>\n\t<td>";
  // Produce a select list of wine types
  selectDistinct($connection,
                 "wine",
                 "type",
```

```php
                        "wineType",
                        "All",
                        $wineType);

    echo "</tr>\n</table>\n";

    echo "<table>\n<tr>\n";

    // Show the user the search screen button
    echo "\t<td><input type=\"submit\" " .
        "name=\"search\" value=\"Search\"></td>\n";

    // Show the user the search screen button
    echo "\t<td><input type=\"submit\" " .
        "name=\"home\" value=\"Home\"></td>\n";

    // If the cart has contents, offer the opportunity
    // to view the cart or empty the cart.
    if (session_is_registered("order_no"))
    {
        echo "\t<td><input type=\"submit\" " .
            "name=\"empty\" value=\"Empty Cart\"></td>\n";
        echo "\t<td><input type=\"submit\" " .
            "name=\"view\" value=\"View Cart\"></td>\n";
    }

    // Show the user either a login or logout button
    loginButtons( );

    echo "\n</tr>\n</table>\n";
    echo "</form>\n";
?>
<br><a href="http://validator.w3.org/check/referer">
    <img src="http://www.w3.org/Icons/valid-html401"
    height="31" width="88" align="right" border="0"
    alt="Valid HTML 4.01!"></a>
</body>
</html>
```

Installation Guide

This appendix is a guide to installing the software used in the book. The first section presents the steps to install and configure MySQL, Apache, and PHP under the Linux operating system environment. We then present a short guide to downloading and installing the PHP script examples used in this book. The last major section shows how a secure Apache web server can be installed using the Secure Sockets Layer library. We conclude with a list of installation resources for Microsoft Windows, Linux, and other environments.

Installing MySQL, Apache, and PHP

There are three approaches to installing MySQL, Apache, and PHP:

- Install a distribution of the Linux operating system that includes the software as precompiled packages. This is the easiest approach.

- Purchase or obtain an installation package; pointers to PHP Triad for the Microsoft Windows environment, and NuSphere for most platforms—including Linux and Sun Solaris—are included at the end of this appendix. This is an easy approach.

- Obtain and build the software from source code. This is the most difficult approach, but it has the advantage that the latest software is installed and the configuration layout and options are controlled in the process.

This section focuses on the third approach, obtaining and building the software from source code. Specifically, this section is a short guide to installation under the Linux operating system, and the result is an installation of Apache with PHP as a *static module* and a complete MySQL installation. We don't provide detailed information on the configuration of the components, installation on other platforms, or choices that can be made in installation. A short list of more detailed installation resources is presented at the end of this appendix.

Before we begin, several basic components are required:

- An ANSI-compliant C programming language compiler such as *gcc*; included in almost all Linux distributions
- *flex*, the fast lexical analyzer, included in almost all Linux distributions
- *bison*, the GNU project parser generator; included in most Linux distributions
- Superuser, that is, root access to the Linux machine on which the software is to be installed
- Common Linux utilities such as *gzip*, *tar*, and *gmake*

Installing MySQL

The instructions here are for installing MySQL 3. MySQL is bundled with only some Linux installations. We assume that MySQL isn't installed or, if it is installed, that a new version is to be installed to replace the current installation.

1. Download the latest version of MySQL from *http://www.mysql.com/downloads/mysql.html*. Choose the latest stable release and, from the stable release page, choose the option under "Source Downloads" marked "tarball (.tar.gz)". Download the file into a directory where files can be created and there is sufficient disk space. A good location is */tmp*. Change directory to this location using:

   ```
   % cd /tmp
   ```

   Note that the % character should not be typed in; this represents the Linux shell prompt and indicates that the command should be entered at the shell prompt.

2. Uncompress the package in the new installation directory by running:

   ```
   % gzip -d mysql-<version>.tar.gz
   ```

   If MySQL 3.23.42 has been downloaded, the command is:

   ```
   % gzip -d mysql-3.23.42.tar.gz
   ```

3. Un-*tar* the tape archive file by running:

   ```
   % tar xvf mysql-<version_number>.tar
   ```

   A list of files that are extracted is shown.

   If the version downloaded is MySQL 3.23.42, the command is:

   ```
   % tar xvf mysql-3.23.42.tar
   ```

4. Change directory to the MySQL distribution directory:

   ```
   % cd mysql-<version>
   ```

   If the version is MySQL 3.23.42, type:

   ```
   % cd mysql-3.23.42
   ```

5. Add a new Unix group account for the MySQL files:

   ```
   % groupadd mysql
   ```

6. Add a new Unix user who is a member of the newly created Unix group `mysql`:

    ```
    % useradd -g mysql mysql
    ```

7. Decide on an installation directory. Later, we recommend that PHP and Apache be installed in */usr/local/*, so a good choice is */usr/local/mysql/*. We assume throughout these steps that */usr/local/mysql/* is used; if another directory is chosen, replace */usr/local/mysql/* with the alternative choice in the remaining steps.

8. Configure the MySQL installation by running the *configure* script. This detects the available Linux tools and the installation environment for the MySQL configuration:

    ```
    % ./configure --prefix=/usr/local/mysql
    ```

9. Compile the MySQL DBMS:

    ```
    % make
    ```

10. Install MySQL in the location chosen in Step 7 by running the command:

    ```
    % make install
    ```

11. MySQL is now installed but isn't yet configured. Now, run the *mysql_install_db* script to initialize the system databases used by MySQL:

    ```
    % ./scripts/mysql_install_db
    ```

12. Change the owner of the MySQL program files to be the root user:

    ```
    % chown -R root /usr/local/mysql
    ```

13. Change the owner of the MySQL databases and log files to be the `mysql` user created in Step 6:

    ```
    % chown -R mysql /usr/local/mysql/var
    ```

14. Change the group of the MySQL installation files to be the `mysql` group:

    ```
    % chgrp -R mysql /usr/local/mysql
    ```

15. Copy the default medium-scale parameter configuration file to the default location of */etc*. These parameters are read when MySQL is started. The copy command is:

    ```
    % cp support-files/my-medium.cnf /etc/my.cnf
    ```

16. Edit the configuration file and adjust the default number of maximum connections to match the default value for the maximum Apache web server connections. Using a text editor, edit the file */etc/my.cnf*, and find the section beginning with the following text:

    ```
    # The MySQL server
    [mysqld]
    ```

    In this section, add the following line, then save the file, and exit the editor:

    ```
    set-variable    = max_connections=150
    ```

17. The MySQL configuration is now complete, and MySQL is ready to be started. Start the MySQL DBMS with the following command:

    ```
    % /usr/local/mysql/bin/safe_mysqld --user=mysql &
    ```

18. Check that the MySQL DBMS is running with the *mysqladmin* utility. The following command reports statistics about the MySQL DBMS version and usage:

```
% /usr/local/mysql/bin/mysqladmin version
```

19. Choose and set a password for root user access to the MySQL DBMS. To set a password of *secret*, use:

```
% /usr/local/mysql/bin/mysqladmin -uroot password secret
```

Record the password for later use.

20. The MySQL server is currently running. However, when the machine is rebooted, MySQL doesn't restart automatically.

After reboot, the command in Step 17 can be used to restart MySQL or, alternatively, this process can be made automatic. To make the process automatic, find the file *rc.local* (normally either in or below the directory */etc*). This file is used to list locally installed software that should be run on startup. Using an editor, add the following line to the bottom of the *rc.local* file:

```
/usr/local/mysql/bin/safe_mysqld --user=mysql &
```

The installation of MySQL is now complete.

These steps install MySQL and start the DBMS server but don't configure a user or user databases. The steps to add a user are the subject of the next section.

Configuring MySQL

The following steps create a user for the MySQL installation that is used in PHP scripts to access the DBMS. The user can carry out all actions required in Chapter 4 to 13 on the *winestore* database but has no access to other databases and can't change database access privileges. In addition, the new user can't access the DBMS from a remote server, under the assumption that the MySQL DBMS and Apache are installed on the same machine through following the instructions in this appendix.

The steps are as follows:

1. Check that MySQL is running using the password defined in Step 19 of the MySQL installation instructions:

```
% /usr/local/mysql/bin/mysqladmin -psecret version
```

If it isn't, then log in as the root user and start the MySQL DBMS using:

```
% /usr/local/mysql/bin/safe_mysqld --user=mysql &
```

2. Start the MySQL command line interpreter using the same password as in the last step:

```
% /usr/local/mysql/bin/mysql -psecret
```

3. Add a new user to the *user* table in the *mysql* database. Choose a username to replace *username* and a password to replace *secret* in the following command:

```
GRANT ALL PRIVILEGES ON winestore.* TO username@localhost
IDENTIFIED BY 'secret';
```

MySQL responds with:

```
Query OK, 0 rows affected (0.00 sec)
```

Record the username and password for use in the examples in Chapter 3 to 13.

4. Quit the MySQL command interpreter with the command:

```
quit
```

MySQL responds with:

```
Bye
```

5. Test the user created in Step 3 by running the MySQL command interpreter using the username and password:

```
% /usr/local/mysql/bin/mysql -uusername -psecret
```

MySQL responds with a message beginning:

```
Welcome to the MySQL monitor.
```

6. Quit the MySQL interpreter again with:

```
quit
```

The MySQL DBMS is now configured with a user who can access the *winestore* database from the database server machine localhost. The *winestore* database can't be tested yet; the *winestore* database is loaded and tested in the section "Quick Start Guide" in Chapter 3.

Installing Apache

The Apache web server is usually installed with most common Linux installations. However, we assume that it isn't installed or that an upgrade is required. In any case, it is essential that the source of Apache is available so that it can be recompiled to include PHP as a module.

If a current version is running, kill the process or stop the web server by running the script *apachectl stop*, usually found in the directory */usr/local/apache/bin*.

Here are the steps to install Apache:

1. Get the latest version of the Apache HTTP Server from *http://www.apache.org/ dist/httpd/*. Choose the latest source code version ending in the suffix *.tar.gz* and save the file in the */tmp* directory. However, if a secure Apache web server with SSL is required instead of the usual installation, find out which is the latest version of Apache that has SSL support by first following the instructions in the section "Installing Apache and ApacheSSL," later in this chapter.

2. Move the Apache distribution file to the base directory of the desired installation. The most common location is */usr/local/* and, assuming the distribution downloaded is Apache 1.3.20, and it was downloaded in the first step into the */tmp* directory, the command is:

```
% mv /tmp/apache_1.3.20.tar.gz /usr/local/
```

After moving the distribution to the desired location, change the directory to that location using:

```
% cd /usr/local
```

3. Uncompress the package in the new installation directory by running:

```
% gzip -d apache_<version_number>.tar.gz
```

If the distribution downloaded is Apache 1.3.20, the command is:

```
% gzip -d apache_1.3.20.tar.gz
```

4. Un-*tar* the archive file by running:

```
% tar xvf apache_<version_number>.tar
```

The list of files extracted is shown.

If the version downloaded was Apache 1.3.20, then the command is:

```
% tar xvf apache_1.3.20.tar
```

5. Change directory to the Apache installation:

```
% cd apache_<version_number>
```

If the Apache version is 1.3.20, type:

```
% cd apache_1.3.20
```

6. Configure the Apache installation by running the *configure* script. This detects the available Linux tools, the installation environment, and other details for the Apache configuration:

```
% ./configure --with-layout=Apache
```

7. Apache has not yet been compiled or installed. The next step is to configure and build the PHP installation, and then to complete the Apache installation. Go ahead to Step 1 in the section "Installing PHP," and return to Step 8 when the PHP steps are complete.

8. The PHP module is now ready to be installed as part of the Apache web server. The following command reconfigures Apache to activate the PHP module support. However, the library referred to in the *activate-module* command doesn't yet exist (it is built in the next step):

```
% ./configure --with-layout=Apache --activate-module=src/modules/php4/libphp4.a
```

9. Compile the Apache web server using the command:

```
% make
```

10. Install the Apache server using the command:

```
% make install
```

If the installation of Apache with PHP support has been successful, the following message is shown:

```
+---------------------------------------------------------+
|You now have successfully built and installed the        |
|Apache 1.3 HTTP server. To verify that Apache actually    |
|works correctly you now should first check the           |
|(initially created or preserved) configuration files     |
|                                                         |
|   /usr/local/apache/conf/httpd.conf                     |
|                                                         |
|                                                         |
| and then you should be able to immediately fire up      |
| Apache the first time by running:                       |
|                                                         |
|   /usr/local/apache/bin/apachectl start                 |
|                                                         |
| Thanks for using Apache.       The Apache Group         |
|                                http://www.apache.org/   |
+---------------------------------------------------------+
```

11. Edit the Apache configuration file and enable PHP script engine support for files that have the suffix *.php*. To do this, edit the file */usr/local/apache/conf/httpd.conf* and remove the # character from the beginning of the following line:

    ```
    AddType application/x-httpd-php .php
    ```

    After removing the comment character #, save the file and exit the editor.

12. Start the Apache web server by running the command indicated by the installation process in Step 10:

    ```
    % /usr/local/apache/bin/apachectl start
    ```

    After the Apache server starts up, the following is displayed:

    ```
    /usr/local/apache/bin/apachectl start: httpd started
    ```

13. Check that the server is responding to HTTP requests by accessing it using a web browser. The simplest way to check is to use a web browser to load the URL *http://localhost/*. If Apache is serving correctly, an Apache test page is shown; if a previously installed Apache has been upgraded, another page may be displayed.

14. To test the PHP module, change the directory to the Apache document root:

    ```
    % cd /usr/local/apache/htdocs
    ```

15. Create a file with the name *phpinfo.php* using a text editor. In the file, type the following, then save the script, and exit the editor:

    ```
    <? phpinfo( ); ?>
    ```

16. Test the newly created PHP script by retrieving with a browser the following URL *http://localhost/phpinfo.php*.

    A web page of information about the Apache and PHP installation is shown. If the page isn't shown—and this is a common installation problem—check that Step 11 of these instructions was correctly completed. If a problem is found, edit and correct the problem, and restart Apache with the following command:

    ```
    % /usr/local/apache/bin/apachectl restart
    ```

17. Apache is now running and serving both static HTML and PHP scripts, and this installation process is complete.

However, when the machine is rebooted, Apache will not be restarted automatically. After reboot, the command in Step 12 can be used to restart Apache or, alternatively, this process can be made automatic. To make the process automatic, find the file *rc.local,* normally either in or below the directory */etc.* This file is used to list locally installed software that should be run on start up. Using an editor, add the following line to the bottom of the *rc.local* file:

```
/usr/local/apache/bin/apachectl start
```

If Apache needs to be stopped at any time, this can by achieved by running:

```
/usr/local/apache/bin/apachectl stop
```

The installation of Apache, PHP, and MySQL is now complete. Instructions to optionally install the winestore source code examples can be found in the later section "Installing the Winestore Examples."

Installing PHP

The instructions here are for installing PHP4. PHP is bundled with most Linux installations. However, we assume PHP isn't installed or, if it is installed, that a newer version is required to replace the existing installation. If Apache is being reinstalled, PHP needs to be reinstalled also.

Here are the steps to installing PHP:

1. Steps 1 to 7 of the Apache installation instructions should be completed.

2. Get the latest version of PHP from *http://www.php.net/downloads.php.* Download the "Complete Source Code" version into the */tmp* directory.

3. Choose an installation directory. If the Apache installation was begun in */usr/ local/,* the same location can also be used for PHP. We assume in the following steps that the base directory of the Apache installation and PHP installation are the same. Move the PHP source code file to the base directory of the desired installation. Assuming this is */usr/local/* and, assuming the distribution downloaded is PHP 4.0.6 and it was downloaded into the */tmp* directory, the command is:

```
% mv /tmp/php-4.0.6.tar.gz /usr/local/
```

After moving the distribution to the desired location, change directory to that location using:

```
% cd /usr/local
```

4. Uncompress the package in the new installation directory by running:

```
% gzip -d php-<version_number>.tar.gz
```

If the version downloaded is PHP 4.0.6, the command is:

```
% gzip -d php-4.0.6.tar.gz
```

5. Un-*tar* the distribution by running:

```
% tar xvf php-<version_number>.tar
```

A list of files extracted is displayed.

If the version downloaded is PHP 4.0.6, the command is:

```
% tar xvf php-4.0.6.tar
```

6. Change directory to the PHP installation:

```
% cd php-<version_number>
```

If the version is PHP 4.0.6, type:

```
% cd php-4.0.6
```

7. Configure the PHP installation by running the *configure* script. This detects the available Linux tools, the installation environment, adds MySQL support, and prepares for Apache integration. It assumes that MySQL has been installed previously in the directory */usr/local/mysql*:

```
% ./configure --with-mysql=/usr/local/mysql --with-apache=../apache_<vers>
```

If Apache 1.3.20 is being used, type:

```
% ./configure --with-mysql=/usr/local/mysql --with-apache=../apache_1.3.20
```

8. Compile the PHP scripting engine by running:

```
% make
```

9. Now that the PHP scripting engine is built, install the PHP engine using:

```
% make install
```

10. The PHP installation is almost complete. Now copy across the default PHP configuration file to the default location, This file, *php.ini*, contains the settings that control the behavior of PHP and includes, for example, how variables are initialized, how sessions are managed, and what scripting tags can be used. The command to copy the file is:

```
% cp php.ini-dist /usr/local/lib/php.ini
```

11. Change directory to the Apache installation:

```
% cd ../apache_<version_number>
```

If Apache 1.3.20 is being installed, type:

```
% cd ../apache_1.3.20
```

12. The initial configuration of the PHP scripting engine module is now complete. Return to Step 8 of the Apache installation procedure and complete the installation of Apache, which includes a test of the PHP module.

Installing the Winestore Examples

The *winestore* example PHP scripts are available from the author's web site, *http://www.webdatabasebook.com*. To install the example scripts that are presented in Chapter 4 to 10, perform the following steps.

1. Download the file *http://www.webdatabasebook.com/wda.tar.gz* into the */tmp* directory

2. Log in as the root user, make a directory for the file below the document root of the Apache installation, and copy the file to that location:

```
% mkdir /usr/local/apache/htdocs/wda
% cp /tmp/wda.tar.gz /usr/local/apache/htdocs/wda
```

3. Change directory to the new location and install the files:

```
% cd /usr/local/apache/htdocs/wda
% gzip -d wda.tar.gz
% tar xvf wda.tar
```

4. Edit the file *db.inc* and modify the first two lines so that the password and user-name match those selected in the previous section "Configuring MySQL." Save the file and exit the editor.

5. Load the book homepage by requesting the URL: *http://localhost/wda/*.

Many of the examples run only if the *winestore* database has been loaded into the MySQL DBMS by following the instructions in the section "Quick Start Guide" in Chapter 3.

Installing Apache to Use SSL

This section describes how to install a secure version of the Apache web server. There are three major differences encountered when installing Apache to use SSL versus installing Apache normally:

Secure Sockets Layer software is required.
There are several sources of Secure Sockets Layer software. The OpenSSL is probably the most-commonly used with Apache

SSL patches must be applied to the Apache code before it is configured and compiled.
Unlike installing other Apache modules, SSL installation requires that the core Apache source code be modified or patched. Normal Apache modules—such as the PHP module—interact with Apache using a defined application programming interface or API. The Apache API provides functions that hide the details of dealing with HTTP from Apache module developers.

However, the code that implements SSL needs to encrypt and decrypt HTTP requests and responses. The Apache API is aimed at the wrong level, and SSL patches need to be applied to Apache. There are several open source and commercial SSL extensions and patches to Apache available. ApacheSSL (*http://www.apache-ssl.org*) and mod_ssl (*http://www.mod_ssl.org*) are both open source and easy to install. We describe the installation of ApacheSSL in this section.

A site certificate needs to be obtained and configured.
A self-signed certificate can be created, but it needs to replaced with a purchased certificate from a Certification Authority when an application goes live.

There are dozens of organizations that can provide authoritative certificates, including companies such as Verisign and Thawte.

Installing OpenSSL

1. Get the latest version of the OpenSSL from *http://www.openssl.org/source/*. Download the Unix *tar*-ed and *gzip*-ed file under the heading "Tarball." For example, download the file *openssl-0.9.6a.tar.gz*.

2. Put the distribution file in a directory that can be used to build the OpenSSL libraries. In our installation instructions, we use */usr/local/*. The default installation process installs OpenSSL in */usr/local/ssl*. To use */usr/local/*, log in as the root user of the Linux installation; in any case, root access is required in Step 5 to install in the default location.

3. Uncompress and un-*tar* the distribution file in the new installation directory using *gzip* and *tar*. If the version downloaded was 0.9.6a, the commands are:

```
% gzip -d openssl-0.9.6a.tar.gz
% tar xvf openssl-0.9.6a.tar
```

The distribution files are listed as they are extracted from the *tar* file.

4. Change the directory to the *openssl* source directory, run the *config* script, and then *make* the installation. Assuming the version downloaded is 0.9.6a, the commands are:

```
% cd openssl-0.9.6a
% ./config
% make
% make test
```

To install OpenSSL in a directory other than */usr/local/ssl*, run *config* with the openssldir=*<directory-path>* directive.

5. Build the install binaries of SSL. To do this, log in as the root user, and then run the *make install* script:

```
% make install
```

This creates an installation of SSL in the directory */usr/local/ssl*.

Installing Apache and ApacheSSL

Both Apache and ApacheSSL need to be installed together, and the ApacheSSL version must match the Apache version. ApacheSSL may not always be available for the latest version of Apache, so it is worth checking out the latest ApacheSSL version first. The current version of ApacheSSL is applied to Apache 1.3.19.

1. Get the latest version of ApacheSSL by selecting a download site from *http://www.apache-ssl.org/* Download the *tar*-ed and *gzip*-ed distribution file. For example, *apache_1.3.19+ssl_1.44.tar.gz*.

2. Get the matching version of the Apache web server source code that also ends with *.tar.gz* from *http://www.apache.org/dist/httpd/*. For example, if the ApacheSSL version downloaded in Step 1 was *apache_1.3.19+ssl_1.44.tar.gz*, retrieve *apache_1.3.19.tar.gz*.

3. Put the Apache distribution file in the base directory where the installation is to be performed. For these instructions, use */usr/local/* as in the Apache installation instructions earlier in this appendix.

4. Unpack the Apache package first by running gzip -d *<filename>* and tar xvf *<filename>*. With Apache Version 1.3.19:

```
% cd /usr/local
% gzip -d apache_1.3.19.tar.gz
% tar xvf apache_1.3.19.tar
```

This creates an *apache_1.3.19* source directory. Record the directory name that was created to use in the next steps. It's assumed from here on that the version is 1.3.19, and the directory is *apache_1.3.19*.

5. Copy the ApacheSSL distribution into the directory created in Step 4 that already contains the Apache source:

```
% cp apache_1.3.19+ssl_1.44.tar.gz /usr/local/apache_1.3.19
```

6. Unpack the ApacheSSL distribution:

```
% cd /usr/local/apache_1.3.19
% gzip -d apache_1.3.19+ssl_1.44.tar.gz
% tar xvf apache_1.3.19+ssl_1.44.tar
```

7. Apply the patches using the *FixPatch* script that comes with ApacheSSL. This script copies the appropriate files from the OpenSSL installation:

```
% ./FixPatch /usr/local/ssl
```

8. Type yes when prompted:

```
Do you want me to apply the fixed-up Apache-SSL patch for you? [n] yes
```

9. You've now applied the patches to Apache and can continue with the normal installation by following Steps 6 to 10 in the Apache installation instructions earlier in this appendix.

Creating a Key and Certificate

For ApacheSSL to operate, it needs to be configured with a private key and a certificate. ApacheSSL comes with a script that runs the *openssl* utility to create a key and a self-signed certificate. This is the easiest way to get started. Once the key and certificate have been created, they need to be configured into Apache. Again, the version of Apache and the patch applied are assumed to be Version 1.3.19; if a different version is used, the following steps need to be changed to include the correct directories based on the version number.

1. Create the key and signed certificate.

```
% cd /usr/local/apache_1.3.19/src
% make certificate
```

2. The *make certificate* script asks for several fields including country, state, organization name, and the machine hostname encoded into the certificate. The script produces a file that contains both the private key and the signed certificate:

```
/usr/local/apache_1.3.19/SSLconf/conf/httpsd.pem
```

3. After logging in as the root user, copy the key and certificate file into the Apache installation:

```
% cd /usr/local/apache_1.3.19/SSLconf/conf
% cp httpsd.pem /usr/local/apache/conf/default.pem
```

4. Modify the *httpsd.conf* file with a text editor so that PHP files are processed by the PHP scripting engine. The configuration file is found in the directory */usr/local/apache/conf/*. Remove the initial # character from the following line:

```
AddType application/x-httpd-php .php
```

5. Modify the *httpsd.conf* file by changing the Port from 80 to the secure web server port 443:

```
Port 443
```

6. Add the following lines to the end of the *httpsd.conf* file:

```
#
# SSL Parameters
#
SSLCACertificateFile /usr/local/apache/conf/default.pem
SSLCertificateFile /usr/local/apache/conf/default.pem
SSLCacheServerPath /usr/local/apache/bin/gcache
SSLCacheServerPort 18698
SSLSessionCacheTimeout 3600
```

7. Start Apache. Unlike a normal Apache installation, ApacheSSL creates an *httpsdctl* script:

```
% /usr/local/apache/bin/httpsdctl start
```

In some cases, this doesn't correctly start Apache. If this happens, use the following alternative commands to explicitly specify the configuration file to use with the secure Apache:

```
% cd /usr/local/apache/
% bin/httpsd -f conf/httpsd.conf
```

8. A secure Apache is now running and serving requests on port 443—the default HTTPS port—with SSL. This can be tested by requesting the resource *https://localhost/* with a web browser. The installation process is now complete.

When a resource such as *https://localhost/* is requested with a browser, the browser alerts the user to an unknown certificate. To obtain a certificate that will be trusted by users, the *openssl* utility needs to be run to create a private key and a certificate request. The certificate request is then sent to a Certification Authority to be signed using their authoritative certificates. There is a fee for this service. While the Apache configuration allows both the key and the certificate to be placed in the one file, the private key should not be sent to anyone, not even the Certification Authority.

If a trusted certificate is required, consult the OpenSSL documentation that describes how to create keys and Certificate Signing Requests. This documentation can be found at *http://www.openssl.org/docs/apps/openssl.html*.

Installation Resources

For more information on installing and configuring, there are several resources:

- For Microsoft Windows installation, we recommend the PHP Triad for Windows installation package available from *http://sourceforge.net/projects/phptriad/*. The package contains MySQL, PHP, Apache, and PHPMyAdmin for MySQL maintenance through a web browser interface.

- *NuSphere* sells integrated Apache, PHP, and MySQL bundles with simple installation procedures and software support. A free download of the installation package without support is also available for Linux, Sun Solaris, and Microsoft Windows environments. Under the Linux environment, NuSphere is installed by following simple steps in a web browser.

- The PHP online manual has instructions for installing PHP with most web servers and platforms, but these instructions are concise. They are located at *http://www.php.net/manual*.

- Many of the online resources accessible from *http://www.php.net/links.php* have installation tutorials or guides.

- The MySQL manual provides an excellent step-by-step guide to installing and configuring MySQL in many environments. The MySQL web site URL is: *http://www.mysql.com*.

Internet and Web Protocols

In this appendix, we introduce the networking protocols and standards of the Internet. The first part give a brief overview of the networking protocol TCP/IP and its basic principles. The second, larger part of this appendix is a discussion of HTTP.

The introduction is brief, and we don't attempt to cover these topics completely. Appendix E provides pointers to selected resources on the topics of the Internet and web protocols.

The Internet

The Internet had its beginnings in the late 1960s with the development of ARPAnet. A primary goal of ARPAnet was to provide a decentralized network of computing resources that did not rely on any one machine or system to operate; that is, no single point of failure could bring the network down. For a network to achieve this, the topology has to provide multiple paths between the computers connected to the network. Such a topology is shown in Figure B-1. Computers are connected to nodes in the network—or form nodes themselves—and so long as a path can be followed through the links between nodes, the computers can communicate.

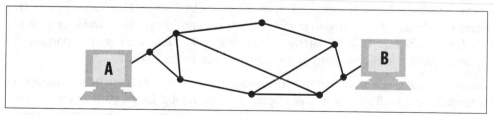

Figure B-1. A network topology that provides multiple communication paths

Another feature of ARPAnet was the use of packet switching. Unlike telephone networks, where a dedicated circuit is established to carry the conversation between two parties, ARPAnet carried data between two communicating systems as a stream of packets, each sent as an individual transmission over the network. Sending a message as a stream of packets allows valuable network bandwidth—the amount of data that can be transmitted for a given period of time—to be shared between different communications.

Packet switching adds complexity. The process of breaking a message into small packets, deciding on the path to send packets, and reassembling of the message before presenting the data to the receiving computer system required the development of network protocols. One of the first protocols was the Network Control Protocol (NCP); it was replaced in 1982 by the Transmission Control Protocol (TCP) and the Internet Protocol (IP). The protocol suite is commonly known as TCP/IP.

Other networks using packet technologies were also being developed and, with the introduction of TCP/IP, interconnections between these networks were possible. Small office-based networks could be connected to main backbone networks such as ARPAnet or the CSNET, the university-based Computer Science Network. These backbone networks were connected to similar networks in other countries over satellite links and submarine cables, and the Internet was born. The Internet isn't one single network: it is many *inter*connected *net*works.

An Analogy

Before we discuss the TCP and IP protocols further, we present a broader picture of how data is transmitted over the Internet by drawing an analogy to the service provided by a courier company.

Imagine that we want to send some hand-drawn illustrations from our office in Melbourne, Australia, to the O'Reilly & Associates, Inc. office in Cambridge, Massachusetts, U.S.A. We would put our drawings into an envelope addressed to our editor Lorrie at O'Reilly's Cambridge office, and a courier would carry the envelope back to the courier company's city office. At the courier's city office our envelope would be sorted from the locally bound envelopes and packed into an air freight bag for Los Angeles and then on to Boston. A similar process would happen, but in reverse, once the bag was unloaded from the plane in Boston. Not knowing exactly where Cambridge is, the envelope may be put on another plane, a train, or a donkey. Eventually, our drawings arrive on Lorrie's desk. This detail isn't important to us, because the courier company is providing a door-to-door service.

Our courier analogy demonstrates a message service over *heterogeneous* transport technologies. The details on the envelope are understood by all courier companies regardless of how they operate. At each point in the network of courier offices, someone reads the details and makes a decision about where the envelope should go next, and how. The Internet is many networks interconnected and a set of protocols—just like the addresses and serial numbers on the envelope—that provide an end-to-end service over the heterogeneous transport technologies.

Our analogy fails to demonstrate one other network characteristic. The set of draw-ings make up one message as far as we and our editor are concerned. If it were not for privacy expectations, our courier company could have opened the envelope and repackaged each sheet of paper into individual envelopes and sent some by air via Sydney, some via Auckland, and even some by sea. No doubt these separate mes-sages would not arrive at the courier's office at Cambridge in order—some might not arrive at all and would have to be sent again—but as long as there was information on each envelope that related them, the original message could be reassembled. The courier's Cambridge office would have to hold on to messages that arrived out of order, decide when to ask for missing envelopes to be resent, then reassemble them into the one envelope and deliver the original message as if nothing had happened. Of course, if a courier company did this, they would go out of business, but this is what happens when applications such as web browsers and servers send a message on the Internet.

TCP/IP

The Transmission Control Protocol and the Internet Protocol manage the sending and receiving of messages as packets over the Internet. The two protocols together provide a service to applications that use the Internet: communication through a network.

The World Wide Web is a network application that uses the services of TCP and IP to communicate over the Internet. When a web browser requests a page from a web server, the TCP/IP services provide a virtual connection—a virtual circuit—between the two communicating systems. Remember that packet-switched networks don't operate like telephone networks that create an actual circuit dedicated to a particu-lar call.

Once a connection is established and acknowledged, the two systems can communi-cate by sending messages. These messages can be large, such as the binary represen-tation of an image, and TCP may fragment the data into a series of IP *datagrams*. An IP datagram is equivalent to the couriers' envelope in that it holds the fragment of the message along with the destination address and several other fields that manage its transmission through the network.

Each node in the network runs IP software, and IP moves the datagrams through the network, one node at a time. When an IP node receives a datagram, it inspects the address and other header fields, looks up a table of routing information, and sends it on to the next node. Often these nodes are dedicated routers—systems that form interconnections between networks—but the nodes can also include the computer systems on which the applications are running. IP datagrams are totally independent of each other as far as IP is concerned: the IP software just moves them from node to node through a network.

The size of a datagram is primarily determined by the largest size message that can be sent by any part of the network. Going back to our courier example: if Lorrie at O'Reilly wanted to send three dozen books to our office, a single package would be fine for air freight but would have to be broken up into smaller packages if the last leg of the journey was by bicycle.

TCP software performs the function of gluing the fragments together at the destination using the *fragment identifier* field in the IP datagram header. Because IP datagrams are transmitted through the network independently, there is no guarantee they will arrive at the destination in order, and TCP stores the fragments in a buffer until all preceding fragments are received.

IP doesn't guarantee that datagrams are delivered. If an IP node receives a corrupt datagram, it throws it away. Datagrams may be missing from the stream the TCP software receives because a datagram was corrupt and not passed on from the IP software or was delayed in the network. TCP buffers the fragments to allow the out-of-order datagrams to arrive. If a missing datagram fails to arrive, TCP eventually requests that it be resent. This can cause datagrams to be received twice; however TCP recognizes and discards the duplicate datagram when it arrives.

IP addresses

To allow communication over heterogeneous networks, each with its own addressing standard, every location in a network needs a globally unique IP address. A computer that is connected to the Internet needs at least one IP address; a node that interconnects two networks needs two.

IP addresses are 32-bit numbers that are commonly represented as a series of four decimal numbers between 0 and 255, separated by a period. An example IP address is 134.148.250.28. Some IP addresses have special meanings; for example, the IP addresses 127.0.0.0 and 127.0.0.1 are reserved for loopback testing on a host. If a connection is to be made from a client to server, both running on the same machine, the address 127.0.0.1 can be used. This address loops back to 127.0.0.0, the localhost. The address 0.0.0.0 is used by IP to identify the default route out of a node.

A system's network file contains the links between network devices and IP addresses. The IP network information can usually be found in the file */etc/networks* on a Linux system.

Ports

When a virtual connection is set up between two communicating systems, each end is tied to a port. The port is an identifier used by the TCP software rather than an actual physical device, and it allows multiple network connections to be made on one machine by different applications.

When a message is received by the TCP software running on a host computer, the data is sent to the correct application based on the port number. By convention, a *well-known port* is normally used by a server providing a well-known service. A list of well-known ports for various applications is maintained by Internet Assigned Number-ber Authority (IANA) and can be found at *http://www.isi.edu/in-notes/iana/ assignments/port-numbers*. For example, the File Transfer Protocol (FTP) uses port 21, and a web server uses port 80.

Systems with TCP/IP software installed have a services file that lists the ports used on that machine. This file is often preconfigured for well-known applications and is maintained by the system administrator to reflect the actual port usage on the machine. This file is usually */etc/services* on a Linux system.

Hypertext Transfer Protocol

As discussed in Chapter 1, HTTP is the standard that allows documents to be communicated and shared over the Web. From a network perspective, HTTP is an *application-layer* protocol that is built on top of TCP/IP. Using our courier analogy from the previous section, HTTP is a kind of cover letter—like a fax cover sheet—that is stored in the envelope and tells the receiver what language the document is in, instructions on how to read the letter, and how to reply.

Since the original version, HTTP/0.9, there have only been two revisions of the HTTP standard. HTTP/1.0 was released as RFC-1945[*] in May 1996 and HTTP/1.1 as RFC-2616 in June 1999.

Request and Response Model

HTTP is simple: a client—most conspicuously a web browser—sends a request for some resource to a HTTP server, and the server sends back a response. The HTTP response carries the resource—the HTML document or image or whatever—as its payload back to the client. This simple request-response model is shown in Figure B-2.

The term *HTTP server* is the correct description for what is more commonly called a web server. Technically, a web browser is an example of a user agent. Other user agents include proxy servers, applications that can provide services such as caching of responses, and access control.

---

[*] Request for Comments, or RFCs, are submitted to the RFC editor (*http://www.rfc-editor.org*) usually by authors attached to organizations such as the Internet Engineering Task Force (IETF at *http://www.ietf.org*). RFCs date back to the early ARPAnet days and are used to present networking protocols, procedures, programs, and concepts. They also include meeting notes, opinions, bad poems, and other humor: RFC-2324 describes the Hypertext Coffee Pot Control Protocol.

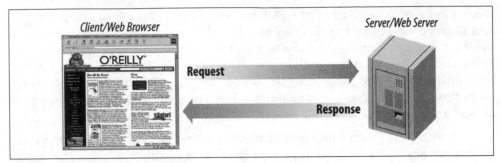

Client/Web Browser

O'REILLY®

Request

Response

Server/Web Server

Figure B-2. Browser makes a request and the HTTP server responds

Simulating an HTTP request

A good way to understand the mechanics of HTTP is to simulate a request and observe the response using the program *telnet*. From a command prompt, the *telnet* program is run with the domain name component of the URL and the port number 80. This instructs the *telnet* program to connect to the host machine on port 80, the port that the web server usually listens on. Then an HTTP request is sent by typing in a request line followed by a blank line (pressing the Enter key twice).

Example B-1 shows the request line:

```
HEAD / HTTP/1.0
```

followed by the server response. The HEAD keyword asks the server to respond with only the HTTP response header fields and not the whole requested document, which is useful if the requested page is large, or the request is for an image. The HEAD keyword is followed by the resource component of the URL and the version of HTTP that the client supports. To see a full response, the request line:

```
GET / HTTP/1.1
```

is entered followed by a blank line.

Example B-1. A simulated HTTP request using telnet

```
% telnet www.w3.org 80
Trying 18.29.1.35...
Connected to www.w3.org.
Escape character is '^]'.
HEAD / HTTP/1.1

HTTP/1.1 200 OK
Date: Wed, 26 Sep 2001 03:42:32 GMT
Server: Apache/1.3.6 (Unix) PHP/3.0.11
P3P: policyref="http://www.w3.org/2001/05/P3P/p3p.xml"
Cache-Control: max-age=600
Expires: Wed, 26 Sep 2001 03:52:32 GMT
Last-Modified: Tue, 25 Sep 2001 21:08:00 GMT
ETag: "5b42a7-4b06-3bb0f230"
```

```
Accept-Ranges: bytes
Content-Length: 19206
Connection: close
Content-Type: text/html; charset=us-ascii

Connection closed by foreign host.
%
```

Uniform Resource Locators

Uniform resource locators—more commonly known as URLs—are used as the primary naming and addressing method of the Web. URLs belong to the larger class of uniform resource identifiers; both identify resources, but URLs include specific host details that allow connection to a server that holds the resource.

A URL can be broken into three basic parts: the protocol identifier; the host and service identifier; and a resource identifier, a path with optional parameters and an optional query that identifies the resource. The following example shows a URL that identifies an HTTP resource:

```
http://host_domain_name:8080/absolute_path?query
```

The HTTP standard doesn't place any limit on the length of a URL, however, some older browsers and proxy servers do. The structure of a URL is formally described by RFC-2396: Uniform Resource Identifiers (URI): Generic Syntax.

Protocol

The first part of the URL identifies the application protocol. HTTP URLs start with the familiar *http://*. Other applications that use URLs to locate resources identify different protocols; for example, URLs used with the File Transfer Protocol (FTP) begin with *ftp://*. URLs that identify HTTP resources served over connections that are encrypted using the Secure Sockets Layer start with *https://*. We discussed the use of the Secure Sockets Layer to protect data transmitted over the Internet in Chapter 9.

Host and service identification

The next part of the HTTP URL identifies the host on which the web server is running, and the port on which the server listens for HTTP requests. The domain name or the IP address can identify the host component. Using the domain name allows user-friendly web addresses such as:

```
http://www.w3.org/Protocols/
```

The equivalent URL using the IP address is more difficult to remember:

```
http://18.29.1.35/Protocols/
```

Nonstandard TCP ports

By convention, servers running well-known Internet applications use standard, well-known TCP port numbers. By default, a HTTP server listens for requests on port 80, an FTP server listens on port 21, and so on. The port number can be omitted from a URL if the well-known port is used. Clients—such as web browsers—determine which well-known port to connect to by the protocol indicated in the URL. For example, requests for the URL *http://www.ora.com* are made to the host machine *www.ora.com* on port 80. When a nonstandard port is used, the URL must include the port number so the browser can successfully connect to the service. For example, the URL *http://www.example.com:8080* connects to the web server running on port 8080 on the host *www.example.com*.

Resource identification

The remaining URL components help locate a specific resource. The path, with optional parameters, and an optional query are processed by the web server to locate or compute a response. The path often corresponds to an actual file path on the host's filesystem. For example, an Apache web server running on *www.example.com* may store all the web content under the directory */usr/local/apache/htdocs* and be configured to use the path component of the URL relative to that directory. The HTTP response to the URL *http://www.example.com/marketing/home.php* contains the file */usr/local/apache/htdocs/marketing/home.php*.

Parameters and queries

The path component of a URL can include parameters and queries that are used by the web server. A common example is to include a query as part of the URL that runs a search script. The following example shows the string q=red as a query that the script *search.php* can use:

```
http://example.com/search.php?q=red
```

Multiple query terms can be encoded using the & character as a separator:

```
http://example.com/search.php?q=red&r=victoria
```

Parameters allow other information not related to a query to be encoded. For example, consider the parameter lines=10 in the URL:

```
http://example.com/search.php;lines=10?q=red
```

This can be used by the *search.php* script to modify the number of lines to display in a result screen.

While HTTP provides the distinction between parameters and queries, parameters are more complex than what we have described here and are not commonly used in practice. We discussed how PHP can use query variables encoded into URLs in Chapter 5.

Fragment identifiers

A URL can include a *fragment identifier* that is interpreted by the client once a requested resource has been received. A fragment identifier is included at the end of a URL separated from the path by the # character. The meaning of the fragment identifier depends on the type of the resource. For example, the following URL includes the fragment identifier tannin for a HTML document:

```
http://example.com/documents/glossary.html#tannin
```

When a web browser receives the HTML resource, it then positions the rendered document in the display to start at the anchor element <a name="tannin"> if the named anchor exists.

Absolute and relative URLs

The URI general syntax allows a resource to be specified as an absolute or a relative URL. Absolute URLs identify the protocol *http://*, the host, and the path of the resource, and can be used alone to locate a resource. Here's an example absolute URL:

```
http://example.com/documents/glossary.html
```

Relative URLs don't contain all the components and are always considered with respect to a *base URL*. A relative URL is resolved to an absolute URL, with respect to the base URL. Typically, a relative URL contains the path components of a resource and allows related sets of resources to reference each other in a relative way. This allows path hierarchies to be readily changed without the need to change every URL embedded in a set of documents.

A web browser has two ways to set base URLs when resolving relative URLs. The first method allows a base URL to be encoded into the HTML using the <base> element. The second method sets the base URL to that of the current document; this is the default. For example, the following HTML document contains three relative URLs embedded into <a> elements:

```
<html>
<body>
<h2>My Home Page</h2>
<p>Read my <a href="cv.html">Curriculum Vitae</a>
<p>Read my
    <a href="work/emp.html">employment history</a>
<p>Visit
    <a href="/admin/fred.html">Fred's home page</a>
</body>
</html>
```

Consider what happens if the example is requested with the following URL:

```
http://example.com/development/dave/home.html
```

The three relative URLs are resolved to the following absolute URLs by the browser:

```
http://example.com/development/dave/cv.html
http://example.com/development/dave/work/emp.html
http://example.com/admin/fred.html
```

Table B-1 shows several relative URLs and how they are resolved to the corresponding absolute URLs given the base URL *http://example.com/a/b/c.html?foo=bar*.

Table B-1. Example relative URLs resolved to absolute URLs

Relative URL	Absolute URL with respect to http://example.com/a/b/c.html?foo=bar
d.html	http://example.com/a/b/d.html
e/d.html	http://example.com/a/b/e/d.html
/d.html	http://example.com/d.html
../d.html	http://example.com/a/d.html
#xyz	http://example.com/a/b/c.html?foo=bar#xyz
./	http://example.com/a/b/
../	http://example.com/a/

URL encoding

The characters used in resource names, query strings, and parameters must not conflict with the characters that have special meanings or can't allowed in a URL. For example, a question mark character identifies the beginning of a query, and an ampersand (&) character separates multiple terms in a query. The meanings of these characters can be escaped using a hexadecimal encoding consisting of the percent character (%) followed by the two hexadecimal digits representing the ASCII encoded of the character. For example, an ampersand (&) character is encoded as %26.

The characters that need to be escape-encoded are the control, space, and reserved characters:

```
; / ? : @ & = + $ ,
```

Delimiter characters must also be encoded:

```
< > # % "
```

The following characters can cause problems with gateways and network agents, and should also be encoded:

```
{ } | \ ^ [ ] `
```

PHP provides the `rawurlencode()` function to protect them. For example, `rawurlencode()` can build the `href` attribute of an embedded link:

```
echo '<a href="search.php?q=' .
     rawurlencode("100% + more") .
     '">';
```

The result is an `<a>` element with an embedded URL correctly encoded:

```
<a href="search.php?q=100%25%20%2B%20more">
```

PHP also provides the `urlencode()` function that differs from the `rawurlencode()` function in that the former encodes spaces as a + sign whereas the latter encodes spaces as %20. The use of the + character to encode a space was an early HTTP way to encode spaces.

HTTP Requests

The model used for HTTP requests is to apply *methods* to identified *resources*. A HTTP request message contains a method name, a URL to which the method is to be applied, and header fields. Some requests can include a body—for example, the data collected in a `<form>`—that is referred to in the HTTP standard as the entity-body.

Example B-2 shows the request message sent from a Netscape browser applying the GET method to the *grapes.gif* resource. The action is to retrieve the image stored in the file *grapes.gif*.

Example B-2. An example HTTP request message

```
GET /grapes.gif HTTP/1.0
Accept: image/gif, image/jpeg, image/png, */*;
Accept-Charset: iso-8859-1,*,utf-8;
Accept-Encoding: gzip;
Accept-Language: en;
Connection: Keep-Alive;
Host: www.webdatabasebook.com;
User-Agent = Mozilla/4.51 [en] (WinNT; I);
```

The first line of the message is the request-line and contains the method name GET, the request URL /grapes.gif, and the HTTP version HTTP/1.0, each separated by a space character. The request-line is followed by a list of header fields. Each field is represented as a name and value pair separated with a colon character, and lines are separated with semicolons.

The header fields are followed by a blank line and then by the optional body of the message. The POST method request usually contains a body of text, as we discuss in the next section.

Request methods

There are six request methods, but only three are used in practice:

GET

> Retrieves a resource. A query can be used to add extra information to the GET request and, as we discussed in our introduction to URLs, these are appended to the URL itself. A database search is a good example of an application of the GET

request: the resource is likely to be a web script, and the query component of the URL is the search conditions.

POST
Sends data to a server. Rather than appending data to the URL, the data is sent in the body of the HTTP request.

HEAD
Returns only the header fields in a response, not the resource itself. This can be used for lightweight retrieval, so that the modification date of a resource can be checked before the full resource is retrieved with GET.

DELETE
Allows a resource identified by the URL to be deleted from a server. This is the counterpart to the PUT method and allows an author to remove a resource from the specified URL. Usually not implemented.

PUT
Similar to the POST method, this method is designed to put a resource onto a server that can be later retrieved with the URL in the PUT request. Some HTML editors and web servers support the PUT methods allowing authors to put resources onto a web site at the specified URL. Usually not implemented.

TRACE
Produces diagnostic information.

The HTTP standard divides these methods into those that are safe and those that aren't. The safe methods—GET and HEAD—don't have any persistent side effects on the server. The unsafe methods—POST, PUT, and DELETE—by their nature are designed to have persistent effects on the server. The standard allows for clients to warn users that a request may be unsafe, and a browser should not resend a request with the POST method without user confirmation.

The HTTP standard further classifies methods as *idempotent* when a request can be repeated many times and have the same effect as if the method was called once. The GET, HEAD, PUT, and DELETE methods are classified as idempotent; the POST method isn't.

GET versus POST

Both the GET and POST methods send data to the server, but which method should you use?

The HTTP standard includes the two methods to achieve different goals. The POST method was intended to create a resource. The contents of the resource would be encoded into the body of the HTTP request. For example, an order <form> might be processed and a new row in a database created.

The GET method is used when a request has no side effects such as performing a search, and the POST method is used when a request has side effects such as adding a new row to a database. A more practical issue is that the GET method may result in long URLs, and may even exceed some browser and server limits on URL length.

Use the POST method if any of the following are true:

- The result of the request has persistent side effects such as adding a new database row.
- If the data collected on the form is likely to result in a large URL if implemented using the GET method.
- The data to be sent is in any encoding other than seven-bit ASCII.

Use the GET method if all the following are true:

- If the request is essentially finding a resource, and HTML <form> data is to help that search.
- The result of the request has no persistent side effects.
- If the data collected and the input field names in a HTML <form> are less than 1,024 characters in length.

HTTP Responses

When a web server processes a request from a browser, it attempts to apply the method to the identified resource and create a response. The action of the request may succeed, or it may fail for a variety of reasons, but the web server always sends a response message back to the browser.

A HTTP response message contains a status line, header fields, and the requested entity as the body of the message. The body of the response is usually the resource requested in the request message. Example B-3 shows the result of a GET method on a small HTML file.

Example B-3. An example HTTP response message

```
HTTP/1.1 200 OK
Date: Tue, 24 Oct 2001 02:54:37 GMT
Server: Apache/1.3.19
Last-Modified: Tue, 24 Oct 2001 02:53:08 GMT
ETag: "4445f-bf-39f4f994"
Content-Length: 321
Accept-Ranges: bytes
Connection: close
Content-Type: text/html

<!DOCTYPE HTML PUBLIC
    "-//W3C//DTD HTML 4.0 Transitional//EN"
    "http://www.w3.org/TR/html4/loose.dtd" >
<html>
<head><title>Grapes and Glass</title></head>
<body>
```

```
<img src="http://example.com/grapes.gif">
<p>Welcome to my simple page
<p><img src="http://example.com/glass.gif">
</body>
</html>
```

The status line—the first line of the message—starts with the protocol version of the message, followed by a status code and a reason phrase, each separated by a space character. The status line is followed by the header fields. As with the request, each field is represented as a name and value pair separated with a colon character. A blank line separates the header fields and the body of the response.

Status codes

HTTP status codes are used to classify responses to requests. The HTTP status code system is extensible, with a set of codes described in the standard that are "generally recognized in current practice." HTTP defines a status code as a three-digit number; the first digit is the class of response. The following list shows the five classes of codes defined by HTTP:

1xx
> Informational. HTTP 1.0 reserves this class of code for future use. HTTP 1.1 uses codes in this class to indicate the request has been received by the server and that processing is continuing.

2xx
> Success. The request was successfully received, and the action successfully performed.

3xx
> Redirection. When a response has a redirection code, the client needs to make a further request to actually get the specified resource. The URL of the actual resource is included in the response header field Location. When the status code is set to 301, the browser automatically makes the request for the URL specified in the Location header field. The use of the Location header field is discussed further in Chapter 5, and used in many examples throughout this book.

4xx
> Client error. The request can't be processed due to bad syntax of the message, the sender is unauthorized or forbidden to access the resource, or the resource can't be found.

5xx
> Server error. The server failed to fulfill an apparently valid request.

The actual code used for a particular response is largely determined by the configuration of the web server, and not by a scripting environment that might create a web application. Some scripting environments allow the web developer to explicitly set these codes. For example, a script associated with a URL might simply set the response code to 501 to indicate the requested function hasn't been implemented.

Caching

Most user agents, such as web browsers, allow HTTP responses to be cached, which can significantly reduce the number of requests sent to a web server and thus improve the performance of a web application. HTTP responses are cached by saving a response to a request in memory. When a browser considers a request, it first looks to its local cache to see if it has an up-to-date copy of the response before sending the request to the web server. Consider a web site that includes a company logo on the top of each page in an image element such as:

```
<img src="/images/logo.gif">
```

When the browser requests a page that contains the image, a separate request is sent to retrieve the image */images/logo.gif*. If the image resource is *cacheable*, and browser caching is enabled, the browser saves the response in a cache. A subsequent request for the image is recognized, and the local copy from the cache is used rather than sending the request for the resource to a web server.

A browser uses a cached response until the response becomes *stale*, or the cache becomes full and the response is displaced by the resources from other requests. The primary mechanism for determining if a response is stale is comparing the date and time set in the Expires header field with the date and time of the host running the user agent. If the date and time are incorrectly set on the user agent's host, a cached response may expire immediately or be cached longer than expected. HTTP/1.1 is more sophisticated than HTTP/1.0 in controlling the life of a cached response using other parameters not discussed here.

Not all responses are *cacheable*. HTTP describes the conditions that allow a user agent to cache a response in some detail; essentially most responses are cacheable unless a *cache-control* header directs otherwise. There are many situations in which an application may wish to prevent a page from being cached, particularly when the content of a response is dynamically generated, such as in a web database application.

HTTP/1.0 cache control

HTTP/1.0 uses the Pragma header set to the value no-cache to prevent caching. Some old user agents don't support the use of the Pragma header to control the caching of a response. The only way to prevent caching of a page with these older user agents is to set the Expires header field to 0, which instructs many user agents to immediately expire the response or change it to a past date and time. This practice is recognized, but not formally supported by the HTTP standard.

HTTP/1.1 cache control

HTTP/1.1 uses the Cache-Control header field as its basic caching control mechanism. The Cache-Control header can be used in both HTTP requests and responses, however, we consider only HTTP responses here. Setting the Cache-Control header field to no-cache in a HTTP response prevents the response from being cached by a HTTP/1.1 user agent.

Some HTTP/1.1 Cache-Control settings are directed to user agents that maintain caches for more that one user, such as a proxy server. Proxy servers are used to achieve several goals; one is to provide caching of responses for a group of users. A local network, such as that found in a university department, can be configured to send all HTTP requests to a proxy server. The proxy server forwards requests to the destination web server and passes back the responses to the originating client. Proxy servers can cache responses and thus reduce requests sent outside the local network. Setting the Cache-Control header field to public allows a user agent to make the cached response available to any request. Setting the Cache-Control header field to private allows a user agent to make the cached response available only to the client who made the initial request.

Setting the Cache-Control header to no-store prevents a user agent from storing the response in nonvolatile storage, such as a hard disk. This prevents sensitive information from being inadvertently saved beyond the life of a browser session. HTTP/1.1 defines several other Cache-Control header fields not described here.

The HTTP/1.1 standard is relatively new, and there are several user agents that aren't HTTP/1.1-aware or -compliant. While HTTP/1.1 provides better cache control directives, it is wise to include header fields that are understood by HTTP/1.0 browsers, proxy servers, and other user agents.

HTTP and TCP/IP

Each time a HTTP request is sent, a TCP/IP connection is made. When a browser makes a request, the following network activity results:

1. The browser initiates a TCP/IP connection to the web server on the host and port identified in the URL of the request.
2. The host sends back a TCP acknowledgment to indicate a virtual circuit has successfully been established.
3. The browser sends the HTTP request in full to the server using the established connection.
4. The server acknowledges the receipt of the request and starts to generate a response. The browser waits for the response and times out if the response doesn't arrive within a preset time limit.
5. The server sends the HTTP response message to the browser.

6. The browser acknowledges the receipt of the complete HTTP response.

7. The server disconnects the virtual circuit.

Each HTTP request-response sequence is a completely separate network connection: each request message sent by a web browser—or any other HTTP user agent—is totally independent of any other request. Every request message a web server receives has its own separate response. This independence of requests is what makes the HTTP protocol stateless.

Simultaneous request model

The stateless nature of the HTTP protocol allows applications that use HTTP to scale well and also allows for some performance optimizations. Because the protocol is stateless, one such optimization is that a web browser can make multiple HTTP requests in parallel. Consider the HTML document shown in Example B-4 that encodes references to two images.

Example B-4. The HTML document http://example.com/wine.html

```
<!DOCTYPE HTML PUBLIC
    "-//W3C//DTD HTML 4.0 Transitional//EN"
    "http://www.w3.org/TR/html4/loose.dtd" >
<html>
<head><title>Grapes and Glass</title></head>
<body>
<img src="http://example.com/grapes.gif">
<p>Welcome to my simple page
<p><img src="http://example.com/glass.gif">
</body>
</html>
```

After requesting the HTML document and processing it, the browser makes two additional requests for the resources *grapes.gif* and *glass.gif*. In all, three separate HTTP requests must be made to display the page. However, the browser can make the two requests for the images simultaneously. The browser isn't concerned about the order in which the images are retrieved and, because each request is independent, TCP/IP can't guarantee that the requests are responded to in any particular order.

Sending requests in parallel allows a browser to maximize the use of available network bandwidth. However, a browser can make only a limited number of parallel requests with improvements to performance and, typically, a limit of four simultaneous requests provides the best results. The ability to send requests simultaneously allows a web browser to use more network capacity relative to other applications. An application such as FTP communicates through one TCP connection and therefore has access to less bandwidth when a web browser makes four TCP connections in parallel.

At the server end, simultaneous requests can be treated independently and may not even be processed by the same web server. A common way to handle high volumes of requests is to use specialized network hardware to balance connections across multiple web servers running on different machines. The stateless nature of HTTP allows for such configurations. We discussed the issues of session management and the stateless nature of HTTP in Chapter 8.

Persistent connections

Web pages that consist of text alone are retrieved from a web server with one HTTP request. However, many web pages contain images and other objects that require additional HTTP requests; some corporate home pages contain more that 60 images, each requiring a separate HTTP request. The page shown in Example B-4 requires three requests: the first to get the page and then two more to get the images. While the browser is usually configured to make up to four parallel requests, with HTTP/1.0, each request must open a separate TCP connection to the server. This is expensive as each request adds to the cost of the TCP dialog required to open the virtual connection.

As a result, browsers and web servers often support a keep-alive capability to reduce the time taken to load web pages that contain images. This feature allows multiple requests to be made in succession using the one TCP connection. After a specified idle period, the connection is assumed to be no longer required and is closed by the server. HTTP/1.1 uses persistent TCP connections as the default behavior. Persistent connections not only improve the performance of the browser but reduce the load on a HTTP server and on the network, because fewer TCP connections need to be established.

In the same way as the simultaneous request model, a browser can send multiple requests on a persistent connection without waiting for each response. This behavior is called pipelining.

MIME

Originally, web pages were solely HTML documents encoding text and hypertext links to other pages. The first version of HTTP, HTTP/0.9, was not much more than a way to wrap HTML documents. However, web pages today are made up of a variety of resources including images, Java applets, sounds, movies, and the HTML that glues them all together.

To allow the transfer of other resources, HTTP/1.0 has borrowed the concepts of Multipurpose Internet Mail Extensions (MIME) as a way to encode objects. As the name suggests, MIME attaches content with encoding other that plain text to electronic mail. HTTP's use of MIME is almost identical to its use in electronic mail.

MIME includes several header fields that describe the enclosed data and are included in the HTTP messages that contain a body. If the response message is carrying a HTML file, the Content-Type field is set to text/html. Web browsers examine the media type in the Content-Type field to help decide how to render the body of a response. They can also be configured to use particular helper applications for those media types that can't be directly displayed. The Content-Length field is also set to the number of bytes that make up the original content.

MIME uses media types to describe content. Media types are divided into a content-type and subtype pairs. The MIME standard defines seven content-types and several basic subtypes. The subtypes can be extended to specifically define different media. A list of well-known subtypes for each content-type is maintained by the Internet Assigned Number Authority (IANA) and can be found at *http://www.isi.edu/in-notes/iana/assignments/media-types/media-types/*.

Media types are also used to describe browser and server capabilities, and preferences. The Accept request header field informs the web server of browser capabilities and preferences. This field carries a list of types in preference order and can include weighting factors.

APPENDIX C
Modeling and Designing Relational Databases

Planning and designing a database is the essential first step to developing a web database application. In this appendix, we introduce database modeling and the techniques to convert a model into the SQL statements needed to create a database.

This appendix isn't intended to replace a course or book on relational databases. Modeling requirements with an entity-relationship model requires both patience and experience. Instead, we detail our thought processes in a case study that models the winestore requirements and converts these to SQL CREATE TABLE statements. Pointers to resources on modeling and database design are included in Appendix E.

The Relational Model

Relational database management systems, or RDBMSs, maintain, enforce, and use relationships between data. To illustrate the principles of relational databases, we use the winestore system requirements and descriptions from Chapter 1 as the basis for our examples.

Case Study: Relations in the Winestore

There are three essential types of data or entities that form the basis of the winestore. First, there is the wine itself: each wine has characteristics or attributes such as a name, a type, and a variety. Second, there is the customer, who has attributes such as a name, an address, and a phone number. Last, and importantly in selling wine online, is a customer purchase order. It is the order that forms a relationship between customers and wines.

An order is made when a customer purchases a quantity of wine. Consider an example. One of our customers, customer #37—we give our customers a number, so as not to confuse two customers who have the same name—purchases two bottles of wine #168, our 1996 Cape Mentelle Cabernet Merlot. The database stores this relationship as an order: customer #37 placed their fifth order with us, ordered wine

#168, and required a quantity of two bottles. Figure C-1 shows a simple representation of this relationship.

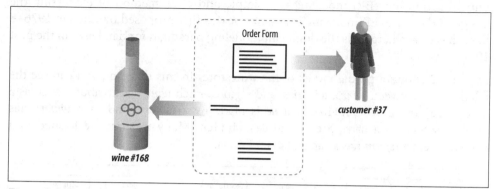

Figure C-1. Customer #37 purchases two bottles of wine #168

There are several constraints in the order that may be obvious but are worth stating: there is only one customer #37, there is one wine we refer to as #168, and the next time the customer orders with us, it will be their sixth order. Relational databases can enforce many constraints on data stored, including ensuring in the example that an order can be made only by a valid customer and that only wines we stock can be ordered. When you represent data in a database, entities such as wine, customers, and orders are represented as tables or relations that group together related data.

There are some limitations to this model. One limitation is that an order consists of only one wine. There are several ways this problem can be resolved. Perhaps the most obvious approach is to create additional attributes in the order, such as wine2, quantity2, wine3, quantity3, and so on. The problem is where to stop: what is the maximum number of wines per order? And, if an order contains only one wine, how are the unused attributes processed? Indeed, just as if you were designing a spreadsheet, any report works only for that number of wines; any change means redevelopment of the report.

Another solution to the problem is to introduce a new table that stores the items that make up an order. This approach is subtle but solves the problems with the initial approach. How, then, do you know when to add attributes or when to add tables? Traditionally, this answer has been the somewhat technical explanation that the database should be normalized according to a set of rules; most acceptably designed databases are in the third-normal form. Fortunately, with the advent and refinement of simpler modeling techniques for designing databases—such as entity-relationship (ER) modeling—a well-designed database can be achieved by following simple rules.

We discuss ER modeling in the next section, as we focus on designing a workable winestore.

Entity-Relationship Modeling

Entity-relationship (ER) modeling is a simple and clear method of expressing the design of database. ER modeling isn't new—it was first proposed by Chen in 1976—but it has only emerged as the dominant modeling paradigm for databases in the past 10 or 12 years.

Figure C-2 shows a partial model of the winestore. In this diagram, you can see the relationship between *wines*, *wineries*, and *regions*. Each *wine* has attributes such as a name, type, and a description. A *wine* is made by a *winery*, and each *winery* has attributes such as a name, phone, and description. Many *wineries* are located in a *region*, where a *region* has a map and description.

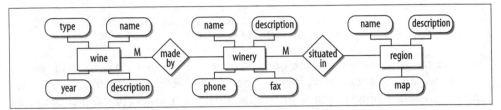

Figure C-2. A simple ER model showing the relationship between wines, wineries, and regions

ER diagrams aren't complicated, and we have already illustrated most of the features of ER modeling in Figure C-2. These features include:

Rectangles
> Represent entities—that is, objects being modeled. Each entity is labeled with a meaningful title.

Diamonds
> Represent relationships between entities; a relationship is labeled with a descriptive title that represents how the entities interact.

Ellipses
> Represent attributes that describe an entity.

Lines
> Connect entities to relationships. Lines may be without any annotation, be annotated with an M and an N, or annotated with an M and a 1 (or an N and a 1). Annotations indicate the cardinality of the relationship; we discuss cardinality later in this section.

Lines
> Connect attributes to entities. These lines are never labeled.

Other ER modeling tools include *double ellipses*, *dashed ellipses*, and *double lines*; we use some of these advanced features later in this appendix. Useful references for more advanced ER modeling—and enhanced ER (EER) modeling—are provided in Appendix E.

Case Study: Modeling the Online Winestore

To illustrate how ER modeling can be used to effectively design a database, we return to our online winestore.

System requirements analysis

The first step in developing a database model using ER modeling is to consider the requirements of the system. The requirements for the online winestore were described in Chapter 1 and are typically gathered from a scope document, customer interviews, user requirements documents, and so on.

Many of the requirements affect development of the ER model, while others are more general system requirements used to develop the web database application. One of the skills of ER modeling is extracting the requirements that impact on the database design from those that are functional elements of the system.

Once a system requirements analysis is complete, and the detailed requirements written down, you can proceed to the conceptual database design using the ER modeling techniques.

Identifying entities in ER modeling

Having identified the general requirements of the system, the first phase in conceptual modeling and creating an ER model is to identify the entities in the system.

Entities are objects or things that can be described by their characteristics. As we identify entities, we list the attributes that describe the entity. For example, a *customer* is an entity that has a *name*, an *address*, a *phone*, and other details.

Be careful when choosing entities. A *customer* or a *wine* is an entity. Reducing the stock in the inventory and adding it to a shopping cart is a function or process, not an entity. The basic rule is that an entity is an object or thing.

Five entities and their attributes have already been identified earlier in this appendix. Four are easy to determine from our requirements:

- The *wine* entity has the attributes type, name, year, and description.
- The *customer* entity has the attributes surname, firstname, initial, title, addressline1, addressline2, addressline3, city, state, zipcode, country, phone, fax, salary, birthdate, email address, and discount.
- The *winery* entity has the attributes name, description, phone, and fax.
- The *region* entity has the attributes name, description, and map.

We add a *users* entity to this list in order to maintain user account details at the winestore:

- The *users* entity has the attributes user_name and password. The user_name is the same as the *customer* email address.

The remaining entities—and, in two cases, the distinction between the entities—are harder to identify.

We have earlier identified the *order* entity in our introduction to ER modeling, but an order is hard to precisely define. One description might be:

> An *order* is an object created by a customer when they agree to purchase one or more (possibly different) bottles of wine.

We can then say that an *order* is created on a date, and the system requirements in Chapter 1 identify that an *order* has a discount, a delivery cost, and a delivery note.

We can also say that this model of an *order* consists of one or more different *wines* and, for each different *wine*, a quantity of that wine is purchased. The subparts in each order—the different kinds of wines—are the *items* that make up the *order*. But is the *wine* itself part of an *item*? The distinction is hard, but the correct answer is probably no: this is a relationship, the *items* that make up an *order* are related to *wines*.

There are now two more entities—*orders* and *items*—and two relationships, which illustrates how difficult it is to reason about entities without considering how they are related. Determining entities isn't always easy, and many different drafts of an ER model are often required before a final, correct model is achieved. The ER model for the winestore took several attempts to get right.

Here are the *item* and *order* entities:

- The *item* entity—which is related to an *order*—has the attributes quantity and price.
- The *order* entity has attributes date, discount percentage, delivery cost, and delivery note.

The system requirements in Chapter 1 showed that *wines* are delivered in shipments. Each shipment is on a date and consists of a number of bottles, at a per-bottle and per-case price. How is this incorporated into the model? Perhaps the most obvious solution is to add quantity and price attributes to the *wine* entity. This doesn't work well: it is difficult to maintain the possibly different prices for different shipments and to maintain the correct shipment dates.

A good solution to the inventory problem is an *inventory* entity. This entity is related to the *wine*, and maintains different sets of data for each shipment of each *wine*:

- The *inventory* entity has an on-hand quantity, an item cost, a dateadded, and a case cost (for a dozen bottles).

The final entity is somewhat of an oddity. If a wine is a Cabernet Merlot, you can simply store the string Cabernet Merlot in an attribute in the *wine* entity. Another approach is to have a *grape_variety* entity, where each different grape variety is described individually. So, *Cabernet* is one instance of a *grape_variety* entity, and *Merlot* is another. The *grape_variety* entity is then related to the *wine* entity. This approach does seem overly complicated, but let's opt for it anyway because it introduces an instructive twist to our modeling, a many-to-many relationship discussed in the next section.

Let's add two attributes to the *grape_variety* entity, variety (the description) and ID (a counter used to, for example, record that *Cabernet* is the first word in *Cabernet Merlot*, and *Merlot* is the second word.

- The *grape_variety* entity has two attributes, ID and variety.

There are other possible entities. For example, the shopping basket could be an entity: the shopping cart is an object that contains items that will be ordered. However, a shopping cart is an incomplete *order* and, hence, it's omitted from the entity list. Including it is perhaps valid, and depends on how the entities are interpreted from the requirements.

There are also other entities that are outside the scope of our requirements. For example, a country might contain many regions, but there is no requirement for countries to be modeled in our system. Also, the winestore itself is an entity, but we are actually interested in the entities that make up the winestore, not really the whole concept itself. Selecting entities is all about getting the granularity and scope of choice right.

We have hinted at but not explicitly identified the relationships between the entities. For example, a *winery* is part of a *region*, a *wine* is made by a *winery*, and an *item* is related to a *wine*. The first step is to identify the entities and their attributes; the second step is to identify how the entities are related.

Identifying relationships in ER modeling

Before identifying the relationships between the entities we have identified, we noted earlier in this section that:

Lines connect entities to relationships. Lines may be without any annotation, be annotated with an M and an N, or annotated with an M and a 1 (or an N and a 1). Annotations indicate the cardinality of the relationship.

Cardinality refers to the three possible relationships between two entities* and, before you can consider how the entities are related, you need to explore the possible kinds of relationship:

One-to-one
A one-to-one relationship is represented by a line without any annotations that joins two entities. One-to-one means that for the two entities connected by the line, there is exactly one instance of the first entity for each one instance of the second entity. An example might be *customers* and *user* details: each *customer* has exactly one *username* and *password*, and that particular *username* and password is only for that *customer*.

One-to-many (or many-to-one)
A one-to-many relationship is represented by a line annotated with a 1 and an M (or a 1 and an N). One-to-many means that for the two entities connected by the line, there are one or more instances of the second entity for each one instance of the first entity. From the perspective of the second entity, any instance of the second entity is related to only one instance of the first entity. An example is *wineries* and *wines*: each *winery* sells many *wines*, but each *wine* is made by exactly one *winery*. Many-to-one relationships are the most common relationships between entities.

Many-to-many
A many-to-many relationship is represented by a line annotated with an M and an N. Many-to-many means that for the two entities connected by the line, each instance of the first entity is related to one or more instances of the second entity and, from the other perspective, each instance of the second entity is related to one or more instances of the first entity. An example is the relationship between *wineries* and delivery firms: a *winery* may use many delivery firms to freight *wine* to *customers*, while a delivery firm may work for many different *wineries*.

It isn't surprising that many database modelers make mistakes with cardinalities. Determining the cardinalities of the relationships between the entities is the most difficult skill in ER modeling, but one that, when performed correctly, results in a well-designed database. To illustrate how cardinality is determined, let's consider the relationships between the entities in the winestore and present arguments for their cardinalities.

---

* Actually, relationships can exist between as many entities as there are in the model. Also, we have deliberately omitted the distinction with relationships that are optional, that is, where one instance of an entity—such as a *customer*—can exist without a related entity—such as an *order*. However, we avoid complex relationships in this appendix; more detail can be found in the books listed in Appendix E.

Correctly assigning cardinalities is essential. Mistakes in cardinalities of relationships lead to duplicated data, inconsistencies, and redundancy in the database. All lead to poor performance and a hard-to-maintain database.

Relationships in the winestore ER model

Before considering cardinalities, you need to consider what entities are related. You know from previous discussion that a *region* is related to a *winery*, and that a *winery* is related to a *wine*. There are other relationships that are implicitly identified: an *order* contains *items*, a *customer* places an *order*, *users* have *customer details*, and a *wine* has an *inventory*.

There is also one crucial relationship that links the *wines* sold to the *customer*, that is, the relationship between an *order item* and the *inventory*. Last, a *wine* contains one or more different *grape variety* entities.

To assign cardinalities—which crucially affect the database design—start with the relationship of *wines* to *wineries*. To begin, you need to decide what sort of relationship these entities have and assign a descriptive term. A good description of the relationship between *wines* and *wineries* is that a winery makes wine. Now draw a diamond labeled *makes* between the entities *wine* and *winery*, and connect the relationship to the two entities with an unannotated line. This process is shown in Figure C-3 (A).

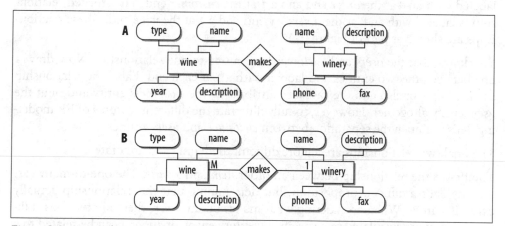

Figure C-3. A partial ER model showing the relationship between wines and wineries

The next step is to determine what cardinality to assign to this relationship. The most effective approach to determining cardinality is to consider the relationship from the perspective of both entities. From the perspective of a *winery*, the question to ask is:

Does a *winery* make exactly one *wine* or one or more *wines*?

The answer is the latter, so you write M at the *wine*-end of the relationship. From the other perspective—that of the *wine*—you can ask a second simple question:

Is a *wine* made by exactly one or more than one *winery*?

This answer is the former—that limitation is noted in the system requirements—and you can write a 1 at the *winery*-end of the relationship. The annotated, one-to-many relationship is shown in Figure C-3 (B).

Dealing with the relationship between *wineries* and *regions* involves similar arguments. You begin by describing the relationship. In this case, an appropriate label might be that a *winery* is situated in a *region*. After drawing the diamond and labeling it, now consider the cardinalities. A *winery* belongs in exactly one *region*, so label the *region* end with a 1. A *region* contains one or more *wineries*, so you label the *winery* end with an M.

There are three more relationships that can be completed using the same one-to-many arguments:

- The consists-of relationship between *orders* and *items*
- The purchase relationship between *customers* and *orders*
- The stocked relationship between *wines* and *inventories*

You can label all three with a 1 and an M (or N). The consists-of relationship is labeled with a 1 at the *order* end and an M at the *item* end. The purchase relationship is labeled with an M at the *order* end and a 1 at the *customer* end. The stocked relationship is labeled with an M at the *inventory* end and a 1 at the *wine* end. These relationships are shown as part of Figure C-4.

You know that the *users* and *customer* have a one-to-one relationship. Now draw a line between the two entities and label it with a 1 at each end. Label the relationship as *has*. You can also add the password attribute to the *customers* entity and omit the *users* entity altogether. However, to fully illustrate the different features of ER modeling, let's maintain the separation between *customer* and *users* entities.

The final two relationships are a more difficult to identify and annotate.

The first is the relationship between an order *item* and a *wine*. The one-to-many cardinality isn't a difficult proposition, but determining that this relationship actually exists is harder. When considering what makes up an *order*, there are two possibilities: an *item* can be related to a specific *inventory* entry, or an *item* can be related to a *wine*. The former is possibly more intuitive because the *item* that is delivered is a bottle from our *inventory*. However, the latter works better when modeling the system's data requirements.

In our design, a customer *order* is made up of quantities of *wines*. You can label this relationship as *sells*. The price of the wine is copied from the inventory and stored in the *order*. This design is appropriate because the relationship between a *customer*

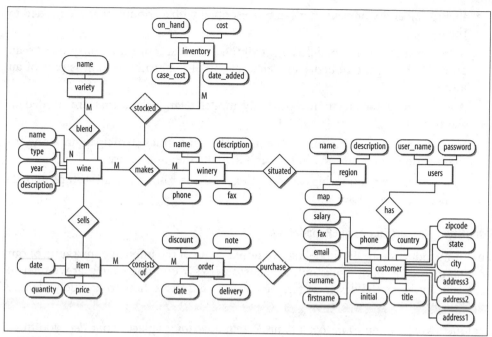

Figure C-4. An almost complete ER model for the winestore

and a specific bottle is uninteresting once the order is shipped and, arguably, it is uninteresting even as the order is packed.

The second difficult—and final—relationship is that between *wines* and *grape varieties*. Naming the relationship is easy: let's call this relationship *blend*. Determining the cardinality is harder. First, consider the relationship from the *wine* perspective. A *wine* can contain more than one *grape variety* when it is a blend, so you label the *grape variety* end of the relationship with an M. Now consider the relationship from the *grape variety* perspective. A *grape variety*, such as *semillon*, may be in many different *wines*. So, let's settle on a many-to-many relationship and label the *wine* end with an N.

Our ER model is almost complete, and Figure C-4 shows it with all its entities and relationships. What remains is to consider the key attributes in each of the entities, which are discussed in the next section. As you consider these, you can adjust the types of relationships slightly.

There are a few rules that determine what relationships, entities, and attributes are, and what cardinalities should be used:

- Expect to draft a model several times.
- Begin modeling with entities, add attributes, and then determine relationships.

- Include an entity only when it can be described with attributes that are needed in the model.
- Some entities can be modeled as attributes. For example, a country can be an entity, but it might be better modeled as one of the attributes that is part of an address.
- Avoid unnecessary relationships. Only model relationships that are needed in the system.
- One-to-one relationships are uncommon. If two entities participate in a one-to-one relationship, check that they aren't actually the same entity.
- Many-to-many relationships are complex. Use one-to-many relationships in preference where possible.

Identifying key attributes in ER modeling

In our introduction to ER modeling, we noted some of the implicit constraints of our model, including that there is only one customer #37 and one wine that we refer to as #168. In the model design so far, we haven't considered how to uniquely identify each entity.

Uniqueness is an important constraint. When a *customer* places an *order*, you must be able to uniquely identify that *customer* and associate the unique *order* with that unique *customer*. You also need to be able to uniquely identify the *wines* the *customer* purchases. In fact, all entities must be uniquely identifiable; this is true for all relational databases.

The next step is to identify the attributes or sets of attributes that uniquely identify an entity. Begin with the *customer*. A surname (or any combination of names) doesn't uniquely identify a customer. A surname, firstname, initial, and a complete address may work, although there are some cases where children and parents share the same name and address.

A less complicated approach for unique identification—and a common one that's guaranteed to work—is to add an identifier number (ID) attribute to the entity. A short unique identifier also leads to better database performance, as discussed in Chapter 3. Using this approach, assign ID #1 to the first customer, ID #2 to the second customer, and so on. In the model, this new attribute is underlined to indicate that it uniquely identifies the customer as shown in Figure C-5.

You can take the same approach with *wine* as for *customers*—for the same reasons—and add an ID field.

For *wineries* and *regions*, the name is most likely unique or, at least, it can be made so. However, for simplicity, you should also use the ID attribute approach to prevent any ambiguity or need for the winestore administrator to create unique names for *wineries* or *regions*. The same argument can be applied to *grape varieties*.

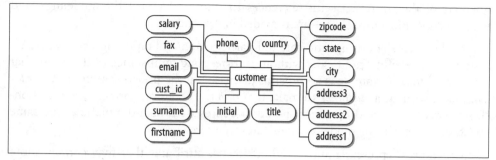

Figure C-5. The customer entity with all attributes; the primary key is shown underlined

Orders can also be dealt with by a unique ID, as can *items* and *inventory*. However, the uniqueness of this ID may be questionable. To illustrate, consider an example. You can number each *order* across the whole system uniquely, beginning with the system's first *order* #1. Alternatively, you can combine the *customer* ID with an *order* ID and begin each different *customer's orders* with *order* ID #1. The combination of *customer* ID and *order* ID is still unique, e.g., *customer* #37, *order* #1 is different from *customer* #15, *order* #1. This latter scheme is an example of a full participation relationship by a weak entity: an *order* isn't possible without a *customer* (hence, the term *full participation*) and the *customer* ID forms part of the *order* entity's unique identifier, hence the term weak entity.

You can use the scheme of full participation by a weak entity for *orders*; the other approach of numbering *orders* across the whole collection also works well. An advantage of this scheme is that the *order* number is more meaningful to the user—for example, a user can tell from their *order* number how many *orders* they have placed—and the *order* number provides a convenient counting tool for reporting. Participation is discussed briefly in the next section and weak entities are discussed in more detail later in the "Completing the ER model" section.

You can follow similar arguments with *items*. An *item* can be uniquely numbered across the whole system or can be numbered from #1 within an *order*. Again, this depends on the participation and, as with *orders*, we follow the latter approach. The same applies for *inventory*, which is numbered within a *wine*.

Because *customer* and *users* have a one-to-one relationship, the customer ID can be used to uniquely identify a user. Therefore, the *users* entity has full participation as a weak entity in the relationship with *customer*.

Other ER modeling tools

Other ER modeling tools include double ellipses and double lines. These tools permit the representation of other constraints, multivalued attributes, and the specification of full participation. In addition, it is possible for a relationship to have an attribute, that is, for a diamond to have attributes that are part of the relationship, not part of the entities. Useful references for more advanced ER modeling—and enhanced ER (EER) modeling—are provided in Appendix E.

Double lines as relationships indicate full participation and represent cases where an instance of one entity can't exist without a corresponding instance of the entity that it is related to. An example is an *order* as discussed in the previous section. An *order* can't exist without a *customer* to make that *order*. Therefore, correctly, the relationship between *order* and *customer* should be represented as a double line; the same constraints apply in the model to *items* and *inventories*.

Dashed ellipses represent multivalued attributes, attributes that may contain more than one instance. For example, the attribute address can be multivalued, because there could be a business address, a postal address, and a home address. Multivalued attributes aren't used in our model.

In addition, there are other extensions to the modeling techniques that have already been applied. For example, more than two entities can be related in a relationship (that is, more than two entities can be connected to a diamond). For example, the sale of a wine can be described as a three-way relationship between a *wine*, a *customer*, and an *order*. A second complex technique is the composite attribute; for example, an attribute of *customer* is address and the attribute address has its own attributes, a street, city, and zipcode. We don't explore complex relationships in this book.

Completing the ER model

Figure C-6 shows the final ER model with the unique key constraints shown. Notice that for *items*, *orders*, *users*, and *inventories,* the attributes from other entities aren't included. They are instead indicated as weak entities with a double rectangle and they participate fully in the related entities as indicated by double lines.

If *items*, *orders*, and *inventories* are numbered across the whole system, you can omit the double rectangles. The double lines can be omitted if any entities can exist without the related entity.

A summary of ER notation tools is shown in Figure C-7.

Converting an Entity-Relationship Model to SQL

There are five steps to convert an ER model to a set of SQL CREATE TABLE statements.

Step 1: Convert regular entities to tables

The first step is the simplest. Here's what you do:

1. For each non-weak entity in the ER model, write out a CREATE TABLE statement with the same name as the entity.

2. Include all attributes of the entity and assign appropriate types to the attributes.

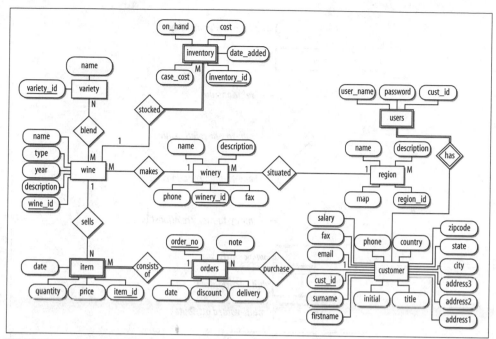

Figure C-6. The complete ER model for the winestore database

3. Include the PRIMARY KEY of the entity.

4. Add any modifiers to attributes and any additional keys as required.

To perform this step, you need to make decisions about attribute types in the SQL CREATE TABLE statements. Attribute types are discussed in Chapter 3.

There are several non-weak entities in the model. Begin with the region entity, which has the attributes region_id, region_name, description, and map. You might anticipate no more than 100 different regions, but being cautious is important if more than 1,000 regions need to be stored. Accordingly, a type of int(4) allows up to 10,000 regions. Using a similar argument, define region_name as a varchar(100). Because descriptions may be long, let's define description as a blob. A map—which is an image—is defined as a mediumblob.

As decided earlier in the chapter, the unique key of the *region* table is an ID, which is now called region_id. Accordingly, you define a PRIMARY KEY of region_id. A requirement of all primary keys is that they are specified as NOT NULL, and this is added to the attribute. Now automate the creation of the values by adding the auto_increment clause and a DEFAULT '0'. (Recall from Chapter 3 that storing NULL or 0 in an auto_increment attribute is a MySQL feature that automatically stores a unique ID larger than all other IDs for this table.)

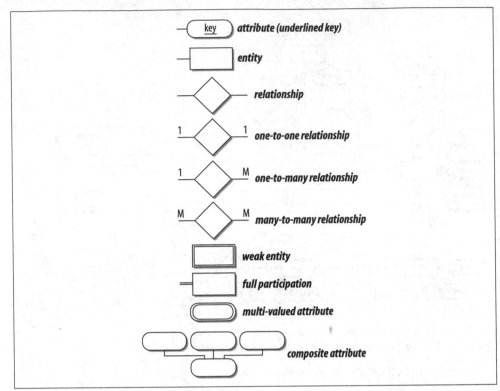

key — attribute (underlined key)

— entity

— relationship

1 — 1 one-to-one relationship

1 — M one-to-many relationship

M — M many-to-many relationship

weak entity

full participation

multi-valued attribute

composite attribute

Figure C-7. Tools used in ER modeling

The resulting definition for the region table is then as follows:

```
CREATE TABLE region (
    region_id int(4) DEFAULT '0' NOT NULL auto_increment,
    region_name varchar(100) DEFAULT '' NOT NULL,
    description blob,
    map mediumblob,
    PRIMARY KEY (region_id),
    KEY region (region_name)
);
```

Notice an additional KEY on the region_name named region. By adding this key, you anticipate that a common query is a search by region_name. Also, a region must have a name, so a NOT NULL is added to the region_name attribute.

The CREATE TABLE statements for the other non-weak entities are listed in Example C-1. Remember, however, that this is only the first step: some of these CREATE TABLE statements are altered by the processes in later steps.

Example C-1. CREATE TABLE commands for non-weak entities

```
CREATE TABLE wine (
  wine_id int(5) DEFAULT '0' NOT NULL auto_increment,
```

Example C-1. CREATE TABLE commands for non-weak entities (continued)

```
    wine_name varchar(50) DEFAULT '' NOT NULL,
    type varchar(10) DEFAULT '' NOT NULL,
    year int(4) DEFAULT '0' NOT NULL,
    description blob,
    PRIMARY KEY (wine_id)
);

CREATE TABLE winery (
    winery_id int(4) DEFAULT '0' NOT NULL auto_increment,
    winery_name varchar(100) DEFAULT '' NOT NULL,
    description blob,
    phone varchar(15),
    fax varchar(15),
    PRIMARY KEY (winery_id)
);

CREATE TABLE customer (
    cust_id int(5) NOT NULL auto_increment,
    surname varchar(50) NOT NULL,
    firstname varchar(50) NOT NULL,
    initial char(1),
    title varchar(10),
    addressline1 varchar(50) NOT NULL,
    addressline2 varchar(50),
    addressline3 varchar(50),
    city varchar(20) NOT NULL,
    state varchar(20),
    zipcode varchar(5),
    country varchar(20),
    phone varchar(15),
    fax varchar(15),
    email varchar(30) NOT NULL,
    birth_date date( ),
    salary int(7),
    PRIMARY KEY (cust_id),
    KEY names (surname,firstname)
);

CREATE TABLE grape_variety (
    variety_id int(3),
    variety_name varchar(20)
    PRIMARY KEY (variety_id)
);
```

Step 2: Convert weak entities to tables

The second step is almost identical to the first but is used for weak entities. Here's what you do:

1. For each weak entity in the model—there are three: *inventory*, *order*, and *item*—translate the entity directly to a CREATE TABLE statement as in Step 1.

2. Include all attributes as in Step 1.

3. Include as attributes the primary key attributes of the *owning* entity; that is, the entity the weak entity is related to. These attributes are in the table and are also included as part of the primary key of the weak entity.

For example, for the *inventory* entity, create the following:

```
CREATE TABLE inventory (
    wine_id int(5) DEFAULT '0' NOT NULL,
    inventory_id int(3) NOT NULL,
    on_hand int(5) NOT NULL,
    cost float(5,2) NOT NULL,
    case_cost float(5,2) NOT NULL,
    dateadded timestamp(12) DEFAULT NULL,
    PRIMARY KEY (wine_id,inventory_id)
);
```

The wine_id is included from the *wine* table and forms part of the PRIMARY KEY definition. All attributes can't be NULL in this *inventory* table, so you'll note liberal use of NOT NULL. The dateadded attribute has a DEFAULT NULL, which if no value is inserted, is automatically filled with the current date and time.

A similar approach is taken with *orders*, in which cust_id is included from the *customer* table as an attribute and as part of the PRIMARY KEY definition:

```
CREATE TABLE orders (
    cust_id int(5) DEFAULT '0' NOT NULL,
    order_id int(5) DEFAULT '0' NOT NULL,
    date timestamp(12),
    discount float(3,1) DEFAULT '0.0',
    delivery float(4,2) DEFAULT '0.00',
    note varchar(120),
    PRIMARY KEY (cust_id,order_no)
);
```

The *items* table is slightly more complex, but made easier because *orders* has already been defined. The *items* table includes the PRIMARY KEY attributes of the entity it is related to (that is, *orders*). Because the PRIMARY KEY of *orders* is already resolved, the resolution is as follows:

```
CREATE TABLE items (
    cust_id int(5) DEFAULT '0' NOT NULL,
    order_id int(5) DEFAULT '0' NOT NULL,
    item_id int(3) DEFAULT '1' NOT NULL,
    qty int(3),
    price float(5,2),
    date timestamp(12),
    PRIMARY KEY (cust_id,order_no,item_id)
);
```

Step 3: One-to-one relationships

There is a one-to-one relationship between *customer* and *users* in our model. The process for conversion is as follows:

1. Choose one of the two tables that participates in the relationship (this table has already been identified and written out as part of Steps 1 or 2). If the relationship involves total participation, choose the entity that totally participates.

2. In the chosen table, include as an attribute (or attributes) the primary key of the other table.

3. If the entities totally participate in each other and neither participates in another relationship, consider removing one of the tables and merging the attributes into a single table.

As *users* is the entity that totally participates in *customer*, the identifier cust_id from *customer* is added to the *users* table and defined as the primary key attribute:

```
CREATE TABLE users (
  cust_id int(4) DEFAULT '0' NOT NULL,
  user_name varchar(50) DEFAULT '' NOT NULL,
  password varchar(15) DEFAULT '' NOT NULL,
  PRIMARY KEY (user_name),
);
```

Step 4: Regular one-to-many relationships

For a regular one-to-many relationship, here's the procedure:

1. Identify the table representing the many (M or N) side of the relationship.

2. Add to the many-side (M or N) table the primary key of the 1-side table.

3. Optionally, add NOT NULL to any attributes added.

In the model, this means adding a winery_id to the *wine* table:

```
CREATE TABLE wine (
  wine_id int(5) DEFAULT '0' NOT NULL auto_increment,
  wine_name varchar(50) DEFAULT '' NOT NULL,
  winery_id int(4),
  type varchar(10) DEFAULT '' NOT NULL,
  year int(4) DEFAULT '0' NOT NULL,
  description blob,
  PRIMARY KEY (wine_id)
);
```

For the *winery* table, it means adding a region_id:

```
CREATE TABLE winery (
  winery_id int(4) DEFAULT '0' NOT NULL auto_increment,
  winery_name varchar(100) DEFAULT '' NOT NULL,
  region_id int(4),
  description blob,
  phone varchar(15),
```

```
    fax varchar(15),
    PRIMARY KEY (winery_id)
);
```

The final regular one-to-many relationship is between *wine* and *item*. For this, add a wine_id to *items*:

```
CREATE TABLE items (
    cust_id int(5) DEFAULT '0' NOT NULL,
    order_id int(5) DEFAULT '0' NOT NULL,
    item_id int(3) DEFAULT '1' NOT NULL,
    wine_id int(4) DEFAULT '0' NOT NULL,
    qty int(3),
    date timestamp(12),
    price float(5,2),
    PRIMARY KEY (cust_id,order_no,item_id)
);
```

In cases where you wish to prevent a row being inserted without a corresponding value, you can add a NOT NULL to the attribute added in this step.

Step 5: Many-to-many relationships

For many-to-many relationships—there is one in our model between *wine* and *variety*—the following procedure is used:

1. Create a new table with a composite name made of the two entities that are related.
2. Add the primary keys of the two related entities to this new table.
3. Add an ID attribute if the order of relationship is important. For example, in the winestore, a Cabernet Merlot Shiraz is different from a Shiraz Merlot Cabernet, so an ID is required.
4. Define the primary key of this new table to be all attributes that form part of the table.

In the example, create the following table:

```
CREATE TABLE wine_variety (
    wine_id int(5) DEFAULT '0' NOT NULL,
    variety_id int(3) DEFAULT '0' NOT NULL,
    id int(1) DEFAULT '0' NOT NULL
    PRIMARY KEY (wine_id, variety_id)
);
```

The table contains the primary keys of the *wine* and *grape_variety* and defines these—along with the ID attribute—as the PRIMARY KEY. No change is required to the *wine* or *grape_variety* tables.

Managing Sessions
in the Database Tier

In Chapter 8 we discussed the development of session-based applications using the PHP session management features. In this appendix, we:

- Discuss the motivation for storing session variables in the database tier of a web database application

- Show how PHP session handlers are written to implement user-defined methods

- Develop a fully functional set of PHP handlers that use a table in a MySQL database to store session variables

Using a Database to Keep State

HTTP is a stateless protocol that allows applications to distribute resources across more that one web server. This allows an application to distribute requests across many web servers, thus dividing the load and permitting scaling of the application.

One of the main problems for session-based web applications is scalability. Implementing session management in the middle tier of an application forces all HTTP requests to be processed by a particular web server. To provide session support, all HTTP requests that belong to a session must be processed in the context of the session variables. Consider an application that holds the contents of a shopping cart using session variables. An HTTP request that submits an order must be processed by reading the session variables that hold the state of the cart. Figure D-1 shows the three-tier architecture of a web database application, with the session store in the web server environment. This is the approach described in Chapter 8.

Moving the session data to the database allows an application to scale horizontally at the middle tier as shown in Figure D-2. The web server doesn't have to keep session variables, so HTTP requests can be processed by different web servers. The PHP scripts on each web server still implement the application logic, but session variables are retrieved from a central database. In many applications, the middle tier—the layer that implements the application logic—is the performance bottleneck. By

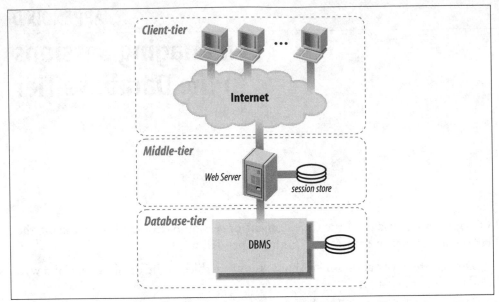

Figure D-1. Three-tier architecture using a web server to store session variables

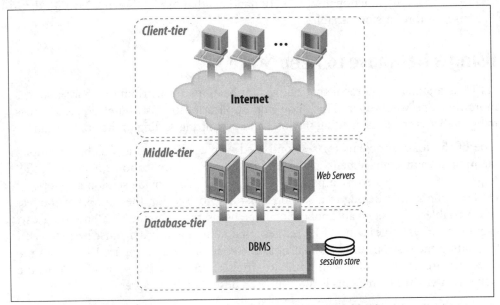

Figure D-2. Three-tier architecture using a database to store session variables

deploying multiple web servers, HTTP load balancing can be achieved and the database server better utilized. However, there is a point at which the performance of the DBMS becomes the bottleneck. Also, allowing multiple web servers to access a central database server requires strategies to control concurrent access, a topic discussed in Chapter 6.

PHP Session Management

In Chapter 8 we showed how to build session-based applications using the PHP session management functions. Applications use these functions to initialize sessions and register session variables as shown in Example D-1. This simple script initializes a session and registers two session variables: count and start.

Example D-1. A simple PHP script that uses a session

```php
<?php
    // Initialize a session. This call either creates
    // a new session or re-establishes an existing one.
    session_start();

    // If this is a new session, then the variable
    // $count is not registered
    if (!session_is_registered("count"))
    {
        session_register("count");
        session_register("start");

        $count = 0;
        $start = time();
    }
    else
    {
        $count++;
    }

    $sessionId = session_id();
?>
<!DOCTYPE HTML PUBLIC
    "-//W3C//DTD HTML 4.0 Transitional//EN"
    "http://www.w3.org/TR/html4/loose.dtd" >
<html>
    <body>
        <p>This page points at a session
            (<?=$sessionId ?>)
        <br>count = <?=$count ?>.
        <br>start = <?=$start ?>.
        <p>This session has lasted
            <?php
                $duration = time() - $start;
```

```
        echo "$duration";
    ?>
    seconds.
  </body>
</html>
```

By default, PHP manages sessions by storing session variables in files on disk and uses the session ID as part of the filename. The session management functions and file storage are discussed in more detail in Chapter 8.

PHP allows user-defined handlers to be written that change how sessions are managed. The handlers define how PHP starts and terminates sessions, stores and retrieves session variables, and removes idle sessions with garbage collection. By implementing user-defined handlers, a developer can modify how PHP sessions are stored, without needing to change any application logic. PHP scripts, such as that shown in Example D-1, don't need to be modified except for an additional include directive to use the user-defined session management handlers.

PHP Session Management Storage Methods

Because PHP abstracts the storage method from the programmatic interface to session management, different storage strategies can be used. PHP can be configured to store session variables in files on disk (the default method), in memory, or in a user-defined way. The method used is configured by the session.save_handler parameter in the *php.ini* file. Here are the values the session.save_handler parameter can be set to:

files
: This is the default storage method for PHP, where session variables are serialized and written to a session file.

mm
: The memory management storage method allows session variables to be stored in Apache's runtime memory. Using memory has the advantage of better performance than files on disk. However, if many sessions must be supported, and each session uses a large volume of data, the memory used by the Apache process may be high. To use memory to store session variables, Apache must be configured and compiled to use an installed memory management module (--with-mm).

user
: The user-defined method allows an application to save session variables to systems other than file or memory, such as to a table in a database. By defining several handler prototypes, PHP allows the developer to define the behavior of the low-level session management. A full explanation is given in the next section.

Building User-Defined Session Handlers

When the PHP session.save_handler parameter is set to user, PHP expects to find functions that provide the low-level session management support. These are the functions the developer needs to write. The functions must conform to the defined prototypes:

Boolean open(string *save_path*, string *session_name*)
> Called by PHP when session_start( ) or session_register( ) is called to access the session store. PHP passes the *php.ini* parameters session.save_path and session.name as arguments to this function, and these arguments are used to locate the session store. By default, session.save_path is set to /tmp to indicate the directory for the files storage method, and session.name is set to PHPSESSID as the name of the session ID cookie. These parameters select the database and table used to store session variables.

Boolean close( )
> Called by PHP at the end of a script when a session is closed. The function should return false if an error occurs during the close operation and true on success.

mixed read(string *session_id*)
> Called by PHP to read the variables for the session identified by *session_id* when a session is initialized. The function returns a string that contains the serialized session variables. The PHP engine converts the string to the individual session variables and sets up the $HTTP_SESSION_VARS array. If no session is found, the function should return a blank string. The function should return false if an error occurs during the read operation and true on success.

Boolean write(string *session_id*, string *values*)
> This function is called by PHP when session variables are updated and when a session is initialized. This function is passed the ID of the session, and the session variables serialized into a single string by PHP. The implementation of write( ) must store the serialized string associated with the session, and record the time the session was last accessed. The serialized string stored for the session is returned by the read( ) handler. PHP uses this function not only to update session variables but to record the last access time when a session is initialized. The function should return false if an error occurs during the write operation and true on success.

Boolean destroy(string *session_id*)
> Called by PHP when the session identified by *session_id* is destroyed. Removes storage dedicated to the identified session. The function should return false if an error occurs during the destroy operation and true on success.

Boolean gc(int *max_lifetime*)
> Called by PHP with a probability set by session.gc_probability when a session is initialized. Removes the data and variables stored by dormant sessions. The

value of session.gc_maxlifetime is passed to this function and is used to determine which are idle sessions. If the garbage collection handler is executed without error, it should return true.

While the return types and the parameters passed to the functions must conform to the prototypes listed here, the actual function names can be different. These functions need to be registered with PHP using session_set_save_handler( ):

session_set_save_handler(string *open*, string *close*, string *read*, string *write*, string *destroy*, string *gc*)

Registers a set of PHP function names as the callback functions for user-defined session management. The arguments to this function are the names of the functions. The six parameters passed to session_set_save_handler( ) are interpreted as the names of the *open*, *close*, *read*, *write*, *destroy*, and *gc* functions.

Once registered, PHP uses these handler functions when the PHP session management calls are made. The handler functions aren't called directly by scripts that use session management. More detail about these handlers is given later when we describe the MySQL storage implementations.

MySQL Session Store

In this section we develop a set of user-defined handlers that store session variables in a MySQL table.

Session Table Structure

For the session handler code that stores session variables, a table is needed to hold sessions. The following SQL CREATE TABLE statement creates a table to hold the session ID, the serialized session variables, and a timestamp to indicate when the session was last accessed:

```
CREATE TABLE PHPSESSION(
  session_id varchar(50) NOT NULL,
  session_variable text,
  last_accessed decimal(15, 3) NOT NULL,
  PRIMARY KEY (session_id),
  KEY last_acc (last_accessed)
);
```

There is an additional index that allows fast deletion of dormant sessions using custom garbage-collection code described later.

When the code is up and running, the *PHPSESSION* table can be examined to see the current sessions:

```
mysql> SELECT * FROM PHPSESSION;
+-----------------------------+----------------------------------+-----------------+
| session_id                  | session_variable                 | last_updated    |
+-----------------------------+----------------------------------+-----------------+
| d003a284fbbf982c90aade5485  | count|i:39;start|i:1000900585;   | 1000900661.575  |
| b74e720d5395800d5fabe7eab8  | count|i:0;start|i:1000900677;    | 1000900678.705  |
+-----------------------------+----------------------------------+-----------------+
2 rows in set (0.02 sec)
```

Handler Implementations

The best way to arrange the functions that implement the session handlers is to place them in a single support file. By placing the functions shown in Example D-2 through D-9 in the one file, you can include that file at the beginning of any PHP script using sessions. The support file containing the handler implementations—for example *mysql_sessions.inc*—must be included before any session calls are made as shown in the following example:

```php
<?php
    include("mysql_sessions.inc");
    start_session();

    //... rest of script ...

?>
```

Support functions

The MySQL-based session handlers use the showerror( ) function implemented in the *error.inc* include file, and the $hostName, $username, and $password variables set in the *db.inc* include file. The showerror( ) function is used by the handler implementations to display details about MySQL errors. The *db.inc* file provides a central location for maintaining connection details. The *error.inc* and *db.inc* files are described in Chapter 4.

Example D-2 shows the function getMicroTime( ), which generates a timestamp. The timestamp records the last session access in the sessionWrite( ) handler and creates a query that identifies idle sessions in the sessionGC( ) handler. The sessionWrite( ) handler and the sessionGC( ) handler are developed later in this section.

Example D-2. The support function getMicroTime()

```
include("error.inc");
include("db.inc");

// Returns current time as a number.
// Used for recording the last session access.

function getMicroTime( )
{
```

Example D-2. The support function getMicroTime() (continued)

```
// microtime( ) returns the number of seconds
// since 0:00:00 January 1, 1970 GMT as a
// microsecond part and a second part.
// e.g.: 0.08344800 1000952237
// Convert the two parts into an array
$mtime = explode(" ", microtime( ));

// Return the addition of the two parts
// e.g.: 1000952237.08344800
return($mtime[1] + $mtime[0]);
}
```

sessionOpen

Example D-3 shows the first of the session handlers required by PHP session management. The sessionOpen( ) function sets two global variables to hold the database connection and the table that manages the session variables. PHP passes the *php.ini* file values of session.save_path and *session.name* as $database_name and $table_name, respectively. The $database_name parameter selects the database, and the $table_name parameter is stored in the global variable $session_table. The global variables $session_table and $connection formulate and execute SELECT, INSERT, UPDATE, and DELETE queries in the other handlers.

Example D-3. The sessionOpen handler

```
// The database connection
$connection;

// The global variable that holds the table name
$session_table;

// The session open handler called by PHP whenever
// a session is initialized. Always returns true.

function sessionOpen($database_name, $table_name)
{

    // Save the database name in a global variable
    global $connection;
    global $hostName;
    global $username;
    global $password;

    if (!($connection = @ mysql_pconnect($hostName,
                                         $username,
                                         $password)))
        showerror( );

    if (!mysql_select_db($database_name, $connection))
        showerror( );
```

Example D-3. The sessionOpen handler (continued)

```
    // Save the table name in a global variable
    global $session_table;
    $session_table = $table_name;

    return true;
}
```

Using the values of session.save_path and session.name as the database name and the table name respectively, the MySQL session handlers developed in this appendix can be configured to use any database and table as a session store. With the handler shown in Example D-3, the name of the table is the same as the name of the cookie used to hold the session ID. For example, consider the following *php.ini* file settings:

```
    session.save_path = winestore
    session.name = PHPSESSION
```

With these settings, our module uses the *PHPSESSION* table in the *winestore* database.

sessionRead

The sessionRead( ) handler function—shown in Example D-4—is called by PHP each time a session is initialized. The handler returns the serialized string that holds the session variables for the given session ID $sess_id. The function executes a query to find the row with a session_id equal to $sess_id and, if the row is found, the session_variable attribute is returned. If no session is found, sessionRead( ) returns a blank string. If an error occurs when the SELECT query is executed, showerror( ) is called.

The query is constructed using the global variables $session_table and executed using the global variable $connection set up by the sessionOpen( ) handler. Note that this function returns all the session variables in the one serialized string. The calling PHP code converts the string to the individual session variables and sets up the $HTTP_SESSION_VARS array and the associated global variables if register_globals has been enabled.

Example D-4. The sessionRead handler

```
// This function is called whenever a session_start()
// call is made and reads the session variables
// Returns "" when a session is not found
//          (serialized)string - session exists

function sessionRead($sess_id)
{
  // Access the DBMS connection
  global $connection;
```

Example D-4. The sessionRead handler (continued)

```
// Access the global variable that holds the name
// of the table that holds the session variables
global $session_table;

// Formulate a query to find the session
// identified by $sess_id
$search_query =
  "SELECT * FROM $session_table
    WHERE session_id = '$sess_id'";

// Execute the query
if (!($result = @ mysql_query($search_query,
                             $connection)))
  showerror();

if(mysql_num_rows($result) == 0)
  // No session found - return an empty string
  return "";
else
{
  // Found a session - return the serialized string
  $row = mysql_fetch_array($result);
  return $row["session_variable"];
}
}
```

sessionWrite

The sessionWrite() handler function isn't responsible only for writing variables to the session store but also records when session variables are read. sessionWrite() is called by PHP each time a variable is registered, when session variables change, and when a session is initialized. It's important that the last_access time-stamp is updated each time a session is initialized; that is, when session_start() is called. If the last access time isn't updated, a session may be seen as dormant by the garbage collection handler and destroyed even though the variables have recently been read.

Example D-5 starts by executing a SELECT query to determine if a session exists. If a session is found, then an UPDATE query is executed, otherwise a new session row is created with an INSERT query. Both the INSERT and UPDATE queries set the last_ accessed field with the timestamp created by the support function getMicroTime() that is shown in Example D-2.

Example D-5. The sessionWrite handler

```
// This function is called when a session is initialized
// with a session_start() call, when variables are
// registered or unregistered, and when session variables
// are modified. Returns true on success.
```

Example D-5. The sessionWrite handler (continued)

```
function sessionWrite($sess_id, $val)
{
  global $connection;
  global $session_table;

  $time_stamp = getMicroTime( );

  $search_query =
    "SELECT session_id FROM $session_table
      WHERE session_id = '$sess_id'";

  // Execute the query
  if (!($result = @ mysql_query($search_query,
                                $connection)))
    showerror( );

  if(mysql_num_rows($result) == 0)
  {
    // No session found, insert a new one
    $insert_query =
      "INSERT INTO $session_table
      (session_id, session_variable, last_accessed)
      VALUES ('$sess_id', '$val', $time_stamp)";

    if (!mysql_query($insert_query,
                     $connection))
      showerror( );
  }
  else
  {
    // Existing session found - Update the
    // session variables
    $update_query =
      "UPDATE $session_table
      SET session_variable = '$val',
          last_accessed = $time_stamp
      WHERE session_id = '$sess_id'";

    if (!mysql_query($update_query,
                     $connection))
      showerror( );
  }
  return true;
}
```

sessionClose

The sessionClose( ) handler can perform any housekeeping functions that need to be executed before a script ends. In the handler implementation shown in Example D-6, the connection setup returned by the sessionOpen( ) is true.

Example D-6. The sessionClose handler

```
// This function is executed on shutdown of the session.
// Always returns true.

function sessionClose($sess_id)
{
    return true;
}
```

sessionDestroy

When session_destroy( ) is called, the sessionDestroy( ) handler shown in Example D-7 is called. This function deletes the row identified by the $sess_id argument from the table that holds the session variables.

Example D-7. The sessionDestroy handler

```
// This is called whenever the session_destroy( )
// function call is made. Returns true if the session
// has successfully been deleted.

function sessionDestroy($sess_id)
{
  global $connection;
  global $session_table;

  $delete_query =
    "DELETE FROM $session_table
      WHERE session_id = '$sess_id'";

  if (!($result = @ mysql_query($delete_query,
                               $connection)))
    showerror( );

  return true;
}
```

Garbage collection

The last handler to be defined is the garbage collection function. Example D-8 shows the implementation of sessionGC( ), which queries for all session rows that have been dormant for $max_lifetime seconds. PHP passes the value set in the session.gc_maxlifetime parameter of the *php.ini* file. The time a session has been dormant is calculated by subtracting the last update time—held in the session row—from the current time.

Example D-8. Garbage collection handler

```
// This function is called on a session's start up with
// the probability specified in session.gc_probability.
// Performs garbage collection by removing all sessions
```

Example D-8. Garbage collection handler (continued)

```
// that haven't been updated in the last $max_lifetime
// seconds as set in session.gc_maxlifetime.
// Returns true if the DELETE query succeeded.

function sessionGC($max_lifetime)
{
  global $connection;
  global $session_table;

  $time_stamp = getMicroTime( );

  $delete_query =
    "DELETE FROM $session_table
      WHERE last_accessed < ($time_stamp - $max_lifetime)";

  if (!($result = @ mysql_query($delete_query,
                                $connection)))
    showerror( );

  return true;
}
```

Registering session handlers

Finally, the handlers implemented in Example D-3 through D-8 need to be registered as callback functions with PHP. Example D-9 shows the call to session_set_save_handler( ) with the names of each handler function.

Example D-9. Registering the user-defined session handlers with PHP

```
// Call to register user call back functions.

session_set_save_handler("sessionOpen",
                         "sessionClose",
                         "sessionRead",
                         "sessionWrite",
                         "sessionDestroy",
                         "sessionGC");
```

Using the User-Defined Session Handler Code

Once the user-defined session handler code is implemented, it can be used by setting up the session configuration in the *php.ini* file and including the library at the top of PHP scripts that use sessions. The session.save_handler parameter needs to be set to user, indicating that user-defined handlers are used; the session.save_path parameter is set to the name of the database; and session.name parameter is set to the name of the table. The following example settings are used if session variables are stored in the *PHPSESSION* table of the *winestore* database:

```
session.save_handler = user
session.save_path = winestore
session.name = PHPSESSION
```

Example D-10 shows how application scripts are modified to use the MySQL session store; the script is a copy of Example D-1, with the addition of the directive to include *mysql_session.inc*.

Example D-10. A simple PHP script that uses the MySQL session store

```php
<?php
  // Include the MySQL session handlers
  include("mysql_session.inc");

  // Initialize a session. This call either creates
  // a new session or re-establishes an existing one.
  session_start();

  // If this is a new session, then the variable
  // $count is not registered
  if (!session_is_registered("count"))
  {
    session_register("count");
    session_register("start");

    $count = 0;
    $start = time();
  }
  else
  {
    $count++;
  }

  $sessionId = session_id();

?>
<!DOCTYPE HTML PUBLIC
    "-//W3C//DTD HTML 4.0 Transitional//EN"
    "http://www.w3.org/TR/html4/loose.dtd" >
<html>
  <body>
    <p>This page points at a session
        (<?=$sessionId ?>)
    <br>count = <?=$count ?>.
    <br>start = <?=$start ?>.
    <p>This session has lasted
      <?php
        $duration = time() - $start;
        echo "$duration";
      ?>
      seconds.
  </body>
</html>
```

Resources

This appendix contains lists of books and online resources that cover many of the topics discussed in this book. The appendix is divided into four sections:

Client-tier resources
> HTML, XML, XHTML, CSS, and JavaScript resources.

Middle-tier resources
> Web server, web technology, and PHP resources. In particular, we include pointers to third-party PHP development tools, an introduction to the PHP libraries, and open source projects.

Database-tier resources
> Database theory, SQL, and DBMS-specific resources.

Security and cryptography resources

Software installation resources are listed at the end of Appendix A.

Client Tier Resources

More information on HTML, the related topic of CSS, JavaScript, and directions in the standards that web browsers support can be found in the following resources:

- The W3C web site *http://www.w3.org* has links to many of the web standards, including HTML 4 (*http://www.w3.org/TR/html4/*), Cascading Style Sheets, XML, and XHTML. The HTML validator—which was used to validate all examples in this book—can be found at *http://validator.w3.org*.

- The HTML Writer's Guild (HWG) is an organization that provides many useful resources to web developers, including links to lists of browser features and HTML validators. Trial membership is free for the first year. The HWG web site is *http://www.hwg.org*.

- *HTML & XHTML: The Definitive Guide,* C. Musciano and B. Kennedy (O'Reilly). This book is a comprehensive guide to writing HTML web pages, and covers HTML 4 features including Cascading Style Sheets.

- *Cascading Style Sheets: The Definitive Guide,* E. A. Meyer (O'Reilly). Besides presenting the CSS material with many examples and case studies, this book provides a CSS support chart that shows which browsers support which features.

- *JavaScript: The Definitive Guide,* D. Flanagan (O'Reilly). Provides an in-depth reference to JavaScript with selected code examples; this book is ideal for the intermediate audience who can program and understand the requirements of JavaScript for a web database application.

- The original cookie specification was developed by Netscape and can be found at *http://www.netscape.com/newsref/std/cookie_spec.html.*

- XHTML 1.0 Recommendations can be found from the W3C site at *http://www.w3.org/TR/2000/REC-xhtml1-20000126/.*

Middle Tier Resources

This section lists resources that contain more information on the Apache web server, web performance tuning, networking, PHP programming, and third-party PHP add-ons including Integrated Development Environments (IDEs), script optimization tools, and commercially supported installation packages.

Web Server and Web Technology Resources

More information on the Apache web server can be found in the following resources:

- The local documentation installed with the Apache web server. After following the Apache installation instructions in Appendix A, the Apache manual is accessible as *http://localhost/manual/.*

- The Apache HTTP Server web site: *http://httpd.apache.org.*

- *Apache: The Definitive Guide,* B. Laurie and P. Laurie (O'Reilly). Oriented around the directives that can be used in the *httpd.conf* file.

More information on web servers, web performance tuning, and web performance modeling and traffic characteristics can be found in the following resources:

- *Web Performance Tuning,* P. Killelea (O'Reilly).

- *Capacity Planning for Web Performance: Metrics, Models, and Methods,* D. A. Menascé and V. A. F. Almeida (Prentice-Hall).

Here are some good background books that cover a range of topics in the middle tier, focusing on web servers and web technology, but are slightly out of date:

- *How to Set Up and Maintain a Web Site,* L.D. Stein (Addison Wesley).
- *Web Server Technology: The Advanced Guide for World Wide Web Information Providers,* N.J. Yeager and R. E. McGrath (Morgan Kaufmann Publishers).

Networking and Web Resources

- The W3C web site: *http://www.w3.org/History.html.* This URL provides a good starting point that includes pages containing many links, time lines, growth statistics, and other useful resources.
- *Internet Core Protocols,* E. Hall and V. Cerf (O'Reilly). This book offers a good introduction to the protocols of the Web.
- The HTTP/1.0 specification is contained in RFC-1945 and is found on the IETF web site at *http://www.ietf.org/rfc/rfc1945.txt.*
- The HTTP/1.1 specification is contained in RFC-2616 and is found on the IETF web site at *http://www.ietf.org/rfc/rfc2616.txt.*
- The Uniform Resource Identifiers (URI): Generic Syntax specification is contained in RFC-2396 and is found on the IETF web site at *http://www.ietf.org/rfc/rfc2396.txt.*
- RFC-1180: *TCP/IP Tutorial,* T. Socolofsky and C. Kale. This RFC provides a tutorial on how data is passed through a TCP/IP network and can be found at: *ftp://ftp.rfc-editor.org/in-notes/rfc1180.txt.*

More About PHP

This book can't replace an introductory programming book or any of the excellent PHP resources that are available in add-on products or from the Web. This section is a brief overview of those resources.

Books

There are now more than 20 books covering PHP, and many of these also introduce interaction with the MySQL DBMS. We recommend the following books—in no particular order—as offering good coverage of PHP scripting topics:

- *A Programmer's Introduction to PHP 4.0,* W. Gilmore (Apress Publishing). Designed for moderately experienced programmers who are new to PHP.
- *Beginning PHP4,* C. Lea, W. Choi, A. Kent, G. Prasad, and C. Ullman (WROX Press). Recommended for novice programmers.
- *PHP Essentials,* J. Meloni (Prima Publishing). Recommended for novice developers who are interested in introductory web database topics as well as PHP.
- *PHP Bible,* T. Converse and J. Park (Hungry Minds, Inc.). Recommended for novice programmers. More than half the 689 pages cover PHP programming.

- *PHP Fast & Easy Web Development*, J. Meloni (Prima Publishing). Recommended for beginners.
- *PHP3: Programming Browser-Based Applications with PHP*, D. Medinets and D. Medinets (McGraw-Hill). Recommended for intermediate programmers, but the book is written about PHP3 and doesn't include many of the new features that are core to development in PHP4
  - *Programming PHP*, by R. Lerdorf and K. Tatroe (O'Reilly). A good introduction to PHP.

Many books omitted from this list are also excellent books, but they may focus more on web database topics than on PHP, or they overlap significantly with the content of this book. A detailed and frequently updated list of all PHP and related books can be found at: *http://www.php.net/books.php.*

Web resources

The best place to start is to check the list of links at the official PHP site, *http://www.php.net/links.php.*

Here are some resources we frequently use:

http://www.php.net/manual/
  The annotated online PHP manual at the official PHP site. Includes many comments for each library and function and tips on use and common problems encountered.

http://www.zend.com
  Site of the commercial company held by long-term developers of PHP. Includes articles, resources, free code, and tutorials.

http://www.hotscripts.com/PHP/
  Articles, tips, tutorials, and scripts; includes many tutorials on installation in a variety of environments.

http://php.resourceindex.com
  Scripts, code fragments, and documentation.

http://www.phpbuilder.com
  Articles, documentation, and code fragments.

http://www.devshed.com/Server_Side/PHP/
  Tutorial-style articles on a range of PHP topics.

http://px.sklar.com
  A simple, low-bandwidth site that contains PHP code fragments and some complete applications.

http://www.thickbook.com
  Julie Meloni's site that supports her two books described in the last section. Includes code and tutorials, some of which aren't covered in the books.

Libraries

PHP has many libraries available for most common tasks in web database applications. In this section, we list most of the PHP libraries and point to other chapters in which selected libraries are discussed in more detail. For most libraries, we provide brief or only partial information.

The following is an alphabetically sorted list of the libraries:

Apache HTTP server functions
> Includes a function to retrieve all HTTP headers, getallheaders( ).

Array functions
> There are almost 50 functions to sort, merge, split, iteratively process, and return information about arrays. We discuss many of these functions in detail in Chapter 2.

BCMath arbitrary precision mathematics functions
> A library of functions to perform high-precision calculations with large numbers.

Bzip compression functions
> Tools to read and write files compressed with Julian Seward's highly effective compression algorithm; however, it's a bit slow compared to *gzip*.

Calendar functions
> For conversion between various calendars, including the Jewish and Gregorian calendars, and for finding the date of Easter.

CCVS API functions
> RedHat's solution for credit card transaction processing.

Character type functions
> Additional string functions to check what characters are contained within a string. These can be used as a replacement for or in addition to the validation methods described in Chapter 7.

ClibPDF function library
> Requires purchase of a license if used for commercial applications: The ClibPDF library accesses a set of C functions for creating Adobe PDF documents. The C library ClibPDF is available from *http://www.fastio.com* along with a licensing agreement.

CURL (client URL library) functions
> Functions that communicate with resources using the FTP, gopher, HTTP, LDAP, Telnet, and other protocols.

Database functions
> The MySQL library functions are discussed in detail in Chapter 4, with additional information on some functions in Chapter 5 and 6. Techniques for using the other DBMS libraries to connect to selected DBMSs are discussed briefly at the end of Chapter 4. Many other DBMS libraries are also available and detailed in the PHP manual; we don't discuss them here.

Date and time functions

The basics of date and time functions are described in Chapter 2. Examples are also discussed in Chapter 7.

Direct IO functions

A function library that accesses a file descriptor. The library is C-like in functionality, and C programmers will feel at home with the functions.

Directory functions

Changes directories in the filesystem, list files in a directory, etc.

Error handling and logging functions

Functions to change error reporting. Controlling the severity of PHP errors that are detected for debugging purposes is discussed in Chapter 2, and custom error handlers are discussed in Chapter 10.

Encryption functions

Selected encryption functions for producing cipher-text from plain text—and reversing the process—are discussed in Chapter 9.

eXtensible Markup Language (XML) functions

XML is a data format for structured document interchange, and this library provides tools to parse and retrieve components of XML documents.

Filesystem functions

Retrieves information about files, creates and modifies attributes of files, reads and writes files, and performs many other low-level file operations.

Forms Data Format functions

Tools to handle form data sent using the Forms Data Format (FDF) that's part of Adobe's PDF standard.

FTP

Functions that implement the File Transfer Protocol.

Functions functions

Seriously! A set of functions that inspects whether a function exists and returns details, such as the number of parameters to a function.

GNU teletext

A GNU project to internationalize programs by making substitution of program output messages in different languages easier.

GMP functions

More math functions for arbitrary-length integers using the GNU MP library; an alternative to the BCMath library described earlier in this section.

HTTP functions

The header( ) function creates HTTP headers in a response to a web browser. It is discussed and used in examples in Chapter 5 to Chapter 13. The function setcookie( ) sets a cookie in a web browser and is discussed in Chapter 8.

Hyperwave functions

This library offers functions to access the Hyperwave information system or document database. Use of the library requires purchase of the enterprise Hyperwave Information Server.

Image and graphics functions

Contains over 50 functions to draw images and render true-type fonts using the GD library.

IMAP, POP3, and NNTP functions

Network-oriented functions that use these protocols to retrieve and process email messages and Internet news postings.

IRC gateway

Functions to access an Internet relay chat (IRC) gateway. IRC is an Internet-base chat room.

Lightweight Directory Access Protocol (LDAP) functions

Tools to connect to and retrieve information from servers that store hierarchical directory information using LDAP.

Mail functions

Really one function, `mail( )`, to send an email to a destination; discussed in Chapter 12.

Mathematical functions

Functions to do just about anything to a number, but not to very large numbers (for those, use the BCMath or the GMP library); for example, the mathematical library includes trigonometry, random number generation, logarithm, and exponential functions. Many of these are discussed in Chapter 2.

Modular Calendar Access Library (MCAL) functions

Tools to access and manage an event calendar, such as a desktop diary, that is managed the underlying MCAL C library.

Ming functions for Flash

Tools that allows creation of Flash format movies.

mnoGoSearch functions

Functions that access the freely available text search engine mnoGoSearch.

Network functions

Networking libraries for high- and low-level network communications; for example, includes functions to check if a domain name exists, and convert numeric IP addresses to domain names and vice versa. A short background on networking can be found in Appendix B

Output control

Manages the buffering of output by PHP, allowing control of the PHP script engine's output.

PDF functions
> Functions that create and manipulate Adobe Portable Document Format (PDF) documents.

POSIX functions
> Functions that get information about processes, users, and other system-oriented aspects of functions defined in the IEEE 1003.1 (POSIX.1) standards document.

Program execution functions
> These are discussed briefly in the context of securing a web database application in Chapter 5.

Pspell functions
> Spelling functions that can not only check spelling but also make suggestions for corrections.

GNU Re-code functions
> Functions that convert strings from one character set to another.

Regular expressions
> Along with the string functions, an introduction to regular expression functions is covered in Chapter 2. (We cover only the native regular expression library that conforms to the POSIX 1003.2 standard, not the Perl-compatible regular expressions functions).

Satellite CORBA client extension functions
> Functions that can access and use CORBA distributed objects.

Semaphore and shared memory functions
> Functions based on Unix System V semaphores that allow multiple users controlled access to shared resources such as global variables in shared memory.

Session management functions
> These functions are covered in detail in Chapter 8; an alternate session management module is discussed in Appendix D.

SHMOP shared memory functions
> These functions duplicate the functionality of the System V shared memory tools described previously, but without some of the overheads in creating and managing shared memory spaces.

Simple Network Management Protocol (SNMP) functions
> Functions that interact with SNMP agents to find available objects and to set those objects.

SWF Shockwave Flash functions
> Another function library to create and use Flash format movies, with overlapping functionality to the Ming library described earlier.

Socket functions

Low-level network libraries to open, send, and receive data, and close network sockets (sockets are often loosely referred to as ports, which are discussed in Appendix B). Has some overlap with the network library, but the socket library is more concerned with low-level networking tasks.

String functions

The popular string functions are discussed in detail in Chapter 2.

URL (Uniform Resource Locator) functions

Tools that encode and decode MIME base64 encoded data used in HTTP and email, that encode and decode special characters from URLs, and that parse a URL and return its components.

Variable functions

Variable functions for determining and setting types are covered in Chapter 2.

Web Distributed Data eXchange (WDDX) libraries

Tools that process the XML-like format used in the open standard WDDX format, a standard that permits interchange of data between web-scripting languages such as PHP, ASP, and ColdFusion. More information about the WDDX Software Development Kit (SDK) can be found at *http://www.openwddx.org*.

XSLT (eXtensible Stylesheet Language Transformations) functions

XSLT is a language for transforming XML documents from one standard XML format to another.

YAZ functions

A library that implements the Z39.50 protocol for information retrieval. Z39.50 can be used, for example, to issue a remote search on a text database and to return results in a standard format.

YP/NIS functions

Tools that manage network functions remotely, such as password files.

Zlib compression functions

A set of functions to read and write *gzip* files compressed using the algorithms of Jean-Loup Gailly and Mark Adler.

Several of these function libraries are immature and are dynamically being improved and changed. New libraries emerge every month. Some libraries are outdated, and the projects that underlie them are inactive. However, for most libraries, several successful installations and uses have been reported, and the latest details can usually be found along with example code at the PHP web site in the annotated manual, *http://www.php.net/manual/*.

We have omitted any discussion of wholly redundant libraries, those used exclusively with Microsoft Windows, very new libraries, unstable libraries, and those libraries that aren't used in web applications.

Third-party products

Zend Optimizer
> A freely available code optimizer that improves the performance of the intermediate code generated by the Zend scripting engine. The Zend web site is *http://www.zend.com.*

DBG: PHP Debugger
> A free interactive debugger for PHP that includes a code profiler that finds code bottlenecks. Available for Microsoft Windows and Linux, and licensed under the same license as PHP. Available from: *http://dd.cron.ru/dbg/.*

afterBurner
> BWare have recently released this free caching tool that caches PHP precompiled scripts in the web server for fast execution when a script is run a second or subsequent time. The afterBurner source code is available from *http://afterburner.bware.it.*

Alternative PHP Cache (APC)
> An alternative free PHP script caching tool that is covered by the same license agreement as PHP itself. The APC source is available from *http://apc.communityconnect.com.*

Zend is a company held by long-term developers of the PHP script engine. Their web site, *http://www.zend.com,* sells several commercial PHP-specific products:

Zend Cache
> Tool that integrates with the Zend engine to better cache scripts, prevent some scripts being cached, and reduce latency. If high-throughput of a web database application is required, Zend Cache is a useful tool.

Zend Encoder
> Tool that converts text scripts to an intermediate format that can be distributed, offering reasonable protection of copyright and the intellectual property in scripts.

Zend IDE
> New integrated development environment for PHP that includes a customizable editor, syntax highlighting, and a debugger.

Zend Launchpad
> Tool that allows systems administrators to maintain their PHP installation through upgrades. It also guides administrators through the PHP installation process and assists in selecting tools

NuSphere market several products that include and support PHP through their web site *http://www.nuspehere.com.* NuSphere products have optional additional email, web, and phone support. Here's a list:

- NuSphere MySQL and NuSphere MySQL Advantage are commercial products that bundle together Apache, MySQL, and PHP with installation tools and other supplementary products. As discussed in Appendix A, a free package is available for download.

- NuSphere PHPEd Advantage is a commercial package that includes PHP, MySQL, and Apache as well as PHPEd, a PHP integrated development environment (IDE) for Microsoft Windows, and other supplementary products.

ActiveState offer an IDE for Microsoft Windows and Linux called ASPN Komodo. Komodo can be used for free under the Linux operating system or for free under the Microsoft Windows environment by students, home users, and nonprofit organizations. A commercial license for Microsoft Windows is required for other uses. Komodo is available from *http://www.activestate.com*. There are several other IDEs for PHP available including the PHPub development environment, K PHP Develop, tsWebEditor, PHP Coder, and BBEdit.

Open source PHP applications

The following are popular examples of open source web database applications. Most either provide good solutions to common application requirements, or make excellent starting points for developing components or systems. The list isn't intended to be comprehensive but instead are representative examples of different application types.

Bookmarker
> A URL bookmarking management system, *http://www.renaghan.com/pcr/bookmarker.html*

Basit
> Web site content management system for managing small- to medium-size web sites, *http://www.fazlamesai.net/basit/eng/*

bplog
> Web-based news and announcement system, *http://bplog.blackplasma.net*

dev/coin online shop
> For building simple online stores, *http://www.devcon.net/software/shop/*

E*reminders
> A system to automatically send out emails about birthdays and other events, *http://sourceforge.net/projects/e-reminders/*

gcdb
> A customer billing and payment management system, *http://sourceforge.net/projects/gcdb/*

HPE
> The Humble Portal Engine that brings together content to build a news portal, *http://sourceforge.net/projects/hpe/*

IPM

The Incyte Project Manager for tracking and managing projects, *http://udpviper.com/project.php?project=ipm*

Les Visiteurs

A web site statistical analysis package for analyzing and producing information about site accesses, *http://www.phpinfo.net/applis/visiteurs/*

Mantis

A software development bug tracking system, *http://mantisbt.sourceforge.net*

Phorecast

An email, calendar, contact, and event management system, *http://phorecast.org*

Phorum

A web-based bulletin board forum, *http://phorum.org*

php3guest

A visitor guestbook, *http://www.bastian-friedrich.de/comp/guestbook/*

phpDVD

A system to track your DVD collection, *http://ugo.scarlata.it/?pid=phpdvd*

phpMyChat

A PHP-based chat room, *http://www.phpheaven.net/projects/phpMyChat/*

phpShop

Reusable components to build an online shop, *http://www.phpshop.org*

postNuke

A self-described rogue content management system, *http://www.postnuke.com*

Database Tier Resources

There are many excellent general database texts available that cover the broad fields of relational databases, E-R modeling, and SQL. Amongst the best are:

- *An Introduction to Database Systems,* C.J. Date (Addison Wesley).
- *Database System Concepts,* A. Silberschatz, H.F. Korth, and S. Sudarshan (McGraw-Hill).
- *Fundamentals of Database Systems*, R. Elmasri and S.B. Navathe (Addison Wesley).
- *Database Management Systems*, R. Ramakrishnan and J. Gehrke (McGraw-Hill).

For a coverage of SQL, there are several good books, but many are out-of-print. Currently available books include:

- *A Guide to the SQL Standard: A User's Guide to the Standard Database Language SQL*, C.J. Date and H. Darwen (Addison Wesley). This book isn't for the beginner but does an excellent job of covering the standard in detail.

- *SQL-99 Complete, Really,* P. Gulutzan and T. Pelzer (CMP Books). MySQL supports the SQL-92 standard, but this book is an excellent and long introduction to SQL with many worked examples.

There are many books that cover the tuning of a specific DBMS. Here's one text that is general in its introductory coverage and devotes a chapter to each DBMS product:

- *Database Performance Tuning Handbook,* J. Dunham (McGraw-Hill).

For MySQL, the *manual.html* file distributed with the installation is an excellent resource. Books include:

- *MySQL and mSQL (Nutshell Series),* R.J. Yarger, G. Reese, and T. King (O'Reilly).
- *MySQL,* P. DuBois (New Riders Publishing).

Security and Cryptography Resources

There are many books on Web security and cryptography. We recommend the following books—in no particular order—which cover topics relevant to those discussed in Chapter 9:

- *Web Security,* L. Stein (Addison Wesley). An excellent, comprehensive book with sufficient technical and nontechnical depth.
- *Web Security and Commerce,* S. Garfinkel and S. Spafford (O'Reilly). A good introductory book that explains the topics in nontechnical language.
- *Applied Cryptography: Protocols, Algorithms, and Source Code in C,* B. Schneier (John Wiley and Sons). Covers the field of cryptography in technical depth.
- *The Code Book,* S. Singh (Anchor Books. An enjoyable popular science book.
- The RSA encryption web site, *http://www.rsa.com.*
- SSL extensions and patches for Apache: *http://www.apache-ssl.org, http://www.mod_ssl.org, http://www.openssl.org/source/.*

Index

Symbols

@ operator prefixing function calls, 176
@ symbol in email addresses, 288, 300
$aCounter->increment( ), 100
$PHPSESSID/PHPSESSID, 315–322

A

absolute value, 89
Access (Microsoft), 197
$aCounter->increment( ), 100
addCase( ), 103
AddSlashes( ), 251
AddType directive, debugging and, 108
aggregation, 133
alert( ), 294
ALTER TABLE statement, 122
alternative patterns, 80
anchors, 78
Apache server, 7, 8
  installing, 475–478
    to use SSL, 480–482
  using for HTTP authentication, 345
Apache Software Foundation, 7
application logic in middle tier, x
  developing with PHP, 28, 162
  for order receipts, 458
  shipping.3 script and, 456
  stored procedures and, 159
applications interface, 13
applications-layer protocols, 3
argument types, 93
arguments, 96–97
arithmetic operators, 147

array( ), 52
array functions, 58–60
array mssql_fetch_row( ), 195
array mysql_fetch_array( ), 168
array mysql_fetch_row( ), 166
array pg_fetch_row( ), 201
array pointers, 57
array_map( ), 65
array_reverse( ), 60
arrays, 52–65
  creating, 52–55
  maximum/minimum values and, 59
  sorting, 61–65
  splitting strings into, 83
array_search( ), 59
array_walk( ), 65
arsort( )/asort( ), 62
assign( ), 460
assignment operator, vs. equality
      operator, 43
assignments, 35
associative arrays, 52, 53
  sorting, 62
asymmetric encryption techniques, 371
at (@) operator prefixing function calls, 176
at (@) symbol in email addresses, 288, 300
attribute names, 121
attributes, 121
  KEY clause and, 153
authenticated( ), 347
authenticateUser( ), 352, 357, 363
authentication, 26, 341–371
  for customers/users, 395–400
    example of, 359–367
  how it works, 342–345

We'd like to hear your suggestions for improving our indexes. Send email to *index@oreilly.com*.

authentication (*continued*)
  script for, 363–365
  using a database for, 350–355
  web database applications and, 355–367
authorization, script for, 365–367
automated housekeeping, 453–455
automatic type conversion, 37
auxiliary tables, locking with, 274–276

B

BDB table type, 278
bold( ), 92
  reusing, 97
bookmarks, restrictions on, 339
Boolean close( ), 527
Boolean destroy( ), 527
Boolean gc( ), 527
Boolean mail ( ), 447
Boolean open( ), 527
Boolean session_destroy( ), 320
Boolean session_is_registered( ), 320
Boolean session_register( ), 319
Boolean session_start( ), 319
Boolean values, 38
Boolean variables, 34
Boolean write( ), 527
BottleCounter( ), 103

 break element, 70
branch statements, 40–45
browse( ), 227–236
  implementing, 230–234
  producing page numbers from, 234
  search1.script and, 463
browsers
  authentication and, 357
  interacting with using JavaScript, 305
  redirection and, 374, 431–434
  which in use by users, 306
browsing, 21, 226–236
  search.1 script for, 463–470
bulk loading of data, 125

C

caching responses, 499
callback functions, 65
calling pages, 224
cart.1 script (winestore home page), 374, 413
cart.2 script (displaying shopping cart), 374, 418–422

cart.3 script (adding items to shopping cart), 374, 422–427
cart.4 script (emptying shopping cart), 374, 427
cart.5 script (browser redirection), 374, 431–434
cart.6 script (updating quantities in shopping cart), 376, 428–431
cartesian product, 135
Cascading Style Sheets (CSS), templates and, 460
case, changing, 69
case study (see winestore application)
caseCount( ), 103
casting operators, 37
ceil( ), 89
certificates, 371
  creating for ApacheSSL, 482–484
challenge method, 343
character lists, 77
characters, 74–81
  escaping, 32, 65
    special characters and, 81
  newline, 70
charAt( ), 294
checkdate( ), 88, 284
checkdnsrr( ), 288
cipher suites, 370
classes, 99–101
clean( ), 210, 214
  preprocessing user data and, 214
  session variables and, 329
  updating shopping cart quantities and, 428
client entry <form>, 326
  script for, 333
client tier, 2, 6
  managing state in, 310
  resources for further reading, 537
  validation in, 22
clients, thick vs. thin, 5, 308
client-server architecture, 6
client-side validation, 291–308
  performance and, 281, 292
cmp_length( ), 65
combined scripts, 219–222
command interpreter for MySQL, 118–119
comments, 31
commit and rollback processing, 278
compare( ), 64
comparison operators, 147
concat( ), 148

floor( ), 89
flush( ), 104
fopen( ), 251
for loop, 47
foreach loop, 47
    using arrays with, 55–57
<form>
    for client entry (see client entry <form>)
    for database writes, 241, 254–258
    for login page, 360–363
    prefilling data and, 304
    processing data and, 288–291
    validating data and, 292–303
<form> validation function, 301–303
formatted output, creating, 67–68
formatting
    dates, 87
    strings, 67–70
fread( ), 251
front-page panel, 180–194
functions (PHP), 82–99
    array, 58–60
    exponential, 90
    float, 88–91
    for accessing sessions, 319
    for database modifications, 253
    for MySQL, 165–176
        error handling and, 174–176
        functions to avoid, 174
    integer, 88–91
    logarithmic, 90
    passing variables to, 95–97
    regular expression, 82–83
    reusing, 97–99
    support, 529
    user-defined, 91–99
functions (SQL), 147–151
functions (for other databases), 195

G

garbage collection, 322
    session handlers for, 534
Gemini table type, 278
GET attribute, cookies and, 321
getCustomerID( ), 386
gethostbyname( ), 288
getmxrr( ), 288
getrandmax( ), 91
global statement/global variables, 94
gmdate( ), 87
gmmktime( ), 84

GRANT statement, 157
GROUP BY clause, 133
grouping output, 131–135
groups, 80

H

handles, 163
HAVING clause, 134
header( ), 225
    browser redirection and, 374
    credentials and, 348
    debugging and, 106
    insertion script and, 246
    starting sessions and, 316
heading( ), 92, 97
heterogeneous arrays, 53
hexadecimal system, 89
hijacking, 358
home page for the winestore
        application, 374, 413–416
housekeeping, 453–455
HTML (Hypertext Markup Language), 3
    embedded links and, 208–210
    templates and, 455–463
    W3C validator for, 104
HTML <form> environment, 206–208
HTML <pre> formatted text tag, 161, 162
HTML receipts, 435, 442
    shipping.2 script and, 376, 448–452
HTML <table> environment, 161, 177
HTTP (Hypertext Transfer Protocol), 3–5,
        489–503
    (see also protocols)
HTTP authentication, 341–350
    PHP and, 345–350
    problems with, 356–358
HTTP redirection, 245
HTTP requests, 489, 495–497
HTTP responses, 489, 497
HTTP servers, 7, 8
$HTTP_POST_VARS, 330
Hypertext Markup Language (see HTML)

I

IBM, SQL and, 16
identifier attributes, 121
identifiers, 314
if...else statement, 41–42
implode( ), 73
in_array( ), 59

M

mail( ), 411, 435
  for order confirmation receipt, 447
mathematical functions, 149–150
mathematical library, 90
max( ), 58
MD5 hashing algorithm, 358
memory, performance and, 339
metacharacters, 82
microseconds, 86
Microsoft Access, 197
Microsoft SQL server, 195–196
microtime( ), 86
middle tier, 2, 7–11
  components of, 7
  resources for further reading, 538–548
  validation in, 22
MIME (Multipurpose Internet Mail
      Extensions), 502
min( ), 58
mixed OCIResult( ), 199
mixed read( ), 527
mixed types, 33
mktime( ), 84
modifiers, 121
mod_ssl, 480
mouse rollovers, 292, 303
mssql_query( ), 195
mssql_select_db( ), 195
multidimensional arrays, 54
MULTIPLE attribute, 289
multiple queries, 188
Multipurpose Internet Mail Extensions
      (MIME), 502
MyISAM table, 277
MySQL, 12, 16, 113–117
  command interpreter for, 118–119
  connecting to, 162–176
  functions for, 165–176
    encrypting and, 354
    error handling and, 174–176
    functions to avoid, 174
  installing/configuring, 471–475
  limitations of, 158
  LOCK TABLES /UNLOCK TABLES
      statements in, 270
  manual for, 147, 484
  modifying, 141–146
  querying
    database-driven, 160–201
    with join queries, 135–141
    with SELECT statement, 128–135

    user-driven, 202–240
  table-locking paradigm in, 277
  techniques for fine-tuning, 154–157
  working with, 119–128
mysql_affected_rows( ), 169, 253
mysql_close( ), 164, 170
mysql_connect( ), 163–167, 411
  error handling and, 175
mysql_data_seek( ), 233
mysql_errno( ), 411
mysql_error( ), 175, 411
mysql_errorno( ), 175
mysql_fetch_array( ), 167, 185, 233
  second or subsequent queries and, 189
  tricks to using, 168
mysql_fetch_field( ), 171, 177
mysql_fetch_object( ), 167, 169, 171
mysql_fetch_row( ), 164, 166–168
mysql_insert_id( ), 253, 270
mysql_list_tables( ), 174
mysql_num_fields( ), 164
mysql_num_rows( ), 169, 174
  error handling and, 175
  mysql_unbuffered_query( ) and, 170
  using instead of int mysql_affected_
      rows( ), 253
mysql_pconnect( ), 167, 169, 170
  error handling and, 175
mysql_query( ), 163, 166–168, 170
  error handling and, 175
  second or subsequent queries and, 189
mysql_select_db( ), 163
mysql_tablename( ), 173
mysql_unbuffered_query( ), 170
  error handling and, 175

N

natural joins, 137–139
nested queries, 16
  not supported in MySQL, 158
newline characters, 70
next( ), 57
nl2br( ), 70
normalization/normalized databases, 113
not equals operator, 43
numbered arrays, 52
numbers
  random, 91
  systems of, 89
  validating, 286
  (see also integers)
numeric assignments, 35

numeric attributes, 121
NuSphere, 484

O

object mysql_fetch_field( ), 171–173
object mysql_fetch_object( ), 168
objects, 99–104
OCIExecute( ), 199
OCIFetch( ), 199
OCILogon( ), 199
OCIParse( ), 199
OCIResult( ), 199
octal system, 89
ODBC functions, 197
odbc_connect( ), 197
odbc_exec( ), 197
one-component querying, 203, 223–226
Open DataBase Connectivity functions, 197
OpenSSL
    certificates and, 484
    downloading/installing, 481
operator precedence, 36
operators, 147–151
<option selected> element, 238
optional characters, 78–80
Oracle 7/8, 198–200
ORDER BY clause, 132, 136
order.1 script (logon), 374, 395–399
order.2 script (logout), 374, 400
order.3 script (finalizing orders), 376,
    436–442
ordering wines, 435–452
    receipts for, 376, 392–395, 442–452,
      456–463
output
    debugging and, 104, 106
    with echo/print statements, 31
    formatting, 67–68
    sorting/grouping, 131–135
    variable substitution and, 66

P

padded strings, 69
page numbers/page links, 234
panel (front-page panel), 180–194
parameters, 204
    for changing session management
      behavior, 323–326
password( ), 354
performance
    client-side validation and, 281, 292

locking tables and, 271
MySQL and, 154–158
server-side validation and, 282
sessions and, 337, 338
synchronization problems and, 339
user-defined functions and, 91
permissions, 158
persistent connections, 167, 169
personalizing web sites, 338
pg_connect( ), 200
pg_exec( ), 201
PHP: Hypertext Preprocessor, 28
PHP scripting language, 7, 9–11, 27–108
    arrays and, 52–65
    benefits for writing web-enabled scripts
      and, 208
    branch statements and, 40–45
    conditional statements and, 40–45
    functions (see functions (PHP))
    HTTP authentication and, 345–350
    initializing variables and, 214–216
    installing, 478
    loops and, 45–48
    objects and, 99–104
    online manual for, 484
    regular expressions and, 76–83
    scripting environment of, 10
    session management and, 314–326, 525
    strings and, 65–76
    using to access non-MySQL
      databases, 195–201
PHP scripts
    for authentication, 363–365
    creating, 30
    debugging, 104–108
    example of, 49–51
    for login <form>, 361–363
    for logout, 365
    managing HTTP authentication
      with, 346–348
    of examples for the winestore, 479
    reusing functions and, 97–99
$PHPSESSID/PHPSESSID, 315–322
.php suffix, debugging and, 108
PHP Triad for Windows, 484
ports, 488
POST attribute, cookies and, 321
PostgreSQL, 16, 200–201
post-validation error finding, 280
powers, 90
precedence of operators, 36
prev( ), 57

primary keys, 112, 151–154
print statement, 31
printf( ), 67–68
print_r( ), 39, 61–63
private keys, 482–484
privileges, 158
protocols, 485–503
    applications-layer, 3
    SSL, 368–371, 480–482
    TCP/IP, 487–489
proxy caches, 7
pseudo-random numbers, 91

Q

query evaluator, 13
query results, 177–180
querying
    automated, for housekeeping, 453–455
    database-driven, 21, 160–201
        five steps to, 163
        INSERT INTO ... SELECT statement
            and, 146
    with join queries, 135–141
    multiple queries and, 188
    one-component, 203, 223–226
    with SELECT statement, 128–135
    table aliases for, 138
    techniques of, 16
    two-component, 202
    user-driven, 21, 202–240
quick start guide for MySQL, 113–117

R

rand( ), 91
random numbers, 91
rawurlencode( ), 228, 234
RDBMS (relational database management
        system), 12, 110, 112
read locks, 269
read-lock queue, 270, 271
receipts for orders placed, 376, 392–395,
        442–452, 456–463
records, 128
recovery, 278
redirection, 374, 431–434
references, 96
regular expression functions, 82–83
regular expressions, 76–83
    metacharacters as, 82
relational database management system
        (see RDBMS)

relational databases, 12, 110
    accessing, 195–201
    planning/designing, 504–522
relational model, 112
reload problem, 243–250
repeating characters, 78–80
requests, HTTP and, 3
require directive, 97–99
reset( ), 57
resource mssql_connect( ), 195
resource mssql_query( ), 195
resource mysql_connect( ), 165
resource mysql_list_tables( ), 173
resource mysql_pconnect( ), 169
resource mysql_query( ), 166
resource mysql_unbuffered_query( ), 170
resource OCILogon( ), 199
resource OCIParse( ), 199
resource odbc_connect( ), 197
resource odbc_exec( ), 197
resource pg_connect( ), 200
resource pg_exec( ), 200
resources for further reading, 537–549
    MySQL manual, 147
    software installation and
        configuration, 484
responses, HTTP and, 3
result sets
    displaying, 226
    limiting, 135
results (query results), 177–180
return( ), 294
return types, 93
REVOKE statement, 158
rollover feature, 292, 303
root user, 9
round( ), 89
rows, 12
rsort( ), 61–63
rtrim( ), 70, 148

S

salt string, 350, 363
scope, 93–95
script tags, debugging and, 108
scripting languages, 9
    engine for, 10
    (see also PHP scripting language)
scripts
    adding multiple queries to, 188
    combined, 219–222
    for customer management, 378–395

sprintf( ), 67–68
SQL (Structured Query Language), 16, 112,
    151–158
    components of, 17
    converting E/R model to, 516–522
    queries and, 128–146
    winestore application, creating
        with, 115–117
    working with MySQL and, 119–128
SQL interpreter, 13
SQL server (Microsoft), 195–196
srand( ), 86, 91
SSL (Secure Socket Layer) protocol, 368–371
    installing Apache to use, 480–482
start/end tags
    include statement and, 98
    omitting, 30
starvation problem, 271
state, 5
    building applications to
        maintain, 310–313
stateless applications, building, 355
stored procedures, 159
strcasecmp( ), 71
strcmp( ), 45, 71, 148
strftime( ), 88
string assignments, 35
string clean( ), 408
string comparison operators/functions, 147
string crypt( ), 350
string getCustomerID( ), 408
string literals, 32, 65–67
string mysql_tablename( ), 174
string session_id( ), 319
string showWine( ), 408
strings, 65–76
    comparing, 71
    converting to timestamp, 86, 285
    converting to/from integers, 284
    splitting into an array, 83
stristr( ), 73
strlen( ), 67
strncasecmp( ), 71
strncmp( ), 71
str_pad( ), 69
strpos( ), 72, 74
strrchr( ), 73
str_replace( ), 75
strrpos( ), 72
strstr( ), 73
strtotime( ), 86, 285
strtr( ), 75

Structured Query Language (see SQL)
strval( ), 285
subject string, 69
subsecond times, 86
substr( ), 71, 214
substring( ), 148
substrings, 71–76
    replacing, 74–76, 83
substr_replace( ), 74
superuser, 9
support functions, 529
swapping memory, 339
switch statement, 42
synchronization, problems with caused by
        sessions, 339
system( ), 212
system requirements for the winestore
        application, 19–21

T

table aliases, 138, 182
tables
    creating, 120–122
        with visual appeal, 182–185
    displaying details of, 122
    locking, 268–278
    temporary, 269
    working with, 122
tainted data, 214
TCP/IP protocol, 487–489
    HTTP and, 500–502
templates, 455–463
temporary tables, 269
terminology for databases, 110–113
testing variables, 39
text files
    bulk loading data from, 125
    vs. databases, 14
thesame( ), 301
thick clients, 6, 308
thin clients, 5
threads, 9
three-tier architectures, 2–17
    reasons for using, 5
time (see date and time)
time( ), 313, 317
time-outs, 314, 339
time string, 85
timestamp, 84–86
tracking (see session management)
transaction management, 17

void showCart( ), 408
void showLogin( ), 386, 408
void showMessage( ), 386, 408
void showPricing( ), 408
void showVarieties( ), 408
volumeDiscount( ), 103

W

W3C validator for HTML, 104
web browsers (see browsers)
web database applications
  authentication and, 355–367
  building, 355–359
  case study illustrating (see winestore
    application)
  components of, 18, 21–25
  locking tables and, 272–278
web pages, reload problem and, 243–250
web scripting languages, 9
  (see also PHP scripting language)
web servers, 7, 8
web sites, personalizing, 338
web spiders, 7
Web (the), 3
  protocols and, 485–503
WHERE clause, 129–131
  join queries and, 135
while loop, 46
whitespace, 70
wildcards, 77
window.close( ), 306
window.open( ), 306
window.print( ), 306

windows.history.go(-1), 306
winestore application, 17–25
  components of, 18, 21–25
  creating with SQL, 115–117
  customer authentication for, 359–367
  customer management for, 372–411
  customer validation for, 282–288
  database for, 113–117
    loading, 113
  ER modeling for, 506–522
  front-page panel for, 180–194
  home page for, 413–416
  ordering and shipping wines
    from, 143–145, 435–452
  regions, adding to, 242
  relations in, 504
  sample PHP scripts for,
    downloading/installing, 479
  scripts for, 374–378, 413, 418–434
  sessions, adding to, 326–336
  shopping cart for, 412–434
  system requirements for, 19–21
  wines, adding to, 142–143
wizards, 337
write-lock queue, 270, 271

X

XTemplate class library, 455

Z

Zend engine, 8, 10

About the Authors

Hugh E. Williams is a senior lecturer in the School of Computer Science and IT at RMIT University in Melbourne, Australia, where he has taught for seven years. He currently teaches in two areas—database technology and web technology—and is the coordinator of a masters program that focuses on the Internet and the Web. His research interests include building better search engines, bioinformatics, and designing faster data structures. When not at work Hugh likes to go running, watch Richmond play footy, and follow the cricket. Hugh has a Ph.D. from RMIT University.

David Lane works as a software engineer and IT manager with the Multimedia Database Systems group at RMIT University in Melbourne, Australia. In that group he has helped develop and commercialize the Structured Information Manager, a large-scale SGML/XML document repository, and a high performance web server. David has also worked with Australia's largest telecommunications company, Telstra, in areas as diverse as satellite communications, human factors research, and electronic document interchange (EDI). David has a bachelor's degree in applied science (majoring in mathematics and computer science) from Swinburne University.

Colophon

Our look is the result of reader comments, our own experimentation, and feedback from distribution channels. Distinctive covers complement our distinctive approach to technical topics, breathing personality and life into potentially dry subjects.

The animal on the cover of *Web Database Applications with PHP and MySQL* is a platypus. The platypus (*Ornithorhynchus anatinus*) of Australia and Tasmania has been described as a living fossil. Its earliest known remains date back 100,000 years, and it combines mammalian and reptilian features. It is aquatic, furry, warm-blooded, and lays eggs. It sports webbed feet, a beaverlike tail, and a ducklike bill.

The preferred plural of platypus is either "platypus" or "platypuses," and a baby platypus has been referred to as a "platapup."

The platypus was first described by Dr. George Shaw, a British scientist. He thought the animal was a hoax and took a pair of scissors to the pelt, expecting to find stitches attaching appendages to skin.

The platypus is an air-breathing mammal that spends most of its day resting in an underground burrow. However, it feeds only in the water and is rarely observed on land. The platypus hunts mostly at night for such food as shrimp, worms, and aquatic insects. Because the animal doesn't need to hear or see its intended food, a platypus protects its eyes and ears by automatically closing them underwater and relies on its bill to locate prey. While diving, the platypus temporarily stores food in special cheek pouches. When the animal returns to the surface to breathe, the food is ground up between rough pads located inside the bill.

A female platypus produces a clutch of one to three eggs in late winter or spring. The mother is believed to incubate them between her lower belly and curled-up tail for about 10 days as she rests in an underground nest made of vegetation collected from the water. She doesn't have nipples; her milk is instead secreted from two patches of skin midway along her belly. It's believed that a platypup feeds by slurping up milk with sweeps of its stubby bill. When juveniles enter the water at about four months, they are nearly as long as an adult.

The platypus is the only Australian mammal known to be venomous. Adult males have a pointed spur located above the heel of each hind leg that can inject poison produced by a gland in the thigh. Platypus venom isn't considered life-threatening to humans. However, spurring is painful, because platypus spurs are sharp and can be driven in with great force; the poison itself triggers severe pain in the affected limb.

The platypus is officially classified as "common but vulnerable" in Australia. As a species, it isn't currently considered endangered. However, platypus populations are believed to have declined or disappeared, particularly in urban and agricultural settings; the specific underlying reasons for this decline is unknown.

Mary Anne Weeks Mayo was the production editor and copyeditor for *Web Database Applications with PHP and MySQL*. Rachel Wheeler, Colleen Gorman, Emily Quill, and Jane Ellin provided quality control. Leanne Soylemez and Phil Dangler provided production assistance. Brenda Miller wrote the index.

Ellie Volckhausen designed the cover of this book, based on a series design by Edie Freedman. The cover image is an original engraving from Johnson's Natural History. Emma Colby produced the cover layout with QuarkXPress 4.1 using Adobe's ITC Garamond font.

Melanie Wang designed the interior layout, based on a series design by David Futato. Mihaela Maier converted the files from Microsoft Word to FrameMaker 5.5.6 using tools created by Mike Sierra. The text font is Linotype Birka; the heading font is Adobe Myriad Condensed; and the code font is LucasFont's The Sans Mono Condensed. The illustrations that appear in the book were produced by Robert Romano and Jessamyn Read using Macromedia FreeHand 9 and Adobe Photoshop 6. The tip and warning icons were drawn by Christopher Bing. This colophon was compiled by Mary Anne Weeks Mayo.

More Titles from O'Reilly

Linux

Using Samba

By Peter Kelly, Perry Donham &
David Collier-Brown
1st Edition November 1999
416 pages, Includes CD-ROM
ISBN 1-56592-449-5

Samba turns a Unix or Linux system into a
file and print server for Microsoft Windows
network clients. This complete guide to
Samba administration covers basic 2.0 con-
figuration, security, logging, and troubleshooting. Whether you're
playing on one note or a full three-octave range, this book will
help you maintain an efficient and secure server. Includes a
CD-ROM of sources and ready-to-install binaries.

Managing & Using MySQL, 2nd Edition

By George Reese, Randy Jay Yarger & Tim King
2nd Edition April 2002
448 pages, ISBN 0-596-00211-4

This edition retains the best features of the
first edition, while adding the latest on
MySQL and the relevant programming language interfaces, with more complete reference information. The administration section
is greatly enhanced; the programming lan-
guage chapters have been updated—especially the Perl and PHP
chapters—and new additions include chapters on security and
extending MySQL and a system tables reference.

Linux Network Administrator's Guide, 2nd Edition

By Olaf Kirch & Terry Dawson
2nd Edition June 2000
506 pages, ISBN 1-56592-400-2

Fully updated, this comprehensive, impres-
sive introduction to networking on Linux
now covers firewalls, including the use of
ipchains and iptables (netfilter), masquerad-
ing, and accounting. Other new topics
include Novell (NCP/IPX) support and INN
(news administration). Original material on serial connections,
UUCP, routing and DNS, mail and News, SLIP and PPP, NFS, and
NIS has been thoroughly updated.

Understanding the Linux Kernel

By Daniel P. Bovet & Marco Cesati
1st Edition October 2000
650 pages, ISBN 0-596-00002-2

Understanding the Linux Kernel helps read-
ers understand how Linux performs best and
how it meets the challenge of different environments. The authors introduce each topic
by explaining its importance, and show how
kernel operations relate to the utilities that
are familiar to Unix programmers and users.

UNIX Power Tools, 2nd Edition

By Jerry Peek, Tim O'Reilly & Mike Loukides
2nd Edition August 1997
1120 pages, Includes CD-ROM
ISBN 1-56592-260-3

Loaded with practical advice about almost
every aspect of Unix, this second edition of
UNIX Power Tools addresses the technology
that Unix users face today. You'll find thor-
ough coverage of POSIX utilities, including
GNU versions, detailed bash and tcsh shell coverage, a strong
emphasis on Perl, and a CD-ROM that contains the best freeware
available.

Linux Device Drivers, 2nd Edition

By Alessandro Rubini & Jonathan Corbet
2nd Edition June 2001
586 pages, ISBN 0-59600-008-1

This practical guide is for anyone who wants
to support computer peripherals under the
Linux operating system. It shows step-by-step
how to write a driver for character devices,
block devices, and network interfaces, illustrating with examples you can compile and
run. The second edition covers Kernel 2.4 and adds discussions
of symmetric multiprocessing (SMP), Universal Serial Bus (USB),
and some new platforms.

Web Programming

ActionScript: The Definitive Guide

By Colin Moock
1st Edition May 2001
720 pages, ISBN 1-56592-852-0

ActionScript: The Definitive Guide is for web developers and web authors who want to go beyond simple Flash animations to create enhanced Flash-driven sites. Regardless of your level of programming expertise, this combination of ActionScript fundamentals, applications, and handy quick-reference will have you scripting like a pro.

CGI Programming with Perl, 2nd Edition

By Shishir Gundavaram
2nd Edition July 2000
470 pages, ISBN 1-56592-419-3

The Common Gateway Interface (CGI) is one of the most powerful methods of providing dynamic content on the Web. CGI is a generic interface for calling external programs to crunch numbers, query databases, generate customized graphics, or perform any other server-side task. Based on the best-selling *CGI Programming on the World Wide Web*, this edition has been completely rewritten to demonstrate current techniques available with the CGI.pm module and the latest versions of Perl.

Dynamic HTML: The Definitive Reference

By Danny Goodman
1st Edition July 1998
1088 pages, ISBN 1-56592-494-0

Dynamic HTML: The Definitive Reference is an indispensable compendium for web content developers. It contains complete reference material for all of the HTML tags, CSS style attributes, browser document objects, and JavaScript objects supported by the various standards and the latest versions of Netscape Navigator and Microsoft Internet Explorer.

JavaScript: The Definitive Guide, 4th Edition

By David Flanagan
4th Edition November 2001
936 pages, ISBN 0-596-00048-0

To stay on top of their work, web professionals need the most up-to-date, complete reference available on the core JavaScript language, which is growing more and more essential for effective web design and development. This new edition covers JavaScript 1.5, the latest version of the language. The book's comprehensive reference section documents every object, property, method, event handler, function and constructor used by client-side JavaScript.

Programming ColdFusion

By Rob Brooks-Bilson
1st Edition August 2001
974 pages, ISBN 1-56592-698-6

Programming ColdFusion covers everything you need to know to create effective web applications with ColdFusion, a powerful tool for rapid web site development. The book starts with the basics and quickly moves to more advanced topics, providing numerous examples of common web application tasks, so you can learn by example.

Programming Web Services with SOAP

By James Snell, Doug Tidwell & Pavel Kulchenko
1st Edition December 2001
264 pages, ISBN 0-596-00095-2

In typical O'Reilly fashion this book moves beyond the theoretical and explains how to build and implement SOAP web services. The book begins with a solid introduction to SOAP, detailing its history and structure, followed by an introduction to the three major types of SOAP applications: SOAP-RPC, SOAP-Messaging, and SOAP-Intermediaries. Each SOAP application is illustrated with an in-depth implementation.

O'REILLY®

TO ORDER: **800-998-9938** • order@oreilly.com • www.oreilly.com
ONLINE EDITIONS OF MOST O'REILLY TITLES ARE AVAILABLE BY SUBSCRIPTION AT safari.oreilly.com
ALSO AVAILABLE AT MOST RETAIL AND ONLINE BOOKSTORES

How to stay in touch with O'Reilly

1. Visit our award-winning web site

> *http://www.oreilly.com/*

★ "Top 100 Sites on the Web"—PC Magazine
★ CIO Magazine's Web Business 50 Awards

Our web site contains a library of comprehensive product information (including book excerpts and tables of contents), downloadable software, background articles, interviews with technology leaders, links to relevant sites, book cover art, and more. File us in your bookmarks or favorites!

2. Join our email mailing lists

Sign up to get email announcements of new books and conferences, special offers, and O'Reilly Network technology newsletters at:

> *http://www.elists.oreilly.com*

It's easy to customize your free elists subscription so you'll get exactly the O'Reilly news you want.

3. Get examples from our books

To find example files for a book, go to:

> *http://www.oreilly.com/catalog*

select the book, and follow the "Examples" link.

4. Work with us

Check out our web site for current employment opportunites:

> *http://jobs.oreilly.com/*

5. Register your book

Register your book at:

> *http://register.oreilly.com*

6. Contact us

O'Reilly & Associates, Inc.
1005 Gravenstein Hwy North
Sebastopol, CA 95472 USA
TEL: 707-827-7000 or 800-998-9938
         (6am to 5pm PST)
FAX: 707-829-0104

order@oreilly.com
For answers to problems regarding your order or our products. To place a book order online visit:
http://www.oreilly.com/order_new/

catalog@oreilly.com
To request a copy of our latest catalog.

booktech@oreilly.com
For book content technical questions or corrections.

proposals@oreilly.com
To submit new book proposals to our editors and product managers.

international@oreilly.com
For information about our international distributors or translation queries. For a list of our distributors outside of North America check out:
http://international.oreilly.com/distributors.html

3336